THE USE
OF FORCE

Brief Contents

Contents

Preface

In the fourth edition of this book, we have retained the perspective of the first three editions. We have continued to emphasize the relation between technology on the one hand and military strategy and foreign policy on the other. The selections reprinted here are of two types. Some treat general principles guiding the direct use of force; others deal with specific applications of force and, in doing so, illustrate the general principles. In choosing either type of selection, we have continued to keep four questions in mind: (1) What role has the threatened or actual use of military force played in international politics? (2) How has military power changed in the twentieth century? (3) How have changes in the instruments of force affected the use of force by twentieth century statesmen? (4) What are the implications of the recent profound changes in the structure of international politics?

We have also made significant changes in this edition. First, we have reorganized the book into four major divisions that deal, respectively, with strategies for the use of force (or what is often termed "grand strategy"), with case studies about some significant twentieth century applications of force, with contemporary dilemmas and disputes about how force should be used in the nuclear era, and with military and political issues of the post Cold-War world. More than the first three editions, the fourth provides a broad, although still not comprehensive, survey of the impact that new technologies have had on military strategy and statecraft in this century. The fourth edition continues to combine classic pieces with contemporary analyses and thereby yields historical perspective.

Second, we have dropped many selections from Part III of the third edition. The disappearance of the Soviet Union radically changed the problems and purposes of NATO and the problems and purposes of projecting American power abroad. Major controversies of the Reagan era, for example, over the "maritime strategy" and "horizontal escalation" have become historical curiosities. The new Part III retains selections on the development of nuclear strategy, but concentrates on questions about the political utility of nuclear forces. Part IV looks at problems that have long been with us but that take on a new character because of the changed, and changing, structure of international politics. The problems considered are those of projecting power, of controlling nuclear weapons, of defending against nuclear weapons as they spread to smaller and less stable states, and of finding alternatives to reliance on national military power. Part IV emphasizes issues that America and the world will face in this decade and beyond.

Third, new selections have replaced some old ones, especially in Parts III and IV, but without loss of continuity both in materials used and in problems treated. In the new edition, twenty selections are carried over from the previous one, and eighteen are new. Our introduction to each major division sets forth its important themes and draws attention to the important points covered.

We hope that both beginning and advanced students will find that this edition helps them to understand the dilemmas that political and military leaders face when contemplating the use of force.

Part I
Strategies for the Use of Force

Military power plays a crucial role in international politics because states coexist in a condition of anarchy. If a state is attacked, it has to defend itself with whatever means it can muster. Because no authoritative agency can be called on to resolve disputes among states, leaders often find it convenient, and sometimes find it necessary, to threaten the use of force or actually to employ it. Though its importance varies from era to era, military power brings some order out of chaos and helps to make and enforce the rules of the game.

Because force is so important internationally, four central questions arise about the role that national military power plays in statecraft: What are the ways in which states can use their military power? What determines how they use it? Under what conditions are they likely to use it? And how can they control the competition in armaments that frequently arises among them?

The essays in Part I deal with these questions. Robert J. Art analyzes the four ways that force can be used. Barry Posen examines the factors that influence the strategies that states develop for using force and devises a set of propositions about the determinants of grand strategy. Robert Jervis looks at the different ways defensive and offensive strategies affect the probabilities that cooperation and peace or conflict and war will prevail. And Bernard Brodie and Samuel P. Huntington lay out what should be the objectives of arms control and whether quantitative or qualitative arms races are the more unstable.

The Four Functions of Force

ROBERT J. ART

WHAT ARE THE USES OF FORCE?

The goals that states pursue range widely and vary considerably from case to case. Military power is more useful for realizing some goals than others, though it is generally considered of some use by most states for all of the goals that they hold. If we attempt, however, to be descriptively accurate, to enumerate all of the purposes for which states use force, we shall simply end up with a bewildering list. Descriptive accuracy is not a virtue *per se* for analysis. In fact, descriptive accuracy is generally bought at the cost of analytical utility. (A concept that is descriptively accurate is usually analytically useless.) Therefore, rather than compile an exhaustive list of such purposes, I have selected four categories that themselves analytically exhaust the functions that force can serve: defense, deterrence, compellence, and "swaggering".

Not all four functions are necessarily well or equally served by a given military posture. In fact, usually only the great powers have the wherewithall to develop military forces that can serve more than two functions at once. Even then, this is achieved only vis à vis smaller powers, not vis à vis the other great ones. The measure of the capabilities of a state's military forces must be made relative to those of another state, not with reference to some absolute scale. A state that can compel another state can also defend against it and usually deter it. A state that can defend against another state cannot thereby automatically deter or compel it. A state can deter another state without having the ability to either defend against or compel it. A state that can swagger vis à vis another may or may not be able to perform any of the other three functions relative to it. Where feasible, defense is the goal that all states aim for first. If defense is not possible, deterrence is generally the next priority. Swaggering is the function most difficult to pin down analytically; deterrence, the one whose achievement is the most difficult to demonstrate; compellence, the easiest to demonstrate but among the hardest to achieve. The following discussion develops these points more fully.

From "To What Ends Military Power" by Robert J. Art, in *International Security*, vol. 4 (Spring 1980), pp. 4–35. Reprinted by permission of The MIT Press, Cambridge, Massachusetts. Portions of the text and some footnotes have been omitted.

The *defensive* use of force is the deployment of military power so as to be able to do two things—to ward off an attack and to minimize damage to oneself if attacked. For defensive purposes, a state will direct its forces against those of a potential or actual attacker, but not against his unarmed population. For defensive purposes, a state can deploy its forces in place prior to an attack, use them after an attack has occurred to repel it, or strike first if it believes that an attack upon it is imminent or inevitable. The defensive use of force can thus involve both peaceful and physical employment and both repellent (second) strikes and offensive (first) strikes. If a state strikes first when it believes an attack upon it is imminent, it is launching a preemptive blow. If it strikes first when it believes an attack is inevitable but not momentary, it is launching a preventive blow. Preemptive and preventive blows are undertaken when a state calculates, first, that others plan to attack it and, second, that to delay in striking offensively is against its interests. A state preempts in order to wrest the advantage of the first strike from an opponent. A state launches a preventive attack because it believes that others will attack it when the balance of forces turns in their favor and therefore attacks while the balance of forces is in its favor. In both cases it is better to strike first than to be struck first. The major distinction between preemption and prevention is the calculation about when an opponent's attack will occur. For preemption, it is a matter of hours, days, or even a few weeks at the most; for prevention, months or even a few years. In the case of preemption, the state has almost no control over the timing of its attack; in the case of prevention, the state can in a more leisurely way contemplate the timing of its attack. For both cases, it is the belief in the certainty of war that governs the offensive, defensive attack. For both cases, the maxim, "the best defense is a good offense," makes good sense.

The *deterrent* use of force is the deployment of military power so as to be able to prevent an adversary from doing something that one does not want him to do and that he might otherwise be tempted to do by threatening him with unacceptable punishment if he does it. Deterrence is thus the threat of retaliation. Its purpose is to prevent something undesirable from happening. The threat of punishment is directed at the adversary's population and/or industrial infrastructure. The effectiveness of the threat depends upon a state's ability to convince a potential adversary that it has both the will and power to punish him severely if he undertakes the undesirable action in question. Deterrence therefore employs force peacefully. It is the threat to resort to force in order to punish that is the essence of deterrence. If the threat has to be carried out, deterrence by definition has failed. A deterrent threat is made precisely with the intent that it will not have to be carried out. Threats are made to prevent actions from being undertaken. If the threat has to be implemented, the action has already been undertaken. Hence deterrence can be judged successful only if the retaliatory threats have not been implemented.

Deterrence and defense are alike in that both are intended to protect the state or its closest allies from physical attacks. The purpose of both is dissuasion—persuading others *not* to undertake actions harmful to oneself. The defensive use of force dissuades by convincing an adversary that he cannot conquer one's military forces. The deterrent use of force dissuades by convincing the adversary that his population and territory will suffer terrible damage if he initiates the undesirable action. Defense dissuades by presenting an unvanquishable military force. Deterrence dissuades by presenting the certainty of retaliatory devastation.

Defense is possible without deterrence, and deterrence is possible without defense. A state can have the military wherewithall to repel an invasion without also being able to threaten devastation to the invader's population or territory. Similarly, a state can have the wherewithall credibly to threaten an adversary with such devastation and yet be unable to repel his invading force. Defense, therefore, does not necessarily buy deterrence, nor deterrence defense. A state that can defend itself from attack, moreover, will have little need to develop the wherewithall to deter. If physical attacks can be repelled or if the damage from them drastically minimized, the incentive to develop a retaliatory capability is low. A state that cannot defend itself, however, will try to develop an effective deterrent if that be possible. No state will leave its population and territory open to attack if it has the means to redress the situation. Whether a given state can defend or deter or do both vis à vis another depends upon two factors: (1) the quantitative balance of forces between it and its adversary; and (2) the qualitative balance of forces, that is, whether the extant military technology favors the offense or the defense. These two factors are situation-specific and therefore require careful analysis of the case at hand.

The *compellent* use of force is the deployment of military power so as to be able either to stop an adversary from doing something that he has already undertaken or to get him to do something that he has not yet undertaken. Compellence, in Schelling's words, "involves initiating an action . . . that can cease, or become harmless, only if the opponent responds." Compellence can employ force either physically or peacefully. A state can start actually harming another with physical destruction until the latter abides by the former's wishes. Or, a state can take actions against another that do not cause physical harm but that require the latter to pay some type of significant price until it changes its behavior. America's bombing of North Vietnam in early 1965 was an example of physical compellence; Tirpitz's building of a German fleet aimed against England's in the two decades before World War I, an example of peaceful compellence. In the first case, the United States started bombing North Vietnam in order to compel it to stop assisting the Vietcong forces in South Vietnam. In the latter case, Germany built a battlefleet that in an engagement threatened to cripple England's in order to compel her to make a general political settlement advantageous to Germany. In both cases, one state initiated some type of action against another precisely so as to be able to stop it, to bargain it away for the appropriate response from the "put upon" state.

The distinction between compellence and deterrence is one between the active and passive use of force. The success of a deterrent threat is measured by its not having to be used. The success of a compellent action is measured by how closely and quickly the adversary conforms to one's stipulated wishes. In the case of successful deterrence, one is trying to demonstrate a negative, to show why something did not happen. It can never be clear whether one's actions were crucial to, or irrelevant to, why another state chose *not* to do something. In the case of successful compellence, the clear sequence of actions and reactions lends a compelling plausibility to the centrality of one's actions. Figure 1 illustrates the distinction. In successful compellence, state B can claim that its pressure deflected state A from its course of action. In successful deterrence, state B has no change in state A's behavior to point to, but instead must resort to claiming that its threats were responsible for the continuity in A's behavior. State A may have changed its behavior for reasons other than state B's compellent action. State A may have continued with its same behavior for reasons other than state B's deterrent threat. "Proving" the importance of B's influence on A for either case is not easy, but it is more plausible to claim that B influenced A when there is a change in A's behavior than when there is not. Explaining why something did not happen is more difficult than explaining why something did.

Compellence may be easier to demonstrate than deterrence, but

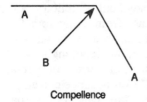

Compellence

(1) A is doing something that B cannot tolerate

(2) B initiates action against A in order to get him to stop his intolerable actions

(3) A stops his tolerable actions and B stops his (or both cease simultaneously)

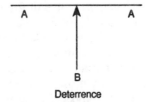

Deterrence

(1) A is presently not doing anything that B finds intolerable

(2) B tells A that if A changes his behavior and does something intolerable, B will punish him

(3) A continues not to do anything B finds intolerable

it is harder to achieve. Schelling argues that compellent actions tend to be vaguer in their objectives than deterrent threats and for that reason more difficult to attain. If an adversary has a hard time understanding what it is that one wished him to do, his compliance with one's wishes is made more difficult. There is, however, no inherent reason why a compellent action must be vaguer than a deterrent threat with regard to how clearly the adversary understands what is wanted from him. "Do not attack me" is not any clearer in its ultimate meaning than "stop attacking my friend." A state can be as confused or as clear about what it wishes to prevent as it can be about what it wishes to stop. The clarity, or lack of it, of the objectives of compellent actions and deterrent threats does not vary according to whether the given action is compellent or deterrent in nature, but rather according to a welter of particularities associated with the given action. Some objectives, for example, are inherently clearer and hence easier to perceive than others. Some statesmen communicate more clearly than others. Some states have more power to bring to bear for a given objective than others. It is the specifics of a given situation, not any intrinsic difference between compellence and deterrence, that determines the clarity with which an objective is perceived.

We must, therefore, look elsewhere for the reason as to why compellence is comparatively harder to achieve than deterrence. It lies, not in what one asks another to do, but in *how* one asks. With deterrence, state B asks something of state A in this fashion: "Do not take action X; for if you do, I will bash you over the head with this club." With compellence, state B asks something of state A in this fashion: "I am now going to bash you over the head with this club and will continue to do so until you do what I want." In the former case, state A can easily deny with great plausibility any intention of having planned to take action X. In the latter case, state A cannot deny either that it is engaged in a given course of action or that it is being subjected to pressure by state B. If they are to be successful, compellent actions require a state to alter its behavior in a manner quite visible to all in response to an equally visible forceful initiative taken by another state. In contrast to compellent actions, deterrent threats are both easier to appear to have ignored or easier to acquiesce to without great loss of face. In contrast to deterrent threats, compellent actions more directly engage the prestige and the passions of the put-upon state. Less prestige is lost in not doing something than in clearly altering behavior due to pressure from another. In the case of compellence, a state has publicly committed its prestige and resources to a given line of conduct that it is now asked to give up. This is not so for deterrence. Thus, compellence is intrinsically harder to attain than deterrence, not because its objectives are vaguer, but because it demands more humiliation from the compelled state.

The fourth purpose to which military power can be put is the most difficult to be precise about. *Swaggering* is in part a residual category, the deployment of military power for purposes other than defense, deterrence, or compellence. Force is not aimed directly at dissuading another state from attacking, at repelling attacks, nor at compelling it to do something specific. The objectives for swaggering are more diffuse, ill-defined, and problematic than that. Swaggering almost always involves only the peaceful use of force and is expressed usually in one of two ways: displaying one's military might at military exercises and national demonstrations and buying or building the era's most prestigious weapons. The swagger use of force is the most egoistic: It aims to enhance the national pride of a people or to satisfy the personal ambitions of its ruler. A state or statesman swaggers in order to look and feel more powerful and important, to be taken seriously by others in the councils of international decision making, to enhance the nation's image in the eyes of others. If its image is enhanced, the nation's defense, deterrent, and compellent capabilities may also be enhanced; but swaggering is not undertaken solely or even primarily for these specific purposes. Swaggering is pursued because it offers to bring prestige "on the cheap." Swaggering is pursued because of the fundamental yearning of states and statesmen for respect and prestige. Swaggering is more something to be enjoyed for itself than to be employed for a specific, consciously thought-out end.

And yet, the instrumental role of swaggering cannot be totally discounted because of the fundamental relation between force and foreign policy that obtains in an anarchic environment. Because there is a connection between the military might that a nation is thought to possess and the success that it achieves in attaining its objectives, the enhancement of a state's stature in the eyes of others can always be justified on *realpolitik* lines. If swaggering causes other states to take one's interests more seriously into account, then the general interests of the state will benefit. Even in its instrumental role, however, swaggering is undertaken less for any given end than for all ends. The swaggering function of military power is thus at one and the same time the most comprehensive and the most diffuse, the most versatile in its effects and the least focused in its immediate aims, the most instrumental in the long run and the least instrumental in the short run, easy to justify on hardheaded grounds and often undertaken on emotional grounds. Swaggering mixes the rational and irrational more than the other three functions of military power and, for that reason, remains both pervasive in international relations and elusive to describe.

Defense, deterrence, compellence, and swaggering—these are the four general purposes for which force can be employed. Discriminating among them analytically, however, is easier than applying them in practice. This is due to two factors. First, we need to know the motives behind an act in order to judge its purpose; but the problem is that motives cannot be readily inferred from actions because several motives can be served by the same action. But neither can one readily infer the motives of a state from what it publicly or officially proclaims them to be. Such statements should not necessarily be taken at face value because of the role that bluff and dissimulation play in statecraft. Such statements are also often concocted with domestic political, not foreign audiences in mind, or else are deliberate exercises in studied ambiguity. Motives are important in order to interpret actions, but neither actions nor words always clearly delineate motives.

It is, moreover, especially difficult to distinguish defensive from compellent actions and deterrent from swaggering ones unless we know the reasons for which they were undertaken. Peaceful defensive preparations often look largely the same as peaceful compellent ones. Defensive attacks are nearly indistinguishable from compellent ones. Is he who attacks first the defender or the compeller? Deterrence and swaggering both involve the acquisition and display of an era's prestigious weapons. Are such weapons acquired to enhance prestige or to dissuade an attack?

Second, to make matters worse, consider the following example. Germany launched an attack upon France and Russia at the end of July 1914 and thereby began World War I. There are two schools of thought as to why Germany did this. One holds that its motives were aggressive—territorial aggrandizement, economic gain, and elevation to the status of a world empire. Another holds that her motives were preventive and hence defensive. She struck first because she feared encirclement, slow strangulation, and then inevitable attack by her two powerful neighbors, foes whom she felt were daily increasing their military might faster than she was. She struck while she had the chance to win.

It is not simple to decide which school is the more nearly correct because both can marshall evidence to build a powerful case. Assume for the moment, though, that the second is closer to the truth. There are then two possibilities to consider: (1) Germany launched an attack because it *was* the case that her foes were planning to attack her ultimately, and Germany had the evidence to prove it; or (2) Germany felt she had reasonable evidence of her foes' *intent* to attack her eventually, but in fact her evidence was wrong because she misperceived their intent from their actions. If the first was the case, then we must ask this question: How responsible was Germany's diplomacy in the fifteen years before 1914, aggressive and blundering as it was, in breeding hostility in her neighbors? Germany attacked in the knowledge that they would eventually have struck her, but if her fifteen-year diplomatic record was a significant factor in causing them to lay these plans, must we conclude that Germany in 1914 was merely acting defensively? Must

we confine our judgment about the defensive or aggressive nature of
the act to the month or even the year in which it occurred? If not,
how many years back in history do we go in order to make a
judgment? If the second was the case, then we must ask this
question: If Germany attacked in the belief, mistakenly as it turns
out, that she would be attacked, must we conclude that Germany
was acting defensively? Must we confine our judgment about the
defensive or aggressive nature of the act simply to Germany's beliefs
about others' intent, without reference to their actual intent?

It is not easy to answer these questions. Fortunately, we do not
have to. Asking them is enough because it illustrates that an assessment of the *legitimacy* of a state's motives in using force is integral
to the task of determining what its motives are. One cannot, that is,
specify motives without at the same time making judgments about
their legitimacy. The root cause of this need lies in the nature of
state action. In anarchy every state is a valid judge of the legitimacy
of its goals because there is no supranational authority to enforce
agreed upon rules. Because of the lack of universal standards, we
are forced to examine each case within its given context and to
make individual judgments about the meaning of the particulars.
When individual judgment is exercised, individuals may well differ.
Definitive answers are more likely to be the exception rather than
the rule.

Where does all of this leave us? Our four categories tell us what
are the four possible purposes for which states can employ military
power. The attributes of each alert us to the types of evidence for
which to search. But because the context of an action is crucial in
order to judge its ultimate purpose, these four categories cannot be
applied mindlessly and ahistorically. Each state's purpose in using
force in a given instance must fall into one of these four categories.
We know *a priori* what the possibilities are. Which one it is, is an
exercise in judgment, an exercise that depends as much upon the
particulars of the given case as it does upon the general features of
the given category. . . . (See Table 1).

Table 1 THE PURPOSES OF FORCE

Type	Purpose	Mode	Targets	Characteristics
Defensive	Fend off attacks and/or reduce damage of an attack	Peaceful and physical	Primarily military Secondarily industrial	Defensive preparations can have dissuasion value; Defensive preparations can look aggressive; First strikes can be taken for defense.
Deterrent	Prevent adversary from initiating an action	Peaceful	Primarily civilian Secondarily industrial Tertiarily military	Threats of retaliation made so as not to have to be carried out; Second strike preparations can be viewed as first strike preparations.
Compellent	Get adversary to stop doing something or start doing something	Peaceful and physical	All three with no clear ranking	Easy to recognize but hard to achieve; Compellent actions can be justified on defensive grounds.
Swaggering	Enhance prestige	Peaceful	None	Difficult to describe because of instrumental and irrational nature; Swaggering can be threatening.

Explaining Military Doctrine

BARRY POSEN

MILITARY ORGANIZATIONS AND MILITARY DOCTRINE

Hypotheses—Offense, Defense, and Deterrence

Most soldiers and many civilians are intuitively attracted to the offense as somehow the stronger form of war. Clausewitz, often misconstrued as the apostle of the offensive, was very mindful of the advantages of a defensive strategy. He called defense "the stronger form of war." However, every aspect of his work that *could be taken* as offensive advocacy has been so taken. What accounts for such systematic misinterpretation?

Uncertainty Reduction

Military organizations will generally prefer offensive doctrines because they *reduce uncertainty* in important ways.

1. The need for standard scenarios encourages military organizations to prefer offensive doctrines. In order to have a set of SOPs* and programs, they must plan for a "standard scenario." Once SOPs and programs have been tailored to such a scenario, the organization, in order to be "fought"—used in combat—must be used with those SOPs and programs. If the organization is to be "fought" successfully, it must respond to command in predictable ways. Commanders must have orders to give that generate predictable responses. Thus, it is strongly in the interests of a military organization to impose its "standard scenario" on the adversary through offensive action before the adversary does the same to it.

2. Warfare is an extremely competitive endeavor. Its most successful practitioners strive for even the smallest advantages. Thus, military organizations seem to prefer offensive doctrines not only because they appear to guarantee the side on the offense its standard scenario, but because they also *deny* the enemy his standard scenario. A military organization prefers to fight its own war and

prevent its adversary from doing so. Taking the offensive, exercising the initiative, is a way of structuring the battle. The advantages seen to lie with surprise are more than psychological. An organization fighting the war that it planned is likely to do better than one that is not. For example, in the Arab attack on Israel in 1973, Egyptian and Syrian preparations were aimed at imposing an uncongenial style of warfare on Israel.

Defensive warfare might also seem to allow an organization to structure the battle. However, the defending organization is often in a reactive position, improvising new programs to cope with the adversary's initiative. If the defending organization is, for whatever reasons, a fast learner, it may rapidly improvise countermeasures that destroy the offender's programs. (The Israel Defense Forces achieved this with their Suez Canal crossing in 1973.) This leaves both organizations fighting a battle of improvisation which both would probably prefer to avoid. Victory goes to the most flexible command structure. Generally, however, professional soldiers appear to believe that striking the first blow is beneficial because, at least initially, it reduces the attacker's necessity to improvise and the defender's ability to improvise. This military judgment may reflect an implicit understanding that military organizations are not fast learners, precisely because they are the structured systems portrayed earlier. The perceived advantage of taking the offensive is thus magnified.

3. Because predicting whose national will can be broken first is a political task, not susceptible to the analytical skills of a military organization, military organizations dislike deterrent doctrines. Punishment warfare, conventional or nuclear, tends not to address an adversary's capabilities, but his will. Calculating in advance of a war whose will is likely to break first is inherently somewhat more difficult for a military organization than devising plausible scenarios for destroying enemy capabilities. Calculations of enemy determination demand an entirely different set of skills than those commanded by a military organization. Calculations about military outcomes are at least somewhat susceptible to "engineering" criteria; calculations of relative will are not. However, this argument may be a weak one. There are more powerful reasons why military organizations do not favor deterrent doctrines.

4. Military organizations will prefer offensive doctrines because they help increase organizational size and wealth. Size and wealth help reduce internal uncertainty by increasing the rewards that the organization can distribute to its members. Size and wealth help reduce external uncertainty by providing a buffer against unforeseen events such as huge losses or partial defeats.

While the offensive allows the attacking force to be more certain of how its organization will perform, and to deny that certainty to an adversary, the offensive is likely to be technically more complex, quantitatively more demanding. There are many extra contingencies for which an offensive military instrument must be prepared. An attacking army encounters natural obstacles that must be crossed, creating a demand for engineers. Fortifications encountered may demand more and heavier artillery for their reduction. The offensive army may have to go anywhere, requiring special technical capabilities in its equipment. Nothing can be specialized for the environment of the home country. Aircraft need greater range and payload. All of these factors require an extensive logistics capability to uncoil behind the advancing military force. Troops will be required to guard and defend this line of communication. Operations at range will impose greater wear and tear on the equipment—demanding large numbers in reserve, and still more support capability. While various characteristics of geography, politics, and technology might place these same demands on a defensive force, as a general rule offensive doctrines impose them to a greater extent. Deterrent doctrines offer the most minimal material opportunities for military organizations. This is partly because they are more dependent on political will than on military capabilities. Partly it is a result of the clarity of the punishment mission, which allows rather extreme specialization.

5. Military organizations will prefer offensive doctrines because they enhance military autonomy. As noted earlier, civilian intervention in operational matters can be a key source of uncertainty for military organizations. Offensive doctrines tend to be more complicated than defensive or deterrent doctrines, and thus increase the difficulties for civilians who wish to understand military matters. Defense and deterrence are relatively easy for civilians to master. Deterrent warfare with nuclear weapons has consistently proved to be the easiest form of warfare for civilian analysts to understand in the post-war period. Deterrent warfare by means of popular resistance—extended guerrilla action, for example—depends so heavily on the legitimacy of the government and its authority over its people that it may be the highest form of political-military warfare. Defense or denial does not present the complications of the offensive, and again includes such strong cooperation with civilian authorities as to restrict the operational autonomy of the army. The offensive, however, can be waged off national soil, and therefore immediately involves less civilian interference. Offensive operations are elaborate combinations of forces and strategems—more art than science. Denial is more straightforward, and punishment is simplest of all. From specialists in victory, defense turns soldiers into specialists in attrition, and deterrence makes them specialists in slaughter.

There is little in organization theory or the civil-military relations literature to suggest that modern militaries will prefer anything but offensive doctrines, if such doctrines are in any way feasible.

Geography

6. Organization theory suggests a somewhat muted geographical influence on military doctrine. (The influence of technology will be discussed below.) Where geography can plausibly be argued to favor an offensive doctrine, it reinforces the organizational tendencies outlined above. For instance, it has become commonplace to explain the affinity of Prussia-Germany (in the past) and Israel (in the present) for offensive doctrines by their a) being surrounded and outnumbered by powerful enemies and b) enjoying the advantage of interior lines (with the ability to shift forces quickly from one front to another). Thus, the sequential defeat of the members of an enemy coalition with a series of rapid offensives, before they can pull their forces together and coordinate an attack, is deemed to be very attractive. Presumably, any state finding itself in a similar position would agree.

One less often finds the reverse argued—that some particular geographic configuration generally and sensibly leads to a defensive military doctrine. At the level of grand strategy, of course, both Britain and the United States have exploited the defensive advantage bestowed by ocean barriers. Yet, the navies of both powers have periodically argued for offensive military strategies to achieve "command of the sea." They usually have been constrained to operate in a more limited fashion, but the preference for the offensive, even in situations where it seems unreasonable, is striking.

Numerous examples of military organizations that undervalue the defensive utility of geography can be found. British colonial soldiers in India viewed Afghanistan as a potential Russian invasion route, and sought to control it. Yet, one British military expedition after another met with disaster brought on by wild Afghan raiders, treacherous terrain and weather, and long distances. This stark evidence of the area's unsuitability as an invasion route was ignored, as subsequent expeditions were deemed necessary. In World War I the Russians underrated the defensive value of the Masurian Lakes to the Germans. The lakes ultimately split the large Russian force, allowing a smaller German army to defeat it piecemeal. At the outset of World War I the British dispatched a small force to Persia, to guard the Abadan oil facilities. Its commanders opted for an attack on Baghdad, a distant objective for which the force was woefully inadequate. Currently, the U.S. Navy advocates an offensive strategy against Soviet Naval forces based in the Barents Sea and Murmansk—a tough and distant target. NATO has geographic choke points off the Norwegian North Cape, and in the Greenland-Iceland-United Kingdom Gap, that provide a powerful defensive advantage against any Soviet naval offensive, and all but obviate the need for an offensive against the north. In short, organization theory suggests that geographic factors that support offensive doctrines will more often be correctly assessed than those that support a defensive doctrine. History seems to confirm this observation.

Hypotheses—Integration*

It was over a century and a half ago that Clausewitz made his now famous remarks on the relationship of war to policy. Most simply, "war is not a mere act of policy but a true political instrument, a continuation of political activity by other means." Political considerations reach into the military means, to influence *"the planning of war, of the campaign, and often even of the battle"* (my emphasis). Clausewitz clearly believed that statesmen could and should ensure that policy infuse military operations. Those in charge of policy require "a certain grasp of military affairs." They need not be soldiers, however. "What is needed in the post is distinguished intellect and character. He [the statesman] can always get the necessary military information somehow or other." Clausewitz was over-optimistic on this score. Few have challenged his judgment that policy must infuse acts of war, but the achievement of this goal has proven more difficult than he imagined. . . .

Functional specialization between soldiers and statesmen, and the tendency of soldiers to seek as much independence from civilian interference as possible, combine to make political-military integration an uncertain prospect. These two fundamental aspects of state structure and organization lead to the following deductions:

1. As a rule, soldiers are not going to go out of their way to reconcile the means they employ with the ends of state policy. This is not necessarily to argue that they deliberately try to disconnect their means from political ends. Often, however, soldiers will elevate the narrow technical requirements of preferred operations above the needs of civilian policy. In the case of the European militaries prior to World War I, the single-minded pursuit of battlefield advantage closed off diplomatic options for statesmen.

2. This cause of disintegration is exacerbated because military organizations are unwilling to provide civilian authorities with information that relates to doctrinal questions, especially those having the most to do with the actual conduct of operations. Thus, civilians

---

*Editors' Note: By integration (and disintegration), Posen means how well (and how poorly) suited a nation's military forces and doctrine are to its foreign policy goals.

are simply unaware of the ways military doctrine may conflict with the ends of state policy. Policy-makers may simply not know enough about the operational practices of their military organizations to either alter their political strategy or force changes in military doctrine that would bring it in line with the existing political strategy. Nevertheless, in spite of the limits of information, organization theory would seem to suggest that if political-military integration is to be achieved, civilian intervention into doctrinal matters is essential. The question is, given the obstacles, what is sufficient to cause civilian intervention? This is a question better answered by balance of power theory.

3. The setting of priorities among military forces and missions is a key aspect of political-military integration. In multiservice military organizations, civilian intervention is critical to the setting of priorities. This is another way civilian intervention causes integration. In chapter 1 it was argued that one of the tasks of grand strategy is to set priorities among threats and opportunities in the environment, and to set priorities among forces to match these threats and opportunities. Interpreting the external environment is the specialty of civilians. Building and operating military forces is the task of services. Setting priorities among the services, and among forces or branches within services, is a central task of grand strategy. Yet, the tendency of individuals within organizations to preserve the task and power of their organization or sub-organization suggests that *among* or *within* services the goal of autonomy should be just as strong as it is for the military as a whole. Thus, it is very difficult for a group of services to accomplish the task of setting priorities. The inclination of a group of services or sub-services to set priorities among themselves is going to be low.

In the absence of civilian intervention, and the exercise of the legitimate authority that only the civilians possess, militaries will arrange a "negotiated environment." This is likely to take the form of either preserving a customary budgetary split or dividing shares equally. Each service will prepare for its own war. Forces will not cooperate effectively. Neither will they be well balanced. A tendency will emerge for each service to set requirements as if it were fighting the war alone. This can easily result in misallocation of the scarce security resources of the state.

Left to themselves, a group of services cannot make a military doctrine that will be well integrated with the political aspects of the state's grand strategy. They can simply assemble a batch of service doctrines. This is less true within services, where higher authority can make allocation decisions. Even within services, priorities may not be set according to strategic criteria. A service doctrine may be as difficult to produce as an overall grand strategy. . . .

Hypotheses—Innovation in Military Doctrine

Obstacles

1. Because of the process of institutionalization, innovation in military doctrine should be rare. It will only occasionally be sponsored by the military organization itself. As already remarked, according to organization theory organizations try to control the behavior of their members in order to achieve purposes. One way of doing this is by distributing power through the organization so as to ensure that certain tasks will be accomplished. Individuals develop a vested interest in the distribution of power and in the purposes it protects. Generally, it is not in the interests of most of an organization's members to promote or succumb to radical change.

2. Innovations in military doctrine will be rare because they increase operational uncertainty. While innovation is in process, the organization's SOPs and programs will be in turmoil. The ability of commanders to "fight" the organization with confidence will decline. Should a war come during the transition, the organization will find itself between doctrines. Under combat conditions, even a bad doctrine may be better than no doctrine. It is possible to argue that the Prussians at Jena, the French in 1940, and the Russians in 1941 were taken in the midst of doctrinal transition.

3. Because of the obstacles to innovation discussed above, a technology that has not been tested in war can seldom function by itself as the catalyst for doctrinal innovation. Military organizations often graft new pieces of technology on to old doctrines. As Bernard Brodie has noted, "Conservatism of the military, about which we hear so much, seems always to have been confined to their adaptation to new weaponry rather than their acceptance of it."[1] . . . A new technology will normally be assimilated to an old doctrine rather than stimulate change to a new one. . . . This problem stems from the difficulty of proving anything about a new military technology without using it in a major war.

Causes of Innovation

In the military sphere, there are two exceptions to the preceding proposition that military organizations generally fail to innovate in response to new technology:

4. Military organizations do seem willing to learn from wars fought by their client states—with the weapons and perhaps the doctrine of the patron. Both the U.S. and Soviet militaries are willing to draw lessons from the 1973 Arab-Israeli war, although many of the "lessons" are not entirely clear.

[1] Bernard Brodie, "Technological Change, Strategic Doctrine, and Political Outcomes," in *Historical Dimensions*, ed. Knorr, p. 299.

5. Military organizations are even better able to learn about technology by using it in their own wars. Perhaps the best example of direct experience leading to correct appraisal of technology is found in the evolution of Prussian doctrine from 1850 to 1870. Prussia's attempted railroad mobilization against Austria in 1850 was a fiasco. Learning from the experience, the Prussians turned the railroad into an efficient war instrument by 1866.

There are limits to the power of this proposition. In the American Civil War, frontline soldiers adjusted rapidly to the technological facts of modern firepower. They "dug in" whenever they had the chance. The generals understood the least, ordering frontal assaults against prepared positions throughout the war. The same occurred in World War I, with generals ordering repeated costly offensives. Bernard Brodie notes that the generals "seemed incapable of learning from experience, largely because of the unprecedented separation of the high command from the front lines." This seems a plausible explanation, and again is entirely consistent with organization theory. . . .

The preceding examples also offer insights into the relationship between technology and the offensive, defensive, or deterrent character of military doctrine. Most simply, if a military organization has adopted an offensive doctrine, or is bent on adopting one, technological lessons on the advantage of defense are likely to be ignored, corrupted, or suppressed. This is consistent with the argument advanced earlier concerning the probable offensive preferences of most military organizations.

Organization theory predicts at least two causes of innovation that are much stronger and more reliable in their operation than experience with new technology: (6) military organizations innovate when they have failed—suffered a defeat—and (7) they innovate when civilians intervene from without. These hypotheses can be deduced from the basic survival motive of large organizations. Failure to achieve their organizational purpose, the successful defense of the state, can cause military organizations to reexamine their basic doctrinal preferences. Similarly, soldiers may respond to the civilian intervention that defeat often precipitates in order to defend the organization's autonomy, which is under attack.

Failure and civilian intervention often go hand in hand. Soldiers fail; civilians get angry and scared; pressure is put on the military. Sometimes the pressure is indirect. Civilian leaders become disenchanted with the performance of one service and shift resources to another. These resources may provide the "slack" for the newly favored service to attempt some innovations. The loser strives to win back his lost position. Interservice rivalry in postwar America may have produced some benefits—a menu of innovations for policymakers. Arguably, interservice rivalry has been a major factor in the growth of the "Triad," which has on the whole increased U.S. security. Similarly, aggrandizement at the expense of another service may be a motive for innovation.

Although civilian intervention into military doctrine would seem to be a key determinant of innovation, it involves special problems. The division of labor between civilians and soldiers is intense. Civilians are not likely to have the capability to dream up whole new doctrines. Thus, civil intervention is dependent on finding sources of military knowledge. Civil intervention should take the form of choosing from the thin innovation menu thrown up by the services. In multiservice defense establishments, civilians have the possibility, depending on the strategic position of the state, of choosing among competing services. Within services, hierarchy and the chain of command should tend to suppress the emergence of new doctrinal alternatives at levels where the civilians cannot find them. None of this is to say that innovation in military doctrine is impossible. These are merely tendencies. . . .

Summary: Organization Theory Hypotheses

Offense, Defense, and Deterrence

1. The need for standard scenarios to reduce operational uncertainty encourages military organizations to prefer offensive doctrines.

2. The incentive, arising from the highly competitive nature of warfare, to deny an adversary his "standard scenario" encourages offensive doctrines.

3. The inability of military organizations to calculate comparative national will causes them to dislike deterrent doctrines.

4. Offensive doctrines will be preferred by military organizations because they increase organizational size and wealth.

5. Offensive doctrines will be preferred by military organizations because they enhance organizational independence from civilian authority.

6. Because the organizational incentives to pursue offensive doctrines are strong, military organizations will generally fix on geographic and technological factors that favor the offensive, but underrate or overlook such factors that favor defense or deterrence.

Integration

1. Because military organizations seek independence from civilian authority in order to reduce the uncertainties of combat, military doctrines tend to be poorly integrated with the political aspects of grand strategy. Soldiers will avoid including political criteria in their

military doctrine if such criteria interfere with strictly instrumental military logic.

2. Because of functional specialization, civilians and soldiers tend to know too little about each other's affairs. Soldiers, again in the quest for autonomy, will exacerbate this problem by withholding important military information from civilians. Inadequate civilian understanding of military matters creates obstacles to political-military integration.

3. Technical specialization within military organizations works against a strategically rational setting of priorities among different services, further contributing to disintegration.

In spite of the obstacles, civilian intervention into military doctrine is likely to be the primary cause of political-military integration of grand strategy, simply because civilians alone have the interest and the authority to reconcile political ends with military means and set priorities among military services according to some rational calculus.

Innovation

Most propositions about military innovation are negative.

1. Because of the process of institutionalization, which gives most members of an organization a stake in the way things are, doctrinal innovation will only rarely be sponsored by the organization itself.

2. Because doctrinal innovation increases operational uncertainty, it will rarely be sponsored by the organization itself.

3. New technology, when it has not been tried in combat, is seldom by itself a catalyst of doctrinal innovation.

4. A client state's combat experience with a new technology can cause innovation.

5. Direct combat experience with a new technology can cause innovation.

6. Failure on the battlefield can cause doctrinal innovation.

7. Civilian intervention can cause military innovation.

BALANCE OF POWER THEORY AND MILITARY DOCTRINE

Organization theory suggests a tendency toward offensive, stagnant military doctrines, poorly integrated with the political elements of a state's grand strategy. Balance of power theory predicts greater heterogeneity in military doctrine, dependent on reasonable appraisals by each state of its political, technological, economic, and geographical problems and possibilities in the international political system. The three case studies will show that although organization theory does accurately predict certain tendencies in military doctrine, overall outcomes are more consistent with balance of power theory predictions.

From balance of power theory specific propositions about the variables offense-defense-deterrence, innovation-stagnation, and integration-disintegration can be deduced. Balance of power theory also describes the circumstances under which these propositions are most likely to hold true. In times of relative international calm, when statesmen and soldiers perceive the probability of war as remote, the organizational dynamics outlined above tend to operate. When threats appear greater, or war appears more probable, balancing behavior occurs. A key element of that behavior is greater civilian attention to matters military.

Such attention puts the more ossified, organizationally self-serving, and politically unacceptable aspects of military doctrine under a harsher light. Fear of disaster or defeat prompts statesmen to question long-standing beliefs, to challenge service preferences, to alter budget shares, and to find new sources of military advice and leadership. Civilians intervene to change details, including posture and doctrine, not merely general principles. Organization theory would view civilian influence at such a level as unlikely. Moreover, soldiers, fearful that policies long preferred for their peacetime utility may be found wanting in war, are (according to balance of power theory) somewhat more amenable to outside criticism than in times of international calm. Soldiers themselves are more likely to examine their traditional premises. They will not abandon them, but they may hedge against their failure. These military tendencies are insufficiently strong in their own right to produce military doctrines consistent with balance of power theory predictions. It is the combination of civilian intervention and increased military open-mindedness that produces the results predicted. . . .

Hypotheses—Offense, Deterrence, and Defense

Discussion of individual hypotheses on the causes of offensive, defensive, and deterrent doctrines must be prefaced with a defense of the overarching hypothesis that balance of power theory implies heterogeneity rather than homogeneity on this dimension. I have argued that organization theory suggests that most militaries will prefer the offensive. If balance of power theory also suggested homogeneity on this dimension—the predominance among doctrines of *one* of the three categories—that could make the task of competitive theory testing either simpler or more difficult. The task would be simple if balance of power theory implied that states would prefer defensive doctrines, since we could easily examine a large number of military doctrines and discover if they were usually offensive or usually defensive. On the other hand, if balance of power theory predicted offensive doctrines, then both theories would be predicting the same outcome, and one could hardly test them against each other. In cases where we found offensive doctrines, we would have an "overdetermination" problem—explanation of over 100 percent of the outcome. Of course, in cases where defensive or deterrent doctrines were found, both theories would be discredited. Balance of power theory does not predict homogeneous outcomes, however, although a misreading of the theory might suggest this.

Several students of state behavior whose analyses reflect the balance of power perspective have predicted state policies that would seem to demand offensive doctrines. Hans Morgenthau, John Herz, and to a lesser extent Robert Gilpin predict that states will generally try to expand their power. States will seek not simply equality, but superiority. States are likely to behave this way because power is the key to survival in an anarchical system; since relative power is difficult to measure, the state never knows when it has enough, and it should therefore logically strive for a fairly wide margin of superiority. Basically, these theorists argue, as I have argued, that the security dilemma is always present. Effectively, they also argue, as I have *not*, that the security dilemma is usually quite intense. If this view of the system and its effects on actors were complete, then it would seem logical to deduce that all states will prefer offensive doctrines in order to be ready to expand their power. Because an offensive doctrine may allow the conquest of one's neighbors and the seizure of power assets that lie beyond one's borders, it might appear to be the military option that provides the most security.

This view, however, is not complete. It is *ahistorical* in the most fundamental sense, assuming that states are effectively newborn children, thrust into the jungle of international politics with nothing more than an orientation briefing on the "law of tooth and claw" to guide their actions. Under such conditions the security dilemma might indeed operate with extraordinary intensity. Robert Gilpin, however, admits that states make cost-benefit calculations when deliberating about whether or not to attempt expansion, and that perceptions of cost are affected by the state's historical experience. Of particular importance are the consequences of its own or others' attempts at expansion, and the lessons learned from those episodes. While states, or those who act for them, frequently misread the lessons of history, balance of power theory itself suggests that expanding hegemons will be opposed and stopped. *We have ample historical evidence that this is the case.* This is a lesson that is easy to learn. Indeed, such learning is consistent with Kenneth Waltz's prediction that states will become socialized to the norms of the system that they inhabit. Not all states learn the lesson—not well enough to sustain perpetual peace—but enough learning takes place to make violent, unlimited, expansionist policies the exception rather than the rule. Status quo policies are the rule rather than the exception. France under Louis XIV and Napoleon, Germany under the Kaiser and Hitler, are already too many would-be European hegemons for those who have had to oppose them, but surprisingly few for a three-century game that has often involved as many as six major players.

A status quo policy, of course, need not lead to a defensive military doctrine, but it certainly need not lead to an offensive one either. Instead, status quo powers will assess their political, geographical, and technological positions and possibilities, and devise a military doctrine that preserves their interests at the lowest costs and risks. Thus, an inference from balance of power theory is that military doctrines will be heterogeneous along the dimension of offense-defense deterrence.

Offense

1. States bent on conquest will prefer offensive military doctrines. This proposition is not deduced from balance of power theory, but rather is a matter of common sense. Louis XIV, Napoleon Bonaparte, and Adolph Hitler all had expansionist foreign policies, and required offensive instruments to pursue those policies.

2. States will try to pass on the costs of war to others. Offensive operations are one way to accomplish this. If war seems to involve high collateral damage, states will try to arrange that the war will be fought on the territory of the enemy, of neutrals, or even of allies. Nicholas Spykman once admonished, "Only in periods of weakness and decline have states fought at home. In periods of vitality and strength, they fight on other people's territory."[2] Of course, not all states have the option of fighting abroad, but those that do tend to avail themselves of it. . . .

3. States will support offensive doctrines when power appears to be shifting against them. Offensive doctrines are necessary to fight "preventive" wars. It also seems probable that in environments where power might rapidly shift, statesmen will want to keep an offensive capability "in the hole." A particularly intense arms race would seem to promote offensive doctrines. (We have already seen how the reverse can be true.) Preventive war is a peculiar sort of balancing behavior. "Because I cannot keep you from catching up I will cut you down now." Israel's cooperation in the Franco-British

[2] Spykman, *America's Strategy in World Politics*. New York: Harcourt, Brace, and World, 1942 p. 29.

attack on Egypt in 1956 is explained in part by the fear that Egypt's new claim on the arsenals of the Eastern bloc would give her a permanent arms-race advantage. Hitler preferred an offensive doctrine partly because he believed that he had rearmed more quickly than his putative adversaries, but that they would soon catch up. An offensive doctrine would allow him to prevent this by permitting Germany to strike the Allies before they could remedy their military deficiencies.

4. Similarly, states without allies, *facing multiple threats*, will be attracted to offensive doctrines. An offensive doctrine allows the state to choose the time and place of battle. If the joint capabilities of the adversaries are superior, offensive doctrines will be particularly attractive. In an offensive move, an isolated state can attack and defeat its adversaries sequentially, minimizing the effect of the imbalance of capabilities. This is a variety of preventive war. Instead of waging one dangerous war against a superior coalition, the offender elects to wage what amounts to a separate war against each of the members of the opposing coalition in turn. An offensive doctrine is thus a method of power balancing.

5. The force of the preceding hypothesis is increased if the geographic factor of encirclement is added. The military history of Prussia and later of Germany reveals a constant affinity for offensive doctrines. This is explained in part by the frequent threats of multifront wars. Israel's offensive doctrine allows her to defeat the Arab states sequentially. It may be that the offensiveness of the Soviet military doctrine—both in the rocket forces and in the ground forces—is partially a response to the existence of hostile states on every border.

6. Statesmen will prefer offensive military doctrines if they lack powerful allies, because such doctrines allow them to manipulate the threat of war with credibility. Offensive doctrines are best for making threats. States can use both the threat of alliance and the threat of military force to aid diplomacy in communicating power and will. In the absence of strong allies, the full burden of this task falls on the state's military capabilities. This was the major characteristic of Hitler's early diplomacy. It provided the motivation for former Secretary of Defense James Schlesinger's merchandising of substantial nuclear counterforce capability in the guise of "flexible strategic options." To some extent, this motivation appears to have been behind the offensive aspects of Strategic Air Command doctrine in the 1950s. Military demonstrations and an offensive doctrine are also important elements of Israeli grand strategy.

7. A state need not be politically isolated or geographically encircled to find defensive doctrines unattractive. States with far-flung security dependencies may find it advisable to defend such

allies by concentrating offensive, disarming military power, or deterrent, punitive military power, against its adversary (or adversaries) rather than dispersing its scarce military capabilities in futile
denial efforts in many places. Such dependencies, like NATO Europe in the 1950s, may be far from the guarantor, close to a major
power adversary, and too weak to contribute much to their own
defense. The security of such states is difficult to guarantee by
defensive/denial means alone. If the United States had had to secure
postwar Europe with conventional denial means, there would probably have been a great many more American troops in Europe than
there were. The Soviet adversary had to be dissuaded from going to
war against U.S. dependencies. The same was true if French allies
in eastern Europe were going to be protected during the interwar
period.

How is dissuasion to be accomplished if defensive/denial means
are ruled out? Only deterrence and offense remain. While the United
States has relied mainly on deterrence in the Cold War, offense has
also played an important role. Many have argued against reliance
on deterrence alone, since the adversary could punish the United
States in return for any strike we might deliver. Extended deterrence
is difficult because, whereas a state's readiness to inflict punishment
on an adversary that aggresses directly against it might be unques-
tionable, its willingness to punish the same adversary for offenses
against far-removed dependencies, and so to draw fresh fire and
suffering on itself, is less likely to be credited. The credibility of the
commitment is believed to go up with an ability to limit damage to
ourselves by disarming the adversary. . . .

Deterrence

8. Far-flung security dependencies and powerful adversaries can
lead a great power to either deterrent or offensive doctrines. Offensive doctrines will be preferred, but often the sheer scope of the
problem and the capabilities of the adversary (or adversaries) make
offensive capabilities hard to get. Technology and geography are
frequently the key determinants of the scope of the problem. Before
World War II Britain hoped to hold possessions half a globe away.
She lacked the raw capability to project much power such a distance—particularly after ensuring the homeland against more immediate adversaries. Even if she could have mustered the capabilities and mastered the distances, Britain lacked a military technology
that could disarm Japan and keep her disarmed. When states face
such a situation, they will accept, although they may not embrace,
deterrent doctrines.

The political organisms that most often find themselves in this
situation seem to be the great empires of history. The British found

it advantageous in the 1920s and '30s to police Arabian tribesmen not by pitched battle, but by bombing from the air. They could either obey the rules or be punished. A close examination of British defense policy in the 1930s shows a pronounced inclination toward deterrence. The politicians of the period frequently used the term. Due to economic, industrial, and technological constraints, the actual operations envisioned were more of the denial than the punishment variety. However, dissuasion was the goal, and one finds a constant concern with the manipulation of military capability and potential military capability to discourage aggression. Only with the short-lived commitment to the population bombing doctrine of Bomber Command were any punitive operations planned in the 1930s. . . .

9. As noted previously, small states threatened by powerful adversaries often make recourse to deterrent doctrines. The peculiar coincidence of doctrines among the very strong and the very weak is easy to explain. In both cases, insufficient capabilities drive states to such doctrines. When a state's capabilities fall short of its aims or needs, it may throw its political "will" into the balance. Will is as much a product of a state's political cohesion as it is a product of any material source. Thus, whenever states face security threats and are, by reason of the magnitude of the task or their own poverty, short of resources, we can expect to see deterrent doctrines.

Defense

I have argued that coalition formation is a common method both of enhancing perceived power for diplomacy and mustering real power for war. Yet, coalition management has its problems. Napoleon once declared that if he had to make war, he would prefer to make it against a coalition. Alfred Vagts observes, "Of all types of war, this is the one in which it is most likely that political aims will crowd out and repress strategic aims. And even if this is not intended, the other partner or partners will still suspect it, will try to spare their own forces and sacrifice those of the ally."

10. Defensive doctrines, or doctrines with strong defensive elements, will be preferred by statesmen with status quo policies who are preparing to fight in coalitions. Such doctrines give the states in the coalition more time to settle the division of costs and benefits of the war. This phenomenon will be particularly pronounced if the costs of going on the offensive are seen to be high. One paradoxical example is found in Egyptian behavior during the 1973 Arab-Israeli war. Although the Egyptians had mounted a successful offensive to cross the Suez Canal, after crossing they chose a low-risk strategy of staying behind their air and anti-tank defenses. By so doing, they allowed Israel the luxury of concentrating the bulk of her military

capability on the dangerous Syrian offensive. Egypt passed on the costs of the war to the Syrians. Egypt only left her defensive positions when frenzied Syrian protests suggested Israel's imminent victory. When Egypt finally attacked, its offensive was shattered. Britain and France were guilty of similar "buck-passing" in the 1930s. In both the Egyptian-Syrian case and the British-French case, the costs of going on the offensive were seen to be high. In the case of the 1914 powers, the cost of the offensive was seen to be low. This explains the less cautious behavior in the earlier period.

11. The preceding hypothesis may be attenuated by another constraint. Although states may seek military doctrines that allow them to pass some of their defense costs onto coalition partners, they must in some measure please these present or potential allies in order to attract them. Thus, alliance suitors may adopt the doctrines of their intended allies. A given military doctrine may fail to achieve both the goal of buck-passing and the goal of alliance-making, and when it does, a state can face difficult choices. In 1973, Egypt appears to have portrayed her military doctrine one way to achieve Syrian cooperation in the initial attack; operated another to spare her own forces early in the war; and finally shifted back to a strategy móre accommodating to the Syrians in the abortive offensive against Israeli forces in the Sinai passes. France in the 1930s, on the other hand, could both attract British support and control her own contribution to any ultimate war effort with a defensive doctrine. Britain did not want any provocation of Germany, and that was fine with France.

12. Status quo states will generally prefer defensive doctrines if geography or technology makes such doctrines attractive. They are more likely to correctly interpret such factors than are non-status quo states, and since their goal is to conserve power, they are more likely to exploit them militarily.

13. Status quo states may prefer defensive doctrines simply because those states know that they are unlikely to strike the first blow. Since they expect to suffer the first blow, it is reasonable for them to expend their military effort learning how to parry it.

Hypotheses—The Causes of Civilian Intervention and Its Effects on Integration and Innovation

I have discussed some causes of the character of military doctrine. Organization theory identifies external intervention as a key source of integration and innovation, but also predicts that such intervention will be very difficult. Balance of power theory predicts that, difficult or not, such intervention will occur if it is necessary to secure the state. If balance of power theory successfully predicts not only intervention, but also the circumstances under which it occurs, then the theory gains in credibility relative to organization theory. Thus, it is important to address the causes of civilian intervention into military matters.

1. Political leaders with aggression in mind will often take a look at their military forces to see if they are ready to go. Hitler was most attentive to his military capabilities and, as we shall see, was a prime mover in the development of Blitzkrieg. This is not so much a proposition deduced from balance of power theory as a matter of common sense. The anarchy of international politics permits mischief. The military value of the object in view may or may not be a motive for mischief. If political leaders contemplate aggression for the purpose of expanding their resources for security, then their intervention can be loosely explained in terms of structural constraints. Otherwise, we must fall back on avarice and "bloody-mindedness" as an explanation.

For whatever reasons civilian policy-makers choose a path of aggression, soldiers must either carry out the orders of their chiefs or resign. The prospect of war can have a catalytic effect on the behavior of soldiers whose lives or careers will inevitably be put into jeopardy. The final steps to the Blitzkrieg doctrine were taken by the commanders of the Germany Army only late in 1939 and early in 1940, when it became clear that Hitler was committed to an offensive against the Allies.

2. If planned aggression for political ends is one general cause of civilian intervention in military matters, the other is fear. This is consistent with balance of power theory. It is easy for statesmen to become frightened by events in the international environment. Many different kinds of events may threaten the state's security. Just as states "balance" materially by arms-racing or coalition formation, they "balance" qualitatively by taking a close look at the doctrine, competence, and readiness of their military organizations. They do not do so all the time, but when they do, fear is most often the driving force.

3. The same fear increases military organizations' receptivity to outside criticism and also sharpens their own self-critical faculties. The force of this proposition is attenuated in multipolar systems, however, if a given state perceives itself to have alliance possibilities. Under conditions of threat, civilians may divide their energies between chasing allies and reviewing their military posture. This may so reduce the pressure on a given military organization as to allow organizational dynamics to triumph. More specific propositions on this matter can be generated.

4. In the face of any sort of security problem, states without allies will tend to pay a good deal of attention to their military organizations. This is true of states that are politically isolated.

Israel is a good current example: military leaders retire to become key political leaders, and politicians are generally well versed in military matters. This sort of attention is also characteristic of both poles in a bipolar system. Since the dawn of the Cold War American leaders have paid more attention to military matters than in any prior period of our history.

Examples of military innovation caused by civilian intervention and stimulated by political isolation are the development of the standing army in France under Louis XIV and the mass army during the French Revolution. Recall the important role played by Cardinal Richelieu and the civilian war minister Michel Le Tellier in the development of France's first all-professional, standing army. What had driven France in this direction? Historian Michael Howard writes, "On the death of Gustavus, . . . Richelieu saw himself faced with the necessity of improvising an army and entering the field himself if Habsburg power, Spanish and Austrian, was not to become dominant in Europe." Le Tellier's son, the Marquis de Louvois, completed his father's work, creating the army with which Louis XIV waged war on nearly all of Europe.

The case of Revolutionary France is similar. The Directory had accumulated six major adversaries, and by August 23, 1793, the danger had become so great that the Committee on Public Safety ordered universal conscription for the first time in any modern European state. By the following summer, the French army fielded three-quarters of a million men, the largest armed force in Europe since the barbarian invasions. The Committee did not simply invent the mass army. Lazare Carnot, a former military professional and a man with new ideas about military organizations and tactics, had joined the Revolution. It was his hand that guided French military innovation.

While political isolation provides an added spur to civilian intervention, even states with alliance possibilities show tendencies to civilian intervention in the face of new or growing threats. The best example of this is found in British behavior in 1934–1940. The rising military power of Germany brought not only a return to substantial defense spending, but greater civilian attention to the plans of the military. In spite of a military organization committed to an offensive doctrine, civilians intervened to promote a major defensive innovation—the development of the country's integrated air defense system, the first of its kind in history. . . . While the RAF did not wholeheartedly embrace air defense, and jealously guarded Bomber Command, that organization's support for air defense increased as the possibility of war loomed larger.

5. Disasters fresh in a state's memory are great promoters of civilian intervention, even if no immediate threat appears on the

horizon. (This proposition and those that follow have their counterparts at the organizational level.) If a threat is apparent, the tendency will be more pronounced. The most recent example is the apparently very thorough review by Israel's Agranat Commission of all the events leading up to and including the 1973 war. While the Commission included two former chiefs of staff, the chairman and the other two members were civilians. Most of the report remains secret, but it is known to have generated wide-ranging reform in Israel's armed forces.

Another example is found in the case of Prussia. Between October 7 and November 7, 1806, Napoleon Bonaparte completely destroyed the armies of the heirs of Frederick the Great. The "army with a country" was swept aside by the superior numbers and methods of the French. Following this disaster, both civilian and military reformers came to the fore. Before the war, reforms of either bureaucracy or army were practically impossible. After the war, under the leadership of the soldiers Gerhard Scharnhorst and Count August Gneisenau, a commission was set up to reform the army. Opposition was not wanting, and in fact was suppressed only by the direct intervention of the king, who removed the opponents of reform from the commission.

6. Some civilian intervention is produced not by disaster but by the high costs expected of a particular military exercise. A victorious but very costly war can substantially weaken a state. Even in the context of a superiority that provided some damage-limiting capability, U.S. civilian policy-makers in the 1950s watched their nuclear forces more closely than they had ever watched military forces before. Though the United States might have "prevailed" in a nuclear conflict, the game was not likely to be worth the candle. . . .

The experience or expectation of military disaster provides a key avenue by which technology can influence military doctrine. Civilians especially are moved to interpret new technology and integrate such interpretations into military doctrine when the technology presents some very clear and unambiguous threat to the state's survival. The threat may be of defeat or the probability of high collateral damage. Civilian intervention is unlikely unless demonstration of the technology, by test or combat-use, is sufficiently stark and frightening to shake civilians' faith in the ability of their own military organizations to handle it. The attitudes of French civilians to any chance of a replay of World War I, British civilians to the spectre of bombs falling on London, and American civilians to nuclear weapons are all good examples. Even here, though, the impact of technology is not determinative. In the French case technology was seen to be largely immutable, a force to be accepted and dealt with. In the British case, technology was seen as something to be changed.

Simple fear of defeat provides another motivation for civilian intervention. If an adversary appears particularly impressive, potentially capable of a decisive victory, civilians will pay considerable attention to their military instrument. The intervention of British civilians into the doctrine of the RAF, for instance, was driven by fear of the German "knock-out-blow-from-the-air."

Summary: Balance of Power Theory Hypotheses

Offense, Defense, and Deterrence

In general, the theory predicts heterogeneity along the dimension offense-defense-deterrence.

1. Expansionist powers will prefer offensive doctrines.

2. States will prefer offensive doctrines when war appears to involve very high collateral damage, because offense allows the state to take the war somewhere else.

3. States with a favorable power position that is suffering erosion will prefer offensive doctrines. (Offensive doctrines are a vehicle for preventive war.)

4. States that face several adversaries may prefer offensive doctrines. (Again, offensive doctrines are the vehicle for preventive war.)

5. Similarly, geographically encircled states may prefer offensive doctrines.

6. States without allies will prefer offensive doctrines because they must exploit military power for diplomacy, a purpose best served by offensive capabilities.

7. States with widely distributed security dependencies will prefer offensive doctrines because they allow the concentration of scarce military assets.

8. States with far-flung security dependencies will accept deterrent doctrines when it is not feasible to sustain offensive or defensive doctrines. Deterrent doctrines are a vehicle for throwing political will into the military balance.

9. Similarly, small states may opt for deterrent doctrines because their capabilities are insufficient to support any other kind.

10. The possibility of coalition warfare can lead a state to a defensive doctrine because such doctrines permit a pace of warfare that allows allies to settle the division of the risks, costs, and benefits of war.

11. States preparing to fight in coalitions must also please their prospective coalition partners. This dilutes the power of proposition

10. If, for its own special reasons, a state adopts an offensive doctrine, its suitors may find it necessary to conform. By the same token, however, conformity to a defensive doctrine is likely if the state being wooed adopts a defensive doctrine.

12. Status quo states will generally prefer defensive doctrines if geography or technology makes such doctrines attractive.

13. Status quo states may prefer defensive doctrines simply because they know that they are unlikely to strike first.

Integration and Innovation

1. Statesmen contemplating aggression will tend to intervene in their military organizations.

2. Generally, anything that increases the perceived threat to state security is a cause of civilian intervention in military matters and hence a possible cause of integration and innovation.

3. Soldiers themselves tend to be more amenable to external prodding when the threat of war looms larger.

4. In states that are either politically isolated or geographically surrounded, civilians tend to intervene in military matters more frequently, and soldiers tend to approach war more seriously than in states with more favorable security conditions. Thus, both integration and innovation should be more frequent in such states.

5. Recent military disasters can be causes of integration and innovation.

6. Anticipated high costs of warfare can be a cause of civilian intervention. Because new technology (e.g., nuclear weapons) can greatly affect anticipated costs, this is one way technology can exert an influence on integration and innovation.

All of the preceding possible causes can be weakened in multipolar systems, where allies appear to be easy to come by. States and statesmen may spend too much time chasing allies, and not enough time auditing their war machines.

SUMMARY

In this chapter I have offered brief surveys of organization theory and balance of power theory, and from these theories I have inferred hypotheses about what causes military doctrine to vary along the dimensions offense-defense-deterrence, innovation-stagnation, and integration-disintegration. I have integrated with these hypotheses a small group of propositions that concern the influence of technology and geography upon military doctrine. Most of these propositions are consistent with one or the other of the two theories introduced.

As argued in the opening pages of this chapter, these are structural theories. They are appropriate for the examination of the cases that follow. These theories will be used in combination to explain the military doctrines of France, Britain, and Germany. Because in some of the cases contradictory hypotheses about doctrine are generated by the two theories, a comparison of these military doctrines allows us to examine and weigh the explanatory power of each theory.

In the broadest sense military doctrine should, according to *organization theory,* show a tendency to be offensive, disintegrated, and stagnant. This is suggested both by the character of military organizations and by their functional separation from the political decision-makers of the state. *Balance of power theory* predicts somewhat different outcomes, depending on the state's situation. In general, anything that makes the civilian leaders of a state more fearful should encourage political-military integration and operational innovation. Civilian preferences for offense, defense, or deterrence will be influenced by the international environment. Finally, if the two theories introduced here have any validity at all, we should find that *technology* and *geography* are rarely determinative in their own right, although they should often have an important effect on doctrine.

Under what conditions will organization theory enjoy its greatest explanatory power? Under what conditions will the international environment have the greatest influence? In times of relative international calm we should expect a high degree of organizational determinism. In times of threat we should see greater accommodation of doctrine to the international system—integration should be more pronounced, innovation more likely. Among states, doctrines should show more heterogeneity. However, even under such circumstances all will not necessarily be well. Multipolar structures, although they exert an important influence on doctrine, may so confuse decisionmakers as to allow organizational determinants to come to the fore once again. The effects can be disastrous.

Cooperation Under The
Security Dilemma

ROBERT JERVIS

I. ANARCHY AND THE SECURITY DILEMMA

The lack of an international sovereign not only permits wars to occur, but also makes it difficult for states that are satisfied with the
status quo to arrive at goals that they recognize as being in their common interest. Because there are no institutions or authorities that can
make and enforce international laws, the policies of cooperation that
will bring mutual rewards if others cooperate may bring disaster if
they do not. Because states are aware of this, anarchy encourages
behavior that leaves all concerned worse off than they could be, even
in the extreme case in which all states would like to freeze the status
quo. This is true of the men in Rousseau's "Stag Hunt." If they
cooperate to trap the stag, they will all eat well. But if one person
defects to chase a rabbit—which he likes less than stag—none of the
others will get anything. Thus, all actors have the same preference
order, and there is a solution that gives each his first choice: (1)
cooperate and trap the stag (the international analogue being cooperation and disarmament); (2) chase a rabbit while others remain at their
posts (maintain a high level of arms while others are disarmed); (3) all
chase rabbits (arms competition and high risk of war); and (4) stay at
the original position while another chases a rabbit (being disarmed
while others are armed).[1] Unless each person thinks that the others
will cooperate, he himself will not. And why might he fear that any
other person would do something that would sacrifice his own first
choice? The other might not understand the situation, or might not be
able to control his impulses if he saw a rabbit, or might fear that some

From "Cooperation Under the Security Dilemma," *World Politics,* Vol. 30, no. 2
(January 78). Copyright © 1978 by Princeton University Press. Excerpts, pp. 167–
170, 186–214. Reprinted by permission of Johns Hopkins University Press.
   * I am grateful to Robert Art, Bernard Brodie, and Glenn Snyder for comments,
and to the Committee on Research of the UCLA Academic Senate for financial
support. An earlier version of this essay appeared as Working Paper No. 5, UCLA
Program in Arms Control and International Security.
   [1] This kind of rank-ordering is not entirely an analyst's invention, as is shown by
the following section of a British army memo of 1903 dealing with British and Russian
railroad construction near the Persia-Afghanistan border:

other member of the group is unreliable. If the person voices any of these suspicions, others are more likely to fear that he will defect, thus making them more likely to defect, thus making it more rational for him to defect. Of course in this simple case—and in many that are more realistic—there are a number of arrangements that could permit cooperation. But the main point remains: although actors may know that they seek a common goal, they may not be able to reach it.

Even when there is a solution that is everyone's first choice, the international case is characterized by three difficulties not present in the Stag Hunt. First, to the incentives to defect given above must be added the potent fear that even if the other state now supports the status quo, it may become dissatisfied later. No matter how much decision makers are committed to the status quo, they cannot bind themselves and their successors to the same path. Minds can be changed, new leaders can come to power, values can shift, new opportunities and dangers can arise.

The second problem arises from a possible solution. In order to protect their possessions, states often seek to control resources or land outside their own territory. Countries that are not self-sufficient must try to assure that the necessary supplies will continue to flow in wartime. This was part of the explanation for Japan's drive into China and Southeast Asia before World War II. If there were an international authority that could guarantee access, this motive for control would disappear. But since there is not, even a state that would prefer the status quo to increasing its area of control may pursue the latter policy.

When there are believed to be tight linkages between domestic and foreign policy or between the domestic politics of two states, the quest for security may drive states to interfere pre-emptively in the domestic politics of others in order to provide an ideological buffer zone. Thus, Metternich's justification for supervising the politics of the Italian states has been summarized as follows:

The conditions of the problem may . . . be briefly summarized as follows:

a) If we make a railway to Seistan while Russia remains inactive, we gain a considerable defensive advantage at considerable financial cost;

b) If Russia makes a railway to Seistan, while we remain inactive, she gains a considerable offensive advantage at considerable financial cost;

c) If both we and Russia make railways to Seistan, the defensive and offensive advantages may be held to neutralize each other; in other words, we shall have spent a good deal of money and be no better off than we are at present. On the other hand, we shall be no worse off, whereas under alternative (b) we shall be much worse off. Consequently, the theoretical balance of advantage lies with the proposed railway extension from Quetta to Seistan.

W. G. Nicholson, "Memorandum on Seistan and Other Points Raised in the Discussion on the Defence of India," (Committee of Imperial Defence, March 20, 1903). It should be noted that the possibility of neither side building railways was not mentioned, thus strongly biasing the analysis.

Every state is absolutely sovereign in its internal affairs But this implies that every state must do nothing to interfere in the internal affairs of any other. However, any false or pernicious step taken by any state in its internal affairs may disturb the repose of another state, and this consequent disturbance of another state's repose constitutes an interference in that state's internal affairs. Therefore, every state—or rather, every sovereign of a great power—has the duty, in the name of the sacred right of independence of every state, to supervise the governments of smaller states and to prevent them from taking false and pernicious steps in their internal affairs.[2]

More frequently, the concern is with direct attack. In order to protect themselves, states seek to control, or at least to neutralize, areas on their borders. But attempts to establish buffer zones can alarm others who have stakes there, who fear that undesirable precedents will be set, or who believe that their own vulnerability will be increased. When buffers are sought in areas empty of great powers, expansion tends to feed on itself in order to protect what is acquired, as was often noted by those who opposed colonial expansion. Balfour's complaint was typical: "Every time I come to a discussion—at intervals of, say, five years—I find there is a new sphere which we have got to guard, which is supposed to protect the gateways of India. Those gateways are getting further and further away from India, and I do not know how far west they are going to be brought by the General Staff."[3]

Though this process is most clearly visible when it involves territorial expansion, it often operates with the increase of less tangible power and influence. The expansion of power usually brings with it an expansion of responsibilities and commitments; to meet them, still greater power is required. The state will take many positions that are subject to challenge. It will be involved with a wide range of controversial issues unrelated to its core values. And retreats that would be seen as normal if made by a small power would be taken as an index of weakness inviting predation if made by a large one.

The third problem present in international politics but not in the Stag Hunt is the security dilemma: many of the means by which a state tries to increase its security decrease the security of others. In domestic society, there are several ways to increase the safety of one's person and property without endangering others. One can move to a safer neighborhood, put bars on the windows, avoid dark streets, and keep a distance from suspicious-looking characters. Of course these

---

[2] Paul Schroeder, *Metternich's Diplomacy at Its Zenith, 1820–1823* (Westport, Conn.: Greenwood Press 1969), 126.

[3] Quoted in Michael Howard, *The Continental Commitment* (Harmondsworth, England: Penguin 1974), 67.

measures are not convenient, cheap, or certain of success. But no one save criminals need be alarmed if a person takes them. In international politics, however, one state's gain in security often inadvertently threatens others. In explaining British policy on naval disarmament in the interwar period to the Japanese, Ramsey MacDonald said that "Nobody wanted Japan to be insecure."[4] But the problem was not with British desires, but with the consequences of her policy. In earlier periods, too, Britain had needed a navy large enough to keep the shipping lanes open. But such a navy could not avoid being a menace to any other state with a coast that could be raided, trade that could be interdicted, or colonies that could be isolated. When Germany started building a powerful navy before World War I, Britain objected that it could only be an offensive weapon aimed at her. As Sir Edward Grey, the Foreign Secretary, put it to King Edward VII: "If the German Fleet ever becomes superior to ours, the German Army can conquer this country. There is no corresponding risk of this kind to Germany; for however superior our Fleet was, no naval victory could bring us any nearer to Berlin." The English position was half correct: Germany's navy was an anti-British instrument. But the British often overlooked what the Germans knew full well: "in every quarrel with England, German colonies and trade were . . . hostages from England to take." Thus, whether she intended it or not, the British Navy constituted an important instrument of coercion. . . .[5]

II. OFFENSE, DEFENSE, AND THE SECURITY DILEMMA

Another approach starts with the central point of the security dilemma—that an increase in one state's security decreases the security of others—and examines the conditions under which this proposition holds. Two crucial variables are involved: whether defensive weapons and policies can be distinguished from offensive ones, and whether the defense or the offense has the advantage. The definitions are not always clear, and many cases are difficult to judge, but these two variables shed a great deal of light on the question of whether status-quo powers will adopt compatible security policies. All the variables discussed so far leave the heart of the problem untouched. But when defensive weapons differ from offensive ones, it is possible for a state

---

[4] Quoted in Gerald Wheeler, *Prelude to Pearl Harbor* (Columbia: University of Missouri Press 1963), 167.

[5] Quoted in Leonard Wainstein, "The Dreadnought Gap," in Robert Art and Kenneth Waltz, eds., *The Use of Force* (Boston: Little, Brown 1971), 155; Raymond Sontag, *European Diplomatic History, 1871-1932* (New York: Appleton-Century-Croits 1933), 147. The French had made a similar argument 50 years earlier; see James Phinney Baxter III, *The Introduction of the Ironclad Warship* (Cambridge: Harvard University Press 1933), 149. For a more detailed discussion of the security dilemma, see Jervis, *Perception and Misperception in International Politics* (Princeton: Princeton University Press 1976), 62-76.

to make itself more secure without making others less secure. And when the defense has the advantage over the offense, a large increase in one state's security only slightly decreases the security of the others, and status-quo powers can all enjoy a high level of security and largely escape from the state of nature.

OFFENSE-DEFENSE BALANCE

When we say that the offense has the advantage, we simply mean that it is easier to destroy the other's army and take its territory than it is to defend one's own. When the defense has the advantage, it is easier to protect and to hold than it is to move forward, destroy, and take. If effective defenses can be erected quickly, an attacker may be able to keep territory he has taken in an initial victory. Thus, the dominance of the defense made it very hard for Britain and France to push Germany out of France in World War I. But when superior defenses are difficult for an aggressor to improvise on the battlefield and must be constructed during peacetime, they provide no direct assistance to him.

The security dilemma is at its most vicious when commitments, strategy, or technology dictate that the only route to security lies through expansion. Status-quo powers must then act like aggressors; the fact that they would gladly agree to forego the opportunity for expansion in return for guarantees for their security has no implications for their behavior. Even if expansion is not sought as a goal in itself, there will be quick and drastic changes in the distribution of territory and influence. Conversely, when the defense has the advantage, status-quo states can make themselves more secure without gravely endangering others.[6] Indeed, if the defense has enough of an advantage and if the states are of roughly equal size, not only will the security dilemma cease to inhibit status-quo states from cooperating, but aggression will be next to impossible, thus rendering international anarchy relatively unimportant. If states cannot conquer each other, then the lack of sovereignty, although it presents problems of collective goods in a number of areas, no longer forces states to devote their primary attention to self-preservation. Although, if force were not usable, there would be fewer restraints on the use of nonmilitary instruments, these are rarely powerful enough to threaten the vital interests of a major state.

Two questions of the offense-defense balance can be separated. First, does the state have to spend more or less than one dollar on defensive forces to offset each dollar spent by the other side on forces

---

[6] Thus, when Wolfers (fn. 10) 126, argues that a status-quo state that settles for rough equality of power with its adversary, rather than seeking preponderance, may be able to convince the other to reciprocate by showing that it wants only to protect itself, not menace the other, he assumes that the defense has an advantage.

that could be used to attack? If the state has one dollar to spend on increasing its security, should it put it into offensive or defensive forces? Second, with a given inventory of forces, is it better to attack or to defend? Is there an incentive to strike first or to absorb the other's blow? These two aspects are often linked: if each dollar spent on offense can overcome each dollar spent on defense, and if both sides have the same defense budgets, then both are likely to build offensive forces and find it attractive to attack rather than to wait for the adversary to strike.

These aspects affect the security dilemma in different ways. The first has its greatest impact on arms races. If the defense has the advantage, and if the status-quo powers have reasonable subjective security requirements, they can probably avoid an arms race. Although an increase in one side's arms and security will still decrease the other's security, the former's increase will be larger than the latter's decrease. So if one side increases its arms, the other can bring its security back up to its previous level by adding a smaller amount to its forces. And if the first side reacts to this change, its increase will also be smaller than the stimulus that produced it. Thus a stable equilibrium will be reached. Shifting from dynamics to statics, each side can be quite secure with forces roughly equal to those of the other. Indeed, if the defense is much more potent than the offense, each side can be willing to have forces much smaller than the other's, and can be indifferent to a wide range of the other's defense policies.

The second aspect—whether it is better to attack or to defend—influences short-run stability. When the offense has the advantage, a state's reaction to international tension will increase the chances of war. The incentives for pre-emption and the "reciprocal fear of surprise attack" in this situation have been made clear by analyses of the dangers that exist when two countries have first-strike capabilities.[7] There is no way for the state to increase its security without menacing, or even attacking, the other. Even Bismarck, who once called preventive war "committing suicide from fear of death," said that "no government, if it regards war as inevitable even if it does not want it, would be so foolish as to leave to the enemy the choice of time and occasion and to wait for the moment which is most convenient for the enemy."[8] In another arena, the same dilemma applies to the policeman in a dark alley confronting a suspected criminal who appears to be holding a weapon. Though racism may indeed be present, the security dilemma can account for many of the tragic shootings of innocent people in the ghettos.

[7] Schelling (fn. 20), chap. 9.
[8] Quoted in Fritz Fischer, *War of Illusions* (New York: Norton 1975), 377, 461.

Beliefs about the course of a war in which the offense has the advantage further deepen the security dilemma. When there are incentives to strike first, a successful attack will usually so weaken the other side that victory will be relatively quick, bloodless, and decisive. It is in these periods when conquest is possible and attractive that states consolidate power internally—for instance, by destroying the feudal barons—and expand externally. There are several consequences that decrease the chance of cooperation among status-quo states. First, war will be profitable for the winner. The costs will be low and the benefits high. Of course, losers will suffer; the fear of losing could induce states to try to form stable cooperative arrangements, but the temptation of victory will make this particularly difficult. Second, because wars are expected to be both frequent and short, there will be incentives for high levels of arms, and quick and strong reaction to the other's increases in arms. The state cannot afford to wait until there is unambiguous evidence that the other is building new weapons. Even large states that have faith in their economic strength cannot wait, because the war will be over before their products can reach the army. Third, when wars are quick, states will have to recruit allies in advance.[9] Without the opportunity for bargaining and re-alignments during the opening stages of hostilities, peacetime diplomacy loses a degree of the fluidity that facilitates balance-of-power policies. Because alliances must be secured during peacetime, the international system is more likely to become bipolar. It is hard to say whether war therefore becomes more or less likely, but this bipolarity increases tension between the two camps and makes it harder for status-quo states to gain the benefits of cooperation. Fourth, if wars are frequent, statesmen's perceptual thresholds will be adjusted accordingly and they will be quick to perceive ambiguous evidence as indicating that others are aggressive. Thus, there will be more cases of status-quo powers arming against each other in the incorrect belief that the other is hostile.

When the defense has the advantage, all the foregoing is reversed. The state that fears attack does not pre-empt—since that would be a wasteful use of its military resources—but rather prepares to receive an attack. Doing so does not decrease the security of others, and several states can do it simultaneously; the situation will therefore be stable, and status-quo powers will be able to cooperate. When Herman Kahn argues that ultimatums "are vastly too dangerous to give because . . . they are quite likely to touch off a pre-emptive strike,"[10] he incorrectly assumes that it is always advantageous to strike first.

[9] George Quester, *Offense and Defense in the International System* (New York: John Wiley 1977), 105–06; Sontag (fn. 5), 4–5.
[10] Kahn (fn. 23), 211 (also see 144).

More is involved than short-run dynamics. When the defense is dominant, wars are likely to become stalemates and can be won only at enormous cost. Relatively small and weak states can hold off larger and stronger ones, or can deter attack by raising the costs of conquest to an unacceptable level. States then approach equality in what they can do to each other. Like the .45-caliber pistol in the American West, fortifications were the "great equalizer" in some periods. Changes in the status quo are less frequent and cooperation is more common wherever the security dilemma is thereby reduced.

Many of these arguments can be illustrated by the major powers' policies in the periods preceding the two world wars. Bismarck's wars surprised statesmen by showing that the offense had the advantage, and by being quick, relatively cheap, and quite decisive. Falling into a common error, observers projected this pattern into the future.[11] The resulting expectations had several effects. First, states sought semipermanent allies. In the early stages of the Franco-Prussian War, Napoleon III had thought that there would be plenty of time to recruit Austria to his side. Now, others were not going to repeat this mistake. Second, defense budgets were high and reacted quite sharply to increases on the other side. It is not surprising that Richardson's theory of arms races fits this period well. Third, most decision makers thought that the next European war would not cost much blood and treasure.[12] That is one reason why war was generally seen as inevitable and why mass opinion was so bellicose. Fourth, once war seemed likely, there were strong pressures to pre-empt. Both sides believed that whoever moved first could penetrate the other deep enough to disrupt mobilization and thus gain an insurmountable advantage. (There was no such belief about the use of naval forces. Although Churchill made an ill-advised speech saying that if German ships "do not come out and fight in time of war they will be dug out like rats in a hole,"[13] everyone knew that submarines, mines, and coastal fortifications made this impossible. So at the start of the war each navy prepared to

[11] For a general discussion of such mistaken learning from the past, see Jervis (fn. 5), chap. 6. The important and still not completely understood question of why this belief formed and was maintained throughout the war is examined in Bernard Brodie, *War and Politics* (New York: Macmillan 1973), 262–70; Brodie, "Technological Change, Strategic Doctrine, and Political Outcomes," in Klaus Knorr, ed., *Historical Dimensions of National Security Problems* (Lawrence: University Press of Kansas 1976), 290–92; and Douglas Porch, "The French Army and the Spirit of the Offensive, 1900–14," in Brian Bond and Ian Roy, eds,. *War and Society* (New York: Holmes & Meier 1975), 117–43.

[12] Some were not so optimistic. Gray's remark is well-known: "The lamps are going out all over Europe; we shall not see them lit again in our life-time." The German Prime Minister, Bethmann Hollweg, also feared the consequences of the war. But the controlling view was that it would certainly pay for the winner.

[13] Quoted in Martin Gilbert, *Winston S. Churchill, III, The Challenge of War, 1914–1916* (Boston: Houghton Mifflin 1971), 84.

defend itself rather than attack, and the short-run destabilizing forces that launched the armies toward each other did not operate.)[14] Furthermore, each side knew that the other saw the situation the same way, thus increasing the perceived danger that the other would attack, and giving each added reasons to precipitate a war if conditions seemed favorable. In the long and the short run, there were thus both offensive and defensive incentives to strike. This situation casts light on the common question about German motives in 1914: "Did Germany unleash the war deliberately to become a world power or did she support Austria merely to defend a weakening ally," thereby protecting her own position?[15] To some extent, this question is misleading. Because of the perceived advantage of the offense, war was seen as the best route both to gaining expansion and to avoiding drastic loss of influence. There seemed to be no way for Germany merely to retain and safeguard her existing position.

Of course the war showed these beliefs to have been wrong on all points. Trenches and machine guns gave the defense an overwhelming advantage. The fighting became deadlocked and produced horrendous casualties. It made no sense for the combatants to bleed themselves to death. If they had known the power of the defense beforehand, they would have rushed for their own trenches rather than for the enemy's territory. Each side could have done this without increasing the other's incentives to strike. War might have broken out anyway, just as DD is a possible outcome of Chicken, but at least the pressures of time and the fear of allowing the other to get the first blow would not have contributed to this end. And, had both sides known the costs of the war, they would have negotiated much more seriously. The obvious question is why the states did not seek a negotiated settlement as soon as the shape of the war became clear. Schlieffen had said that if his plan failed, peace should be sought.[16] The answer is complex, uncertain, and largely outside of the scope of our concerns. But part of the reason was the hope and sometimes the expectation that breakthroughs could be made and the dominance of the offensive restored. Without that hope, the political and psychological pressures to fight to a decisive victory might have been overcome.

The politics of the interwar period were shaped by the memories of the previous conflict and the belief that any future war would resemble it. Political and military lessons reinforced each other in ameliorating the security dilemma. Because it was believed that the First World War had been a mistake that could have been avoided by

---

[14] Quester (fn. 33), 98–99. Robert Art, *The Influence of Foreign Policy on Seapower*, II (Beverly Hills: Sage Professional Papers in International Studies Series, 1973), 14–18, 26–28.

[15] Konrad Jarausch, "The Illusion of Limited War: Chancellor Bethmann Hollweg's Calculated Risk, July 1914," *Central European History, II* (March 1969), 50.

[16] Brodie (fn. 8), 58.

skillful conciliation, both Britain and, to a lesser extent, France were highly sensitive to the possibility that interwar Germany was not a real threat to peace, and alert to the danger that reacting quickly and strongly to her arms could create unnecessary conflict. And because Britain and France expected the defense to continue to dominate, they concluded that it was safe to adopt a more relaxed and nonthreatening military posture.[17] Britain also felt less need to maintain tight alliance bonds. The Allies' military posture then constituted only a slight danger to Germany; had the latter been content with the status quo, it would have been easy for both sides to have felt secure behind their lines of fortifications. Of course the Germans were not content, so it is not surprising that they devoted their money and attention to finding ways out of a defense-dominated stalemate. *Blitzkrieg* tactics were necessary if they were to use force to change the status quo.

The initial stages of the war on the Western Front also contrasted with the First World War. Only with the new air arm were there any incentives to strike first, and these forces were too weak to carry out the grandiose plans that had been both dreamed and feared. The armies, still the main instrument, rushed to defensive positions. Perhaps the allies could have successfully attacked while the Germans were occupied in Poland.[18] But belief in the defense was so great that this was never seriously contemplated. Three months after the start of the war, the French Prime Minister summed up the view held by almost everyone but Hitler: on the Western Front there is "deadlock. Two Forces of equal strength and the one that attacks seeing such enormous casualties that it cannot move without endangering the continuation of the war or of the aftermath."[19] The Allies were caught in a dilemma they never fully recognized, let alone solved. On the one hand, they had very high war aims; although unconditional surrender had not yet been adopted, the British had decided from the start that the removal of Hitler was a necessary condition for peace.[20] On the other hand, there were no realistic plans or instruments for allowing the Allies to

---

[17] President Roosevelt and the American delegates to the League of Nations Disarmament Conference maintained that the tank and mobile heavy artillery had reestablished the dominance of the offensive, thus making disarmament more urgent (Boggs, fn. 28, pp. 31, 108), but this was a minority position and may not even have been believed by the Americans. The reduced prestige and influence of the military, and the high pressures to cut government spending throughout this period also contributed to the lowering of defense budgets.

[18] Jon Kimche, *The Unfought Battle* (New York: Stein 1968); Nicholas William Bethell, *The War Hitler Won: The Fall of Poland, September 1939* (New York: Holt 1972); Alan Alexandroff and Richard Rosecrance, "Deterrence in 1939," *World Politics*, XXIX (April 1977), 404–24.

[19] Roderick Macleod and Denis Kelly, eds., *Time Unguarded: The Ironside Diaries, 1937–1940* (New York: McKay 1962), 173.

[20] For a short time, as France was falling, the British Cabinet did discuss reaching a negotiated peace with Hitler. The official history ignores this, but it is covered in P. M. H. Bell, *A Certain Eventuality* (Farnborough, England: Saxon House 1974), 40–48.

impose their will on the other side. The British Chief of the Imperial General Staff noted, "The French have no intention of carrying out an offensive for years, if at all"; the British were only slightly bolder.[21] So the Allies looked to a long war that would wear the Germans down, cause civilian suffering through shortages, and eventually undermine Hitler. There was little analysis to support this view—and indeed it probably was not supportable—but as long as the defense was dominant and the numbers on each side relatively equal, what else could the Allies do?

To summarize, the security dilemma was much less powerful after World War I than it had been before. In the later period, the expected power of the defense allowed status-quo states to pursue compatible security policies and avoid arms races. Furthermore, high tension and fear of war did not set off short-run dynamics by which each state, trying to increase its security, inadvertently acted to make war more likely. The expected high costs of war, however, led the Allies to believe that no sane German leader would run the risks entailed in an attempt to dominate the Continent, and discouraged them from risking war themselves.

Technology and Geography. Technology and geography are the two main factors that determine whether the offense or the defense has the advantage. As Brodie notes, "On the tactical level, as a rule, few physical factors favor the attacker but many favor the defender. The defender usually has the advantage of cover. He characteristically fires from behind some form of shelter while his opponent crosses open ground."[22] Anything that increases the amount of ground the attacker has to cross, or impedes his progress across it, or makes him more vulnerable while crossing, increases the advantage accruing to the defense. When states are separated by barriers that produce these effects, the security dilemma is eased, since both can have forces adequate for defense without being able to attack. Impenetrable barriers would actually prevent war; in reality, decision makers have to settle for a good deal less. Buffer zones slow the attacker's progress; they thereby give the defender time to prepare, increase problems of logistics, and reduce the number of soldiers available for the final assault. At the end of the 19th century, Arthur Balfour noted Afghanistan's "non-conducting" qualities. "So long as it possesses

---

[21] Macleod and Kelly (fn. 43), 174. In flat contradiction to common sense and almost everything they believed about modern warfare, the Allies planned an expedition to Scandinavia to cut the supply of iron ore to Germany and to aid Finland against the Russians. But the dominant mood was the one described above.

[22] Brodie (fn. 8), 179.

few roads, and no railroads, it will be impossible for Russia to make effective use of her great numerical superiority at any point immediately vital to the Empire." The Russians valued buffers for the same reasons; it is not surprising that when Persia was being divided into Russian and British spheres of influence some years later, the Russians sought assurances that the British would refrain from building potentially menacing railroads in their sphere. Indeed, since railroad construction radically altered the abilities of countries to defend themselves and to attack others, many diplomatic notes and much intelligence activity in the late 19th century centered on this subject.[23]

Oceans, large rivers, and mountain ranges serve the same function as buffer zones. Being hard to cross, they allow defense against superior numbers. The defender has merely to stay on his side of the barrier and so can utilize all the men he can bring up to it. The attacker's men, however, can cross only a few at a time, and they are very vulnerable when doing so. If all states were self-sufficient islands, anarchy would be much less of a problem. A small investment in shore defenses and a small army would be sufficient to repel invasion. Only very weak states would be vulnerable, and only very large ones could menace others. As noted above, the United States, and to a lesser extent Great Britain, have partly been able to escape from the state of nature because their geographical positions approximated this ideal.

Although geography cannot be changed to conform to borders, borders can and do change to conform to geography. Borders across which an attack is easy tend to be unstable. States living within them are likely to expand or be absorbed. Frequent wars are almost inevitable since attacking will often seem the best way to protect what one has. This process will stop, or at least slow down, when the state's borders reach—by expansion or contraction—a line of natural obstacles. Security without attack will then be possible. Furthermore, these lines constitute salient solutions to bargaining problems and, to the extent that they are barriers to migration, are likely to divide ethnic groups, thereby raising the costs and lowering the incentives for conquest.

Attachment to one's state and its land reinforce one quasi-geographical aid to the defense. Conquest usually becomes more difficult the deeper the attacker pushes into the other's territory. Nationalism spurs the defenders to fight harder; advancing not only

---

[23] Arthur Balfour, "Memorandum," Committee on Imperial Defence, April 30, 1903, pp. 2-3; see the telegrams by Sir Arthur Nicolson, in G. P. Gooch and Harold Temperley, eds., *British Documents on the Origins of the War*, Vol. 4 (London: H.M.S.O. 1929), 429, 524. These barriers do not prevent the passage of long-range aircraft; but even in the air, distance usually aids the defender.

lengthens the attacker's supply lines, but takes him through un-familiar and often devastated lands that require troops for garrison duty. These stabilizing dynamics will not operate, however, if the defender's war materiel is situated near its borders, or if the people do not care about their state, but only about being on the winning side. In such cases, positive feedback will be at work and initial defeats will be insurmountable.[24]

Imitating geography, men have tried to create barriers. Treaties may provide for demilitarized zones on both sides of the border, although such zones will rarely be deep enough to provide more than warning. Even this was not possible in Europe, but the Russians adopted a gauge for their railroads that was broader than that of the neighboring states, thereby complicating the logistics problems of any attacker—including Russia.

Perhaps the most ambitious and at least temporarily successful at-tempts to construct a system that would aid the defenses of both sides were the interwar naval treaties, as they affected Japanese-American relations. As mentioned earlier, the problem was that the United States could not defend the Philippines without denying Japan the ability to protect her home islands.[25] (In 1941 this dilemma became in-soluble when Japan sought to extend her control to Malaya and the Dutch East Indies. If the Philippines had been invulnerable, they could have provided a secure base from which the U.S. could interdict Japanese shipping between the homeland and the areas she was trying to conquer.) In the 1920's and early 1930's each side would have been willing to grant the other security for its possessions in return for a reciprocal grant, and the Washington Naval Conference agreements were designed to approach this goal. As a Japanese diplomat later put it, their country's "fundamental principle" was to have "a strength insufficient for attack and adequate for defense."[26] Thus, Japan agreed in 1922 to accept a navy only three-fifths as large as that of the United States, and the U.S. agreed not to fortify its Pacific islands.[27] (Japan had earlier been forced to agree not to fortify the islands she had taken from Germany in World War I.) Japan's navy would not be large enough to defeat America's anywhere other than close to the home islands. Although the Japanese could still take the Philippines,

<hr/>

[24] See, for example, the discussion of warfare among Chinese warlords in Hsi-Sheng Chi, "The Chinese Warlord System as an International System," in Morton Kaplan, ed., *New Approaches to International Relations* (New York: St. Martin's 1968), 405–25.

[25] Some American decision makers, including military officers, thought that the best way out of the dilemma was to abandon the Philippines.

[26] Quoted in Elting Morrison, *Turmoil and Tradition: A Study of the Life and Times of Henry L. Stimson* (Boston: Houghton Mifflin 1960), 326.

[27] The U.S. "refused to consider limitations on Hawaiian defenses, since these works posed no threat to Japan." Braisted (fn. 27), 612.

not only would they be unable to move farther, but they might be weakened enough by their efforts to be vulnerable to counterattack. Japan, however, gained security. An American attack was rendered more difficult because the American bases were unprotected and because, until 1930, Japan was allowed unlimited numbers of cruisers, destroyers, and submarines that could weaken the American fleet as it made its way across the ocean.[28]

The other major determinant of the offense-defense balance is technology. When weapons are highly vulnerable, they must be employed before they are attacked. Others can remain quite invulnerable in their bases. The former characteristics are embodied in unprotected missiles and many kinds of bombers. (It should be noted that it is not vulnerability *per se* that is crucial, but the location of the vulnerability. Bombers and missiles that are easy to destroy only after having been launched toward their targets do not create destabilizing dynamics.) Incentives to strike first are usually absent for naval forces that are threatened by a naval attack. Like missiles in hardened silos, they are usually well protected when in their bases. Both sides can then simultaneously be prepared to defend themselves successfully.

In ground warfare under some conditions, forts, trenches, and small groups of men in prepared positions can hold off large numbers of attackers. Less frequently, a few attackers can storm the defenses. By and large, it is a contest between fortifications and supporting light weapons on the one hand, and mobility and heavier weapons that clear the way for the attack on the other. As the erroneous views held before the two world wars show, there is no simple way to determine which is dominant. "[T]hese oscillations are not smooth and predictable like those of a swinging pendulum. They are uneven in both extent and time. Some occur in the course of a single battle or campaign, others in the course of a war, still others during a series of wars." Longer-term oscillations can also be detected:

> The early Gothic age, from the twelfth to the late thirteenth century, with its wonderful cathedrals and fortified places, was a period during which the attackers in Europe generally met serious and increasing difficulties, because the improvement in the strength of fortresses outran the advance in the power of destruction. Later, with the spread of firearms at the end of the fifteenth century, old fortresses lost their power to resist. An age ensued during which the offense possessed, apart from short-term setbacks, new advantages. Then, during the seventeenth century, especially after about 1660, and until at least at the outbreak of the War of the Austrian Succession in 1740, the defense regained much of the ground it had lost

---

[28] That is part of the reason why the Japanese admirals strongly objected when the civilian leaders decided to accept a seven-to-ten ratio in lighter craft in 1930. Stephen Pelz, *Race to Pearl Harbor* (Cambridge: Harvard University Press 1974), 3.

since the great medieval fortresses had proved unable to meet the bombardment of the new and more numerous artillery.[29]

Another scholar has continued the agrument: "The offensive gained an advantage with new forms of heavy mobile artillery in the nineteenth century, but the stalemate of World War I created the impression that the defense again had an advantage; the German invasion in World War II, however, indicated the offensive superiority of highly mechanized armies in the field."[30]

The situation today with respect to conventional weapons is unclear. Until recently it was believed that tanks and tactical air power gave the attacker an advantage. The initial analyses of the 1973 Arab-Israeli war indicated that new anti-tank and anti-aircraft weapons have restored the primacy of the defense. These weapons are cheap, easy to use, and can destroy a high proportion of the attacking vehicles and planes that are sighted. It then would make sense for a status-quo power to buy lots of $20,000 missiles rather than buy a few half-million dollar tanks and multi-million dollar fighter-bombers. Defense would be possible even against a large and well-equipped force; states that care primarily about self-protection would not need to engage in arms races. But further examinations of the new technologies and the history of the October War cast doubt on these optimistic conclusions and leave us unable to render any firm judgment.[31]

Concerning nuclear weapons, it is generally agreed that defense is impossible—a triumph not of the offense, but of deterrence. Attack makes no sense, not because it can be beaten off, but because the attacker will be destroyed in turn. In terms of the questions under consideration here, the result is the equivalent of the primacy of the defense. First, security is relatively cheap. Less than one percent of the G.N.P. is devoted to deterring a direct attack on the United States; most of it is spent on acquiring redundant systems to provide a lot of insurance against the worst conceivable contingencies. Second, both sides can simultaneously gain security in the form of second-strike

[29] John Nef, *War and Human Progress* (New York: Norton 1963), 185. Also see *ibid.*, 237, 242–43, and 323; C. W. Oman, *The Art of War in the Middle Ages* (Ithaca, N.Y.: Cornell University Press 1953), 70–72; John Beeler, *Warfare in Feudal Europe, 730–1200* (Ithaca, N.Y.: Cornell University Press 1971), 212–14; Michael Howard, *War in European History* (London: Oxford University Press 1976), 33–37.

[30] Quincy Wright, *A Study of War* (abridged ed.; Chicago: University of Chicago Press 1964), 142. Also see 63–70, 74–75. There are important exceptions to these generalizations—the American Civil War, for instance, falls in the middle of the period Wright says is dominated by the offense.

[31] Geoffrey Kemp, Robert Pfaltzgraff, and Uri Ra'anan, eds., *The Other Arms Race* (Lexington, Mass.: D. C. Heath 1975); James Foster, "The Future of Conventional Arms Control," *Policy Sciences*, No. 8 (Spring 1977), 1–19.

capability. Third, and related to the foregoing, second-strike capability can be maintained in the face of wide variations in the other side's military posture. There is no purely military reason why each side has to react quickly and strongly to the other's increases in arms. Any spending that the other devotes to trying to achieve first-strike capability can be neutralized by the state's spending much smaller sums on protecting its second-strike capability. Fourth, there are no incentives to strike first in a crisis.

Important problems remain, of course. Both sides have interests that go well beyond defense of the homeland. The protection of these interests creates conflicts even if neither side desires expansion. Furthermore, the shift from defense to deterrence has greatly increased the importance and perceptions of resolve. Security now rests on each side's belief that the other would prefer to run high risks of total destruction rather than sacrifice its vital interests. Aspects of the security dilemma thus appear in a new form. Are weapons procurements used as an index of resolve? Must they be so used? If one side fails to respond to the other's buildup, will it appear weak and thereby invite predation? Can both sides simultaneously have images of high resolve or is there a zero-sum element involved? Although these problems are real, they are not as severe as those in the prenuclear era: there are many indices of resolve, and states do not so much judge images of resolve in the abstract as ask how likely it is that the other will stand firm in a particular dispute. Since states are most likely to stand firm on matters which concern them most, it is quite possible for both to demonstrate their resolve to protect their own security simultaneously.

OFFENSE-DEFENSE DIFFERENTIATION

The other major variable that affects how strongly the security dilemma operates is whether weapons and policies that protect the state also provide the capability for attack. If they do not, the basic postulate of the security dilemma no longer applies. A state can increase its own security without decreasing that of others. The advantage of the defense can only ameliorate the security dilemma. A differentiation between offensive and defensive stances comes close to abolishing it. Such differentiation does not mean, however, that all security problems will be abolished. If the offense has the advantage, conquest and aggression will still be possible. And if the offense's advantage is great enough, status-quo powers may find it too expensive to protect themselves by defensive forces and decide to procure offensive weapons even though this will menace others. Furthermore, states will still have to worry that even if the other's military posture shows that it is peaceful now, it may develop aggressive intentions in the future.

Assuming that the defense is at least as potent as the offense, the differentiation between them allows status-quo states to behave in ways that are clearly different from those of aggressors. Three beneficial consequences follow. First, status-quo powers can identify each other, thus laying the foundations for cooperation. Conflicts growing out of the mistaken belief that the other side is expansionist will be less frequent. Second, status-quo states will obtain advance warning when others plan aggression. Before a state can attack, it has to develop and deploy offensive weapons. If procurement of these weapons cannot be disguised and takes a fair amount of time, as it almost always does, a status-quo state will have the time to take countermeasures. It need not maintain a high level of defensive arms as long as its potential adversaries are adopting a peaceful posture. (Although being so armed should not, with the one important exception noted below, alarm other status-quo powers.) States do, in fact, pay special attention to actions that they believe would not be taken by a status-quo state because they feel that states exhibiting such behavior are aggressive. Thus the seizure or development of transportation facilities will alarm others more if these facilities have no commercial value, and therefore can only be wanted for military reasons. In 1906, the British rejected a Russian protest about their activities in a district of Persia by claiming that this area was "only of [strategic] importance [to the Russians] if they wished to attack the Indian frontier, or to put pressure upon us by making us think that they intend to attack it."[32]

The same inferences are drawn when a state acquires more weapons than observers feel are needed for defense. Thus, the Japanese spokesman at the 1930 London naval conference said that his country was alarmed by the American refusal to give Japan a 70 percent ratio (in place of a 60 percent ratio) in heavy cruisers: "As long as America held that ten percent advantage, it was possible for her to attack. So when America insisted on sixty percent instead of seventy percent, the idea would exist that they were trying to keep that possibility, and the Japanese people could not accept that."[33] Similarly, when Mussolini told Chamberlain in January 1939 that Hitler's arms program was motivated by defensive considerations, the Prime Minister replied that "German military forces were now so strong as to make it impossible for any Power or combination of Powers to attack her successfully.

---

[32] Richard Challener, *Admirals, Generals, and American Foreign Policy, 1898–1914* (Princeton: Princeton University Press 1973), 273; Grey to Nicolson, in Gooch and Temperley (fn. 47), 414.

[33] Quoted in James Crowley, *Japan's Quest for Autonomy* (Princeton: Princeton University Press 1966), 49. American naval officers agreed with the Japanese that a ten-to-six ratio would endanger Japan's supremacy in her home waters.

She could not want any further armaments for defensive purposes; what then did she want them for?"[34]

Of course these inferences can be wrong—as they are especially likely to be because states underestimate the degree to which they menace others.[35] And when they are wrong, the security dilemma is deepened. Because the state thinks it has received notice that the other is aggressive, its own arms building will be less restrained and the chances of cooperation will be decreased. But the dangers of incorrect inferences should not obscure the main point: when offensive and defensive postures are different, much of the uncertainty about the other's intentions that contributes to the security dilemma is removed.

The third beneficial consequence of a difference between offensive and defensive weapons is that if all states support the status quo, an obvious arms control agreement is a ban on weapons that are useful for attacking. As President Roosevelt put it in his message to the Geneva Disarmament Conference in 1933: "If all nations will agree wholly to eliminate from possession and use the weapons which make possible a successful attack, defenses automatically will become impregnable, and the frontiers and independence of every nation will become secure."[36] The fact that such treaties have been rare—the Washington naval agreements discussed above and the anti-ABM treaty can be cited as examples—shows either that states are not always willing to guarantee the security of others, or that it is hard to distinguish offensive from defensive weapons.

Is such a distinction possible? Salvador de Madariaga, the Spanish statesman active in the disarmament negotiations of the interwar years, thought not: "A weapon is either offensive or defensive according to which end of it you are looking at." The French Foreign Minister agreed (although French policy did not always follow this view): "Every arm can be employed offensively or defensively in turn . . . The only way to discover whether arms are intended for purely defensive purposes or are held in a spirit of aggression is in all cases to enquire into the intentions of the country concerned." Some evidence for the validity of this argument is provided by the fact that much time in these unsuccessful negotiations was devoted to separating offensive from defensive weapons. Indeed, no simple and unambiguous definition is possible and in many cases no judgment can be reached. Before the American entry into World War I, Woodrow Wilson wanted to arm merchantmen only with guns in the back of the

---

[34] E. L. Woodward and R. Butler, eds., *Documents on British Foreign Policy, 1919-1939*, Third series, III (London: H.M.S.O. 1950), 526.

[35] Jervis (fn. 5), 69-72, 352-55.

[36] Quoted in Merze Tate, *The United States and Armaments* (Cambridge: Harvard University Press 1948), 108.

ship so they could not initiate a fight, but this expedient cannot be applied to more common forms of armaments.[37]

There are several problems. Even when a differentiation is possible,
a status-quo power will want offensive arms under any of three conditions. (1) If the offense has a great advantage over the defense, protection through defensive forces will be too expensive. (2) Status-quo
states may need offensive weapons to regain territory lost in the
opening stages of a war. It might be possible, however, for a state to
wait to procure these weapons until war seems likely, and they might
be needed only in relatively small numbers, unless the aggressor was
able to construct strong defenses quickly in the occupied areas. (3) The
state may feel that it must be prepared to take the offensive either
because the other side will make peace only if it loses territory or
because the state has commitments to attack if the other makes war on
a third party. As noted above, status-quo states with extensive
commitments are often forced to behave like aggressors. Even when
they lack such commitments, status-quo states must worry about the
possibility that if they are able to hold off an attack, they will still not
be able to end the war unless they move into the other's territory to
damage its military forces and inflict pain. Many American naval
officers after the Civil War, for example, believed that "only by destroying the commerce of the opponent could the United States bring
him to terms."[38]

A further complication is introduced by the fact that aggressors as
well as status-quo powers require defensive forces as a prelude to
acquiring offensive ones, to protect one frontier while attacking
another, or for insurance in case the war goes badly. Criminals as well
as policemen can use bulletproof vests. Hitler as well as Maginot built
a line of forts. Indeed, Churchill reports that in 1936 the German
Foreign Minister said: "As soon as our fortifications are constructed
[on our western borders] and the countries in Central Europe realize
that France cannot enter German territory, all these countries will
begin to feel very differently about their foreign policies, and a new
constellation will develop."[39] So a state may not necessarily be
reassured if its neighbor constructs strong defenses.

More central difficulties are created by the fact that whether a
weapon is offensive or defensive often depends on the particular
situation—for instance, the geographical setting and the way in which
the weapon is used. "Tanks . . . spearheaded the fateful German
thrust through the Ardennes in 1940, but if the French had disposed of

[37] Boggs (fn. 28), 15, 40.

[38] Kenneth Hagan, *American Gunboat Diplomacy and the Old Navy, 1877-1889*
(Westport, Conn.: Greenwood Press 1973), 20.

[39] Winston Churchill, *The Gathering Storm* (Boston: Houghton 1948), 206.

a properly concentrated armored reserve, it would have provided the best means for their cutting off the penetration and turning into a disaster for the Germans what became instead an overwhelming victory."[40] Anti-aircraft weapons seem obviously defensive—to be used, they must wait for the other side to come to them. But the Egyptian attack on Israel in 1973 would have been impossible without effective air defenses that covered the battlefield. Nevertheless, some distinctions are possible. Sir John Simon, then the British Foreign Secretary, in response to the views cited earlier, stated that just because a fine line could not be drawn, "that was no reason for saying that there were not stretches of territory on either side which all practical men and women knew to be well on this or that side of the line." Although there are almost no weapons and strategies that are useful only for attacking, there are some that are almost exclusively defensive. Aggressors could want them for protection, but a state that relied mostly on them could not menace others. More frequently, we cannot "determine the absolute character of a weapon, but [we can] make a comparison . . . [and] discover whether or not the offensive potentialities predominate, whether a weapon is more useful in attack or in defense."[41]

The essence of defense is keeping the other side out of your territory. A purely defensive weapon is one that can do this without being able to penetrate the enemy's land. Thus a committee of military experts in an interwar disarmament conference declared that armaments "incapable of mobility by means of self-contained power," or movable only after long delay, were "only capable of being used for the defense of a State's territory."[42] The most obvious examples are fortifications. They can shelter attacking forces, especially when they are built right along the frontier,[43] but they cannot occupy enemy territory. A state with only a strong line of forts, fixed guns, and a small army to man them would not be much of a menace. Anything else that can serve only as a barrier against attacking troops is similarly defensive. In this category are systems that provide warning of an attack, the Russian's adoption of a different railroad gauge, and nuclear land mines that can seal off invasion routes.

If total immobility clearly defines a system that is defensive only, limited mobility is unfortunately ambiguous. As noted above, short-

[40] Brodie, *War and Politics* (fn. 35), 325.
[41] Boggs (fn. 28), 42, 83. For a good argument about the possible differentiation between offensive and defensive weapons in the 1930's, see Basil Liddell Hart, "Aggression and the Problem of Weapons," *English Review*, Vol. 55 (July 1932), 71-78.
[42] Quoted in Boggs (fn. 28), 39.
[43] On these grounds, the Germans claimed in 1932 that the French forts were offensive (*ibid.*, 49). Similarly, fortified forward naval bases can be necessary for launching an attack; see Braisted (fn. 27), 643.

range fighter aircraft and anti-aircraft missiles can be used to cover an attack. And, unlike forts, they can advance with the troops. Still, their inability to reach deep into enemy territory does make them more useful for the defense than for the offense. Thus, the United States and Israel would have been more alarmed in the early 1970's had the Russians provided the Egyptians with long-range instead of short-range aircraft. Naval forces are particularly difficult to classify in these terms, but those that are very short-legged can be used only for coastal defense.

Any forces that for various reasons fight well only when on their own soil in effect lack mobility and therefore are defensive. The most extreme example would be passive resistance. Noncooperation can thwart an aggressor, but it is very hard for large numbers of people to cross the border and stage a sit-in on another's territory. Morocco's recent march on the Spanish Sahara approached this tactic, but its success depended on special circumstances. Similarly, guerrilla warfare is defensive to the extent to which it requires civilian support that is likely to be forthcoming only in opposition to a foreign invasion. Indeed, if guerrilla warfare were easily exportable and if it took ten defenders to destroy each guerrilla, then this weapon would not only be one which could be used as easily to attack the other's territory as to defend one's own, but one in which the offense had the advantage: so the security dilemma would operate especially strongly.

If guerrillas are unable to fight on foreign soil, other kinds of armies may be unwilling to do so. An army imbued with the idea that only defensive wars were just would fight less effectively, if at all, if the goal were conquest. Citizen militias may lack both the ability and the will for aggression. The weapons employed, the short term of service, the time required for mobilization, and the spirit of repelling attacks on the homeland, all lend themselves much more to defense than to attacks on foreign territory.[44]

Less idealistic motives can produce the same result. A leading student of medieval warfare has described the armies of that period as follows: "Assembled with difficulty, insubordinate, unable to maneuver, ready to melt away from its standard the moment that its short period of service was over, a feudal force presented an assemblage of unsoldierlike qualities such as have seldom been known to coexist. Primarily intended to defend its own borders from the Magyar, the Northman, or the Saracen . . . , the institution was utterly unadapted to take the offensive."[45] Some political groupings can be similarly

[44] The French made this argument in the interwar period; see Richard Challener, *The French Theory of the Nation in Arms* (New York: Columbia University Press 1955), 181–82. The Germans disagreed; see Boggs (fn. 28), 44–45.
[45] Oman (fn. 53), 57–58.

described. International coalitions are more readily held together by fear than by hope of gain. Thus Castlereagh was not being entirely self-serving when in 1816 he argued that the Quadruple Alliance "could only have owed its origin to a sense of common danger; in its very nature it must be conservative; it cannot threaten either the security or the liberties of other States."[46] It is no accident that most of the major campaigns of expansion have been waged by one dominant nation (for example, Napoleon's France and Hitler's Germany), and that coalitions among relative equals are usually found defending the status quo. Most gains from conquest are too uncertain and raise too many questions of future squabbles among the victors to hold an alliance together for long. Although defensive coalitions are by no means easy to maintain—conflicting national objectives and the free-rider problem partly explain why three of them dissolved before Napoleon was defeated—the common interest of seeing that no state dominates provides a strong incentive for solidarity.

Weapons that are particularly effective in reducing fortifications and barriers are of great value to the offense. This is not to deny that a defensive power will want some of those weapons if the other side has them: Brodie is certainly correct to argue that while their tanks allowed the Germans to conquer France, properly used French tanks could have halted the attack. But France would not have needed these weapons if Germany had not acquired them, whereas even if France had no tanks, Germany could not have foregone them since they provided the only chance of breaking through the French lines. Mobile heavy artillery is, similarly, especially useful in destroying fortifications. The defender, while needing artillery to fight off attacking troops or to counterattack, can usually use lighter guns since they do not need to penetrate such massive obstacles. So it is not surprising that one of the few things that most nations at the interwar disarmament conferences were able to agree on was that heavy tanks and mobile heavy guns were particularly valuable to a state planning an attack.[47]

Weapons and strategies that depend for their effectiveness on surprise are almost always offensive. That fact was recognized by some of the delegates to the interwar disarmament conferences and is the principle behind the common national ban on concealed weapons. An earlier representative of this widespread view was the mid-19th-century Philadelphia newspaper that argued: "As a measure of defense, knives, dirks, and sword canes are entirely useless. They are fit only for attack, and all such attacks are of murderous character.

---

[46] Quoted in Charles Webster, *The Foreign Policy of Castlereagh, II, 1815-1822* (London: G. Bell and Sons 1963), 510.
[47] Boggs (fn. 28), 14–15, 47–48, 60.

Whoever carries such a weapon has prepared himself for homicide."[48]

It is, of course, not always possible to distinguish between forces that are most effective for holding territory and forces optimally designed for taking it. Such a distinction could not have been made for the strategies and weapons in Europe during most of the period between the Franco-Prussian War and World War I. Neither naval forces nor tactical air forces can be readily classified in these terms. But the point here is that when such a distinction is possible, the central characteristic of the security dilemma no longer holds, and one of the most troublesome consequences of anarchy is removed.

Offense-Defense Differentiation and Strategic Nuclear Weapons. In the interwar period, most statesmen held the reasonable position that weapons that threatened civilians were offensive.[49] But when neither side can protect its civilians, a counter-city posture is defensive because the state can credibly threaten to retaliate only in response to an attack on itself or its closest allies. The costs of this strike are so high that the state could not threaten to use it for the less-than-vital interest of compelling the other to abandon an established position.

In the context of deterrence, offensive weapons are those that provide defense. In the now familiar reversal of common sense, the state that could take its population out of hostage, either by active or passive defense or by destroying the other's strategic weapons on the ground, would be able to alter the status quo. The desire to prevent such a situation was one of the rationales for the anti-ABM agreements; it explains why some arms controllers opposed building ABM's to protect cities, but favored sites that covered ICBM fields. Similarly, many analysts want to limit warhead accuracy and favor multiple re-entry vehicles (MRV's), but oppose multiple independently targetable re-entry vehicles (MIRV's). The former are more useful than single warheads for penetrating city defenses, and ensure that the state has a second-strike capability. MIRV's enhance counterforce capabilities. Some arms controllers argue that this is also true of cruise missiles, and therefore do not want them to be deployed either. There is some evidence that the Russians are not satisfied with deterrence and are seeking to regain the capability for defense. Such an effort, even if not inspired by aggressive designs, would create a severe security dilemma.

What is most important for the argument here is that land-based ICBM's are both offensive and defensive, but when both sides rely on Polaris-type systems (SLBM's), offense and defense use different weapons. ICBM's can be used either to destroy the other's cities in

[48] Quoted in Philip Jordan, *Frontier Law and Order* (London: University of Nebraska Press 1970), 7; also see 16–17.

[49] Boggs (fn. 28), 20, 28.

retaliation or to initiate hostilities by attacking the other's strategic missiles. Some measures—for instance, hardening of missile sites and warning systems—are purely defensive, since they do not make a first strike easier. Others are predominantly offensive—for instance, passive or active city defenses, and highly accurate warheads. But ICBM's themselves are useful for both purposes. And because states seek a high level of insurance, the desire for protection as well as the contemplation of a counterforce strike can explain the acquisition of extremely large numbers of missiles. So it is very difficult to infer the other's intentions from its military posture. Each side's efforts to increase its own security by procuring more missiles decreases, to an extent determined by the relative efficacy of the offense and the defense, the other side's security. That is not the case when both sides use SLBM's. The point is not that sea-based systems are less vulnerable than land-based ones (this bears on the offense-defense ratio) but that SLBM's are defensive, retaliatory weapons. First, they are probably not accurate enough to destroy many military targets.[50] Second, and more important, SLBM's are not the main instrument of attack against other SLBM's. The hardest problem confronting a state that wants to take its cities out of hostage is to locate the other's SLBM's, a job that requires not SLBM's but anti-submarine weapons. A state might use SLBM's to attack the other's submarines (although other weapons would probably be more efficient), but without anti-submarine warfare (ASW) capability the task cannot be performed. A status-quo state that wanted to forego offensive capability could simply forego ASW research and procurement.

There are two difficulties with this argument, however. First, since the state's SLBM's are potentially threatened by the other's ASW capabilities, the state may want to pursue ASW research in order to know what the other might be able to do and to design defenses. Unless it does this, it cannot be confident that its submarines are safe. Second, because some submarines are designed to attack surface ships, not launch missiles, ASW forces have missions other than taking cities out of hostage. Some U.S. officials plan for a long war in Europe which would require keeping the sea lanes open against Russian submarines. Designing an ASW force and strategy that would meet this threat without endangering Soviet SLBM's would be difficult but not impossible, since the two missions are somewhat different.[51] Furthermore, the Russians do not need ASW forces to combat submarines carrying out conventional missions; it might be in

[50] See, however, Desmond Ball, "The Counterforce Potential of American SLBM Systems," *Journal of Peace Research*, XIV (No. 1, 1977), 23–40.
[51] Richard Garwin, "Anti-Submarine Warfare and National Security," *Scientific American*, Vol. 227 (July 1972), 14–25.

America's interest to sacrifice the ability to meet a threat that is not likely to materialize in order to reassure the Russians that we are not menacing their retaliatory capability.

When both sides rely on ICBM's, one side's missiles can attack the other's, and so the state cannot be indifferent to the other's building program. But because one side's SLBM's do not menace the other's, each side can build as many as it wants and the other need not respond. Each side's decision on the size of its force depends on technical questions, its judgment about how much destruction is enough to deter, and the amount of insurance it is willing to pay for—and these considerations are independent of the size of the other's strategic force. Thus the crucial nexus in the arms race is severed.

Here two objections not only can be raised but have been, by those who feel that even if American second-strike capability is in no danger, the United States must respond to a Soviet buildup. First, the relative numbers of missiles and warheads may be used as an index of each side's power and will. Even if there is no military need to increase American arms as the Russians increase theirs, a failure to respond may lead third parties to think that the U.S. has abandoned the competition with the U.S.S.R. and is no longer willing to pay the price of world leadership. Furthermore, if either side believes that nuclear "superiority" matters, then, through the bargaining logic, it will matter. The side with "superiority" will be more likely to stand firm in a confrontation if it thinks its "stronger" military position helps it, or if it thinks that the other thinks its own "weaker" military position is a handicap. To allow the other side to have more SLBM's—even if one's own second-strike capability is unimpaired—will give the other an advantage that can be translated into political gains.

The second objection is that superiority *does* matter, and not only because of mistaken beliefs. If nuclear weapons are used in an all-or-none fashion, then all that is needed is second-strike capability. But limited, gradual, and controlled strikes are possible. If the other side has superiority, it can reduce the state's forces by a slow-motion war of attrition. For the state to strike at the other's cities would invite retaliation; for it to reply with a limited counterforce attack would further deplete its supply of missiles. Alternatively, the other could employ demonstration attacks—such as taking out an isolated military base or exploding a warhead high over a city—in order to demonstrate its resolve. In either of these scenarios, the state will suffer unless it matches the other's arms posture.[52]

These two objections, if valid, mean that even with SLBM's one

---

[52] The latter scenario, however, does not require that the state closely match the number of missiles the other deploys.

cannot distinguish offensive from defensive strategic nuclear weapons. Compellence may be more difficult than deterrence,[53] but if decision makers believe that numbers of missiles or of warheads influence outcomes, or if these weapons can be used in limited manner, then the posture and policy that would be needed for self-protection is similar to that useful for aggression. If the second objection has merit, security would require the ability to hit selected targets on the other side, enough ammunition to wage a controlled counterforce war, and the willingness to absorb limited countervalue strikes. Secretary Schlesinger was correct in arguing that this capability would not constitute a first-strike capability. But because the "Schlesinger Doctrine" could be used not only to cope with a parallel Russian policy, but also to support an American attempt to change the status quo, the new American stance would decrease Russian security. Even if the U.S.S.R. were reassured that the present U.S. Government lacked the desire or courage to do this, there could be no guarantee that future governments would not use the new instruments for expansion. Once we move away from the simple idea that nuclear weapons can only be used for all-out strikes, half the advantage of having both sides rely on a sea-based force would disappear because of the lack of an offensive-defensive differentiation. To the extent that military policy affects political relations, it would be harder for the United States and the Soviet Union to cooperate even if both supported the status quo.

Although a full exploration of these questions is beyond the scope of this paper, it should be noted that the objections rest on decision makers' beliefs—beliefs, furthermore, that can be strongly influenced by American policy and American statements. The perceptions of third nations of whether the details of the nuclear balance affect political conflicts—and, to a lesser extent, Russian beliefs about whether superiority is meaningful—are largely derived from the American strategic debate. If most American spokesmen were to take the position that a secure second-strike capability was sufficient and that increments over that (short of a first-strike capability) would only be a waste of money, it is doubtful whether America's allies or the neutrals would judge the superpowers' useful military might or political will by the size of their stockpiles. Although the Russians stress war-fighting ability, they have not contended that marginal increases in strategic forces bring political gains; any attempt to do so could be rendered less effective by an American assertion that this is

---

[53] Thomas Schelling, *Arms and Influence* (New Haven: Yale University Press 1966), 69–78. Schelling's arguments are not entirely convincing, however. For further discussion, see Jervis, "Deterrence Theory Re-Visited," Working Paper No. 14, UCLA Program in Arms Control and International Security.

nonsense. The bargaining advantages of possessing nuclear "superiority" work best when both sides acknowledge them. If the "weaker" side convinces the other that it does not believe there is any meaningful difference in strength, then the "stronger" side cannot safely stand firm because there is no increased chance that the other will back down.

This kind of argument applies at least as strongly to the second objection. Neither side can employ limited nuclear options unless it is quite confident that the other accepts the rules of the game. For if the other believes that nuclear war cannot be controlled, it will either refrain from responding—which would be fine—or launch all-out retaliation. Although a state might be ready to engage in limited nuclear war without acknowledging this possibility—and indeed, that would be a reasonable policy for the United States—it is not likely that the other would have sufficient faith in that prospect to initiate limited strikes unless the state had openly avowed its willingness to fight this kind of war. So the United States, by patiently and consistently explaining that it considers such ideas to be mad and that any nuclear wars will inevitably get out of control, could gain a large measure of protection against the danger that the Soviet Union might seek to employ a "Schlesinger Doctrine" against an America that lacked the military ability or political will to respond in kind. Such a position is made more convincing by the inherent implausibility of the arguments for the possibility of a limited nuclear war.

In summary, as long as states believe that all that is needed is second-strike capability, then the differentiation between offensive and defensive forces that is provided by reliance on SLBM's allows each side to increase its security without menacing the other, permits some inferences about intentions to be drawn from military posture, and removes the main incentive for status-quo powers to engage in arms races.

IV. FOUR WORLDS

The two variables we have been discussing—whether the offense or the defense has the advantage, and whether offensive postures can be distinguished from defensive ones—can be combined to yield four possible worlds.

	OFFENSE HAS THE ADVANTAGE	DEFENSE HAS THE ADVANTAGE
OFFENSIVE POSTURE NOT DISTINGUISHABLE FROM DEFENSIVE ONE	1 Doubly dangerous	2 Security dilemma, but security requirements may be compatible.
OFFENSIVE POSTURE DISTINGUISHABLE FROM DEFENSIVE ONE	3 No security dilemma, but aggression possible. Status-quo states can follow different policy than aggressors. Warning given.	4 Doubly stable

The first world is the worst for status-quo states. There is no way to get security without menacing others, and security through defense is terribly difficult to obtain. Because offensive and defensive postures are the same, status-quo states acquire the same kind of arms that are sought by aggressors. And because the offense has the advantage over the defense, attacking is the best route to protecting what you have; status-quo states will therefore behave like aggressors. The situation will be unstable. Arms races are likely. Incentives to strike first will turn crises into wars. Decisive victories and conquests will be common. States will grow and shrink rapidly, and it will be hard for any state to maintain its size and influence without trying to increase them. Cooperation among status-quo powers will be extremely hard to achieve.

There are no cases that totally fit this picture, but it bears more than a passing resemblance to Europe before World War I. Britain and Germany, although in many respects natural allies, ended up as enemies. Of course much of the explanation lies in Germany's ill-chosen policy. And from the perspective of our theory, the powers' ability to avoid war in a series of earlier crises cannot be easily explained. Nevertheless, much of the behavior in this period was the product of technology and beliefs that magnified the security dilemma. Decision makers thought that the offense had a big advantage and saw little difference between offensive and defensive military postures. The era was characterized by arms races. And once war seemed likely, mobilization races created powerful incentives to strike first.

In the nuclear era, the first world would be one in which each side relied on vulnerable weapons that were aimed at similar forces and each side understood the situation. In this case, the incentives to strike first would be very high—so high that status-quo powers as well as aggressors would be sorely tempted to pre-empt. And since the forces could be used to change the status-quo as well as to preserve it, there would be no way for both sides to increase their security simultaneously. Now the familiar logic of deterrence leads both sides to see the dangers in this world. Indeed, the new understanding of this situation was one reason why vulnerable bombers and missiles were replaced. Ironically, the 1950's would have been more hazardous if the decision makers had been aware of the dangers of their posture and had therefore felt greater pressure to strike first. This situation could be recreated if both sides were to rely on MIRVed ICBM's.

In the second world, the security dilemma operates because offensive and defensive postures cannot be distinguished; but it does not operate as strongly as in the first world because the defense has the advantage, and so an increment in one side's strength increases its security more than it decreases the other's. So, if both sides have reasonable subjective security requirements, are of roughly equal power, and the variables discussed earlier are favorable, it is quite likely that status-quo states can adopt compatible security policies. Although a state will not be able to judge the other's intentions from the kinds of weapons it procures, the level of arms spending will give important evidence. Of course a state that seeks a high level of arms might be not an aggressor but merely an insecure state, which if conciliated will reduce its arms, and if confronted will reply in kind. To assume that the apparently excessive level of arms indicates aggressiveness could therefore lead to a response that would deepen the dilemma and create needless conflict. But empathy and skillful statesmanship can reduce this danger. Furthermore, the advantageous position of the defense means that a status-quo state can often maintain a high degree of security with a level of arms lower than that of its expected adversary. Such a state demonstrates that it lacks the ability or desire to alter the status-quo, at least at the present time. The strength of the defense also allows states to react slowly and with restraint when they fear that others are menacing them. So, although status-quo powers will to some extent be threatening to others, that extent will be limited.

This world is the one that comes closest to matching most periods in history. Attacking is usually harder than defending because of the strength of fortifications and obstacles. But purely defensive postures are rarely possible because fortifications are usually supplemented by armies and mobile guns which can support an attack. In the nuclear era, this world would be one in which both sides relied on relatively invulnerable ICBM's and believed that limited nuclear war was impossible. Assuming no MIRV's, it would take more than one attacking missile to destroy one of the adversary's. Pre-emption is therefore unattractive. If both sides have large inventories, they can ignore all but drastic increases on the other side. A world of either ICBM's or SLBM's in which both sides adopted the "Schlesinger Doctrine" would probably fit in this category too. The means of preserving the status quo would also be the means of changing it, as we discussed earlier. And the defense usually would have the advantage, because compellence is more difficult than deterrence. Although a state might succeed in changing the status-quo on issues that matter much more to it than to others, status-quo powers could deter major provocations under most circumstances.

In the third world there may be no security dilemma, but there are security problems. Because states can procure defensive systems that do not threaten others, the dilemma need not operate. But because the offense has the advantage, aggression is possible, and perhaps easy. If the offense has enough of an advantage, even a status-quo state may take the initiative rather than risk being attacked and defeated. If the offense has less of an advantage, stability and cooperation are likely because the status-quo states will procure defensive forces. They need not react to others who are similarly armed, but can wait for the warning they would receive if others started to deploy offensive weapons. But each state will have to watch the others carefully, and there is room for false suspicions. The costliness of the defense and the allure of the offense can lead to unnecessary mistrust, hostility, and war, unless some of the variables discussed earlier are operating to restrain defection.

A hypothetical nuclear world that would fit this description would be one in which both sides relied on SLBM's, but in which ASW techniques were very effective. Offense and defense would be different, but the former would have the advantage. This situation is not likely to occur; but if it did, a status-quo state could show its lack of desire to exploit the other by refraining from threatening its submarines. The desire to have more protecting you than merely the other side's fear of retaliation is a strong one, however, and a state that knows that it would not expand even if its cities were safe is likely to believe that the other would not feel threatened by its ASW program. It is easy to see how such a world could become unstable, and how spirals of tensions and conflict could develop.

The fourth world is doubly safe. The differentiation between offensive and defensive systems permits a way out of the security dilemma; the advantage of the defense disposes of the problems discussed in the previous paragraphs. There is no reason for a status-quo power to be tempted to procure offensive forces, and aggressors give notice of their intentions by the posture they adopt. Indeed, if the advantage of the defense is great enough, there are no security problems. The loss of the ultimate form of the power to alter the status quo would allow greater scope for the exercise of nonmilitary means and probably would tend to freeze the distribution of values.

This world would have existed in the first decade of the 20th century if the decision makers had understood the available technology. In that case, the European powers would have followed different policies both in the long run and in the summer of 1914. Even Germany, facing powerful enemies on both sides, could have made herself secure by developing strong defenses. France could also have made her frontier almost impregnable. Furthermore, when crises arose, no one would have had incentives to strike first. There would have been no competitive mobilization races reducing the time available for negotiations.

In the nuclear era, this world would be one in which the superpowers relied on SLBM's, ASW technology was not up to its task, and limited nuclear options were not taken seriously. We have discussed this situation earlier; here we need only add that, even if our analysis is correct and even if the policies and postures of both sides were to move in this direction, the problem of violence below the nuclear threshold would remain. On issues other than defense of the homeland, there would still be security dilemmas and security problems. But the world would nevertheless be safer than it has usually been.

On the Objectives
of Arms Control

BERNARD BRODIE

.

The volume of literature on arms control contrasts sharply with the dearth of results in actual armaments limitation or control. Thus huge disparity between fullness of advice and leanness of practical results suggests a good deal about both the character of that advice and the magnitude of the practical difficulties—and especially about the failure of the former to adjust to the latter.

The ample quantity of the writing on arms control in the face of what would seem to be such poor prospects of realization reflects also an aspiration, amounting often to religiosity, in much of the motivation for that writing. Although we must be grateful for whatever propels motivation in what we feel intuitively to be a good cause, we must also be suspicious of that kind of motivation which corrupts the endeavor.[1]

All but a minute proportion of the works that I have seen on the general subject of arms control fail to be of any utility for the policymaker, and thus also for the student of policy making, except insofar as some of those writings conveniently provide for the interested layman some technical knowledge about weaponry. That failure is naturally due to various characteristics, but one common characteristic that I should put at the top of the list is *persistent failure to clarify and analyze objectives,* which of course precludes any rigorous and consistent adherence to the soundest objectives. Naturally, this clarification should not have to be done over and over again, but it would be useful to have it be done occasionally.

ARMS CONTROL OBJECTIVES AND PERCEPTIONS

An appropriate analysis of objectives would inevitably entail a pragmatic approach—we want our objectives to be mutually consistent, to be worth achieving, and to be in some degree achievable—and

From *International Security,* Vol. 1:1, Summer, 1976, p. 17–36. Reprinted by permission of the MIT Press, Cambridge, Massachusetts.
[1] I can only hope that what I have seen is a fair and representative sampling. A manuscript for a bibliography of items related to and about arms control, prepared by Professor Richard Dean Burns, comes to some 900 pages of double-spaced typing. It will be published in 1976 or 1977 by the Clio Press of Santa Barbara, California.

that in turn entails a properly empirical utilization of our experience. We have had much relevant experience with arms control negotiations, with the armaments competitions that have stimulated efforts at control, and above all with war, the prospect of which ultimately dominates everything having to do with arms competitions and the efforts to control them.

Inasmuch as arms control efforts seek to affect future events, we have to be conscious of the degree of our uncertainty about the future, in which we are instructed by our experience with surprise in the past. Perhaps an appreciation for this uncertainty will inhibit our choice of arms control objectives, but if so, that is simply the way the ball bounces.

I am using the term "arms control" in a sense which accords with the popular conception but which some would regard as unduly restrictive. It was right once to make the point that the kind of arms control that may be most important in the long run is that which depends on tacit rather than explicit agreement—also that arms control for the purpose of enhancing security does not usually imply reducing the overall costs of our armaments but may in particular respects mean raising them.[2] Though of some perennial application, those points were more pertinent to the Eisenhower years than to the present. Anyway, the more common and narrower conception, which I accept, identifies the term "arms control" with some degree of limitation or reduction of particular armaments, and it implies also explicit rather than merely tacit international agreement. There is indeed substantial extra value in the relevant agreements being explicit.

The objectives of arms control are usually not stated, but when they are stated, they are only rarely if ever reflectively considered. Apparently this is because most writers feel that the merit of their implied or declared objectives is too obvious to need consideration.[3] Not only are some two, three, or four objectives usually held to be obviously desirable, but even the order of their priority seems to be a matter for declaration rather than examination. Among the numerous statements that might be quoted to illustrate this point, I choose one which I find specially provocative but which reflects fairly the view most commonly held by the vast majority of those who write on arms control. Herman Kahn and Anthony Weiner say that the purpose of arms control is:

---

[2] These ideas were prominent in the work of Thomas C. Schelling. See especially the book by him and Morton H. Halperin, *Strategy and Arms Control* (New York: Twentieth Century Fund, 1961).

[3] Hedley Bull's *The Control of the Arms Race* (New York: Praeger, 1961) does indeed devote the first chapter to "The Objectives of Arms Control," but I find it exploratory rather than analytical. This and the above-mentioned book by Schelling and Halperin, both published in the same year, both short, remain to this date the landmark books in the field.

. . . to improve the inherent stability of the situation, decrease the occasions or the approximate causes of war within the system, and decrease the destructiveness and other disutilities of any wars that actually occur. One may also add to this last, 'decrease the cost of defense preparation,' but we would argue that this would take a rather low priority to the first three objectives.[4]

This statement puts the aim of saving money not only last but in a separate sub-category of lesser worthiness than the other three. Those three in turn really boil down to only two, because the first two mentioned refer to the common aim of reducing the probability of war, and the third, which thus becomes the second, has to do with reducing the destructiveness of war if it should occur.

One notices in passing that giving priority to the twin aims of reducing the probability of war and of reducing its destructiveness if it occurs—the reference is almost always to war between the two superpowers—reflects an implicit appraisal of the existing probability of war. Some would protest that if war breaks out the penalties are so vast that *any* possibility of its occurring warrants whatever efforts we can make to counteract that possibility. Still, we know that few would greatly bestir themselves to cope with an evil that they regard as having only a miniscule probability of occurring. Individual views on armaments and arms control cover a wide range, and it is important to establish that one prime factor accounting for the differences is the individual's appraisal of the probability of war—an appraisal that is usually vaguely felt and nearly always implicit rather than explicit.

I find the Kahn-Weiner statement provocative because of their view of priorities. My own contrary view is that in a pragmatic approach to arms control the object of saving money really deserves a superior rating to that of saving the world. This conclusion must imply, among other things, either a high confidence that the probability of war between the two superpowers will continue to be extremely low, or the conviction that in any case we cannot do much about that probability through arms control. To make explicit and thus also to clarify what is otherwise ambiguous, let me record that I subscribe to both propositions.

Although one can defend a low expectation of superpower conflict by citing only objective factors, one must admit that the *weighting* of those factors depends upon a substantial increment of subjective and thus intuitive judgement.[5] Besides obliging one to be tolerant of differing opinions, this fact throws the main burden of the argument on the

---

[4] Herman Kahn and Anthony Weiner, "Technological Innovation and the Future of Strategic Warfare," *Astronautics and Aeronautics* (December, 1967), p. 28.

[5] I have dealt at greater length with the question of the probability of war between the United States and the Soviet Union in my *War and Politics* (New York: Macmillan, 1973), especially in chapters 6 and 9.

latter of the two above propositions—that arms control negotiations and the resulting agreements, if any, will rarely make important contributions to reducing either the probability of war or its destructiveness. There are several reasons for this, of which two stand out particularly: (1) each party is extremely suspicious of the adversary's efforts to disarm him in weaponry regarded as truly important, and (2) apart from a few simple and obvious devices like the "hot line" between Washington and Moscow, experience assures us that it is not at all a simple matter to determine objectively, let alone get international agreement upon, those arms limitation measures that will really advance the ends of greater stability and lesser destructiveness.

That leaves us with the mere matter of saving money, on which governments, unlike amateur observers, never look askance. Governments are at all times coping intensively with a number of recalcitrant economic problems, which in recent years have included marked inflationary pressures and also growing alternative demands for the monies raised from public restive about taxes. Competitive pressures from the chief foreign rival will at times force a commitment to expenditures which government leaders may feel to be of doubtful utility from the military point of view, or changed conditions will make less necessary or desirable what was previously considered essential. Yet political reasons may militate against cutting back unilaterally. Each government also finds itself pressed by its own military in a conflict where the rival government, which has similar problems, may occasionally be a useful ally.

We have already noticed that every participant in the national debate on arms control carries with him as part of his intellectual and emotional baggage some kind of appraisal of war-probability which inevitably affects his relevant attitudes. Obviously it will affect his feelings on how much one should try to accommodate to the views of the bargaining partner. It is an old story that one important reason why arms limitation conferences have so often failed or yielded only the most meager results is that both sides bring with them to the conference a contingent of experts, whether in uniform or not, whose whole professional predisposition is to look upon that bargaining partner as the prospective military adversary. They also feel a pronounced distaste for giving up any of those armaments with which they individually identify themselves and which they may have fought for on the domestic scene. There are also those left at home who can be counted upon to influence the debate that will precede any ratification. Depending on the moods of the time these experts may feel obliged to give lip service to arms limitation, but they will bring to the process a tight and often arbitrary measure of proportionality.

All that is of course familiar, but there is another less observed facet of the problem. Those who entertain a low estimate of superpower war probability will incline towards the idea that for deterrence purposes the fact of being powerful is much more important than the exact character or structure of that power. This attitude makes for more flexibility in the critical negotiations, and also for acceptance as a matter of course of the important distinction between deterrence capabilities and war-fighting capabilities. The former capabilities are those which are menacing enough, under expected conditions of low mutual motivation for war, to preclude the adversary's giving serious consideration to exploiting the means and paying the price of defeating them.

Those persons, on the other hand, who regard the danger of super-power war as appreciable are consistent in arguing that the best deterrence force is the optimum fighting force. They will run into difficulties with their insistence on this point when they contemplate the ultimate in strategic nuclear deterrence, where war-fighting capabilities seem to dissolve into irrelevance. Herman Kahn's well-known parable of the doomsday machine (designed by Americans to blow up the world if it should detect some five nuclear weapons exploding anywhere over the United States) demonstrated hypothetically that deterrence and war-fighting capabilities are *not* the same thing, at least at the maximum levels of warfare.[6] At theater levels of warfare, however, war-fighting capabilities are much more relevant to deterrence, and anyway, one wants the monies allocated to fighting forces to be spent efficiently, which means efficiently for fighting purposes. Even so, it is likely that an effort concentrated on deterrence will be less costly by wide margins than one concentrated on matching or outdoing the opponent in war-fighting capabilities.

All sorts of slogans get in the way of a reasonable handling of this problem, such as the common assertion that our efforts should be guided exclusively by the opponent's capabilities, not by our estimate of his intentions. This slogan is not likely to be fully followed in practice, because our sense of threat is inevitably qualified by our operating image of the opponent, which may be of one who wants to be strong but also wants desperately to avoid war. Nevertheless, the slogan does act to exacerbate competitive pressures.[7] These pressures certainly increase the disposition to match the rival's military efforts in degree, and they also to some extent dispose us to imitate him in kind. Obviously our military have their own ideas in some matters, but they and we will be uneasy with too radical a departure from the major pattern the rival is following. Thus both sides build up huge conventional forces in an age of nuclear weapons.

[6] See Herman Kahn, *On Thermonuclear War* (Princeton: Princeton University Press, 1960), pp. 145–151.

[7] I discuss the issue of "capabilities versus intentions" at greater length in my *Escalation and the Nuclear Option* (Princeton: Princeton University Press, 1966), ch. 7.

AGREEING UPON ARMS CONTROL OBJECTIVES

We turn now to some examples which will illustrate and perhaps also elaborate the various points made above. On the general issue of the difficulty of winning acceptance even of agreements that would seem to be obviously in the security interests of the participants, a recent and conspicuous example is the history of the effort to avoid proliferation of nuclear weapons. There is little overt dissension anywhere to the belief, which is almost universal within the United States, that the general proliferation of nuclear weapons among non-possessing nations would be a threat to world peace. This view seems to be held even by some governments that have refused to sign the Non- Proliferation Treaty of 1968, including the French government—which has, however, not hesitated to attempt to sell to governments like that of South Korea not only nuclear power plants but also plutonium reprocessing plants to go with them. In this case we do have a treaty, the achievement of which was one of the leading aims of American foreign policy for several years before its accomplishment. Still, the considerable resistances to the adoption of that treaty are well known. At this writing 98 nations are parties to it and 12 that have signed have not yet ratified. Both figures leave out some quite important states.[*] What is more, the treaty itself has more than its share of legal escape hatches, quite apart from the fact that it is more than usually subject to evasion or violation.

Ah, one protests, but is not this too blatant an example of inequality, where nations are being asked to sign a self-denying ordinance not subscribed to by some nations including our own, and where the compensation is all too abstract? No doubt, but when are the benefits of an arms limitation treaty not abstract—except insofar as they directly result in the saving of money? The fact remains that a proposition that commends itself overwhelmingly to virtually all interested citizens in the United States—and most arms limitation proposals do not meet that criterion—quite clearly does not commend itself universally. The treaty we do have is not worthless but neither is it worth very much. The actual plans of signatory nations concerning their own military nuclear programs have probably been little if at all affected by that treaty. The objective of the treaty is still worth pursuing, certainly in the direction of curbing the almost wanton distribution of nuclear power reactors and especially of plutonium reprocessing plants, but we have reason to be aware of the limited prospects of its success. In other examples we shall be considering, it is much less clear whether the objective is worth pursuing.

---

[*] Japan became the 98th party to the treaty with the deposit of its instrument of ratification on June 8, 1976.

DETERMINING WHAT IS NEGOTIABLE:
THE CASE OF TACTICAL NUCLEAR WEAPONS

One critical example of an arms limitation objective that we are in danger of pursuing too hastily involves tactical nuclear weapons (TNWs). These are commonly believed to be the most ill-begotten of a noisome race of weapons, particularly objectionable because they are unnecessary. In this view they should not be used even in the event of a major attack by the Soviet Union upon our own and allied forces in Europe and at sea. To use them, the argument goes, is to wipe out the only meaningful stop (or "firebreak") between theater warfare and the suicidal strategic kind. Why the slide from one to the other should be so steep and slippery is not explained, no doubt because the reasons are considered too obvious to require explanation.

The notion that TNWs are on the whole more dangerous than useful to their possessor derives from an idea developed and advocated in the early 1960s, mostly by a group of analysts then at the RAND Corporation.[9] If the United States and its NATO allies built up their conventional ground and air forces to something like parity with those of the Warsaw Pact, these men argued, the "nuclear threshold" would be raised to so high a level as virtually to eliminate the chances of its being breached even in an outbreak of major military action in Europe—which, everyone agreed, could be initiated only by a Soviet attack. They further insisted that inasmuch as everyone would understand that our European allies would be much more willing to resist Soviet aggression if they were highly confident that the resulting battle would remain non-nuclear, the proposed posture would greatly enhance real deterrence.

Thus, the 7,000 American TNWs reported to be stationed in Europe are held to be exceptionally available tokens to be offered in any arms reduction proposals to the Soviet Union. Secretary of State Henry A. Kissinger has already offered to reduce them by 1,000 if the Soviet Union will make an offsetting—though not similar—reduction in its armed forces in Europe. Whatever Kissinger's own beliefs on the subject may be—and he is on record as being dubious of the views of the conventional-war enthusiasts—he is aware that an offer of this kind meets the minimum of objections from the Pentagon, the Congress, and other relevant agencies. Alain Enthoven, however, would go much further than Kissinger. He would reduce their number unilaterally without offsetting concessions, and not *by* 1,000 but *to* 1,000.[10]

---

[9] Leadership of this group within RAND must be credited to Albert Wohlstetter, though Alain C. Enthoven has been the most frequent spokesman in print for their position. Others among them known for their publications include Malcolm Hoag, W. W. Kaufmann, and Henry Rowen.

[10] See Alain C. Enthoven, "U. S. Forces in Europe: How Many? Doing What?" *Foreign Affairs*, (April 1975), pp. 512–532.

To the layman 1,000 nuclear weapons will seem like an adequate number for any purpose, but if those retained are ever really adapted to tactical uses, which would mean among other things greatly reducing the yields on most of them, 1,000 would certainly not be adequate. Enthoven would reduce the number of TNWs in Europe primarily to free for conventional war purposes the men now assigned to guarding them, which he numbers at 30,000. And he would retain the 1,000 strictly to deter the Soviet Union from using TNWs in its attack.

Whether the Europeans could ever have high confidence that a major war in Europe would remain non-nuclear, or whether such confidence ought under any circumstances to be entertained, are among the vital questions which have not been scrutinized. The group that originated this mode of thought believed the logic of the new idea to be so compelling that it would be quickly accepted by the Soviet military leaders as well as allied ones, not to mention our own. To be sure, involved Americans were determined not to lose a war in Europe. There would be no first use by us *unless we found ourselves losing.* The Russians were apparently expected to accommodate to this rigidity on our part, which they would no doubt consider somewhat peculiar, and to do so without using nuclear weapons.

One notes a complete absence of empirical inquiry about various of the radical assumptions that went into this doctrine. *What* Europeans were meant by *the* Europeans who would supposedly resist under one set of circumstances but not under another? Did anyone try to find out whether that was really the opinion of those few Europeans who would make the critical decisions? Would the Russians launch a large-scale attack without the determination to win, swiftly, and would they expose themselves to the hazards of such a duel while leaving entirely to us the choice of weapons? What did their overt doctrine tell us on these matters? These and comparable questions which were subject to fruitful investigation were not in fact investigated. One notices also that the original protagonists of this view harbored a sufficiently high expectation of a Soviet attack in Europe to advocate with some urgency a considerable and costly improvement of NATO forces, though they seemed to find it forensically necessary to insist that in military manpower the NATO forces were already very nearly equal to those of the Warsaw Pact.[11]

The theory was attractive enough to win ready converts in the

[11] Dr. Enthoven has been consistently arguing this point in several publications, the most recent being his aforementioned *Foreign Affairs* article. On page 516 Enthoven holds that Warsaw Pact forces on M-Day plus 60 would be only 1,241,000 (as compared with NATO's 1,105,000). One wonders what happened to that Soviet Union which, without allies, suffered the loss of five to six million troops in the first 5½ months of war in 1941, and then went on to win. The estimate is Albert Seaton's in his *The Russo-German War, 1941-1945* (New York: Praeger, 1971), p. 208n.

highest reaches of the Kennedy Administration, including the President himself and his vigorous Secretary of Defense, Robert S. McNamara. And what was a novel and radical doctrine 15 years ago has now in the mid-1970s become the conventional wisdom of the interested public and of most of the defense community. Professional military officers tend today to be ambivalent on the use of TNWs, being ready in principle to use them if the other side uses them first, or, as something of an afterthought, in the event we find ourselves losing without them. But whether their forces are organized, equipped, and trained to make so swift a shift from one form of warfare to another is a pertinent question—to which the answer almost certainly is "no". The military did, after all, like that part of the theory which justified their requesting a good deal more of the kind of equipment they were accustomed to, albeit modernized. And, as some of them have frankly admitted, they have simply stopped thinking much about the problem. The most extraordinary example of how one service has adjusted to the idea that TNWs would surely not be used in a war with the Soviet Union is the manner in which our surface combat fleet has developed around huge attack carriers, any one of which could be volatilized by one small nuclear weapon, deliverable by aircraft, surface vessel, submarine, or even shore-based missile launcher.

Thus, a theory has been accepted almost without challenge simply because it is a seductive one. One wants to believe it, especially if one can be persuaded that forces organized for the non-use of nuclear weapons make for more rather than less deterrence. Some theories are of course self-fulfilling, and this one might be so if we were not talking about war—which always presupposes an adversary with intentions and drives of his own. Under the circumstances, however, it is a dangerous theory as well as a costly one. The conventional forces it calls for in NATO have not been provided, and would be of dubious utility if they were. Our NATO allies were never impressed with the American idea, and besides they felt the threat from the Soviet Union to be diminishing. That situation was not conducive to spending more on defense. Anyway, European policymakers have a long-standing fondness for nuclear *deterrence,* and if the strategic variety seems less dependable to them than formerly, as it clearly (and perhaps fortunately) does, they are that much less willing to relinquish the theater kind. Since 1967 they have found it expedient to give lip service within NATO to the concept of "graduated response," but they are far from fleshing our their purely conventional capabilities. They have indeed been tending in the opposite direction.

One of the primary ideas upon which the whole conventional war construct is based is that large-scale conflict between the superpowers can be the result of accident. By "accidental war" is presumably meant that which comes despite neither side wanting it, and with neither side realizing until war is actually upon it that the policy it is pursuing makes that war unavoidable. This notion has given rise to the concept of the "pause," intended to permit the enemy to reconsider his behavior before one introduces nuclear weapons against him. Presumably this kind of accident is made possible by the very existence of nuclear weapons, for within the definition of the term given above, no such thing as accidental war has happened within the last three hundred years, if ever. And it really is bizarre to think that the presence of nuclear weapons can make nations more reckless and disportive in bearding their opponents than ever before, in a word more ready to risk war in the conviction that it will not come. Thus we pay heavy extra premiums in our defenses simply because most of those who currently philosophize about strategy have made no effort to acquaint themselves with the history of war.

In the context of TNWs, what about the aim of diminishing the destructiveness of war? The answers, in diminishing order of importance, are about as follows: First, the surest way of reducing the destructiveness of war is to deter it, and insofar as theater forces are required for deterrence they should be as effective in that role as possible. For *any* given sum of expenditures the best theater deterrence force is the most efficient fighting force, and that means a force organized, trained, and equipped for using the most modern weapons, certainly including nuclear ones. The prevailing assumption is, of course, that an attack upon it will *not* be an accident. Second, the decision to use nuclear weapons would in any case not be primarily ours to make, especially with the basic premise in all our war plans being that the opponent is the aggressor; defense plans have to consider not the most desired but the most likely mode of enemy attack. Third, there is no *prima facie* evidence that a battle fought with TNWs would be more destructive to the terrain over which it is fought or to noncombatants in the theater than the conventional battles we have known in the two world wars. It might well be the other way round. The critical factor in destructiveness to the terrain is usually the rate of movement of the contending armies, the destructiveness tending to be inversely proportional to the swiftness with which one side pushes back or destroys the other. Also, with nuclear weapons it is very much a matter of the types most used and the manner in which they are employed—something that should be studied intensively in advance, largely for the sake of minimizing undesired collateral damage.

DECIDING ON WEAPON NUMBERS

Leaving now the matter of TNWs, but pursuing the important objective of "limiting the destructiveness of war if it comes," we might briefly consider the views of Herbert York, who has been active in efforts to get agreements to reduce the size of nuclear stockpiles, especially of strategic nuclear weapons.[12] There can be little question that American and Soviet strategic nuclear weapons already deployed or otherwise available for use have grown in numbers far beyond any reasonable conception of military need and certainly of deterrence. This has been a result mainly of competitive pressures and of such technological advances as MIRV. The requirement to escape the threat of having one's retaliatory force obliterated by surprise attack is solved far better by the manner of its deployment than by multiplying its weapons. Though the long-term viability of our silo-protected ICBMs may be in doubt, alternative means of deployment, such as submarine-launched missiles, make it absurd to sound alarms about the imminent danger of the Russians developing a "first-strike capability"—a complaint frequently voiced by former Secretary of Defense Melvin Laird. Equally dubious were the public expressions of another recent Secretary of Defense, James R. Schlesinger, who argued that with the kind of accuracy that promises to become available in the cruise missile we should develop what was formerly called a "damage-limiting" capability, that is, limiting damage to ourselves by destroying enemy missiles in their silos.

Why then, has it been so difficult for York to get a sympathetic hearing for his views, even in such milieus as the Arms Control and Disarmament Agency (ACDA)? One of the reasons, no doubt, is that nuclear weapons already produced and deployed are so much sunk capital, not especially costly to maintain in their land-based missile configurations and certainly not when stockpiled. The budget for all American strategic nuclear forces, which includes bombers and missile submarines and all monies spent on related research and development, was in FY 1976 about 18 percent of our entire defense budget. Those costs would not be substantially reduced simply by phasing out warheads. Also, with the passing of the years the possibility of a strategic nuclear exchange seems to have become in most people's minds more and more remote, and one reason for that is precisely the horrendous number of weapons. It is one thing to say that we have far more than enough weapons for deterrence, but who is to say—and to persuade others—how far that number can reasonably drop before deterrence is in fact diminished? Who wants to rock the boat, especially since large numbers are also a protection against the alleged "destabilization" that tends to result from various kinds of technological innovation? Many people show a deep concern about "superiority," about relative "throw-weights" and all the rest, and although these fears do point to the importance of fruitful negotiation

---

[12] Of his many writings on the subject, one of the most comprehensive is *Race to Oblivion* (New York: Simon and Schuster, 1970).

to find mutual limits, they also reflect an abiding confidence in numbers which has to be, if not honored, at least humored.

Most important of all, however, in accounting for the lack of receptiveness to York's ideas is the fact that, precisely because the number of weapons is so huge, the realization of his ideas would require a *drastic* reduction in those numbers—not just 10 or 20 percent but something well over 90 percent! If the object is to retain the kind of deterrence which strategic nuclear weapons provide against any kind of war with the rival superpower, but to decrease materially the grimness that would follow a failure of deterrence—we should have to know how to draw the curve for the marginal utility of weapons. We should than have to hunt for something like an optimum balance between deterrence on the one hand, and on the other hand reasonable (?) limits to destructiveness if deterrence fails. We should then have to develop a consensus within the country, at least among relevant bureaucracies and the Congress, that we had found the optimum zone of figures, following which we should have to embark upon appropriate negotiations abroad. And because the figure to be aimed at is now so much lower than before, negotiations would have to include not only the Soviet Union but also China, France, and Britain. No one should presume to say that the day will never arrive when such a chain of events is possible, but it is certainly not on the horizon.

ASSESSING THE ARMS RACE

The competitive pressures mentioned above bring us to another of the alleged major causes of war which arms control is supposed to curb—the arms race. It is an article of faith among most of those who write on arms control that curbing the arms race in order to keep the peace of the world is what arms control is all about, or at least mostly about. Among these writers arms competitions or "races" are alleged to be by themselves the most potent—the word "inevitable" is frequently in evidence—of the causes of war.

The idea is on the face of it somewhat illogical. Why the pressures of an arms competition, however costly, irritating, or even alarming they may become, should move one of the competitors to try to resolve it all by resorting to the immeasurably more costly and hazardous arbitrament of war is not easy to see, unless he happens to be greatly superior, in which case the competition should not bother him. If the competition is downgraded to being only a potent contributing cause, then we should focus on what comes first and consider how much the arms competition really contributes. It may in fact derive from the prime cause, which we must assume to be political, in which case it is simply part of the working out of the animosity, that is, it is more an effect than a cause.

The arms competition we have been witnessing in the Middle East is clearly of the latter kind. We see both sides frantically attempting between wars to rearm themselves against another outbreak that both sides believe highly likely if not inevitable. In such situations, however, the major provocations to violence clearly lie outside the arms competition itself and almost totally account for that competition. Conditions of the moment which the aggressor finds favorable to himself *may* help to trigger a war, but that does not alter the basic quality we see in the competition, which is that it is entirely derivative from the hostility and not the other way round.

What may be called the "classical" arms race, on the other hand, follows a model where the rivals measure their arms progress against each other, out of considerations of status and of ultimate security against *conceivable* warlike situations, but where the focus is more on competition itself than on any high or imminent expectation of war. The latter situation fairly describes the competition between the United States and the Soviet Union during at least the last decade—which is in some contrast to the situation of the 1950s when the expectation of war was considerably higher.[13]

Arms races of this latter type are fairly recent phenomena. In older times the size of the military forces of the prince depended on his wealth, pride, and territorial ambitions, but a number of factors were missing then that seem to be essential in the modern type of competition. Among them are rapid technological progress and also a level of productivity of the national economy which makes for a good deal of "fat"—as contrasted with the subsistence-level economy that characterized most nations before the 19th century. There are in modern times vast resources free for competitive military buildups that were not comparably free at an earlier time.

Probably the most celebrated arms race in history is the Anglo-German naval race that began with the German naval laws of 1898 and 1900. It stands out as the stereotype of the modern arms race, and it was indeed hard and furious. It has for that reason often been charged with being a primary cause of Britain's entry into World War I.

There is much instruction in studying that race, particularly in seeing how the Germans rationalized a vain and improvident policy and how badly they misjudged the British. There can be no doubt that

---

[13] We should note here Albert Wohlstetter's denial that there is an arms race between the two superpowers, though he concedes there is an arms competition which raises costs on both sides. I have assumed above that the two terms were sufficiently imprecise to be virtually interchangeable. See Wohlstetter's "Is There a Strategic Arms Race?," *Foreign Policy*, No. 15 (Summer, 1974), pp. 3–20 and No. 16 (Fall, 1974), pp. 48–81. See also Michael L. Nacht's critique of Wohlstetter's view in the same journal, No. 19 (Summer, 1975), pp. 163–177, and Wohlstetter's reply to Nacht and others in No. 20 (Fall, 1975), pp. 170–198.

it caused much irritation and even some alarm in Britain. But we know now a good deal about the motivations of Britain's pre-war diplomacy and also about that week of groping in the Cabinet that finally brought Britain's declaration of war in August 1914. The evidence is overwhelming that the German naval competition was of far less than prime significance in provoking the British decision. It had had virtually nothing to do with Britain's departing "splendid isolation" to conclude its alliance with Japan in 1902 and its *entente* with France in 1904. In subsequent events, including the *entente* with Russia in 1907, it had loomed somewhat larger, but it was still only part of the whole image of Germany that the several pre-war crises and the posturing of a vainglorious kaiser helped to produce. Finally there was the clear and blatant violation of the Belgium Neutralization Treaty of 1839.[14]

No doubt the British tolerance for the German competition derived from their confidence that they could maintain the naval fighting superiority that was so important to them. To outbuild the Germans was costly but feasible, and far less costly than fighting them. That fact, too, points to something instructive about that race and especially to how it differed from any kind of armaments race that could possibly exist today between the United States and the Soviet Union.

The unit of account for fleet fighting power at the time of that race was the battleship—after 1906 the Dreadnought-type battleship— designed and built primarily for fighting its like on the high seas. Once built it might also be used for other purposes, like shore bombardment, but it was never put in hazard for such purposes if there was a chance that it might be needed for contending with enemy battleships. Because the British succeeded in building more battleships than the Germans and because they also built ships with bigger guns, they maintained a battle superiority which both sides knew to be overwhelming. When it came to the contest of battle fleets in World War I, the British Grand Fleet simply contained the German High Seas Fleet for four years of war and made the latter quite useless. It did so while being mostly silent and at anchor. On the one occasion that the two fleets met, off Jutland, the entire preoccupation of the German commander was with escape.

Thus, with surface fleets even more than with armies, the fact that the military units of each side fought comparable military units of the

---

[14] On official British attitudes towards Germany, a number of fascinating once-secret memoranda are reprinted in Kenneth Bourne's *The Foreign Policy of Victorian England*, 1830–1902 (London: Oxford University Press, 1970). Despite the terminal date in the book's title, the memoranda which are especially interesting cover the period from 1901 to 1914 (pp. 462–504). See especially the long extract from the major policy memorandum of 1 January 1907 by Eyre Crowe, who bore the misleading title of Senior Clerk in the Foreign Office, pp. 481–493.

other gave real meaning to a margin of superiority. Such meaning is lost in the present armaments rivalry with the Soviet Union, in which it is basic that we are dealing with weaponry where the units are *not* primarily intended to fight each other. Certainly that is characteristic of the whole family of nuclear weapons which, despite frequent allegations to the contrary, are the weapons most effective in keeping the two nations firmly on course—that is, on the course of avoiding war with each other. Also, there is between the superpowers nothing comparable now to the peculiar and one-sided vulnerability of Britain to the interruption of her sea-borne communications, a vulnerability which absolutely obliged her to insist on clear superiority on the seas.

That nuclear weapons are not intended primarily to fight each other may be denied by proponents of counterforce targeting. Until the conclusion of the SALT I agreements, some were excited also by the qualified capability of ABMs to destroy incoming nuclear warheads high above the ground—a possibility that seemed to promise to make warfare once more a duel, to be fought this time in space. However, few students of the problem can deny that success for a counterforce strategy must depend on some quite unpredictable variables and, especially because of the several alternative means of retaliatory attack, *is bound always to be critically limited.*

In the present situation there is even less reason than before to worry about the alleged provocatory nature of arms races. We may even allow ourselves some astonishment at how little such provocations seem to matter, either in diplomacy or in everyday life. Both superpowers have weapons aimed at each other that could spell for each something approaching obliteration. Neither side has anything remotely resembling a defense except its power of retaliation. It is a circumstance that, at the dawn of the nuclear age, people predicted would be quite intolerable. But the feared condition arrived gradually, and as people came to live with it, proved not only tolerable but also not without its own peculiar comforts. There developed a sense that no issue existed to induce the superpowers to go to war with each other when such a penalty for doing so hung over them mutually—a condition quite new in the world's history.

There are now, as there always have been, the habitual sounders of alarm about losing some margin of superiority, either in ships at sea, in throw-weight of missiles, or whatnot. But despite the jingoism on the far right evoked by the 1976 primaries, the national audience seems to be lacking something in responsiveness. When before has a secretary of state, who incidentally enjoyed a considerable and unusual reputation for understanding strategic issues, replied to some fulminations from the Defense Department, as Kissinger did in 1974, with the exclamation: "What in the name of God is strategic superiority? What is the significance of it politically, militarily, operationally, at this level of numbers?"

For our purposes we are not obliged to determine whether Kissinger is right or wrong in the sentiment reflected in his exclamation. What it does tell us incontrovertibly is that whatever arms race is going on currently, and however costly it may be, it is not in itself adding very much to the irritations and provocations that arise from time to time between the two major rivals. An arms race may indeed cause them to treat each other with more respect than they otherwise would, but that too has its net utilities.

We have learned over the three decades that nuclear weapons have been with us that the balance of terror is *not* delicate. For either superpower to attack the other because of an optimistic guess of the latter's vulnerabilities is obviously to take a risk of cataclysmic proportions. Neither can be seduced into such an error by some apparent shift in the relationship of forces—usually more apparent to technicians than to politicians. Nor will either superpower be seduced by the appearance of some new mechanical contrivance which at best affects only a part of the whole scheme of things, usually a small part.

The terms "destabilizing" and "stabilizing" have become fashionable in referring to various technological developments. Their use commonly reflects a limited perception of how each development alters or fits into the entire technological *and* political universe in which we live. No doubt a prolonged somnolescence by the United States concerning qualitative and quantitative changes in the arms balance would in time prove dangerous, especially if it were not accompanied by a drastic downward reassessment of our foreign policy interests. But the fate of ourselves and of the world is not going to hang on what we do or fail to do about some object like the cruise missile. Not long ago the alleged fate-determining object was the ABM. It sometimes helps to remember the several invasion panics in England in the mid-19th century, when the adoption of steam propulsion by warships was supposed to have created "a steam bridge across the Channel."

BUDGETING FOR DEFENSE

If arms competitions are not in themselves dangerous, which is to say significantly provocative of an inclination to war, they are certainly costly. An international agreement which succeeds in limiting that competition is an important and welcome way of limiting those costs. Naturally one does not wish to save money at the cost of a significant impairment of security, but the role for intelligent arms control is precisely to find and exploit instances where there is no such conflict.

There are some, to be sure, who argue that the arms race, if there is one, is not too costly. Many, including President Ford, have pointed to our current defense budget as being "only" 6 percent of our GNP, which they call an historically low proportion that should be considered a floor on our military expenditures. Some, like former Secretary of Defense Schlesinger, make statements arguing a positive value for their own sake in high military expenditures, claiming that any attempt to reduce them sends the "wrong signals" to the Soviet leaders. Reasoning from the 6 percent figure Schlesinger was looking forward with no apparent pain to annual defense budgets of $150 billion by 1980.

One might point out that 6 percent of GNP is historically a low peacetime figure for the United States only since the Korean War. One could suggest also that national and indeed worldwide trends make governments more responsible for social welfare than formerly, and these trends, which appear politically irreversible at least for the United States, make 6 percent of GNP for military expenditures considerably more burden than it used to be. This percentage currently represents approximately $100 billion. We are also becoming increasingly aware that percentage of GNP is a much less meaningful figure than percentage of the national budget, for the latter represents monies being raised by taxation and by deficit financing, and we are becoming acutely aware of the limits, disutilities, and special pains associated with both. The defense budget is still by far the largest single category in the national budget, and it accounts for roughly 35 percent of it.

But is all this relevant? The notion that it pays to spend extra billions just to send the "right" signals abroad ought to be rejected as most unlikely to be "cost-effective" compared with other means of signaling. What are the "right signals" supposed to be anyway? What signals are in fact sent by simply boosting military expenditures? If these and related questions are not in the narrow sense researchable, they are certainly worth more thought than they usually get by those who urge the Schlesinger view. That view, while not necessarily in conflict with efficient military expenditure, is not likely to be conducive to it either.

The merit of explicit, mutual agreements on arms control is that both sides are committed to the same course of action, usually for the same or at least similar reasons. That makes the signals mutual. Just as cost-effectiveness analysis was devised and pursued for the sake of avoiding sheer waste in military expenditures (it is usually expressed in other ways, but they amount to the same thing), so arms control should be conceived as an important and fruitful means of avoiding waste. For that we should not have to make apologies.

Two examples should suffice to illustrate the practical application of our argument. The first is the Washington Naval Limitation Treaty of 1922, later supplemented by the London Naval Treaty of 1930. These treaties are among the very few in history—if there are indeed others of comparable weight—in which the several great powers succeeded by free mutual agreement not only in limiting future building in a primary military category but actually in reducing significantly levels already reached. The motivation on all sides was entirely economic, though naturally in the speeches applauding the signing ceremonies the benign consequences for world peace were duly rung in.[15]

The other, more recent example was the effective demolition of the ABM programs of the United States and the Soviet Union as a result of the SALT 1 agreements of 1972. To anyone who had followed the ABM debate in the United States, this result was astonishing. Few historical debates on armaments had aroused the passions that this one did, with experts in the related technologies arrayed on both sides. The substance of the debate was mostly over the efficacy of the Sentinel system, a name changed to "Safeguard" by President Nixon, who showed himself to be one of its most ardent champions. In pushing the necessary supporting acts through a once-reluctant Senate, Nixon did indeed use the "bargaining chip" argument along with several others, but his obvious ardor for the system itself made it difficult to give credence to this explanation.

The fact that it ultimately did prove to be a bargining chip does not quite dispel one's doubts as to whether it was so conceived all along. It appears likely that President Nixon underwent a real change of heart about ABM, the rapidly growing problem with inflation no doubt having much to do with his change. Inflation clearly made him look harder at the data that brought into question the efficacy and utility of the system, including new developments like MIRVs, the cruise missile, and alternatives to fixed silos for ICBMs, especially land-mobile systems.

In any case, the motivation and justification for doing away mutually with the ABM (actually, in the first instance, limiting it) were almost entirely economic. It cannot plausibly be argued that it enhanced our security to accomplish this result; neither does it make much sense to say that it diminished it.[16] The ABM lent itself ideally to the action taken for the following basic reasons: (1) it was not yet acquired and deployed; (2) its efficacy was always questionable and becoming more so; (3) it would be an extraordinarily expensive system to build,

---

[15] The standard monograph on the first and most important of these treaties, that of Washington in 1922, is still Harold and Margaret Sprout, *Toward a New Order of Sea Power* (Princeton: Princeton University Press, 2nd ed., 1943.)

[16] One of the few hold-outs on the latter view is Dr. Donald G. Brennan, in his "When the SALT Hit the Fan," *National Review*, vol. 24, (June 23, 1972) pp. 685–692. See also his testimony in the ratification hearings of the SALT 1 agreements. It is important to notice that Dr. Brennan never thought that the ABM would be effective in protecting cities unless offensive forces were suitably limited. In his current view, the massive buildup of offensive forces since the late 1960s has diminished the feasibility (though not the desirability) of such a posture, at least based on current technology, to near the vanishing point.

deploy, and maintain; and (4) it would be difficult domestically to win a consensus on dropping it except through an instrument that obliged the Soviet Union to do likewise.

The original SALT agreement limited each side to two sites, one being the capital or "national command authority," the other being a single field site containing no more than 100 interceptor missiles of all types (in the United States the Spartan and the Sprint missiles). It quickly became obvious that the Congress would never support a system for the single city of Washington. An amendment in 1974 to the SALT agreement limited each side to one site only. The United States by then had built such a site, at Grand Forks, North Dakota, but in 1975 the Congress, facing the choice of appropriating $60 million to continuing it for another year or $40 million for liquidating it, chose the latter course. It is difficult to tell what the total expenditure had been at that time—it had cost about $4 billion to develop just the Spartan missile with its special nuclear warhead, of which some 30 were built—but there is no doubt that many times that sum was saved by abandoning it.

It retrospect the ABM may look like a system that virtually cried out for mutual abrogation, but it certainly did not look so at the time. The support for it within the defense community was intense. Now the ABM appears to have been a target of opportunity, torpedoed at just the right time and by the right means.

It should be the prime function of an intelligently directed arms control program always to be looking out for more such targets. They will be found especially among emerging systems, but also among those existing ones which are costly to maintain and of dubious marginal utility. One might, for example, nominate for consideration our aircraft bombing force, including both the proposed B-1 and the existing 400 B-52s. What is the marginal utility of this force *along with* our submarine-launched and our land-based missiles? If some bombers are desirable, do we need all those proposed? It would indeed take some stout-hearted men to explore this issue together with, or perhaps in the face of, the Air Force, but such a course is not unprecedented. The naval treaties of 1922 and 1930 were bitterly opposed by the chief naval officers and the navy leagues of virtually all the countries involved, which makes their achievement all the more remarkable. Perhaps the required stout-heartedness *is* what arms control is all about.

Arms Races:
Prerequisites and Results

SAMUEL P. HUNTINGTON

INTRODUCTION

Si vis pacem, para bellum, is an ancient and authoritative adage of military policy. Of no less acceptance, however, is the other, more modern, proposition: "Armaments races inevitably lead to war." Juxtaposed, these two advices suggest that the maxims of social science, like the proverbs of folklore, reflect a many-sided truth. The social scientist, however, cannot escape with so easy an observation. He has the scholar's responsibility to determine as fully as possible to what extent and under what conditions his conflicting truths are true. The principal aim of this essay is to attempt some resolution of the issue: When are arms races a prelude to war and when are they a substitute for war?

Throughout history states have sought to maintain their peace and security by means of military strength. The arms race in which the military preparations of two states are intimately and directly inter-related is, however, a relatively modern phenomenon. The conflict between the apparent feasibility of preserving peace by arming for war and the apparent inevitability of competitive arms increases resulting in war is, therefore, a comparatively new one. The second purpose of this essay is to explore some of the circumstances which have brought about this uncertainty as to the relationship between war, peace and arms increases. The problem here is: What were the prerequisites to the emergence of the arms race as a significant form of international rivalry in the nineteenth and twentieth centuries?

For the purposes of this essay, an arms race is defined as a progressive, competitive peacetime increase in armaments by two states or coalition of states resulting from conflicting purposes or mutual fears. An arms race is thus a form of reciprocal interaction between two states or coalitions. A race cannot exist without an increase in arms, quantitatively or qualitatively, but every peacetime increase in arms is not necessarily the result of an arms race. A nation may expand its armmaments for the domestic purposes of aiding industry or curbing

From *Public Policy,* 1958, pp. 41–83. Copyright © 1958 by John Wiley & Sons, Inc. Reprinted with permission of John Wiley & Sons, Inc.

unemployment, or because it believes an absolute need exists for such an increase regardless of the actions of other states. In the 1880s and 1890s, for instance, the expansion of the United States Navy was apparently unrelated to the actions of any other power, and hence not part of an arms race. An arms race reflects disagreement between two states as to the proper balance of power between them. The concept of a "general" arms race in which a number of powers increase their armaments simultaneously is, consequently, a fallacious one. Such general increases either are not the result of self-conscious reciprocal interaction or are simply the sum of a number of two-state antagonisms. In so far as the arms policy of any one state is related to the armaments of other states, it is a function of concrete, specific goals, needs, or threats arising out of the political relations among the states. Even Britain's vaunted two-power naval standard will be found, on close analysis, to be rooted in specific threats rather than in abstract considerations of general policy.

PREREQUISITES FOR AN ARMS RACE

. . . Certain conditions peculiarly present in the nineteenth and twentieth centuries would appear to be responsible for the emergence of the arms race as a frequent and distinct form of international rivalry. Among the more significant of these conditions are: a state system which facilitates the balancing of power by internal rather than external means; the preeminence of military force-in-being over territory or other factors as an element of national power; the capacity within each state to increase its military strength through quantitative or qualitative means; and the conscious awareness by each state of the dependence of its own arms policy upon that of another state.[1]

[1] Since an arms race is necessarily a matter of degree, differences of opinion will exist as to whether any given relationship constitutes an arms race and as to what are the precise opening and closing dates of any given arms race. At the risk of seeming arbitrary, the following relationships are assumed to be arms races for the purposes of this essay:

1. France v. England	naval	1840–1866
2. France v. Germany	land	1874–1894
3. England v. France & Russia	naval	1884–1904
4. Argentina v. Chile	naval	1890–1902
5. England v. Germany	naval	1898–1912
6. France v. Germany	land	1911–1914
7. England v. United States	naval	1916–1930
8. Japan v. United States	naval	1916–1922
9. France v. Germany	land	1934–1939
10. Soviet Union v. Germany	land	1934–1941
11. Germany v. England	air	1934–1939
12. United States v. Japan	naval	1934–1941
13. Soviet Union v. United States	nuclear	1946–

Balancing power: external and internal means. Arms races are an integral part of the international balance of power. From the viewpoint of a participant, an arms race is an effort to achieve a favorable international distribution of power. Viewed as a whole, a sustained arms race is a means of achieving a dynamic equilibrium of power between two states or coalitions of states. Arms races only take place between states in the same balance of power system. The more isolated a nation is from any balance of power system the less likely it is to become involved in an arms race. Within any such system, power may in general be balanced in two ways: externally through a realignment of the units participating in the system (diplomacy), or internally by changes in the inherent power of the units. The extent to which the balancing process operates through external or internal means usually depends upon the number of states participating in the system, the opportunity for new states to join the system, and the relative distribution of power among the participating states.

The relations among the states in a balance of power system may tend toward any one of three patterns, each of which assigns somewhat different roles to the external and internal means of balancing power. A situation of *bellum omnium contra omnes* exists when there are a large number of states approximately equal in power and when there is an approximately equal distribution of grievances and antagonisms among the states. In such a system, which was perhaps most closely approximated by the city-states of the Italian Renaissance, primary reliance is placed upon wily diplomacy, treachery and surprise attack. Since no bilateral antagonisms continue for any length of time, a sustained arms race is very unlikely. A second balance of power pattern involves an all-against-one relationship: the coalition of a number of weaker states against a single *grande nation*. The fears and grievances of the weaker states are concentrated against the stronger, and here again primary reliance is placed upon diplomatic means of maintaining or restoring the balance. European politics assumed this pattern in the successive coalitions to restrain the Hapsburgs, Louis XIV, Frederick II, Napoleon and Hitler. At times, efforts may be made to bring in other states normally outside the system to aid in restoring the balance.

A third pattern of balance of power politics involves bilateral antagonisms between states or coalitions of states roughly equal in strength. Such bilateral antagonisms have been a continuing phenomenon in the western balance of power system: France vs. England, Austria vs. France and then Prussia (Germany) vs. France, Austria-Hungary vs. Russia, the Triple Alliance vs. the Triple Entente, and now, the United States vs. the Soviet Union. In these relationships the principal grievances and antagonisms of any two states become concentrated upon each other, and as a result, this antagonism becomes the primary focus of their respective foreign policies. In this situation, diplomacy and alliances may play a significant role if a "balancer" exists who can shift his weight to whichever side appears to be weaker. But no balancing state can exist if all the major powers are involved in bilateral antagonisms or if a single overriding antagonism forces virtually all the states in the system to choose one side or the other (bipolarization). In these circumstances, the balancing of power by rearranging the units of power becomes difficult. Diplomatic maneuvering gives way to the massing of military force. Each state relies more on armaments and less on alliances. Other factors being equal, the pressures toward an arms race are greatest when international relations assume this form.

In the past century the relative importance of the internal means of balancing power has tended to increase. A single worldwide balance of power system has tended to develop, thereby eliminating the possibility of bringing in outside powers to restore the balance. At the same time, however, the number of great powers has fairly constantly decreased, and bilateral antagonisms have consequently become of greater importance. Small powers have tended to seek security either through neutrality (Switzerland, Sweden) or through reliance upon broadly organized efforts at collective security. The growth of the latter idea has tended to make military alliances aimed at a specific common foe less reputable and justifiable. . . . Alliances were perhaps the primary means of balancing power in Europe before 1870. Between 1870 and 1914, both alliances and armaments played important roles. Since 1918 the relative importance of armaments has probably increased. The primary purpose of the military pacts of the post-World War II period, with the possible exception of NATO, generally has been the extension of the protection of a great power to a series of minor powers, rather than the uniting of a number of more or less equal powers in pursuit of a common objective. In addition, the development of democractic control over foreign policy has made alliances more difficult. Alignments dictated by balance of power considerations may be impossible to carry out due to public opinion. Rapid shifts in alliances from friends to enemies also are difficult to execute in a democratic society. Perhaps, too, a decline in the arts of diplomacy has contributed to the desire to rest one's security upon resources which are "owned" rather than "pledged."

Elements of power: money, territory, armaments. Arms races only take place when military forces-in-being are of direct and prime importance to the power of a state. During the age of mercantilism, for instance, monetary resources were highly valued as an index of power, and, consequently, governmental policy was directed toward the accumulation of economic wealth which could then be transformed into military and political power. These actions, which might take a variety of forms, were in some respects the seventeenth century equivalents of the nineteenth and twentieth century arms races. In the eighteenth century, territory was of key importance as a measure of power. The size of the armies which a state could maintain was roughly proportional to its population, and, in an agrarian age, its population was roughly proportional to its territory. Consequently, an increase in military power required an increase in territory. Within Europe, territory could be acquired either by conquest, in which case a surprise attack was probably desirable in order to forestall intervention by other states, or by agreement among the great powers to partition a smaller power. Outside of Europe, colonial territories might contribute wealth if not manpower to the mother country, and these could be acquired either by discovery and settlement or by conquest. Consequently, territorial compensations were a primary means of balancing power, and through the acquisition of colonies, states jealous of their relative power could strive to improve their position without directly challenging another major state and thereby provoking a war.

During the nineteenth century territory bacame less important as an index of power, and industry and armaments more important. By the end of the century all the available colonial lands had been occupied by the major powers. In addition, the rise of nationalism and of self-determination made it increasingly difficult to settle differences by the division and bartering of provinces, small powers and colonies. By expanding its armaments, however, a state could still increase its relative power without decreasing the absolute power of another state. Reciprocal increases in armaments made possible an unstable and dynamic, but none the less real equilibrium among the major powers. The race for armaments tended to replace the race for colonies as the "escape hatch" through which major states could enhance their power without directly challenging each other.

The increased importance of armaments as a measure of national power was reflected in the new emphasis upon disarmament in the efforts to resolve antagonisms among nations. The early peace writers, prior to the eighteenth century, placed primary stress upon a federation of European states rather than upon disarmament measures. It was not until Kant's essay on "Eternal Peace" that the dangers inherent in an arms race were emphasized, and the reduction of armaments made a primary goal. In 1766 Austria made the first proposal for a bilateral reduction in forces to Frederick the Great, who rejected it. In 1787 France and England agreed not to increase their naval establishments. In 1816 the Czar made the first proposal for a general reduction in armaments. Thenceforth, throughout the nineteenth century problems of armament and disarmament played an increasingly significant role in diplomatic negotiations.[2]

[2] Merze Tate, *The Disarmament Illusion* (New York, 1942), p. 7.

Capacity for qualitative and quantitative increases in military power. An arms race requires the progressive increase from domestic sources of the absolute military power of a state. This may be done quantitatively, by expanding the numerical strength of its existing forms of military force, or qualitatively, by replacing its existing forms of military force (usually weapons systems) with new and more effective forms of force. The latter requires a dynamic technology, and the former the social, political and economic capacity to reallocate resources from civilian to military purposes. Before the nineteenth century the European states possessed only a limited capacity for either quantitative or qualitative increases in military strength. Naval technology, for instance, had been virtually static for almost three centuries: the sailing ship of 1850 was not fundamentally different from that of 1650, the naval gun of 1860 not very much removed from that of 1560.[3] As a result, the ratio of construction time to use time was extremely low: a ship built in a few months could be used for the better part of a century. Similarly, with land armaments, progress was slow, and only rarely could a power hope to achieve a decisive edge by a "technological breakthrough". Beginning with the Industrial Revolution, however, the pace of innovation in military technology constantly quickened, and the new weapons systems inevitably stimulated arms races. The introduction, first, of the steam warship and then of the ironclad, for instance, directly intensified the naval competition between England and France in the 1850s and 1860s. Throughout the nineteenth century, the importance of the weapons technician constantly increased relative to the importance of the strategist.

Broad changes in economic and political structure were at the same time making quantitative arms races feasible. The social system of the *ancien régime* did not permit a full mobilization of the economic and manpower resources of a nation. So long as participation in war was limited to a small class, competitive increases in the size of armies could not proceed very far. The destruction of the old system, the spread of democracy and liberalism, the increasing popularity among all groups of the "nation in arms" concept, all permitted a much more complete mobilization of resources for military purposes than had been possible previously. In particular, the introduction of universal military service raised the ceiling on the size of the army to the point where the limiting factor was the civilian manpower necessary to support the army. In addition, the development of industry permitted the mass production and mass accumulation of the new weapons which the new technology had invented. The countries which lagged behind

[3] Bernard Brodie, *Sea Power in the Machine Age* (Princeton, 2nd ed., 1944), p. 181; Arthur J. Marder, *The Anatomy of British Sea Power* (New York, 1940), pp. 3–4.

in the twin processes of democratization and industrialization were severely handicapped in the race for armaments.

In the age of limited wars little difference existed between a nation's military strength in peace and its military strength in war. During the nineteenth century, however, the impact of democracy and industrialism made wars more total, victory or defeat in them became more significant (and final), military superiority became more critically important, and consequently a government had to be more fully assured of the prospect of victory before embarking upon war. In addition, the professional officer corps which developed during the nineteenth century felt a direct responsibility for the military security of the state and emphasized the desirability of obtaining a safe superiority in armaments As a result, unless one of the participants possessed extensive staying power due to geography or resources, the outcome of a war depended almost as much upon what happened before the declarations of war as after. By achieving superiority in armaments it might be possible for a state to achieve the fruits of war without suffering the risks and liabilities of war. Governments piled up armaments in peacetime with the hope either of averting war or of insuring success in it should it come.

Absolute and relative armaments goals. A state may define its armaments goals in one of two ways. It can specify a certain *absolute* level or type of armaments which it believes necessary for it to possess irrespective of the level or type possessed by other states. Or, it can define its goal in *relative* terms as a function of the armaments of other states. Undoubtedly, in any specific case, a state's armaments reflect a combination of both absolute and relative considerations. Normally, however, one or the other will be dominant and embodied in offical statements of the state's armaments goals in the form of an "absolute need" or a ratio-goal. Thus, historically Great Britain followed a relative policy with respect to the capital ships in its navy but an absolute policy with respect to its cruisers, the need for which, it was held, stemmed from the unique nature of the British Empire.

If every state had absolute goals, arms races would be impossible: each state would go its separate way uninfluenced by the actions of its neighbors. Nor would a full scale arms race develop if an absolute goal were pursued consistently by only one power in an antagonistic realtionship: whatever relative advantage the second power demanded would be simply a function of the constant absolute figure demanded by the first power. An arms race only arises when two or more powers consciously determine the quantitative or qualitative aspects of their armaments as functions of the armaments of the other power. Absolute goals, however, are only really feasible when a state is not a member of or only on the periphery of a balance of power system. Except in these rare cases, the formulation by a state of its armaments goal in absolute terms is more likely to reflect the desire to obscure from its rivals the true relative superiority which it wishes to achieve or to obscure from itself the need to participate actively in the balancing process. Thus, its Army Law of 1893 was thought to give Germany a force which in quantity and quality would be unsurpassable by any other power. Hence Germany

> was, in the eyes of her rulers, too powerful to be affected by a balancing movement restricted only to the continent. . . . From this time on Germany considered herself militarily invulnerable, as if in a state of splendid isolation, owing to the excellence of her amalgam army.[4]

As a result, Germany let her army rest, turned her energies to the construction of a navy, and then suddenly in 1911 became aware of her landpower inferiority to the Dual Alliance and had to make strenuous last minute efforts to increase the size of her forces. Somewhat similarly, states may define absolute qualitative goals, such as the erection of an impenetrable system of defenses (Maginot Line) or the possession of an "ultimate" or "absolute" weapon, which will render superfluous further military effort regardless of what other states may do. In 1956 American airpower policy was consciously shaped not to the achievement of any particular level of air strength relative to that of the Soviet Union, but rather to obtaining an absolute "sufficiency of airpower" which would permit the United States to wreak havoc in the Soviet Union in the event of an all-out war.[5] The danger involved in an absolute policy is that, if carried to an extreme, it may lead to a complacent isolationism blind to the relative nature of power.

The armaments of two states can be functionally interrelated only if they are also similar or complementary. An arms race is impossible between a power which possesses only a navy and one which possesses only an army: no one can match divisions against battleships. A functional realtionship between armaments is complementary when two

---

[4] Arpad Kovacs, "Nation in Arms and Balance of Power: The Interaction of German Military Legislation and European Politics, 1866–1914" (Ph.D. Thesis, University of Chicago, 1934), p. 159.

[5] For the most complete statement of the sufficiency theory, see Donald A. Quarles, Secretary of the Air Force, "How Much is 'Enough'?" *Air Force*, XLIX (September, 1956), pp. 51–52: ". . . there comes a time in the course of increasing our airpower when we must make a determination of sufficiency. . . .

"Sufficiency of airpower, to my mind, must be determined period by period on the basis of the force required to accomplish the mission assigned. . . . Neither side can hope by a mere margin of superiority in airplanes or other means of delivery of atomic weapons to escape the catastrophe of such a [total] war. Beyond a certain point, this prospect is not the result of *relative* strength of the two opposed forces. It is the *absolute* power in the hands of each, and in the substantial invulnerability of this power to interdiction."

See also H. Rept. 2104, 84th Cong., 2d Sess., p. 40 (1956).

military forces possessing different weapons systems are designed for combat with each other. In this sense, an air defense fighter command complements an opposing strategic bombing force or one side's submarine force complements the other's antisubmarine destroyers and hunter-killer groups. A functional relationship is similar when two military forces are not only designed for combat with each other but also possess similar weapons systems, as has been very largely the case with land armies and with battle fleets of capital ships. In most instances in history, arms races have involved similar forces rather than complementary forces, but no reason exists why there should not be an arms race in the latter. The only special problem posed by a complementary arms race is that of measuring the relative strengths of the opposing forces. In a race involving similar forces, a purely quantitative measurement usually suffices; in one of complementary forces, qualitative judgments are necessary as to the effectiveness of one type of weapons system against another.

Even if both parties to an arms race possess similar land, sea and air forces, normally the race itself is focused on only one of these components or even on only one weapons system within one component, usually that type of military force with which they are best able to harm each other.[6] This component or weapons system is viewed by the states as the decisive form of military force in their mutual relationship, and competition in other forces or components is subordinated to the race in this decisive force. The simple principles of concentration and economy of force require states to put their major efforts where they will count most The arms race between Germany and England before World War I was in capital ships. The arms race between the same two countries before World War II was in bombers and fighters. The current race between the Soviet Union and the United States has largely focused upon nuclear weapons and their means of delivery, and has not extended to the massing of conventional weapons and manpower. In general, economic considerations also preclude a state from becoming involved at the same time in two separate arms races with two different powers in two different forms of military force. When her race in land forces with France slackened in the middle 1890s, Germany embarked upon her naval race with Great Britain, and for the first decade of the twentieth century the requirements of this enterprise prevented any substantial increase in the size of the army. When the naval race in turn slackened in 1912, Germany returned to the rebuilding of her ground forces and to her military manpower race with France.

[6] Other things being equal, this will probably be the "dominant weapon" in Fuller's sense, that is, the weapon with the longest effective range. See J. F. C. Fuller, *Armament and History* (New York, 1945), pp. 7-8.

Two governments can consciously follow relative arms policies only if they are well informed of their respective military capabilities. The general availability of information concerning armaments is thus a precondition for an arms race. Prior to the nineteenth century when communication and transportation were slow and haphazard, a state would frequently have only the vaguest notions of the military programs of its potential rivals. Often it was possible for one state to make extensive secret preparations for war. In the modern world, information with respect to military capabilities has become much more widespread and has been one of the factors increasing the likelihood of arms races. Even now, however, many difficulties exist in getting information concerning the arms of a rival which is sufficiently accurate to serve as the basis for one's own policy. At times misconceptions as to the military strengths and policies of other states become deeply ingrained, and at other times governments simply choose to be blind to significant changes in armaments. Any modern government involved in an arms race, moreover, is confronted with conflicting estimates of its opponent's strength. Politicians, governmental agencies and private groups all tend to give primary credit to intelligence estimates which confirm military policies which they have already espoused for other reasons. The armed services inevitably overstate the military capabilities of the opponent: in 1914, for instance, the Germans estimated the French army to have 121,000 more men than the German army, the French estimated the German army to have 134,000 more men than the French army, but both countries agreed in their estimates of the military forces of third powers.[7] Governments anxious to reduce expenditures and taxes pooh-pooh warnings as to enemy strength: the reluctance of the Baldwin government to credit reports of the German air build-up seriously delayed British rearmament in the 1930s. At other times, exaggerated reports as to enemy forces may lead a government to take extraordinary measures which are subsequently revealed to have been unnecessary. Suspicions that the Germans were exceeding their announced program of naval construction led the English government in 1909 to authorize and construct four "contingency" Dreadnoughts. Subsequently revelations proved British fears to be groundless. Similarly, in 1956 reports of Soviet aircraft production, later asserted to be considerably exaggerated, influenced Congress to appropriate an extra $900 million for the Air Force. At times, the sudden revelation of a considerable increase in an enemy's capabilities may produce a panic, such as the invasion panics of England in 1847–48, 1951–53, and 1959–61. The tense atmosphere of an arms race also tends to encourage reports of

---

[7] Bernadotte E. Schmitt, *The Coming of the War: 1914* (New York, 2 vols., 1930), I, 54n.

mysterious forces possessed by the opponent and of his development of secret new weapons of unprecedented power. Nonetheless, fragmentary and uncertain though information may be, its availability in one form or another is what makes the arms race possible.

ABORTIVE AND SUSTAINED ARMS RACES

An arms race may end in war, formal or informal agreement be-tween the two states to call off the race, or victory for one state which achieves and maintains the distribution of power which it desires and ultimately causes its rival to give up the struggle. The likelihood of war arising from an arms race depends in the first instance upon the relation between the power and grievances of one state to the power and grievances of the other. War is least likely when grievances are low, or, if grievances are high, the sum of the grievances and power of one state approximates the sum of the grievances and power of the other. An equality of power and an equality of grievances will thus reduce the chances of war, as will a situation in which one state has a marked superiority in power and the other in grievances. Assuming a fairly equal distribution of grievances, the likelihood of an arms race ending in war tends to vary inversely with the length of the arms race and directly with the extent to which it is quantitative rather than qualitative in character. This section deals with the first of these relationships and the next section with the second.

An arms race is a series of interrelated increases in armaments which if continued over a period of time produces a dynamic equilibrium of power between two states. A race in which this dynamic equilibrium fails to develop may be termed an abortive arms race. In these instances, the previously existing static equilibrium between the two states is disrupted without being replaced by a new equilibrium reflecting their relative competitive efforts in the race. Instead, rapid shifts take place or appear about to take place in the distribution of power which enhance the willingness of one state or the other to precipitate a conflict. At least one and sometimes two danger points occur at the beginning of every arms race. The first point arises with the response of the challenged state to the initial increases in armaments by the challenging state. The second danger point is the reaction of the challenger who has been successful in initially achieving his goal to the frantic belated efforts of the challenged state to retrieve its former position.

The formal beginning of an arms race is the first increase in armaments by one state—the challenger—caused by a desire to alter the existing balance of power between it and another state. Prior to this initial action, a pre-arms race static equilibrium may be said to exist. This equilibrium does not necessarily mean an equality of power. It simply reflects the satisfaction of each state with the existing distribution of power in the light of its grievances and antagonisms with the other state. Some of the most stable equilibriums in history have also been ones which embodied an unbalance of power. From the middle of the eighteenth century down to the 1840s, a static equilibrium existed between the French and British navies in which the former was kept roughly two-thirds as strong as the latter. After the naval race of 1841–1865 when this ratio was challenged, the two powers returned to it for another twenty year period. From 1865 to 1884 both British and French naval expenditures were amazingly constant, England's expenditures varying between 9.5 and 10.5 million pounds (with the exception of the crisis years of 1876–77 when they reached 11 and 12 million pounds) and France's expenditures varying from 6.5 to 7.5 million pounds.[8] In some instances the equilibrium may receive the formal sanction of a treaty such as the Washington arms agreement of 1922 or the treaty of Versailles. In each of these cases, the equilibrium lasted until 1934 when the two powers—Germany and Japan—who had been relegated to a lower level of armaments decided that continued inferiority was incompatible with their national goals and ambitions. In both cases, however, it was not the disparity of power in itself which caused the destruction of the equilibrium, but rather the fact that this disparity was unacceptable to the particular groups which assumed control of those countries in the early 1930s. In other instances, the static equilibrium may last for only a passing moment, as when France began reconstructing its army almost immediately after its defeat by Germany in 1871.

For the purposes of analysis it is necessary to specify a particular increase in armaments by one state as marking the formal beginning of the arms race. This is done not to pass judgment on the desirability or wisdom of the increase, but simply to identify the start of the action and reaction which constitute the race. In most instances, this initial challenge is not hard to locate. It normally involves a major change in the policy of the challenging state, and more likely than not it is formally announced to the world. The reasons for the challenging state's discontent with the status quo may stem from a variety of causes. It may feel that the growth of its economy, commerce, and population should be reflected in changes in the military balance of power (Germany, 1898; United States, 1916; Soviet Union, 1946). Nationalistic, bellicose, or militaristic individuals or parties may come to power who are unwilling to accept an equilibrium which other groups in their society had been willing to live with or negotiate about (Germany and Japan, 1934). New political issues may arise which cause a deterioration in the relationships of the state with another power and which consequently lead it to change its estimate of the arms balance necessary for its security (France, 1841, 1875; England, 1884).

Normally the challenging state sets a goal for itself which derives from the relation between the military strengths of the two countries prior to the race. If the relation was one of disparity, the initial challenge usually comes from the weaker power which aspires to parity or better. Conceivably a stronger power could initiate an arms race by deciding that it required an even higher ratio of superiority over the weaker power. But in actual practice this is seldom the case: the gain in security achieved in upping a 2:1 ratio to 3:1, for instance, rarely is worth the increased economic costs and political tensions. If parity of military power existed between the two countries, the arms race begins when one state determines that it requires military force superior to that of the other country.

In nine out of ten races the slogan of the challenging state is either "parity" or superiority." Only in rare cases does the challenger aim for less than this, for unless equality or superiority is achieved, the arms race is hardly likely to be worthwhile. The most prominent exception to the "parity or superiority" rule is the Anglo-German naval race of 1898–1912. In its initial phase, German policy was directed not to the construction of a navy equal to England's but rather to something between that and the very minor navy which she possessed prior to the race. The rationale for building such a force was provided by Tirpitz's "risk theory": Germany should have a navy large enough so that Britain could not fight her without risking damage to the British navy to such an extent that it would fall prey to the naval forces of third powers (i.e., France and Russia). The fallacies in this policy became obvious in the following decade. On the one hand, for technical reasons it was unlikely that an inferior German navy could do serious damage to a superior British fleet, and, on the other hand, instead of making Britain wary of France and Russia the expansion of the German navy tended to drive her into their arms and consequently to remove the hostile third powers who were supposed to pounce upon a Britain weakened by Germany.[9] One can only conclude that it is seldom worthwhile either for a superior power to attempt significantly to increase its superiority or for a weaker power to attempt only to reduce its degree of inferiority. The rational goals in an arms race are parity or superiority.

In many respects the most critical aspect of a race is the initial response which the challenged state makes to the new goals posited by the challenger. In general, these responses can be divided into four

---

[9] For the risk theory, see Alfred von Tirpitz, *My Memoirs* (New York, 2 vols., 1919), I, pp. 79, 84, 121, 159–160, and for a trenchant criticism, E. L. Woodward, *Great Britain and the German Navy* (Oxford, 1935), pp. 31–39.

categories, two of which preserve the possibility of peace, two of which make war virtually inevitable. The challenged state may, first, attempt to counterbalance the increased armaments of its rival through diplomatic means or it may, secondly, immediately increase its own armaments in an effort to maintain or directly to restore the previously existing balance of military power. While neither of these responses guarantees the maintenance of peace, they at least do not precipitate war. The diplomatic avenue of action, if it exists, is generally the preferred one. It may be necessary, however, for the state to enhance its own armaments as well as attempting to secure reliable allies. Or, if alliances are impossible or undesirable for reasons of state policy, the challenged state must rely upon its own increases in armaments as the way of achieving its goal. In this case a sustained arms race is likely to result. During her period of splendid isolation, for instance, England met the French naval challenge of the 1840s by increasing the size and effectiveness of her own navy. At the end of the century when confronted by the Russo-French challenge, she both increased her navy and made tentative unsuccessful efforts to form an alliance with Germany. In response to the German challenge a decade later, she again increased her navy and also arrived at a rapprochement with France and Russia.

If new alliances or increased armaments appear impossible or undesirable, a state which sees its superiority or equality in military power menaced by the actions of another state may initiate preventive action while still strong enough to forestall the change in the balance of power. The factors which enter into the decision to wage preventive war are complex and intangible, but, conceivably, if the state had no diplomatic opportunities and if it was dubious of its ability to hold its own in an arms race, this might well be a rational course of behavior.[10] Tirpitz explicitly recognized this in his concept of a "danger zone" through which the German navy would pass and during which a strong likelihood would exist that the British would take preventive action to destroy the German fleet. Such an attack might be avoided, he felt, by a German diplomatic "peace offensive" designed to calm British fears and to assure them of the harmless character of German intentions. Throughout the decade after 1898 the Germans suffered periodic scares of an imminent British attack. Although preventive action was never seriously considered by the British government, enough talk went on in high British circles of "Copenhagening" the German fleet to give the Germans some cause for alarm. In the "war in sight"

---

[10] On the considerations going into the waging of preventive war, see my "To Choose Peace or War," *United States Naval Institute Proceedings*, LXXXIII (April, 1957), pp. 360–62.

crisis of 1875, the initial success of French rearmament efforts aimed at restoring an equality of military power with Germany stimulated German statesmen and military leaders carefully to consider the desirability of preventive war. Similarly, the actions of the Nazis in overthrowing the restrictions of the Treaty of Versailles in the early 1930s and starting the European arms build-up produced arguments in Poland and France favoring preventive war. After World War II at the beginning of the arms race between the United States and the Soviet Union a small but articulate segment of opinion urged the United States to take preventive action before the Soviet Union developed nuclear weapons.[11] To a certain extent, the Japanese attack on the United States in 1941 can be considered a preventive action designed to forestall the inevitable loss of Japanese naval superiority in the western Pacific which would have resulted from the two-ocean navy program begun by the United States in 1939. In 1956 the Egyptians began to rebuild their armaments from Soviet sources and thus to disturb the equilibrium which had existed with Israel since 1949. This development was undoubtedly one factor leading Israel to attack Egypt and thereby attempt to resolve at least some of the outstanding issues between them before the increase in Egyptian military power.

At the other extreme from preventive action, a challenged state simply may not make any immediate response to the upset of the existing balance of power. The challenger may then actually achieve or come close to achieving the new balance of military force which it considers necessary. In this event, roles are reversed, the challenged suddenly awakens to its weakened position and becomes the challenger, engaging in frantic and strenuous last-ditch efforts to restore the previously existing military ratio. In general, the likelihood of war increases just prior to a change in military superiority from one side to the other. If the challenged state averts this change by alliances or increased armaments, war is avoidable. On the other hand, the challenged state may precipitate war in order to prevent the change, or it may provoke war by allowing the change to take place and then attempting to undo it. In the latter case, the original challenger, having achieved parity or superiority, is in no mood or position to back down; the anxious efforts of its opponent to regain its military strength appear to be obvious war preparation; and consequently the original challenger normally will not hesitate to risk or provoke a war while it may still benefit from its recent gains.

Belated responses resulting in last-gasp arms races are most clearly seen in the French and British reactions to German rearmament in the

<hr />

[11] *Ibid.*, pp. 363–66.

1930s. The coming-to-power of the Nazis and their subsequent rearmament efforts initially provoked little military response in France. In part, this reflected confidence in the qualitative superiority of the French army and the defensive strength of the Maginot Line. In part, too, it reflected the French political situation in which these groups most fearful of Nazi Germany were generally those most opposed to large armies and militarism, while the usual right-wing supporters of the French army were those to whom Hitler appeared least dangerous. As a result, the French army and the War Ministry budget remained fairly constant between 1933 and 1936. Significant increases in French armaments were not made until 1937 and 1938, and the real French rearmament effort got under way in 1939. France proposed to spend more on armaments in that single year than the total of her expenditures during the preceding five years. By then, however, the five-to-one superiority in military effectives which she had possessed over Germany in 1933 had turned into a four-to-three inferiority.[12]

Roughly the same process was going on with respect to the ratio between the British and German air forces. At the beginning of the 1930s the Royal Air Force, although a relatively small force, was undoubtedly much stronger than anything which the Germans had managed to create surreptitiously. During the period from 1934 to 1938, however, the strength of the RAF in comparison to the Luftwaffe steadily declined. In July 1934, Churchill warned Parliament that the German air force had then reached two-thirds the strength of the British Home Defense Air Force, and that if present and proposed programs were continued, the Germans would achieve parity by December 1935. Baldwin assured the Commons that Britain would maintain a fifty per cent superiority over Germany. Subsequently, however, Churchill's estimates proved to be more correct than those of the Government, and the air program had to be drastically increased in 1936 and 1937. By then, however, two years had been lost. In 1936 Germany achieved parity with Britain. In the spring of 1937 the Luftwaffe exceeded the RAF in first-line strength and reserves. By September 1938 it was almost twice as large as the RAF, and the production of aircraft in Germany was double that in England. The British vigorously pushed their efforts to make up for lost time: British aviation expenditures which had amounted to 16.8 million pounds in 1934–35 rose to 131.4 millions in 1937–38, and were budgeted at 242.7 millions for 1939–40. The Germans were now on top and the British the challengers moving to close the gap. The

---

[12] N. M. Sloutzski, *World Armaments Race, 1919–1939* (Geneva Studies, Vol. XII, No.1, July 1941), pp. 45–46, 99–101. In 1933 the French army numbered approximately 508,000 men, the German army roughly 100,000. In 1939 the French army numbered 629,000 men, the German army 800-900,000.

readiness of the Germans to go to war consequently was not un-
natural. As far back as 1936, the British Joint Planning Staff had
picked September 1939 as the most likely date for the beginning of a
war because in the fall of 1939 Germany's armed strength would reach
its peak in comparison with that of the allies. This forecast proved
true on both points, and it was not until after the start of the war that
the British began seriously to catch up with the head start of the Luftwaffe. British aircraft production first equalled that of the Germans in
the spring of 1940.

A slightly different example of a belated, last minute arms race is
found in the German-French and German-Russian competitions of
1911–1914. In this instance, deteriorating relations between the two
countries led both to make strenuous efforts to increase their forces in
a short time and enhanced the willingness of each to go to war. For a
decade or more prior to 1911, German and French armaments had
been relatively stable, and during the years 1908–1911 relations between the two countries had generally improved. The Agadir crisis of
1911 and the Balkan War of the following year stimulated the Germans to reconsider their armaments position. Fear of a Franco-
Russian surprise attack and concern over the quantitative superiority
of the French army led the Germans to make a moderate increase in
their forces in 1912. In the spring of 1913 a much larger increase of
117,000 men was voted. Simultaneously, the French extended their
term of military service from two to three years, thereby increasing
their peacetime army by some 200,000 men. The Russians also had an
extensive program of military reorganization under way. During the
three year period 1911–14 the French army increased from 638,500
men to 846,000, and the German army from 626,732 to 806,026 men.
If war had not broken out in 1914, the French would have been faced
with an acute problem in maintaining a military balance with
Germany. The population of France was about 39,000,000, that of
Germany 65,000,000. During the twenty years prior to 1914 the
French trained 82 per cent of their men liable for military service, the
Germans 55 per cent of theirs. As a result, the two armies were approximately equal in size. If the Germans had continued to expand
their army, the French inevitably would have fallen behind in the race:
the extension of service in 1913 was a sign that they were reaching the
limit of their manpower resources. Their alternatives would have been
either to have provoked a war before Germany gained a decisive
superiority, to have surrendered their goal of parity with Germany
and with it any hope of retrieving Alsace-Lorraine, or to have
stimulated further improvement of the military forces of their Russian
ally and further expansion of the military forces of their British ally—
perhaps putting pressure on Great Britain to institute universal
military service. The Germans, on the other hand, felt themselves

menaced by the reorganization of the Russian army. Already significantly outnumbered by the combined Franco-Russian armies, the Germans could hardly view with equanimity a significant increase in the efficiency of the Tsarist forces. Thus each side tended to see itself losing out in the arms race in the future and hence each side was more willing to risk a test of arms when the opportunity presented itself in 1914.

The danger of war is highest in the opening phases of an arms race, at which time the greatest elements of instability and uncertainty are present. If the challenged state neither resorts to preventive war nor fails to make an immediate response to the challenger's activities, a sustained arms race is likely to result with the probability of war decreasing as the initial action and counteraction fade into the past. Once the initial disturbances to the pre-arms race static equilibrium are surmounted, the reciprocal increases of the two states tend to produce a new, dynamic equilibrium reflecting their relative strength and participation in the race. In all probability, the relative military power of the two states in this dynamic equilibrium will fall somewhere between the previous status quo and the ratio-goal of the challenger. The sustained regularity of the increases in itself becomes an accepted and anticipated stabilizing factor in the relations between the two countries. A sustained quantitative race still may produce a war, but a greater likelihood exists that either the two states will arrive at a mutual accommodation reducing the political tensions which started the race or that one state over the long haul will gradually but substantially achieve its objective while the other will accept defeat in the race if this does not damage its vital interests. Thus, a twenty-five year sporadic naval race between France and England ended in the middle 1860s when France gave up any serious effort to challenge the 3 : 2 ratio which England had demonstrated the will and the capacity to maintain. Similarly, the Anglo-German naval race slackened after 1912 when, despite failure to reach formal agreement, relations improved between the two countries and even Tirpitz acquiesced in the British 16 : 10 ratio in capital ships.[13] Britain also successfully maintained her two-power standard against France and Russia for twenty years until changes in the international scene ended her arms competition with those two powers. Germany and France successively

---

[13] Some question might be raised as to whether the Anglo-German naval race ended before World War I or in World War I. It would appear, however, that the race was substantially over before the war began. The race went through two phases. During the first phase, 1898–1905, German policy was directed toward the construction of a "risk" navy. During the second phase, 1906–1912, the Anglo-French entente had removed the basis for a risk navy, and the introduction of the Dreadnought opened to the Germans the possibility of naval parity with Britain. By 1912, however, it was apparent to all that Britain had the will and the determination to maintain the 60 percent superiority which she desired over Germany, and to lay "two keels for one" if this should be necessary. In

increased their armies from the middle 1870s to the middle 1890s when tensions eased and the arms build-up in each country slackened. The incipient naval races among the United States, Britain, and Japan growing out of World War I were restricted by the Washington naval agreement; the ten-year cruiser competition between the United States and England ended in the London Treaty of 1930; and eventually the rise of more dangerous threats in the mid-1930s removed any remaining vestiges of Anglo-American naval rivalry. The twelve-year arms race between Chile and Argentina ended in 1902 with a comprehensive agreement between the two countries settling their boundary disputes and restricting their armaments. While generalizations are both difficult and dangerous, it would appear that a sustained arms race is much more likely to have a peaceful ending than a bloody one.

QUANTITATIVE AND QUALITATIVE ARMS RACES

A state may increase its military power quantitatively, by expanding the numerical strength of its existing military forces, or qualitatively, by replacing its existing forms of military force (normally weapons systems) with new and more effective forms of force. Expansion and innovation are thus possible characteristics of any arms race, and to some extent both are present in most races. Initially and fundamentally every arms race is quantitative in nature. The race begins when two states develop conflicting goals as to what should be the distribution of military power between them and give these goals explicit statement in quantitative ratios of the relative strenghts which each hopes to achieve in the decisive form of military force. The formal start of the race is the decision of the challenger to upset the existing balance and to expand its forces quantitatively. If at some point in the race a qualitative change produces a new decisive form of military force, the quantitative goals of the two states still remain roughly the same. The relative balance of power which each state desires to achieve is independent of the specific weapons and forces which enter into the balance. Despite the underlying adherence of both states to their original ratio-goals, however, a complex qualitative race

---

addition, increased tension with France and Russia over Morocco and the Balkans turned German attention to her army. In 1912 Bethmann-Hollweg accepted as the basis for negotiation a British memorandum the first point of which was: "Fundamental. Naval superiority recognized as essential to Great Britain." Relations between the two countries generally improved between 1912 and 1914: they cooperated in their efforts to limit the Balkan wars of 1912–13 and in the spring of 1914 arrived an agreement concerning the Baghdad railway and the Portuguese colonies. By June 1914 rivalry had abated to such an extent that the visit of a squadron of British battleships to Kiel became the occasion for warm expressions of friendship. "In a sense," as Bernadotte Schmitt says, "potential foes had become potential friends." *The Coming of the War: 1914*, I, pp. 72–73; Sidney B. Fay, *The Origins of the World War* (New York, 2 vols., 1928), I, pp. 299ff.; Tirpitz, *Memoirs*, I, pp. 271–72.

produced by rapid technological innovation is a very different phenomenon from a race which remains simply quantitative.

Probably the best examples of races which were primarily quantitative in nature are those between Germany and France between 1871 and 1914. The decisive element was the number of effectives each power maintained in its peacetime army and the number of reserves it could call to the colors in an emergency. Quantitative increases by one state invariably produced comparable increases by the other. The German army bill of 1880, for instance, added 25,000 men to the army and declared in its preamble that "far-reaching military reforms had been carried out outside of Germany which cannot remain without influence upon the military power of the neighboring countries." These increases it was alleged would produce "too considerable a numerical superiority of the enemy's forces."[14] Again in 1887 Bismarck used Boulanger's agitation for an increase in the French army as a means of putting through an expansion of the German one. After the French reorganized their army in 1889 and drastically increased the proportion of young men liable to military service, the Germans added 20,000 men to their force in 1890. Three years later a still larger increase was made in the German army and justified by reference to recent French and Russian expansions. Similarly, the naval race of 1884–1905 between England, on the one hand, and France and Russia, on the other, was primarily quantitative in nature. Naval budgets and numerical strengths of the two sides tended to fluctuate in direct relation with each other.

A qualitative arms race is more complex than a quantitative one because at some point it involves the decision by one side to introduce a new weapons system or form of military force. Where the capacity for technological innovation exists, the natural tendency is for the arms race to become qualitative. The introduction of a new weapons system obviously is normally desirable from the viewpoint of the state which is behind in the quantitative race. The English-French naval rivalry of 1841–1865 grew out of the deteriorating relations between the two countries over Syria, Tahiti and Spain. Its first manifestation was quantitative: in 1841 the number of seamen in the French navy which for nearly a century had been about two-thirds the number in the British navy was suddenly increased so as to almost equal the British strength. Subsequently the large expansions which the French proposed to make in their dockyards, especially at Toulon, caused even Cobden to observe that " a serious effort seemed really to be made to rival us at sea."[15] The Anglo-French quantitative rivalry subsided with the departure of Louis Philippe in 1848, but shortly

---

14 Kovacs, "Nation in Arms," p. 36.
15 Cobden, "Three Panics," p. 224.

thereafter it resumed on a new qualitative level with the determination of Napoleon III to push the construction of steam warships. The *Napoléon*, a screw propelled ship of the line of 92 guns, launched by the French in 1850 was significantly superior to anything the British could bring against it, until the *Agamemnon* was launched two years later. The alliance of the two countries in the Crimean War only temporarily suspended the naval race, and by 1858 the French had achieved parity with the British in fast screw ships of the line. In that year the French had 114 fewer sailing vessels in their navy than they had in 1852, while the number of British sailing ships had declined only from 299 to 296. On the other hand, the British in 1852 had a superiority of 73 sailing ships of the line to 45 for the French. By 1858, however, both England and France had 29 steam ships of the line while England had an enhanced superiority of 35 to 10 in sailing ships. A head start in steam construction and conversion plus the concentration of effort on this program had enabled the French, who had been hopelessly outnumbered in the previously decisive form of naval power, to establish a rough parity in the new form. In view of the British determination to restore their quantitative superiority and the superior industrial resources at their disposal, however, parity could only be temporary. In 1861 the British had 53 screw battleships afloat and 14 building while the French had only 35 afloat and two building.[16]

By the time that the British had reestablished their superiority in steam warships, their opponents had brought forward another innovation which again threatened British control of the seas. The French laid down four ironclads in 1858 and two in 1859. The first was launched in November 1859 and the next in March 1860. The British launched their first ironclad in December 1860. The British program, however, was hampered by the Admiralty's insistence upon continuing to build wooden warships. The French stopped laying down wooden line of battleships in 1856, yet the British, despite warnings that wooden walls were obsolete, continued building wooden ships down through 1860, and in 1861 the Admiralty brought in the largest request in its history for the purchase of timber.[17] Meanwhile, in the fall of 1860 the French started a new construction program for ten more ironclads to supplement the six they already had underway. The British learned of these projects in February 1861 and responded with a program to add nine new ironclads to their fleet. In May 1861, the French had a total of fifteen ironclads built or building, the British only seven. From 1860 until 1865 the French possessed superiority or parity with the British in

---

[16] *Ibid.*, pp. 304–308, 392–93.
[17] *Ibid.*, pp. 343, 403; Robert G. Albion, *Forests and Sea Power* (Cambridge, 1926), p. 408.

ironclad warships. In February 1863, for instance, the French had
four ironclads mounting 146 guns ready for action, the British four
ironclads mounting 116 guns. Thanks to the genius and initiative of
the director of French naval construction, Dupuy de Lôme, and the
support of Napoleon III, there had occurred, as one British military
historian put it,

> an astonishing change in the balance of power which might have been
> epoch-making had it not been so brief, or if France and Britain had gone to
> war, a reversal which finds no place in any but technical histories and which
> is almost entirely unknown in either country today. In a word, supremacy
> at sea passed from Britain to France.[18]

This was not a supremacy, however, which France could long maintain. By 1866, Britannia had retrieved the trident. In that year
England possessed nineteen ironclads, France thirteen, and the
English superiority was enhanced by heavier guns. Thereafter the
naval strengths of the two powers resumed the $3:2$ ratio which had
existed prior to 1841.

In general, as this sequence of events indicates, technological innovation favors, at least temporarily, the numerically weaker power.
Its long-run effects, however, depend upon factors other than the currently prevailing balance of military strength. It was indeed paradoxical that France should make the innovations which she did make in
her naval race with England. In the 1850s and 1860s France normally
had twice as much timber on hand in her dockyards as had the British,
and she was, of course, inferior to England in her coal and iron
resources. Nonetheless she led the way in the introduction of steam
and iron, while the Royal Navy, which was acutely hampered by a
timber shortage clung to the wooden ships.[19] In this instance, on both
sides, immediate needs and the prospects of immediate success
prevailed over a careful considerarion of long-term benefits.

The problem which technological innovation presents to the quantitatively superior power is somewhat more complex. The natural
tendencies for such a state are toward conservatism: any significant innovation will undermine the usefulness of the current type of weapons
system in which it possesses a superiority. What, however, should be
the policy of a superior power with respect to making a technological
change which its inferior rivals are likely to make in the near future?
The British navy had a traditional answer to this problem: never introduce any development which will render existing ships obsolete but
be prepared if any other state does make an innovation to push ahead

[18] Cyril Falls, *A Hundred Years of War* (London, 1953), p. 102.
[19] Albion, *Forests and Sea Power*, pp. 406–07; Brodie, *Sea Power in the Machine
Age*, p. 441.

an emergency construction program which will restore the previously existing ratio. While this policy resulted, as we have seen above, in some close shaves, by the beginning of the twentieth century it had become a fundamental maxim of British naval doctrine. Consequently, Sir John Fisher's proposal in 1904 to revolutionize naval construction by introducing the "all big gun ship" which would render existing capital ships obsolete was also a revolution in British policy. In terms of its impact upon the Anglo-German naval balance, Fisher's decision was welcomed by many Germans and condemned by many British. Although the construction of Dreadnoughts would force Germany to enlarge the Kiel Canal, the Germans seized the opportunity to start the naval race afresh in a class of vessels in which the British did not have an overwhelming numerical superiority. For the first few years the British by virtue of their headstart would have a larger number of Dreadnoughts, but then the German yards would start producing and the gap which had to be closed would be much smaller in the Dreadnoughts than in the pre-Dreadnought battleships. The introduction of the Dreadnought permitted the Germans to raise their sight from a "risk" navy (which had become meaningless since the Anglo-French entente in any event) to the possibility of parity with Britain. To many Britishers, on the other hand, construction of the Dreadnought seemed to be tantamount to sinking voluntarily a large portion of the British navy. The tremendous number of pre-Dreadnought capital ships which the Royal Navy possessed suddenly decreased in value. Great Britain, one British naval expert subsequently argued, had to write off seventy-five warships, the Germans only twenty-eight. British naval superiority fell by 40 or 50 per cent: in 1908 England had authorized twelve Dreadnoughts and the Germans nine; in pre-Dreadnought battleships the British had 63 and the Germans 26.[20]

Fisher's policy, however, was undoubtedly the correct one. Plans for an all-big-gun ship had been under consideration by various navies since 1903. The Russo-Japanese War underwrote the desirability of heavy armaments. The United States authorized the construction of two comparable vessels in March, 1905, and the Germans themselves were moving in that direction. The all-big-gun ship was inevitable, and this consideration led Fisher to insist that Britain must take the lead. While the superiority of the Royal Navy over the German fleet was significantly reduced, nonetheless at no time in the eight years after 1905 did the Germans approach the British in terms of numerical equality. Their highest point was in 1911 when their Dreadnought battleship and battle-cruiser strength amounted to 64 per cent of the

[20] Hector C. Bywater, *Navies and Nations* (London, 1927), pp. 27–28; Fay, *Origins of the World War*, I, p. 236.

British strength.[21] Thus, by reversing the nineteenth century policy of the British navy, Fisher avoided the British experience of the 1850s and 1860s when technological innovations by an inferior power temporarily suspended Britain's supremacy on the seas.

The very incentive which an inferior power has to make a technological innovation is reason for the superior power to take the lead, if it can, in bringing in the innovation itself. The British-Dreadnought debate of 1904–1905 had its parallels in the problem confronting the American government in 1949–1950 concerning the construction of a hydrogen bomb. Like the British, the Americans possessed a superiority in the existing decisive type of weapons system. As in the British government, opinion was divided, and the arguments pro and con of the technicians and military experts had to be weighed against budgetary considerations. As with the Dreadnought, the new weapons system was pushed by a small group of zealots convinced of the inevitability and necessity of its development. In both cases, humanitarian statesmen and conservative experts wished to go slow. In each case, the government eventually decided to proceed with the innovation, and, in each case, the wisdom of its policy was demonstrated by the subsequent actions of its rival. In an arms race, what is technically possible tends to become politically necessary.

Whether an arms race is primarily quantitative or primarily qualitative in nature has a determining influence upon its outcome. This influence is manifested in the different impacts which the two types of races have on the balance of military power between the two states and on the relative demands which they make on state resources.

Qualitative and quantitative races and the balance of power. In a simple quantitative race one state is very likely to develop a definite superiority in the long run. The issue is simply who has the greater determination and the greater resources. Once a state falls significantly behind, it is most unlikely that it will ever be able to overcome the lead of its rival. A qualitative race, on the other hand, in which there is a series of major technological innovations in reality consists of a number of distinct races. Each time a new weapons system is introduced a new race takes place in the development and accumulation of that weapon. As the rate of technological innovation increases each separate component race decreases in time and extent. The simple quantitative race is like a marathon of undetermined distance which can only end with the exhaustion of one state or both, or with the state which is about to fall behind in the race pulling out its

[21] I am indebted to a paper by Mr. Peter E. Weil on "The Dreadnought and the Anglo-German Naval Race, 1905-1909" for statistics on British and German naval strengths.

firearms and attempting to despatch its rival. The qualitative race, on the other hand, resembles a series of hundred yard dashes, each beginning from a fresh starting line. Consequently, in a qualitative race hope springs anew with each phase. Quantitative superiority is the product of effort, energy, resources, and time. Once achieved it is rarely lost. Qualitative superiority is the product of discovery, luck, and circumstance. Once achieved it is always lost. Safety exists only in numbers. While a quantitative race tends to produce inequality between the two competing powers, a qualitative race tends toward equality irrespective of what may be the ratio-goals of the two rival states. Each new weapon instead of increasing the distance between the two states reduces it. The more rapid the rate of innovation the more pronounced is the tendency toward equality. Prior to 1905, for instance, Great Britain possessed a superiority in pre-Dreadnought battleships. By 1912 she had also established a clear and unassailable superiority in Dreadnoughts over Germany. But if Germany had introduced a super-Dreadnought in 1909, Great Britain could never have established its clear superiority in Dreadnoughts. She would have had to start over again in the new race. A rapid rate of innovation means that arms races are always beginning, never ending. In so far as the likelihood of war is decreased by the existence of an equality of power between rival states, a qualitative arms race tends to have this result. A quantitative arms race, on the other hand, tends to have the opposite effect. If in a qualitative race one power stopped technological innovation and instead shifted its resources to the multiplication of existing weapons systems, this would be a fairly clear sign that it was intending to go to war in the immediate future.

Undoubtedly many will question the proposition that rapid technological innovation tends to produce an equality of power. In an arms race each state lives in constant fear that its opponent will score a "technological breakthrough" and achieve a decisive qualitative superiority. This anxiety is a continuing feature of arms races but it is one which has virtually no basis in recent experience. The tendency toward simultaneity of innovation is overwhelming. Prior to World War I simultaneity was primarily the result of the common pool of knowledge among the advanced nations with respect to weapons technology. The development of weapons was largely the province of private firms who made their wares available to any state which was interested. As a result at any given time the armaments of the major powers all strikingly resembled one another.[22] During and after World

[22] See Victor Lefebure, "The Decisive Aggressive Value of the New Agencies of War," in The Inter-Parliamentary Union, *What Would Be the Character of a New War?* (New York, 1933), pp. 97–101. See also Marion W. Boggs, *Attempts to Define and Limit "Aggressive" Armament in Diplomacy and Strategy* (Columbia, Mo., 1941),

War I military research and development became more and more a governmental activity, and, as a result, more and more enshrouded in secrecy. Nonetheless relative equality in technological innovation continued among the major powers. The reason for this was now not so much access to common knowledge as an equal ability and opportunity to develop that knowledge. The logic of scientific development is such that separate groups of men working in separate laboratories on the same problem are likely to arrive at the same answer to the problem at about the same time. Even if this were not the case, the greatly increased ratio of production time to use time in recent years has tended to diminish the opportunity of the power which has pioneered an innovation to produce it in sufficient quantity in sufficient time to be militarily decisive. When it takes several years to move a weapons system from original design to quantity operation, knowledge of it is bound to leak out, and the second power in the arms race will be able to get its own program under way before the first state can capitalize on its lead. The *Merrimac* reigned supreme for a day, but it was only for a day and it could be only for a day.

The fact that for four years from 1945 to 1949 the United States possessed a marked qualitative superiority over the Soviet Union has tended to obscure how rare this event normally is. American superiority, however, was fundamentally the result of carrying over into a new competitive rivalry a weapons system which had been developed in a previous conflict. In the latter rivalry the tendency toward simultaneity of development soon manifested itself. The Soviet Union developed an atomic bomb four years after the United States had done so. Soviet explosion of a hydrogen weapon lagged only ten months behind that of the United States. At a still later date in the arms race, both powers in 1957 were neck and neck in their efforts to develop long-range ballistic missiles.

The ending of an arms race in a distinct quantitative victory for one side is perhaps best exemplified in the success of the British in maintaining their supremacy on the seas. Three times within the course of a hundred years the British were challenged by continental rivals, and three times the British outbuilt their competitors. In each case, also, implicitly or explicitly, the bested rivals recognized their defeat and abandoned their efforts to challenge the resources, skill and determination of the British. At this point in a quantitative race when it appears that one power is establishing its superiority over the other, proposals

---

p. 76: ". . . the history of war inventions tends to emphasize the slowness and distinctively international character of peacetime improvements; no weapon has been perfected with secrecy and rapidity as the exclusive national property of any one state. At an early stage all nations secure access to the information, and develop not only the armament, but measures against it."

are frequently brought forward for some sort of "disarmament" agreement. These are as likely to come from the superior side as from the inferior one. The stronger power desires to clothe its *de facto* supremacy in *de jure* acceptance and legitimacy so that it may slacken its own arms efforts. From 1905 to 1912, for instance, virtually all the initiatives for Anglo-German naval agreement came from the British. Quite properly, the Germans regarded those advances as British efforts to compel "naval competition to cease at the moment of its own greatest preponderance." Such proposals only heightened German suspicion and bitterness. Similarly, after World War II the Soviet Union naturally described the American nuclear disarmament proposal as a device to prevent the Soviet Union from developing its own nuclear capability. A decade later a greater common interest existed between the Soviet Union and the United States in reaching an arms agreement which would permanently exclude "fourth powers" from the exclusive nuclear club. In disarmament discussions the superior power commonly attempts to persuade the inferior one to accept as permanent the existing ratio of strength, or, failing in this effort, the superior power proposes a temporary suspension of the race, a "holiday" during which period neither power will increase its armaments. In 1899 the Russians, with the largest army in Europe, proposed that for five years no increases be made in military budgets. In 1912–14 Churchill repeatedly suggested the desirability of a naval building holiday to the Germans who were quite unable to perceive its advantages. In 1936 the United States could easily agree to a six year holiday in 10,000 ton cruisers since it had already underway all the cruisers it was permitted by the London Treaty of 1930. Similarly, in its 1957 negotiations with the Soviet Union the United States could also safely propose an end to the production of nuclear weapons. The inferior participant in disarmament negotiations, on the other hand, inevitably supports measures based not upon the existing situation but either upon the abstract principle of "parity" or upon the inherent evil of large armaments as such and the desirability of reducing all arms down to a common low level. Thus, in most instances, a disarmament proposal is simply a maneuver in the arms race: the attempt by a state to achieve the ratio-goal it desires by means other than an increase in its armaments.

The domestic burden of quantitative and qualitative races. Quantitative and qualitative arms races have markedly different effects upon the countries participating in them. In a quantitative race the decisive ratio is between the resources which a nation devotes to military purposes and those which it devotes to civilian ones. A quantitative race of any intensity requires a steady shift of resources from the latter to the former. As the forms of military force are multiplied a larger and larger proportion of the national product is devoted to the purposes of the race, and, if it is a race in military manpower, an increasing proportion of the population serves a longer and longer time in the armed forces. A quantitative race of any duration thus imposes ever increasing burdens upon the countries involved in it. As a result, it becomes necessary for governments to resort to various means of stimulating popular support and eliciting a willingness to sacrifice other goods and values. Enthusiasm is mobilized, hostility aroused and directed against the potential enemy. Suspicion and fear multiply with the armaments. Such was the result of the quantitative races between the Triple Alliance and the Triple Entente between 1907 and 1914:

> In both groups of powers there was a rapid increase of military and naval armaments. This caused increasing suspicions, fears, and newspaper recriminations in the opposite camp. This in turn led to more armaments and so to the vicious circle of ever growing war preparations and mutual fears and suspicions.[23]

Eventually a time is reached when the increasing costs and tensions of a continued arms race seem worse than the costs and the risks of war. Public opinion once aroused cannot be quieted. The economic, military and psychological pressures previously generated permit only further expansion or conflict. The extent to which an arms race is likely to lead to war thus varies with the burdens it imposes on the peoples and the extent to which it involves them psychologically and emotionally in the race. Prolonged sufficiently, a quantitative race must necessarily reach a point where opinion in one country or the other will demand that it be ended, if not by negotiation, then by war. The logical result of a quantitative arms race is a "nation in arms," and a nation in arms for any length of time must be a nation at war.

A qualitative arms race, however, does not have this effect. In such a race the essential relationship is not between the military and the civilian, but rather between the old and the new forms of military force. In a quantitative race the principal policy issue is the extent to which resources and manpower should be diverted from civilian to military use. In a qualitative race, the principal issue is the extent to which the new weapons systems should replace the old "conventional" ones. In a quantitative race the key question is "How much?" In a qualitative race, it is "How soon?" A quantitative race requires continuous expansion of military resources, a qualitative race continuous redeployment of them. A qualitative race does not normally increase arms budgets, even when, as usually happens, the new forms of military force are more expensive than the old ones. The costs of a qualitative race only increase significantly when an effort is made to maintain both old and new forms of military force: steam and sail;

ironclads and wooden walls; nuclear and nonnuclear weapons. Transitions from old to new weapons systems have not normally been accompanied by marked increases in military expenditures. During the decade in which the ironclad replaced the wooden ship of the line British naval expenditures declined from £12,779,000 in 1859 to less than eleven million pounds in 1867.[24] Similarly, the five years after the introduction of the Dreadnought saw British naval expenditures drop from £35,476,000 in 1903–04 to £32,188,000 in 1908–09. During the same period estimates for shipbuilding and repairs dropped from £17,350,000 to £14,313,900. The years 1953–1956 saw the progressive adoption of nuclear weapons in the American armed forces, yet military budgets during this period at first dropped considerably and then recovered only slightly, as the increased expenditures for the new weapons were more than compensated for by reductions in expenditures for nonnuclear forces.

Quantitative and qualitative arms races differ also in the interests they mobilize and the leadership they stimulate. In the long run, a quantitative race makes extensive demands on a broad segment of the population. A qualitative race, however, tends to be a competition of elites rather than masses. No need exists for the bulk of the population to become directly involved. In a quantitative arms race, the users of the weapons—the military leaders—assume the key role. In a qualitative race, the creators of the weapons—the scientists—rival them for preeminence. Similarly, the most important private interests in a quantitative race are the large mass production industrial corporations, while in a qualitative race they tend to be the smaller firms specializing in the innovation and development of weapons systems rather than in their mass output.

While the rising costs of a quantitative race may increase the likelihood of war, they may also enhance efforts to end the race by means of an arms agreement. Undoubtedly the most powerful motive (prior to the feasiblity of utter annihilation) leading states to arms limitations has been the economic one. The desire for economy was an important factor leading Louis Philippe to propose a general reduction in European armaments in 1831. In the 1860s similar motives stimulated Napoleon III to push disarmament plans. They also prompted various British governments to be receptive to arms limitation proposals, provided, of course, that they did not endanger Britain's supremacy on the seas: the advent of the Liberal government in 1905, for instance, resulted in renewed efforts to reach accommodation with the Germans. In 1898 the troubled state of Russian finances was largely responsible

[24] James Phinney Baxter, 3rd, *The Introduction of the Ironclad Warship* (Cambridge, 1933), p. 321.

for the Tsar's surprise move in sponsoring the first Hague Conference. Eight years later it was the British who, for economic reasons, wished to include the question of arms limitation on the agenda of the second Hague Conference.

The success of rising economic costs in bringing about the negotiated end of an arms race depends upon their incidence being relatively equal on each participant. A state which is well able to bear the economic burden normally spurns the efforts of weaker powers to call off the race. Thus, the Kaiser was scornful of the Russian economic debility which led to the proposal for the first Hague Conference, and a German delegate to that conference, in explaining German opposition to limitation, took pains to assure the participants that:

> The German people are not crushed beneath the weight of expenditures and taxes; they are not hanging on the edge of the precipice; they are not hastening towards exhaustion and ruin. Quite the contrary; public and private wealth is increasing, the general welfare, and standard of life, are rising from year to year.[25]

On the other hand, the relatively equal burdens of their arms race in the last decade of the nineteenth century eventually forced Argentina and Chile to call the race off in 1902. The victory of Chile in the War of the Pacific had brought her into conflict with an "expanding and prosperous Argentina" in the 1880s, and a whole series of boundary disputes exacerbated the rivalry which developed between the two powers for hegemony on the South American continent. As a result, after 1892 both countries consistently expanded their military and naval forces, and relations between them staggered from one war crisis to another. Despite efforts made to arbitrate the boundary disputes,

> an uneasy feeling still prevailed that hostilities might break out, and neither State made any pretence of stopping military and naval preparations. Orders for arms, ammunition, and warships were not countermanded, and men on both sides of the Andes began to declaim strongly against the heavy expenditure thus entailed. The reply to such remonstrances invariably was that until the question of the boundary was settled, it was necessary to maintain both powers on a war footing. Thus the resources of Argentina and Chile were strained to the utmost, and public works neglected in order that funds might be forthcoming to pay for guns and ships bought in Europe.[26]

These economic burdens led the presidents of the two countries to arrive at an agreement in 1899 restricting additional expenditures on armaments. Two years later, however, the boundary issue again flared

---

[25] Quoted in Tate, *Disarmament Illusion*, p. 281. See also pp. 193–94, 251–52.
[26] Charles E. Akers, *A History of South America* (New York, new ed., 1930), p. 112.

up, and both sides recommenced preparations for war. But again the resources of the countries were taxed beyond their limit. In August 1901 the Chilean president declared to the United States minister "that the burden which Chile is carrying . . . is abnormal and beyond her capacity and that the hour has come to either make use of her armaments or reduce them to the lowest level compatible with the dignity and safety of the country."[27] Argentina was also suffering from severe economic strain, and as a result, the two countries concluded their famous *Pactos de Mayo* in 1902 which limited their naval armaments and provided for the arbitration of the remaining boundary issues.

In summary, two general conclusions emerge as to the relations between arms races and war:

(1) War is more likely to develop in the early phases of an arms race than in its later phases.

(2) A quantitative race is more likely than a qualitative one to come to a definite end in war, arms agreement, or victory for one side.

ARMS RACES, DISARMAMENT, AND PEACE

In discussions of disarmament, a distinction has frequently been drawn between the presumably technical problem of arms limitation, on the one hand, and political problems, on the other. Considerable energy has been devoted to arguments as to whether it is necessary to settle political issues before disarming or whether disarmament is a prerequisite to the settlement of political issues. The distinction between arms limitation and politics, however, is a fallacious one. The achievement of an arms agreement cannot be made an end in itself. Arms limitation is the essence of politics and inseparable from other political issues. What, indeed, is more political than the relative balance of power between two distinct entities? Whether they be political parties competing for votes, lobbyists lining up legislative blocs, or states piling up armaments, the power ratio between the units is a decisive factor in their relationship. Virtually every effort (such as the Hague Conferences and the League of Nations) to reach agreement on arms apart from the resolution of other diplomatic and political issues has failed. Inevitably attempts to arrive at arms agreements have tended to broaden into discussions of all the significant political issues between the competing powers. On the other hand, it cannot be assumed that arms negotiations are hopeless, and that they only add another issue to those already disrupting the relations between the two countries and stimulating passion and suspicion. Just as the problem of armaments cannot be settled without

[27] Quoted in Robert N. Burr, "The Balance of Power in Nineteenth-Century South America: An Exploratory Essay," *Hispanic American Historical Review*, XXXV (February, 1955), 58n.

reference to other political issues, so is it also impossible to resolve these issues without facing up to the relative balance of military power. The most notable successes in arms limitation agreements have been combined, implicitly or explicitly, with a resolution of other controversies. The Rush-Bagot Agreement, for instance, simply confirmed the settlement which had been reached in the Treaty of Paris. The *Pactos de Mayo* dealt with both armaments and boundaries and implicitly recognized that Argentina would not intervene in west coast politics and that Chile would not become involved in the disputes of the Plata region. The Washington naval agreements necessarily were part and parcel of a general Far Eastern settlement involving the end of the Anglo-Japanese alliance and at least a temporary resolution of the diplomatic issues concerning China. As has been suggested previously, in one sense armaments are to the twentieth century what territory was to the eighteenth. Just as divisions of territory were then the essence of general diplomatic agreements, so today are arrangements on armaments. If both sides are to give up their conflicting ratio-goals and compromise the difference, this arrangement must coincide with a settlement of the other issues which stimulated them to develop the conflicting ratio-goals in the first place. If one state is to retreat further from its ratio-goal than the other, it will have to receive compensations with respect to other points in dispute.

While arms limitation is seldom possible except as part of a broader political settlement, it is also seldom possible if the scope of the arms limitation is itself too broad. One of the corollaries of the belief that arms races produce wars is the assumption that disarmament agreements are necessary to peace. Too frequently it has been made to appear that failure to reach a disarmament agreement leaves war as the only recourse between the powers. In particular, it is false and dangerous to assume that any disarmament to be effective must be total disarmament. The latter is an impossible goal. Military force is inherent in national power and national power is inherent in the existence of independent states. In one way or another all the resources of a state contribute to its military strength. The discussions in the 1920s under the auspices of the League conclusively demonstrated that what are armaments for one state are the pacific instruments of domestic well-being and tranquility for another. The history of general disarmament conferences persuasively suggests the difficulties involved in deciding what elements of power should be weighed in the balance even before the issue is faced as to what the relative weight of the two sides should be. At the first Hague Conference, for instance, the Germans were quick to point out that the Russian proposal for a five year holiday in military budget increases was fine for Russia who had all the men in her army that she needed, but that such a restriction would not prevent Russia from building strategic railways to her western border w⊥ich would constitute a greater menace to Germany than additional Russian soldiers. The demand for total disarmament frequently reflects an unwillingness to live with the problems of power. A feasible arms limitation must be part of the process of politics, not of the abolition of politics.

The narrower the scope of a proposed arms limitation agreement, the more likely it is to be successful. Disarmament agreements seldom actually disarm states. What they do is to exclude certain specified areas from the competition and thereby direct that competion into other channels. The likelihood of reaching such an agreement is greater if the states can have a clear vision of the impact of the agreement on the balance of power. The more restricted the range of armaments covered by the agreement, the easier it is for them to foresee its likely effects. In general, also, the less important the area in the balance of power between the two states, the easier it is to secure agreement on that area. Part of the success of the Washington agreements was that they were limited to capital ships, and, at that time, particularly in the United States the feeling existed that existing battleships were obsolete and that in any event the battleship had passed its peak as the supreme weapon of naval power. Similarly, in 1935 Germany and England were able to arrive at an agreement (which lasted until April 1939) fixing the relative size of their navies—something which had been beyond the capability of sincere and well-meaning diplomats of both powers before World War I— because air power had replaced sea power as the decisive factor in the arms balance between Germany and England. Restrictions on land armaments have generally been harder to arrive at than naval agreements because the continental European nations usually felt that their large armies were directly essential to their national existence and might have to be used at a moment's notice.

Successful disarmament agreements (and a disarmament agreement is sucessful if it remains in force for a half decade or more) generally establish quantitative restrictions on armaments. The quantitative ratio is the crucial one between the powers, and the quantitative element is much more subject to the control of governments than is the course of scientific development. Furthermore, a quantitative agreement tends to channel competition into qualitative areas, while an agreement on innovation tends to do just the reverse. Consequently, quantitative agreement tends to reduce the likelihood of war, qualitative agreement to enhance it. In the current arms race, for instance, some sort of quantitative agreement might be both feasible, since the race is primarily qualitative in nature, and desirable, since such an agreement would formally prohibit the more dangerous type of arms race. On the other hand, a qualitative agreement between the two countries prohibiting, say, the construction and testing of intercontinental ballistic missiles, might well be disastrous if it should stimulate a quantitative race in aircraft production, the construction of bases, and the multiplication of other forms of military force. In addition, the next phase in the arms race, for instance, may well be the development of defenses against ballistic missiles. A qualitative answer to this problem, such as an effective anti-missile missile, would, in the long run, be much less expensive and much less disturbing to peace than a quantitative answer, such as a mammoth shelter construction program, which would tax public resources, infringe on many established interests, and arouse popular concern and fear. Continued technological innovation could well be essential to the avoidance of war. Peace, in short, may depend less upon the ingenuity of the rival statesmen than upon the ingenuity of the rival scientists.

The balancing of power in any bipolar situation is inherently difficult due to the absence of a "balancer." In such a situation, however, a qualitative arms race may be the most effective means of achieving and maintaining parity of power over a long period of time. The inherent tendency toward parity of such a race may to some extent provide a substitute for the missing balancer. In particular, a qualitative race tends to equalize the differences which might otherwise exist between the ability and willingness of a democracy to compete with a totalitarian dictatorship. The great problem of international politics now is to develop forms of international competition to replace the total wars of the first half of the twentieth century. One such alternative is limited war. Another is the qualitative arms race. The emerging pattern of rivalry between the West and the Soviet bloc suggests that these may well be the primary forms of military activity which the two coalitions will employ. As wars become more frightening and less frequent, arms races may become longer and less disastrous. The substitution of the one for the other is certainly no mean step forward in the restriction of violence. In this respect the arms race may serve the same function which war served: "the intensely sharp competitive *preparation* for war by the nations," could become, as William James suggested, *"the real war,* permanent, unceasing. . . ."[28] A qualitative race regularizes this preparation and introduces an element of stability into the relations between the two powers. Even if it were true, as Sir Edward Grey argued, that arms races inevitably foster suspicion and insecurity, these would be small prices to pay for the avoidance of destruction. Until fundamental changes take place in the structure of world politics, a qualitative arms race may well be a most desirable form of competition between the Soviet Union and the United States.

[28] *Memories and Studies* (New York, 1912), p. 273.

Part II
Case Studies in the Twentieth Century Use of Force

The ten studies in Part II are taken from the twentieth century and are arranged in chronological order. The cases under the heading "The Great Power Era" deal with the use of force amongst the great powers prior to 1945. Those under the heading "The Superpower Era" examine instances in which the superpowers were involved in using either conventional forces or nuclear weapons (or nuclear threats). All of the studies illustrate the general principles explained in Part I. The cases deal with different types of military technologies, ranging from chemical to nuclear weapons, and treat the use of military force in both wartime and peacetime. In all of the examples, military power was essential to the successful pursuit of national goals, or was thought to be so. Each of these selections either demonstrates a specific way of using military power—in an offensive, defensive, or deterrent fashion—or identifies the factors that restrained states in their use of force.

Stephen Van Evera looks at how belief in the virtue of the offensive affected the great powers' foreign policies in the decades before World War I and how it caused the July 1914 crisis to spiral out of control. Frederic J. Brown shows why restraint prevailed in the use of chemical weapons in World War I and II, contrary to the expectations of the time. Edward L. Katzenbach, Jr., describes the innumerable rationalizations used to extend the life of the horse cavalry well into the twentieth century and, in doing so, shows that military organizations may strongly resist technological change. Sir George Sansom explains why the Japanese decided to launch what they considered to be a preventive war against the United States and indicates why their strategic calculations were faulty.

Louis Morton discusses the reasons why the United States used the atomic bomb against Japan. Morton H. Halperin details the evolution of a system of mutual restraints in the American and Chinese use of force during the Korean War and speculates on why the two countries accepted the restraints. David Welch, James G. Blight and Bruce J. Allyn explain the reasons why the Soviet Union put missiles into Cuba in September of 1962 and why it took them out in October and November of the same year. John Lewis Gaddis tests the strategy of flexible response in its application to Vietnam by the Kennedy and Johnson administrations and finds it wanting.

Barry M. Blechman and Douglas M. Hart show why the Nixon Administration felt it necessary to make veiled nuclear threats against the Soviet Union during the 1973 Middle East War and ask whether the threats prevented the Soviets from sending troops to aid Egypt against Israel. Finally, Lawrence Freedman and Efraim Karsh analyze the military strategies employed by Iraq and the U.S.-led coalition and show why the latter prevailed with so few casualties over the former.

The Cult of the Offensive
and World War I

STEPHEN VAN EVERA

During the decades before the First World War a phenomenon which may be called a "cult of the offensive" swept through Europe. Militaries glorified the offensive and adopted offensive military doctrines, while civilian elites and publics assumed that the offense had the advantage in warfare, and that offensive solutions to security problems were the most effective.

This article will argue that the cult of the offensive was a principal cause of the First World War, creating or magnifying many of the dangers which historians blame for causing the July crisis and rendering it uncontrollable. The following section will first outline the growth of the cult of the offensive in Europe in the years before the war, and then sketch the consequences which international relations theory suggests should follow from it. The second section will outline consequences which the cult produced in 1914, and the final section will suggest conclusions and implications for current American policy.

THE CULT OF THE OFFENSIVE AND INTERNATIONAL RELATIONS THEORY

The Growth of the Cult

The gulf between myth and the realities of warfare has never been greater than in the years before World War I. Despite the large and growing advantage which defenders gained against attackers as a result of the invention of rifled and repeating small arms, the machine gun, barbed wire, and the development of railroads, Europeans increasingly believed that attackers would hold the advantage on the battlefield, and that wars would be short and "decisive"—a

From "The Cult of the Offensive and the Origins of the First World War" by Stephen Van Evera, *International Security*, Summer 1984 (Vol. 9, No. 1) pp. 58–107. © 1984 by the President and Fellows of Harvard College and of the Massachusetts Institute of Technology. Reprinted by permission of MIT Press, Cambridge, Massachusetts, and the copyright holders. Portions of the text have been omitted; all referential and some explanatory footnotes have also been omitted.

I would like to thank Jack Snyder, Richard Ned Lebow, Barry Posen, Marc Trachtenberg, and Stephen Walt for their thoughtful comments on earlier drafts of this paper.

"brief storm," in the words of the German Chancellor, Bethmann Hollweg. They largely overlooked the lessons of the American Civil War, the Russo–Turkish War of 1877–78, the Boer War, and the Russo-Japanese War, which had demonstrated the power of the new defensive technologies. Instead, Europeans embraced a set of political and military myths which obscured both the defender's advantages and the obstacles an aggressor would confront. The mindset helped to mold the offensive military doctrines which every European power adopted during the period 1892–1913.

In Germany, the military glorified the offense in strident terms, and inculcated German society with similar views. General Alfred von Schlieffen, author of the 1914 German war plan, declared that "Attack is the best defense," while the popular publicist Friedrich von Bernhardi proclaimed that "the offensive mode of action is by far superior to the defensive mode," and that "the superiority of offensive warfare under modern conditions is greater than formerly." German Chief of Staff General Helmuth von Moltke also endorsed "the principle that the offensive is the best defense," while General August von Keim, founder of the Army League, argued that "Germany ought to be armed for attack," since "the offensive is the only way of insuring victory." These assumptions guided the Schlieffen Plan, which envisaged rapid and decisive attacks on Belgium, France, and Russia.

In France, the army became "Obsessed with the virtues of the offensive," in the words of B. H. Liddell Hart, an obsession which also spread to French civilians. The French army, declared Chief of Staff Joffre, "no longer knows any other law than the offensive. . . . Any other conception ought to be rejected as contrary to the very nature of war," while the President of the French Republic, Clément Fallières, announced that "The offensive alone is suited to the temperament of French soldiers. . . . We are determined to march straight against the enemy without hesitation." . . . French military doctrine reflected these offensive biases. In Marshall Foch's words, the French army adopted "a single formula for success, a single combat doctrine, namely, the decisive power of offensive action undertaken with the resolute determination to march on the enemy, reach and destroy him."

Other European states displayed milder symptoms of the same virus. The British military resolutely rejected defensive strategies despite their experience in the Boer War which demonstrated the power of entrenched defenders against exposed attackers. General W. G. Knox wrote, "The defensive is never an acceptable role to the Briton, and he makes little or no study of it," and General R. C. B. Haking argued that the offensive "will win as sure as there is a sun in the heavens." The Russian Minister of War, General V.

A. Sukhomlinov, observed that Russia's enemies were directing their armies "towards guaranteeing the possibility of dealing rapid and decisive blows. . . . We also must follow this example." Even in Belgium the offensive found proponents: under the influence of French ideas, some Belgian officers favored an offensive strategy, proposing the remarkable argument that "To ensure against our being ignored it was essential that we should attack," and declaring that "We must hit them where it hurts."

Mythical or mystical arguments obscured the technical dominion of the defense, giving this faith in the offense aspects of a cult, or a mystique, as Marshall Joffre remarked in his memoirs. . . . British and French officers suggested that superior morale on the attacking side could overcome superior defensive firepower, and that this superiority in morale could be achieved simply by assuming the role of attacker, since offense was a morale-building activity. One French officer contended that "the offensive doubles the energy of the troops" and "concentrates the thoughts of the commander on a single objective," while British officers declared that "Modern [war] conditions have enormously increased the value of moral quality," and "the moral attributes [are] the primary causes of all great success." In short, mind would prevail over matter; morale would triumph over machine guns.

Europeans also tended to discount the power of political factors which would favor defenders. Many Germans believed that "band-wagoning" with a powerful state rather than "balancing" against it was the guiding principle in international alliance-formation. Aggressors would gather momentum as they gained power, because opponents would be intimidated into acquiescence and neutrals would rally to the stronger side. Such thinking led German Chancellor Bethmann Hollweg to hope that "Germany's growing strength . . . might force England to realize that [the balance of power] principle had become untenable and impracticable and to opt for a peaceful settlement with Germany," and German Secretary of State Gottlieb von Jagow to forecast British neutrality in a future European war: "We have not built our fleet in vain," and "people in England will seriously ask themselves whether it will be just that simple and without danger to play the role of France's guardian angel against us." German leaders also thought they might frighten Belgium into surrender: during the July crisis Moltke was "counting on the possibility of being able to come to an understanding [with Belgium] when the Belgian Government realizes the seriousness of the situation." This ill-founded belief in bandwagoning reinforced the general belief that conquest was relatively easy.

The belief in easy conquest eventually pervaded public images of international politics, manifesting itself most prominently in the widespread application of Darwinist notions to international affairs. In this image, states competed in a decisive struggle for survival which weeded out the weak and ended in the triumph of stronger states and races—an image which assumed a powerful offense. . . . This Darwinist foreign policy thought reflected and rested upon the implicit assumption that the offense was strong, since "grow or die" dynamics would be impeded in a defense-dominant world where growth could be stopped and death prevented by self-defense.

Consequences of Offense-Dominance

Recent theoretical writing in international relations emphasizes the dangers that arise when the offense is strong relative to the defense. If the theory outlined in these writings is valid, it follows that the cult of the offensive was a reason for the outbreak of the war.

Five major dangers relevant to the 1914 case may develop when the offense is strong, according to this recent writing. First, states adopt more aggressive foreign policies, both to exploit new opportunities and to avert new dangers which appear when the offense is strong. Expansion is more tempting, because the cost of aggression declines when the offense has the advantage. States are also driven to expand by the need to control assets and create the conditions they require to secure themselves against aggressors, because security becomes a scarcer asset. Alliances widen and tighten as states grow more dependent on one another for security, a circumstance which fosters the spreading of local conflicts. Moreover, each state is more likely to be menaced by aggressive neighbors who are governed by the same logic, creating an even more competitive atmosphere and giving states further reason to seek security in alliances and expansion.

Second, the size of the advantage accruing to the side mobilizing or striking first increases, raising the risk of preemptive war.* When

---

* In a "preemptive" war, either side gains by moving first; hence, one side moves to exploit the advantage of moving first, or to prevent the other side from doing so. By contrast, in a "preventive" war, one side foresees an adverse shift in the balance of power, and attacks to avoid a more difficult fight later.

"Moving first" in a preemptive war can consist of striking first or *mobilizing* first, if mobilization sets in train events which cause war, as in 1914. Thus a war is preemptive if statesmen attack because they believe that it pays to strike first; or if they mobilize because they believe that it pays to mobilize first, even if they do not also believe that it pays to strike first, if mobilizations open "windows" which spur attacks for "preventive" reasons, or if they produce other effects which cause war. Under such circumstances war is caused by preemptive actions which are not acts of war, but which are their equivalent since they produce conditions which cause war.

A preemptive war could also involve an attack by one side and mobilization by the other—for instance, one side might mobilize to forestall an attack, or might attack to forestall a mobilization, as the Germans apparently attacked Liège to forestall Belgian preparations to defend it (see below). Thus four classes of preemp-

the offense is strong, smaller shifts in ratios of forces between states create greater shifts in their relative capacity to conquer territory. As a result states have greater incentive to mobilize first or strike first, if they can change the force ratio in their favor by doing so. This incentive leads states to mobilize or attack to seize the initiative or deny it to adversaries, and to conceal plans, demands, and grievances to avoid setting off such a strike by their enemies, with deleterious effects on diplomacy.

Third, "windows" of opportunity and vulnerability open wider, forcing faster diplomacy and raising the risk of preventive war. Since smaller shifts in force ratios have larger effects on relative capacity to conquer territory, smaller prospective shifts in force ratios cause greater hope and alarm, open bigger windows of opportunity and vulnerability, and enhance the attractiveness of exploiting a window by launching a preventive attack.

Fourth, states adopt more competitive styles of diplomacy—brinkmanship and presenting opponents with *faits accomplis,* for instance—since the gains promised by such tactics can more easily justify the risks they entail. At the same time, however, the risks of adopting such strategies also increase, because they tend to threaten the vital interests of other states more directly. Because the security of states is more precarious and more tightly interdependent, threatening actions force stronger and faster reactions, and the political ripple effects of *faits accomplis* are larger and harder to control.

Fifth, states enforce tighter political and military secrecy, since national security is threatened more directly if enemies win the contest for information. As with all security assets, the marginal utility of information is magnified when the offense is strong; hence states compete harder to gain the advantage and avoid the disadvantage of disclosure, leading states to conceal their political and military planning and decision-making more carefully.

The following section suggests that many of the proximate causes of the war of 1914 represent various guises of these consequences of offense-dominance: either they were generated or exacerbated by the assumption that the offense was strong, or their effects were

---

tion are possible: an attack to forestall an attack, an attack to forestall a mobilization, a mobilization to forestall an attack, or a mobilization to forestall a mobilization (such as the Russian mobilizations in 1914).

The size of the incentive to preempt is a function of three factors: the degree of secrecy with which each side could mobilize its forces or mount an attack; the change in the ratio of forces which a secret mobilization or attack would produce; and the size and value of the additional territory which this changed ratio would allow the attacker to conquer or defend. If secret action is impossible, or if it would not change force ratios in favor of the side moving first, or if changes in force ratios would not change relative ability to conquer territory, then there is no first-strike or first-mobilization advantage. Otherwise, states have some inducement to move first.

rendered more dangerous by this assumption. These causes include: German and Austrian expansionism; the belief that the side which mobilized or struck first would have the advantage; the German and Austrian belief that they faced "windows of vulnerability"; the nature and inflexibility of the Russian and German war plans and the tight nature of the European alliance system, both of which spread the war from the Balkans to the rest of Europe; the imperative that "mobilization meant war" for Germany; the failure of Britain to take effective measures to deter Germany; the uncommon number of blunders and mistakes committed by statesmen during the July crisis; and the ability of the Central powers to evade blame for the war. Without the cult of the offensive these problems probably would have been less acute, and their effects would have posed smaller risks. Thus the cult of the offensive was a mainspring driving many of the mechanisms which brought about the First World War.

THE CULT OF THE OFFENSIVE AND THE CAUSES OF THE WAR

German Expansion and Entente Resistance

Before 1914 Germany sought a wider sphere of influence or empire, and the war grew largely from the political collision between expansionist Germany and a resistant Europe. Germans differed on whether their empire should be formal or informal, whether they should seek it in Europe or overseas, and whether they should try to acquire it peacefully or by violence, but a broad consensus favored expansion of some kind. The logic behind this expansionism, in turn, rested on two widespread beliefs which reflected the cult of the offensive: first, that German security required a wider empire; and second, that such an empire was readily attainable, either by coercion or conquest. Thus German expansionism reflected the assumption that conquest would be easy both for Germany and for its enemies . . . and most German officers and civilians believed they could win a spectacular, decisive victory if they struck at the right moment.

Bandwagon logic fed hopes that British and Belgian opposition to German expansion could be overcome. . . . Victory, moreover, would be decisive and final. . . . The presumed power of the offense made empire appear both feasible and necessary. Had Germans recognized the real power of the defense, the notion of gaining wider empire would have lost both its urgency and its plausibility.

Security was not Germany's only concern, nor was it always a genuine one. In Germany, as elsewhere, security sometimes served as a pretext for expansion undertaken for other reasons. Thus proponents of the "social imperialism" theory of German expansion note that German elites endorsed imperialism, often using security arguments, partly to strengthen their domestic political and social position. Likewise, spokesmen for the German military establishment exaggerated the threat to Germany and the benefits of empire for organizationally self-serving reasons. Indeed, members of the German elite sometimes privately acknowledged that Germany was under less threat than the public was being told. For example, the Secretary of State in the Foreign Office, Kiderlen-Wächter, admitted, "If we do not conjure up a war into being, no one else certainly will do so," since "The Republican government of France is certainly peace-minded. The British do not want war. They will never give cause for it. . . . "

Nevertheless, the German public believed that German security was precarious, and security arguments formed the core of the public case for expansion. Moreover, these arguments proved persuasive, and the chauvinist public climate which they created enabled the elite to pursue expansion, whatever elite motivation might actually have been. . . . The same mixture of insecurity and perceived opportunity stiffened resistance to German expansion and fuelled a milder expansionism elsewhere in Europe, intensifying the conflict between Germany and its neighbors. In France the nationalist revival and French endorsement of a firm Russian policy in the Balkans were inspired partly by a growing fear of the German threat after 1911, partly by an associated concern that Austrian expansion in the Balkans could shift the European balance of power in favor of the Central Powers and thereby threaten French security, and partly by belief that a war could create opportunities for French expansion. . . .

Russian policy in the Balkans was driven both by fear that Austrian expansion could threaten Russian security and by hopes that Russia could destroy its enemies if war developed under the right conditions. Sazonov saw a German–Austrian Balkan program to "deliver the Slavonic East, bound hand and foot, into the power of Austria–Hungary," followed by the German seizure of Constantinople, which would gravely threaten Russian security by placing all of Southern Russia at the mercy of German power. Eventually a "German Khalifate" would be established, "extending from the banks of the Rhine to the mouth of the Tigris and Euphrates," which would reduce "Russia to a pitiful dependence upon the arbitrary will of the Central Powers." At the same time some Russians believed these threats could be addressed by offensive action: Russian leaders spoke of the day when "the moment for the downfall of Austria–Hungary arrives," and the occasion when "The Austro-Hungarian ulcer, which today is not yet so ripe as the Turkish, may be cut up." Russian military officers contended that "the Austrian army represents a serious force. . . . But on the occasion of the first great defeats all of this multi-national and artificially united mass ought to disintegrate."

In short, the belief that conquest was easy and security scarce was an important source of German–Entente conflict. Without it, both sides could have adopted less aggressive and more accommodative policies.

The Incentive to Preempt

American strategists have long assumed that World War I was a preemptive war, but they have not clarified whether or how this was true. Hence two questions should be resolved to assess the consequences of the cult of the offensive: did the states of Europe perceive an incentive to move first in 1914, which helped spur them to mobilize or attack? If so, did the cult of the offensive help to give rise to this perception?

The question of whether the war was preemptive reduces to the question of why five principal actions in the July crisis were taken. These actions are: the Russian preliminary mobilization ordered on July 25–26; the partial Russian mobilization against Austria–Hungary ordered on July 29; the Russian full mobilization ordered on July 30; French preliminary mobilization measures ordered during July 25–30; and the German attack on the Belgian fortress at Liège at the beginning of the war. The war was preemptive if Russia and France mobilized preemptively, since these mobilizations spurred German and Austrian mobilization, opening windows which helped cause war. Thus while the mobilizations were not acts of war, they caused effects which caused war. The war was also preemptive if Germany struck Liège preemptively, since the imperative to strike Liège was one reason why "mobilization meant war" to Germany.

The motives for these acts cannot be determined with finality; testimony by the actors is spotty and other direct evidence is scarce. Instead, motives must be surmised from preexisting beliefs, deduced from circumstances, and inferred from clues which may by themselves be inconclusive. However, three pieces of evidence suggest that important preemptive incentives existed, and helped to shape conduct. First, most European leaders apparently believed that mobilization by either side which was not answered within a very few days, or even hours, could affect the outcome of the war. This judgment is reflected both in the length of time which officials assumed would constitute a militarily significant delay between mobilization and offsetting counter-mobilization, and in the severity of the consequences which they assumed would follow if they mobilized later than their opponents.

Second, many officials apparently assumed that significant mobilization measures and preparations to attack could be kept secret for a brief but significant period. Since most officials also believed that a brief unanswered mobilization could be decisive, they concluded that the side which mobilized first would have the upper hand.

Third, governments carried out some of their mobilization measures in secrecy, suggesting that they believed secret measures were feasible and worthwhile.

THE PERCEIVED SIGNIFICANCE OF SHORT DELAYS. Before and during the July crisis European leaders used language suggesting that they believed a lead in ordering mobilization of roughly one to three days would be significant. In Austria, General Conrad believed that "every day was of far-reaching importance," since "any delay might leave the [Austrian] forces now assembling in Galicia open to being struck by the full weight of a Russian offensive in the midst of their deployment." In France, Marshall Joffre warned the French cabinet that "any delay of twenty-four hours in calling up our reservists" once German preparations began would cost France "ten to twelve miles for each day of delay; in other words, the initial abandonment of much of our territory." In Britain, one official believed that France "cannot possibly delay her own mobilization for even the fraction of a day" once Germany began to mobilize. In Germany, one analyst wrote that "A delay of a single day . . . can scarcely ever be rectified." Likewise Moltke, on receiving reports of preparations in France and Russia during the July crisis, warned that "the military situation is becoming from day to day more unfavorable for us," and would "lead to fateful consequences for us" if Germany did not respond. . . .

Germans also placed a high value on gaining the initiative at Liège, since Liège controlled a vital Belgian railroad junction, and German forces could not seize Liège with its tunnels and bridges intact unless they surprised the Belgians. As Moltke wrote before the war, the advance through Belgium "will hardly be possible unless Liège is in our hands . . . the possession of Liège is the *sine qua non* of our advance." But seizing Liège would require "meticulous preparation and surprise" and "is only possible if the attack is made at once, before the areas between the forts are fortified," "immediately" after the declaration of war. In short, the entire German war plan would be ruined if Germany allowed Belgium to prepare the defense of Liège.

This belief that brief unanswered preparations and actions could be decisive reflected the implicit assumption that the offense had the advantage. Late mobilization would cost Germany control of East and West Prussia only if Russian offensive power were strong, and German defensive power were weak; mobilizing late could only be a "crime against the safety" of Germany if numerically superior enemies could destroy it; lateness could only confront Russia with "certain catastrophe" or leave it in danger of "losing before we have time to unsheath our sword" if Germany could develop a powerful offensive with the material advantage it would gain by preparing first; and lateness could only condemn France to "irreparable inferiority" if small material inferiority translated into large territorial losses. Had statesmen understood that in reality the defense had the advantage, they also would have known that the possession of the initiative could not be decisive, and could have conceded it more easily.

WAS SECRET PREPARATION BELIEVED FEASIBLE? The belief that delay could be fatal would have created no impulse to go first had European leaders believed that they could detect and offset their opponents' preparations immediately. However, many officials believed that secret action for a short time was possible. Russian officials apparently lacked confidence in their own ability to detect German or Austrian mobilization, and their decisions to mobilize seem to have been motivated partly by the desire to forestall surprise preparation by their adversaries. Sazonov reportedly requested full mobilization on July 30 partly from fear that otherwise Germany would "gain time to complete her preparations in secret." Sazonov offers confirmation in his memoirs, explaining that he had advised mobilization believing that "The perfection of the German military organization made it possible by means of personal notices to the reservists to accomplish a great part of the work quietly." Germany could then "complete the mobilization in a very short time. This circumstance gave a tremendous advantage to Germany, but we could counteract it to a certain extent by taking measures for our own mobilization in good time."

Similar reasoning contributed to the Russian decision to mobilize against Austria on July 29. Sazonov explains that the mobilization was undertaken in part "so as to avoid the danger of being taken unawares by the Austrian preparations." Moreover, recent experience had fuelled Russian fears of an Austrian surprise: during the Balkan crisis of 1912, the Russian army had been horrified to discover that Austria had secretly mobilized in Galicia, without detection by Russian intelligence; and this experience resolved the Russian command not to be caught napping again. In one observer's opinion, "the experience of 1912 . . . was not without influence as regards Russia's unwillingness to put off her mobilization in the July days of 1914." Top Russian officials also apparently believed that Russia could itself mobilize secretly, and some historians ascribe the Russian decision to mobilize partly to this erroneous belief. . . .

Like their Russian counterparts, top French officials also apparently feared that Germany might mobilize in secret, which spurred the French to their own measures. Thus during the July crisis General Joffre spoke of "the concealments [of mobilization] which are possible in Germany," and referred to "information from excellent sources [which] led us to fear that on the Russian front a sort of secret mobilization was taking place [in Germany]." In his memoirs, Joffre quotes a German military planning document acquired by the French government before the July crisis, which he apparently took to indicate German capabilities, and which suggested that Germany could take "quiet measures . . . in preparation for mobilization," including "a discreet assembly of complementary personnel and materiel" which would "assure us advantages very difficult for other armies to realize in the same degree." . . .

To sum up, then, French policymakers feared that Germany could mobilize secretly; Russians feared secret mobilization by Germany or Austria, and hoped Russian mobilization could be secret; while Central Powers planners saw less possibility for preemptive mobilization by either side, but hoped to mount a surprise attack on Belgium.*

DID STATESMEN ACT SECRETLY? During the July crisis European statesmen sometimes informed their opponents before they took military measures, but on other occasions they acted secretly, suggesting that they believed the initiative was both attainable and worth attaining, and indicating that the desire to seize the initiative may have entered into their decisions to mobilize. German leaders warned the French of their preliminary measures taken on July 29, and their pre-mobilization and mobilization measures taken on July 31; and they openly warned the Russians on July 29 that they would mobilize if Russia conducted a partial mobilization. Russia openly warned Austria on July 27 that it would mobilize if Austria crossed the Serbian frontier, and then on July 28 and July 29 openly announced to Germany and Austria its partial mobilization of July 29, and France delayed full mobilization until after Germany had taken the onus on itself by issuing ultimata to Russia and France. However, Russia, France, and Germany tried to conceal four of the five major preemptive actions of the crisis: the Russians hid both their preliminary measures of July 25–26 and their general mobilization of July 30, the French attempted to conceal their preliminary mobilization measures of July 25–29, and the Germans took great care to conceal their planned *coup de main* against Liège. Thus

---

* During the July crisis, adversaries actually detected signs of most major secret mobilization activity in roughly 6–18 hours, and took responsive decisions in 1–2 days. Accordingly, the maximum "first mobilization advantage" which a state could gain by forestalling an adversary who otherwise would have begun mobilizing first was roughly 2–4 days.

states sometimes conceded the initiative, but sought it at critical junctures.

Overall, evidence suggests that European leaders saw some advantage to moving first in 1914: the lags which they believed significant lay in the same range as the lags they believed they could gain or forestall by mobilizing first. These perceptions probably helped spur French and Russian decisions to mobilize, which in turn helped set in train the German mobilization, which in turn meant war partly because the Germans were determined to preempt Liège. Hence the war was in some modest measure preemptive.

If so, the cult of the offensive bears some responsibility. Without it, statesmen would not have thought that secret mobilization or preemptive attack could be decisive. The cult was not the sole cause of the perceived incentive to preempt; rather, three causes acted together, the others being the belief that mobilization could briefly be conducted secretly, and the systems of reserve manpower mobilization which enabled armies to multiply their strength in two weeks. The cult had its effect by magnifying the importance of these other factors in the minds of statesmen, which magnified the incentive to preempt which these factors caused them to perceive. The danger that Germany might gain time to complete preparations in secret could only alarm France and Russia if Germany could follow up these preparations with an effective offensive; otherwise, early secret mobilization could *not* give "a tremendous advantage" to Germany, and such a prospect would not require a forestalling response. Sazonov could have been tempted to mobilize secretly only if early Russian mobilization would forestall important German gains, or could provide important gains for Russia, as could only have happened if the offense were powerful.

"Windows" and Preventive War

Germany and Austria pursued bellicose policies in 1914 partly to shut the looming "windows" of vulnerability which they envisioned ₁ying ahead, and partly to exploit the brief window of opportunity which they thought the summer crisis opened. This window logic, in turn, grew partly from the cult of the offensive, since it depended upon the implicit assumption that the offense was strong. The shifts in the relative sizes of armies, economies, and alliances which fascinated and frightened statesmen in 1914 could have cast such a long shadow only in a world where material advantage promised decisive results in warfare, as it could only in an offense-dominant world.

The official communications of German leaders are filled with warnings that German power was in relative decline, and that Germany was doomed unless it took drastic action—such as provoking and winning a great crisis which would shatter the Entente, or directly instigating a "great liquidation" (as one general put it). German officials repeatedly warned that Russian military power would expand rapidly between 1914 and 1917, as Russia carried out its 1913–1914 Great Program, and that in the long run Russian power would further outstrip German power because Russian resources were greater. In German eyes this threat forced Germany to act. Secretary of State Jagow summarized a view common in Germany in a telegram to one of his ambassadors just before the July crisis broke:

> Russia will be ready to fight in a few years. Then she will crush us by the number of her soldiers; then she will have built her Baltic fleet and her strategic railways. Our group in the meantime will have become steadily weaker. . . . I do not desire a preventive war, but if the conflict should offer itself, we ought not to shirk it.

. . . During the war, Chancellor Bethmann Hollweg confessed that the "window" argument had driven German policy in 1914: "Lord yes, in a certain sense it was a preventive war," motivated by "the constant threat of attack, the greater likelihood of its inevitability in the future, and by the military's claim: today war is still possible without defeat, but not in two years!"

Window logic was especially prevalent among the German military officers, many of whom openly argued for preventive war during the years before the July crisis. . . . After the war Jagow recalled a conversation with Moltke in May 1914, in which Moltke had spelled out his reasoning:

> In two–three years Russia would have completed her armaments. The military superiority of our enemies would then be so great that he did not know how we could overcome them. Today we would still be a match for them. In his opinion there was no alternative to making preventive war in order to defeat the enemy while we still had a chance of victory. The Chief of General Staff therefore proposed that I should conduct a policy with the aim of provoking a war in the near future.

. . . German leaders also saw a tactical window of opportunity in the political constellation of July 1914, encouraging them to shut their strategic window of vulnerability. In German eyes, the Sarajevo assassination created favorable conditions for a confrontation, since it guaranteed that Austria would join Germany against Russia and France (as it might not if war broke out over a colonial conflict or a dispute in Western Europe), and it provided the Central powers with a plausible excuse, which raised hopes that Britain might remain neutral. . . .

Whether the Germans were aggressive or restrained depended on whether at a given moment they thought windows were open or closed. Germany courted war on the Balkan question after Sarajevo because window logic led German leaders to conclude that war could not be much worse than peace, and might even be better, if Germany could provoke the right war under the right conditions against the right opponents. German leaders probably preferred the status quo to a world war against the entire Entente, but evidence suggests that they also preferred a continental war against France and Russia to the status quo—as long as Austria joined the war, and as long as they could also find a suitable pretext which they could use to persuade the German public that Germany fought for a just cause. This, in turn, required that Germany engineer a war which engaged Austrian interests, and in which Germany could cast itself as the attacked, in order to involve the Austrian army, to persuade Britain to remain neutral, and to win German public support. These window considerations help explain both the German decision to force the Balkan crisis to a head and German efforts to defuse the crisis after it realized that it had failed to gain British neutrality. The German peace efforts after July 29 probably represent a belated effort to reverse course after it became clear that the July crisis was not such an opportune war window after all.

Window logic also helped to persuade Austria to play the provocateur for Germany. Like their German counterparts, many Austrian officials believed that the relative strength of the central powers was declining, and saw in Sarajevo a rare opportunity to halt this decline by force. . . . the Austrian foreign ministry reportedly believed that, "if Russia would not permit the localization of the conflict with Serbia, the present moment was more favorable for a reckoning than a later one would be." . . .

Thus the First World War was in part a "preventive" war, launched by the Central powers in the belief that they were saving themselves from a worse fate in later years. The cult of the offensive bears some responsibility for that belief, for in a defense-dominated world the windows which underlie the logic of preventive war are shrunken in size, as the balance of power grows less elastic to the relative sizes of armies and economies; and windows cannot be shut as easily by military action. Only in a world taken by the cult of the offensive could the window logic which governed German and Austrian conduct have proved so persuasive: Germans could only have feared that an unchecked Russia could eventually "crush us by the numbers of her soldiers," or have seen a "singularly favorable situation" in 1914 which could be "exploited by military action" if material superiority would endow the German and Russian armies with the ability to conduct decisive offensive operations against one another. Moltke claimed he saw "no alternative to making preventive war," but had he believed that the defense dominated, better alternatives would have been obvious. . . .

The Scope and Inflexibility of Mobilization Plans

The spreading of World War I outward from the Balkans is often ascribed to the scope of rigidity of the Russian and German plans for mobilization, which required that Russia must also mobilize armies against Germany when it mobilized against Austria–Hungary, and that Germany also attack France and Belgium if it fought Russia. Barbara Tuchman writes that Europe was swept into war by "the pull of military schedules," and recalls Moltke's famous answer when the Kaiser asked if the German armies could be mobilized to the East: "Your Majesty, it cannot be done. The deployment of millions cannot be improvised. If Your Majesty insists on leading the whole army to the East it will not be an army ready for battle but a disorganized mob of armed men with no arrangements for supply." . . .

The scope and character of these plans in turn reflected the assumption that the offense was strong. In an offense-dominant world Russia would have been prudent to mobilize against Germany if it mobilized against Austria–Hungary; and Germany probably would have been prudent to attack Belgium and France at the start of any Russo–German war. Thus the troublesome railroad schedules of 1914 reflected the offense-dominant world in which the schedulers believed they lived. Had they known that the defense was powerful, they would have been drawn towards flexible plans for limited deployment on single frontiers; and had such planning prevailed, the war might have been confined to Eastern Europe or the Balkans.

Moreover, the "inflexibility" of the war plans may have reflected the same offensive assumptions which determined their shape. Russian and German soldiers understandably developed only options which they believed prudent to exercise, while omitting plans which they believed would be dangerous to implement. These judgments in turn reflected their own and their adversaries' offensive ideas. Options were few because these offensive ideas seemed to narrow the range of prudent choice.

Lastly, the assumption of offense-dominance gave preset plans greater influence over the conduct of the July crisis, by raising the cost of improvisation if statesmen insisted on adjusting plans at the last minute. Russian statesmen were told that an improvised partial mobilization would place Russia in an "extremely dangerous situation," and German civilians were warned against improvisation in similar terms. This in turn reflected the size of the "windows" which improvised partial mobilizations would open for the adversary on the frontier which the partial mobilization left unguarded, which in turn reflected the assumption that the offense was strong (since if defenses were strong a bungled mobilization would create less opportunity for others to exploit). Thus the cult of the offensive gave planners greater power to bind statesmen to the plans they had prepared.

RUSSIAN MOBILIZATION PLANS. On July 28, 1914, Russian leaders announced that partial Russian mobilization against Austria would be ordered on July 29. They took this step to address threats emanating from Austria, acting partly to lend emphasis to their warnings to Austria that Russia would fight if Serbia were invaded, partly to offset Austrian mobilization against Serbia, and partly to offset or forestall Austrian mobilization measures which they believed were taking place or which they feared might eventually take place against Russia in Galicia. However, after this announcement was made, Russian military officers advised their civilian superiors that no plans for partial mobilization existed, that such a mobilization would be a "pure improvisation," as General Denikin later wrote, and that sowing confusion in the Russian railway timetables would impede Russia's ability to mobilize later on its northern frontier. . . . Thus Russian leaders were forced to choose between full mobilization or complete retreat, choosing full mobilization on July 30.

The cult of the offensive set the stage for this decision by buttressing Russian military calculations that full mobilization was safer than partial. We have little direct evidence explaining why Russian officers had prepared no plan for partial mobilization, but we can deduce their reasoning from their opinions on related subjects. These suggest that Russian officers believed that Germany would attack Russia if Russia fought Austria, and that the side mobilizing first would have the upper hand in a Russo–German war (as I have outlined above). Accordingly, it followed logically that Russia should launch any war with Austria by preempting Germany.

Russian leaders had three principal reasons to fear that Germany would not stand aside in an Austro–Russian conflict. First, the Russians were aware of the international Social Darwinism then sweeping Germany, and the expansionist attitude toward Russia which this worldview engendered. . . . Second, the Russians were aware of German alarm about windows and the talk of preventive war which this alarm engendered in Germany. Accordingly, Russian leaders expected that Germany might seize the excuse offered by a Balkan war to mount a preventive strike against Russia, especially since a war arising from the Balkans was a "best case" scenario for Germany, involving Austria on the side of Germany as it did. Thus General Yanushkevich explained Russia's decision to mobilize against Germany in 1914: "We knew well that Germany was ready for war, that she was longing for it at that moment, because our big armaments program was not yet completed . . . and because our war potential was not as great as it might be." Accordingly, Russia had to expect war with Germany: "We knew that war was inevitable, not only against Austria, but also against Germany. For this reason partial mobilization against Austria alone, which would have left our front towards Germany open . . . might have brought about a disaster, a terrible disaster." In short, Russia had to strike to preempt a German preventive strike against Russia.

Third, the Russians knew that the Germans believed that German and Austrian security were closely linked. Germany would therefore feel compelled to intervene in any Austro–Russian war, because a Russian victory against Austria would threaten German safety. German leaders had widely advertised this intention: for instance, Bethmann Hollweg had warned the Reichstag in 1912 that if the Austrians "while asserting their interests should against all expectations be attacked by a third party, then we would have to come resolutely to their aid. And then we would fight for the maintenance of our own position in Europe and in defense of our future and security." And in fact this was precisely what happened in 1914: Germany apparently decided to attack on learning of Russian *partial* mobilization, before Russian full mobilization was known in Germany. This suggests that the role of "inflexible" Russian plans in causing the war is overblown—Russian full mobilization was sufficient but not necessary to cause the war; but it also helps explain why these plans were drawn as they were, and supports the view that some of the logic behind them was correct, given the German state of mind with which Russia had to contend.

In sum, Russians had to fear that expansionist, preventive, and alliance concerns might induce Germany to attack, which in turn reflected the German assumption that the offense was strong. The Russian belief that it paid to mobilize first reflected the effects of the same assumption in Russia. Had Europe known that the defense dominated, Russians would have had less reason to fear that an Austro–Russian war would spark a German attack, since the logic of expansionism and preventive war would presumably have been weaker in Germany, and Germany could more easily have tolerated some reduction in Austrian power without feeling that German safety was also threatened. At the same time, Russian soldiers would presumably have been slower to assume that they could improve their position in a Russo–German war by mobilizing preemptively. In short, the logic of general mobilization in Russia largely reflected and depended upon conclusions deduced from the cult of the offensive, or from its various manifestations. Without the cult of the offensive, a partial southern mobilization would have been the better option for Russia.

It also seems probable that the same logic helped persuade the Russian General Staff to eschew planning for a partial mobilization. If circumstances argued against a partial mobilization, they also argued against planning for one, since this would raise the risk that Russian civilians might actually implement the plan. This interpretation fits with suggestions that Russian officers exaggerated the difficulties of partial mobilization in their representations to Russian civilians. If Russian soldiers left a partial mobilization option undeveloped because they believed that it would be dangerous to exercise, it follows that they also would emphasize the difficulty of improvising a southern option, since they also opposed it on other grounds.

GERMAN MOBILIZATION PLANS. The Schlieffen Plan was a disastrous scheme which only approached success because the French war plan was equally foolish: had the French army stood on the defensive instead of lunging into Alsace–Lorraine, it would have smashed the German army at the French frontier. Yet General Schlieffen's plan was a sensible response to the offense-dominant world imagined by many Germans. The plan was flawed because it grew from a fundamentally flawed image of warfare.

In retrospect, Germany should have retained the later war plan of the elder Moltke (Chief of Staff from 1857 to 1888), who would have conducted a limited offensive in the east against Russia while standing on the defensive in the west. However, several considerations pushed German planners instead toward Schlieffen's grandiose scheme, which envisioned a quick victory against Belgium and France, followed by an offensive against Russia.

First, German planners assumed that France would attack Germany if Germany fought Russia, leaving Germany no option for a one-front war. By tying down German troops in Poland, an eastern war would create a yawning window of opportunity for France to recover its lost territories, and a decisive German victory over Russia would threaten French security by leaving France to face Germany alone. For these reasons they believed that France would be both too tempted and too threatened to stand aside. . . .

Second, German planners assumed that "window" considerations required a German offensive against either France or Russia at the outset of any war against the Entente. German armies could mobilize faster than the combined entente armies; hence, the ratio of forces would most favor Germany at the beginning of the war. Therefore, Germany would do best to force an early decision, which in turn required that it assume the offensive, since otherwise its enemies would play a waiting game. As one observer explained,

Germany "has the speed and Russia has the numbers, and the safety of the German Empire forbade that Germany should allow Russia time to bring up masses of troops from all parts of her wide dominions." Germans believed that the window created by these differential mobilization rates was big, in turn, because they believed that both Germany and its enemies could mount a decisive offensive against the other with a small margin of superiority. If Germany struck at the right time, it could win easily—Germans hoped for victory in several weeks, as noted above—while if it waited it was doomed by Entente numerical superiority, which German defenses would be too weak to resist.

Third, German planners believed that an offensive against France would net them more than an offensive against Russia, which explains the western bias of the Schlieffen Plan. France could be attacked more easily than Russia, because French forces and resources lay within closer reach of German power; hence, as Moltke wrote before the war, "A speedy decision may be hoped for [against France], while an offensive against Russia would be an interminable affair." Moreover, France was the more dangerous opponent not to attack, because it could take the offensive against Germany more quickly than Russia, and could threaten more important German territories if Germany left its frontier unguarded. Thus Moltke explained that they struck westward because "Germany could not afford to expose herself to the danger of attack by strong French forces in the direction of the Lower Rhine," and Alfred von Wegerer wrote later that the German strike was compelled by the need to protect the German industrial region from French attack. In German eyes these considerations made it too dangerous to stand on the defensive in the West in hopes that war with France could be avoided.

Finally, German planners believed that Britain would not have time to bring decisive power to bear on the continent before the German army overran France. Accordingly, they discounted the British opposition which their attack on France and Belgium would elicit: Schlieffen declared that if the British army landed, it would be "securely billeted" at Antwerp or "arrested" by the German armies, while Moltke said he hoped that it would land so that the German army "could take care of it." In accordance with their "bandwagon" worldview, German leaders also hoped that German power might cow Britain into neutrality; or that Britain might hesitate before entering the war, and then might quit in discouragement once the French were beaten—Schlieffen expected that, "If the battle [in France] goes in favor of the Germans, the English are likely to abandon their enterprise as hopeless"—which led them to further discount the extra political costs of attacking westward.

Given these four assumptions, an attack westward, even one through Belgium which provoked British intervention, was the most sensible thing for Germany to do. Each assumption, in turn, was a manifestation of the belief that the offense was strong. Thus while the Schlieffen Plan has been widely criticized for its political and military naiveté, it would have been a prudent plan had Germans actually lived in the offense-dominant world they imagined. Under these circumstances quick mobilization would have in fact given them a chance to win a decisive victory during their window of opportunity, and if they had failed to exploit this window by attacking, they would eventually have lost; the risk of standing on the defense in the West in hopes that France would not fight would have been too great; and the invasion of France and Belgium would have been worth the price, because British power probably could not have affected the outcome of the war.

Thus the belief in the power of the offense was the linchpin which held Schlieffen's logic together, and the main criticisms which can be levelled at the German war plan flow from the falsehood of this belief. German interests would have been better served by a limited, flexible, east-only plan which conformed to the defensive realities of 1914. Moreover, had Germany adopted such a plan, the First World War might well have been confined to Eastern Europe, never becoming a world war.

"Mobilization Means War"

"Mobilization meant war" in 1914 because mobilization meant war to Germany: the German war plan mandated that special units of the German standing army would attack Belgium and Luxemburg immediately after mobilization was ordered, and long before it was completed. (In fact Germany invaded Luxemburg on August 1, the same day on which it ordered full mobilization.) Thus Germany had no pure "mobilization" plan, but rather had a "mobilization and attack" plan under which mobilizing and attacking would be undertaken simultaneously. As a result, Europe would cascade into war if any European state mobilized in a manner which eventually forced German mobilization.

This melding of mobilization and attack in Germany reflected two decisions to which I have already alluded. First, Germans believed that they would lose their chance for victory and create a grave danger for themselves if they gave the Entente time to mobilize its superior numbers. In German eyes, German defenses would be too weak to defeat this superiority. . . . Second, the German war plan depended on the quick seizure of Liège. Germany could only secure Liège quickly if German troops arrived before Belgium prepared its defense, and this in turn depended on achieving surprise against

Belgium. Accordingly, German military planners enshrouded the planned Liège attack in such dark secrecy that Bethmann Hollweg, Admiral Tirpitz, and possibly even the Kaiser were unaware of it. They also felt compelled to strike as soon as mobilization was authorized, both because Belgium would strengthen the defenses of Liège as a normal part of the Belgian mobilization which German mobilization would engender, and because otherwise Belgium eventually might divine German intentions towards Liège and focus upon preparing its defense and destroying the critical bridges and tunnels which it controlled.

Both of these decisions in turn reflected German faith in the power of the offense, and were not appropriate to a defense-dominant world. Had Germans recognized the actual power of the defense, they might have recognized that neither Germany nor its enemies could win decisively even by exploiting a fleeting material advantage, and decided instead to mobilize without attacking. The tactical windows that drove Germany to strike in 1914 were a mirage, as events demonstrated during 1914–1918, and Germans would have known this in advance had they understood the power of the defense. Likewise, the Liège *coup de main* was an artifact of Schlieffen's offensive plan; if the Germans had stuck with the elder Moltke's plan, they could have abandoned both the Liège attack and the compulsion to strike quickly which it helped to engender.

Brinkmanship and Faits Accomplis

Two *faits accomplis* by the Central powers set the stage for the outbreak of the war: the Austrian ultimatum to Serbia on July 23, and the Austrian declaration of war against Serbia on July 28. The Central powers also planned to follow these with a third *fait accompli*, by quickly smashing Serbia on the battlefield before the Entente could intervene. These plans and actions reflected the German strategy for the crisis: "*fait accompli* and then friendly towards the Entente, the shock can be endured," as Kurt Riezler had summarized.

This *fait accompli* strategy deprived German leaders of warning that their actions would plunge Germany into a world war, by depriving the Entente of the chance to warn Germany that it would respond if Austria attacked Serbia. It also deprived diplomats of the chance to resolve the Austro-Serbian dispute in a manner acceptable to Russia. Whether this affected the outcome of the crisis depends on German intentions—if Germany sought a pretext for a world war, then this missed opportunity had no importance, but if it preferred the status quo to world war, as I believe it narrowly did, then the decision to adopt *fait accompli* tactics was a crucial step on the road to war. Had Germany not done so, it might have recognized where its policies led before it took irrevocable steps, and have drawn back.

The influence of the cult of the offensive is seen both in the German adoption of this *fait accompli* strategy and in the disastrous scope of the results which followed in its train. Some Germans, such as Kurt Riezler, apparently favored brinkmanship and *fait accompli* diplomacy as a means of peaceful expansion. Others probably saw it as a means to provoke a continental war. In either case it reflected a German willingness to trade peace for territory, which reflected German expansionism—which in turn reflected security concerns fuelled by the cult of the offensive. Even those who saw *faits accomplis* as tools of peaceful imperialism recognized their risks, believing that necessity justified the risk. . . . *Faits accomplis* were dangerous tools whose adoption reflected the dangerous circumstances which Germans believed they faced.

The cult of the offensive also stiffened the resistance of the Entente to the Austro–German *fait accompli,* by magnifying the dangers they believed it posed to their own security. Thus Russian leaders believed that Russian security would be directly jeopardized if Austria crushed Serbia, because they valued the power which Serbia added to their alliance, and because they feared a domino effect, running to Constantinople and beyond, if Serbia were overrun. Sazonov believed that Serbian and Bulgarian military power was a vital Russian resource, "five hundred thousand bayonets to guard the Balkans" which "would bar the road forever to German penetration, Austrian invasion." If this asset were lost, Russia's defense of its own territories would be jeopardized by the German approach to Constantinople: Sazonov warned the Czar, "First Serbia would be gobbled up; then will come Bulgaria's turn, and then we shall have her on the Black Sea." This would be "the death-warrant of Russia" since in such an event "the whole of southern Russia would be subject to [Germany]."

Similar views could be found in France. During the July crisis one French observer warned that French and Serbian security were closely intertwined, and the demise of Serbia would directly threaten French security:

> To do away with Serbia means to double the strength which Austria can send against Russia: to double Austro–Hungarian resistance to the Russian Army means to enable Germany to send some more army corps against France. For every Serbian soldier killed by a bullet on the Morava one more Prussian soldier can be sent to the Moselle. . . . It is for us to grasp this truth and draw the consequences from it before disaster overtakes Serbia.

These considerations helped spur the Russian and French decisions to begin military preparations on July 25, which set in train a
further sequence of events: German preliminary preparations,
which were detected and exaggerated by French and Russian officials, spurring them on to further measures, which helped spur the
Germans to their decision to mobilize on July 30. The effects of the
original *fait accompli* rippled outward in ever-wider circles, because
the reactions of each state perturbed the safety of others—forcing
them to react or preempt, and ultimately forcing Germany to launch
a world war which even it preferred to avoid.

Had Europe known that, in reality, the defense dominated, these
dynamics might have been dampened: the compulsion to resort to
faits accomplis, the scope of the dangers they raised for others, and
the rippling effects engendered by others' reactions all would have
been lessened. States still might have acted as they did, but they
would have been less pressured in this direction.

Problems of Alliances: Unconditionality and Ambiguity

Two aspects of the European alliance system fostered the outbreak of World War I and helped spread the war. First, both
alliances had an unconditional, offensive character—allies supported one another unreservedly, regardless of whether their behavior was defensive or provocative. As a result a local war would tend
to spread throughout Europe. And second, German leaders were
not convinced that Britain would fight as an Entente member, which
encouraged Germany to confront the Entente. In both cases the cult
of the offensive contributed to the problem.

UNCONDITIONAL ("TIGHT") ALLIANCES. Many scholars contend
that the mere existence of the Triple Alliance and the Triple Entente
caused and spread the war. . . . But the problem with the alliances
of 1914 lay less with their existence than with their nature. A
network of defensive alliances, such as Bismarck's alliances of the
1880s, would have lowered the risk of war by facing aggressors with
many enemies, and by making status quo powers secure in the
knowledge that they had many allies. Wars also would have tended
to remain localized, because the allies of an aggressor would have
stood aside from any war that aggressor had provoked. Thus the
unconditional nature of alliances rather than their mere existence
was the true source of their danger in 1914.

The Austro–German alliance was offensive chiefly and simply
because its members had compatible aggressive aims. Moreover,
German and Russian mobilization plans left their neighbors no
choice but to behave as allies by putting them all under threat of
attack. But the Entente also operated more unconditionally, or

"tightly," because Britain and France failed to restrain Russia from undertaking mobilization measures during the July crisis. This was a failure in alliance diplomacy, which in turn reflected constraints imposed upon the Western allies by the offensive assumptions and preparations with which they had to work.

First, they were hamstrung by the offensive nature of Russian military doctrine, which left them unable to demand that Russia confine itself to defensive preparations. All Russian preparations were inherently offensive, because Russian war plans were offensive. This put Russia's allies in an "all or nothing" situation—either they could demand that Russia stand unprepared, or they could consent to provocative preparations. Thus the British ambassador to St. Petersburg warned that Britain faced a painful decision, to "choose between giving Russia our active support or renouncing her friendship." Had Russia confined itself to preparing its own defense, it would have sacrificed its Balkan interests by leaving Austria free to attack Serbia, and this it would have been very reluctant to do. However, the British government was probably willing to sacrifice Russia's Balkan interests to preserve peace; what Britain was unable to do was to frame a request to Russia which would achieve this, because there was no obvious class of defensive activity that it could demand. . . .

Second, Britain and France were constrained by their dependence upon the strength and unity of the Entente for their own security, which limited their ability to make demands on Russia. Because they feared they might fracture the Entente if they pressed Russia too hard, they tempered their demands to preserve the alliance. Thus Poincaré wrote later that France had been forced to reconcile its efforts to restrain Russia with the need to preserve the Franco–Russian alliance, "the break up of which would leave us in isolation at the mercy of our rivals." Likewise Winston Churchill recalled that "the one thing [the Entente states] would not do was repudiate each other. To do this might avert the war for the time being. It would leave each of them to face the next crisis alone. They did not dare to separate." These fears were probably overdrawn, since Russia had no other option than alliance with the other Entente states, but apparently they affected French and British behavior. This in turn reflected the assumption in France and Britain that the security of the Entente members was closely interdependent. French leaders felt forced in their own interests to aid Russia if Russia embroiled itself with Germany, because French security depended on the maintenance of Russian power. This in turn undermined the French ability to credibly threaten to discipline a provocative Russia. . . .

Third, British leaders were unaware that German mobilization meant war, hence that peace required Britain to restrain Russia from mobilizing first, as well as attacking. As a result, they took a more relaxed view of Russian mobilization than they otherwise might, while frittering away their energies on schemes to preserve peace which assumed that war could be averted even after the mobilizations began. This British ignorance reflected German failure to explain clearly to the Entente that mobilization did indeed mean war—German leaders had many opportunities during the July crisis to make this plain, but did not do so. We can only guess why Germany was silent, but German desire to avoid throwing a spotlight on the Liège operation probably played a part, leading German soldiers to conceal the plan from German civilians, which led German civilians to conceal the political implications of the plan from the rest of Europe. Thus preemptive planning threw a shroud of secrecy over military matters, which obscured the mechanism that would unleash the war and rendered British statesmen less able to wield British power effectively for peace by obscuring what it was that Britain had to do.

Lastly, the nature of German war plans empowered Russia to involve France, and probably Britain also, in war, since Germany would be likely to start any eastern war by attacking westward, as Russian planners were aware. Hence France and Britain would probably have to fight for Russia even if they preferred to stand aside, because German planners assumed that France would fight eventually and planned accordingly, and the plans they drew would threaten vital British interests. We have no direct evidence that Russian policies were emboldened by these considerations, but it would be surprising if they never occurred to Russian leaders.

These dynamics reflected the general tendency of alliances toward tightness and offensiveness in an offense-dominant world. Had Europe known that the defense had the advantage, the British and French could have more easily afforded to discipline Russia in the interest of peace, and this might have affected Russian calculations. Had Russia had a defensive military strategy, its allies could more easily and legitimately have asked it to confine itself to defensive preparations. Had British leaders better understood German war plans, they might have known to focus their efforts on preventing Russian mobilization. And had German plans been different, Russian leaders would have been more uncertain that Germany would entangle the Western powers in eastern wars, and perhaps proceeded more cautiously.

The importance of the failure of the Western powers to restrain Russia can be exaggerated, since Russia was not the chief provocateur in the July crisis. Moreover, too much can be made of factors which hamstrung French restraint of Russia, since French desire to prevent war was tepid at best, so French inaction probably owed as much to indifference as inability. Nevertheless, Russian mobilization was an important step toward a war which Britain, if not France, urgently wanted to prevent; hence, to that extent, the alliance dynamics which allowed it helped bring on the war.

THE AMBIGUITY OF BRITISH POLICY. The British government is often accused of causing the war by failing to warn Germany that Britain would fight. Thus Albertini concludes that "to act as Grey did was to allow the catastrophe to happen," and Germans themselves later argued that the British had led them on, the Kaiser complaining of "the grossest deception" by the British.

The British government indeed failed to convey a clear threat to the Germans until after the crisis was out of control, and the Germans apparently were misled by this. Jagow declared on July 26 that "we are sure of England's neutrality," while during the war the Kaiser wailed, "If only someone had told me beforehand that England would take up arms against us!" However, this failure was not entirely the fault of British leaders; it also reflected their circumstances. First, they apparently felt hamstrung by the lack of a defensive policy option. Grey voiced fear that if he stood too firmly with France and Russia, they would grow too demanding, while Germany would feel threatened, and "Such a menace would but stiffen her attitude."

Second, British leaders were unaware of the nature of the German policy to which they were forced to react until very late, which left them little time in which to choose and explain their response. Lulled by the Austro–German *fait accompli* strategy, they were unaware until July 23 that a crisis was upon them. . . . They also were apparently unaware that a continental war would begin with a complete German conquest of Belgium, thanks to the dark secrecy surrounding the Liège operation. Britain doubtless would have joined the war even if Germany had not invaded Belgium, but the Belgian invasion provoked a powerful emotional response in Britain which spurred a quick decision on August 4. This reaction suggests that the British decision would have been clearer to the British, hence to the Germans, had the nature of the German operation been known in advance.

Thus the British failure to warn Germany was due as much to German secrecy as to British indecision. Albertini's condemnation of Grey seems unfair: governments cannot easily take national decisions for war in less than a week in response to an uncertain provocation. The ambiguity of British policy should be recognized as an artifact of the secret styles of the Central powers, which reflected the competitive politics and preemptive military doctrines of the times. . . .

CONCLUSION

The cult of the offensive was a major underlying cause of the war of 1914, feeding or magnifying a wide range of secondary dangers which helped pull the world to war. The causes of the war are often catalogued as an unrelated grab-bag of misfortunes which unluckily arose at the same time; but many shared a common source in the cult of the offensive, and should be recognized as its symptoms and artifacts rather than as isolated phenomena.

The consequences of the cult of the offensive are illuminated by imagining the politics of 1914 had European leaders recognized the actual power of the defense. German expansionists then would have met stronger arguments that empire was needless and impossible, and Germany could have more easily let the Russian military buildup run its course, knowing that German defenses could still withstand Russian attack. All European states would have been less tempted to mobilize first, and each could have tolerated more preparations by adversaries before mobilizing themselves, so the spiral of mobilization and counter-mobilization would have operated more slowly, if at all. If armies mobilized, they might have rushed to defend their own trenches and fortifications, instead of crossing frontiers, divorcing mobilization from war. Mobilizations could more easily have been confined to single frontiers, localizing the crisis. Britain could more easily have warned the Germans and restrained the Russians, and all statesmen could more easily have recovered and reversed mistakes made in haste or on false information. Thus the logic that led Germany to provoke the 1914 crisis would have been undermined, and the chain reaction by which the war spread outward from the Balkans would have been very improbable. In all likelihood, the Austro–Serbian conflict would have been a minor and soon-forgotten disturbance on the periphery of European politics. . . .

Chemical Warfare:
A Study in Restraints

FREDERIC J. BROWN

. . . [World War I] was [a] war without limits—the brains and muscle of modern industrial nations applied without restriction to the art of war. In the minds of expert and layman alike, World War I was about to pass a threshold into new levels of violence when it ended. It was the mind that could speculate not the eye that had seen which would project World War I as it could have been in 1919.

MILITARY PERSPECTIVES

Speculation would play a significant role in determining the future of gas warfare; however, there were more substantial factual inputs that would influence subsequent decision-makers—the lessons learned from the experiences of World War I.

Tactical characteristics. The tactical military lessons were mixed, a potpourri of individual or unit experiences extremely difficult to evaluate in the aggregate in order to rate gas as "effective" or "noneffective." More important to military analysts than an imprecise evaluation of effectiveness were the characteristics of poison gas as observed on the battlefield. By November 1918, it was apparent that chemical warfare had three central characteristics: it was an extremely versatile weapon, tractable to almost any tactical situation; the logistic requirements complicated the battlefield enormously; and its employment demanded unprecedented sophistication of individual and unit training.

The tactical versatility of gas was derived from the diverse properties of the gases employed. Gas could be persistent or nonpersistent over a wide range of lethality—from an extremely toxic cyanic compound to a nonlethal, harassing tear or sneezing gas. The effect of the gas could be immediate or delayed for several hours.

These properties gave chemical warfare a role in the offensive or defensive, in mobile or position warfare. A lethal, nonpersistent agent could be placed on enemy positions just before attack and it would be

From *Chemical Warfare: A Study in Restraints* by Frederic J. Brown, pp. 32–48 and 290–298. Copyright © 1968 by Princeton University Press. Reprinted by permission. Portions of the text and some footnotes have been deleted.

dissipated before friendly troops arrived. A persistent agent such as mustard could be placed to protect a flank during an attack, to deny an area to the enemy, or as a very effective barrage in front of a defensive position. Such flexibility applied, of course, to all belligerents, provided that each could support the logistic requirements of gas warfare.

The logistic demands were enormous. Gas substituted for nothing. Its requirements were an additional load to an already overloaded battlefield. To be effective, a high concentration of gas had to be maintained over the enemy position. The Germans found that 12,000 kilograms of Green Cross [nonpersistent] shells were necessary to gas an area one kilometer square. Similar consumption figures were experienced by other belligerents.[1]

Graver problems were presented to both logisticians and tacticians by the requirements for individual and collective protection in a toxic environment. In addition to the other stresses and dangers of war, the very air the soldier breathed and the harmless inanimate objects he touched had become potential weapons against him. The range of problems posed was infinite: How would the soldier eat, drink, sleep, perform bodily functions, use his weapon, give and receive commands; how would he protect horses, pigeons, and watch dogs; how would he know when his immediate area was contaminated? By November 1918, many of these issues had been broached but they had not been solved. The battlefield had experienced a quantum jump in sophistication; it had become too "complicated."

Nothing indicated the spectrum of new problems better than the gas mask. A highly personal symbol of gas warfare, it was awkward, heavy to carry, and uncomfortable to wear. An officer in the 3rd Division, AEF, described it:

> The mask is safe but it is the most uncomfortable thing I ever experienced. If . . . [anyone wants to] know how a gas mask feels, let him seize his nose with a pair of fire tongs, bury his face in a hot feather pillow, then seize a gas pipe with his teeth and breathe through it for a few hours while he performs routine duties. It is safe, but like the deadly poison which forced its invention, it is not sane.[2]

It was not just that the mask was uncomfortable. The survival of the individual was determined by the quality of the mask. Either it worked

---

[1] . . . High ammunition expenditure rates were not unique to gas; however, gas required a special infrastructure—meteorological stations, special purpose units with specialized training, etc.—that was not required for conventional warfare.

[2] R. Cochrane, *Gas Warfare in World War I*, 20 Studies (Army Chemical Center: Chemical Corps Historical Office, 1957-1960), Study 14, p. 34. . . . The mask also reduced vision and muffled the voice—two essential requirements to command on the battlefield. . . .

faultlessly or the soldier died. Life was dependent upon 100 per cent reliability. This unique and disquieting reliance on science and industry, was not the only psychological problem related to wearing the mask. There was the added trauma of divorcement from the external environment. The gas mask "makes the soldier blind and deaf when he enters into material warfare, despoils him of his feed and drink, his nicotine and alcohol, and then makes war a fearful means for the destruction of morale."[3]

As well as indirect psychological effects derived from protective measures, fears of gas warfare produced other reactions. One was a psychoneurosis, "Gas Fright." Soldiers, hearing a report that gas was in the area, would acquire all of the symptoms of gas poisoning although they had not been gassed. Gas could induce severe morale problems among troops already fatigued and dispirited by a difficult tactical situation. The First Army of the AEF was in such a situation facing the Kriemhilde Stellung in October 1918. The history of the 42nd Division commented:

. . . an important cause of the low morale was the mounting fear of the enemy's use of gas . . . it was largely responsible for creating so great a straggler problem that, as Bullard said, a solid line of MP's back of the fighting front had become necessary to keep the men in the line. The basis of that fear was the gas atmosphere that the enemy maintained over much of the front by his regulated gas fire each day. When it did not cause real casualties, it supported apprehension and panic, and hastened the onset of battle fatigue and gas mask exhaustion.[4]

The combined effects of tactical flexibility, logistical complexity, and adverse psychological response to an alien environment required highly trained units. For front-line troops, instantaneous reaction was required twenty-four hours per day. If the unit was not properly trained, it suffered debilitating casualties.[5]

In summary, chemical warfare was an enigma from the perspective of tactical military employment. If it could be used unilaterally, there was no question that it was effective. Unfortunately, however, it could not be used unilaterally. Once the enemy retaliated, the game did not appear worth the candle. No transitory advantage justified the difficulties of a chemical battlefield. The problems of fighting in an alien

[3] Maj. G. Soldan, *Der Mensch und die Schlacht der Zunkuft* (Oldenberg: Verlag Stalling, 1925). . . .

[4] Cochrane, *op. cit.*, Study 17, pp. 40–41. . . .

[5] All armies experienced roughly equivalent gas-casualty rates, dependent upon the training of troops. Casualties at Ypres in 1915 were estimated at over 30 per cent. Later in the year, the gas-casualty rate declined to less than 3 per cent as training improved. Yet the first attack on U.S. troops in 1918 produced over 30 per cent casualties—not a glowing testimonial to U.S. preparations. . . .

environment appeared insoluble. Science and technology might develop an answer but this was a mixed blessing at best.

Science and technology. If it can be said that science and the industrial revolution approached the battlefield in the American Civil War, it can be said to have arrived during World War I. In no other area was this as apparent as chemical warfare. A General could improve upon or detract from the capabilities of the chemical warfare equipment given to him; but the life and death decisions of strategic magnitude were made in laboratories and industrial plants.

Throughout the war there was a scientific race between belligerents. The Germans seized the initiative when they introduced chlorine gas at Ypres in April 1915; six months passed before the Allies could retaliate. In July 1917, the Germans introduced mustard gas; it was June 1918 before the Allies could retaliate in kind,[6] and not until the last month of the war that they had sufficient stocks of mustard gas. This provided a significant advantage to the Germans in the spring-summer offenses of 1918.

Thirty different chemical substances were tested in combat during the war,[7] each of which posed a unique problem for defense. Since no army could afford to find itself in a defenseless position due to a new enemy gas, there were continual efforts at improvement. The British alone issued 7 different masks to their troops—a total of 50 million masks. . . .

The role of science was equal to if not greater than the traditional value of physical courage in determining success on the battlefield. As toxic agents and their methods of delivery became more sophisticated in 1917 and 1918, the necessity for professional-military assimilation of science and technology became more pronounced. It was not a comforting thought to realize that an enemy with a superior technical expertise and industrial capability could introduce a weapon which would overcome one's own superior training and leadership. This was a disturbing reality that the military profession faced in looking back at World War I. Chemical warfare was the most striking example.

A question of honor. However, there was more to disturb the military profession than science and technology. Chemical warfare did not fall within the limits of the honor of the profession. The code of war was unwritten, but it was understood. Essentially based upon the code of chivalry, it had varied as mores changed and as the increasing range of weapons changed the nature of the battlefield. In 1914, it was represented by the Rules of Land Warfare in the Hague Conventions. Violation could be tolerated only through necessity of

---

[6] Due to a brilliant manufacturing feat of the French. The British did not have mustard gas until September 1918.

[7] . . . Over 3,000 substances were investigated for war use.

war and even here the accountability rested with the Head of State. Two hallmarks of the profession were that war would be limited in its efforts to combatants only, and that the most honorable and heroic way to defeat the enemy was in hand-to-hand combat. In the minds of certain World War I military leaders, gas violated these customs and typified the contemporary degeneration of the profession in the face of unlimited war.

General Peyton March, the Chief of Staff of the United States Army during and after the war, recalled a visit to a hospital in France:

> [The hospital contained] . . . over one hundred French women and children who had been living in their homes in rear of and near the front and who were gassed. The sufferings of these children, particularly, were horrible and produced a profound impression on me. War is cruel at best, but the use of an instrument of death, which once launched, cannot be controlled, and which may decimate noncombatants—women and children—reduces civilization to savagery.[8]

While March was primarily concerned about the gassing of noncombatants, two general officers more closely connected with the initiation at Ypres condemned the effect on troops. General von Deimling, Commanding General of a German Corps at Ypres, commented: "I must confess that the commission for poisoning the enemy just as one poisons rats struck me as it must any straightforward soldier; it was repulsive to me."[9] Lord French, the British Commander in France, expressed the "deepest regret and some surprise" that the German Army claiming to be "the chief exponent of the chivalry of war should have stooped to employ such devices against brave and gallant foes. . . ."[10] Reactions such as these would be reinforced with time as the rationale of wartime necessity faded from view. A sense of guilt for past actions combined with the natural desire to enhance the image of one's profession could make gas an exceedingly unpopular subject for military discussion.

At the end of World War I, the prospects of military acceptance of chemical warfare were unfavorable. On balance, the military characteristics of gas warfare did not justify its use unless the situation ensured unilateral employment. Unless some nation made a significant technological breakthrough in protection, a mutual exchange of gas would create a toxic battle environment causing more problems to

---

[8] Gen. P. March, *The Nation at War* (Garden City, N.Y.: Doubleday-Doran, 1932), p. 333. This passage was written in 1931, but it was not inconsistent with his immediate postwar attitude.

[9] Gen. von Deimling, *Reminiscences* (Paris: Montaigne, 1931). . . .

[10] *The Despatches of Lord French* (London: Chapman and Hull Ltd., 1917), p. 360. In the British Army, the Gas Brigade and gas itself were referred to as "frightfulness. . . ."

be raised than could be solved. Nevertheless, the rewards for a breakthrough would be high. . . .

The question was complicated, however, by the side issues that gas introduced. Gas symbolized the encroachment of science and technology into military decision-making, and became "an affair of honor" to the military profession. If the military continued to view gas from these perspectives, its future would not be promising.

FEARS FOR THE FUTURE—ESCALATION

The issues that gas posed to the military were dwarfed by the problems it presented to the makers of national security policy. The history of the use of toxic agents in World War I made a near perfect model of escalation: escalation of delivery systems, of weapon capabilities, and of targets selected. . . .

By the time of the 1918 offensive, at least 50 per cent of the artillery shells fired by the Germans were gas shells. The last ominous increment to delivery capability was never employed. In 1918, the British contracted for 250 bombing aircraft each with a 7,500-pound bomb load. . . .

The last and most foreboding input to the model of escalation was target selection. The initial use of gas was confined to a military target, but as the war developed and the use of gas increased in intensity, it was impossible to avoid noncombatants. One of the objections to the release of clouds of gas from cylinders was that the size of the cloud produced significant gas concentrations at undesired locations. In discussing this problem, Hanslian referred to effects as far as 20 kilometers behind the front and deaths at a distance of 15 kilometers. There is no indication, however, that the belligerents did not tacitly agree that a certain "spillover" of gas into towns was an inevitable accompaniment to its tactical use in a congested countryside.

The strategic use of gas was an entirely different question. The delivery system could only be by airplane and the implications were truly frightening. The Germans initiated strategic bombing on Christmas Eve 1914—one aircraft with one bomb. The bombing effort gradually escalated to two serious raids on London (June 13, 1917 and July 7, 1917) causing 832 casualties. After the July 7th raid, the English War Cabinet appointed a committee headed by Jan Christian Smuts to study the air defense of the United Kingdom. In its report, this committee gave serious consideration to the "probability" of the Germans using gas to attack London. Thus by the fall of 1917, the Germans had initiated unrestricted city bombing and the British had matched the capability of gas with the potential of the airplane, at least in defensive contingency planning.

By late 1918, the potential of the airplane was becoming real capability. The bomber force would be available in 1919. There was no shortage of toxic agent. The Allies were prepared.[11] As the capability was being gathered, the Allies made plans for the forthcoming air offensive. The order called for unrestricted bombing. In addition to authorizing the use of high explosives, the order provided a ready case for gas bombing.

There is no indication that a decision was ever made to initiate strategic gas bombing. The mere fact that it had quite obviously been seriously considered was enough to complete a rather terrifying model of escalation that would haunt the makers of postwar policy.

During the war there had been two attempts to halt the spiral of escalation. The first was offered by the United States in May 1915—after German initiation at Ypres but before British retaliation at Loos. President Wilson proposed that Germany discontinue submarine warfare against merchant ships and the use of poison gas, while England would terminate the blockade of neutral ports. The offer was refused by both powers.[12]

The other attempt was an appeal against the use of gas by the International Committee of the Red Cross on February 6, 1918. The Red Cross put its finger on the root of the problem when it predicted that the use of gas "threatens to increase to a never foreseen extent."[13] The appeal was rejected by both sides in notes designed more for propaganda effect than for serious negotiation. The atmosphere of distrust could not be overcome despite a mutual interest in terminating gas warfare.

Viewed in retrospect, the image of gas was no more encouraging to the decision-maker than it was to the military professional. The other group whose impressions would influence the future of poison gas was the general public. It will be recalled that the Allies had changed the focus of gas propaganda several times during the war. By 1918, poison gas was being represented as an unwanted but German-introduced feature of the war in which Allied science and technology were proving their superiority.

---

[11] In the spring of 1918, Colonel Fries suggested to General Pershing that the Allies deliver gas by airplane. As the incident was related by General Harbord, Chief of Staff, AEF, General Pershing refused the idea because the AEF would not initiate and "at that time" the enemy was not using gas against civilian populations, although the situation could change. "While our aviators were not allowed to initiate such warfare, *we were not unprepared to retaliate if it came to that*" (Maj. Gen. J. Harbord, *The American Army in France, 1917–1919* [Boston: Little, Brown, 1936], p. 223 [italics mine]).

[12] E. Franklin, "Chemical Warfare—Its Possibilities and Probabilities," *International Conciliation*, No. 248 (March 1929), p. 57.

[13] Comité International de la Croix-Rouge (CICR), *Documents relatifs à la Guerre Chimique et Aérienne* (Genéve: CICR, 1932), p. 6. Trans. by author.

Under the circumstances, gas was being presented quite rationally, and it apparently was not the subject of any more unfavorable reaction than that directed at all the new weapons of war. The situation could change rapidly, however, if interest groups, including decision-makers and the military, desired to use gas as a *cause célèbre* to promote a particular want.

Only the future would tell. . . .

SUMMARY AND CONCLUSIONS

To advocates of chemical warfare, World War II repeated the pattern of World War I. Toxic agents had been on the verge of acceptance as a major strategic weapons system but then were not employed. In both cases, the war ended before chemical warfare had the opportunity to display its potential. In the former case, realization of the potential effectiveness of gas was impeded due to the unavailability of a delivery system (the long-range bomber) commensurate with the capabilities of the weapon.

The situation was totally different in World War II. The supporting infrastructure required for effective employment had been developed. Non-use resulted from the interaction of a variety of objective and subjective restraints. For the first time since the advent of the nation at arms a major weapon employed in one conflict was not carried forward to be used in a subsequent conflict. Can this be considered a favorable indicator of inhibitions on the employment of nuclear weapons in general war, or is it an accident unlikely to recur?

It is extremely difficult to predict the future employment of nuclear weapons. Nevertheless, I believe that a study of American chemical warfare policy can provide an understanding of the nature of restraints which should prove as valid in the present and future as it has in the past. . . .

Three general areas of restraint have emerged in this study. First, there are those forces which were expected to restrain but which were proven generally ineffective in the heat of war. Second, there is the problem of non-assimilation by the professional military—a significant but little-appreciated subjective inhibition on employment. Last are the agreed components of deterrence—cost, capability, and credibility; this study evaluates their effectiveness as an element of restraint and emphasizes several critical aspects of deterrence developed from the study of chemical warfare.

Overestimation of the influence of public opinion was a serious fallacy of interwar prognostication. In the belief that adverse public sentiment was a major hope of preventing war, the United States actively encouraged anti-gas propaganda in the immediate post-World War I period. During World War II, however, this restraint was ineffective. Without government encouragement, American public attitudes toward the employment of gas shifted from opposition to passive acceptance if not support of initiation. The combination of bitter, costly island invasions in the Pacific Theater, and the identification of the entire enemy population as evil created an environment wherein the primary criterion for weapon use was rapid termination of the conflict rather than the "humanity" of a particular weapon.

Although public opinion per se was not a direct restraint on the use of gas, indirect effects of public attitudes i.. the interwar period were operative throughout the war. Due in significant measure to its awareness of the abhorrence with which the public viewed gas during the twenties and thirties, the Army never seriously pressed for gas warfare readiness; an Army desiring integration into the mainstream of American life would not burnish its image by meaningful support of a weapon so distasteful to the public. Public opinion, therefore, contributed to the nation's low state of readiness for chemical warfare at the outbreak of war.

Public opinion also had an impact on the decision-making elite of World War II. Profoundly influenced by the anti-gas propaganda, President Roosevelt would not even consider the possibilities of American initiation or preparation beyond the minimum amount required for retaliation. Anti-gas propaganda conditioned the attitudes of other leaders, both military and civilian, as well. Chemical warfare was consistently associated with a normative qualifying expression. State Department as well as JCS* papers on chemical warfare referred to "this inhuman method of warfare" or "this particularly inhuman form of warfare."

The other great hope of opponents of gas warfare lay in the creation of legal restraints, which turned out to have no greater direct effect than had public opinion. No power considered any treaty restriction or limiting declaration of a belligerent to be more than a statement of intent, which could be violated if the exigencies of unlimited war required.

The legal restraint was moderately effective; but in an unanticipated sense. The numerous interwar attempts to codify prohibition served to focus public and elite group attention on the problems and prospects of chemical warfare. Due to extensive conferences, specific national decisions had to be made on chemical warfare policy at times when national capability and popular sentiment created environments of unreality. Particularly in the United States, ratification of the chemical warfare prohibition of the Washington Conference established a questionable precedent for future negotiation and made it exceedingly difficult to promote actual chemical warfare readiness.

* [Editors' note: Joint Chiefs of Staff.]

A comparable effect developed in Germany. Readiness was impeded by the legal prohibition of Versailles and the Geneva Protocol; in addition, there were the specific arms control measures of the Peace Treaty. The Germans lost ten years in the international race to develop more effective chemical warfare weapons, and this hiatus provoked a serious "crisis of confidence." Ironically, the Germans made the major offensive chemical warfare breakthrough of the interwar period—nerve agents—yet forfeited the advantage by presuming that the Allies had made a similar advance. Thus, a former legal restraint helped indirectly to negate a major technological breakthrough.

Similar to the case with public attitudes, the legal restraint gained its limited effectiveness in an indirect and unanticipated manner. Based upon this experience, it would appear that the primary value of the legal restraint rests in its tendency to reinforce other existing restraints. Treaty prohibition, though imperfect, reinforced both public and military dislike and fear of chemical warfare and provided a ready excuse for lack of substantive preparation. Any legal restraint derived from custom or a general principle of law prohibiting weapons causing unnecessary suffering—if such exists and can be applied—should be even more effective, in that each would represent a more universal consensus of expert and lay attitudes.

Acceptance of a weapon within the military establishment is a prerequisite to employment. Influenced by the counter-propaganda writings of articulate military proponents of chemical warfare, most civilians assumed that the military accepted and was eager to employ chemical weapons. This assumption was false. Aside from those military leaders institutionally committed to toxic agents, the military establishment as a whole was opposed to their use. As an area weapon developed by scientists to strike insidiously and from afar, gas did not accord with the honor of the profession. In addition, the immense logistical and training burden unique to gas warfare required greater battlefield effect than could be attained with other weapons in order to justify resort to such a high-cost weapon. It could not be proven that the use of gas would provide any quantum jump in probability of battlefield success, particularly when the enemy could be expected to retaliate in kind. With major financial restraints imposed throughout the Depression, no national military establishment was inclined to emphasize weapons of doubtful effectiveness when Artillery, Infantry, and the Air Force were faced with acute shortages in conventional weapons.

Since gas warfare was not assimilated into the military establishment of any major power, its use was precluded in World War II. Without professional support for meaningful gas warfare readiness, no nation was prepared to employ toxic agents when it entered the war. For the Axis Powers, during the successful first half of the war, there was no incentive to commit the resources required for increased chemical warfare preparedness when other weapons of proven utility were in constant demand. The same logic, albeit reversed in its time sequence, applied to the Allied Powers.

This lack of assimilation was particularly evident in the United States response to the extreme asymmetry of readiness existing between the United States and Japan toward the end of World War II. Despite its awareness that the Japanese could not retaliate, the United States did not employ toxic agents. The central reason for this lay in the general military disinterest in gas which had retarded readiness sufficiently to preclude timely, serious consideration of initiation. Decades of conditioning to a second-strike philosophy prevented such logistic preparedness in the forward areas which could have provided an incentive to striking the first blow.

The implication here is that lack of assimilation is a more fundamental inhibition to initiation than fear of retaliation. No major belligerent in World War II accepted gas warfare. As a result, a defensive aura surrounded the entire area of toxic chemical warfare. Aside from Japan, each nation maintained a credible retaliatory capability, yet the capability was in each case more potential than real. There was never sufficient readiness to provide the incentive for immediate initiation.

Even if any nation had developed a material capability adequate to make initiation feasible, fear of the costs of enemy retaliation would have remained as a restraint sufficient to deter it. Whether the prospective victim actually possessed sufficient retaliatory capability to inflict intolerable levels of punishment is essentially irrelevant. Partially due to poor chemical warfare intelligence on the part of all belligerents, which credited the enemy with a capability commensurate with the assumed diabolical nature of his intentions, each nation saw asymmetrical chemical warfare capabilities as favoring the enemy. When the potential initiator realized his superiority and his invulnerability to direct enemy retaliation, as was the case of the United States, in the last stages of the Pacific War, initiation was deterred by threat of retaliation against an ally, China. In World War II, the restraint of enemy retaliation was magnified in effect by the demands of coalition warfare. The presence of allies that were hostages for the good conduct of the coalition leader increased the stability of mutual deterrence.

These restraints, proven in war, varied considerably from interwar predictions. Neither public opinion nor legal restriction was directly effective; but, on the other hand, lack of assimilation and fear of retaliation proved to be significant restraints. In World War II, the lesson was clear; the loci of decision-making with respect to gas warfare lay within the professional military establishments themselves. Military lack of interest kept the issue of initiation from reaching civilian elite groups.

American experience with toxic agents during World War II revealed several general characteristics of successful deterrence. Readiness to retaliate was communicated through statements of heads of government backed up with overt chemical warfare preparations. The unrestricted nature of war, exemplified by the unlimited bombing policy, gave credibility to the threat to employ toxic agents in response to enemy initiation. No nation doubted that the potential target nation possessed a retaliatory capability sufficient to punish the initiator, directly, or indirectly, through a coalition partner, and general military dislike of toxic agents was sufficient to restrain any inclination to develop a possible disarming first-strike capability.

Each belligerent saw escalation of toxic agent employment as an inevitable effect of initiation. Once World War II began, there does not appear to have been any serious consideration of initiation solely for tactical success. It was tacitly assumed that any use of gas would immediately escalate to the strategic level and, therefore, that any initiation should itself be at the strategic level. Essentially the same logic applied to the choice of chemical agents. It was assumed that there was no effective limiting point between the employment of nonlethal and lethal agents. For this reason, nontoxic chemical agents were not employed in a combat environment.

Based upon Japanese actions, however, the validity of both assumptions is questionable. The Japanese employed nontoxic and toxic agents against the Chinese both before and after United States entry in the war, yet the United States ignored the situation. Due to lack of readiness and unwillingness to employ, the United States preferred to overlook a situation that, in terms of declaratory policy, would have required retaliation. As long as Japanese violation of tacitly agreed limits did not affect a core interest of the United States as defined by decision-makers or by reaction of the general public, there was no automaticity of escalation. The effect of this American response was to diminish the credibility of the American policy which enabled the Japanese to reallocate their chemical warfare readiness resources.[14]

World War II also saw in the United Kingdom and Germany the establishment of the most extensive and costly passive defense systems yet developed. In neither case did civil defense measures act as a destabilizing element in the maintenance of mutual deterrence. Each accepted civil protection as a necessary component of readiness for a nation continuously under the threat of surprise strategic attack. If it had any specific effect, the existence of effective civil defense acted as

---

[14] There is no indication that, despite attendance at interwar international conferences, the Japanese thought that in initiating they were doing anything other than field testing a new weapon. One can only speculate that it was their inexperience with chemical warfare which prevented them from realizing the implications of initiating employment.

a stabilizing element by reducing the expected reward, and thus incentive, for a surprise first strike.

A further element of restraint demonstrated in the Second World War was the impact on decision-making of an irrational leader. Hitler was accepted by the Allied Powers as a national leader likely to make irrational decisions. This image was in itself a stimulant to British preparations for gas warfare and thus indirectly contributed to deterrence. With his back to the wall, Hitler apparently decided to initiate gas warfare, but the inevitability of defeat was so obvious by early 1945 that he had lost authority over his key military subordinates. The result was failure to implement his decision.

This development would suggest that the critical time for one belligerent's initiation of a mass-casualty weapon is during that period when it is becoming obvious that eventual victory is improbable unless a new element is introduced into the war to restore the momentum of the offensive, but before it is obvious to the military establishment that the initiative has passed to the enemy and that eventual defeat is certain. In short, the decision would have to be made before the national leader has, by failure, undermined his power to have such a momentous decision implemented.

It remains one of the ironies of the Second World War that toxic agents, considered sufficiently humane to be used for the execution of convicted prisoners, were not employed in a war which saw the extensive use of another weapon with enormous destructive powers—the atomic bomb. The heritage of World War I was responsible—poison gas was a weapon too technologically demanding and psychologically disquieting to be assimilated by the military profession. It was an unacceptable anachronism, born too early out of a unique marriage of science and war. Added to this primary and most effective restraint of nonassimilation was mutual possession of a credible deterrent force. . . .

The Horse Cavalry
in the Twentieth Century

EDWARD L. KATZENBACH, JR.

THE PROBLEM

Lag-time, that lapsed period between innovation and a successful institutional or social response to it, is probably on the increase in military matters. Moreover, as the tempo of technological change continues to quicken, it is likely that lag-time will increase as well. . . .

Of course, at first there would seem to be a paradox here. As weapons systems have become more complex, the lead-time needed to bring them from the drawing board to the assembly line has become markedly longer. On the basis of the longer lead-time one might hypothesize that the institutional lag might lessen inasmuch as prior planning would seem eminently more possible. It might even be surmised that the institutional response might be made to coincide with the operational readiness of new weapons. To date, however, military institutions have not been able to use this lead-time effectively because real change has so outdistanced anticipated change. Moreover, there is not the urgency that there should be in the military to make major institutional adjustments in the face of the challenge of new weapons systems, if for no other reason than that the problem of testing is so difficult. . . . It is quite impossible to *prove* that minor adjustments in a traditional pattern of organization and doctrine will not suffice to absorb technological innovations of genuine magnitude.

Furthermore the absence of any final testing mechanism of the military's institutional adequacy short of war has tended to keep the pace of change to a creep in time of peace, and, conversely, has whipped it into a gallop in time of war. The military history of the past half century is studded with institutions which have managed to dodge the challenge of the obvious. . . . The most curious of all was the Horse Cavalry which maintained a capacity for survival that borders on the miraculous. The war horse survived a series of

From *Public Policy*, 1958, pp. 120–149. Copyright © 1958 by John Wiley & Sons, Inc. Reprinted by permission of John Wiley & Sons, Inc. Portions of the text and some footnotes have been omitted.

challenges each of which was quite as great as those which today's weapons systems present to today's traditional concepts. . . . It continued to live out an expensive and decorous existence with splendor and some spirit straight into an age which thought it a memory. . . .

The horse cavalry has had to review its role in war four times since the end of the nineteenth century in the face of four great changes in the science of war: the development of repeating automatic and semi-automatic weapons, the introduction of gasoline and diesel-fueled engines, the invention of the air-borne weapon, and the coming of the nuclear battlefield. Each new challenge to the horse has been, of necessity, seriously considered. Each has demanded a review of doctrine, a change in role and mission. And in each review there have been, of necessity, assumptions made as to the relevance of experience to some pattern of future war . . . [for] the paradox of military planning is that it must be reasonably precise as to quite imprecise future contingencies.

THE WEAPONS PROBLEM

By the year 1900, or thereabouts, the clip-fed breech-loading repeating rifle was in the hands of the troops of all the major powers. . . . Self-firing automatic weapons were also on the assembly lines of the world's armament makers. Hiram Maxim had registered the last of a famous series of machine gun patents in 1885. By the time (1904–1905) of the Russo-Japanese War the guns of Maxim and Hotchkiss were in national arsenals everywhere, or almost everywhere, for the expense of new weapons was rapidly shrinking the ranks of those powers which could be considered "great." At roughly the same time it had been found that the use of glycerine in the recoil mechanism of artillery pieces enabled these to remain aimed after being fired. This in turn meant that the artillery piece itself became a rapid fire (20 rounds per minute) weapon. . . . Firepower, in short, had a new meaning.

For the elite of the armies of the world, the cavalry, each of these developments would seem to have been nothing short of disaster. For that proud and beautiful animal, the horse, has a thin skin and a high silhouette, and its maximum rate of speed on the attack is only 30 m.p.h. Especially in conjunction with barbed wire, automatically manufactured since 1874 and in military use at the end of the century, it is difficult to imagine a target more susceptible to rapid fire.

The cavalry had always considered itself to have a variety of missions. The cavalry was the good eye of the infantry. It was taught to collect, and if necessary to fight for information about the enemy. The cavalry protected friendly, and harried enemy flanks and rear. It covered any necessary withdrawal. It was used in pursuit of defeated enemy. And above and beyond all else, the cavalry was used to charge the faltering, the weary, or the unwary, to deliver the *coup de grâce* with the *arme blanche:* with cold steel, with saber or lance, to "crown victory" as the proud phrase went.

It was clear that the introduction of the automatic and the semi-automatic weapon would make some cavalry missions more difficult. But there was no doubt in any cavalryman's mind, and there was little doubt in the minds of most others, that most cavalry missions would have to continue simply because there was no viable substitute. The horse was transport, and the horse was mobility. A group of horsemen could cover a hundred miles in twenty-four hours with a load of around 225–250 pounds. The beast was reasonably amphibious; at least it could swim rivers. To scout, to patrol, to cover flank, rear and withdrawal, to raid—these missions remained untouched.

There remained, however, one really great problem area. Did automatic fire relegate the horse to a transport role or should it still be considered as part of a weapons system? At the time the problem was never stated quite this simply. Indeed it was never stated simply at all, but in essence this was the issue from roughly the end of the Boer War until World War I. The reason why the question so divided men was this: Cavalry as an arm was an integrated weapon made up of horse, man and cold steel fighting as one. If horses were to be considered simply as transportation, and if man and horse were to be separated for the fire fight, then the cavalry as an arm would no longer exist. Only mounted infantry would remain.[1]

On the issue of the relationship between horse and man hung a number of subsidiary issues. Should the horseman be armed with the new automatic weapons? If so, he would have to be dismounted in action, for the horse, as differentiated from the elephant, is a most unsatisfactory gun platform. Yet to deprive cavalry of the new weapons would be to deprive the weapons of mobility. And if the horse could no longer be used to charge the new guns, then of what possible use was honed steel, e.g., lance and sword, even if one took into serious account the last ditch defense of it, to wit that it was "always loaded"? Finally, and here one comes to the most burning question in any issue of military policy—the effect of change on morale. If the cavalry were deprived of its cold steel, would it lose that fine edge of morale, that élan without which of course it would not be "cavalry," no matter what its mission?

There should have been some way to learn through experience just what could and could not be done with the cavalry with and

---

[1] Perhaps this will be better understood if a modern analogy is cited—the substitution of missile for manned aircraft, for example.

against the new weapons. There were, after all, two wars of some importance during the period under consideration—the Boer War (1898–1901) and the Russo-Japanese (1904–1905). In both, cavalry and repeating and automatic weapons were used. Each fall, .noreover, there were great maneuvers in each country of Europe. Present at each were foreign observers with, at least by modern standards, a free run of the field of action. Why was it then that there could be no final decisions on these matters?

The answer lies in the number of variables. For instance, before the problem of the cavalry armament could even be tackled, the difficult question had to be answered as to what the rapid-fire weapons could do and should be doing.

. . . For each demonstrable fact there was an awkwardly intangible "if" which could neither be properly accounted for nor possibly forgotten. If into the balance of judgment concerning the machine gun was thrown the urgent problem of its resupply and its vulnerability to long-range artillery fire, then a rational conclusion might be reached that the weapon was primarily defensive in character and should be dug into the earth, into a well sandbagged bunker, there to pour forth its withering fire into an attacking force. Yet if, on the other hand, it was concluded that the withering fire of the weapon made it ideal to use on the surprise target, the target of opportunity on the enemy flank, then the weapon became offensive. If an offensive weapon, then the machine gun could well be designated a cavalry weapon. If defensive, then was it not an infantry, or even an artillery weapon? Of course this initial decision was a serious one for it might well determine the future of the weapon. Once assigned to an organization, a branch or arm of a service, it was at least likely that the weapon's development would be stunted except in line with the mission of the unit to which it was assigned.

Within the military staff of all nations the machine gun raised many more problems than it solved—as can be expected of any new weapons system. These problems were, furthermore, broadly intellectual rather than narrowly technical. Indeed the mechanical improvement of a given weapons system is usually less urgent and almost always less baffling than deciding a proper and fitting target for it, and then solving the galaxy of problems of organization and control which hinge on this basic decision. . . .

So in the period between 1900 and 1914 the immediate problem was to conceptualize the mission or missions of the machine gun and the tactics of the new clip-fed, bolt-action rifle and the automatic gun. The second problem was to decide the future tactics and armament of cavalry in view of the concept arrived at. What actually happened was that the new was absorbed into old organizational and tactical concepts, and nothing of the old was rejected. The reasoning from country to country may, however, be of lasting interest. The matter of the cavalry *charge* provides an excellent focal point.

THE CHARGE

It is hard to see where there was room for claim and counterclaim in so substantive an issue as this—the charge of a wave of horsemen, gaily colored (except in the United States), helmets shining, plumes flying, sabers drawn or lances at the ready. Surely a comprehensive and conclusive study of the charge and its role, if any, in modern war was not outside the bounds of logical possibility. Yet just as it was impossible in the 1930s to analyze the role of the battleship in the air age and is now impossible to assess the relationship between the naval aircraft carrier and the nuclear bomber, so it was impossible to evaluate the charge—and for much the same reasons.

The reasons why the charge was continued varied from one country to another. But basically it was continued because the cavalry liked it. In virtually all countries the cavalry was a club, an exclusive one, made up at the officer level of those who could afford to ride when young, hunt, dress and play polo when older. The impression that one absorbs from contemporary cavalry reviews, from the pictures, the social columns, the interests expressed in the less than serious articles, together with the portrait of the cavalry-man in the contemporary novel, is of a group of men who were at once hard-riding, hard-drinking, and hard-headed. Its leadership was derived from the countryside rather than from the city. The cavalry was the home of tradition, the seat of romance, the haven of the well-connected. New York City's Squadron A, the proud majors in the Prussian Cavalry Reserve, the French Horse Breeders' Association, all had a built-in loyalty to the cavalry, and if the Chief of Cavalry said that the charge was still feasible, he had important backing. So it was that in Europe the charge was still considered not only feasible, but a future way of war.

American cavalrymen, however, thought that European cavalry had much to learn. And in many respects the U.S. "Red Necks" were quite the most realistic of the world's cavalries in the period just prior to World War I. To be sure, they retained the saber charge, executing it with the same straight saber, a thrust weapon, used by the Canadian cavalry. But in the years just before World War I until just after World War II the U.S. Cavalry preferred to practice the charge with the Colt semi-automatic .45 pistol. (The pistol charge was never actually used in battle. The last battle charge of the U.S. Cavalry seems to have been in the Philippines during the insurrection of 1901.) Of course it might be argued that to put a .45 in the hands of a man on a horse was simply to mount the inaccurate on the unstable, but given the argument that the essence of the charge was its psychological impact, the sound of the .45 might have had an effect comparable to the sight of saber or lance.

But what the U.S. Cavalry did have that the others did not was a genuine appreciation of the importance of dismounted action. It is this which is given the more elaborate treatment in the regulations, and it is this that the trooper really expected to be the rule in combat. But was this the result of a thoughtful analysis of the new weapons or something else?

Certainly the articles in the *Journal of the U.S. Cavalry Association* are the most sophisticated in regard to the new repeating arms and their impact on cavalry. In the years just after the turn of the century the great argument in U.S. Cavalry circles was whether or not the saber should be retained at all. But it seems to have been generally admitted that while "Mounted charges may yet be used on rare occasions when the enemy is demoralized, out of ammunition, or completely taken by surprise . . . ," nonetheless "for cavalry to make a mounted charge against enemy troops who are dismounted and armed with the present magazine gun, would be to seek disaster." The corollary that ". . . the trooper must bear in mind that in fighting his carbine is his main reliance"[2] was also accepted.

Were it not that certain European cavalry groups were at the time tending to reject the thesis to which the U.S. subscribed, there would be nothing in any way remarkable about the U.S. position, so patently obvious and right does it seem in retrospect. Yet in the early nineteen hundreds U.S. doctrine was different, and hence needs a word of explanation.

The U.S. cavalryman had a tradition quite different from that of any of the Europeans. He had always done the bulk of his fighting on his feet. Therefore there was no break in tradition for him to recognize the revolution in firepower for the great change it was. Cavalry during the Civil War most frequently fought dismounted, although clashes between cavalry were fought with the sword, and in the wars against the Indians cavalrymen also dismounted to fight with the aimed accurate fire quite unattainable on horseback. Horses were considered transportation, and the ground was considered a respectable substance on which to fight a battle. U.S. cavalrymen did not feel morally obligated to die on a horse—which European cavalrymen did. In short, the U.S. Cavalry reacted to the new firepower as it did because its history and its tradition made it quite natural for it to do so. In Europe the cavalry history of the U.S. Civil War was scarcely known until the very late nineteen

    [2] "Comment and Criticism," *Journal of the U.S. Cavalry Association (JUSCA)*, Vol. 13, No. 48, April 1903, pp. 720, 721.

hundreds, and hence the relevance of that war to cavalry problems was largely overlooked. Or given European experience and tradition, would a study of the Civil War have made any real difference?

Of all the cavalry arms of the world that which seems in retrospect to have been the furthest behind the times was that of the German Empire. The German Cavalry had adopted the lance for all ninety-three of its cavalry regiments in 1890 instead, as was true in the mid-nineteenth century, of having only one in four so armed. The lance was, of course, much more than a shaft of wood taller than a man, one tipped with steel and pennant decked: a lance was a state of mind. And it was a reminder that those who carried it still believed that the cavalry really was an arm to be reckoned with. . . .

Why was it that such serious students of war as the Germans are reputed to have been were in general quite so oblivious to the impact of the new firepower? There seem to have been several reasons. The first and most important was the attitude of Emperor William II towards cavalry. A young U.S. Cavalry lieutenant who witnessed German maneuvers in the fall of 1903 was frankly appalled by it. He noted the total lack of realism in the great rolling charges of the cavalry against both rifle and artillery. And he noted too the fact that the Kaiser was so proud of his cavalry that his umpires, knowing their place, pronounced the charges successful!! In Germany, in short, the well-known penchant of the Emperor for the charge undoubtedly did much to insulate the Germans from any serious thought of change.

There was, however, another reason as well. Even after seeing machine guns fired in the late 1880s, the German General Staff refused to take them seriously. Their reason lay in their mis-reading of their own experience with the *mitrailleuses* during the war of 1870–71 when these were badly misused. The fact that past experience happened to be irrelevant did not make it any less important, however, and it was not until 1908 that the machine gun was given the serious attention in Germany that it so obviously deserved. Even then it was only the infantry that recognized the importance of the new automatic weapons. Cavalry units, although armed with them, did not take them very seriously. German cavalry went trotting off to war in 1914, pennons flying from their lances, just as units of French infantry went off to war in red trousers, and for much the same reason: psychological effect. For the real effect of cavalry was, when on the charge, a psychological one, and was generally admitted as such. It was the role of the charge to break the enemy's will, and what could do this more effectively than a charge by lancers? The same argument was used by those who wanted to keep the infantry in red pants. They advanced the proposition that the sense of belonging was the essence of group spirit, and group spirit in turn was the touchstone of the will to fight, the ingredient that won battles. They added the corollary that nothing gave units the sense of oneness that did red trousers, and that therefore camouflaged material would actually sabotage national security. . . .

So tradition, personal predilection, and misinterpreted past experience kept the cavalry charge alive in Germany. The experience of the British after the Boer War likewise suggests how difficult it is to test the relevance of one's own experience in war.

THE RELEVANCE OF EXPERIENCE

From the end of the Boer War to the beginning of World War I the great debate in the British Cavalry, as in other countries, dealt with the retention of the lance and the charge. The arguments put forward for their retention inevitably raise the question of whether faith was not interfering with reason. . . .

A U.S. Cavalry officer noted on a trip to Aldershot in 1903 that "Every change is made entirely with reference to the Boer War and the Boer country, as though future wars would be fought under the same conditions."[3] But what this observer should also have noted was that there was a wide division of opinion as to just what that war proved, and how genuinely relevant it really was. . . .

Like other modern wars the Boer War was made up of a series of actions no one of which was decisive. The Boers, fine shots and fine horsemen, used their horses as transportation. In effect they fought as mounted infantry, employing the mobility of the horse in combination with the aimed firepower of infantry. They possessed all the advantages of great space and a friendly and embattled population, and the British were hard put to it to bring them to terms. But these were virtually the only points on which there was any agreement whatsoever. What did the facts mean, if anything?

Two of Great Britain's best known military figures, Lord Roberts, the British Chief of Staff, and Field-Marshal Sir John D. P. French, Cavalry Commander in Africa and, in 1914, Commander-in-Chief of the British Expeditionary Forces, led two factions within the army whose views of the future of cavalry were in direct opposition.

The Right Honorable Field-Marshal Earl Roberts placed the *imprimatur* of his authority on a book called *War and the Arme Blanche* by one Erskine Childers. In his introduction to this book Lord Roberts set forth his basic beliefs. . . . Lord Roberts believed simply that the "main lesson" to be learned from the Boer War and the Russo-Japanese War was that "knee to knee, close order charg-

---

[3] Frank R. McCoy, "Notes of the German Maneuvers," *JUSCA*, Vol. 14, No. 49, January 1904, pp. 30, 31.

ing is practically a thing of the past." He qualified his opinion somewhat. "There may be, there probably will be, mounted attacks, preferably in open order against Cavalry caught unawares, or against broken Infantry," he wrote. But even these mounted attacks, he said, should be carried out with the rifle, rather than with steel.[4] These ideas he actually wrote into the British regulations, *Cavalry Training,* in 1904.

... The general argument, as one can imagine, was first that lances and sabers were not killing men in war, and second, that infantry and mounted infantry were killing, when dismounted, cavalrymen. Three wars, the U.S. Civil War, the Boer War, and the Russo-Japanese War, were cited as proof of the contention. In retrospect this point of view hardly needs explanation. It seems quite obvious to think that the armaments which took the warrior off his feet and put him on his belly would by the same token take him off his charger and put him on the ground.

For a time Lord Roberts was Commander-in-Chief of the British Army, and his views were thus imposed for a brief moment on the generals. What this meant in effect was that the lance disappeared in Britain between 1903 and 1906. But Lord Roberts proved unpopular, and as is the way with unpopular leaders, he was eased gently out of office in quite short order, to become a disturbing shadow amongst their eminences in the House of Lords. And the lance came back into use in 1906 to remain for better than two decades—until 1927, to be precise.

Sir John French, an officer whom one of the most distinguished of Great Britain's War Secretaries, Lord Haldane, called "a real soldier of the modern type"[5] was an old Hussar. He had entered the army through the Militia and had thus avoided Sandhurst and the mental training this would have involved. For Sir John the experience of the Boer War was disturbing only because a number of his colleagues had been disturbed by it. As he thought over this experience, his final assessment as of the very eve of World War I was that "It passes comprehension that some critics in England should gravely assure us that the war in South Africa should be our chief source of inspiration and guidance, and that it was not normal."[6]

The Field-Marshal's reasoning was very simple. First, he said, "The composition and tactics of the Boer forces were as dissimilar from those of European armies as possible," and he added that "Such tactics in Europe would lead to the disruption and disbandment of any army that attempted them."[7] Second, he noted that in

[4] Erskine Childers, *War and the Arme Blanche* (London, 1910). With an introduction by the Right Hon. Field-Marshal Earl Roberts, V.C., K.G., p. xii.

[5] Richard Burdon Halden, *An Autobiography* (London, 1929), p. 295.

[6] General Friedrich von Bernhardi, *Cavalry* (New York, 1914), with a preface by Field-Marshal Sir J. D. P. French, p. 9.

[7] *Ibid.,* p. 9.

South Africa both unlimited space and the objective of complete submission of the enemy made it a most unusual war. Third, he maintained that the British had not at the time developed proper means for remounting the cavalry with trained horses. But to say this is really to say nothing at all. It is only by uncovering Sir John's basic premises that there is really any possibility of understanding his view of his own experience.

Perhaps Sir John summarized his own thinking best when he wrote sometime during the course of 1908 that "The Boers did all that could be expected of Mounted Infantry, but were powerless to crown victory as only the dash of Cavalry can do."[8] It was the "dash of Cavalry" of which Sir John was thinking. There is ample evidence to document the point. If cold steel were thrown away as "useless lumber," he wrote, ". . . we should invert the role of cavalry, turn it into a defensive arm, and make it a prey to the first foreign cavalry that it meets, for good cavalry can always compel a dismounted force of mounted riflemen to mount and ride away, and when such riflemen are caught on their horses they have power neither of offence nor of defence and are lost."[9] Based on this analysis of the effect of rapid fire on mounted cavalry action, he deduced that the proper role of cavalry was first to fight the battlefield's greatest threat, i.e., the enemy cavalry. "The successful cavalry fight confers upon the victor command of the ground."[10] This, he said, was a job for cold steel. Only when the enemy cavalry was out of action did he think that the cavalry would rely more on the rifle than on steel—which is not to say that he ruled "out as impossible, or even unlikely, attacks by great bodies of mounted men against other arms on the battlefield."[11]

So it was that Sir John and his followers decided that the experience of recent wars was irrelevant. The Boer War was not relevant because it had not been fought in Europe and because the Boers had not been armed with steel as were cavalries in Europe. The war in Manchuria between the Russians and the Japanese was irrelevant not only because it had not been fought in Europe, but also because the cavalry used there had been badly mounted, rode indifferently, and, above all, were poorly trained, i.e., in dismounted principles. "They were," wrote Sir John, "devoid of real Cavalry training, they thought of nothing but of getting off their horses and shooting. . . ."[12] From one principle, note, Sir John never deviated: *Unless the enemy cavalry was defeated, the cavalry could not carry out its*

[8] From his introduction to the English edition of Lt. Gen. Friedrich von Bernhardi, *Cavalry in Future Wars* (London, 1909), p. x.
[9] Bernhardi, *Cavalry, op. cit.*, p. 11.
[10] *Ibid.*, p. 13.
[11] *Ibid.*, p. 15. See also A. P. Ryan, *Mutiny at the Curragh* (London, 1956), pp. 97–100 for a further elaboration of Sir John's views.
[12] Bernhardi, *Cavalry in Future Wars, op. cit.* p. xxiii.

other responsibilities. And there was a corollary of this, to wit: *"Only cavalry can defeat cavalry,"* cavalry being defined of course as "a body of horsemen armed with steel."

Sir John, however wrong he may have been in his estimate of the firepower revolution of his day, made one point of real consequence when he insisted that the cavalry should keep its mind on a war likely to be fought—which a war in Manchuria, the United States, or South Africa was not. To talk about wars which are likely seems eminently sensible, although there are times when the unlikely ones are given rather more attention than they warrant depending on what set of premises are in search of some wider acceptance. To cite a recent example, the war in Korea in 1950–1952 provided what seemed to the U.S. Air Force to be irrelevant experience because bombers were not effectively used. To the U.S. Navy and Marine Corps, on the other hand, it seemed very relevant indeed because Korea was a peninsula admirably suited to the projection of naval power. To the U.S. Army it presented a whole new way of thinking: that limited war involving ground troops might well be the way of the future despite and because of the horrors of nuclear exchange.

THE LIMITS OF A WEAPONS SYSTEM EVALUATION

But even if history in terms of recent war experience seemed irrelevant for one reason or another to the problem of the charge, it is hard to believe that war is a science so limited that means could not be found to test in practice the effectiveness of the charge, that a conclusive study could not be made of charges made in a variety of patterns, in different formations, and with different weapons against simulated "enemy formations." But the simple truth is that nothing is more difficult to test than a weapon's effectiveness. . . .

There is a grievously large number of intellectual stumbling blocks in first setting up and then later evaluating any test experience. For example, during the summer of 1936[13] the U.S. Infantry maneuvered against the U.S. Cavalry at Fort Benning, Georgia. As the problem started, the cavalry rode and the infantry trucked to the given maneuver area. The motor vehicles being rather faster than the horses the infantry had ample time to get into position first. This proved a most frightening advantage. The infantry, well camouflaged, waited with some excitement while the cavalry were allowed to pass concealed forward infantry units. Only when the advance units of cavalry hit the main units of infantry did the infantry's stratagem become apparent. It was at that moment that the infantrymen rose shouting from entrenched positions waving bed sheets. The horses thought their Day of Judgment had arrived

---

[13] The story is from eye-witness reports and there is a date problem.

as ghosts rose over the battlefield, and what followed is best left to the imagination.

To infantrymen the maneuver proved conclusively that trucks gave the infantry a mobility with which the cavalry could not hope to compete and that when minus multicolored uniforms and not drawn up in drill formation, the infantry made unsatisfactory cavalry targets. Yet to the cavalrymen—and this raised a furor that still stays in men's minds—the whole exercise only proved that infantrymen were practical jokers. The problem, that is to say, of "proving out" doctrine in the field of maneuver is distressingly difficult.

Essentially the problem lies in one's estimate of that appalling obscurity, "the nature of man." The cavalryman knows, as he charges "the enemy designate," that if this were really the enemy, he would be quite too frightened to fire accurately. And he knows this because it is part of a credo without which he would never be induced to charge in the first place. Therefore the "effect of fire" becomes a subjective instead of an objective judgment, mitigated by one's belief in a concatenation of other effects—of surprise, of fear, of the use of the defilade. So while all will call for more realism in testing, getting a consensus as to what "realism" is, more frequently than not, quite outside the realm of possibility.

FACTORS IN INSTITUTIONAL SURVIVAL

The role of history. On the morrow of victory after World War I, a member of the House of Commons rose to criticize the Secretary of War, Mr. Winston Churchill. He noted that the cavalry was at "practically the same figure as before the war, and yet if I should have thought anything had been proved by the War, it was that cavalry was less useful (than) we had previously thought it was going to be."[14]

Shortly thereafter, in 1930 to be precise, there appeared a history of the French Cavalry in the World War by a Professor of Tactics at l'École Militaire et d'Application du Génie, a most prolific writer by the name of Capitaine F. Gazin. The next to the last paragraph reads as follows:

> Today, really more than yesterday, if the cavalry is to have power and flexibility, following along with technical progress, it must have horses with better blood lines, cadres filled with burning faith, and above all well trained troops conscious of the heavy weight of past glory.[15]

There would seem to be no reasonable doubt but that in the minds of the doughboy, the *poilu* or Tommy Atkins, the day of the

[14] *125 H.C. Deb. 25*, pp. 1366 ff.
[15] F. Gazin, *La Cavalerie dans la Guerre Mondiale* (Paris, 1930), p. 325.

horse was over. The cavalryman had been called a number of things during the war, "Pigsticker," the "Rocking Horseman," etc., which indicated what the infantry thought of his contribution. But to the cavalryman himself the cavalry was not dead, and the history of the Great War was never written really in meaningful terms. To him the role of the horseman in the victory became swollen with the yeast of time. Indeed, in cavalry historiography, the role of the horse in World War I was most emphasized at that moment in time when the cavalry was most threatened in army reorganization plans, between 1934 and 1939.

The cavalry had been used in the First World War. The Germans used it extensively on that last stronghold of the cavalryman, the eastern frontier. The British and French used it extensively in 1914 during the retreat from Le Mans during late August and early September. Indeed the largest item of export from Great Britain to its forces on the Continent for the war as a whole was horse fodder. . . . For the most part the cavalry fought dismounted, but it did fight mounted as well. It did charge machine guns. In one case the Canadians charged a group of German machine guns, and came out unscathed, so great was the surprise achieved when the horsemen charged, blades bared. And it was used mounted as late as 1918. Indeed this claim has been made for its work at that time—by a cavalryman: "It may or may not be true to say that we (the allies) should have defeated the Germans just the same in the autumn of 1918, even without our cavalry. But it is certainly true that, had it not been for that same cavalry, there would have been no autumn advance at all for the Germans would have defeated us in the spring."[16]

But the campaign which did more to save the horse cavalry than any other was not fought in Europe at all. It was fought on the sands of Palestine, at Gaza, at Beersheba, at Jerusalem, and it was fought in part, and indeed in large part, with the lance. It was as dashingly romantic as anything that happened during that singularly drab war, and strong drink it was to the cavalry. In a sense, it kept the cavalry going for another quarter century. There was irony in this for the most eager of the cavalrymen, men of the stamp of Sir John French, had for a decade defended the cavalry regulations on the basis of the forecast of their utility for the big war on the continent, only to have the cavalry successfully used only on the periphery of the great battlefields.

So experience, that most revered of teachers, continued to couch the "lessons" of war in a certain studied ambiguity. The horse

[16] Lt. Col. T. Preston, "Cavalry in France," *Cavalry Journal* (British), No. 26 (1936), p. 19.

retained that place in warfare which it had had for a thousand years—in the minds of its military riders.

Mission justification for the future, 1920–1940. On the eve of World War II the General Officers of the U.S. Army were, next to those of Poland, Rumania and possibly the USSR, most convinced of the continuing utility of the horse. The French had four divisions of mixed horse and mechanized cavalry. The Germans had a debated number of horses and mechanized cavalry, for use largely as reconnaissance. The British were converting from oats to oil as rapidly as possible.

A number of problems immediately present themselves. A first very general question must be asked of the cavalrymen themselves: What did they consider their mission to be in the period between 1920 and roughly 1935 when the development of both plane and tank had reached the stage at which their future development could be foreseen with some clarity, and at which therefore some reasonable readjustment of forces to the fact of their existence could be expected? How can one account for those great differences in thinking between the responsible staffs of the larger nations during the years between 1935 and the outbreak of war in 1939? . . .

The basic argument of the cavalrymen in their journals and in their manuals in the period between the great wars was an absolutely sound one. They argued in essence that new weapons obviated only those with like characteristics. They argued that while a better tank scrapped a worse one, the tank as a weapons system could not replace the horse until such time as it could perform all the missions of a horse. Whether these missions were worthwhile was seldom considered.

Many of the arguments which cavalrymen of all nations advanced to substantiate their claims as to their future role in war will be recognized by any student of recent military history as a version of what one can only describe as standardized clap-trap. One was the argument that, since most of the world was roadless, "To base our transportation needs solely upon conditions existent in the comparatively tiny proportion of the earth's surface containing roads . . . is putting too many eggs in the same basket."[17] This will be recognized as a cavalry variant on the navy contention that "since the world is 60 per cent water . . . ," and the air contention that "since air surrounds the earth and the shortest distance between two points. . . ." Another argument familiar to all military historians came up again and again in the journals. This one was to the effect that mechanical aids and auxiliaries end by neutralizing each other, an argument which in its most outrageous form had the anti-tank

[17] Major Malcolm Wheeler-Nicholson, *Modern Cavalry* (New York, 1922), p. vii.

weapon returning the battlefield to the horse.[18] "It is quite within the bounds of possibility that an infantry anti-tank weapon may be produced which will make tanks useless as weapons of attack," wrote one enthusiast[19] in a vein not unlike that used by airmen against seamen at roughly the same moment in time. The difficulty of supplying tanks was brought up as the supply problem is brought up as a limitation on each new weapons system.[20] And, of course, the essentially experimental nature of tanks—"as yet untried" is the term—raised its head perennially and everywhere.

But there were other problems and more serious ones. If the tank could be made to replace the cavalry on the charge, did that mean that the tank could take over all the other cavalry missions: reconnaissance, raids, flank protection in rough country? Could the plane be made to supplement the tank in such a way that the two used in combination could effectuate a complete substitution for the horse? Or would some kind of combination of horse and tank, and plane and tank be a future necessity? And if this were so with whom would the control lie, with tankmen or horsemen or pilots? And finally if this was a problem of phasing out the horse, what factors should govern the timing of this phasing?

These questions do not seem to have been asked with any precision largely perhaps because they edged too closely on the emotion-packed matter of prestige, on the one hand, and on an essentially insoluble organization problem on the other. Naturally armor wanted maximum independence as do those who service and fire any weapon. The tankman wanted a command of his own, just as the machinegunner wanted his own battalion, the artillery its own regiment, the horse cavalry its own division and the airman his own service. And this is logical for in a decentralized structure growth is faster as imagination is given a freer rein. But the difficulty is that, war being all of one cloth, each weapon component also wishes to control elements of the others. And this is why the sparks flew between arms in the period between the World Wars, and before the First and after the Second. Where, as in Germany and Great Britain, armor was given its independence, it thrived. Where, as in the United States and Poland, the Cavalry (Horse) remained in control, tank doctrine never grew roots. But where, as in France, mechanized and horse were joined together in what at first blush seemed to be a happy marriage, a unity was forced which was pitifully inadequate from every standpoint.

[18] Anonymous, "Oil and Oats," *Cavalry Journal* (British), Vol. 28, No. 107, Jan. 1938, p. 31; Col. Sir Hereward Wake, "The Infantry Anti-Tank Weapon," *Army Quarterly*, Vol. 17, No. 2, Jan. 1929.

[19] Wake, *op. cit.*, p. 349.

[20] Lt. F. A. S. Clark, "Some Further Problems of Mechanical Warfare," *Army Quarterly*, Vol. 6, No. 2, July 1923, p. 379.

For the man on the horse there was much greater difficulty in understanding the tank than in understanding the rapid fire weapon. Perhaps this could be expected since tank and horse were competitors for the same missions. Certainly the limpid eye and high spirit of the one and the crass impersonal power of the other was enough to render partisans of the one quite helpless when it came to understanding the military views of the other, quite as helpless indeed as the seabased fighter is to understand the landbased or the airbased and their view of world geography.

Practicality and the concept of the balanced force. One finds the horse cavalryman making the same points over and over again. He stressed the tanks' need for spare parts, without taking into consideration that one of the greatest difficulties of the cavalry was that horses do not have spare parts. He stressed the lack of mobility of the tank along mountain trails without mention of the appalling problem of getting horses overseas—they have a tendency to pneumonia, together with a soft breast which becomes raw and infected with the roll and pitch of the ship. Whereas the point was occasionally made that the Lord took care of the resupply of horses—i.e., that while factories could be bombed out, sex could not—no mention was ever made that in wartime as in peace He still took four or five years to produce each animal. And, finally, although the horse was claimed to have certain immunities to gas warfare, the peculiar problems of getting gas masks on the poor beasts were omitted.

Yet whether partisans were ankle deep in the sands of prejudice or not, there were certain aspects of the relationship between horses and planes, and horses and tanks which were so obvious that they could hardly be missed. However low and slow it flew, the plane would not be a substitute for a still lower and still slower man on a horse. And the plane could not penetrate forests and neither, within limits, could tanks. So there was, and indeed there still is, a gap between what the horse can do and what the plane and tank can do. But admitting the gap, there still remained the most vexing problem of all, to wit whether that gap was worth filling and if so how. And this was something which each general staff decided somewhat differently and for itself.

The U.S. Cavalry was, in retrospect, as retrogressive in 1940 as it had been progressive in the years before World War I. It had never crossed the sea during World War I due to transportation difficulties, and spent its war chasing Mexicans. But it shared every confidence that its future role would be everything that it had not been in the recent past. As of 1940 it labored under the most embarrassing of illusions. The U.S. Cavalry believed that it had modernized itself. And it defended its horse cavalry on the sacred ground of "balanced force." "Each arm has powers and limitations," explained Major General John K. Herr, Chief of Cavalry, before the Subcommittee on Military Affairs of the House Committee on Appropriations on March 11, 1940. "The proper combination is that which arranges the whole so that the powers of each offset the limitations of the others." It was because the Poles did not have that balance that they were, said General Herr, overrun by the Germans.

> Judging from Spain, had Poland's cavalry possessed modern armament in every respect and been united in one big cavalry command with adequate mechanized forces included, and supported by adequate aviation, the German light and mechanized forces might have been defeated.

Then General Herr went on to add these words of comfort:

> Mechanized cavalry is valuable and an important adjunct but is not the main part of the cavalry and cannot be. Our cavalry is not the medieval cavalry of popular imagination but is cavalry which is modernized and keeping pace with all developments.[21]

Yet it certainly does not seem that the U.S. cavalry was "keeping pace with all developments." Putting horses in trucks to give them mobility (this was the so-called "portée cavalry"), and adding inadequate anti-tank batteries can hardly be called modernizing. Is there any reasonable explanation for the illusion?

Concepts of modernization. One cannot help but be impressed with the intellectual isolation in which the U.S. armed forces operated in the 1930's. *The Journal of the U.S. Cavalry Association* paid almost no attention to mechanization throughout the period. Compared to the military periodicals on the continent, the U.S. journal seems curiously antiquated. And because there was so little critical thinking going on within the service, it is not surprising that there was virtually no thinking going on in Army ordnance either, for ordnance, after all, works on a demand basis and if there is no demand, there is likely to be no new hardware. In the United States there was in short no intellectual challenge.

Not only were there no pressures to change cavalry thinking from inside the arm, there were no pressures from outside either. United States industry was never anxious to sell to the services during the depression years or before. They were no more willing to put money into military research and development than were the services or the Congress. The few Secretaries of War who can be considered adequate were interested in the managerial aspects of their office

---

[21] The text of General Herr's testimony before Congress may be found reprinted in *JUSCA*, Vol. 49, No. 3, May–June 1940. See p. 206. . . .

and not in matters which they considered "purely military." And finally there was a not inconsiderable pressure for the *status quo* in the Congress. The U.S. had some ten millions of horses, and government spending in this direction, little though it was, was a chief source of revenue to all the many horse breeders, hay growers, and saddlemakers.

In Great Britain, the situation was markedly different. Although the British had their branch journals,—the tankers founded their own in 1937—they also had great advantage in having two journals which were more generally read. The first was the *Army Quarterly* which published on all topics of concern to the army as a whole, and the other was *The Journal of the Royal United Service Institution* which crossed service lines. Into these journals there poured articles from a singularly able, and remarkably prolific and dedicated group of publicists of whom J. F. C. Fuller and Captain Basil H. Liddell Hart are simply the best known. Officers in the British Empire were simply unable to escape, as were U.S. officers, from challenge. Thus from 1936 onwards there was an increasingly strong movement in favor of conversion to oil. Furthermore this was helped rather than hindered by the stand taken by many in Parliament. For Parliament was at least conscious of *The Times* military correspondent, Liddell Hart, and the battle he was waging for mechanized warfare, a form of warfare which would, so he thought, limit and shorten future wars by making them more rapid, hence shorter and cheaper than the war of the trenches. To be sure there were those who, like Admiral of the Fleet Sir Roger Keyes, took a position against the reduction of cavalry. But they were in the minority. Most felt that the Household Cavalry and two mounted regiments still left in Egypt in 1939 were probably two too many. . . .

After World War II the French, as is the wont of democracies, held an inquiry into the military disasters of some five years before. But the questions which were put to the generals and the questions which they wanted to answer were all in terms of why they had not understood and appreciated the role of the tank and the plane. Never does the question seem to have been asked in the converse, i.e., why was the horse thought to have been so useful circa 1939? It would have been interesting to know too what thinking had been done as to the circumstances under which Cavalry divisions, offensive forces, were to be used in conjunction with the Maginot Line, a defensive ideal. Perhaps they were to have been used in the second phase of the struggle in a counter-offensive after the enemy had partially defeated himself by throwing his troops against the defensive fires of the Line. . . .

However, the overall development of French cavalry thinking between the wars is plain enough. What they did was to absorb the new machines of war into old doctrine. Instead of allowing the characteristics of new weapons to create new doctrine, the French General Staff simply gave them missions to fulfill that were within the old framework. Thus tanks were made subordinate and supporting weapons to the infantry, and subordinate and supporting weapons to the cavalry. In a sense the French achieved what General Herr of the U.S. Cavalry wanted to achieve, except that the French did look forward to complete mechanization at some future date, which Herr did not. And the *Revue de Cavalerie*, a strange hodgepodge of oats, history and oil, reflects that point of view.

The German experience was somewhat different again. Whereas the French looked back to the stalemate at Verdun, the great achievement of defensive weapons, the Germans looked back to the great offensives of 1918 and to the very near miss of the Schlieffen plan in 1914. Particularly in the case of the younger officers the great objective was regaining the lost means of offensive. A defeated army, the Germans were in a position to start once more from the beginning. To be sure there was a very difficult period of struggle with German horse cavalrymen, but those in Germany with an interest in tanks had an advantage which those in the democracies did not. They had the interest of the Chief of State. When Hitler saw Panzer units in action, he said repeatedly, "That's what I need! That's what I want to have!"[22] To Hitler they were the keystone in a concept of total war.

The *Revue de Cavalerie* stopped publication during the war and never appeared again. The British *Cavalry Journal* disappeared forever as well. Only the *Journal of the U.S. Cavalry Association* continued to appear. Its heroes were the horse-drawn artillery which landed on Guadalcanal, the animals flown over the Burma "Hump" into China, the U.S. units which were remounted on Italian Cavalry horses in Italy and German horses in Germany; the great heroes were the only real cavalry left—the Cossacks. Duly noted was how greatly needed were horse cavalry during the battles in Normandy and elsewhere.

In his closing chapter of *He's in the Cavalry Now*, Brig. Gen. Rufus S. Ramey, a former commander of the U.S. Cavalry School, concluded in 1944, "Currently we are organizing and training adequate mechanized horse cavalry for field employment."[23] His was the final testament. The last old Army mule, except for the West Point Mascot, was retired in 1956. The horse cavalry had been disbanded five years before.

New Item. In 1956 the Belgian General Staff suggested that for

---

[22] General Heinz Guderian, *Panzer Leader* (New York, 1952), p. 30.
[23] Brig. Gen. Rufus S. Ramey, *He's in the Cavalry Now* (New York, 1944), p. 190. There were 60,170 animals in the U.S. Forces on December 31, 1943.

the kind of dispersed war which low yield atomic weapons necessarily create, the horse, which in Europe could be independent of depots, should be reintroduced into the weapons system.[24]

CONCLUSION

The military profession, dealing as it does with life and death, should be utterly realistic, ruthless in discarding the old for the new, forward-thinking in the adoption of new means of violence. But equally needed is a romanticism which, while perhaps stultifying realistic thought, gives a man that belief in the value of the weapons system he is operating that is so necessary to his willingness to use it in battle. Whether a man rides a horse, a plane or a battleship into war, he cannot be expected to operate without faith in his weapons system. But faith breeds distrust of change. Furthermore there is need for discipline, for hierarchy, for standardization within the military structure. These things create pressures for conformity, and conformity too is the enemy of change. Nor is there generally the pressure for the adoption of the new that is found in other walks of life. There is no profit motive, and the challenge of actual practice, in the ultimate sense of war, is very intermittent. Finally, change is expensive, and some part of the civilian population has to agree that the change is worth the expense before it can take place. What factors then make for change in situations short of war?

Surely the greatest instigation of new weapons development has in the past come from civilian interest plus industrial pressure. The civilian governors get the weapons system *they* want. Hitler gets his tanks, the French public their line of forts. When society shows an interest in things military, weapons are adopted—apparently in great part because of the appeal they make to a set of social values and economic necessities. The abolition of the horse cavalry came about first in those countries which could not afford to raise the horses and in which there were those with a hungry intellectual interest in the ways of war. When there was no interest in the military, as in the United States, there was no pressure to change and the professional was given tacit leave to romanticize an untenable situation. Thus the U.S. Horse Cavalry remained a sort of monument to public irresponsibility in this, the most mechanized nation on earth.

[24] "Belgians Hit U.S. Concept of Atomic War," *Christian Science Monitor*, August 25, 1956.

Japan's Fatal Blunder

SIR GEORGE SANSOM

In the light of what we know today the decision of the leaders of Japan to make war upon the United States appears as an act of folly, by which they committed themselves to a hopeless struggle against a Power with perhaps ten times their own potential industrial and military strength. But was that decision in fact as reckless as it now seems, or can it be regarded as the taking of a justifiable risk in the circumstances in which it was made?

Perhaps it is too soon to expect a complete answer to this question, but there is already available a good deal of useful information upon which a preliminary judgement can be based. There is, for instance, an interesting series of reports published by the United States Strategic Bombing Survey,* which was conducted (by civilians) primarily for the purpose of ascertaining the degree to which air-power contributed to the defeat of Japan. During this enquiry there was collected a mass of statistical and other information regarding political and economic conditions in Japan prior to and during the war. These studies, together with two volumes of Interrogations compiled by the United States Navy,† include valuable data based upon oral and documentary evidence obtained in Japan in 1945, not long after the surrender, when memories were fresh. It should be understood that the answers elicited by interrogations cannot all be taken at face value. Allowance must be made for certain factors of error. Thus, the "Summaries" of the Bombing Survey, in which general conclusions are drawn, naturally tend to place emphasis on the part played by aircraft in reducing Japan to the point of surrender and, by implication, to underestimate the importance of the general strategic conduct of the war and the particular effectiveness of submarine action on vital Japanese lines of communication by sea. Moreover, the interrogations were not always skillfully conducted and the replies sometimes betray a

Reprinted by permission from *International Affairs*, October 1948, pp. 543–555. One footnote has been omitted.

*[*Editors' note:* United States Strategic Bombing Survey, *Japan's Struggle to End the War* (Washington, D.C.: Government Printing Office, 1946).]

†[*Editors' note:* United States Strategic Bombing Survey, *Interrogations of Japanese Officials*, 2 vols. (Washington, D.C.: Government Printing Office, 1946).]

desire to please the questioners, if not to mislead them. Different and more reliable results might have been obtained from really searching cross-examination by experienced persons. Nevertheless, the documents are extremely interesting and suffice to establish beyond reasonable doubt a number of important facts. The following tentative appraisal draws freely upon information which they contain, though it is supplemented at a few points by knowledge derived by the writer from other sources during a visit to Japan early in 1946.

There is no doubt that Japan was preparing for war at least a decade before 1941, but this does not necessarily mean that she had decided before that year to make war upon the United States or the British Commonwealth. The most that can be safely said is that certain influential army leaders and their civilian supporters contemplated war if the European situation should so develop as to make it feasible and advantageous. There was no concealment of Japan's intention to get ready for war. But during 1940 there was still no agreement in influential circles as to the course which Japan should take in international affairs, or even as to the lines upon which her economy should be further developed and controlled. The full powers which the Government had progressively acquired in preceding years were exercised only partially; a medley of State controls existed side by side with autonomous direction in separate branches of production and trade; and, in general, conflict between the military and the leaders of industry and finance continued unabated and unresolved.

It is sometimes stated by British and American writers that Big Business in Japan—the so-called *Zaibatsu*—co-operated enthusiastically in preparations for war or at least meekly gave way to military pressure. The evidence for this view is poor. On the contrary, during the early part of 1940 the influential Economic Federation of Japan (*Nihon Keizai Remmei*) resisted the Government's plans for industrial expansion, arguing that they were basically unsound. Their opposition was, it is true, based on technical rather than political grounds, but it cannot be said that they co-operated freely with the military leaders in the development of an economy designed for warlike purposes.

In fact, under the Yonai Government, which was in power until July 1940, there were still elements in the Cabinet that favoured a cautious if not a pacific foreign policy, and were inclined to take the side of the industrialists in resisting totalitarian trends. It was at this point that the military used their strongest political weapon. By withdrawing the War Minister, they forced the resignation of the Yonai Cabinet, in which the relatively liberal Mr. Arita was Foreign Minister. The second Konoye Cabinet was then formed, with Tojo, a convinced expansionist, as War Minister. Its announced policy was the development of a highly organized National Defence State and the consolidation of an Asiatic "Co-Prosperity Sphere." This was definitely a war Cabinet, and its immediate purpose was to bring the industrialists to heel. Once the Government reached a firm decision the resistance of the industrialists was sooner or later bound to collapse. The close concentration of industrial power in Japan, having historically been achieved largely under official direction or with official support, had never acquired true independence or substantial political strength. It could struggle against this measure or that, but in matters of high policy it could not successfully challenge the authority of the bureaucracy with which it was so organically related.

In September 1940, Tojo let it be known that national mobilization required an intensified control which was inconsistent with the old liberal economic structure. But still the struggle continued and, surprisingly, the resistance of the industrial and financial leaders, represented by the Economic Federation, increased rather than diminished. The planned economy which was the object of Hoshino and Ohashi—two officials who had gained experience in Manchuria—was fought with some success by members of the *Zaibatsu* who, whatever their views as to war and peace, realized the limitations of the Japanese economy. But they were at length forced to execute plans in which they had little faith.

These facts are cited as showing that as late as 1941, despite long preparation, there was yet no effective centralized control of the Japanese industrial structure; and, quite apart from the conflict between Government and private enterprise, there was another defect in the country's war-making capacity, for the administrative machine, seemingly so efficient in normal times, turned out to be rigid and unmanageable. It was even necessary for Tojo, when he became Prime Minister in 1941, to seek legislation which would compel the various ministries to obey his orders. Such a diagnosis of the radical weaknesses in Japan's governmental structure at a juncture when her national existence was about to be staked upon its efficiency may seem too sweeping, but it could be supported by further evidence. It is sufficient to say here that the subsequent course of events, in both the economic and military spheres, shows that part of the failure of the Japanese economy to meet the demands made upon it in time of war can be traced back to faulty arrangements in time of peace. That governments or individuals should contract bad habits is not surprising, but it is surprising that the rulers of Japan should not have realized how inadequate, even by their own standards, was their country's organization for a war of their own choosing against powerful enemies.

The degree of their economic miscalculations is easy to measure by results. More difficult is an assessment of their political judgement. There can be no doubt that the coalition which began to rule Japan in July 1940 was determined to make use of the European war to further an expansionist policy in Asia and, if possible, to settle the conflict with China on favorable terms. When France was defeated and England appeared to the Japanese to be about to follow her in disaster, the Konoye Government began to feel confident enough to probe the weaknesses of possible antagonists by such measures as flouting British and American interests in China, blackmailing the United Kingdom into closing the Burma Road, pressing the Netherland Indies for economic concessions and moving troops into northern Indo-China. In the summer of 1940 it even looked as if an attack upon British possessions in the Far East was imminent. But action was postponed, partly because the progress of the Battle of Britain raised doubts about the expected collapse of the United Kingdom, but also because the Japanese army and navy wished to complete their armament and to collect further stocks of basic materials. They appear to have decided that, tempting as it was, an attack upon British and Dutch territories alone would be strategically unsound, because it would leave on their flank unimpaired American strength which might intervene at a moment chosen by the United States. They were, moreover, not yet satisfied that they had the whole country with them, for despite their vigorous domestic propaganda there were still dissidents in high places and doubtless also among the people. The distribution of political influence within Japan was traditionally such that any decisive move required much bargaining and persuasion. The firmly established system of checks and balances was customary rather than constitutional, but it had the effect of delaying political action. Even within the ruling coalition there were differences of opinion on the timing and the length of each step taken on the road to war, and there were cautious or conservative elements whose hesitations had to be overcome.

This was the condition reached by the summer of 1941. The extremists continued to strengthen their position step by step, by committing Japan to engagements from which it was difficult if not impossible to withdraw. Perhaps this period was the most crucial in Japanese history, since a vital decision on war or peace is not a simple choice of alternatives at a given moment, but is influenced by the cumulative effect of previous commitments, none of which is separately decisive. The extremists had in July 1941, by a series of gradual manoeuvres, gone far towards creating a situation in which their voice would be dominant. They then took a long step by establishing bases in Southern Indo-China. All available evidence goes to show that they did not expect this move to evoke strong reactions from the United States or the United Kingdom. It was represented as nothing but a strategical development in the war against China, but its implications were perfectly clear. It was the first phase of a projected southward movement. It is interesting to note, from the captured German documents published in January 1948 by the United States Government, that the draft secret protocol of November 1940 to the agreement between the U.S.S.R. and the Tripartite Powers states that "Japan declares that her territorial aspirations centre in the area of Eastern Asia to the south of the Island Empire of Japan."[1] The sharp counter-measures of the United States and the United Kingdom came as a surprise to the extremists and threw the moderates into confusion, though they must have had some warning from the Japanese Embassy in Washington. The situation is well described in the Summary Report of the United States Bombing Survey, as follows:

> Though the conservative wing of the ruling coalition had endorsed each move of its coalition partners, it hoped at each stage that the current step would not be the breaking-point leading to war. It arranged and concluded the Tripartite Pact (September 1940) and hoped that the Western Powers would be sufficiently impressed with the might and solidarity of the Axis to understand the futility of further resistance. It approved of the Indo-China adventure, assuming that Japan would get away with this act of aggression as easily as with previous ones.

But while the freezing of Japanese assets and the embargo upon the export of strategic materials to Japan imposed by the Western Powers shocked the conservatives and frightened the moderates, they had already gone too far in their acquiescence. They could not now suggest any course but negotiations with the United States, and over the terms of these negotiations they could exercise no control, since the power of final decision had already passed into the hands of the extremists. All they could now hope for was that the extremists would make enough concessions to satisfy the United States, and this was a vain hope, because to make any effective concessions would be to admit that the whole of Japanese policy since 1931 had been a blunder, for which the military party and its civilian allies were responsible. The Army's prestige would never recover from such a blow. War was inevitable. The only question now was what kind of war.

Such in broad outline was the political background of the decision to go to war. It remains to consider on what grounds the military

[1] J. Sontag and J. S. Beddie, eds., Declaration 3, Draft Secret Protocol No. 1, *Nazi Soviet Relations*, 1939–40 (U.S.A. Department of State, 1948), p. 257.

leaders of Japan based their judgement that Japan could successfully challenge the United States and the British Commonwealth. It cannot be assumed that they blindly led their country into war with no prospect of success. Theirs was a considered policy, attended by calculated risks. Examined in retrospect it proves to have been based upon mistaken assumptions, and executed with insufficient skill and foresight; but it was not, as conceived, irrational. It must also be remembered that the economic sanctions imposed upon Japan in 1941 were such as to make war appear a reasonable, if dangerous, alternative.

The planners who decided that the risk of war could be taken were not blind to the frightful disparity between their own strength and that of their enemies. They counted upon certain favourable circumstances to balance their own deficiencies. Late in the summer of 1941 they were convinced that Germany would be victorious and that within a few months, Russia having been defeated, the United States and the United Kingdom would be obliged to accept supremacy of Germany in Europe. This outlook, though it promised them membership of a successful alliance, was in one respect not entirely pleasing to them, since they felt some distrust of their Axis partners, which the Germans in Japan by their arrogant behavior did nothing to diminish. Some Japanese expansionists therefore felt that their plans might be upset by a premature settlement of the European conflict, which would leave them without any spoils of war in the Pacific; and this fear probably, though not certainly, was an additional motive for the rapid seizure of territories in Asia from which they could derive supplies of oil and rubber, and strategic bargaining power. As they saw the position, those objectives—stepping stones to further expansion—could be attained by a short and restricted campaign. They would engage in hostilities in the Pacific for a strictly limited purpose. First they would conquer an area enclosed within a perimeter including Burma, Malaya, Sumatra, Java, Northern New Guinea, the Bismarck Archipelago, the Gilbert and Marshall Islands, Wake and the Kuriles. This, they calculated, could be achieved in a few months if American sea and air power could be weakened by surprise attacks upon Pearl Harbor and the Philippines. The United States, preoccupied with the European situation, would be unable to take the offensive before Japan had accomplished the necessary strengthening of the perimeter and established forward air and sea bases. Once firmly entrenched on that perimeter they could obtain from the occupied areas what they required to sustain and expand their deficient economy—oil, rubber, bauxite, metals, food. Thus supplied, they could wage defensive warfare which, it was supposed, would within a year or two weaken the American purpose and so lead to a compromise peace. Negotiation would leave to Japan a substantial portion of her gains and a dominant position in Eastern Asia.

This was not at that time a strategy which could be condemned out of hand as unrealistic. It could be regarded, and presented to the Japanese people, as a reasonable and honourable alternative to submitting to sanctions. It aroused misgivings in some circles in Japan, and even its proponents knew that it would throw a great strain upon Japan's capacity; but they counted upon the shock of rapid conquests, and upon the fighting qualities of their soldiers and sailors. Certainly in the first few months of the war nothing happened to make them revise their opinions. Their successes were greater and easier than they had foreseen.

So encouraged were they by their achievement that they began to consider an extension of their perimeter. They planned an advance into the Solomons and Port Moresby, to be followed by a further advance into New Caledonia, Samoa, and the Fijis, the capture of Midway and the occupation of the Aleutians. It was here that they made their first cardinal blunder, for . . . "by stretching and overextending her line of advance, Japan was committed to an expensive and exacting supply problem. She delayed the fortification of the perimeter originally decided upon, jeopardised her economic program for exploiting the resources of the area already captured and laid herself open to early counter-attack in far advanced and, as yet, weak positions."[2]

This blunder in execution also laid bare certain weaknesses in the original conceptions of the Japanese planners. Perhaps the most important of these was their misjudgement of the temper of the United States, for the attack on Pearl Harbor had a stimulating psychological effect upon the American people which in military importance far outweighed the losses sustained at Pearl Harbor. The Japanese army had persuaded the Japanese people that the democratic states were materialistic, irresolute, incapable of matching the unique Japanese spirit. They had argued, not without some plausibility, that the United States had for a decade or more shown a strong aversion to protecting its interests in the Far East by warlike measures, despite repeated provocation. They inferred that those interests were not regarded as of vital importance and that consequently in the long run a spirit of compromise would prevail. They seem to have been deceived by their own propaganda, for even after their initial reverses in the first half of 1942 at Midway and towards the end of the year at Guadalcanal, they appear still to have supposed that they could fight the war on their own terms. They did not yet realize that their original plan of restricted warfare, which

[2] United States Strategic Bombing Survey, Summary Report, *Pacific War* (Washington, United States Government Printing Office, 1946), p. 4.

could be sustained for a limited period by their 1941 economy was no longer feasible.

It was not until 1943 that they had fully grasped the fact that they could no longer dictate the scale or location of hostilities, but were involved in total war in which the initiative had already passed to the American forces. That they made this mistake is indicated by their failure to carry out complete economic mobilization until 1943. An index of the gross national product (computed by the United States Bombing Survey with the assistance of Japanese experts) shows a rise from 100 in 1940 to only 101 in 1941 and 102 in 1942. It was not until 1943 that a substantial increase was gained by a production drive which raised the figure to 113 for 1943 and 124 for 1944. This was the peak of Japanese production, and it was reached by forcing an ever-growing proportion of the total economy into direct war purposes, while straining the civilian population almost to breaking point. It was a remarkable performance, but it was too little and too late. No effort was made to carry out a coherent plan of overall expansion of the Japanese economy, perhaps because a balanced development was impossible in view of its previous distortion. Even if the foregoing explanation of the delay in carrying out full economic mobilization errs in placing too much emphasis upon a tardy appreciation of the strategic position, it is clear that the Japanese tradition of government depending upon slow and cautious compromise was ill-adapted for times of emergency that demanded bold decision and quick performance.

The subsequent course of the Pacific war needs no detailed recital here. It is enough to say that although the Japanese made after 1942 immense military and economic efforts to meet conditions for which they had not originally planned, both were insufficient to stem the tide which began to flow against them. Nearly all their calculations had gone wrong. The British Isles were not invaded, the Soviet Union did not collapse, the United States showed not the least disposition to compromise, but began to plan the outright defeat of Japan. The prospect of a negotiated peace vanished. Plans to draw upon the occupied territories for essential materials could not be executed, because submarine and air attacks upon Japanese shipping prevented not only the carriage of needed supplies to Japan, but also the full support of Japanese forces in the field. Japanese commanders have testified that only 20 per cent of the supplies dispatched to Guadalcanal reached their destination, and that of 30,000 troops landed, 10,000 died of starvation or disease and 10,000 were evacuated early in 1943 in a debilitated condition. Though Japanese troops everywhere fought stubbornly and well, inflicting heavy losses upon their opponents, by the opening months of 1943 not only had the Japanese advance been stopped, but their overall strategic plan had been upset. This was the result of an overwhelming superiority of American power, and it revealed a basic error in the initial premises of that plan. It had been supposed that the perimeter could be held indefinitely, but American experience showed after the engagements of 1942 that it was not necessary to reduce the whole perimeter. The widely spread Japanese positions were dependent upon supply by sea, and it was necessary to destroy them only at points selected by the American command. So long as attacks upon Japanese shipping were maintained, other points could be by-passed as a general advance was begun towards bases within striking distance of Japan.

It was after the evacuation of Guadalcanal, in February 1943, that thoughtful Japanese began to suspect that their prospects of victory had disappeared, while those who knew all the facts saw that the situation was desperate. It is surprising that, to quote the words of Hoshino, Chief Secretary of the Tojo Cabinet, "the real Japanese war economy only began after Guadalcanal." Perhaps even more surprising is the confusion which is revealed in the direction both of the war economy and the national strategy after that date. Full credit must be given to the Japanese people for their efforts to restore and develop their war potential after 1942, but their leaders seem never to have reached a clear and comprehensive view of their country's situation. Some rough estimates of national strength were compiled before the war. They were tentative and incomplete, and perhaps this was in the circumstances unavoidable.

But it is strange that, so far as is known, a full re-appraisal in the light of the new conditions was not attempted until September 1943. This was made not by the Government for its own purposes, but by Takagi, an officer of the Naval General Staff, at the request of Admiral Yonai, who had been out of office since his Cabinet fell in 1940. This influential statesman, when asked in 1945 what he considered the turning point of the war replied: "To be very frank, I think the turning point was the start. I felt from the very beginning that there was no chance of success." Takagi's report strengthened Admiral Yonai's fears that the prosecution of the war by the Tojo Government was unsatisfactory. It confirmed his judgement that Japan should seek a compromise peace before she suffered a crushing defeat. Yonai was not alone in this feeling. It was shared by certain influential persons outside the Government and a number of naval officers. They had indeed good reason for their anxiety. The circumstances beyond Japan's control were grave enough—the growing shortages of materials, losses of aircraft, warships and merchant vessels, and the certainty of long-range air attacks upon the centres of production at home. And, added to these, was growing confusion within Japan.

Nominally, by 1943 the Japanese Government had achieved full control of all national organs and activities, but Japan had evidently not become a solid authoritarian state. Animosity between Army and Navy was such that the submarine service resented the diversion of its vessels from combatant functions to army transport duties, and towards the end of the war the Army began to build submarines for its own use and declined naval advice. Army and Navy details, it is said, would fight outside factories for supplies designated for one or the other service. Ginjiro Fujihara, an industrial magnate who at a critical juncture became director of aircraft production, even alleged (no doubt untruthfully) that army and navy rivalry was responsible for keeping down the total output by about 50 per cent. In addition to their inter-service quarrels, the armed forces displayed hostility towards civilian organs. The director of the General Mobilization Bureau testified on interrogation that they would never disclose their stocks or discuss their requirements with him, would not submit demands through the appropriate ministry and thus thwarted all attempts at co-ordination of supply. Control bodies set up by the Government for key materials tried to enforce a system of priorities, but the Army and Navy would help themselves to supplies without troubling to obtain priority-certificates. Civilian manufacturing firms were, it is reported, obliged to resort to black market transactions in order to secure material or machines. It is of course easy to exaggerate the extent and importance of such abuses, which are common enough in all countries at war; but it is clear that there was a serious lack of harmony between the two fighting services. Admiral Toyoda (Commander-in-Chief Combined Fleet, and later Chief of Naval General Staff) said upon interrogation: "There was not full understanding and agreement between Army and Navy prior to and during the war." This discord he ascribed to the great political power of the Army, which the Navy did not share. It showed itself, he thought, not so much in operational matters as in the division of supplies. But General Yamashita, the Japanese commander in the Philippines, was only apprised of the intended naval strike on Leyte Gulf in a *written* communication from Tokyo which was two weeks on the way and reached him on the day of the operation.

Uneasy relations between Army and Navy were paralleled by quarrels between civilian organs. It is remarkable that, despite their reputed gift for careful and strict organization, the Japanese authorities were not in practice able to exercise their unlimited powers of control. Under a surface appearance of national unity, old divisions of opinions, old patterns of influence, persisted with very little change. It is perhaps comforting to discover that what appears to be a solid monolithic state can hide grave structural weaknesses behind a forbidding exterior.

By July 1944, the invasion of Saipan had succeeded and Tojo's Cabinet had collapsed. The strenuous efforts made to raise production in Japan had led to a considerable increase in capacity, yet by late in the summer output had begun to decline because shipping losses had cut down essential imports. National morale was still high but by the autumn of 1944 Japan was on the verge of economic collapse, and that was before the heavy strategical bombing of the home islands. Tojo was succeeded as Prime Minister by Koiso, a retired general, whose Government set up a Supreme War Direction Council intended ostensibly to strengthen national defence, but in fact obliged to consider ways of terminating the war. The story of the steps by which most of its members at length reached a decision in favour of surrender is a long and complicated one. Not much progress was made at first, but certain members of the Cabinet were cautiously working for peace and carrying on discussions with senior statesmen who, though out of office, retained great personal influence. High naval officers were predominant among the service men who favoured attempts to secure a negotiated peace, while the Army command still thought in terms of prolonged resistance, hoping that they could inflict such losses upon an invading force that a compromise could be secured, which would leave to Japan something better than the prospect of unconditional surrender. The peace party was growing in confidence, but only slowly, and was hampered by the fear that, since the Japanese people were still ignorant of the true state of affairs, a premature move might bring about internal chaos.

Meanwhile, with the loss of the Philippines and the intensification of bombing, which affected both military targets and urban populations, the situation became more and more desperate in the eyes of the peace party, less and less hopeful in the eyes of the last-ditchers. But it seems that there was little prospect of obtaining the agreement of any substantial portion of the Army leaders so long as Germany continued to resist. It was not until April 8, 1945 that the Koiso Government fell and was succeeded by a Cabinet under Admiral Suzuki, whose mission was to bring the war to an end, though publicly both Government and people were still committed to a continued resistance. Progress towards peace was still slow, for nobody would come out with an open declaration that the war was lost. Early in May, however—shortly after the end of the European war—the balance began to turn in favour of peace. Appraisals of the economic situation showed that the country was utterly incapable of continuing effective resistance, and there were even some signs of a decline in public morale. Still no specific proposals for ending the war were made, though on June 6 the Supreme War Council definitely stated to the Emperor that it was necessary to bring it to an end. On June 20, the Emperor summoned the Council, and showed himself in favour of positive steps, including an approach to the Soviet Union with a request for mediation. Discussions with Russia made no progress, the Soviet Government temporized and the Japanese ambassador in Moscow reported that in his opinion there was no alternative to unconditional surrender.

Time went by, and still no firm decision had been reached when the Potsdam Declaration was issued on July 26, 1945. The Prime Minister, the Foreign Minister and the Navy Minister (Yonai) were in favour of accepting its terms, the War Minister and the Chiefs of Staff were opposed. It is interesting to note, as illustrating the nature of the opposition, that Toyoda had not approved of the War from the beginning, yet was unable to agree to unconditional surrender, which he thought dishonourable. A strong military group still held out for resistance to invasion. Differences of opinion continued until August 9, 1945, by which time an atomic bomb had been dropped on Hiroshima (August 6) and the Soviet Union had declared war upon Japan (August 9). After repeated meetings on August 9, just before midnight the Inner Cabinet appealed to the Emperor for a final expression of his wish and the Emperor declared in favour of peace. There were further cabinet discussions as to the interpretation of the Potsdam terms, but they were finally accepted on August 14. This was more than twelve months after the fall of the Tojo Government, and four months after the formation of the Suzuki Cabinet, which was certainly intended to bring an end to hostilities. It may well be asked why, in the light of Japan's inability, so manifest after the end of 1944, to carry the war to a successful conclusion, the discussion was prolonged well into 1945, while her factories and her houses were being destroyed, her warships sunk and her armies cut off from their homes? The answer is not clear, but it seems as if the delay was something dictated by the nature of Japanese institutions. The slow process by which an apparently unanimous will to war was created before 1941 had to be repeated in reverse before a will to peace could be announced.

The fact that the decision to accept the Potsdam terms was reached soon after the explosion of the atomic bomb and the Russian declaration of war has been interpreted as showing that the bomb and the Russian action were what produced Japan's surrender. This is a view which it is difficult to accept. It might be correct to say that these two menacing events accelerated a decision which was being reached by slow and devious processes characteristic of Japanese political life. But it cannot be truthfully said that any one single cause brought about the surrender; at the same time there is good reason for thinking that, even had no atomic bombing attacks been delivered, the disintegration of Japan's economic life, under sustained blockade and continued aerial and naval bombardment, would within a few months—perhaps weeks—after June 1945 have brought about unconditional surrender, even without the need for invasion. But all this is in the realm of conjecture, and not even the participants themselves can say with certainty what course the debates in the War Council would have taken in hypothetical conditions. Even if we were today certain that it was not the atomic bomb which caused the surrender, it would not follow that the decision to use the bomb was wrong. That decision was necessarily taken in the light of such sure knowledge as was then at the disposal of our Governments; and although intelligence reports on conditions in Japan were remarkably good, that knowledge was not sufficient to justify abstaining from the use of a weapon which might end the war quickly, and save the lives of thousands of allied prisoners, possibly hundreds of thousands of allied soldiers, to say nothing of great numbers of enemy soldiers and civilians. Discussion of the rights and wrongs of the use of the atomic bomb at Hiroshima frequently confuses two separate issues. If the question is whether it was immoral to use such a destructive weapon, then one must bring into consideration incendiary raids, such as that of the night of March 9, 1945, which killed probably 100,000 people and destroyed over 250,000 homes, in circumstances of appalling terror. If the question is whether the use of the atomic bomb was strategically unnecessary or (in the light of subsequent history) politically mistaken, then moral considerations are irrelevant so long as the right of a belligerent to attack civilian targets is admitted. There cannot by any rational standard of morals be a valid distinction between methods of killing civilians in which one is right and the other is wrong because it is quicker and more effective.

The Decision to Use
the Atomic Bomb

LOUIS MORTON

It is now more than ten years since the atomic bomb exploded over Hiroshima and revealed to the world in one blinding flash of light the start of the atomic age. As the meaning of this explosion and the nature of the force unleashed became apparent, a chorus of voices rose in protest against the decision that had opened the Pandora's box of atomic warfare.

The justification for using the atomic bomb was that it had ended the war, or at least ended it sooner and thereby saved countless American—and Japanese—lives. But had it? Had not Japan already been defeated and was she not already on the verge of surrender? What circumstances, it was asked, justified the fateful decision that "blasted the web of history and, like the discovery of fire, severed past from present"?[1]

The first authoritative explanation of how and why it was decided to use the bomb came in February 1947 from Henry L. Stimson, wartime Secretary of War and the man who more than any other was responsible for advising the President.[2] This explanation did not answer all the questions or still the critics. During the years that have followed others have revealed their part in the decision and in the events shaping it. These explanations have not ended the controversy, but they have brought to light additional facts bearing on the decision to use the bomb. With this information and with the perspective of ten years, it may be profitable to look again at the decision that opened the age of atomic warfare.

Reprinted by special permission from *Foreign Affairs*, January 1957, pp. 334–353. Copyright © 1956 by the Council on Foreign Relations, Inc., New York. Some footnotes have been omitted.

[1] James Phinney Baxter, 3rd, *Scientists Against Time* (Boston: Little, Brown, 1946), p. 419.

[2] Henry L. Stimson, "The Decision to Use the Atomic Bomb," *Harper's*, February 1947. The article is reproduced with additional comments in Henry L. Stimson and McGeorge Bundy, *On Active Service in Peace and War* (New York: Harper, 1948), chapter 13, and in *Bulletin of the Atomic Scientists*, February 1947.

THE INTERIM COMMITTEE

The epic story of the development of the atomic bomb is by now well known. It began in 1939 when a small group of eminent scientists in this country called to the attention of the United States Government the vast potentialities of atomic energy for military purposes and warned that the Germans were already carrying on experiments in this field. The program initiated in October of that year with a very modest appropriation and later expanded into the two-billion-dollar Manhattan Project had only one purpose—to harness the energy of the atom in a chain reaction to produce a bomb that could be carried by aircraft if possible, and to produce it before the Germans could.[3] That such a bomb, if produced, would be used, no responsible official even questioned. "At no time from 1941 to 1945," declared Mr. Stimson, "did I ever hear it suggested by the President, or by another responsible member of the Government, that atomic energy should not be used in the war." And Dr. J. Robert Oppenheimer recalled in 1954 that "we always assumed if they [atomic bombs] were needed, they would be used."[4]

So long as the success of the project remained in doubt there seems to have been little or no discussion of the effects of an atomic weapon or the circumstances under which it would be used. "During the early days of the project," one scientist recalled, "we spent little time thinking about the possible effects of the bomb we were trying to make"[5] It was a "neck-and-neck race with the Germans," the outcome of which might well determine who would be the victor in World War II. But as Germany approached defeat and as the effort to produce an atomic bomb offered increasing promise of successs, those few men who knew what was being done and who appreciated the enormous implications of atomic energy became more and more concerned. Most of this concern came from the scientists in the Metallurgical Laboratory at Chicago, where by early 1945 small groups began to question the advisability of using the weapon they were trying so hard to build. It was almost as if they hoped the bomb would not work after it was completed.

On the military side, the realization that a bomb would probably be ready for testing in the summer of 1945 led to concrete planning for the use of the new weapon, on the assumption that the bomb when

[3] The one exception was the Navy's work in the field of atomic energy as a source of power for naval vessels. *Hearings Before the Special Committee on Atomic Energy*, Senate, 79th Cong., 1st Sess., S.R. 179, pt. 3, pp. 364–389, testimony of Dr. Ross Gunn.

[4] Stimson, *Harper's*, p. 98; U.S. Atomic Energy Commission, *Transcript of Hearings Before Personnel Security Board in the Matter of Dr. J. Robert Oppenheimer, 12 April–6 May 1954* (Washington: G.P.O., 1954), p. 33.

[5] *Senate Hearings*, pt. 2, p. 302, testimony of Dr. John A. Simpson.

completed would work. By the end of 1944 a list of possible targets in Japan had been selected and a B-29 squadron was trained for the specific job of delivering the bomb. It was also necessary to inform certain commanders in the Pacific about the project, and on December 30, 1944, Major-General Leslie R. Groves, head of the Manhattan District, recommended that this be done.[6]

Even at this stage of development no one could estimate accurately when the bomb would be ready or guarantee that, when ready, it would work. It is perhaps for this reason—and because of the complete secrecy surrounding the project—that the possibility of an atomic weapon never entered into the deliberations of the strategic planners. It was, said Admiral William Leahy, "the best kept secret of the entire war" and only a handful of the top civilian and military officials in Washington knew about the bomb.[7] As a matter of fact, one bright brigadier-general who innocently suggested that the Army might do well to look into the possibilities of atomic energy suddenly found himself the object of the most intensive investigation. So secret was the project, says John J. McCloy, that when he raised the subject at a White House meeting of the Joint Chiefs of Staff in June 1945 it "caused a sense of shock, even among that select group."[8]

It was not until March 1945 that it became possible to predict with certainty that the bomb would be completed in time for testing in July. On March 15, Mr. Stimson discussed the project for the last time with President Roosevelt, but their conversation dealt mainly with the effects of the use of the bomb, not with the question of whether it ought to be used. Even at this late date, there does not seem to have been any doubt at the highest levels that the bomb would be used against Japan if it would help bring the war to an early end. But on lower levels, and especially among the scientists at the Chicago laboratory, there was considerable reservation about the advisability of using the bomb.

After President Roosevelt's death, it fell to Stimson to brief the new President about the atomic weapon. At a White House meeting on April 25, he outlined the history and status of the program and predicted that "within four months we shall in all probability have completed the most terrible weapon ever known in human history."[9] This meeting, like Stimson's last meeting with Roosevelt, dealt largely

---

[6] "Memo, Groves for CofS, 30 Dec. 1944 sub: Atomic Fission Bombs," printed in *Foreign Relations of the United States: The Conferences at Malta-Yalta, 1945* (Washington: G.P.O., 1955). . . .

[7] Admiral William D. Leahy, *I Was There* (New York: Whittlesey House, 1950), p. 434.

[8] John J. McCloy, *The Challenge to American Foreign Policy* (Cambridge: Harvard University Press, 1953), p. 42. See also . . . James F. Byrnes, *Speaking Frankly* (New York: Harper, 1947), p. 257.

[9] Stimson's memorandum of this meeting is printed in *Harper's*, pp. 99-100.

with the political and diplomatic consequences of the use of such a weapon rather than with the timing and manner of employment, the circumstances under which it would be used, or whether it would be used at all. The answers to these questions depended on factors not yet known. But Stimson recommended, and the President approved, the appointment of a special committee to consider them.

This special committee, known as the Interim Committee, played a vital role in the decision to use the bomb. Secretary Stimson was chairman, and George L. Harrison, President of the New York Life Insurance Company and special consultant in the Secretary's office, took the chair when he was absent. James F. Byrnes, who held no official position at the time, was President Truman's personal representative. Other members were Ralph A. Bard, Under Secretary of the Navy, William L. Clayton, Assistant Secretary of State, and Drs. Vannevar Bush, Karl T. Compton and James B. Conant. Generals Marshall and Groves attended at least one and possibly more of the meetings of the committee.

The work of the Interim Committee, in Stimson's words, "ranged over the whole field of atomic energy, in its political, military, and scientific aspects."[10] During the first meeting the scientific members reviewed for their colleagues the development of the Manhattan Project and described vividly the destructive power of the atomic bomb. They made it clear also that there was no known defense against this kind of attack. Another day was spent with the engineers and industrialists who had designed and built the huge plants at Oak Ridge and Hanford. Of particular concern to the committee was the question of how long it would take another country, particularly the Soviet Union, to produce an atomic bomb. "Much of the discussion," recalled Dr. Oppenheimer, who attended the meeting of June 1 as a member of a scientific panel, "revolved around the question raised by Secretary Stimson as to whether there was any hope at all of using this development to get less barbarous [sic] relations with the Russians."[11]

The work of the Interim Committee was completed June 1, 1945, when it submitted its report to the President, recommending unanimously that:

1. The bomb should be used against Japan as soon as possible.

2. It should be used against a military target surrounded by other buildings.

[10] Stimson, *Harper's*, p. 100.
[11] *Oppenheimer Hearings*, pp. 34, 257, testimony of Dr. Oppenheimer and Dr. Compton; Byrnes, *op. cit.*, pp. 260–261; Stimson, *Harper's*, pp. 100–101.

3. It should be used without prior warning of the nature of the weapon.

(One member, Ralph A. Bard, later dissented from this portion of the committee's recommendation.)

"The conclusions of the Committee," wrote Stimson, "were similar to my own, although I reached mine independently. I felt that to extract a genuine surrender from the Emperor and his military advisers, they must be administered a tremendous shock which would carry convincing proof of our power to destroy the empire. Such an effective shock would save many times the number of lives, both American and Japanese, than it would cost."[12]

Among the scientists working on the Manhattan Project were many who did not agree. To them, the "wave of horror and repulsion" that might follow the sudden use of an atomic bomb would more than outweigh its military advantages. "It may be very difficult," they declared, "to persuade the world that a nation which was capable of secretly preparing and suddenly releasing a new weapon, as indiscriminate as the rocket bomb and a thousand times more destructive, is to be trusted in its proclaimed desire of having such weapons abolished by international agreement."[13] The procedure these scientists recommended was, first, to demonstrate the new weapon "before the eyes of representatives of all the United Nations on the desert or a barren island," and then to issue "a preliminary ultimatum" to Japan. If this ultimatum was rejected, and "if the sanction of the United Nations (and of public opinion at home) were obtained," then and only then, said the scientists, should the United States consider using the bomb. "This may sound fantastic," they said, "but in nuclear weapons we have something entirely new in order of magnitude of destructive power, and if we want to capitalize fully on the advantage their possession gives us, we must use new and imaginative methods."[14]

These views, which were forwarded to the Secretary of War on June 11, 1945, were strongly supported by 64 of the scientists in the Chicago Metallurgical Laboratory in a petition sent directly to the President. At about the same time, at the request of Dr. Arthur H. Compton, a poll was taken of the views of more than 150 scientists at the Chicago Laboratory. Five alternatives ranging from all-out use of

---

[12] Stimson, *Harper's*, p. 101. The same idea is expressed by Sir Winston Churchill, *Triumph and Tragedy* (Cambridge: Houghton, 1953), pp. 638–639.
[13] "Report of the Committee on Social and Political Implications," signed by Professor James Franck of the University of Chicago and submitted to the Secretary of War, June 11, 1945, *Bulletin of Atomic Scientists*, May 1, 1946, p. 3.
[14] *Ibid.*, pp. 3–4.

the bomb to "keeping the existence of the bomb a secret" were presented. Of those polled, about two-thirds voted for a preliminary demonstration, either on a military objective or an uninhabited locality; the rest were split on all-out use and no use at all.[15]

These views, and presumably others, were referred by Secretary Stimson to a distinguished Scientific Panel consisting of Drs. Arthur H. Compton, Enrico Fermi, E. O. Lawrence and J. Robert Oppenheimer, all nuclear physicists of the first rank. "We didn't know beans about the military situation," Oppenheimer later said. "We didn't know whether they [the Japanese] could be caused to surrender by other means or whether the invasion [of Japan] was really inevitable. . . . We thought the two overriding considerations were the saving of lives in the war and the effect of our actions on the stability of the postwar world."[16] On June 16 the panel reported that it had studied carefully the proposals made by the scientists but could see no practical way of ending the war by a technical demonstration. Almost regretfully, it seemed, the four members of the panel concluded that there was "no acceptable alternative to direct military use."[17] "Nothing would have been more damaging to our effort," wrote Stimson, ". . . than a warning or demonstration followed by a dud—and this was a real possibility." With this went the fear, expressed by Byrnes, that if the Japanese were warned that an atomic bomb would be exploded over a military target in Japan as a demonstration, "they might bring our boys who were prisoners of war to that area."[18] Furthermore, only two bombs would be available by August, the number General Groves estimated would be needed to end the war; these two would have to obtain the desired effect quickly. And no one yet knew, nor would the scheduled ground test in New Mexico prove, whether a bomb dropped from an airplane would explode.[19]

Nor, for that matter, were all those concerned certain that the bomb would work at all, on the ground or in the air. Of these doubters, the greatest was Admiral Leahy, who until the end remained unconvinced. "This is the biggest fool thing we have ever done," he told Truman after Vannevar Bush had explained to the President how the bomb worked. "The bomb will never go off, and I speak as an expert on explosives."[20]

---

[15] *Ibid.*, p. 1; Leo Szilard, "A Personal History of the Bomb," in *The Atlantic Community Faces the Bomb*, University of Chicago Roundtable, No. 601, Sept. 25, 1949, p. 15. See also P. M. S. Blackett, *Fear, War, and the Bomb* (New York: Whittlesey House, 1949), pp. 114–116.

[16] *Oppenheimer Hearings*, p. 34.

[17] Quoted in Stimson, *Harper's*, p. 101. The Scientific Panel was established to advise the Interim Committee and its report was made to that body.

[18] *Ibid.*, Byrnes, p. 261.

[19] *Ibid., Oppenheimer Hearings*, p. 163, testimony of General Groves.

[20] Harry S. Truman, *Year of Decisions* (Garden City: Doubleday, 1955), p. 11. Leahy in his memoirs frankly admits this error.

Thus, by mid-June 1945, there was virtual unanimity among the President's civilian advisers on the use of the bomb. The arguments of the opponents had been considered and rejected. So far as is known the President did not solicit the views of the military or naval staffs, nor were they offered.

MILITARY CONSIDERATIONS

The military situation on June 1, 1945, when the Interim Committee submitted its recommendations on the use of the atomic bomb, was distinctly favorable to the Allied cause. Germany had surrendered in May and troops from Europe would soon be available for redeployment in the Pacific. Manila had fallen in February; Iwo Jima was in American hands; and the success of the Okinawa invasion was assured. Air and submarine attacks had virtually cut off Japan from the resources of the Indies, and B-29s from the Marianas were pulverizing Japan's cities and factories. The Pacific Fleet had virtually driven the Imperial Navy from the ocean, and planes of the fast carrier forces were striking Japanese naval bases in the Inland Sea. Clearly, Japan was a defeated nation.

Though defeated in a military sense, Japan showed no disposition to surrender unconditionally. And Japanese troops had demonstrated time and again that they could fight hard and inflict heavy casualties even when the outlook was hopeless. Allied plans in the spring of 1945 took these facts into account and proceeded on the assumption that an invasion of the home islands would be required to achieve at the earliest possible date the unconditional surrender of Japan—the announced objective of the war and the basic assumption of all strategic planning.

Other means of achieving this objective had been considered and, in early June, had not yet been entirely discarded. One of these called for the occupation of a string of bases around Japan in order to increase the intensity of air bombardment. Combined with a tight naval blockade, such a course would, many believed, produce the same results as an invasion and at far less cost of lives. "I was unable to see any justification," Admiral Leahy later wrote, ". . . for an invasion of an already thoroughly defeated Japan. I feared the cost would be enormous in both lives and treasure." Admiral King and other senior naval officers agreed. To them it had always seemed, in King's words, "that the defeat of Japan could be accomplished by sea and air power alone, without the necessity of actual invasion of the Japanese home islands by ground troops."[21]

The main arguments for an invasion of Japan—the plans called for an assault against Kyushu (Olympic) on November 1, 1945, and

[21] Leahy, *op. cit.*, pp. 384–385. . . .

against Honshu (Coronet) five months later—are perhaps best summarized by General Douglas MacArthur. Writing to the Chief of Staff on April 20, 1945, he declared that this course was the only one that would permit application of the full power of our combined resources —ground, naval and air—on the decisive objective. Japan, he believed, would probably be more difficult to invade the following year. An invasion of Kyushu at an early date would, moreover, place United States forces in the most favorable position for the decisive assault against Honshu in 1946, and would "continue the offensive methods which have proved so successful in Pacific campaigns."[22] Reliance upon bombing alone, MacArthur asserted, was still an unproved formula for success, as was evidenced by the bomber offensive against Germany. The seizure of a ring of bases around Japan would disperse Allied forces even more than they already were, MacArthur pointed out, and (if an attempt was made to seize positions on the China coast) might very well lead to long drawn-out operations on the Asiatic mainland.

Though the Joint Chiefs had accepted the invasion concept as the basis for preparations, and had issued a directive for the Kyushu assault on May 25, it was well understood that the final decision was yet to be made. By mid-June the time had come for such a decision and during that period the Joint Chiefs reviewed the whole problem of Japanese strategy. Finally, on June 18, at a meeting in the White House, they presented the alternatives to President Truman. Also present (according to the minutes) were Secretaries Stimson and Forrestal and Assistant Secretary of War John J. McCloy.[23]

General Marshall presented the case for invasion and carried his colleagues with him, although both Admirals Leahy and King later declared they did not favor the plan. After considerable discussion of casualties and of the difficulties ahead, President Truman made his decision. Kyushu would be invaded as planned and preparations for the landing were to be pushed through to completion. Preparations for the Honshu assault would continue, but no final decision would be made until preparations had reached the point "beyond which there would not be opportunity for a free choice."[24] The program thus approved by Truman called for:

1. Air bombardment and blockade of Japan from bases in Okinawa, Iwo Jima, the Marianas and the Philippines.

---

[22] This message is reproduced in *The Entry of the Soviet Union Into the War Against Japan: Military Plans, 1941-1945* (Department of Defense Press Release, September 1955), pp. 55-57.

[23] Forrestal says in his *Diaries* that neither he nor Stimson was present, while McCloy's definite recollection is that Stimson was present but Forrestal was not. A summary of this meeting is contained in *The Entry of the Soviet Union . . .*, pp. 77-85. . . .

[24] McCloy, *op. cit.*, p. 41. . . .

2. Assault of Kyushu on November 1, 1945, and intensification of blockade and air bombardment.

3. Invasion of the industrial heart of Japan through the Tokyo Plain in central Honshu, tentative target date March 1, 1946.

During the White House meeting of June 18, there was dicussion of the possibility of ending the war by political means. The President displayed a deep interest in the subject and both Stimson and McCloy emphasized the importance of the "large submerged class in Japan who do not favor the present war and whose full opinion and influence had never yet been felt."[25] There was discussion also of the atomic bomb, since everyone present knew about the bomb and the recommendations of the Interim Committee. The suggestion was made that before the bomb was dropped, the Japanese should be warned that the United States had such a weapon. "Not one of the Chiefs nor the Secretary," recalled Mr. McCloy, "thought well of a bomb warning, an effective argument being that no one could be certain, in spite of the assurances of the scientists, that the 'thing would go off.'"[26]

Though the defeat of the enemy's armed forces in the Japanese homeland was considered a prerequisite to Japan's surrender, it did not follow that Japanese forces elsewhere, especially those on the Asiatic mainland, would surrender also. It was to provide for just this contingency, as well as to pin down those forces during the invasion of the home islands, that the Joint Chiefs had recommended Soviet entry into the war against Japan.

Soviet participation was a goal long pursued by the Americans. Both political and military authorities seem to have been convinced from the start that Soviet assistance, conceived in various ways, would shorten the war and lessen the cost. In October 1943, Marshal Stalin had told Cordell Hull, then in Moscow for a conference, that the Soviet Union would eventually declare war on Japan. At the Tehran Conference in November of that year, Stalin had given the Allies formal notice of this intention and reaffirmed it in October 1944. In February 1945, at the Yalta Conference, Roosevelt and Stalin had agreed on the terms of Soviet participation in the Far Eastern war. Thus, by June 1945, the Americans could look forward to Soviet intervention at a date estimated as three months after the defeat of Germany.

But by the summer of 1945 the Americans had undergone a change of heart. Though the official position of the War Department still held that "Russian entry will have a profound military effect in that almost

---

[25] *The Entry of the Soviet Union. . .*, p. 83. . . . .
[26] McCloy, p. 43. . . . .

certainly it will materially shorten the war and thus save American lives,"[27] few responsible American officials were eager for Soviet intervention or as willing to make concessions as they had been at an earlier period. What had once appeared extremely desirable appeared less so now that the war in Europe was over and Japan was virtually defeated. President Truman, one official recalled, stated during a meeting devoted to the question of Soviet policy that agreements with Stalin had up to that time been "a one-way street" and that "he intended thereafter to be firm in his dealings with the Russians."[28] And at the June 18 meeting of the Joint Chiefs of Staff with the President, Admiral King had declared that "regardless of the desirability of the Russians entering the war, they were not indispensable and he did not think we should go so far as to beg them to come in."[29] Though the cost would be greater he had no doubt "we could handle it alone."

The failure of the Soviets to abide by agreements at Yalta had also done much to discourage the American desire for further cooperation with them. But after urging Stalin for three years to declare war on Japan, the United States Government could hardly ask him now to remain neutral. Moreover, there was no way of keeping the Russians out even if there had been a will to do so. In Harriman's view, "Russia would come into the war regardless of what we might do."[30]

A further difficulty was that Allied intelligence still indicated that Soviet intervention would be desirable, if not necessary, for the success of the invasion strategy. In Allied intelligence, Japan was portrayed as a defeated nation whose military leaders were blind to defeat. Though her industries had been seriously crippled by air bombardment and naval blockade and her armed forces were critically deficient in many of the resources of war, Japan was still far from surrender. She had ample reserves of weapons and ammunition and an army of 5,000,000 troops, 2,000,000 of them in the home islands. The latter could be expected to put up a strong resistance to invasion. In the opinion of the intelligence experts, neither blockade nor bombing alone would produce unconditional surrender before the date set for invasion. And the invasion itself, they believed, would be costly and possibly prolonged.[31]

According to these intelligence reports, the Japanese leaders were fully aware of their desperate situation but would continue to fight in the hope of avoiding complete defeat by securing a better bargaining

[27] Letter, Stimson to Grew, May 21, 1945, reproduced . . . in *The Entry of the Soviet Union* . . ., pp. 70–71.

[28] Walter Millis, ed., *The Forrestal Diaries* (New York: Viking, 1951), p. 78.

[29] *The Entry of the Soviet Union* . . ., p. 85. . . .

[30] Statement to Leahy quoted in Leahy, p. 369. . . .

[31] *The Entry of the Soviet Union* . . ., pp. 85–88. . . .

position. Allied war-weariness and disunity, or some miracle, they hoped, would offer them a way out. "The Japanese believe," declared an intelligence estimate of June 30, ". . . that unconditional surrender would be the equivalent of national extinction, and there are as yet no indications that they are ready to accept such terms."[32] It appeared also to the intelligence experts that Japan might surrender at any time "depending upon the conditions of surrender" the Allies might offer. Clearly these conditions, to have any chance of acceptance, would have to include retention of the imperial system.[33]

How accurate were these estimates? Judging from postwar accounts of Japan, they were very close to the truth. Since the defeat at Saipan, when Tojo had been forced to resign, the strength of the "peace party" had been increasing. In September 1944 the Swedish Minister in Tokyo had been approached unofficially, presumably in the name of Prince Konoye, to sound out the Allies on terms for peace. This overture came to naught, as did another the following March. But the Swedish Minister did learn that those who advocated peace in Japan regarded the Allied demand for unconditional surrender as their greatest obstacle.[34]

The Suzuki Cabinet that came into power in April 1945 had an unspoken mandate from the Emperor to end the war as quickly as possible. But it was faced immediately with another problem when the Soviet Government announced it would not renew the neutrality pact after April 1946. The German surrender in May produced another crisis in the Japanese Government and led, after considerable discussion, to a decision to seek Soviet mediation. But the first approach, made on June 3 to Jacob Malik, the Soviet Ambassador, produced no results. Malik was noncommittal and merely said the problem needed further study. Another overture to Malik later in the month also came to naught.

At the end of June, the Japanese finally approached the Soviet Government directly through Ambassador Sato in Moscow, asking that it mediate with the Allies to bring the Far Eastern war to an end. In a series of messages between Tokyo and Moscow, which the Americans intercepted and decoded, the Japanese Foreign Office

---

[32] G-2 memorandum prepared for ODP and quoted in Ray S. Cline, *United States Army in World War II. The War Department. Washington Command Post: The Operations Division* (Washington: Department of the Army, Office of Military History, 1951), p. 347. . . .

[33] *Ibid.* . . .

[34] Robert J. C. Butow, *Japan's Decision to Surrender* (Stanford: Stanford University Press, 1954), pp. 40, 54–57. Other accounts of the situation in Japan are Toshikazu Kase, *Journey to the Missouri* (New Haven: Yale University Press, 1950); U.S. Strategic Bombing Survey, *Japan's Struggle to End the War* (Washington: G.P.O., 1946); Takushiro Hattori, *Complete History of the Greater East Asia War* (Japan: Masu Shobo Co., 1953), v. 4.

outlined the position of the government and instructed Ambassador Sato to make arrangements for a special envoy from the Emperor who would be empowered to make terms for Soviet mediation. Unconditional surrender, he was told, was completely unacceptable, and time was of the essence. But the Russians, on one pretext and another, delayed their answer until mid-July when Stalin and Molotov left for Potsdam. Thus, the Japanese Government had by then accepted defeat and was seeking desperately for a way out; but it was not willing even at this late date to surrender unconditionally, and would accept no terms that did not include the preservation of the imperial system.

Allied intelligence thus had estimated the situation in Japan correctly. Allied invasion strategy had been reexamined and confirmed in mid-June, and the date for the invasion fixed. The desirability of Soviet assistance had been confirmed also and plans for her entry into the war during August could now be made. No decision had been reached on the use of the atomic bomb, but the President's advisers had recommended it. The decision was the President's and he faced it squarely. But before he could make it he would want to know whether the measures already concerted would produce unconditional surrender at the earliest moment and at the lowest cost. If they could not, then he would have to decide whether circumstances warranted employment of a bomb that Stimson had already labeled as "the most terrible weapon ever known in human history."

THE DECISION

Though responsibility for the decision to use the atomic bomb was the President's, he exercised it only after careful study of the recommendations of his senior advisers. Chief among these was the Secretary of War, under whose broad supervision the Manhattan Project had been placed. Already deeply concerned over the cost of the projected invasion, the political effects of Soviet intervention and the potential consequences of the use of the atomic bomb, Stimson sought a course that would avoid all these evils. The difficulty, as he saw it, lay in the requirement for unconditional surrender. It was a phrase that might make the Japanese desperate and lead to a long and unnecessary campaign of attrition that would be extremely costly to both sides. But there was no way of getting around the term; it was firmly rooted in Allied war aims and its renunciation was certain to lead to charges of appeasement.

But if this difficulty could be overcome, would the Japanese respond if terms were offered? The intelligence experts thought so, and the radio intercepts from Tokyo to Moscow bore them out. So far as the Army was concerned there was much to be gained by such a course. Not only might it reduce the enormous cost of the war, but it would also make possible a settlement in the Western Pacific "before too many of our allies are committed there and have made substantial contributions towards the defeat of Japan."[35] In the view of the War Department these aims justified "any concessions which might be attractive to the Japanese, so long as our realistic aims for peace in the Pacific are not adversely affected."[36]

The problem was to formulate terms that would meet these conditions. There was considerable discussion of this problem in Washington in the spring of 1945 by officials in the Department of State and in the War and Navy Departments. Joseph C. Grew, Acting Secretary of State, proposed to the President late in May that he issue a proclamation urging the Japanese to surrender and assuring them that they could keep the Emperor. Though Truman did not act on the suggestion, he thought it "a sound idea" and told Grew to discuss it with his cabinet colleagues and the Joint Chiefs. On June 18, Grew was back with the report that these groups favored the idea, but that there were differences on the timing.

Grew's ideas, as well as those of others concerned, were summarized by Stimson in a long and carefully considered memorandum to the President on July 2. Representing the most informed military and political estimate of the situation at this time, this memorandum constitutes a state paper of the first importance. If any one document can be said to provide the basis for the President's warning to Japan and his final decision to use the atomic bomb, this is it.

The gist of Stimson's argument was that the most promising alternative to the long and costly struggle certain to follow invasion was to warn the Japanese "of what is to come" and to give them an opportunity to surrender. There was, he thought, enough of a chance that such a course would work to make the effort worthwhile. Japan no longer had any allies, her navy was virtually destroyed and she was increasingly vulnerable to air attack and naval blockade. Against her were arrayed the increasingly powerful forces of the Allies, with their "inexhaustible and untouched industrial resources." In these circumstances, Stimson believed the Japanese people would be susceptible to reason if properly approached. "Japan," he pointed out, "is not a nation composed of mad fanatics of an entirely different mentality from ours. On the contrary, she has within the past century shown herself to possess extremely intelligent people. . . ." But any attempt, Stimson added, "to exterminate her armies and her population by gunfire or other means will tend to produce a fusion of race solidity and antipathy. . . ."

[35] OPD Compilation for the Potsdam Conference, quoted in Cline, op. cit., p. 345.
[36] Ibid., pp. 345–346.

A warning to Japan, Stimson contended, should be carefully timed. It should come before the actual invasion, before destruction had reduced the Japanese "to fanatical despair" and, if the Soviet Union had already entered the war, before Russian attack had progressed so far.[37] It should also emphasize, Stimson believed, the inevitability and completeness of the destruction ahead and the determination of the Allies to strip Japan of her conquests and to destroy the influence of the military clique. It should be a strong warning and should leave no doubt in Japanese minds that they would have to surrender unconditionally and submit to Allied occupation.

The warning, as Stimson envisaged it, had a double character. While promising destruction and devastation, it was also to hold out hope to the Japanese if they heeded its message. In his memorandum, therefore, Stimson stressed the positive features of the warning and recommended that it include a disavowal of any intention to destroy the Japanese nation or to occupy the country permanently. Once Japan's military clique had been removed from power and her capacity to wage war destroyed, it was Stimson's belief that the Allies should withdraw and resume normal trade relations with the new and peaceful Japanese Government. "I personally think," he declared, "that if in saying this we should add that we do not exclude a constitutional monarchy under her present dynasty, it would substantially add to the chance of acceptance."

Not once in the course of this lengthy memorandum was mention made of the atomic bomb. There was no need to do so. Everyone concerned understood clearly that the bomb was the instrument that would destroy Japan and impress on the Japanese Government the hopelessness of any course but surrender. As Stimson expressed it, the atomic bomb was "the best possible sanction," the single weapon that would convince the Japanese "of our power to destroy the empire."[38]

Though Stimson considered a warning combined with an offer of terms and backed up by the sanction of the atomic bomb as the most promising means of inducing surrender at any early date, there were other courses that some thought might produce the same result. One was the continuation and intensification of air bombardment coupled with surface and underwater blockade. This course had already been considered and rejected as insufficient to produce surrender, though its advocates were by no means convinced that this decision was a wise one. And Stimson himself later justified the use of the bomb on the

---

[37] In his diary, under the date June 19, Stimson wrote: "The last-chance warning . . . must be given before an actual landing of the ground forces in Japan, and fortunately the plans provide for enough time to bring in the sanctions to our warning in the shape of heavy ordinary bombing attack and an attack of S-1 [the atomic bomb]." Stimson and Bundy, p. 624.

[38] Stimson, *Harper's*, pp. 101, 104.

ground that by November 1 conventional bombardment would have caused greater destruction than the bomb. This apparent contradiction is explained by the fact that the atomic bomb was considered to have a psychological effect entirely apart from the damage wrought.[39]

Nor did Stimson, in his memorandum, consider the effect of the Soviet Union's entry into the war. By itself, this action could not be counted on to force Japan to capitulate, but combined with bombardment and blockade it might do so. At least that was the view of Brigadier-General George A. Lincoln, one of the Army's top planners, who wrote in June that "probably it will take Russian entry into the war, coupled with a landing, or imminent threat of landing, on Japan proper by us, to convince them [the Japanese] of the hopelessness of their position."[40] Why, therefore, was it not possible to issue the warning prior to a Soviet declaration of war against Japan and rely on that event, together with an intensified air bombardment, to produce the desired result? If together they could not secure Japan's surrender, would there not still be time to use the bomb before the scheduled invasion of Kyushu in November?

No final answer to this question is possible with the evidence at hand. But one cannot ignore the fact that some responsible officials feared the political consequences of Soviet intervention and hoped that ultimately it would prove unnecessary. This feeling may unconsciously have made the atom bomb solution more attractive than it might otherwise have been. Some officials may have believed, too, that the bomb could be used as a powerful deterrent to Soviet expansion in Europe, where the Red tide had successfully engulfed Rumania, Bulgaria, Jugoslavia, Czechoslovakia and Hungary. In an interview with three of the top scientists in the Manhattan Project early in June, Mr. Byrnes did not, according to Leo Szilard, argue that the bomb was needed to defeat Japan, but rather that it should be dropped to "make Russia more manageable in Europe."[41]

It has been asserted also that the desire to justify the expenditure of the two billion dollars spent on the Manhattan Project may have disposed some favorably toward the use of the bomb. Already questions had been asked in Congress, and the end of the war would almost certainly bring on a full-scale investigation. What more striking justification of the Manhattan Project than a new weapon that had ended the war in one sudden blow and saved countless American lives? "It was my reaction," wrote Admiral Leahy, "that the scientists and others wanted to make this test because of the vast sums that

---

[39] *Ibid.*, p. 105.
[40] Quoted in Cline, p. 344.
[41] Szilard, *op. cit.*, pp. 14-15.

had been spent on the project. Truman knew that, and so did other people involved."[42]

This explanation hardly does credit to those involved in the Manhattan Project and not even P. M. S. Blackett, one of the severest critics of the decision to use the bomb, accepted it. "The wit of man," he declared, "could hardly devise a theory of the dropping of the bomb, both more insulting to the American people, or more likely to lead to an energetically pursued Soviet defense policy."[43]

But even if the need to justify these huge expenditures is discounted —and certainly by itself it could not have produced the decision—the question still remains whether those who held in their hands a weapon thought capable of ending the war in one stroke could justify withholding that weapon. Would they not be open to criticism for failing to use every means at their disposal to defeat the enemy as quickly as possible, thereby saving many American lives?

And even at that time there were some who believed that the new weapon would ultimately prove the most effective deterrent to war yet produced. How better to outlaw war forever than to demonstrate the tremendous destructive power of this weapon by using it against an actual target?

By early 1945 the stage had been set for the final decision. Stimson's memorandum had been approved in principle and on July 4 the British had given their consent to the use of the bomb against Japan. It remained only to decide on the terms and timing of the warning. This was the situation when the Potsdam Conference opened on July 17, one day after the bomb had been successfully exploded in a spectacular demonstration at Alamogordo, New Mexico. The atomic bomb was a reality and when the news reached Potsdam there was great excitement among those who were let in on the secret. Instead of the prospect of long and bitter months of fighting the Japanese, there was now a vision, "fair and bright indeed it seemed" to Churchill, "of the end of the whole war in one or two violent shocks."[44]

President Truman's first action was to call together his chief advisers—Byrnes, Stimson, Leahy, Marshall, King and Arnold. "I asked for their opinion whether the bomb should be used," he later wrote. The consensus was that it should."[45] Here at last was the miracle to end the war and solve all the perplexing problems posed by the necessity for invasion. But because no one could tell what effect the bomb might have "physically or psychologically," it was decided to

[42] Leahy, p. 441.
[43] Blackett, *op. cit.*, p. 138.
[44] Churchill, *op. cit.*, p. 638.
[45] . . . Truman, *op. cit.*, p. 415. General Eisenhower was at Potsdam and his advice, Truman says, was asked. The various participants differ in their recollections of this meeting. . . .

proceed with the military plans for the invasion.

No one at this time, or later in the conference, raised the question of whether the Japanese should be informed of the existence of the bomb. That question, it will be recalled, had been discussed by the Scientific Panel on June 16 and at the White House meeting with the JCS, the service Secretaries and Mr. McCloy on June 18. For a variety of reasons, including uncertainty as to whether the bomb would work, it had then been decided that the Japanese should not be warned of the existence of the new weapon. The successful explosion of the first bomb on July 17 did not apparently outweigh the reasons advanced earlier for keeping the bomb a secret, and evidently none of the men involved thought the question needed to be reviewed. The Japanese would learn of the atomic bomb only when it was dropped on them.

The secrecy that had shrouded the development of the atomic bomb was torn aside briefly at Potsdam, but with no visible effect. On July 24, on the advice of his chief advisers, Truman informed Marshal Stalin "casually" that the Americans had "a new weapon of unusual destructive force." "The Russian Premier," he recalled, "showed no special interest. All he said was that he was glad to hear it and hoped we would make 'good use of it against the Japanese.'"[46] One cannot but wonder whether the Marshal was preoccupied at the moment or simulating a lack of interest.

On the military side, the Potsdam Conference developed nothing new. The plans already made were noted and approved. Even at this late stage the question of the bomb was divorced entirely from military plans and the final report of the conference accepted as the main effort the invasion of the Japanese home islands. November 15, 1946, was accepted as the planning date for the end of the war against Japan.

During the conference, Stalin told Truman about the Japanese overtures—information that the Americans already had. The Marshal spoke of the matter also to Churchill, who discussed it with Truman, suggesting cautiously that some offer be made to Japan. "Mr. Stimson, General Marshall, and the President," he later wrote, "were evidently searching their hearts, and we had no need to press them. We knew of course that the Japanese were ready to give up all conquests made in the war." That same night, after dining with Stalin and Truman, the Prime Minister wrote that the Russians intended to attack Japan soon after August 8—perhaps within two weeks after that date.[47] Truman presumably received the same information, confirming Harry Hopkin's report of his conversation with Stalin in Moscow in May.

[46] Truman, p. 416. . . .
[47] Truman, p. 396; Churchill, p. 642. See also Byrnes, p. 205; Leahy, p. 420.

All that remained now was to warn Japan and give her an opportunity to surrender. In this matter Stimson's and Grew's views, as outlined in the memorandum of July 2, were accepted, but apparently on the advice of the former Secretary of State Cordell Hull it was decided to omit any reference to the Emperor. Hull's view, solicited by Byrnes before his departure for Potsdam, was that the proposal smacked of appeasement and "seemed to guarantee continuance not only of the Emperor but also of the feudal privileges of a ruling caste." And should the Japanese reject the warning, the proposal to retain the imperial system might well encourage resistance and have "terrible political repercussions" in the United States. For these reasons he recommended that no statement about the Emperor be made until "the climax of Allied bombing and Russia's entry into the war."[48] Thus, the final terms offered to the Japanese in the Potsdam Declaration on July 26 made no mention of the Emperor or of the imperial system. Neither did the declaration contain any reference to the atom bomb but simply warned the Japanese of the consequences of continued resistance. Only those already familiar with the weapon could have read the references to inevitable and complete destruction as a warning of atomic warfare.

The receipt of the Potsdam Declaration in Japan led to frantic meetings to decide what should be done. It was finally decided not to reject the note but to await the results of the Soviet overture. At this point, the military insisted that the government make some statement to the people, and on July 28 Premier Suzuki declared to the press that Japan would ignore the declaration, a statement that was interpreted by the Allies as a rejection.

To the Americans the rejection of the Potsdam Declaration confirmed the view that the military was still in control of Japan and that only a decisive act of violence could remove them. The instrument for such action lay at hand in the atomic bomb; events now seemed to justify its use. But in the hope that the Japanese might still change their minds, Truman held off orders on the use of the bomb for a few days. Only silence came from Tokyo, for the Japanese were waiting for a reply from the Soviet Government, which would not come until the return of Stalin and Molotov from Potsdam on August 6. Prophetically, Foreign Minister Tojo wrote Sato on August 2, the day the Potsdam Conference ended, that he could not afford to lose a single day in his efforts to conclude arrangements with the Russians "if we were to end the war before the assault on our mainland."[49] By that time, President Truman had already decided on the use of the bomb.

[48] *Memoirs of Cordell Hull* (New York: Macmillan, 1948), v. 2, p. 1593.
[49] Kase, *op. cit.*, p. 222.

Preparations for dropping the two atomic bombs produced thus far had been under way for some time. The components of the bombs had been sent by cruiser to Tinian in May and the fissionable material was flown out in mid-July. The B-29s and crews were ready and trained, standing by for orders, which would come through the Commanding General, U. S. Army Strategic Air Forces in the Pacific, General Spaatz. Detailed arrangements and schedules were completed and all that was necessary was to issue orders.

At General Arnold's insistence, the responsibility for selecting the particular target and fixing the exact date and hour of the attack was assigned to the field commander, General Spaatz. In orders issued on July 25 and approved by Stimson and Marshall, Spaatz was ordered to drop the "first special bomb as soon as weather will permit visual bombing after about 3 August 1945 on one of the targets: Hiroshima, Kokura, Niigata, and Nagasaki." He was instructed also to deliver a copy of this order personally to MacArthur and Nimitz. Weather was the critical factor because the bomb had to be dropped by visual means, and Spaatz delegated to his chief of staff, Major-General Curtis E. LeMay, the job of deciding when the weather was right for this most important mission.

From the dating of the order to General Spaatz it has been argued that President Truman was certain the warning would be rejected and had fixed the date for the bombing of Hiroshima even before the issuance of the Potsdam Declaration. But such an argument ignores the military necessities. For operational reasons, the orders had to be issued in sufficient time "to set the military wheels in motion." In a sense, therefore, the decision was made on July 25. It would stand unless the President changed his mind. "I had made the decision," wrote Truman in 1955. "I also instructed Stimson that the order would stand unless I notified him that the Japanese reply to our ultimatum was acceptable."[50] The rejection by the Japanese of the Potsdam Declaration confirmed the orders Spaaz had already received.

THE JAPANESE SURRENDER

On Tinian and Guam, preparations for dropping the bomb had been completed by August 3. The original plan was to carry out the operation on August 4, but General LeMay deferred the attack because of bad weather over the target. On August 5 the forecasts were favorable and he gave the word to proceed with the mission the following day. At 0245 on August 6, the bomb-carrying plane was airborne. Six and a half hours later the bomb was released over Hiroshima, Japan's eighth largest city, to explode 50 seconds later at a height of about 2,000 feet. The age of atomic warfare had opened.

[50] Truman, pp. 420–421.

Aboard the cruiser *Augusta* on his way back to the United States, President Truman received the news by radio. That same day a previously prepared release from Washington announced to the world that an atomic bomb had been dropped on Hiroshima and warned the Japanese that if they did not surrender they could expect "a rain of ruin from the air, the like of which has never been seen on this earth."[51]

On August 7, Ambassador Sato in Moscow received word at last that Molotov would see him the next afternoon. At the appointed hour he arrived at the Kremlin, full of hope that he would receive a favorable reply to the Japanese proposal for Soviet mediation with the Allies to end the war. Instead, he was handed the Soviet declaration of war, effective on August 9, Thus, three months to the day after Germany's surrender, Marshal Stalin had lived up to his promise to the Allies.

Meanwhile, President Truman had authorized the use of the second bomb—the last then available. The objective was Kokura, the date August 9. But the plane carrying the bomb failed to make its run over the primary target and hit the secondary target, Nagasaki, instead. The next day Japan sued for peace.

The close sequence of events between August 6 and 10, combined with the fact that the bomb was dropped almost three months before the scheduled invasion of Kyushu and while the Japanese were trying desperately to get out of the war, has suggested to some that the bombing of Hiroshima had a deeper purpose than the desire to end the war quickly. This purpose, it is claimed, was nothing less than a desire to forestall Soviet intervention into the Far Eastern war. Else why this necessity for speed? Certainly nothing in the military situation seemed to call for such hasty action. But if the purpose was to forestall Soviet intervention, then there was every reason for speed. And even if the Russians could not be kept out of the war, at least they would be prevented from making more than a token contribution to victory over Japan. In this sense it may be argued that the bomb proved a success, for the war ended with the United States in full control of Japan.

This theory leaves several matters unexplained. In the first place, the Americans did not know the exact date on which the Soviet Union would declare war but believed it would be within a week or two of August 8. If they had wished to forestall a Soviet declaration of war, then they could reasonably have been expected to act sooner than they did. Such close timing left little if any margin for error. Secondly, had the United States desired above everything else to keep the Russians out, it could have responded to one of several unofficial Japanese overtures, or made the Potsdam Declaration more attractive to Japan. Certainly the failure to put a time limit on the declaration suggests

---

[51] The statement is published in *The New York Times*, August 7, 1945. . . .

that speed was not of the essence in American calculations. Finally, the date and time of the bombing were left to Generals Spaatz and LeMay, who certainly had no way of knowing Soviet intentions. Bad weather or any other untoward incident could have delayed the attack a week or more.

There is reason to believe that the Russians at the last moved more quickly than they had intended. In his conversations with Harry Hopkins in May 1945 and at Potsdam, Marshal Stalin had linked Soviet entry with negotiations then in progress with Chinese representatives in Moscow. When these were completed, he had said, he would act. On August 8 these negotiations were still in progress.

Did the atomic bomb accomplish its purpose? Was it, in fact, as Stimson said, "the best possible sanction" after Japan rejected the Potsdam Declaration? The sequence of events argues strongly that it was, for bombs were dropped on the 6th and 9th, and on the 10th Japan surrendered. But in the excitement over the announcement of the first use of an atomic bomb and then of Japan's surrender, many overlooked the significance of the Soviet Union's entry into the war on the 9th. The first bomb had produced consternation and confusion among the leaders of Japan, but no disposition to surrender. The Soviet declaration of war, though not entirely unexpected, was a devastating blow and, by removing all hope of Soviet mediation, gave the advocates of peace their first opportunity to come boldly out into the open. When Premier Suzuki arrived at the palace on the morning of the 9th, he was told that the Emperor believed Japan's only course now was to accept the Potsdam Declaration. The militarists could and did minimize the effects of the bomb, but they could not evade the obvious consequences of Soviet intervention, which ended all hope of dividing their enemies and securing softer peace terms.

In this atmosphere, the leaders of Japan held a series of meetings on August 9, but were unable to come to agreement. In the morning came word of the fate of Nagasaki. This additional disaster failed to resolve the issues between the military and those who advocated surrender. Finally the Emperor took the unprecedented step of calling an Imperial Conference, which lasted until 3 o'clock the next morning. When it, too, failed to produce agreement the Emperor told his ministers that he wished the war brought to an end. The constitutional significance of this action is difficult for Westerners to comprehend, but it resolved the crisis and produced in the cabinet a formal decision to accept the Potsdam Declaration, provided it did not prejudice the position of the Emperor.

What finally forced the Japanese to surrender? Was it air bombardment, naval power, the atomic bomb or Soviet entry? The United States Strategic Bombing Survey concluded that Japan would have surrendered by the end of the year, without invasion and without the atomic bomb. Other equally informed opinion maintained that it was the atomic bomb that forced Japan to surrender. "Without its use," Dr. Karl T. Compton asserted, "the war would have continued for many months."[52] Admiral Nimitz believed firmly that the decisive factor was "the complete impunity with which the Pacific Fleet pounded Japan," and General Arnold claimed it was air bombardment that had brought Japan to the verge of collapse.[53] But Major-General Claire Chennault, wartime air commander in China, maintained that Soviet entry into the Far Eastern war brought about the surrender of Japan and would have done so "even if no atomic bombs had been dropped."[54]

It would be a fruitless task to weigh accurately the relative importance of all the factors leading to the Japanese surrender. There is no doubt that Japan had been defeated by the summer of 1945, if not earlier. But defeat did not mean that the military clique had given up; the Army intended to fight on and had made elaborate preparations for the defense of the homeland. Whether air bombardment and naval blockade or the threat of invasion would have produced an early surrender and averted the heavy losses almost certain to accompany the actual landings in Japan is a moot question. Certainly they had a profound effect on the Japanese position. It is equally impossible to assert categorically that the atomic bomb alone or Soviet intervention alone was the decisive factor in bringing the war to an end. All that can be said on the available evidence is that Japan was defeated in the military sense by August 1945 and that the bombing of Hiroshima, followed by the Soviet Union's declaration of war and then the bombing of Nagasaki and the threat of still further bombing, acted as catalytic agents to produce the Japanese decision to surrender. Together they created so extreme a crisis that the Emperor himself, in an unprecedented move, took matters into his own hands and ordered his ministers to surrender. Whether any other set of circumstances would have resolved the crisis and produced the final decision to surrender is a question history cannot yet answer.

[52] Compton, "If the Atomic Bomb Had Not Been Dropped," *Atlantic Monthly*, December, 1946, p. 54.
[53] H. H. Arnold, *Global Mission* (New York: Harper, 1949), p. 598. . . .
[54] *The New York Times*, August 15, 1945. . . .

The Korean War

MORTON H. HALPERIN

FOREIGN-POLICY OBJECTIVES

Prior to the outbreak of the Korean War, the United States believed that a major objective of the Soviet Union was to expand the area under its control. Thus, in responding to the North Korean attack—which had not been anticipated—American objectives were developed in the framework of the belief that the attack was part of a general plan for expansion and perhaps a prelude to general war. The United States sought to prevent the success of this Communist attempt to expand by the use of force in the belief that allowing the Soviets to succeed in Korea would encourage aggression elsewhere. General Omar Bradley expressed this purpose at the MacArthur hearings in describing Korea as "a preventive limited war aimed at avoiding World War III."[1] President Harry Truman later described his objectives in intervening in the Korean War in similar terms:

> Communism was acting in Korea just as Hitler, Mussolini, and the Japanese had acted ten, fifteen, and twenty years earlier. I felt certain that if South Korea was allowed to fall Communist leaders would be emboldened to override nations closer to our own shores. If the Communists were permitted to force their way into the Republic of Korea without opposition from the free world, no small nation would have the courage to resist threats and aggression by stronger Communist neighbors. If this was allowed to go unchallenged it would mean a third world war, just as similar incidents had brought on the second world war.[2]

The defense of Korea was partly motivated by the feeling that the action was necessary to convince the West Europeans that the United States would come to their aid. The Administration was wary of committing its military power, thereby leaving itself exposed to Soviet

From *Limited War in the Nuclear Age* by Morton H. Halperin, pp. 39–58. Reprinted by permission of the author. Some footnotes have been omitted.
[1] Hearings before the Committee on Armed Services and the Committee on Foreign Relations, *Military Situation in the Far East*, U.S. Senate, 82nd Congress, 1st Session, 1951, five parts, p. 154.

[2] Harry S. Truman, *Memoirs*, Vol. II: *Years of Trial and Hope*. Garden City, N.Y.: Doubleday & Co., 1956, p. 333.

aggression in Europe. During the latter stages of the Korean War, in fact, the major American buildup occurred in Europe and not in the Far East. The Administration was also aware of the danger of splitting the NATO alliance in a dispute over Far Eastern policy. A major objective throughout the war was to prevent adverse repercussions in Europe while using the episode to strengthen NATO and build up its military capability. America's NATO allies, particularly the British, constantly applied pressure on the United States to prevent expansion of the war and to bring it swiftly to a conclusion. Following an almost inadvertent reference by President Truman at a press conference to the possibility of using atomic weapons, British Prime Minister Clement Attlee flew to the United States to confer with Truman and to propose the seeking of a cease fire in Korea to be followed by the admission of Communist China to the United Nations. Partly because the defense effort in Korea was carried on under UN auspices, the United States felt obliged constantly to consult its allies on policy and was influenced by their continuous efforts to halt the expansion of the war and to bring about its conclusion.

Soviet objectives were more closely related to the situation in the Far East. The Soviets were interested in the capture of South Korea for its own sake and probably expected a relatively quick and easy North Korean victory. In addition, the Soviets probably hoped to prevent Japan's alignment with the Western powers. Allen Whiting has suggested the nature of the Soviet Far Eastern objective:

> In view of the multiple pressures directed at Japanese foreign policy, the Communist leaders may have conceived the Korean War as serving ends beyond the immediate control of the peninsula. Military victories in Taiwan and Korea could be heralded as ushering in the Communist era in Asia, and as demonstrating the impotence of America's "puppets," Chiang Kai-shek and Syngman Rhee. The resultant effect upon Japan might swing opportunistic groups behind existing neutralist opposition to Yoshida and prevent his supporting American policy.[3]

This interpretation of Soviet strategy in the Korean War was offered by John Foster Dulles right after the North Korean attack. Dulles, who was at the time the State Department planner for the Japanese Peace Treaty, suggested that the Korean attack may have been motivated in part by a desire to block American efforts to make Japan a full member of the free world. He conjectured also that the attack may have been ordered because the Communists could not tolerate the "hopeful, attractive Asiatic experiment in democracy" that was under way in South Korea.[4]

[3] Allen S. Whiting, *China Crosses the Yalu: The Decision to Enter the Korean War.* (New York: Macmillan Co., 1960), p. 37.
[4] *New York Times*, July 2, 1950.

The Chinese objectives in entering the Korean War were also based on general political considerations, but of a defensive nature. According to Whiting the Chinese also hoped to influence the course of United States-Japanese relations. Moreover they were worried about the loss of prestige they would suffer if they allowed the Western "imperialists" to march unhindered to their borders. And they were perhaps most concerned with the beneficial effects of United Nations success in Korea on the many opponents of the Communist regime still active and on Taiwan. Whiting concluded:

> In sum, it was not the particular problems of safeguarding electric-power supplies in North Korea or the industrial base in Manchuria that aroused Peking to military action. Instead, the final step seems to have been prompted in part by general concern over the range of opportunities within China that might be exploited by a determined, powerful enemy on China's doorstep. At the least, a military response might deter the enemy from further adventures. At the most, it might succeed in inflicting sufficient damage to force the enemy to compromise his objectives and to accede to some of Peking's demands. Contrary to some belief, the Chinese Communist leadership did not enter the Korean War either full of self-assertive confidence or for primarily expansionist goals.[5]

The Chinese apparently entered the war with the aim of saving at least some of North Korea. Their minimal objective was to preserve the identity of Communist North Korea rather than its total territorial integrity.

In an effort to secure the political effects discussed, American battlefield objectives and war-termination conditions underwent considerable fluctuation during the course of the war. When the United States first intervened, its objective was simply to restore peace and the South Korean border. Very early in the war and after the Chinese intervention, the United States considered a total withdrawal from Korea.[6] Later its battlefield objective expanded to include the unification of Korea. But in the end, the United States accepted a truce line which closely approximated the *status quo ante*. As Richard Neustadt has pointed out, Truman's original decision to seek the unification of Korea failed to take into account the political-effects objectives that the United States was pursuing, and in the end the recognition of this forced the abandonment of the unification effort.

> Had the unification of Korea been Truman's dearest object, its announcement as a war aim would have been another matter. But it was among the least of the objectives on his mind. In July and August 1950, in

⁵ Whiting, *op. cit.*, p. 159.
⁶ Courtney Whitney, *MacArthur: His Rendezvous with History*. New York: Alfred A. Knopf, 1956, pp. 429–431, 438.

December after Chinese intervention, in his struggles with MacArthur, and thereafter through his last two years of office, his behavior leaves no doubt about the many things he wanted more than that. He wanted to affirm that the UN was not a League of Nations, that aggression would be met with counterforce, that "police actions" were well worth their cost, that the "lesson of the 1930's" had been learned. He wanted to avoid "the wrong war, in the wrong place, at the wrong time," as General Bradley put it— and any "War," if possible. He wanted NATO strengthened fast, both militarily and psychologically. He wanted the United States rearmed without inflation, and prepared, thereafter, to sustain a level of expenditure for military forces and for foreign aid far higher than had seemed achievable before Korea.[7]

Once the Soviets recognized that they could not easily secure their objective of demonstrating American weakness and unwillingness to use force, they seemed to have abandoned the battlefield objective of capturing all of Korea. They may have been willing to accept an end to the war with part or perhaps even all of North Korea in Western hands, and ultimately settled for a virtual restoration of the *status quo ante*.

RISK OF CENTRAL WAR

The Korean War was fought before the era of intercontinental ballistic missiles and fusion weapons. Thus, while both sides could have expanded the war quickly and decisively, there was not the danger that now exists of a sudden unleashing of nuclear missiles which within an hour could destroy a large part of both the United States and the Soviet Union.

Even without this threat of a mutually devastating strategic exchange, the danger of a world war was nevertheless present, and both sides seem to have been determined to prevent its occurrence. Truman has reported that the major American aim in Korea was to prevent a third world war. The Russian decision to remain out of the war seemed to be partly motivated by a fear of igniting a global war. In this situation where neither side could gain a decisive advantage by going first, both sides seemed to recognize that, no matter who started the global war, both would suffer major losses. Though the United States could have attacked the Soviet Union with its very limited stockpile of atomic weapons, it probably could not have presented a Soviet ground attack in Western Europe which might have resulted in Communist domination of the European continent. The Soviets had almost no capacity to attack the United States and could not have prevented an American attack on the Soviet Union. Though both sides avoided forcing the other into starting a global war, neither was

[7] Richard E. Neustadt, *Presidential Power: The Politics of Leadership*. New York: John Wiley and Sons, 1960, p. 126.

constantly concerned with the possibility of "preemption" by its adversary.

The United States, however, was concerned that the Korean War should not lead it to expend those military capabilities which were considered an important deterrent to general war. In Korea the United States was employing the troops and the matériel which it felt were necessary to deter general war. At the MacArthur hearings, Air Force General Vandenburg rejected a senator's suggestion that the United States should commit a major part of the American Air Force to the Korean War effort. He argued instead that the United States must get a cease fire

> without endangering that one potential that we have which has kept the peace so far, which the United States Air Force; which, if utilized in a manner to do what you are suggesting, would [sic], because of attrition and because the size of the Air Force is such and the size of the air force industry is such that we could not still be that deterrent to [general] war which we are today.[1]

Soviet action during the war, including the failure to commit combat forces, suggests that they shared with the United States the desire to avoid a global war.

IMAGES OF THE ROLE OF FORCE

The North Korean attack on South Korea suggested the willingness of the Communists to seek a limited objective by a limited use of force. The Soviets probably intended to seize South Korea with the use of North Korean forces and then to halt their military operations. When the United States intervened, they recognized their miscalculation of American intentions, but proceeded on the assumption that American intervention need not lead to world war. The attack into South Korea, moreover, seems to have been motivated by the Soviet compulsion to fill power vacuums. In view of the specific United States declaration that South Korea was outside its defense perimeter, the Soviets reasonably could have counted on a quick and easy victory by the North Koreans. But, while Communist conduct during the war reflected a doctrine that included the limited use of military force and limited objectives, neither the Chinese nor the Russians seemed to have any idea of the optimum methods of communicating intentions and capabilities to the other side in the course of such a war.

American images of the role of force, on the other hand, seem to have been much less hospitable to the limitation of warfare. It would appear that the United States had not foreseen the possibility of Soviet

---

[1] *Military Situation in the Far East, op. cit.,* p. 1385.

military action in South Korea or any other local area unconnected with a general Soviet military offensive. The result was the American decision not to prepare for the defense of South Korea in view of the low estimate of its value in a general war. Thus the decision of June 1950 to defend South Korea was not based on a reestimate of South Korea's military importance, but on recognition that something had occurred for which American military doctrine had not been prepared. In making its policy decisions throughout the war, the United States was operating without any general theoretical notions of the nature of local war in the atomic age, and its decisions were probably affected by the lack of such theory.

Each side's image of the other's intentions influenced its decisions. The Soviets clearly underestimated the likelihood of American intervention. In the Soviet view American action in withdrawing its troops from Korea and the American declarations that it would defend South Korea only as part of its United Nations obligations had meant that the United States would not in fact defend South Korea. The Soviets failed to anticipate the partly moral and partly political American reaction to aggression. They were insensitive to the importance that the United States would attach to repelling "illegal" aggression, as opposed to less clear-cut violations of international law.

The American decision to intervene in Korea and the subsequent decisions were also based on and influenced by estimates of Soviet intentions.[9] In assessing the motives of the North Korean attack, American policy makers gave consideration and, to some extent, credence to five different interpretations, as follows:

1. The "diversionary move" interpretation. In view of the number of other areas, particularly Western Europe, that appeared more militarily significant than South Korea, the North Korean attack was seen as a diversionary move, aimed to draw American resources away from the areas where they were most important. Truman reports that he shared this view in part and was determined not to leave Europe vulnerable to Soviet aggression.

2. The "soft-spot probing" interpretation. By this image of Soviet doctrine, the Soviet compulsion to fill power vacuums had led to the attack on South Korea which had been abandoned by the United States and which was clearly incapable of defending itself.

3. The "testing" interpretation. This was the view that seemed to influence most Truman's image of the North Korean attack. It recalled the progress of Hitler's aggressive moves and asserted that the

[9] This discussion of the American image of Soviet doctrine is based on Alexander L. George, "American Policy-Making and the North Korean Aggression," *World Politics*, VII (January 1955), pp. 209–232.

North Korean attack should be seen as a prelude to attacks in other areas if that aggression were allowed to succeed. This view differed from the "soft-spot probing" interpretation in its assumption that the Communists' success in Korea would encourage them to attempt aggression in the other areas where Western defense capabilities were far stronger. In short the purpose of the Korean attack was to probe the firmness of Western intentions, and not simply to fill a power vacuum.

4. The "demonstration" interpretation. By this interpretation, the Soviets were mainly concerned with demonstrating their own strength and American weakness in order to promote, on a long-term basis, important shifts in political allegiance throughout the world.

5. The "Soviet-Far-East-strategy" interpretation. This interpretation put emphasis on the idea, already discussed, that the Soviets hoped to prevent the entrance of Japan into the Western camp and to pave the way for further Communist expansion in the Far East.

. . . The inclination of American policy makers toward the "testing" interpretation of Soviet doctrine—in which the Korean attack was equated with Hitler's early expansionist moves—may have reinforced the likelihood that the United States would intervene in Korea. If the "soft-spot probing" interpretation of Soviet conduct had been accepted instead, the United States might have been more prone to cede South Korea while taking steps to prevent the existence of power vacuums elsewhere. The belief that successful aggression would embolden the Soviets made the defense of South Korea seem crucial.

DOMESTIC POLITICAL PRESSURES

During the Korean War the Truman administration continued to pursue its domestic political goals. Despite the war there was politics-as-usual on both sides of the political fence. The President was constantly concerned with promoting his Fair Deal program, consolidating the position of the Democratic Party, strengthening his northern and western liberal support in Congress, and calming the political crises raised by such men as Senator Joseph McCarthy. Nor was the Administration immune to criticism from the Republican Party, which felt that it was possible, necessary, and desirable to attack the Administration's conduct as well as to question the basic concept of limiting war.

After the MacArthur hearings, a Republican minority report declared:

> We believe that a policy of victory must be announced to the American people in order to restore unity and confidence. It is too much to expect

that our people will accept a limited war. Our policy must be to win. Our strategy must be devised to bring about decisive victory.[10]

These few sentences suggest a number of important assumptions about the nature of wartime politics. The first is the notion that the unity of the American people can be achieved only with a declaration that victory is the goal. A further implication is that, after such a declaration, the method of achieving a battlefield victory becomes a "military" problem that is beyond the realm of partisan domestic politics. On the other hand, once the government admits that there are other political considerations that affect and moderate the goal of a strictly military victory, then, according to this Republican statement, it is legitimate to criticize the particular policy adopted. Unity will come only when the country is asked to back an absolute goal. If there is no such goal, then the opposition has a duty to examine and critically appraise the war effort.

Congress, as a whole, also felt itself free to criticize. The hearings into the firing of General Douglas MacArthur were striking in that they required the Administration, *during the war,* to justify its conduct and to explain what it hoped to accomplish in the war and how the war was being conducted, as well as to explicate a host of particulars which must have been of as much interest to the Communists as they were to the senators across the table. Actually the Chinese and the Russians. However, the senators' questions at hearings provided a unique and invaluable opportunity for the Administration to communicate what it wanted to communicate to this hearing did not have that motivation. Congress forced the Administration to discuss its strategy and objectives during the war without any apparent consideration of the effect this would have on the American war effort.

The quotation from the report of the Republican senators also reflects the then still strong American opposition to fighting a local war. The Senators stated flatly that the American people would not accept a strategy of limiting war, and indicated their rejection of the strategy as well. The implication is that during a local war the American government will be subjected to attacks from the political opposition, from Congress, and from public citizens on two grounds: the legitimacy of fighting such a war and the particular strategy employed in the war.

The general public seems to have shared the Republican senators' dissatisfaction with the course of the Korean War, at least in its later stages. On the other hand, the public apparently approved the decision of the Eisenhower administration to end the war short of victory as it had approved the initial decision to intervene. The public's

---

[10] *Military Situation in the Far East, op. cit.,* p. 3590.

frustration with the continuing war probably added to the margin of Eisenhower's victory in 1952; his ending the war enhanced the Republican image as the party of peace and increased the Eisenhower plurality in 1956. The Korean War does not seem to have had a major or lasting impact on popular political attitudes.[11] In this respect, American political leaders seem to have overestimated the effect of the war on the voting public. Korea is taken as demonstrating—as to some extent it did—that extended local wars which cannot be decisively won are not popular with the American public. Leading the United States into a major local war or expanding the war without securing a clear victory is likely to be perceived as a political liability; ending a war on almost any terms may be a political asset.

All these domestic pressures undoubtedly influenced the manner in which the Truman administration conducted its Korean operations, both by hampering its freedom of action and by increasing the costs of various actions.

ATOMIC WEAPONS

The most dramatic limit on the Korean War was that neither side used its atomic weapons. According to Brodie there were four reasons why these weapons were not used by the United States:[12]

1. The Joint Chiefs of Staff and civilian policy makers continued to feel that the war in Korea was basically a Soviet feint. There was, therefore, a strong case for conserving the then relatively limited stockpile of atomic weapons for the principal war which, they thought, would come in Europe. Their fear was not that the employment of nuclear weapons would lead to an expansion of the war and a Soviet attack on Europe, but rather that Korea was deliberately designed as a decoy to get the United States to exhaust its nuclear stockpile and conventional military resources so that the Soviets could later attack with impunity in Europe. It was the desire, then, to save resources and not the fear of provoking the enemy that was one of the main causes of the American decision not to use nuclear weapons in Korea.

2. American policy was also affected by the reports of local Air Force commanders that there were no suitable targets for atomic weapons in Korea. While the impact of this view was considerable, it apparently reflected an uninformed attitude about the possible uses of atomic weapons. Commanders in the field came to think, for example, that atomic bombs were of little use against bridges, a belief which Brodie explained as follows:

[11] Angus Campbell et. al., *The American Voter.* New York: John Wiley and Sons, 1960, pp. 49, 50, 527, 546, 555.
[12] Bernard Brodie, *Strategy in the Missile Age.* Princeton, N.J.: Princeton University Press, 1959.

This odd idea probably resulted from a mis-reading of the results at Hiroshima and Nagasaki. Some bridges were indeed badly damaged at those places and some were not, but for the latter it was generally forgotten that a bridge only 270 feet from ground zero at Hiroshima was actually 2,100 feet from the point of explosion, and also that it received its blast effect from above rather than from the side.[13]

Nuclear weapons were still relatively new and had not been extensively tested, and it is probable that commanders in the field were too busy to search out potential targets for nuclear weapons.

3. American allies, particularly the British, were strongly and emotionally opposed to the use of atomic weapons in the Korean War. This pressure from allies strengthened America's own anxieties and moral doubts about again using these weapons.

4. A subsidiary reason for the failure to use atomic weapons in the Korean War was the fear of the retaliatory employment by the Soviets of the few atomic weapons in their possession against Pusan or Japan, despite the American near monopoly of these weapons. Brodie doubts, however, whether this fear played a conscious part in the relevant decisions.

The first two motives just discussed will not be important in the future. The American stockpile of tactical nuclear weapons is now so great that military commanders may urge their use precisely because they are a nonscarce military resource, and certainly no argument can be made that they should not be used because they are scarce. Military officers now have a much better understanding of the capabilities of nuclear weapons, which, moreover, now come in much smaller packages. Thus it will be clear to military commanders that there would be suitable targets for their use in any conceivable future major limited war. While we can expect continued pressure from our allies against the use of nuclear weapons, certain allies might advocate their use in some situations. There will, however, be other international political pressures—for example, from the uncommitted or neutral states—against nuclear weapons, and the possibility of a Soviet nuclear response will be a much more important determinant of the decision.

We know much less about the details of the Russian decision not to use atomic weapons in Korea. The Russians seemed determined not to supply any matériel to the forces fighting in Korea which could clearly be labeled as having been supplied by them after the war began. This would certainly be the case with atomic weapons.[14] In addition, the

---

[13] *Ibid.,* p. 319n.
[14] It was also true, however, of the MIGs which the Soviets supplied probably with Russian pilots.

Soviet stockpile of such weapons was so small that its use in a localized military encounter might have seemed wasteful.

The limit observed by both sides seems not to have resulted from an attempt—or even an awareness of the need—to bargain with the enemy. However the Soviets were probably more restrained than the United States by the fear that the initiation of nuclear attacks would be met by a response in kind.[15]

The Chinese Communists seem genuinely to have feared the possibility of the American use of atomic weapons when they intervened in the Korean War. According to Whiting the Chinese felt that a nuclear response was a real possibility; intervention was considered risky and every effort was made to delay it and to minimize its consequences. The extent of this Chinese concern was reflected both in its shelter-building program and in domestic Chinese Communist propaganda. But Peking was reassured by the three-week testing period of relatively small Chinese intervention which revealed that United States aircraft, though authorized to bomb the Korean ends of the Yalu bridges, were forbidden to venture into Chinese territory.

The background of the limit on the use of atomic weapons in the Korean War, then, suggests a failure of both sides to understand what the other side was likely to do and what the other side's fears and goals were. It also suggests that, to a large extent, the determination of limits is based on considerations other than those that result from the battlefield interaction. Some of the other limiting points established in the war reveal the same pattern.

CHINESE INTERVENTION

One of the major expansions of the Korean War was the decision of the United Nations Command to cross the thirty-eighth parallel. This decision was based partly on the military consideration that one could not stand by and allow the enemy forces to regroup for renewed attack just beyond the border, but also on political grounds—when the battlefield conditions changed in its favor, the United States decided to pursue the unification of Korea by military means. In crossing the parallel the United States was aware of the risk that it might trigger Chinese Communist intervention, and tried by reassuring statements to prevent it. But it apparently underestimated the Chinese reaction and, at the same time, failed to develop a concurrent strategy which, by retaliatory threats or other sanctions, could succeed in preventing Chinese intervention. As Whiting has suggested the threat to use atomic weapons on the Chinese mainland if the Chinese intervened

[15] However, if the use of atomic weapons had been confined to the Korean theater—that is, if the decision to use these weapons was not coupled with a decision to expand the war in some other way—it is not clear who would have gained from an atomic exchange.

might have been a much more effective deterrent than the attempt to
reassure them that a march to the border did not presage an attack on
mainland China.[16] The threat to use atomic weapons would have involved major political costs for the United States, and the American
government might not have threatened to launch an atomic attack
even if it had recognized that the threat might be effective. Had the
Administration been aware of the fact that the fear of greater expansion might have deterred Chinese intervention, an alternative course
might have been to threaten to expand the war to China with conventional weapons. But even this was not done. In fact, a decision was
made before the intervention that Chinese intervention would not lead
to conventional bombing beyond the Yalu. MacArthur reportedly
believed that this decision had been leaked to the Chinese.[17]

In choosing, instead, to inform the Chinese of its limited objectives, the United States also considered it important to reassure the
Chinese that their hydroelectric plants would not be jeopardized by a
march up to the Yalu. But, as Whiting has pointed out:

> It was widely believed in Western circles that a determining factor in
> Chinese Communist concern over North Korea was the reliance of Man-
> churian industry upon power supplies across the border as well as along the
> Yalu River. This belief prompted explicit reassurances from Western
> spokesmen, both in Washington and at Lake Success, concerning "China's
> legitimate interests" near the frontier. Yet we have seen that Peking ig-
> nored this issue completely in its domestic as well as its foreign communica-
> tions. The absence of propaganda about the protection of the hydroelectric
> installations, despite the need to maximize popular response to mobiliza-
> tion of "volunteers," suggests that this consideration played little if any
> role in motivating Chinese Communist intervention.[18]

In its advance through North Korea, then, the United Nations
Command was attempting to communicate two points to the Chinese
Communists: first, that it was prepared to go up to but not beyond the
Yalu; and second, that it was prepared to respect China's legitimate
interests in the northern regions of North Korea. The United States
sought, therefore, to establish its limited objectives: that United
Nations forces would take all North Korea, that the North Korean
government would cease to exist, but China's legitimate industrial interests would be protected. An effort was made to assure the Chinese
that the capture of North Korea would not be used as a springboard
for an attack into China. The United States assumed that the limits

---

[16] Whiting, *op. cit.,* p. 162. Panikkar, the Indian ambassador in Peking, reported
that the Chinese expected an atomic attack, but were nonetheless prepared to intervene.
[17] Whitney, *op. cit.,* pp. 455–456.
[18] Whiting, *op. cit.,* pp. 151–152.

were ones that the Chinese were interested in, and that these limits would serve to keep the Chinese out of the war. But Chinese interests were different and could only be satisfied by different boundary conditions to the war.

Neustadt argues that the Chinese were not in any way affected by the announcement of the United Nations' aim to destroy the North Korean government.

> To judge from what the Chinese said, and later did, Peking's concern was with MacArthur's military progress, never mind its foreign policy objective. Chinese concern was not confined to anything so simple as a buffer zone along the border; an entity called North Korea, not the border, was at stake (perhaps in roughly the same sense that South Korea, under reverse circumstances, was for Washington). Even had the UN promised restoration of an independent North once all resistance ceased—which, naturally, no one proposed—I know of nothing to suggest that Peking would have withheld intervention. The communist world does not take kindly, it appears, to the dismantling of a member state's facilities for governance: the party and the army. MacArthur's military progress threatened both, no matter what came after. In short, the military risks and diplomatic dangers usually associated with MacArthur's march across the parallel existed independent of the words used in the UN resolution. MacArthur's march was authorized before the words were seen, much less approved, at Lake Success.[19]

Washington was apparently convinced even in retrospect that its declarations did not influence the Chinese decision to enter the war and that no other declaratory policy could have altered the Chinese decision. American policy makers concluded that once the decision was made to cross the thirty-eighth parallel, nothing could be done to affect the Chinese decision. In fact, the State Department reportedly argued in December of 1950 that the Chinese decision to intervene was made prior to the crossing of the thirty-eighth parallel. In one sense, at least, this conclusion may be wrong: the Chinese position might have been altered by threats to expand the war with the use of atomic weapons against China. Moreover it is by no means certain that the Chinese were concerned with the preservation of the total territorial integrity of North Korea. As Whiting suggests an American commitment to advance only part way up the peninsula—that is, to permit the maintenance of the North Korean government in some part of its territory—might have been sufficient to deter the Chinese entrance into the war.

---

[19] Neustadt, *op. cit.*, p. 125.

> Neither before nor during the first three months of war [Whiting wrote]
> did the degree of interest in Pyongyang evinced by Peking warrant accept-
> ance at face value of its concern for a "just" peace, based upon the *status
> quo ante bellum.*
> This is not to say that the Chinese Communist leadership was prepared
> to accept with equanimity the total defeat of North Korea. As a minimal
> goal, intervention must have been attempted to preserve an entity iden-
> tifiable as the DPRK, and to prevent unification of all Korea under U.N.
> supervision. The late date of Chinese Communist entry into the war sug-
> gests that it was the political importance of the North Korean government,
> rather than its territorial integrity, that was at stake. Although intervention
> was officially predicated upon U.N. crossing of the thirty-eighth parallel,
> no Chinese People's Volunteers and Democratic People's Republic of
> Korea defense lines were established during the August-October period,
> not even to protect Pyongyang. To Peking, a "just" Korean peace was not
> an end in itself but rather a means towards fulfilling other related goals of
> policy.[20]

Thus, even after the crossing of the thirty-eighth parallel, Chinese
intervention might have been prevented had the United States acted
differently. Although trying to impose limits on expansion, the United
States failed to grasp adequately either the reasons that the Chinese
felt intervention was necessary or the threats that might have deterred
their intervention. Both sides expanded the war, the United Nations
by crossing the thirty-eighth parallel and the Chinese by entering the
war. Each side failed to convey to the other the kind of counteraction
to be expected which might have deterred expansion. China attempted
to prevent the crossing of the thirty-eighth parallel by declaring her
intention to intervene, but this intention, relayed by the Indian
ambassador, was not taken seriously by the United Nations Command. The United Nations sought to prevent the Chinese entrance,
not be threatening a further expansion but by attempting to satisfy the
Chinese security interests that, it was assumed, might lead her to enter
the war.

PORTS AND TROOPS

Despite the fact that United States planes, taking off from airfields
in South Korea and Japan and from aircraft carriers, consistently
bombed targets in North Korea, the Communists engaged in almost
no bombing south of the thirty-eighth parallel. This was one of the
major asymmetries of the war both from a legalistic point of view and
in terms of interfering with the military operations of the enemy. Both
sides apparently devoted considerable attention to the question of
what targets to attack, and a variety of motives affected the relevant
decisions.

[20] Whiting, *op. cit.,* pp. 155–156.

The American decision to bomb targets in North Korea was made prior to the commitment of American ground troops in June 1950. A month later permission was given to bomb industrial targets in North Korea, but the use of incendiary bombs was not allowed because of the civil damage that would have resulted. The Air Force was not authorized to bomb areas close to the Soviet and Chinese borders. Rashin was the single industrial center within the forbidden area and it was the only industrial target in North Korea which was not destroyed by mid-September when an end to strategic bombing was ordered by the Joint Chiefs. Not until June 1952 were attacks on the hydroelectric plants in North Korea authorized; within two weeks almost 90 percent of the North Korea power capacity was destroyed.[21]

American attacks on targets in North Korea steadily expanded. The attacks were aimed at affecting the immediate military situation. The restraints observed had several motives: (1) to avoid extensive civilian destruction considered undesirable on both humanitarian and propaganda grounds; (2) to avoid a spillover of the war into China or the Soviet Union (the spillover into China prior to her entry into the war probably did not have a major impact on Chinese policy, but the incursion did create propaganda and political difficulties); (3) to avoid damaging, in the case of the hydroelectric plants, targets considered vital to the Chinese so as to avoid their entrance into the war, presumably in retaliation.

The Communists exercised far greater restraint on their air forces. Except for a few night "heckling" attacks from small biplanes in the spring of 1951 no air attacks were made on any targets in South Korea. The Communist restraint was not the result of the absence of inviting military targets. The port of Pusan was an extremely inviting target for bombardment and mining. It was the key to the American logistic effort and frequently was lighted up all night. American logistic convoys and troops in the field also could have been hampered by air attacks. A number of factors seem to have influenced the Communist decision not to respond in kind to United Nations air attacks on North Korea:

1. The Communists might have believed that it would have been very difficult, if not impossible, for the United Nations to continue its operations in Korea if Pusan came under heavy attack, and that, once the United Nations committed itself to the defense of South Korea, it was no longer in a position to accept complete withdrawal. Therefore, if attacks on logistic lines made impossible the continued conduct of an effective ground war in Korea, the United States might have been forced to engage in strategic strikes against the Chinese, if not the

Russian, homeland.[22] If the Communists found this supposition credible, they may have concluded that, once their initial grab for South Korea failed, they could not afford to do anything that would lead to their complete control over South Korea.[23] They may have recognized that American confinement of the war to the Korean peninsula was dependent on her ability to fight there effectively.

2. In order to avoid attacks on Chinese air bases just north of the Yalu, Red airmen were not allowed to attack United Nations positions from these bases. Although the Communists were permitting the United States the sanctuary of bases in Japan and on aircraft carriers, they apparently were afraid that they would not be granted a similar sanctuary for bombing operations. United States planes managed to keep the North Korean airfields out of commission almost continuously throughout the war. Thus, given that the Chinese limited the use of their fields to staging operations and to fighter planes, the Communists were incapable of bombing operations.

3. There is some evidence to suggest that Soviet pilots constituted a significant part of the "Chinese" air force during the Korean War.[24] If this is true the explanation for target restraint may have been the desire to avoid the capture of Soviet airmen. This proof of direct Soviet involvement in the war would at the least have been politically damaging and, from a Soviet point of view, might have created an intolerable risk of American retaliation.

By the end of the war the United States was exercising almost no target restraint in North Korea and the Communists were doing no bombing in South Korea. Each side was guided by a complex series of motives and incentives. However, despite the asymmetry of the actions, there is nothing to suggest that either side treated its decisions on targeting as being closely related to, affected by, or likely to affect, the opponent's decisions on these questions.

EXPANSION AND LIMITATION

Decisions on expanding the United Nations operations resulted from the rejecting or approving of the field commanders' proposals by the Joint Chiefs of Staff or civilian officials. In some cases, particularly on the question of using atomic weapons, the military never

---

[22] The United States had secured British concurrence to bomb bases in China in the event of heavy air attacks from Chinese bases on United Nations troops (*H. C. Debs.,* 5th Series, CDXCVI, 970, Feb. 26, 1952) and this was probably communicated to the Chinese. However, Truman reported that he was convinced that Russia would come in if Manchurian bases were bombed.

[23] This thesis implies that the Chinese would not have driven the United Nations forces off the Korean peninsula by ground action even if they had the capability. There is no evidence to substantiate or invalidate this point.

[24] Futrell, *op. cit.,* pp. 370, 651–652.

made the request, and so, in some sense, no decision was made. On three occasions General MacArthur was refused his requests: to employ Chinese Nationalist troops, to impose a naval blockade on China, and to bomb bases and supply lines in China. But a number of MacArthur's requests for permission to expand the war were approved. These included the commitment of American ground forces, the Inchon offensive, and the crossing of the thirty-eighth parallel.

President Truman states that the National Security Council recommended the consideration of three factors relevant to the decision of whether to go on the offensive: action by the Soviet Union and the Chinese Communists, the views of friendly members of the United Nations, and the risk of general war.[25] These and other decisions were also influenced by American doctrine as well as by domestic political pressures. The balancing of the factors varied from decision to decision, but all played a role in the major decisions to limit or expand the war.

Much less is known about the Communist decision-making process or the factors which influenced their decisions to limit or expand the war. The initial decision to keep the Chinese out of the war seems to have been based largely on domestic conditions in China, particularly the desire of the Chinese to implement their program of economic growth and development, and their desire to avoid military entanglements at a time when they had not yet consolidated their hold over their own country.[26] The reasons for the Russians' abstention from open intervention in the war are less clear. The Soviets were determined not to do anything that directly labeled them as participants; they did not publicize the participation of any Russian "volunteers" in the war, nor provide any atomic capability, although they did supply large amounts of conventional military equipment. One likely explanation is the Russian fear that intervention would lead to general war. The United States had the capability of inflicting great destruction on the Soviet homeland with its stock of atomic weapons, while the Soviets had no capability of directly attacking the United States, although they might have been able to capture a large part of Western Europe with ground forces. Thus the Soviets, aware of their inferior strategic position, were probably determined to keep out of the war and to provide no excuse for a direct American attack on the Soviet Union.

Each side apparently made its decisions to limit the war for different reasons and with minimal attention to the battlefield interaction. In addition the two sides observed very different limits. What the United States did in North Korea was quite different from what the

---

[25] Truman, op. cit., p. 359.

[26] It was probably based also on the belief that the United States would not intervene and that the North Korean army would capture all of South Korea. . . .

Communists did in South Korea, but the Chinese used a much greater percentage of their gross national product than the United States did. Nevertheless, while the United States used naval vessels and airplanes to bomb troops and airfields within Korea, the Communists did not. The United States engaged in logistical interdiction; the Communists did not. Each side, then, observed its own series of limits and restraints only in some very general way related to, and dependent on, the limits of the other side.

At least a few of the limits were symmetrical. Both sides restricted their military operations almost entirely to Korea, and neither used nuclear weapons. There was lack of symmetry in that all the military targets in North Korea were attacked but most in South Korea were not. The United States attacked the Chinese points of entry—the Yalu bridges; but the Chinese did not attack the United States' points of entry—the ports. Both sides observed a number of what Schelling has called "legalistic" limitations.[27] The United Nations carefully observed both the Chinese and Russian borders and tried to avoid crossing them inadvertently. There was symmetry in the absence of official declaration of war. The United Nations troops participated in the war in a "police action" capacity, and none of the countries involved, including the United States, declared war. The Chinese used "volunteers," and the Russians supplied equipment and presumably technicians, but little manpower for the battle.

In some cases the limits represented a recognition of the battlefield interaction. But the origin of many of the limits observed, and part of the explanation for others, lay not within the dynamics of the war itself, but within the domestic and international context in which the war was fought.

---

[27] Thomas C. Schelling, *Nuclear Weapons and Limited War*. RAND P-1620, Feb. 20, 1959, p. 1.

Essence of Revision: Moscow, Havana,
and the Cuban Missile Crisis

DAVID A. WELCH, JAMES G. BLIGHT, AND BRUCE J. ALLYN

The event referred to as the "Cuban missile crisis" in the United States is called the "Caribbean crisis" in the Soviet Union, and the "October crisis" in Cuba; but in all three countries it is widely acknowledged to have been the single most dangerous episode of the Cold War. Analysis of the crisis has heretofore been one-sided. Although information about the American side of the crisis is relatively plentiful, both Cuba and the Soviet Union have closely guarded the histories of their sides of the event. *Glasnost*, however, has led to a series of unprecedented discussions between East and West on the history and significance of the crisis, culminating in a tripartite conference in Moscow in January 1989. Drawing on the evidence and testimony presented at that conference, at the earlier U.S.-Soviet conference in Cambridge, Massachusetts, in October 1987, and in supplemental interviews, we present here a summary and analysis of the new light that has recently been shed on "all three" crises.

New information and testimony illuminate the longstanding debate about Soviet motives for deploying missiles to Cuba; the meaning, significance, and perceptions of American military activities and covert operations in 1962; the genesis, terms, and conduct of the missile deployment; the operational status of the missiles; decision-making during the early phases of the crisis; the origin of Khrushchev's Turkish missile trade proposal; the U-2 shootdown of October 27; the diplomacy leading to a resolution of the crisis; the sources of Khrushchev's sense of urgency at the climax of the confrontation; and the acute tensions in Soviet-Cuban relations

From *International Security*, Winter 1989/90 (Vol. 14, No. 3), ©1989 by the President and Fellows of Harvard College and of the Massachusetts Institute of Technology. Reprinted by permission of MIT Press, Cambridge, Massachusetts. Some footnotes have been omitted.

The authors gratefully acknowledge the assistance of Graham T. Allison, Jr., Jorge Domínguez, Alexander L. George, Joseph S. Nye, Jr., Scott D. Sagan, Georgy Shakhnazarov, and the staffs of the Center for the Study of the Americas (Havana), the Institute of World Economy and International Relations (Moscow), and the National Security Archive (Washington, D.C.). The authors also thank the Carnegie Corporation of New York, George Keros, The John D. and Catherine T. MacArthur Foundation, the Ploughshares Fund, and Carl Sloane.

immediately following its resolution. We organize our treatment by topic—and, where possible, in chronological order—on the assumption that the reader will be familiar with the main events of the crisis itself. We highlight those areas in which recent discussions have most significantly advanced our understanding of the event.

MOTIVES FOR THE SOVIET DEPLOYMENT

The Soviet decision to deploy medium- and intermediate-range ballistic missiles (MRBMs and IRBMs) in Cuba appears to have been a response to three main concerns: first, the perceived need to deter an American invasion of Cuba and prevent the destruction of the Cuban revolution; second, the perceived need to redress the gross imbalance in deliverable strategic nuclear weapons that favored the United States; and third, the desire, born of national pride and prestige, to counter American deployments of nuclear weapons on the Soviet periphery, by exercise of the Soviet Union's "equal right" to deploy its own nuclear missiles on territory adjacent to the United States. According to recent Soviet testimony, the first and second appear to have been the most important motivations, though there is disagreement on the proper assignments of weight to each. Interestingly, Soviets have continued without exception to deny any direct connection between the Cuban missile crisis and the unstable Berlin situation; in Moscow, Andrei Gromyko added his voice to the chorus.

The desire to deter an American invasion of Cuba emerged shortly after the crisis itself as the official Soviet rationale for the deployment. Most Western commentators have dismissed or discounted this motivation, however, because it seemed calculated to justify the public terms on which the crisis was ultimately resolved—the missiles in Cuba were withdrawn in return for an American pledge not to invade the island. But several well-placed Soviets, including Andrei Gromyko, Aleksandr Alekseev, Sergei Khrushchev, and Sergo Mikoyan, have insisted that fears of an American invasion were in fact uppermost in Khrushchev's mind. These fears were grounded in what appeared to be a consistent and deliberate pattern of American activity designed to subvert and overthrow the regime of Fidel Castro, leading up to and including the use of American military force if necessary.[1]

[1] President Kennedy cut off all diplomatic relations with Cuba in January 1961; he eliminated the Cuban sugar quota in March; and most ominously, he approved the abortive Bay of Pigs invasion in April, in which a group of hastily-trained and poorly-armed Cuban exiles, organized and supported by the Central Intelligence Agency (CIA), sought to trigger an anti-Castro revolt by establishing a beach-head on the southern coast of the island. Though the operation was a dismal failure, it did not dissuade the CIA from pursuing a substantial covert action campaign, code-named "Operation Mongoose," ostensibly intended to bring about the liquidation of the Castro regime. Castro's position began to look especially precarious in January 1962, when, at Punta del Este, Uruguay, the United States managed to persuade the Organization of American States to declare the government of Cuba incompatible

When asked by Khrushchev, Defense Minister Rodion Ya. Malinovsky reportedly informed the Soviet premier that Cuba could resist a full-scale American invasion for three or four days—hardly long enough to send reinforcements. According to Ambassador Alekseev, Khrushchev maintained at meetings with Presidium members that "there was no other path" to save the Cuban revolution than through the installation of nuclear missiles. Thus, Khrushchev may have believed that a deployment of conventional forces to the island as a trip wire would not have sufficed (possibly because of the marginal credibility of any explicit or implicit strategic nuclear threat undergirding it), and that the Soviet Union could not credibly deter an American invasion by threats of retaliation elsewhere.

However, at the Moscow conference, Cuban participants sharply contradicted Khrushchev's analysis in several ways. Though stopping short of insisting that Cuba could have held off a full-scale American attack, Cuban Politburo member Jorge Risquet contended that Cuba could have resisted far longer than three days, and expressed indignation at the estimate attributed to Malinovsky. Sergio del Valle, chief of staff of the Cuban army in 1962, claimed that Cuba had armed and mobilized 270,000 people—double Secretary of Defense Robert McNamara's 1962 estimate.[2] If this is correct, then the five American divisions slated for the invasion under 316 OPLAN would certainly have faced stiffer resistance than the United States anticipated. Even more striking, the Cuban delegation maintained that Fidel Castro's grounds for approving the deploy-

---

with the inter-American system, to ostracize Castro diplomatically, and to agree on measures of collective defense against possible Cuban attempts to export revolution to other countries of the Western hemisphere. When Kennedy declared an embargo on all trade with Cuba in February, all of the pieces appeared to the Cubans to be in place for the expected American move: Cuba had been isolated in the Western Hemisphere diplomatically, militarily, and economically. The CIA's involvement in the Bay of Pigs adventure is elaborately reconstructed in Peter Wyden, *Bay of Pigs: The Untold Story* (New York: Simon and Schuster, 1979). On the extent of CIA activities in Florida aimed at destabilizing the Castro regime, see Joan Didion, *Miami* (New York: Simon and Schuster, 1987), pp. 90–91; and the collection of documents on Operation Mongoose available at the National Security Archive, Washington, D.C. See also Nikita Khrushchev, *Khrushchev Remembers*, trans. and ed. by Strobe Talbott (Boston: Little, Brown, 1974), pp. 492–493. Khrushchev's report to the Supreme Soviet, Dec. 12, 1962, in Ronald Pope, *Soviet Views on the Cuban Missile Crisis: Myth and Reality in Foreign Policy Analysis* (Lanham, Md.: University Press of America, 1982), pp. 71–107; and Sergo Mikoyan's remarks, in David A. Welch, ed., *Proceedings of the Cambridge Conference on the Cuban Missile Crisis*, Oct. 11–13, 1987, CSIA Working Paper 89-2, Center for Science and International Affairs, Harvard University (hereafter CCT), p. 42.

[2] In a later interview, del Valle claimed that the 270,000 armed and mobilized troops were divided into fifty-six existing divisions, which had been brought up to full strength from reserves. Although they varied considerably in size, each division had on average 4800 men, considerably smaller than an American division. Twenty-eight divisions deployed on the western side of the island included some of the largest and strongest, since this was where the first wave of an invasion was expected to land. Authors' interview with Sergio del Valle, May 18, 1989, Havana.

ment differed significantly from Khrushchev's grounds for proposing it. Dismissing the utility of Soviet nuclear missiles in Cuba for deterrence or defense (noting that they served primarily to turn Cuba into a target), Emilio Aragonés, one of the six members of the Cuban Communist Party Secretariat in 1962, claimed that Castro and the Cuban leadership accepted the deployment for two reasons: first, because the missiles would have shifted the global correlation of forces in favor of socialism; and second, because Cuba should accept "its share of the risk," since Cuba owed a debt of gratitude to the Soviet Union for efforts made on its behalf. Although the deployment posed certain risks for Cuba, the Soviet Union had already taken risks in support of the Cuban revolution. Castro himself has made similar statements in the past. It is clear, however, that Cuba's national pride is better preserved by these claims than by the admission that Cuba required assistance from another nation, in the form of a nuclear deterrent, to protect her own sovereignty and independence. In subsequent interviews, both del Valle and Aragonés acknowledged that in 1962, they had been attracted to the idea of the deployment largely because of its potential for deterring an American invasion.[3]

The Cubans' argument at the Moscow conference, however, serves to highlight the link between the deployment of missiles to Cuba and the Soviet desire to redress the strategic nuclear imbalance. General Dimitry Volkogonov, who had reviewed the relevant archival materials, stated at the Moscow conference that in 1962, the Soviet Union had succeeded in deploying only twenty ICBMs capable of reaching the United States, far fewer than the seventy-five hitherto estimated by Western intelligence analysts. Thus the disparity in strategic nuclear weapons appears to have been even greater than was appreciated at the time. A successful Cuban deployment could have more than quadrupled the number of warheads that Soviet missiles could have delivered on the United States.[4] Most Western analysts have assumed that some such cal-

---

[3] Del Valle interview, May 18, 1989; James G. Blight (JGB) and David A. Welch (DAW) interview with Emilio Aragonés, May 19, 1989, Havana. In an interesting inversion of public rationales, Aragonés claimed that "even though it seemed to me that the [Soviets'] main goal of the deployment was to change the correlation of forces, the missiles would have had the effect of protecting Cuba, and so I was very much in favor of the idea."

[4] On October 19, the CIA reported that the Soviet Union was installing twenty-four SS-4 (Soviet designation R-12) MRBM launchers in Cuba—four each at four sites near San Cristóbal, and four at two sites near Sagua la Grande. Each launcher could have been equipped with two missiles, for a possible total of forty-eight MRBMs. Twelve SS-5 (R-14) IRBM launchers were observed under construction, four each at two sites near Guanajay, and four at one site near Remedios, suggesting that twenty-four IRBMs could have been deployed to Cuba (including reloads). With one warhead per missile (25 kt-2 MT yield for the SS-4s, 3-5 MT yield for the SS-5s), seventy-two warheads could have been deployed to Cuba. In such a case, the number of land-based missile warheads capable of reaching the United States would have more than quadrupled, increasing from twenty (the ICBMs in the Soviet Union itself) to ninety-

culation was the primary, though not fully articulated, initial motivation for the deployment of missiles.[5] Even if Khrushchev's chief
concern had been the political problem of preserving a socialist
Cuba, the strategic value of the deployment probably contributed to
the attractiveness of the deployment. . . . In short, different individuals within the Soviet decision-making establishment, and different
branches of the Soviet state, seem to have understood the deployment in different ways, which may have complicated Khrushchev's

---

two (twenty on ICBMs, seventy-two on MRBMs and IRBMs in Cuba). See CIA
memorandum on the construction of missile sites in Cuba, October 19, 1962, National
Security Archive, Washington, D.C. According to General Volkogonov, however, the
deployment consisted of three SS-4 regiments (eight launchers each for a total of
twenty-four) and two SS-5 regiments (eight launchers each for a total of sixteen);
MCT. Raymond Garthoff claims that only one warhead was to be provided per
launcher even though two missiles were assigned to each (to offset reliability
problems). Garthoff, *Reflections on the Cuban Missile Crisis*, 2nd ed. (Washington,
D.C.: Brookings, 1989), p. 20. If this is so, the deployment would have tripled the
number of warheads that Soviet land-based missiles could have delivered promptly
on the United States, from twenty (the ICBMs in the Soviet Union) to sixty (twenty
on ICBMs, forty on MRBMS and IRBMs in Cuba). American intelligence estimated
in 1962 that the Soviets had also deployed 155 cruise and ballistic missiles on
submarines, and approximately 200 long-range bombers. Although these were severely constrained operationally (because of geographical, logistical, and technical
factors), and although they did not represent a serious first-strike threat, they might
have succeeded in delivering some number of nuclear warheads on the United States
in the event of war. The missiles in Cuba, therefore, probably no more than doubled
the number of nuclear weapons of all kinds that the Soviets could have delivered,
though an accurate estimate of this increment is impossible to make. See Scott D.
Sagan, "SIOP-62: The Nuclear War Plan Briefing of President Kennedy," *International Security*, Vol. 12, No. 1 (Summer 1987), pp. 27–28; and Raymond L. Garthoff,
*Intelligence Assessment and Policymaking: A Decision Point in the Kennedy Admin-
istration* (Washington, D.C.: Brookings, 1984), p. 55.
[5] Among those in the West who have viewed the deployment primarily or exclusively
as an attempt to redress the strategic nuclear imbalance are Roger Hilsman, *To Move
a Nation: The Politics of Foreign Policy in the Administration of John F. Kennedy*
(New York: Doubleday, 1967), pp. 200–202; Arnold Horelick, "The Cuban Missile
Crisis: An Analysis of Soviet Calculations and Behavior," *World Politics*, Vol. 16,
No. 3 (April 1964), p. 376; Arnold Horelick and Myron Rush, *Strategic Power and
Soviet Foreign Policy* (Chicago: University of Chicago Press, 1965), p. 141; Michel
Tatu, *Power in the Kremlin: From Khrushchev's Decline to Collective Leadership*,
trans. Helen Katel (London: Collins, 1969), p. 231; and Jerome H. Kahan and Anne
K. Long, "The Cuban Missile Crisis: A Study of Its Strategic Context," *Political
Science Quarterly*, Vol. 87, No. 4 (December 1972), pp. 564–590. Sergei Khrushchev
denied at the Moscow conference that the deployment of missiles to Cuba was a
cost-effective solution to the strategic nuclear imbalance, arguing that stationing
ICBMs on Soviet soil, which required nothing extra in the way of conventional
defenses and involved none of the added expense of dismantling, crating, shipping,
and assembling missiles thousands of miles away, would have been a more sensible
solution. He therefore discounts the strategic nuclear rationale behind the deployment of missiles to Cuba. His argument, however, overlooks the difficulties that the
Soviets were experiencing in producing three-stage long-range rockets. There was
simply no long-range option available in 1962. See Horelick and Rush, *Strategic
Power and Soviet Foreign Policy*, pp. 105–106; and Graham T. Allison, *Essence of
Decision: Explaining the Cuban Missile Crisis* (Boston: Little, Brown, 1971). pp. 20–
21.

task of enlisting support for the terms on which the crisis was ultimately resolved.

There is little doubt that Khrushchev was attracted to the idea of deploying missiles to Cuba at least partly because of its apparent symmetry with the deployment of American Jupiter missiles in Turkey. His speeches in Bulgaria in May, 1962—where, he writes in his memoirs, the idea of the deployment first occurred to him—refer repeatedly and vehemently to the presence of American nuclear missiles so close to the Soviet border. Moreover, Fyodor Burlatsky reports that Yuri Andropov gave him a letter to edit from Khrushchev to Castro, in which Khrushchev emphasized the symmetry between the deployment of missiles in Cuba and the deployment of Jupiters in Turkey. But though this seems to have been on Khrushchev's mind, there is no evidence that it rivaled the other motivations in urgency or importance. It is more likely that the perceived symmetry with the Turkish deployment bolstered, rather than led to, the idea in the first place.[6]

In any retrospective discussion, of course, it is appropriate to ask whether the motivations and contingencies were, in the event itself, well-thought-out in advance. Khrushchev's personality was undoubtedly an important factor. Gromyko acknowledged that "Khrushchev was an emotional man. He had enough emotion for ten people—at least." But, not surprisingly, Gromyko argued that the deployment had been decided upon only after a thorough, careful, "cool-headed" evaluation. Jorge Risquet, on the other hand, expressed some doubt, claiming that "Comrade Khrushchev did not think through all the moves in advance." Anatoly Dobrynin agreed to some extent, stating that there was "improvisation as things unfolded; at least, that is what we felt in the embassy."[7] The discussions at the Moscow conference gave little reason for revising the common wisdom that the venture was, in important respects, ill-conceived and subject to insufficient critical examination.

THE AMERICAN THREAT TO CUBA: PERCEPTION AND MISPERCEPTION

American intentions toward Cuba in 1962 have long been the subject of debate, and continue to be so. The crucial question is whether or not the Kennedy administration intended, at some point, to use American military force to oust Fidel Castro and establish a regime more congenial to American interests. Soviet and Cuban

[6] The supposed symmetry between the two deployments was far from obvious to the members of the Kennedy administration, who noted that the Soviet deployment was much larger than the American deployment; it involved no dual-control arrangements; and, perhaps most importantly, it was undertaken in strict secrecy behind the cloak of deception.

[7] Bruce J. Allyn, David G. Welch, and James A. Blight, eds. *Proceedings of the Moscow Conference on the Cuban Missile Crisis*, Jan. 27–28, 1989, CSIA Working Paper, Center for Science and International Affairs, Harvard University. Hereafter referenced as MCT.

fears that this was the case seem to have played an important part in the decision to deploy nuclear missiles; disavowals of any such intention by former Kennedy administration officials have long been received with skepticism by Soviets, Cubans, and revisionist historians in the United States. More is at stake in the debate than simply the accuracy of the historical record or the reputation of the Kennedy administration. The issue sheds important light on the role of perceptions and misperceptions in the genesis of a crisis.

Former Secretary of Defense Robert McNamara insisted at the Moscow conference that, "If I was a Cuban and read the evidence of covert American action against their government, I would be quite ready to believe that the U.S. intended to mount an invasion."[8] His frankness on this point was welcomed by both the Soviet and Cuban delegations. McNamara insisted, however, that despite the extent of American covert operations against Castro, and despite the preparation of military contingencies in October, 1962, the Kennedy administration did not intend to invade Cuba; that is, no political decision to invade Cuba had been taken, and no serious discussions to consider such an operation had taken place among senior policy-makers. The Cuban and Soviet delegations in Moscow expressed skepticism on this point.

Several publications have called into question the veracity of McNamara's disclaimer. Attention has focused on recently declassified documents that show that the Kennedy administration actively sought to destroy the Castro regime.[9] One memorandum, for example—the "Cuba Project" program review dated February 20, 1962, and signed by Chief of Operations Brigadier General Edward G. Lansdale—specified late October 1962 as the target for Castro's ouster, and suggested that American military force might be required to accomplish that objective.[10] CINCLANT (commander in chief, Atlantic fleet) Admiral Robert L. Dennison's official retrospective history of the crisis records that on October 1, more than two weeks before the missiles were discovered, orders were given to prepare the air strike option, 312 OPLAN, for "maximum readiness" by October 20.[11]

These documents show clearly that the United States was increasingly harassing the government of Fidel Castro, and that the Kennedy administration was actively laying the military groundwork for possible contingencies, such as a discovery of nuclear weapons

---

[8] *MCT.*

[9] See, e.g., James G. Hershberg, "Before the 'Missiles of October': Did Kennedy Plan a Military Strike Against Cuba?" Occasional Paper No. 89-1, Nuclear Age History and Humanities Center, Tufts University, October 1989 (forthcoming in *Diplomatic History*); and Pierre Salinger, "Gaps in the Cuban Missile Crisis Story," *New York Times*, February 5, 1989, p. 4–25.

[10] Lansdale, "Program review memorandum, subject: The Cuba Project, 20 Feb., 1962," National Security Archive, Washington, D.C.

[11] *CINCLANT Historical Account*, p. 39.

in Cuba. This much, both McNamara and McGeorge Bundy concede.[12] However, the stronger claim—that such documents show that the Kennedy administration had actually decided to use American military force against Cuba—is entirely speculative. The evidence suggests otherwise. For example, the tapes of the White House discussions on October 16, immediately following the discovery of the missiles in Cuba, strongly evince a belligerent attitude on the part of the president and his advisers, but nowhere refer to any prior decision to invade Cuba, any established intention to invade Cuba, or even any previous exploration of the desirability of such an invasion.[13] If indeed there had been serious consideration of the possibility, one would expect it to be reflected in those early, formative discussions, because an invasion would have been a comparatively well-formulated option already on the table. Instead, the process of option-formation began from scratch. President Kennedy's reluctance to use more than a display of force during the crisis itself further reinforces doubt that he had harbored an intention to initiate serious military action against Cuba before the discovery of the missiles.

Despite the fact that there is no evidence of intent on the part of the Kennedy administration to invade Cuba prior to the deployment of the missiles, it seems clear that Cuba and the Soviet Union quite understandably applied worst-case analyses to the various covert activities of CIA operatives in Cuba and to the activities of the American military in 1961 and 1962. The Cuban participants at the Moscow conference reported that Cuba had well-placed informants in the American defense and intelligence communities who kept them abreast of the various contingencies under consideration. Ambassador Alekseev explicitly claimed that the Cubans had "precise data" about American plans to invade the island.[14] Although operational plans and operational contingencies are not conclusive evidence of political intentions, they are nevertheless strong evidence of the worst possible case, and were apparently interpreted by Cuban and Soviet intelligence as reflecting a policy decision of the Kennedy administration to invade Cuba and to overthrow Castro. When McNamara explicitly refers to these interpretations as Soviet and Cuban "misperceptions," he correctly points out that mistaken conclusions were drawn from the available evidence. But the United States had provided virtually *no* evidence suggesting otherwise. As current Deputy Foreign Minister Viktor Komplektov

---

[12] Bundy, however, said that he viewed American covert operations against Castro as a "psychological salve," and that he had no expectation that they would succeed in their stated goals. Remarks at a news conference at Harvard University, October 13, 1987.

[13] See Marc Trachtenberg, ed., "White House Tapes and Minutes of the Cuban Missile Crisis," *International Security*, Vol. 10, No. 1 (Summer 1985), pp. 171–194.

[14] *MCT.*

argued at the Moscow conference, "Everything suggested that there *were* intentions." Indeed, it was the avowed policy of the United States to destabilize the Castro regime, and part of that effort involved convincing Cuba of its vulnerability to American attack. The Kennedy administration, therefore, actively promoted the very "misperceptions" that led, in part, to the Soviet decision to deploy nuclear missiles to Cuba.

THE GENESIS, TERMS, AND CONDUCT OF THE DEPLOYMENT

In his memoirs, Khrushchev claims that the idea to deploy nuclear missiles in Cuba first occurred to him when he was in Bulgaria, between May 14 and 20, 1962.[15] But, according to Sergo Mikoyan, Khrushchev had already discussed the idea with First Deputy Premier Anastas I. Mikoyan at the end of April, during a walk in the Lenin Hills. The aim, Khrushchev told Mikoyan, would be to deploy the missiles very rapidly under a cloak of secrecy, in September or October, and to reveal their presence to the U.S. president after the mid-term congressional elections in November, by means of a letter delivered to Kennedy by the Soviet ambassador in Washington, Anatoly Dobrynin.[16]

Gromyko reports that Khrushchev first discussed the idea with him on the flight home from Bulgaria.[17] Soon after his return, Khrushchev assembled a small group to consider the matter; its members included Mikoyan, Gromyko, Malinovsky, Biryuzov, and Secretary of the Central Committee Frol R. Kozlov. Shortly thereafter, the whole Presidium was included in the deliberations.[18]

According to Gromyko, the discussions during the formative phase were candid and exploratory, though Khrushchev was clearly the "dominant" figure.[19] Sergei Khrushchev reports that Anastas Mikoyan expressed strong reservations, cautioning that this was "a very dangerous step."[20] According to Sergo Mikoyan, his father had two misgivings: first, he did not believe Castro would agree, and second, he did not believe it would be possible to install the missiles secretly.[21] The only other member reported to have expressed doubt in Presidium meetings was Otto Kuusinen.

Gromyko reports that he told Khrushchev in May that a deployment of nuclear missiles in Cuba would trigger a "political explosion" in the United States, but Khrushchev seemed bent on the plan.[22] Though it was not characteristic of Gromyko to object to an

[15] Khrushchev, *Khrushchev Remembers*, p. 493.
[16] CCT, p. 42–43.
[17] Andrei A. Gromyko, "Karibskii krizis: o glasnosti teper' i skrytosti togda" (The Caribbean Crisis: on openness now and secrecy then), *Izvestia*, April 5, 1989, p. 5.
[18] *CCT*, p. 43.
[19] *MCT*.
[20] *MCT*.
[21] *CCT*, p. 43.
[22] Gromyko, "Karibskii krizis," p. 5. Alekseev reports that Gromyko told him

idea proposed by Khrushchev, it is quite plausible that he voiced pros and cons of the idea. If his testimony is accurate, then Khrushchev ultimately decided to disregard the cautions of both Mikoyan and Gromyko, two of his advisers who knew American politics best. Aleksandr Alekseev was at that time a Soviet press representative in Cuba who was on very friendly terms with both Fidel Castro and his brother, Minister of Defense Raúl Castro. On Mikoyan's recommendation, Alekseev was urgently recalled to Moscow at the beginning of May and informed that he would be the new ambassador to Havana, replacing Sergei M. Kudryavtsev, whom Castro strongly disliked. Alekseev was officially appointed ambassador effective May 31, by order of the Presidium of the Supreme Soviet on May 7. When Khrushchev returned from Bulgaria, Alekseev was informed of the plan to deploy nuclear missiles to Cuba and was included in the decision-making circle. When Khrushchev asked him how Castro would react to the proposal, Alekseev reports that he expressed grave doubts that Castro would agree.[23] Khrushchev decided to send a special mission to Cuba to find out, and to determine whether the missiles could be installed secretly.

A ten-day Soviet "agricultural mission" traveled to Havana at the very end of May. The mission included Alekseev, Sharif Rashidov, an alternate member of the Presidium, Biryuzov, traveling under the pseudonym "engineer Petrov," and two other rocket specialists named Ushakov and Ageyev. The group arrived in Havana even before Kudryavtsev had been informed of his imminent departure, which indicates the secrecy and urgency surrounding the operation.[24] Upon arrival, Alekseev informed Raúl Castro that "engineer Petrov" was actually the commander of the Strategic Rocket Forces, and a meeting was arranged with Fidel Castro for that same evening. According to Alekseev, Fidel Castro expressed immediate interest in the proposal, and left to confer with the other five members of the Cuban secretariat. Aragonés reports that all five— Raúl Castro, Che Guevara, President Osvaldo Dorticós, Blas Roca, and himself—were unanimously in favor of the idea.[25]

---

privately in August 1962 that he had "strong reservations" about the idea, and that he had expressed them to Khrushchev in private. Authors' interview with Aleksandr Alekseev, April 27, 1989, Moscow; and Alekseev, "Uroki karibskogo krizisa."

[23] Alekseev claims that the reason he thought Castro would not accept the missiles was that he would jeopardize his support in Latin America if he were to be perceived as too tightly bound to the Soviet Union, and that in that meeting Malinovsky, evidently strongly in favor of the plan, took exception to his doubts. Alekseev says in retrospect that he underestimated Castro's internationalism, and he now believes Castro was sincere when he said he would accept the missiles to bolster socialism on the world scale. Alekseev interview.

[24] S. A. Mikoyan, "Karibskii krizis: kakim on viditsia na rasstoianii," (The Caribbean Crisis: how it appears from a distance), *Latinskaya amerika*, No. 1 (1988), p. 70.

[25] Aragonés interview.

Much to Mikoyan's surprise, Biryuzov returned to the Soviet Union with Fidel Castro's agreement and with an optimistic assessment of the chances of deploying the missiles secretly. At a meeting of the Presidium on June 10, Biryuzov reported the results of the negotiations. The Presidium officially ordered the Defense Ministry to develop specific plans for the missile deployment, as well as the deployment of associated air and coastal defense forces.

In early July, a Cuban delegation led by Raúl Castro visited Moscow to discuss Soviet arms shipments to Cuba, and to finalize operational details of the missile deployment. Delegations led by Raúl Castro and Marshal Malinovsky met for two weeks, with Khrushchev himself present at meetings on July 3 and 8. The first step would be to install a network of the latest Soviet SA-2 surface-to-air-missiles (SAMs) around the perimeter of the island, and especially near the MRBM and IRBM sites at San Cristóbal, Sagua la Grande, Guanajay, and Remedios.[26] The first SAMs and supporting equipment for the MRBMs were shipped at the very end of July.

While in Moscow, Raúl Castro and Malinovsky drafted an agreement covering various details of the deployment, including the rights and obligations of the host country and of the Soviet forces building and manning the missile sites. The agreement was a formal treaty with the following terms: (1) the Soviets would at all times have complete custody and control of the nuclear missiles in Cuba (but the exact number of missiles was not specified); (2) the Soviets would be given temporary use of the sites as rocket bases for a period of five years, though the sites themselves would remain sovereign Cuban territory; (3) after five years, there would be a further decision to annul or continue the arrangement; (4) all costs associated with the deployment were to be borne by the Soviet Union; and (5) some SAMs were to be provided to the Cubans, though the SA-2 SAMs would initially be installed, manned, and operated by the Soviets until Cuban forces could be trained to operate and maintain them. Raúl Castro and Malinovsky signed each paragraph of the agreement, and space was provided at the end of the document for the signatures of Fidel Castro and Nikita Khrushchev. But the two leaders, intending to sign it at a public ceremony in Havana in November, never did so.

When Raúl Castro returned from Moscow with a draft of the document in hand, his brother elaborated and modified the wording of the preamble. His amended version declared that the purpose of the agreement was "to provide mutual military assistance" rather than "to save the Cuban revolution," and it strongly affirmed the legality of the deployment.[27] Che Guevara and Emilio Aragonés

---

[26] At the time of the crisis, no IRBMs were present in Cuba, and the first IRBM was not expected to become operational until well into December. Central Intelligence Agency memorandum, "Subject: The Crisis USSR/Cuba," October 27, 1962, National Security Archive, Washington D.C.

[27] *MCT;* and Alekseev interview.

traveled to Moscow at the end of the summer (August 27–September 2) to secure Soviet approval for Castro's changes. While there, they proposed that the agreement be made public immediately, prior to the deployment itself, to remove any pretext for a hostile American reaction. The Cubans warned the Soviet leadership that the situation in the United States was becoming increasingly volatile. Concerned by the prospect that rising suspicions in the United States might eventually lead to war hysteria, they sought to draw international attention to the legality of the deployment. Aragonés reported that they told Khrushchev that there might be "a preventive strike with severe consequences for us" if the Americans were not given adequate opportunity to reconcile themselves to the deployment; but Khrushchev assured the Cubans that there would be no problem. Making the deployment public would be a terrible mistake, Khrushchev insisted; it might precipitate the very invasion the missiles were intended to forestall. And if the Americans did attack Cuba in the meantime, Khrushchev proclaimed, then he would promptly send the Baltic Fleet. Though skeptical of Khrushchev's promise of naval support, the Cubans deferred to Khrushchev's assessment of the Americans, because of the Soviets' greater experience in foreign affairs, and agreed to let the matter drop.[28] At the Moscow conference, the Cuban delegation identified Khrushchev's judgment as a serious mistake.[29]

The Soviet expedition to Cuba was under the overall command of General Issa Pliyev, a former cavalry officer with no experience with nuclear missiles. Why Khrushchev chose Pliyev is unclear, though one plausible explanation is offered by Ambassador Alekseev, who suggests that he did so to throw American intelligence off the scent. As part of the operation, according to General Volkogo-

[28] Aragonés reports: "He said to Che and me, with Malinovsky in the room, 'You don't have to worry; there will be no big reaction from the U.S. And if there is a problem, we will send the Baltic Fleet.' " Asked, "Did you think he was joking, or did you think he was serious?" Aragonés replied, "He was totally serious. When he said it, Che and I looked at each other with raised eyebrows. But, you know, we were deferential to the Soviets' judgments, because, after all, they had a great deal of experience with the Americans, and they had superior information than we had. We trusted their judgment." Aragonés interview. Khrushchev may have believed from the start that the United States would react to the news of Soviet missiles in Cuba with moderation. Alekseev reports that in May, Khrushchev "said the Americans are a pragmatic people and would not attack if there were missiles in Cuba." Alekseev interview. The Soviet Baltic fleet, however, would have been completely incapable of providing timely or effective naval support, and it is difficult to credit the claim that Khrushchev was serious on this point.

[29] When asked at the Moscow conference whether the deployment could have been undertaken openly, Gromyko insisted that a secret deployment was the only viable option. His opinion was widely shared among the Soviet delegation, echoed most forcefully by Viktor Komplektov and Georgy Shakhnazarov, who noted that secrecy was "characteristic of the times." Theodore Sorensen asserted that the president would have found it much more difficult to mobilize world opinion on his side if the deployment had been done openly; McGeorge Bundy strongly agreed. MCT.

CASE STUDIES IN THE TWENTIETH CENTURY USE OF FORCE

nov, over 40,000 Soviet troops were sent to Cuba, under secrecy so tight that only the commanding officers of the units dispatched knew where they were headed.[30] Unaware of their destination, Soviet soldiers reportedly brought with them full winter gear, and were only told where they were going after their ships had passed the Strait of Gibraltar. Some Soviet sources claim that the commanders of the vessels involved in the operation were instructed to open sealed orders, at a predetermined point in the voyage, that charged them to scuttle their ships if an attempt was made to stop and search them, and that when American reconnaissance planes flew overhead, Soviet personnel would dance on deck in an attempt to look like tourists.

The first SS-4 MRBMs arrived on September 15, eleven days after President Kennedy's first major warning against the deployment of "offensive weapons" to Cuba, two days after his second warning, and just four days after a denial by TASS that any such deployment was in the offing. Once in Cuban ports, the missiles and their related equipment were off-loaded under cover of darkness, with elaborate precautions to ensure that the shipments went undetected. As part of the deception, Soviet troops wore civilian sport-shirts to disguise their numbers and identities. One of those who came off a Soviet ship was the thirty-nine-year-old commander of a motorized infantry regiment, Lieutenant Colonel Dimitry Yazov, now Soviet Minister of Defense.

Only Soviets were involved in the unloading, transportation, and installation of the missiles; indeed, the Soviets themselves had even chosen the locations of the missile sites. The Cuban armed forces' role in the deployment was limited to guiding the preliminary exploration of the terrain, choosing the routes from the ports to the missile sites, and building roads where necessary.

Camouflage was also a Soviet responsibility; yet the Soviets' failure to camouflage the missile sites permitted American intelligence to discover the deployment prematurely, by means of reconnaissance photographs taken on October 14. It appears that the reason the Soviets failed to camouflage the missiles is that Soviet standard operating procedures for constructing nuclear missile sites did not include the use of camouflage. All previous installations had been on Soviet territory; the installation crews in Cuba simply overlooked the importance of disguising their activities on foreign

[30] Volkogonov's report is consistent with Sergo Mikoyan's claim at the Cambridge conference that 42,000 Soviet troops were involved in the Cuban deployment. Del Valle claims that the total number of Soviet military involved in the deployment was closer to 44,000, of which approximately 20,000 were armed regulars, the remainder being logistics and construction personnel. Del Valle interview. This figure is much higher than previous American intelligence estimates, which ranged from 4,500 to 16,000 in October and November, 1962, and later went to 22,000. See Raymond L. Garthoff, *Reflections on the Cuban Missile Crisis*, first ed. (Washington, D.C.: Brookings, 1987), p. 21 n.

soil under the watchful eyes of the Americans. Castro is reported later to have expressed his astonishment and dismay that Cubans had not been consulted on camouflage measures; the sites could easily have been disguised as agricultural projects, Castro maintained, had the Soviets only asked for help.

SOVIET MISSILES IN CUBA: WARHEADS, TARGETS, AND ORDERS

One of the more persistent puzzles of the Cuban missile crisis concerns whether or not nuclear warheads for the Soviet MRBMs ever reached Cuba. American intelligence never detected nuclear warheads in Cuba, and interpreted the fact that the assembly of likely warhead storage bunkers at the missile sites was incomplete (shown by reconnaissance photographs), as evidence that they had not yet arrived.[31] But the Kennedy administration, in the face of uncertainty, operated on the assumption that they had.[32]

According to General Volkogonov, twenty nuclear warheads had arrived in Cuba in late September or early October, and twenty others were in transit aboard the *Poltava* when the quarantine went into effect. Apparently, the Soviets did not keep the Cubans well-informed of the warhead shipments. General del Valle, the Cuban chief of staff, was informed on October 23 or 24 by General Pliyev merely that "everything was ready," which del Valle interpreted to mean that warheads had arrived. Only later did he learn the details of the warhead shipments, and discover that they were incomplete.[33]

According to Volkogonov, the warheads that had arrived in Cuba were kept "well away" from the missiles themselves, and at no time were measures taken to mate them, even when alert levels were raised following President Kennedy's speech of October 22. Had the order to prepare the missiles come down, Volkogonov claimed, they could have been targeted in four hours, and would have required a subsequent countdown of fifteen minutes.[34]

Sergei Khrushchev claimed at the Moscow conference that the inaccuracy of the SS-4 missiles restricted their useful targets to large cities and industrial centers such as Washington or New York. Contrary to newspaper accounts of the conference, however, at no

[31] See, e.g., Ray S. Cline, "Nuclear War Seemed Remote," *Washington Post*, February 5, 1989, p. D8. The United States had solid intelligence that warheads were on the way to Cuba aboard the freighter *Poltava* (out of Odessa) when the quarantine was imposed. See Garthoff, *Reflections on the Cuban Missile Crisis*, first ed., pp. 20–22. The *Poltava* stopped short of the quarantine line and returned to the Soviet Union.

[32] See, e.g., McGeorge Bundy, *Danger and Survival: Choices About the Bomb in the First Fifty Years* (New York: Random House, 1988), p. 425.

[33] Del Valle interview. The details of the deployment in Cuba evince a high degree of Soviet self-reliance, and an equally high degree of Cuban deference. There may have been a dearth of trust on the one side, and an excess of trust on the other.

[34] *MCT*. American intelligence estimated in 1962 that the fastest an SS-4 missile could have been fired from a cold start was eight hours. CIA memorandum on the construction of missile sites in Cuba, October 19, 1962.

time did Khrushchev suggest that either Washington or New York was actually targeted, because at no time were targeting procedures under way. "My father would not have allowed [the warheads] to be mounted," Sergei Khrushchev insisted. "He felt that would have made it easier for a madman to start a war."[35]

General Volkogonov said that the standing orders given to the three SS-4 and two SS-5 regiments deployed to Cuba were extremely clear. He read from Defense Ministry Archives to the Moscow conferees that: "The rocket forces are to be used only in the event of a U.S. attack, unleashing a war, and under the strict condition of receiving a command from Moscow." Both conditions had to be satisfied before the missiles were to be used.[36] While these orders defined the limits of the local commanders' authority to launch nuclear missiles, however, none of the Soviets interviewed for this study believed that physical mechanisms preventing unauthorized use (such as modern permissive action links) were built into the warheads.

THE EARLY PHASE OF THE CRISIS: OCTOBER 16–26

President Kennedy learned of the Soviet deployment on October 16; he and his advisers spent almost a full week formulating a response before announcing the discovery publicly. During that week, on October 18, Soviet Foreign Minister Gromyko paid a visit to the White House which he described as "the most complex discussion" of his diplomatic career.[37] Kennedy did not ask Gromyko directly about the presence of Soviet missiles in Cuba, nor did Gromyko volunteer any information about them, much to the relief of both. Gromyko has since asserted, however, that he was instructed to be forthcoming if confronted directly. At the Moscow conference, he maintained merely that he would have given a "proper answer" to a direct question from the president; but in a subsequent article, he claimed that he was instructed by Moscow to say that the Soviets were deploying a "small quantity of missiles of a defensive nature" to Cuba, and to encourage quiet diplomacy if Kennedy's reaction were negative.[38]

On October 22, at 7:00 p.m. Eastern time, President Kennedy went on national television to announce the discovery of Soviet missiles in Cuba and his intention to impose a naval quarantine on all shipments of offensive weapons to the island. Just an hour before, Secretary of State Dean Rusk had handed Ambassador Dobrynin an advance copy of the president's speech. Rusk recalls, "I saw him age ten years right in front of my eyes." We now know

---

[35] *MCT.*
[36] *MCT.*
[37] Andrei Gromyko, *Pamiatnoe* (Moscow: Politizdat, 1988), pp. 390–396.
[38] Gromyko, "Karibskii krizis," p. 5.

why: Dobrynin had not been informed by his own government of the deployment.[39]

Khrushchev apparently reacted to Kennedy's speech with anger, ordering work accelerated on construction of the missile sites, and ordering Soviet ships to ignore the naval quarantine, scheduled to take effect at 10:00 a.m. on Wednesday, October 24. The order to ignore the quarantine seems to have been rescinded before the first Soviet vessels reached the quarantine line. But not until October 26 would Khrushchev publicly take a conciliatory, cooperative attitude toward resolving the crisis. The Cuban response to Kennedy's speech was also angry, bellicose, and defiant, but unlike Khrushchev's, it appears not to have mellowed as the days passed.

From Wednesday, October 24, to Friday, October 26, stalemate set in. Neither the United States nor the Soviet Union backed away from its public position, but both sides avoided a confrontation. At 1:00 p.m. on October 26, Aleksandr Fomin, an official at the Soviet embassy in Washington known to be the senior KGB official in Washington, met ABC's State Department correspondent John Scali, at Fomin's request. Fomin asked Scali to determine whether or not the United States would be interested in resolving the crisis by pledging not to invade Cuba in return for the withdrawal of the nuclear missiles. In so doing, Fomin was apparently acting on his own initiative. Scali replied at 7:30 p.m. that the administration was interested in Fomin's suggestion. Dobrynin was uncertain whether this channel reflected the views of the White House, and did not authorize a telegram to Moscow.[40] Fomin may have cabled a report notwithstanding.

The State Department began to receive a private, conciliatory letter from Khrushchev to Kennedy between 6:00 and 9:00 p.m. on Friday, October 26, vaguely proposing to conclude a deal along the same lines as Fomin had suggested to Scali. Most students of the crisis have assumed that the letter merely formalized Fomin's earlier trial balloon; but it appears now that this assumption is incorrect. The American embassy in Moscow had begun to receive the message at 4:43 p.m. Moscow time (early Friday morning in Washington), many hours before Fomin's initiative. The Fomin-Scali communication would have been too late to influence the content of the letter.

Khrushchev's letter clearly evinced exhaustion and anxiety. His

[39] When Dobrynin stated at the Moscow meeting that he did not know about the missiles in Cuba until Dean Rusk told him, Gromyko queried, "What, Anatoly Fyodorovich, you mean I did not tell you, the Ambassador, about the nuclear missiles in Cuba?" Dobrynin responded, "No, you did not tell me." Gromyko wryly replied, "That means it must have been a very big secret." *MCT*.

[40] Dobrynin reports that Robert Kennedy had asked him on October 26 to disregard messages from other channels of communication because they did not reflect the president's views. *MCT*.

tone of somber realism convinced many in the ExComm that Khrushchev was looking for a peaceful way out of the crisis; it convinced many in Cuba that Khrushchev was losing his nerve and that he was about to cave in to American pressure. In his memoirs, Khrushchev acknowledges that his anxiety during this time was "intense."[41] The pressure had led him to look for a relatively quick way out of the confrontation, even on what he himself must surely have recognized as sub-optimal terms. Khrushchev later reported a feeling among some of his military advisers during the crisis that a harder line was in order. But Western suppositions, that Khrushchev at this point faced a divided Presidium and threats to his own authority, have been unequivocally denied by knowledgeable Soviets.[42]

THE ORIGIN OF THE TURKISH MISSILE TRADE

On Saturday, October 27, before President Kennedy could respond to Khrushchev's letter of the day before, a second letter, taking a harder line, was broadcast by Radio Moscow. Khrushchev now insisted that the United States remove its intermediate-range Jupiter missiles in Turkey in return for the removal of Soviet missiles in Cuba. Khrushchev's quick about-face has always puzzled not only Western students of the crisis, but members of the ExComm as well, who show considerable surprise and confusion in the transcripts of the October 27 meetings.

In 1987, Georgy Shakhnazarov conveyed a message from Anatoly Dobrynin to the participants in the Cambridge conference, indicating that the idea for the missile trade had been hatched in the Soviet embassy in Washington. His rather cryptic remark remained unclear until the Moscow conference, where Dobrynin provided further details previously unknown. He and Robert Kennedy met secretly on the night of Friday, October 26, as part of a series of private, late-night back-channel discussions between the two. Dobrynin remarked to the attorney general that the administration's extreme reaction to the deployment of Soviet missiles in Cuba was puzzling in view of the fact that the United States had deployed similar missiles in Turkey, next door to the Soviet Union. In raising the issue, Dobrynin says, he was acting entirely on his own initiative, not expecting it to be interpreted as part of a negotiating position. He was merely attempting to make the point that the Soviet side had an equal right to provide for its own security. Dobrynin reports:

> Robert Kennedy said, "You are interested in the missiles in Turkey?"
> He thought pensively and said, "One minute, I will go and talk to the

---

[41] *Khrushchev Remembers*, p. 492.

[42] See *CCT*, esp. pp. 39–40; and *MCT*. Khrushchev recalled feeling pressured by "military advisers" to take a harder line. In an interview shortly after the crisis with American journalist Norman Cousins, Khrushchev referred to those advisers as "maniacs." See Pope, *Soviet Views on the Cuban Missile Crisis*, p. 92.

President." He went out of the room. . . . [He] came back and said,
"The President said that we are ready to consider the question of
Turkey, to examine favorably the question of Turkey."[43]

Dobrynin immediately reported this conversation to Moscow.
Shortly thereafter, Khrushchev demanded the missile trade. Dobrynin hastened to add that although he believes his cable to have been
the source of the missile trade proposal, it is possible that the idea
arose simultaneously in Moscow. No one at the Moscow conference, however, offered the latter interpretation, even though some,
such as Andrei Gromyko, were presumably in a position to know.

If Dobrynin's story is accurate, then some traditional understandings of the climax of the crisis must give way. The tapes of the
ExComm meetings of October 27 clearly indicate that the question
of the missile trade dominated the discussion, and that the president
himself was its strongest advocate. But at no point in those discussions did the president or his brother discuss Robert Kennedy's
meeting with Dobrynin of the previous day; nor did they reveal that
they had already communicated to the Soviet Union that the Jupiter
missiles in Turkey were negotiable. In conjunction with the recent
revelation of the "Cordier maneuver,"[44] and in view of the secrecy
surrounding Robert Kennedy's October 27 meeting with Ambassador Dobrynin (several members of the ExComm were unaware even
that such a meeting was to take place), the president's reticence in
the transcripts of the October 27 meetings strongly suggests that the
ExComm had become largely irrelevant to the president's decision-
making at the height of the crisis. Crucial decisions were being made
by the president and a few close advisers, well away from—and
unknown to—the ExComm as a whole. The group that had played a
central role in the early option-formation phase of the crisis seems
to have been left out of important aspects of decision-making at its
climax.

THE U-2 SHOOT-DOWN OF OCTOBER 27

As the ExComm puzzled over Khrushchev's new demand on
October 27, word reached Washington that an American U-2 reconnaissance aircraft had been shot down over Cuba by an SA-2

[43] *MCT.* It is worth noting that the idea of a missile trade was not a new one, and
that, indeed, the president seems to have been expecting the Soviets to propose it
for some time. See David A. Welch and James G. Blight, "The Eleventh Hour of the
Cuban Missile Crisis: An Introduction to the ExComm Transcripts," *International
Security,* Vol. 12, No. 3 (Winter 1987/88), pp. 12–13. The missile trade was also
proposed by Walter Lippmann in his October 25 column in the *Washington Post,* and
had been the subject of considerable public debate.
[44] President Kennedy instructed Dean Rusk on the night of October 27 to prepare
a contingency plan whereby Columbia University President Andrew Cordier, upon a
further signal, would contact U Thant, acting secretary general of the United Nations,
to propose a public missile trade. See Welch and Blight, "The Eleventh Hour of the
Cuban Missile Crisis," pp. 15–16.

surface-to-air missile fired from the Los Angeles battery, near the port of Banes. It has generally been supposed in the West that the missile that downed the aircraft was fired by Soviet troops, because the SA-2s were believed to have been under strict Soviet control. But it has always been difficult to imagine why Khrushchev would have risked a serious escalation of the crisis at that point. Some have surmised that the shoot-down was the unauthorized act of a Soviet officer in Cuba. Others have supposed that Cubans had in fact fired the missile, either after seizing control of the SAM site in a firefight with Soviets,[45] or by exercising their discretion in a dual-control arrangement of some kind. Most fantastic is Carlos Franqui's recent report that Castro once claimed that he himself had shot down the aircraft.

At the Moscow conference, the Soviet side released new details confirming that the U-2 shoot-down was indeed an unauthorized act by Soviet air defense forces. According to Alekseev, two generals were involved in the decision-making when the U-2 was detected at approximately 10:00 a.m. on Saturday, October 27. General Volkogonov publicly identified one as Pliyev's deputy for air defense, the late Lieutenant General Stepan N. Grechko. The second general was apparently Leonid S. Garbuz, now retired, then Pliyev's deputy for military training.[46]

Once the U-2 was spotted near Banes, the two generals had twenty minutes to make a decision whether or not to fire. After

[45] Seymour M. Hersh, "Was Castro Out of Control in 1962?" *Washington Post*, October 11, 1987, pp. H1–H2. Cf. Daniel Ellsberg, "The Day Castro Almost Started World War III," *New York Times*, October 31, 1987, p. 27; see also Adrian G. Montoro, "Moscow Was Caught Between Cuba and U.S.," *New York Times*, November 17, 1987. According to Ellsberg, as told to Hersh, an intercepted radio message from the Soviet naval base at Banes indicated that fire had been exchanged with "non-Russians," and that casualties had been taken. The clash was reported to have taken place at the Los Angeles SAM site on Friday, October 26, the day before that very same site shot down the American U-2. Hersh and Ellsberg speculate that Cubans might have seized control of the site and downed the American plane. At the Moscow conference, Ambassador Alekseev claimed that the incident was a mishandling of ammunition, which resulted in an explosion at the SAM site and several Soviet casualties. *MCT*. Sergio del Valle, however, claims that the event occurred in 1964 at Guantana, in Pinar del Río, at the other end of the island. Del Valle interview. Sergo Mikoyan reports that neither he nor, so far as he knows, his father, ever heard of any conflict between Soviet soldiers and Cuban regulars, from either Soviet or Cuban sources. Mikoyan did admit the possibility, however, that there may have been a skirmish at the Los Angeles SAM site between Soviet forces and one of the many bands of anti-Castro "worm squads" known to be operating in the area. Personal communication to DAW. The truth of the matter remains unclear.

[46] BJA discussions at the Soviet Central Committee and the Soviet Defense Ministry Institute for Military History, July 1989. In 1987, General Igor D. Statsenko told Sergo Mikoyan that he personally gave the order to fire on the U-2. But Statsenko was in Cuba with the Strategic Rocket Forces and was not in the air defense decision-making loop. In giving false testimony, Statsenko may have sought to make public the fact that the shoot-down was indeed an unauthorized act by Soviet forces; military secrecy would not then have allowed him to release the identities of those who actually did make the decision.

attempting unsuccessfully to contact General Pliyev, they decided to shoot on their own authority. As recently disclosed by the newspaper of the Cuban armed forces, *Bastión*, the local commander who actually gave the order to fire was General Georgy A. Voronkov, now retired and living in Odessa.

Contrary to previous accounts of the shoot-down, which suggested that Soviet SAM units had standing orders not to fire on American aircraft, Alekseev claims that there was "no direct prohibition" against doing so. Del Valle confirms this, noting that the officer on site was criticized by Khrushchev, but that he defended himself by saying that he had only followed Soviet standing orders "to fire on any aircraft that flies overhead in wartime," an action for which he was later decorated by Fidel Castro personally. From the Cuban point of view, the situation could indeed have been construed as "wartime." Throughout the crisis, Castro had authorized his own anti-aircraft (AA) artillery to fire at groups of two or more low-flying American planes; on October 26, he ordered his AA units to fire on any American aircraft within range. That same day, Voronkov received an order to begin operating the radar stations. Cuban Politburo member Jorge Risquet claimed at the Moscow conference that Soviet air defense forces were willing to fire on American aircraft on October 27 because they had been "inspired by the enthusiasm of the Cubans." Indeed, the downing of the U-2 was a tremendous boost to Cuban morale; news of it spread rapidly throughout the island, and was greeted everywhere with wild celebration. As Risquet put it, "our people felt that we were not defenseless." But many Cuban leaders reportedly felt that the shoot-down was "very dangerous," and worried "that it would inflame the situation."

At the Moscow conference, Volkogonov read from Malinovsky's telegram to Pliyev immediately following the shoot-down, rebuking him for "hastily [shooting] down the U.S. plane" because "an agreement for a peaceful way to deter an invasion of Cuba was already taking shape." This contradicts the English version of Khrushchev's memoirs, which indicate that he believed that it was Cubans who had shot down the American plane. Yet Sergei Khrushchev insists that his father knew at the time that Soviets had shot down the plane, and that in the tape recordings on which Khrushchev's memoirs were based, he clearly stated this. Strobe Talbott, editor and translator of Khrushchev's memoirs, reports the discrepancy in the English edition as a "mistake." The Russian language version of Khrushchev's memoirs published by Progress Publishers (currently in limited special circulation in the Soviet Union) also states that Cubans shot down the plane, because it is a re-translation of Talbott's English version.

There is some evidence to suggest that there may have been a partial, unsuccessful cover-up attempt by the Soviet military. Ambassador Alekseev reported that he did not find out that Soviets were responsible for the shoot-down until over a decade later, and he has speculated that Malinovsky himself may have tried to prevent details of the event from spreading in order to prevent embarrassment to the Ministry of Defense and the responsible Soviet officers in Cuba.

We now know that the ExComm's reaction to the shoot-down was more measured and restrained than the hysteria suggested in many memoirists' previous accounts. Khrushchev, however, must have been seriously shaken by the event, which made it painfully clear that his control over developments in Cuba had significantly eroded. Kennedy's control over events, as it turned out, was equally tenuous. Later that same day, an American U-2 on a routine air sampling mission in the Arctic strayed into Siberian air space as the result of a navigational error. Khrushchev may have read the incident as a provocation, but also seems to have been sensitive to the possibility that it was accidental. According to several Soviets at the Moscow conference, the risks that unintended actions might lead to an escalation of the confrontation were very much in the forefront of Khrushchev's mind as the crisis reached its crescendo.

THE RESOLUTION OF THE CRISIS

At 7:15 p.m. on Saturday, October 27, Robert Kennedy telephoned Dobrynin to request another meeting. The two met at 7:45 in the Department of Justice. The reports of important aspects of the meeting in Robert Kennedy's *Thirteen Days* were starkly contradicted by Ambassador Dobrynin in Moscow. First, Robert Kennedy reported telling Dobrynin that "we had to have a commitment by tomorrow that those bases would be removed. I was not giving them an ultimatum but a statement of fact. He should understand that if they did not remove those bases, we would remove them."[47] Though the attorney general explicitly denied that this was an ultimatum, it has generally been interpreted by Western historians as a clear compellent threat.[48] However, Dobrynin denies that Robert Kennedy issued any ultimatum or made any threats. He further denies that Robert Kennedy warned of an imminent coup or loss of civilian

[47] Robert F. Kennedy, *Thirteen Days: A Memoir of the Cuban Missile Crisis* (New York: Norton, 1969), p. 108.

[48] Daniel Ellsberg interviewed Robert Kennedy in 1964, when Kennedy claimed that he had warned Dobrynin that he had just forty-eight hours to remove the missiles; that if dismantling had not begun by that time, the missiles would be attacked and an invasion would follow; and that any further shoot-downs of American reconnaissance planes would result in an attack on "all the SAM sites immediately and probably the missile sites as well." Hersh, "Was Castro Out of Control in 1962?" p. H2. Ellsberg's conclusion is that, because Khrushchev well understood that he no longer controlled the Cubans, and that he may also have lost control over the SAM batteries, the Soviet leader was compelled to interpret Robert Kennedy's message as an ultimatum, requiring an immediate cessation of the crisis. Personal communication to JGB and DAW.

control of the military, in contradiction to Soviet accounts of the meeting, including Khrushchev's own.[49] In fact, according to Dobrynin, Robert Kennedy soft-pedaled the danger of imminent American action, and Dobrynin claims that his cable to Moscow reporting the meeting was similarly low-key on that point.

The second respect in which Dobrynin contradicts Robert Kennedy's account of the meeting helps explain the first, and concerns the status of the missile trade. Robert Kennedy wrote:

> He asked me what offer the United States was making, and I told him of the letter that President Kennedy had just transmitted to Khrushchev. He raised the question of our removing the missiles from Turkey. I said that there could be no quid pro quo or any arrangement made under this kind of threat or pressure, and that in the last analysis this was a decision that would have to be made by NATO. However, I said, the President had been anxious to remove those missiles from Turkey and Italy for a long period of time. He had ordered their removal some time ago, and it was our judgment that, within a short time after this crisis was over, those missiles would be gone.[50]

Dobrynin insists that it was Robert Kennedy who pursued the idea of an explicit "deal" on the Turkish missiles; that he wished to portray it as a significant concession by the United States; and that he never said that the president had already ordered their removal. Dobrynin's version of the meeting was confirmed in an important respect at the Moscow conference by Theodore Sorensen, who edited *Thirteen Days* prior to its publication. Sorensen confessed that the missile trade had been portrayed as an explicit deal in the diaries on which the book was based, and that he had seen fit to revise that account in view of the fact that the trade was still a secret at the time, known to only six members of the ExComm.

Andrei Gromyko stressed at the Moscow conference that the question of the Turkish missiles was "not trivial," and that the Soviet Union had a solid foundation to consider that their removal was part of the terms on which the crisis was resolved. Indeed, Khrushchev sent the president a letter after the conclusion of the crisis, in which he described the withdrawal of the Jupiter missiles from Turkey as an integral part of the agreement on which the crisis was resolved. In Moscow, Sorensen conceded that this letter had been received, but explained its absence from the collected Kennedy-Khrushchev correspondence by noting that the administration decided against acknowledging the withdrawal of the Jupiters as a quid pro quo, and returned the letter as if it had never been opened.

It appears, therefore, that the withdrawal of the Jupiter missiles from Turkey in the spring of 1963 was indeed part of a private deal

[49] Personal communication to the authors.
[50] Robert Kennedy, *Thirteen Days*, pp. 108–109.

that led to the withdrawal of Soviet missiles from Cuba in November, 1962. However, both the United States and the Soviet Union have subsequently found it expedient not to insist on this point, the United States because of the complications and ill-will it would cause among its NATO allies (and because of the domestic political consequences to the president had he publicly acknowledged the trade of the missiles), and the Soviet Union because of Castro's objection to being treated like a "bargaining chip" on a par with a "minor" NATO ally such as Turkey.

KHRUSHCHEV'S SENSE OF URGENCY

Between the time Dobrynin took his leave of Robert Kennedy on October 27 and the time the ExComm met again at 9:00 on Sunday morning, Khrushchev had decided to bring the confrontation to an end. Western students of the crisis have long wondered what caused Khrushchev to do so at that particular time. Dobrynin's claim that he did not interpret Robert Kennedy's message of October 27 as a threat or an ultimatum only adds to the puzzle, since Robert Kennedy's account of the meeting has been widely regarded as the best explanation of Khrushchev's sense of urgency.

That Khrushchev felt a sense of urgency can hardly be questioned. According to Fyodor Burlatsky, the letter of October 28 accepting Kennedy's non-invasion pledge in return for withdrawal of the missiles from Cuba "was prepared at Khrushchev's dacha [at Kuntsevo] thirty kilometers from Moscow. When the letter was finished, a man was dispatched with it to drive very quickly to the radio station. He was told to have it for transmission before three o'clock. They were very nervous." Sergo Mikoyan added, "At Radio Moscow there are six elevators in the building. Someone had telephoned ahead, and they reserved one elevator just for this letter to arrive."

If indeed Khrushchev's urgency was a reaction to any verbal message, it may have been to that of John Scali, rather than to Robert Kennedy's. At the Moscow conference, Aleksandr Fomin reported that in his meeting with Scali on Saturday, October 27, at which Scali attempted to ascertain the reason why Khrushchev's Friday letter had been so quickly superseded by a letter demanding a missile trade, Scali angrily threatened that there would be an American attack within hours if the missiles were not removed. After the resolution of the crisis, Fomin communicated a personal message from Khrushchev to Scali that his outburst had been "very valuable."

It seems probable, however, that Khrushchev was paying greater attention to his own intelligence sources than to Scali's extracurricular theatrics, since Scali was not the only one who appeared to be speaking for the administration. During the night of October 25–26, Soviet intelligence apparently reported persuasive evidence of an

imminent American attack, leading Khrushchev to propose conciliatory terms in his Friday letter. Later in the day on October 26,
Soviet intelligence reversed its earlier estimate, possibly encouraging Khrushchev to toughen his terms in the second letter. But some
time still later on October 26 or October 27, Soviet and Cuban
intelligence appear once again to have concluded that an American
attack could be expected momentarily. If this indeed was their
assessment, it may have weighed heavily in Khrushchev's decision
to bring the crisis to an end.

Other factors apparently played a significant role. The U-2 shoot-
down and the inadvertent straying of another American U-2 over
Soviet air space on October 27 indicated that events were slipping
out of control. But perhaps as important, it appears that Khrushchev
was influenced by a communication from Castro through Alekseev
on October 27. That message came to light at the Moscow conference, and was reported in the press as Castro's attempt to urge
Khrushchev to fire the nuclear missiles in Cuba against the United
States.

It remains unclear exactly what Castro communicated to Khrushchev. We have reason to believe that in an unpublished passage
of his memoirs, Khrushchev reported it thus: "Suddenly, we received through our Ambassador a cable from Castro. The Ambassador reported that Castro had given him the report face-to-face.
Castro informed him that he had reliable information that an American invasion would take place within a few hours. Therefore, he
was proposing to preempt the invasion and inflict a nuclear strike
on the U.S."[51]

But well-placed Soviets and Cubans deny that Castro's message
urged a nuclear strike. According to both Ambassador Alekseev
(who transmitted the message to Khrushchev) and Emilio Aragonés
(who helped draft it, and who had felt on October 26 that Khrushchev's resolve was weakening), the telegram was intended to
communicate the Cuban people's willingness to fight to the last man
and the last bullet in the event of an American attack, and to urge
Khrushchev to show firmness. Both Alekseev and Aragonés believe
that Khrushchev misinterpreted the telegram as urging a preemptive
strike, an entirely plausible belief given Khrushchev's state of mind
at the climax of the confrontation.

Until the cable itself is made public by the Soviets or Cubans, the
issue cannot be resolved conclusively. A great deal depends upon
the precise wording of the telegram, and whether it accurately
reflects Castro's verbal communication to Alekseev.[52] But if Khru-

[51] This was conveyed to the authors by a knowledgeable source. This passage did
not appear in the manuscripts that were delivered to the West in 1970.
[52] A confidential source informed the authors that in February 1989, Castro
remarked that he believed the missiles should have been fired in the event of a full-
scale American invasion, though not preemptively or in the event of an air strike; del
Valle reports that in 1962, he shared this sentiment (del Valle interview). This is an

shchev did misinterpret the telegram from Castro, then it would stand as one more reminder of the significance of major miscommunications during crises. In this case, a misinterpretation may have facilitated a rapid resolution; in other circumstances, it might have complicated one.

CUBA AND THE CONCLUSION OF THE CRISIS

Castro's displeasure at Khrushchev's failure to consult him before agreeing to withdraw the missiles from Cuba is a matter of record. Apparently, Cuba first heard of Khrushchev's decision on the radio. Ambassador Alekseev reports that upon hearing the news, "I felt myself the most unhappy man on earth, as I imagined what Fidel's reaction to this would be." Indeed, Castro refused to see him for several days.[53]

Part of Castro's fury at not having been consulted may have stemmed from his conviction that Khrushchev did not get as much as he could have from the Americans. At the Moscow conference, Jorge Risquet insisted that the "five conditions" Castro had publicly proclaimed as the price for his assent to the withdrawal of the missiles had indeed been within reach, including American withdrawal from Guantánamo.[54] If indeed Castro was convinced that this was a concession to which the United States would agree, then it bespeaks an appalling ignorance of American political realities on

---

understandable attitude; as del Valle put it, Cuba had "no atomic culture" at the time, meaning Cubans had not yet developed the understanding of the consequences of nuclear explosions that existed in the United States and the Soviet Union. But in any case, the consequences for Cuba of a full-scale American invasion would not have differed from the consequences of a nuclear war in important respects; in either event, Cuba faced devastation. Castro's apparent willingness to see Soviet nuclear missiles fired from Cuban soil in the event of a full-scale invasion must be understood from this perspective.

What does seem clear is that, in the telegram in question, Alekseev communicated to Khrushchev Castro's conviction, based in part on Cuban intelligence sources, that an American attack was imminent. If indeed Cuba had informants well-placed in the American defense and intelligence communities, then the president's instructions on the morning of October 27 to prepare for a possible attack on the morning of October 30 may have been an important factor. Scott Sagan has suggested to the authors that "pathfinder" teams may have been infiltrated into Cuba as part of the contingency planning, and the detection or capture of one of these teams would have been interpreted as strong evidence of a forthcoming invasion. It has also been claimed that Soviet military intelligence had tapped into Washington phone lines in 1962, raising the possibility that the Soviets would have overheard discussion of preparations for an attack the following week. See Harry Rositzke, *The KGB: The Eyes of Russia* (Garden City, N.Y.: Doubleday, 1981), pp. 197–198.

[53] *MCT*; and Alekseev interview.

[54] Castro's five conditions for complying with the U.S.-Soviet agreement were: that the United States (1) lift the naval quarantine; (2) lift its economic blockade of Cuba; (3) discontinue "subversive activities and piratical attacks"; (4) cease violating Cuban airspace and territorial waters; and (5) shut down its naval base at Guantánamo.

Castro's part.[55] Aragonés, however, maintains that Castro's five conditions represented merely a statement of principles, not an attempt to stake out a negotiating position, and that they were intended primarily to serve domestic political purposes. Cuba had been badly treated by both superpowers, and its national honor required a public articulation of Cuban dissent.[56]

Raymond Garthoff has reported that Cuban troops surrounded the missile sites on October 28, and only stood down after the arrival in Havana of Soviet First Deputy Premier Anastas Mikoyan, whose task was to persuade Castro to go along with the U.S.-Soviet agreement. The Moscow conference and subsequent discussions have shed light on the issue and have raised interesting new questions in the process. Ambassador Alekseev believes, for example, that the troops that took up positions around the missile sites were in fact Soviet soldiers in Cuban uniforms, and insists that there was no danger of a Soviet-Cuban clash at that time. Both Sergio del Valle and Emilio Aragonés insist that the troops were Cuban anti-aircraft units deployed to protect the missile sites from low-level attack.[57]

Anastas Mikoyan's success in persuading Castro to accept the U.S. demand for a November withdrawal of the Il-28 light bombers, in addition to the withdrawal of the missiles, was a remarkable achievement. The American demand that Cuba relinquish weapons intended for the Cuban Air Force, wholly independently of the Soviet missile deployment, only added insult to injury. Mikoyan's success was aided by one of those curious interventions of fate: Castro's initial attitude toward the Soviet representative was softened by the sudden death of Mikoyan's wife at the very moment he arrived in Havana. But according to Cuban testimony, the published American views of the negotiations involving the bombers are mistaken in a variety of ways. First, American intelligence believed

[55] Dobrynin reported at the Moscow conference that in a confidential letter to President Kennedy on October 29 or 30, the Soviet Union did raise the issue of Guantánamo, but he added that he doubted that any hopes of American concessions on the base were realistic. Andrei Gromyko further remarked that the agreement concluding the crisis included the crucial concession from the United States: a commitment not to invade Cuba. *MCT*. Alekseev reports that he believes Khrushchev deliberately chose not to consult Castro on the removal of the missiles, because he knew he would not agree. Alekseev interview.

[56] Aragonés interview. The Cuban delegation to the Moscow conference added that Khrushchev's explanation for his failure to consult Castro—that there was simply insufficient time—was wholly plausible. Indeed, Castro's telegram may have been largely responsible for convincing Khrushchev that time was so short. Nevertheless, the Cuban delegation insisted that Khrushchev should at least have made the October 28 deal contingent upon Cuban agreement. *MCT*.

[57] Del Valle interview; Aragonés interview. Del Valle explains that between October 24 and 28, fifty anti-aircraft batteries were mobilized from the reserves and were assigned to protect the missile sites. On October 28, when the dismantling of the nuclear missiles began, these units started to withdraw.

in 1962 that forty-two Il-28s had been delivered to Cuba, of which only seven had been assembled; Sergio del Valle, however, maintains that twelve Il-28s had been delivered, of which only three were to be transferred to the Cuban Air Force. None of the three Cuban bombers had been uncrated during the crisis, and the Soviets simply withdrew them at the same time they withdrew their own bombers, an operation facilitated by the fact that the aircraft were all located at the same bases.[58] It may be, therefore, that none of the bombers had yet been formally transferred to Cuba, and that Mikoyan did not have to persuade Castro to relinquish something he had already been given. Second, some American analysts have believed that Mikoyan's task was abetted by President Kennedy's message to the NATO allies of November 19, warning that if the bombers were not promptly withdrawn, air strikes might be necessary to destroy them. The president reportedly intended the message to leak to the Soviets. However, Emilio Aragonés, who was present throughout the negotiations between Castro and Mikoyan, does not recall any discussion of the American threat and does not believe that it was communicated to Castro. Aragonés recalls that Mikoyan represented the withdrawal of the bombers merely as a request from the Soviet and American negotiators in New York, and persuaded him to go along by appealing to the necessity for a quick solution.

The fact that the Il-28 bombers were a subject of debate at all, according to Sergo Mikoyan, was largely the fault of the Soviet Union itself. Khrushchev, by his letter to the president of October 28 stating that he had given an order "to dismantle the arms which you described as offensive," was attempting to deny that the nuclear missiles in Cuba were, in fact, "offensive," and was indeed attempting to avoid using the word "missiles" publicly. But the effect was to give the United States *carte blanche* to specify which weapon systems were to be withdrawn, and the Kennedy administration chose to insist upon the removal of the Il-28s—obsolete, short-range bombers believed to have a nuclear capability, but for which no nuclear weapons had been supplied. The withdrawal of the Il-28s was a blow to Cuba's national pride, and it further strained Soviet-Cuban relations. As Sergo Mikoyan put it, the Soviets fell victim to their own "propagandistic tendencies."

CONCLUSION

The new testimony from Soviets and Cubans has considerably enriched the story of the Cuban missile crisis, though it has opened as many questions as it has plausibly answered. All of the new evidence assembled here, however, has been testimonial. To date,

---

[58] Del Valle interview. According to del Valle, the Cubans planned to use their Il-28s in a coastal defense role, primarily against mother ships from which smaller craft would carry subversives and counterrevolutionaries attempting to infiltrate the Cuban coast.

Western students of the crisis have not seen a single Soviet or Cuban document against which to check the recollections of Soviet and Cuban participants and scholars. Cuba and the Soviet Union have no history of declassifying diplomatic documents for historical uses, and no procedures for doing so; in any case, the relevant diplomatic archives in both Moscow and Havana are probably sparse by American standards. According to Soviet testimony, no written records of Kremlin decision-making were kept prior to October 22, 1962, precisely to avoid breaches of secrecy. The director of the Institute of Cuban History notes that the Cuban government in 1962 was so young and so disorganized that it had not yet established procedures for handling paperwork; most relevant decisions were made in conversations that were not recorded.

The next major step in the historiography of the Cuban missile crisis will have to await the release of those documents that do exist in Moscow and Havana. In the meantime, we must make what we can of verbal testimonies. The weaknesses of oral history are well known: memories are imperfect and selective; current interests and objectives color recollections of historical events. Perhaps most frustrating is the fact that not all key players have survived to give their testimony, and others, because of advancing age, have little time left in which to do so. But until relatively recently, few historians and political scientists believed that they would have the chance to hear the Soviet and Cuban stories at all. We believe that the Soviets and Cubans who have spoken out have treated the opportunity to do so with due seriousness; in our opinion, therefore—bearing in mind the inherent limitations of oral history—their contributions have greatly improved the understanding of the causes, conduct, and implications of the Cuban missile crisis.

Implementing Flexible Response:
Vietnam as a Test Case

JOHN LEWIS GADDIS

In order to discuss the implementation of "flexible response," it is necessary to make a choice. One can examine in overview a series of events in which that strategy manifested itself: the Bay of Pigs, Laos, Berlin, the Cuban missile crisis, the Dominican Republic. Or, one can focus in detail on the event that because of its duration, divisiveness, and cost, overshadowed them all: the war in Vietnam. There are two good reasons for choosing the second approach. First, American policy in Southeast Asia reflected in microcosm virtually all of the elements of "flexible response" as applied in practice. Second, Kennedy, Johnson, and their advisers regarded Vietnam as a fair test of that strategy: it had been Eisenhower's inability to deal with that and comparable problems that had produced the "flexible response" critique in the first place; if the strategy could not be made to work in Vietnam, then there would be serious grounds upon which to question its applicability elsewhere. American leaders took on this test fully aware of the potential difficulties, but at the same time fully confident of their ability to surmount them through a strategy designed to meet just that kind of situation.

To say that their confidence was misplaced is to understate: rarely have accomplishments turned out so totally at variance with intended objectives. The war did not save South Vietnam, it did not deter future

From *Strategies of Containment: A Critical Appraisal of Postwar American National Security Policy* by John Lewis Gaddis. Copyright © 1982 by Oxford University Press, Inc. Reprinted by permission.

aggression, it did not enhance the credibility of United States commitments elsewhere in the world, it did not prevent recriminations at home. It is too easy to blame these disparities on deficiencies in the postwar national security decision-making structure, substantial though those may have been. There has been, as we have seen, no single or consistent approach to containment; to indict all manifestations of that strategy is only to be vague. Nor is it helpful to ascribe the failure in Vietnam to the shift in leadership at the White House after November 22, 1963, however strikingly the personalities of Kennedy and Johnson may have differed. For the fact is that Johnson followed the stategy of "flexible response" faithfully in Vietnam, perhaps more so than Kennedy himself would have done.

The American defeat there rather grew out of assumptions derived quite logically from that strategy: that the defense of Southeast Asia was crucial to the maintenance of world order; that force could be applied in Vietnam with precision and discrimination; that means existed accurately to evaluate performance; and that the effects would be to enhance American power, prestige, and credibility in the world. These assumptions in turn reflected a curiously myopic preoccupation with process—a disproportionate fascination with means at the expense of ends—with the result that a strategy designed to produce a precise correspondence between intentions and accomplishments in fact produced just the opposite.

I

Officials of the Kennedy and Johnson administrations liked to insist that their policies in Vietnam were consistent with the overall direction of American foreign policy since 1947: that conflict, they maintained, was but another in a long series of steps taken to demonstrate that aggression did not pay. "The challenge that we face today in Southeast Asia," Johnson argued, "is the same challenge that we have faced with courage and that we have met with strength in Greece and Turkey, in Berlin and Korea, in Lebanon and in Cuba." The "great lesson of this generation" was that "wherever we have stood firm, aggression has ultimately been halted."[1] To question the need for a similar commitment to South Vietnam, these statements implied, was to dispute the very assumptions that had sustained the strategy of containment from its beginnings.

[1] Johnson remarks at Syracuse University, August 5, 1964, *JPP:1963-4*, p. 930; Johnson remarks to members of Congressional committees, May 4, 1965, *JPP: 1965*, p. 487. See also Rostow to Kennedy, August 17, 1961, Kennedy Papers, NSC File, Box 231, "Southeast Asia—General"; McNamara statement, "United States Policy in Vietnam," March 26, 1964, *DSB*, (April 13, 1964), p. 566; Johnson address at Johns Hopkins University, April 7, 1965, *JPP: 1965*, p. 395; Johnson remarks to National Rural Electric Cooperative Association, July 14, 1965, *ibid.*, p. 751; Johnson press conference statement, July 28, 1965, *ibid.*, pp. 794-95.

In fact, though, a gradual shift had taken place in those assumptions over the years. Kennan, it will be recalled, had stressed distinctions between vital and peripheral interests, between varieties of threats to them, and between levels of feasible response given available means; the Kennedy and Johnson administrations made no such distinctions. Kennan had sought to maintain the global balance of power by applying a combination of political, economic, military, and psychological leverage in carefully selected pivotal areas; Johnson by 1965 was relying almost exclusively on the use of military force in a theater chosen by adversaries. Kennan had hoped to harness forces of nationalism, even where communist, to contain the expanding power and influence of the Soviet Union; Johnson sought to oppose communism, even where nationalist, for the purpose of preserving American credibility in the world. And, in a final ironic twist, Johnson and later Nixon came to rely with plaintive consistency on the assistance of the Soviet Union; the original target of containment, to extricate the United States from the tangle in which its own strategy had ensnared it.

One might explain these remarkable mutations as the result of obtuseness, short-sightedness, or even absent-mindedness, but there is no evidence these qualities played any more prominent role during the Kennedy-Johnson years than is normally the case. What was distinctive about those administrations, though, was their commitment to symmetrical response, and it is here that one must look to account for an evolution of strategic thinking all the more striking for the fact that those carrying it off seemed unaware that it had occurred.

It had been, of course, NSC-68 that had shifted perceptions of threat from the Soviet Union to the international communist movement; that document had also provided a rationale for expanding means and, as a consequence, interests. Eisenhower had rejected the analysis of means set forward in NSC-68, but not its assessment of threats or interests; for this reason he had been willing to extend an ambiguous commitment to the defense of South Vietnam through the SEATO treaty,* an initiative consistent with his administration's concern to achieve maximum deterrence at minimum cost. Expense was

---

*The SEATO treaty, signed September 8, 1954, provided that in case of "armed attack" against any of the signatories or against states or territories which the signatories "by unanimous agreement may hereafter designate," they would "in that event act to meet the common danger in accordance with [their] constitutional processes." In the event of a threat "other than by armed attack" or "by any fact or situation which might endanger the peace of the area," the signatories would "consult immediately in order to agree on the measures which should be taken for the common defense." South Vietnam was not a signatory to the treaty, but a protocol attached to it did extend its provisions to cover "the States of Cambodia and Laos and the free territory under the jurisdiction of the State of Vietnam," (*American Foreign Policy, 1950-1955: Basic Documents* [Washington: 1957], pp. 913-14, 916.)

of less concern to Kennedy who, confronted with an upsurge of Viet Cong insurgency, reverted to NSC-68's concept of expandable means but coupled it with a determination to honor Eisenhower's commitment, even though it had been extended largely as a substitute for means. At the same time, Kennedy was determined to lower the risks of escalation or humiliation that earlier strategy had run; this resolve led, in time, to the deployment of American ground forces, first as "advisers" to the South Vietnamese, then, under Johnson, as full-fledged combatants.[2]

But what, precisely, was the United States interest in Vietnam? Why was the balance of power at stake there? Walt Rostow had warned in his 1962 "BSNP" draft that "major losses of territory or of resources would make it harder for the U.S. to create the kind of world environment it desires, . . . generate defeatism among governments and peoples in the non-Communist world, or give rise to frustrations at home." But when pressed to explain why the "loss" of such a small and distant country would produce these drastic consequences, Washington officials generally cited the SEATO treaty obligation, which, if not honored, would raise doubts about American commitments elsewhere in the world. "The integrity of the U.S. commitment is the principal pillar of peace throughout the world," Rusk wrote in 1965. "If that commitment becomes unreliable, the communist world would draw conclusions that would lead to our ruin and almost certainly to a catastrophic war."

This was curious reasoning. It required justifying the American commitment to South Vietnam as essential to the maintenance of global stability, but then portraying that stability as endangered by the very vulnerability of Washington's commitment. It involved both deterring aggression and being held hostage to it. The confusion, it would appear, stemmed from the failure of both the Kennedy and Johnson administrations to articulate independently derived conceptions of interest in Southeast Asis; instead, they tended to view the American stake there as determined exclusively by threats and obligations. The security of the United States, indeed of the entire non-communist world, was thought to be imperiled wherever communist challenges came up against American guarantees. Vietnam might be insignificant in itself, but as a point of intersection between threat and commitment, it was everything.

Nothing in this argument required the threat to be centrally directed, or even coordinated with communist activities elsewhere. There were, to be sure, frequent references early in the war to the

[2] Rostow draft, "Basic National Security Policy," March 26, 1962, p. 9; Rusk memorandum, July 1, 1965, *Pentagon Papers*, IV, 23. See also Rusk and McNamara to Kennedy, November 11, 1961, *ibid.*, II, 111; Johnson remarks to members of Congressional committees, May 4, 1965, *JPP: 1965*, p. 486; and Rostow to McNamara, May 2, 1966, Johnson Papers, NSF Agency File, Boxes 11-12, "Defense Department Vol. III."

Sino-Soviet plan for "world domination,"[3] but these became less common as evidence of the Moscow-Peking split became irrefutable. Rationales then shifted to the containment of China, but only briefly; by early 1965 the predominant concern, as Under-Secretary of Defense John McNaughton put it, was simply "to avoid a humiliating US defeat (to our reputation as a guarantor)."[4] Communism need not pose a coordinated threat to the world balance of power, then, but because victories for communism at the expense of the United States, even if uncoordinated, could result in humiliation, the challenge to global stability was no less real. The only difference was that it was now Washington's fear of retreat that linked these threats together, not the internal discipline and control of international communism itself.

Nor did the American commitment in question need to have been prudent. There was a definite sense within the Kennedy administration that Eisenhower had overextended the United States in Southeast Asia: Rostow, as has been seen would have preferred a less formal alliance structure based on offshore strongpoints;[5] Robert Komer, one of his assistants, privately described SEATO in 1961 as a "millstone" directed against non-existent dangers of overt aggression. Nonetheless, Rostow wrote Kennedy later that year: "Surely we are hooked in Viet-Nam; surely we shall honor our . . . SEATO commitment." The problem, simply, was that the dangers of disengagement seemed at each stage to outweigh the costs of pressing on. "The reasons why we went into Vietnam . . . are now largely academic," McNaughton wrote in 1966. "At each decision point we have gambled; at each point, to avoid the damage to our effectiveness of defaulting on our commitment, we have upped the ante. We have not defaulted, and the ante (and commitment) is now very high."[6]

[3] See, for example, the Joint Chiefs of Staff to McNamara, January 13, 1962, *Pentagon Papers*, II, 664; Roger Hilsman address, Tampa, Florida, June 14, 1963, *DSB*, XIX (July 8, 1963), 44; Johnson remarks at the National Cathedral School, Washington, June 1, 1965, *JPP: 1965*, p. 600.

[4] McNaughton memorandum, "Proposed Course, of Action re Vietnam," March 24, 1965, *Pentagon Papers*, III, 695. See also Michael Forrestal to William P. Bundy, November 4, 1964, *ibid.*, p. 592. For further official perceptions of lack of coordination in the international communist movement, see Thomas L. Hughes to Hilsman, April 20, 1963, Kennedy Papers NSC Files, Box 314, Folder 6; Hilsman to Rusk, July 31, 1963, *ibid.*, Folder 10; Johnson to Lodge, March 20, 1964, *Pentagon Papers*, III, 511; Bundy to Johnson, October 21, 1964, Johnson Papers, National Security Files—NSC Staff, Box 2, "Memos for the President, vol. 7; Rostow to Rusk, December 16, 1964, *ibid.*, NSF Country Files—Vietnam, Box 11, "Memos, Vol. XXIII."

[5] See above, p. 223.

[6] Komer memorandum, "A Doctrine of Deterrence for SEA—The Conceptual Framework," May 9, 1961, Kennedy Papers, NSC Files, Box 231, "Southeast Asia—General"; Rostow to Kennedy, August 17, 1961, *ibid.*; McNaughton memorandum, January 18, 1966, *Pentagon Papers*, IV, 47. See also Rostow's draft, "Basic National Security Policy," March 26, 1962, pp. 141–44, and Arthur Schlesinger's account of Kennedy's conversation with Khrushchev at Vienna in June 1961, in *A Thousand Days*, p. 368.

There was a distinct self-reinforcing tendency in all of this. The more the administration defended its Vietnam policies in terms of safeguarding credibility, the more American credibility seemed to depend upon the success of those policies. "To leave Viet-Nam to its fate would shake . . . confidence . . . in the value of an American commitment and in the value of America's word," Johnson proclaimed in April 1965. And again, in May: "There are a hundred other little nations . . . watching what happens. . . . If South Viet-Nam can be gobbled up, the same thing can happen to them." And still again, in July: "If we are driven from the field in Viet-Nam, then no nation can ever again have the same confidence in . . . American protection."' Perceptions in international relations are only in part the product of what people believe; they arise as well from what nations claim. Given the frequency and intensity of these and other comparable pronouncements, it is hardly surprising that they were taken seriously, both at home and abroad. And yet the irony is that the administration made them to stave off pressures for withdrawal that could lead to humiliation; their effect, though, was to widen the very gap between promise and performance from which humiliation springs.

But why this extreme fear of humiliation in the first place? Partly, one suspects, because it might suggest weakness to adversaries: "lessons" of Munich, after all, were still very much alive. Vietnam had also become something of a matter of personal pride: "we have not lost a single nation to communism since 1959," Johnson liked to boast.⁸ But a deeper concern, oddly enough, may have been not so much what the world might think as what the United States might do. There was, within both the Kennedy and Johnson administrations, a strange dread of American irrationality—of the unpredictable and uncontrollable reactions that might ensue if the United States was perceived to have "lost" Vietnam. Rusk and McNamara had warned as early as 1961 that such a development "would stimulate bitter domestic controversies in the United States and would be seized upon by extreme elements to divide the country and harass the Administration." Rostow's "BSNP" draft even raised the possibility that "the U.S. might rashly initiate war" if confronted by a major defeat.⁹ Johnson may well have entertained the strongest fears of all: "I knew that if we let Communist aggression succeed in taking over South Vietnam," he later recalled,

⁷ Johnson Johns Hopkins address, April 7, 1965, *JPP: 1965,* p. 395; Johnson remarks to members of Congressional committees, May 4, 1965, *ibid.,* p. 491; Johnson press conference statement, July 28, 1965, *ibid.,* p. 794.

⁸ Johnson remarks in Hartford, Connecticut, September 28, 1964, *JPP: 1964.* See also Johnson's remarks in Detroit, Michigan, September 7, 1964, *ibid.,* p. 1050; and May, *"Lessons" of the Past,* especially pp. 112–14.

⁹ Rusk and McNamara to Kennedy, November 11, 1961, *Pentagon Papers,* II, 111; Rostow draft, "Basic National Security Policy," March 26, 1962, p. 9. See also William P. Bundy to McNaughton, November 26, 1964, *Pentagon Papers,* III, 658.

there would follow in this country an endless national debate—a mean and destructive debate—that would shatter my Presidency, kill my administration, and damage our democracy. I knew that Harry Truman and Dean Acheson had lost their effectiveness from the day that the Communists took over in China. I believed that the loss of China had played a large role in the rise of Joe McCarthy. And I knew that all these problems, taken together, were chickenshit compared with what might happen if we lost Vietnam.[10]

The ultimate danger, then, was what the United States might do to itself if it failed to meet obligations it itself had established.

Shortly after the Johnson administration left office, William Whitworth, a writer for the *New Yorker,* sought to interview several of the former President's advisers on the underlying geopolitical rationale for the Vietnam War. The only one who would see him was Eugene V. Rostow, Walt Rostow's older brother, who had served as Under-Secretary of State for Political Affairs from 1966 to 1969. The ensuing discussion took on a revealing circularity. Asked why American security depended upon the defense of Southeast Asia, Rostow emphasized the need to maintain a "balance of power" in the world. But when queried as to why it had been necessary to do that, Rostow fell back upon a classic "flexible response" argument: the need to be able to handle, without resort to nuclear weapons, problems such as Vietnam. Whitworth found this puzzling: "We have the balance in order to deal with the problem, and we have to deal with the problem in order to preserve the balance. The theory is eating its own tail." "Well, in a sense, you're right," Rostow replied. "All I can say is that it has always been very dangerous for people when a potentially hostile power establishes hegemony. I can't particularize how that potential hegemony would be exercised, but I would prefer, even at considerable cost, to prevent the risk."[11]

This spectacle of theories eating tails was no rare thing in Vietnam: the expansion of means to honor a commitment made as a substitute for means; the justification of that commitment in terms of a balance of power made shaky by its very existence; the defense, in the interests of credibility, of policies destructive of credibility; the search, ultimately, for domestic consensus by means that destroyed that consensus—all of these reflect the failure of "flexible response" strategy to proceed in an orderly manner through the stages of identifying interests, perceiving threats, and selecting appropriate responses. Instead, both threats and responses became interests in themselves, with

---

[10] Quoted in Doris Kearns, *Lyndon Johnson and the American Dream* (New York: 1976), pp. 252-53. See also Lyndon B. Johnson, *The Vantage Point: Perspectives of the Presidency, 1963-1969* (New York: 1971), pp. 151-52.

[11] William Whitworth, *Naive Questions About War and Peace* (New York; 1970), pp. 105-6, 124.

the result that the United States either ignored or forgot what it had set out to do in Vietnam at just the moment it was resolving, with unprecedented determination, to do it.

II

A second prominent feature of "flexible response" as applied in Vietnam was the belief in "calibration," or "fine tuning"—that by being able to move up or down a range of precisely calculated actions, the United States could deter limited aggression without either extreme escalation or humiliation. "Our military forces must be . . . used in a measured, limited, controlled and deliberate way, as an instrument to carry out our foreign policy," one of McNamara's assistants wrote in late 1964. "Never must military operations become an end in themselves." Johnson made the same point some months later: he would not heed, he insisted, "those who urge us to use our great power in a reckless or casual manner. . . . We will do what must be done. And we will do only what must be done."[12] And yet, since this strategy in the end produced *both* escalation *and* humiliation, it would appear to have contained, as did official thinking on the balance of power, certain deficiencies.

Deterrence, ideally, should involve expressing determination without actually having to exhibit it. John Foster Dulles had attempted this delicate maneuver by threatening to use nuclear weapons to discourage aggression at all levels—an approach that at least had the merit of separating the projection of resolve from its actual demonstration, so long as skill, or luck, held out. Lacking the previous administration's self-confidence in such matters, convinced as well of the ineffectiveness of that strategy in limited war situations, Kennedy and his advisers had ruled out nuclear threats in areas like Southeast Asia, but not the need to manifest American firmness there. "We must produce quickly a course of action which convinces the other side we are dead serious," Rostow had warned Kennedy in August 1961. "What the U.S. does or fails to do," Maxwell Taylor added a few months later, "will be decisive to the end result."[13] The difficulty was that, short of embracing Dulles's strategy, all conceivable projections of resolve seemed to require, in one form or another, actual demonstrations of it.

[12] Joseph Califano draft presidential statement, December 2, 1964, enclosed in Califano to Bundy, December 3, 1964, Johnson Papers, NSF—Agency Files, Box 11-12, "Defense Department, Volume I"; Johnson message to Congress on Vietnam appropriations, May 4, 1965, *JPP: 1965*, p. 497. See also *JPP: 1963-64*, pp. 372, 1174; *JPP: 1965*, p. 489.

[13] Rostow to Kennedy, August 17, 1961, Kennedy Papers, NCS Files, Box 231, "Southeast Asia—General"; Taylor to Kennedy, October 24, 1961, *Pentagon Papers* , II, 88.

This did not bother the Joint Chiefs of Staff, who, as early as May 1961, had recommended the dispatch of United States troops to South Vietnam "to provide a visible deterrent to potential North Vietnamese and/or Chinese Communist action," and to "indicate the firmness of our intent to all Asian nations." An old Vietnam hand, Brigadier General Edward Lansdale, explained the rationale as follows:

> US *combat* forces, even in relatively small units, are the symbol of our national power. If an enemy engages one of our combat units, he is fully aware that he automatically has engaged the entire power of the US. This symbol of real national strength, employed wisely in Germany, Greece, and the Formosa Straits in a manner not unlike that contemplated for Thailand and Vietnam, has "kept the peace." When the mission of such US force is properly announced and followed immediately by a firm action, recent history teaches that the effect is just the reverse of "escalation" and that our action obtains world support outside the [Sino-Soviet] Bloc.

"[T]he point of installing token U.S. forces before the event," Robert Komer added, "is to signal our intentions to the other fellow, and thus hopefully avoid having to face up to the commitment of substantial US forces after a fracas has developed." It was true that the United States might "end up with something approaching another Korea, but I think the best way of avoiding this is to move fast now before the war spreads to the extent that a Korean type commitment is required.[14]* This theory that immediate small-scale involvement could make massive long-term involvement unnecessary formed the basis of recommendations by Maxwell Taylor and Walt Rostow for the introduction of some 8,000 U.S. combat troops into South Vietnam in November 1961. "In our view," Taylor wrote the President, nothing is more calculated to sober the enemy and to discourage escalation ... than the knowledge that the United States has prepared itself soundly to deal with aggression at any level."[15]

---

[14] Joint Chiefs of Staff to Gilpatric, May 10, 1961, *Pentagon Papers,* II, 49; Lansdale to Gilpatric, May 10, 1961, Kennedy Papers, NSC Files, Box 231, "Southeast Asia—General"; Komer to Rostow, August 2, 1961, *ibid.;* Komer to Bundy, October 31, 1961, *ibid.* See also Komer memorandum, "A Doctrine of Deterrence for SEA—The Conceptual Framework," May 9, 1961, *ibid.*

*"I'm no happier than anyone about getting involved in another squalid, secondary theatre in Asia. But we'll end up doing so sooner or later anyway because we won't be willing to accept another defeat. If so, the real question is not whether but how soon and how much!" (Komer to Bundy, October 31, 1961, Kennedy Papers, NSC Files, Box 231, "Southeast Asia—General.")

[15] Taylor to Kennedy, November 3, 1961, *Pentagon Papers,* II, 654. See also, on the Taylor-Rostow report, *ibid.,* II, 73–120; Rostow, *The Diffusion of Power,* pp. 270–71, 274–79; and Maxwell Taylor, *Swords and Ploughshares* (New York: 1972), pp. 225–48.

But Kennedy had long been skeptical about the wisdom of sending American forces to fight in Southeast Asia: he had reminded his advisers the previous July of "the reluctance of the American people and of many distinguished military leaders to see any direct involvement of U.S. troops in that part of the world. . . . [N]othing would be worse than an unsuccessful intervention in this area." State Department assessments reinforced this view:

> We do not think the presence of US troops would serve to deter infiltrations short of overt armed intervention. There is not much reason for supposing the Communists would think our troops would be much more successful against guerrilla operations in South Viet-Nam than French troops were in North Viet-Nam. Counter-guerrilla operations require highly selective application of force; selection requires discrimination; and alien troops simply lack the bases for discriminating between friend and foe, except by the direction in which they shoot.

If the South Vietnamese themselves were not willing to make a "serious national effort," Dean Rusk warned in November, then it was "difficult to see how [a] handful [of] American troops can have [a] decisive influence." Persuaded by these arguments, concerned as well about priorities elsewhere (notably Berlin) and the risk of upsetting negotiations then in progress on Laos, Kennedy deferred implementing the Taylor-Rostow recommendation for combat troops. It would have been "like taking a drink," he explained to Arthur Schlesinger. "The effect wears off, and you have to take another."[16]

It is important to note, though, that Kennedy's decision against sending combat troops to Vietnam was not a rejection of "calibration" —just the opposite. The full Taylor-Rostow recommendations, he thought, would have constituted too abrupt an escalation of pressure; he preferred, instead, a more gradual approach, involving an increase of American economic and military aid to Saigon, together with the introduction of U.S. "advisers." Nothing in this procedure precluded the dispatch of ground troops at a later date if that should become necessary. Nor were there illusions as to the impact of these decisions on American credibility: "We are fully cognizant," the State Department cabled Saigon, "of [the] extent to which [these] decisions if implemented . . . will sharply increase the commitment of our prestige struggle to save SVN."[17] Kennedy's actions reflected doubts only

---

[16] Bundy memorandum, Kennedy meeting with advisers, July 28, 1961, Kennedy Papers, NSC Files, Box 231, "Southeast Asia—General"; Policy Planning Council memorandum, "Security in Southeast Asia," July 27, 1961, enclosed in McGhee to Rostow, July 28, 1961, *ibid.;* Rusk to State Department, November 1, 1961, *Pentagon Papers,* II, 105; Schlesinger, A *Thousand Days,* p. 547.

[17] Rusk to Nolting, November 14, 1961, *Pentagon Papers,* II, 119.

about the appropriate level of response necessary to demonstrate
American resolve, not about the importance of making that demonstration in the first place.

"Calibration" during the next two years took the form primarily of
efforts to transform South Vietnam into a sufficiently self-reliant anti-
communist bastion so that no direct commitment of United States
forces would be necessary. The goal, according to Roger Hilsman,
was to devise "an integrated and systematic military-political-
economic strategic counterinsurgency concept," to orient Saigon's
military and security forces "increasingly toward counter-guerrilla or
unconventional warfare tactics," to "broaden the effective participation of Vietnamese Government officials in the formulation and execution of government policy," and to "identify the populace with the
Vietnamese Government's struggle against the Viet Cong."[18] All of
this required several delicate balancing acts: moderating President
Ngo Dinh Diem's autocratic control enough to win popular support
for his government without at the same time weakening it to the point
that it could not resist Viet Cong pressures; providing the assistance
necessary for Diem to survive without discrediting him as an American
puppet; taking care, simultaneously, to see that Washington's interest
in Diem's survival did not allow him to make a puppet out of the
United States. In the end, the line proved too fine to walk: frustrated
by Diem's repression of Buddhist critics, fearful of a secret deal between his government and North Vietnam, Kennedy in August 1963
authorized a carefully orchestrated effort—in itself an example of
"calibration"—to overthrow him.[19] As it happened, though,
Washington was able to control neither the timing nor the manner of
Diem's removal, nor had it given much thought to what would replace
him; the effect was that the very instability Kennedy had feared
dominated politics in Saigon for the next three years.

The resulting Viet Cong gains led the Johnson administration by
the end of 1964 to approve what Kennedy had rejected—a combat role
for the United States in Vietnam. Even so, though, the principle of
"calibration" would still apply; there would be no sharp, all-out application of force. Rather, the plan, in Johnson's words, was for
military pressures against North Vietnam "progressively mounting in
scope and intensity for the purpose of convincing the leaders of the
DRV that it is to their interest to cease to aid the Viet Cong and to
respect the independence and security of South Vietnam." This "slow
squeeze" strategy contemplated action strong enough to end the existing deteriorating situation, but not so violent as to knit the North

[18] Hilsman to Harriman, June 18, 1962, *Pentagon Papers*, II, 673.
[19] See, for example, Hilsman's elaborate "Action Plan" for South Vietnam, un-
dated, Kennedy Papers, NSC File, Box 317, "Meetings on Vietnam"; also, the *Pentagon Papers*, II, 201–76.

Vietnamese people more closely together, provoke Chinese Communist intervention, arouse world opinion, or preclude opportunities for an eventual negotiated settlement. The objective, Bundy noted on the eve of the first air strikes against the North in February 1965, was "to keep before Hanoi the carrot of our desisting as well as the stick of continued pressure. . . . Once such a policy is put into force, we shall be able to speak in Vietnam on many topics and in many ways, with growing force and effectiveness."[20]*

The bombing campaign against North Vietnam was intended to be the most carefully calibrated military operation in recent history. Great significance was attached to not crossing certain geographic "thresholds" for fear of bringing in the Chinese, as had happened in Korea, to avoiding civilian casualties that might intensify opposition to the war within the United States and elsewhere, and to combining the bombing with various inducements, especially periodic bombing pauses and offers of economic aid, to bring Hanoi to the conference table. Target selection was done in Washington, often in the White House itself, with the President at times personally monitoring the outcome of particular missions. Extraordinary precision was demanded of pilots—one 1966 order specified that piers at Haiphong could be hit only if no tankers were berthed at them, that vessels firing on American planes could be struck only if they were "clearly North Vietnamese," and that no attacks were to be launched on Sunday.[21] Even with such restrictions, though, the scale and intensity of the bombing progressively mounted, from 25,000 sorties** and 63,000 tons of bombs dropped in 1965 to 108,000 sorties and 226,000 tons in 1967, from missions directed initially at military bases in the southern "panhandle" of North Vietnam to infiltration routes, transportation facilities, and petroleum storage areas throughout the country, ultimately to factories and power plants in the Hanoi-Haiphong complex itself.[22] And none of it produced discernible progress toward

[20] Johnson to Taylor, December 3, 1964, Johnson Papers, NSC Staff Files, Box 2, "Memos for the President, Vol. 7"; Bundy memorandum, "A Policy of Sustained Reprisal," February 7, 1965, *Pentagon Papers*, III, 690; Bundy to Johnson, February 7, 1965, *ibid.*, p. 311. See also Kearns, *Johnson and the American Dream*, pp. 264–65. For the evolution of the "slow squeeze" option, see the *Pentagon Papers*, III, 206–51, 587–683.

*Eugene Rostow argued that Johnson's "bold but prudent action in Vietnam had posed two things: that we would risk bombs over New York in order to protect Saigon, and that Moscow would not bomb New York to protect Hanoi. This was an event and a demonstration of capital importance, which should greatly fortify our system of alliances, and weaken that of our enemies." (Rostow memorandum, April 10, 1965, enclosed in Bill Moyers to Bundy, April 13, 1965, Johnson Papers, NSF Country Files: Vietnam, Box 16, "Memos—Vol. XXXII.")

[21] JSC to CINCPAC, June 22, 1966, *Pentagon Papers*, IV, 105–6.

**A sortie is one flight by one plane.

[22] George C. Herring, *America's Longest War: The United States and Vietnam, 1950–1975* (New York: 1979), p. 147.

what it was supposed to accomplish: a tapering off of infiltration into South Vietnam, and movement toward negotiations.

Meanwhile, pressures had been building for the introduction of ground troops. Bundy had recommended this option as early as May 1964: the idea, he wrote Johnson, would be one of "marrying Americans to Vietnamese at every level, both civilian and military . . . to provide what [Saigon] has repeatedly asked for: the tall American at every point of stress and strain." "I do not at all think it is a repetition of Korea," he added in August. "It seems to me at least possible that a couple of brigade-size units put in to do specific jobs . . . might be good medicine everywhere." Rostow agreed, pointing out that such troops could usefully serve as bargaining chips in any future negotiations, and by February 1965 Rusk too had endorsed the idea, along with the bombing, as a way to send "a signal to Hanoi and Peiping that they themselves cannot hope to succeed without a substantial escalation on their part, with all the risks they would have to face."[23] The decisive argument in the end, though, proved to be General William Westmoreland's assertion that troops were needed to guard the air base at Da Nang from which some of the strikes against the north were being launched, a claim almost certainly advanced with a view to securing presidential authorization of a combat mission whose scope could then be widened far beyond the limited purposes for which it was made.[24] This "entering wedge" worked, and by early April 1965 Johnson had approved a combat role for United States forces in Vietnam. The pattern of escalation quickly went beyond Bundy's two brigades: from an initial deployment of 3,500 Marines at Da Nang, U.S. troop strength rose to 184,000 by the end of 1965, 385,000 by the end of 1966, and 486,000 by the end of 1967.[25] Nor, as the Tet offensive of early 1968 seemed to show, was there convincing evidence that those troops had come any closer to accomplishing their mission than had the bombing campaign.

What strikes one in retrospect about the strategy of calibrated escalation is the extent to which, as so often happened in Vietnam, the effects produced were precisely opposite from those intended. The objective of applying incremental pressures beginning in 1961 had been

[23] Bundy to Johnson, May 22 and August 31, 1965, Johnson Papers, NSF-NSC Staff Files, Box 1, "Memos for the President, Vol. 4," and Box 2, "Memos for the President, Vol. 6"; Rostow to McNamara, November 16, 1964, *Pentagon Papers*, III, 632; Rusk memorandum, "Viet-Nam," February 23, 1965, Johnson Papers, NSF Country File: Vietnam, Box 14, "Memos, Vol. XXIX."

[24] See, on this point, Guenter Lewy, *America in Vietnam* (New York: 1978), pp. 42–46; Robert L. Gallucci, *Neither Peace Nor Honor: The Politics of the American Military in Viet-Nam* (Baltimore: 1976), pp. 111–12; and the analysis in the *Pentagon Papers*, III, 429–33.

[25] Figures on troop strength are from Herbert Y. Schandler, *The Unmaking of a President: Lyndon Johnson and Vietnam* (Princeton, 1977), p. 352.

to avoid a massive American military involvement: token commitments, it was thought, would demonstrate resolve, thereby obviating the necessity for larger commitments later. The theory was not unlike that of vaccination, in that exposure to minimum risk was expected to provide immunities against more serious dangers. Another analogy, used at the time, was that of a plate-glass window, insufficiently strong in itself to keep out a thief, but capable of producing such conspicuous consequences if shattered as to discourage attempts from being made in the first place. Getting involved, in short, was the best way to avoid getting involved: "I deeply believe," Rostow had written in August of that year, "that the way to save Southeast Asia and to minimize the chance of deep U.S. military involvement there is for the President to make a bold decision very soon."[26]

Bold decisions were made (admittedly not in as bold a manner as Rostow had wanted), but the effect was hardly to minimize American involvement. United States manpower, resources, and prestige were far more deeply committed by 1968 than even "worst case" scenarios seven years earlier had indicated. McNamara had estimated in November 1961 that in the unlikely event that *both* North Vietnam and Communist China overtly intervened in the war, Washington might have to send six divisions, or 205,000 men. Peking did not intervene, Hanoi kept its own participation below the level of overt acknowledgment, but still the United States had more than doubled McNamara's prediction as to "the ultimate possible extent of our military commitment."[27] Calibrated pressures as a deterrent obviously had not worked.

One reason for this was a persistent lack of clarity as to who, or what, was being deterred. Impressed by Khrushchev's "wars of national liberation" speech, the Kennedy administration had at first located the roots of Viet Cong insurgency in Moscow: Rostow in 1961 had even advocated an early form of "linkage," making it clear to the Kremlin that no progress toward détente could take place while guerilla activity continued in Southeast Asia.[28]* By 1964, though,

[26] Rostow to Robert F. Kennedy, August 18, 1961, Kennedy Papers, NSC Files, Box 231, "Southeast Asia—General." See also Robert Komer, "A Doctrine of Deterrence for SEA—The Conceptual Framework," May 9, 1961, *ibid.*

[27] McNamara to Kennedy, November 8, 1961, *Pentagon Papers,* II, 108.

[28] Rostow to Kennedy, May 11, 1961, Kennedy Papers, NSC Files, Box 231, "Southeast Asia—General."

*Rostow wanted Kennedy to warn Khrushchev at Vienna that if the United States were "drawn deeper and more directly on to the Southeast Asian mainland," this would require a major increase in military spending and difficulties in relations with Moscow because "it is difficult for a democracy simultaneously to gear itself for possible military conflict and also to take the steps necessary to ease tensions and to expand the areas of U.S.-Soviet collaboration." (Rostow to Kennedy, May 11, 1961, Kennedy Papers, NSC Files, Box 231, "Southeast Asia—General.") There is no evidence that Kennedy actually raised this point with Khrushchev at Vienna—perhaps he realized that the Soviet leader might welcome rather than regret an American distraction in Southeast Asia.

Peking, not Moscow, had come to be seen as the culprit: the objective of American policy, National Security Council staff member Michael Forrestal argued late that year, should be to "delay China's swallowing up Southeast Asia until (a) she develops better table manners and (b) the food is somewhat more indigestible." The absence of official relations precluded opportunities for diplomatic "linkage" with Peking, however, and Johnson's advisers, remembering miscalculations during the Korean War, were extremely cautious about applying military pressure in any form. "China is there on the border with 700 million men," Johnson noted; "we could get tied down in a land war in Asia very quickly if we sought to throw our weight around."[29]

The alternative, it would appear, was direct pressure against Hanoi, but things were not quite that simple. John McNaughton in September 1964 identified at least four separate "audiences" aside from Moscow and Peking that the United States would have to influence: "the Communists (who must feel strong pressures), the South Vietnamese (whose morale must be buoyed), our allies (who must trust us as 'underwriters'), and the US public (which must support our risk-taking with US lives and prestige)." The difficulty, of course, was that actions directed at one "audience" might affect others in undesirable ways. Too sharp an escalation aimed at Hanoi risked alienating public opinion in the United States (especially during an election year), and elsewhere in the world, not to mention the danger of Chinese intervention. Moreover, such action would accomplish little as long as instability continued to reign in Saigon, as it had since the overthrow of Diem late in 1963. On the other hand, though, further restraint could only accelerate deterioration of the military situation in the South; it also conveyed the appearance of weakness and indecisiveness, not only in Hanoi and among American allies in Asia, but in Saigon itself, where the resulting low morale produced still more instability. The need, McNaughton argued, was for action taken "with special care—signaling to the DRV that initiatives are being taken, to the GVN that we are behaving energetically . . . , and to the US public that we are behaving with good purpose and restraint."[30]

[29] Forrestal to William P. Bundy, Novermber 23, 1964, *Pentagon Papers,* III, 644; Johnson remarks at the University of Akron, October 21, 1964, *JPP: 1964,* p. 1391. See also *ibid.,* pp. 1164–65.

[30] McNaughton draft, "Plan of Action for South Vietnam," September 3, 1964, *Pentagon Papers,* III, 559. See also Taylor to Rusk, August 18, 1964, *ibid.,* pp. 545–48; Bundy memorandum, meeting with Johnson, September 9, 1964, Johnson Papers, NSF-NSC Staff Files, Box 2, "Memos for the President, Vol. 6"; William H. Sullivan to William P. Bundy, November 6, 1964, *Pentagon Papers,* III, 594; Rostow to Rusk, November 23, 1964, *ibid.,* pp. 645–46; Taylor briefing of November 27, 1964, *ibid.,* pp. 671–72; William P. Bundy memorandum, November 28, 1964, *ibid.,* p. 676; Bundy memorandum, December 28, 1964, Johnson Papers, NSF—NSC Staff Files, Box 2, "Memos for the President, Vol. 7"; Bundy to Johnson, January 27, 1965, *ibid.* See also Leslie H. Gelb and Richard Betts, *The Irony of Vietnam: The System Worked* (Washington, D.C.: 1979), pp. 12–13.

But "calibration" implies a single target: where several exist, in a constantly shifting but interrelated pattern, the attainment of a precise correspondence between intentions and consequences becomes no easy matter.* A second problem flowed directly from the first. By eschewing anything other than gradual escalation, matched carefully to the level of enemy provocation, the Johnson administration was in effect relinquishing the initiative to the other side. This was, of course, a standard military criticism of White House policy: the argument was that if only restraints on air and ground action could be lifted, the war could be ended rapidly.[31]† Given the subsequently demonstrated ability of the North Vietnamese and Viet Cong to hold out for years under much heavier pressures, the claim, in retrospect, seems unconvincing. Still, there was one valid element in the military's argument. Theorists of international relations have suggested that deterrence is more likely to work when a potential aggressor is unsure of his ability to control the risks involved in the action he is contemplating. If that confidence exists, deterrence will probably be ineffective.[32] This idea of cultivating uncertainty in the minds of adversaries had been central to Dulles's strategy of "retaliation"—with what effects it is impossible to say, given the difficulty of trying to prove what deterrence deterred. But uncertainty did not carry over into the strategy of "calibration." To proclaim that one intends to do only what is necessary to counter aggression and no more is, after all, to yield control over one's actions to those undertaking the aggression. Washington officials may have had the illusion that they were making decisions on Vietnam force deployments during the Johnson years, but in fact those choices were

---

*McNamara succinctly summarized the problem of impressing multiple "audiences" in a July 1965 memorandum to Johnson: "Our object in Vietnam is to create conditions for a favorable outcome by demonstrating to the VC/DRV that the odds are against their winning. We want to create these conditions, if possible, without causing the war to expand into one with China or the Soviet Union and in a way which preserves support of the American people and, hopefully, of our allies and friends." (McNamara to Johnson, July 20, 1965, Johnson Papers, NSF Country File: Vietnam, Box 74, "1965 Troop Decision.")

[31] See, for example, the Joint Chiefs of Staff to McNamara, January 22, 1964, *Pentagon Papers*, III, 497-98; also Gallucci, *Neighter Peace Nor Honor*, pp. 38-39

†Perhaps the most pungent expression of this idea came from General Thomas S. Power, Strategic Air Force Commander, who told a Pentagon audience in 1964 that "the task of the military in war was to kill human beings and destroy man-made objects," and to do it "in the quickest way possible." It had been "the moralists who don't want to kill" that had given "Hitler his start and got us into the mess in Cuba and Viet-Nam." The "computer types who were making defense policy don't know their ass from a hole in the ground." (Summary, Power briefing, April 28, 1964, Johnson Papers, NSF Agency File, Box 11-12, "Defense Dept. Vol. I")

[32] George and Smoke, *Deterrence in American Foreign Policy*, p. 529.

being made, as a consequence of the administration's own strategy, in Hanoi.[33]

The alternative, of course, was some kind of negotiated settlement with North Vietnam, an option the administration was careful never to rule out. "[We] should strike to hurt but not to destroy," Bundy noted in May 1964, "for the purpose of changing the North Vietnamese decision on intervention in the South." Taylor seconded the point some months later: "it is well to remind ourselves that 'too much' in this matter of coercing Hanoi may be as bad as 'too little.' At some point, we will need a relatively cooperative leadership in Hanoi willing to wind up the VC insurgency on terms satisfactory to us and our SVN allies."[34] But Johnson and his advisers were wary of a "neutralist" solution for South Vietnam along the lines of the shaky 1962 truce in Laos—perhaps with good reason, given the speed with which Hanoi violated the agreements eventually reached at Paris in 1973. The preferred option was to achieve successes on the battlefield, and then approach North Vietnam: "After, *but only after*, we have established [a] clear pattern [of] pressure hurting DRV and leaving no doubts in South Vietnam of our own resolve, we could . . . accept [a] conference broadened to include [the] Vietnam issue," the State Department cabled Saigon in August 1964; such negotiations, if they did occur, would have to bring "Hanoi (and Peiping) eventually [to] accept idea of getting out."[35] This familiar but elusive position of "negotiation from strength" had two difficulties: it contained no safeguards against attempts by Hanoi to bolster its own negotiating position, or against the progressively deeper American involvement the strategy of "calibration" was supposed to prevent.

Finally, the strategy of "calibration" broke down because it failed to ensure that force, once applied, would be used as a precise and discriminating instrument of policy. It provided no safeguards against the subordination of strategic interests to those of the organizations implementing the strategy. Large bureaucracies all too often develop their own institutional momentum: "standard operating procedures" can make an organization impervious either to instructions from above or feedback from below.[36] One strength of McNamara's

[33] See, on this point, Alain Enthoven to Clark Clifford, March 20, 1968, in Enthoven and Smith, *How Much Is Enough,* pp. 298–99; and Schandler, *The Unmaking of a President,* pp. 31–42, 46.

[34] Bundy to Johnson, May 22, 1964, Johnson Papers, NSF-NSC Staff File, Box 1, "Memos for the President, Vol. I"; Taylor to State Department, November 3, 1964, *Pentagon Papers,* III, 591. See also Taylor to State Department, August 18, 1964, *ibid.,* pp. 546–47.

[35] Rusk to Lodge, August 14, 1964, *ibid.,* II, 330. See also William P. Bundy's first draft of this cable, *ibid.,* III, 526.

[36] See, on this point, Graham T. Allison, *Essence of Decision: Explaining the Cuban Missile Crisis* (Boston: 1971), pp. 83, 89.

reforms in the Pentagon had been the extent to which he had overcome this problem in dealing with the military on nuclear and
budgetary matters. No such successes, however, occurred in Vietnam.
Instead, once American forces were committed, Washington seemed
to lose control, leaving the military with a degree of autonomy surprising in an administration that had prided itself on having reduced
military authority over the conduct of national security affairs.[37]

The generalization may seem out of place applied to a war whose
soldiers complained regularly about civilian-imposed constraints, but
the military's grievances in this regard should be treated with skepticism. It is true that during the early period of American involvement,
there were significant restrictions on the nature and scope of U.S.
military activity, but as time went on without the desired enemy
response, these gradually dropped away. By August of 1967, for example, the White House had authorized for bombing some 95 percent
of the North Vietnamese targets requested by the Joint Chiefs of Staff.
Moreover, the Air Force's perceived institutional interests were
allowed to influence the conduct of the air war in important ways.
Despite its obvious (and widely appreciated) inapplicability to guerilla
warfare, the Air Force insisted successfully on a campaign of strategic
bombing in North Vietnam, and even on the use of B-52's, designed
originally to deliver nuclear weapons against Soviet targets, to hit
suspected Viet Cong emplacements in the south. Similarly, it relied
heavily on high-performance jet aircraft for other bombing missions
in the south, despite studies indicating that slower propeller-driven
models would have been three times as accurate, from five to thirteen
times less costly, but with roughly the same loss ratio.[38] It was, in
retrospect, an adaptation of ends to fit preferred means, rather than
the other way around.

The tendency was even more obvious with regard to the ground
war. Like most of his army colleagues, General Westmoreland had little sympathy for or understanding of the irregular warfare concepts
that had been popular during the early Kennedy administration: the
function of infantry, he insisted, was to seek out, pursue, and destroy
enemy forces. As a consequence, he never seriously considered the
strategy of holding and securing territory recommended by most
counterinsurgency theorists, and implemented with considerable success by the Marines in the area around Da Nang in 1965 and 1966.[39]
Instead he chose to emphasize largescale "search and destroy" operations, designed to wear the enemy down through sheer attrition. These

[37] Gelb and Betts, *The Irony of Vietnam,* pp. 239–40; Lewy, *America in Vietnam,*
pp. 114–16
[38] Gallucci, *Neither Peace Nor Honor,* pp. 73–80; Lewy, *America in Vietnam,* p. 98.
[39] Gallucci, *Neither Peace Nor Honor,* pp. 114–15, 119–20; Lewy, *America in Vietnam,* pp. 43, 51, 117.

not only disrupted efforts at pacification and provided the enemy with sufficient advance warning to escape; they also frequently forced the Americans to destroy villages in order to reach Viet Cong troops and arms caches located deliberately within those villages. Random "harassment and interdiction" fire against "suspected" but unobserved enemy targets did little to convince inhabitants of the regions affected that their security would be enhanced by supporting Saigon. The Westmoreland strategy even involved, in some instances, the deliberate creation of refugees as a means of securing the countryside, as complete a reversal as can be imagined from the original objectives the American commitment in South Vietnam had been intended to serve.[40]

It was left to the Navy, though, to come up with the most striking example of weapons ill-suited to tasks by retrieving from mothballs the U.S.S. *New Jersey*, the world's last functioning battleship, for the purpose of shelling the jungle in a manner reminiscent of nothing so much as an incident in Joseph Conrad's "Heart of Darkness":

> Once, I remember, we came upon a man-of-war anchored off the coast. There wasn't even a shed there, and she was shelling the bush. It appears the French had one of their wars going on thereabouts. . . . In the empty immensity of earth, sky, and water, there she was, incomprehensible, firing into a continent. Pop, would go one of the six-inch guns; a small flame would dart and vanish, a little white smoke would disappear, a tiny projectile would give a feeble screech—and nothing happened. Nothing could happen. There was a touch of insanity in the proceeding, a sense of lugubrious drollery in the sight; and it was not dissipated by somebody on board assuring me earnestly there was a camp of natives—he called them enemies—hidden out of sight somewhere.[41]

It was all a remarkable departure from the injunctions to do just enough, but no more than was necessary, with which the United States had entered the conflict in Vietnam.

"[T]he central object of U.S. military policy is to create an environment of stability in a nuclear age," Rostow wrote in 1966; "this requires as never before that military policy be the servant of political purposes and be woven intimately into civil policy." To be sure, this had been the objective all along of the "calibration" strategy: it reflected the immense confidence in the ability to "manage" crises and control bureaucracies that was characteristic of "flexible response," the concern to integrate force and rationality, to find some

⁴⁰ *Ibid.*, pp. 52, 65, 99–101, 106, 108–14; 118–19; Frances FitzGerald, *Fire in the Lake: The Vietnamese and the Americans in Vietnam* (Boston: 1972), pp. 344–45.
⁴¹ Joseph Conrad, *Heart of Darkness*, edited by Robert Kimbrough (New York: 1971), p. 14.

middle ground between the insanity of nuclear war and the humiliation of appeasement. But it was also a curiously self-centered strategy, vague as to the objects to be deterred, heedless of the extent to which adversaries determined its nature and pace, parochial in its assumption that those adversaries shared its own preoccupations and priorities, blind to the extent to which the indiscriminate use of force had come to replace the measured precision of the original concept. "Despite its violence and difficulties, our commitment to see it through in Vietnam is essentially a stabilizing factor in the world," Rostow had insisted, no doubt with complete sincerity and the best of intentions.[42] But when sincerity and good intentions come to depend upon myopic self-absorption, then the price can be high indeed.

III

One of the curious things about the breakdown of "calibration" was official Washington's chronic inability to detect the fact that it had failed. Gaps between objectives sought and results produced widened with only infrequent attempts to call attention to what was happening; those warnings that were advanced produced few discernible responses. This pattern suggests yet another deficiency in "flexible response" theory as applied in Vietnam: a persistent inability to monitor performance, an absence of mechanisms for ensuring that correspondence between the intent of one's actions and their actual consequences that is essential for an effective strategy.

That such lapses should have occurred is puzzling, given the great emphasis both Kennedy and Johnson placed on management techniques designed to achieve precise adaptations of resources to objectives. Exponents of "systems analysis" have explained that their ideas were not applied in Vietnam until it was too late to avoid involvement, but that, once put to use, they quickly revealed the futility of the existing strategy.[43] This view is correct, but narrow. It is true that the Systems Analysis Office in the Pentagon did not begin making independent evaluations of the war until 1966. But, in a larger sense, the Kennedy-Johnson management techniques had been present all along, in the form of both administrations' confidence that they could control bureaucracies with precision, use force with discrimination, weigh costs against benefits, and relate short-term tactics to long-term objectives. The inability to monitor performance, demonstrated so vividly in the failure of "calibration," suggests difficulties in applying these methods, but not their absence.

One reason these methods broke down in Vietnam was their heavy reliance on easily manipulated statistical indices as measurements of

---

[42] Rostow to McNamara, May 2, 1966, Johnson Papers, NSF Agency File, Boxes 11-12, "Defense Department Vol. III." See also Rostow's 1962 draft "Basic National Security Policy," p. 38.

[43] Enthoven and Smith, *How Much Is Enough*, pp. 270–71.

"progress" in the war. Here the primary responsibility rests with McNamara, who insisted on applying to that complex situation the same emphasis on quantification that had served him so well in the more familiar worlds of big business and the Pentagon.[44]* The difficulty, of course, was that the voluminous calculations McNamara insisted on were no better than the accuracy of the statistics that went into them in the first place: there were few if any safeguards against distortion. *"Ah, les statistiques!"* Roger Hilsman reports one South Vietnamese general as having exclaimed. "Your Secretary of Defense loves statistics. We Vietnamese can give him all he wants. If you want them to go up, they will go up. If you want them to go down, they will go down."[45] Or, in the succinct parlance of a later generation of computer specialists, "garbage in, garbage out."

The problem manifested itself first with regard to South Vietnamese performance following the introduction of United States advisers in 1961. The very presence of the Americans, it had been thought, would make possible more accurate monitoring of the situation,[46] but in fact the opposite occurred. The advisers depended on information furnished them by Diem's officers, many of whom combined a desire to please their powerful ally with a reluctance to risk their own necks in battle. The result was a deliberate inflation of statistical indices, the extent of which became clear only after the fall of Diem in November 1963. Of some 8,600 "strategic hamlets" Diem claimed to have constructed, it turned out that only about 20 percent existed in completed form. A high percentage of military operations initiated by Saigon—possibly as many as one third—were launched in areas where the Viet Cong were known *not* to be. One district chief had listed all twenty-four hamlets in his district as secure when in fact he controlled only three. "[T]he situation has been deteriorating . . . to a far greater extent than we had realized," McNamara acknowledged ruefully, "because of our undue dependence on distorted Vietnamese reporting."[47]**

---

[44] See David Halberstam's evocative portrait of McNamara in *The Best and the Brightest*, pp. 215–50.

*McNamara "has been trying to think of ways of dealing with this problem [Vietnam] for so long that he has gone a little stale," Bundy wrote to Johnson in June 1964. "Also, in a curious way, he has rather mechanized the problem so that he misses some of its real political flavor." (Bundy to Johnson, June 6, 1964, Johnson Papers, NSF—NSC Staff File, Box 2, "Memos for the President, Vol. 5.")

[45] Hilsman, *To Move a Nation,* p.523.

[46] See, on this point, the *Pentagon Papers,* II, 410–11.

[47] McNamara to Johnson, December 21, 1963, *ibid.,* III, 494. See also John McCone to McNamara, December 21, 1963, *ibid.,* p. 32; and Johnson, *The Vantage Point,* p. 63. The examples of distorted South Vietnamese reporting are from Hilsman, *To Move a Nation,* pp. 522–23.

**The difficulties, of course, did not end in 1963. The number of "Viet Cong" turned in under the Third Party Inducement Program, which provided monetary rewards for indentifying "defectors" willing to rally to Saigon's cause, rose from 17,836 in 1968 to

Not all such misrepresentations came from the South Vietnamese, though. Anxious to meet Washington's expectations of success, General Paul D. Harkins, commander of U.S. advisers in Vietnam, systematically ignored or suppressed reports from his own subordinates questioning Saigon's optimistic assessments of the war. As a result, Taylor and McNamara could report with conviction as late as October 1963 that "the tactics and techniques employed by the Vietnamese under U.S. monitorship are sound and give promise of ultimate victory."[48] Evidence that the situation was not in fact that rosy did occasionally surface, whether from the rare official visitor who managed to evade Harkins's packaged briefings and carefully guided tours, or from the more fequent published reporting of skeptical American correspondents in Saigon, among them Neil Sheehan and David Halberstam. But although Kennedy worried about these discrepancies, he at no point gave up primary reliance on official channels as a means of monitoring progress in the war; Johnson, if anything, depended on them more heavily.[49] It has been suggested that the accuracy of information tends to decline as the level of its classification rises, if for no other reason than that opportunities for independent verification are diminished thereby.[50] The proposition may not be universally applicable, but that the White House would have been better off reading Halberstam than Harkins seems beyond dispute.

These problems did not disappear with the onset of active American military involvement in Vietnam. The most notorious example, of course, was the use of enemy "body counts" as the chief indicator of "progress" in the ground war. The argument has been made that in such a conflict, where conventional indices—territory taken, distances covered, cities occupied—meant little, emphasis on these kinds of macabre statistics was unavoidable.[51]* That may be,

---

47,088 in 1969, at which point it was discovered that many of the alleged "defectors" were not Viet Cong at all, but South Vietnamese who had made a deal with friends to report them, and then split the reward. (Lewy, *America in Vietnam*, pp. 91–92.)

[48] Taylor and McNamara to Kennedy, October 2, 1963, *Pentagon Papers*, II, 187. See also Halberstam, *The Best and the Brightest*, pp. 200–205.

[49] Bundy memorandum, Kennedy meeting with Taylor and McNamara, September 23, 1963, Kennedy Papers, NSC Files, Box 200. "Vietnam Memos & Misc." See also Hilsman, *To Move a Nation* pp. 446–47, 502–4.

[50] Gallucci, *Neither Peace Nor Honor*, pp. 132–35; Gelb and Betts, *The Irony of Vietnam*, pp. 304–5. See also Roberta Wohlstetter, *Pearl Harbor: Warning and Decision* (Stanford: 1962), pp. 122–24.

[51] Dave Richard Palmer, *Summons of the Trumpet: U.S.-Vietnam in Perspective* (San Rafael, Cal.: 1978), pp. 119–20.

*The body count phenomenon even extended, at times, to digging up bodies for counting from freshly dug graves. (Lewy, *America in Vietnam*, p. 80.)

but what seems odd is the importance accorded them, given their widely acknowledged inaccuracy. Contemporary evaluations identified a margin of error of from 30 to 100 percent in these statistics, partly as the result of double or triple counting, partly because of the difficulty of distinguishing combatants from non-combatants, partly because of pressure from field commanders for higher and higher levels of "performance."[52] A more reliable index of success in the war was available—the number of North Vietnamese-Viet Cong weapons captured—but this was never given the significance of the body counts, probably because the figures were much less impressive. "It is possible that our attrition estimates substantially overstate actual VC/NVA losses," McNamara admitted in 1966. "For example, the VC/NVA apparently lose only about one-sixth as many weapons as people, suggesting the possibility that many of the killed are unarmed porters or bystanders."[53]

Similar statistical inflation occurred in the air war as well. Despite its acknowledged unreliability in an age of high-performance jet aircraft, pilot instead of photographic reconnaissance was generally used to measure the effectiveness of bombing in the North, presumably because damage claims tended to be higher. Photographic confirmation, when requested, was often not for the purpose of verifying pilot reports but to boost "sortie rates." Allocations of fuel and ordnance depended on these rates; they inevitably became an object of competition between the Air Force and the Navy, both of which shared the task of bombing North Vietnam. The results were predictable: a preference for aircraft with small bomb-load capacities which necessitated more frequent missions; the expenditure of bombs on marginal or already destroyed targets; even, during periods of munitions shortages, the flying of sorties without bombs. As one Air Force colonel put it: "bombs or no bombs, you've got to have more Air Force over the target than Navy."[54]

A second reason for the failure to monitor performance was a persistent tendency to disregard discouraging intelligence. It is a myth that the United States stumbled blindly into the Vietnam War. At every stage in the long process of escalation informed estimates were available which accurately (and pessimistically) predicted the outcome.* As early as November 1961, for example, the CIA was

[52] Lewy, *America in Vietnam*, pp. 78–82; Enthoven and Smith, *How Much Is Enough*, pp. 295–96.

[53] McNamara to Johnson, November 17, 1966, *Pentagon Papers*, IV, 371.

[54] Quoted in Gallucci, *Neither Peace Nor Honor*, p. 84; see also *ibid.*, pp. 80–85; Gelb and Betts, *The Irony of Vietnam*, pp. 309–10.

*"The information I received [on Vietnam] was more complete and balanced than anyone outside the mainstream of official reporting could possibly realize." (Johnson, *The Vantage Point*, p. 64.)

forecasting that North Vietnam would be able to match, through increased infiltration, any U.S. troop commitment to South Vietnam, and that bombing the North would not significantly impede that process. Two-and-a-half years later, a series of war games in which several key officials of the Johnson administration took part produced precisely the same conclusion.[55] Despite his own enthusiasm for this alternative in 1961 and 1964, Maxwell Taylor by 1965 was strongly opposing the introduction of ground combat forces on the grounds that a "white-faced soldier armed, equipped and trained as he is [is] not [a] suitable guerrilla fighter for Asian forests and jungles." Clark Clifford, Johnson's long-time personal friend and future Defense Secretary, was warning in May 1965 that Vietnam "could be a quagmire. It could turn into an open end commitment on our part that would take more and more ground troops, without a realistic hope of ultimate victory." George Ball, in a series of eloquent dissents from official policy, stressed that "a deep commitment of United States forces in a land war in South Viet-Nam would be a catastrophic error. If there ever was an occasion for a tactical withdrawal, this is it." Even William P. Bundy, one of the original architects of "calibration," had concluded by June of 1965 that any level of commitment beyond 70,000 to 100,000 troops would pass "a point of sharply diminishing returns and adverse consequences."[56]

"There are no signs that we have throttled the inflow of supplies for the VC," McNamara acknowledged after five months of bombing. "Nor have our air attacks on North Vietnam produced tangible evidence of willingness on the part of Hanoi to come to the conference table in a reasonable mood." And even if military successes on the ground could be achieved, there was no guarantee that these would not simply "drive the VC back into the trees" from which they could launch attacks at some future date. "[I]t is not obvious," the Secretary of Defense admitted, "how we will be able to disengage our forces from Vietnam." And yet, despite this gloomy appraisal, McNamara recommended a continuation of the bombing and an increase in troop strength from 75,000 to 175,000-200,000 men. Early in 1966, on the basis of no more encouraging signs of progress in ground or air operations, he endorsed a new troop ceiling of 400,000

[55] Special National Intelligence Estimate 10-4-61. November 5, 1961, *Pentagon Papers,* II, 107; Robert H. Johnson to William P. Bundy, March 31, 1965, Johnson Papers, NSF Country Files: Vietnam, Box 16, "Memos Vol. XXXII." See also Gelb and Betts, *The Irony of Vietnam,* pp. 25-26; Halberstam, *The Best and the Brightest,* pp. 460-62; and Johnson, *The Vantage Point,* pp. 147-49.

[56] Taylor to State Department, February 22, 1965, *Pentagon Papers,* III, 419; Clifford to Johnson, May 17, 1965, Johnson Papers, NSF Country Files: Vietnam, Box 74, "1965 Troop Decision"; Ball memorandum, "Cutting Our Losses in South Viet-Nam," June 28, 1965, *ibid.,* Box 18, "Memos (B) Vol. XXV"; William P. Bundy memorandum, "Holding On in South Vietnam," June 30, 1965, *ibid.*

men, acknowledging at the same time that the North Vietnamese and Viet Cong could probably match those increases. It might be possible, he thought, eventually to contain the enemy with 600,000 men, but that would risk bringing in the Chinese Communists. "It follows, therefore, that the odds are about even that, even with the recommended deployments, we will be faced in early 1967 with a military stand-off at a much higher level, with pacification hardly underway and with the requirement for the deployment of still more U.S. forces."[57]

McNamara's perserverance in the face of pessimism was not atypical—indeed, the Defense Secretary allowed the second sentiment to overwhelm the first sooner than most officials did. Westmoreland, in December 1965, for example, admitted that "notwithstanding the heavy pressures on their transportaion system in the past 9 months, they [the North Vietnamese] have demonstrated an ability to deploy forces into South Vietnam at a greater rate than we are deploying U.S. forces." Nevertheless, "our only hope of a major impact on the ability of the DRV to support the war in Vietnam is continuous air attack . . . from the Chinese border to South Vietnam." The CIA, whose assessments of the consequences of escalation had been especially discouraging, acknowledged in March 1966 that the bombing so far had been ineffective, but then recommended more of it, with fewer restraints. Later that year, in a comment characteristic of the resolute optimism of Johnson administration officials, Robert Komer argued that "by themselves, none of our Vietnam programs offer high confidence of a successful outcome. . . . Cumulatively, however, they *can* produce enough of a *bandwagon psychology* among the southerners to lead to such results by end-1967 or sometime in 1968. At any rate, do we have a better alternative?"[58]

The problem, as Komer suggested, was that however unpromising the prospects of continued escalation, the alternatives seemed even worse. Withdrawal would constitute humiliation, with all that implied for the maintenance of world order. Negotiations prior to establishing a "position of strength" could only lead to appeasement. Continuation of the status quo would not work because the status quo was too delicate. Public opinion remained solidly behind escalation until 1968; indeed, Johnson saw himself as applying the brake, not the accelerator.[59] As a result, there developed a curious mixture of gloom

[57] McNamara to Johnson, July 20, 1965, Johnson Papers, NSF Country File: Vietnam, Box 74, "1965 Troop Decision"; McNamara to Johnson, January 24, 1966, *Pentagon Papers*, IV, 49–51.

[58] Westmoreland cable, December 27, 1965, *Pentagon Papers*, IV, 39. The CIA and Komer reports are discussed in *ibid.*, pp. 71–71, 389–91. (Emphases in orginal.)

[59] Gelb and Betts, *The Irony of Vietnam*, pp. 159–60. See also Johnson, *The Vantage Point*, p. 147; and Kearns, *Lyndon Johnson and the American Dream*, p. 282.

and optimism: things were bad, they were likely to get worse before they got better, but since the alternatives to the existing strategy appeared even more forbidding, there seemed to be little choice but to "press on."

What has not been satisfactorily explained, though, is how the Johnson administration came to define its options so narrowly. In retrospect, quite a lot—negotiations on Hanoi's terms, a gradual relinquishment of responsibility for the war to the South Vietnamese, even a phased withdrawal in the anticipation of an eventual North Vietnamese-Viet Cong victory—would have been preferable to the strategy actually followed, which produced those same results but at vastly greater costs than if they had been sought in the mid-1960's. As George Kennan told the Senate Foreign Relations Committee in 1966, "there is more respect to be won in the opinion of this world by a resolute and courageous liquidation of unsound positions than by the most stubborn pursuit of extravagant and unpromising objectives."[60] But Johnson and his advisers could never bring themselves to consider "heretical" options, despite abundant evidence that their strategy was not working. Their hesitancy suggests still another reason for the failure to monitor performance in Vietnam: an absence of mechanisms for forcing the consideration of unpalatable but necessary alternatives.

Several explanations have been advanced to account for this lapse. It has been argued that there was a premium on "toughness" during the Kennedy-Johnson years; that advocates of a compromise settlement bore a far heavier burden of proof than did supporters of escalation.[61] But this view fails to explain Johnson's tenacious search for a negotiated settlement with Hanoi, carried on not just for the purpose of defusing opposition to the war at home but also in the genuine hope of finding a way out consistent with American credibility.[62] It has been pointed out that Johnson's circle of close advisers narrowed as critics of the war proliferated, and that this limited the Chief Executive's exposure to dissenting points of view.[63] But the President did keep on and listen to "house heretics" like George Ball; more significantly, he paid close attention to McNamara's growing doubts about the war in 1966 and 1967, but still refused to change the strategy.[64] It has recently been suggested that the whole national security decision-making system was at fault: the system "worked" in that it produced the results it had been "programmed" to produce, given prevailing assumptions about containment and the balance of

[60] Senate Committee on Foreign Relations, Hearings, *Supplemental Foreign Assistance Fiscal Year 1966—Vietnam* (Washington: 1966), pp. 335–36.

[61] Richard. J. Barnet, *Roots of War* (Baltimore: 1972), pp. 109–15.

[62] See the list of American peace initiatives and Hanoi's responses in Appendix A to Johnson, *The Vantage Point*, pp. 579–89.

[63] Gallucci, *Neither Peace Nor Honor,* pp. 132–34.

[64] See Johnson's personally drafted memorandum on McNamara's recommendations, December 18, 1967, in Johnson, *The Vantage Point*, pp. 600–601.

power since 1945; the error was in the "programming."[65] But this argument oversimplifies variations in perceptions of interests and threats over the years: while it is true that all postwar administrations have committed themselves to the general objective of containment, they have differed significantly over what was to be contained, and over the means available to do it.

It is this problem of perceived means that best explains the Johnson administration's inability to come up with alternatives in Vietnam. The mechanism that has most often forced the consideration of unpalatable options in the postwar years has been budgetary: when one knows one has only limited resources to work with, then distinctions between what is vital and peripheral, between the feasible and unfeasible, come more easily, if not less painfully. The Eisenhower administration found this out in 1954, when it decided that the "unacceptable" prospect of a communist North Vietnam was in fact preferable to the more costly alternative of direct U.S. military involvement. But, as has been seen, budgetary concerns carried little weight during the Kennedy and Johnson administrations. The theory of "flexible response" implied unlimited means and, hence, little incentive to make hard choices among distasteful alternatives.

Kennedy did from time to time emphasize the existence of limits beyond which Washington could not go in aiding other countries. "[T]he United States is neither omnipotent or omniscient," he pointed out in 1961: "we are only 6 percent of the world's population . . . we cannot right every wrong or reverse each adversary." It has been argued that the abortive 1963 plan for a phased withdrawal of American advisers from South Vietnam reflected Kennedy's sense that the limits of feasible involvement in that country were approaching.[66] But there is no conclusive evidence that Kennedy, on fiscal grounds, was considering a diminished American role there; certainly Johnson did not do so. The new President dutifully stressed the need for economy during his first months in office, but more for the purpose of enhancing his reputation with the business community than from any great concern about the limits of American power in the world scene.[67] And, as the Vietnam crisis intensified, so too did the conviction of Johnson and his advisers that the United States could afford whatever it would take to prevail there.

"[L]et no one doubt for a moment," Johnson proclaimed in August 1964, "that we have the resources and we have the will to

[65] Gelb and Betts, *The Irony of Vietnam*, pp. 2–3.
[66] Kennedy address at the University of Washington, November 16, 1961, *KPP: 1961*, p. 726. See also *ibid.*, pp. 340–41, 359; *KPP: 1963*, pp. 659–60, 735; and the *Pentagon Papers*, II, 161.
[67] *JPP: 1963–64*, pp. 44, 89, 122, 150.

follow this course as long as it may take." In a White House meeting the following month, Rusk pointed out that it had cost $50,000 per guerilla to suppress the insurgency in Greece in the late 1940's; in Vietnam "it would be worth any amount to win." Johnson agreed, emphasizing the need for all to understand "that it was not necessary to spare the horses." "Our assets, as I see them, are sufficient to see this thing through if we enter the exercise with adequate determination to succeed," Rostow wrote in November 1964; "at this stage in history we are the greatest power in the world—if we behave like it." Five months later, as direct American military involvement in Vietnam was beginning, McNamara informed the Joint Chiefs of Staff and the service secretaries that "there is an unlimited appropriation available for the financing of aid to Vietnam. Under no circumstances is a lack of money to stand in the way of aid to that nation." There were always costs in meeting "commitments of honor," Rusk commented in August of that year. "But I would suggest, if we look at the history of the last 30 or 40 years, that the costs of *not* meeting your obligations are far greater than those of meeting your obligations."[68]

"The world's most affluent society can surely afford to spend whatever must be spent for its freedom and security," Johnson told the Congress early in 1965. This assumption of virtually unlimited resources goes far toward explaining the persistence of what was acknowledged to be a costly and inefficient strategy: the idea was that if the United States could simply stay the course, regardless of the expense, it would prevail. "I see no choice," the President added, later that year, "but to continue the course we are on, filled as it is with peril and uncertainty and cost in both money and lives." It might take "months or years or decades," but whatever troops General Westmoreland required would be sent "as requested." "Wastefully, expensively, but nonetheless indisputably, we are winning the war in the South," Robert Komer concluded late in 1966. "Few of our programs—civil or military—are very efficient, but we are grinding the enemy down by sheer weight and mass." Westmoreland agreed. "We'll just go on bleeding them until Hanoi wakes up to the fact that they have bled their country to the point of national disaster for generations. Then they will have to reassess their position."[69]

[68] Johnson remarks to American Bar Association meeting, New York, August 12, 1964, *ibid.*, p. 953; Bundy memorandum, Johnson conference with advisers, September 9, 1964, Johnson Papers, NSF—NSC Files, Box 2, "Memos for the President, Vol. 6"; Rostow to Rusk, November 23, 1964, *Pentagon Papers*, III, 647; McNamara to the Joint Chiefs of Staff and service secretaries, March 1, 1965, *ibid.*, p. 94; Rusk CBS-TV interview, August 9, 1965, *DSB*, LIII (August 30, 1965), 344. (Emphasis in original.)

[69] Johnson report to Congress on national defense, January 18, 1965, *JPP: 1965*, p. 69; Johnson remarks to members of Congressional delegations, May 4, 1965, *ibid.*, p. 487; Johnson press conference, July 28, 1965, *ibid.*, pp. 795, 799; Komer memorandum, date not given, *Pentagon Papers*, II, 575; Westmoreland statement to press, April 14, 1967, quoted in Lewy, *America in Vietnam*, p. 73.

But McNamara's "systems analysis" specialists had reached the conclusion, by 1966, that it might take generations to bring the North Vietnamese to that point. Their studies showed, for example, that although enemy attacks tended to produce significant enemy casualties, operations launched by U.S. and South Vietnamese forces produced few if any. This suggested that despite the massive American military presence in the south, the North Vietnamese and Viet Cong still retained the initiative, and hence could control their losses. Other studies indicated that while bombing raids against North Vietnam had increased four times between 1965 and 1968, they had not significantly impaired Hanoi's ability to supply its forces in the south: enemy attacks there had increased on the average five times, and in places eight times, during the same period. The bombing was estimated to have done some $600 million worth of damage in the north, but at a cost in lost aircraft alone of $6 billion. Sixty-five percent of the bombs and artillery rounds expended in Vietnam were being used against unobserved targets, at a cost of around $2 billion a year. Such strikes, the analysts concluded, probably killed about 100 North Vietnamese or Viet Cong in 1966, but in the process provided 27,000 tons of dud bombs and shells which the enemy could use to make booby traps, which that same year accounted for 1,000 American deaths. But most devastating of all, the systems analysts demonstrated in 1968 that despite the presence of 500,000 American troops, despite the expenditure of more bomb tonnage than the United States had dropped in all of World War II, despite estimated enemy casualties of up to 140,000 men in 1967, the North Vietnamese could continue to funnel at least 200,000 men a year into South Vietnam indefinitely. As one analyst wrote, "the notion that we can 'win' this war by driving the VC/NVA from the country or by inflicting an unacceptable rate of casualties on them is false."[70]

Only the last of these studies had any noticeable impact outside the Office of the Secretary of Defense, though: persuasive though they were, there was little incentive, in an administration confident that it could sustain the costs of the war indefinitely, to pay any attention to them.[71] It was not until Johnson personally became convinced that the costs of further escalation would outweigh conceivable benefits that the discipline of stringency could begin to take hold. That did not happen until after the Tet offensive of February 1968, when the President received Westmoreland's request for an additional 206,000 troops, a figure that could not have been met without calling up Reserves and without major domestic and international economic dislocations.*

---

[70] Enthoven and Smith, *How Much Is Enough,* pp. 290–306.

[71] *Ibid.,* pp. 292–93.

*Curiously, Westmoreland's request was apparently prompted by the Chairman of the Joint Chiefs of Staff, General Earle G. Wheeler, as a means of forcing the reluctant Johnson to call up the Reserves. (Schandler, *The Unmaking of a President,* pp. 116, 138.)

Johnson had always regarded these as limits beyond which he would not go, not on the basis of rigorous statistical analysis, but rather from the gut political instinct that if he passed those points, public support for the war would quickly deteriorate.[72] In the end, then, the Johnson administration based its ultimate calculation of costs and benefits on criteria no more sophisticated than those employed by Eisenhower prior to 1961, or by Truman prior to 1950. The techniques of systems analysis, which had been designed to avoid the need for such arbitrary judgments, in fact only deferred but did not eliminate them.

Several circumstances discouraged the objective evaluation of performance in Vietnam. The military's relative autonomy gave it a large degree of control over the statistical indices used to measure "progress" in the war; this, combined with the organizationally driven compulsion to demonstrate success and the traditional reluctance of civilians in wartime to challenge military authority, made it difficult to verify charges of ineffectiveness.[73] Such accurate intelligence as did get through tended to be disregarded because the alternative courses of action thereby indicated seemed worse than the option of "pressing on." And the perception of unlimited means made perseverance even in the face of unpromising signals seem feasible: far from widening alternatives, the abundance of means, and the consequent lack of incentives to make hard decisions, actually narrowed them. As a result, the postwar administration most sensitive to the need to monitor its own performance found itself ensnared inextricably in a war it did not understand, could not win, but would not leave.

IV

But effectiveness in strategy requires not only the ability to identify interests and threats, calibrate responses, and monitor implementation; it also demands a sense of proportion, an awareness of how commitments in one sphere compare with, and can distract attention and resources away from, obligations elsewhere. Johnson and his subordinates thought they had this larger perspective: Vietnam, they repeatedly insisted, was important not just in itself, but as a symbol of American resolve throughout the world.* The line between a symbol and a fixation is a fine one, though; once it is crossed, perspectives

---

[72] Schandler, *The Unmaking of a President*, pp. 39, 56, 100–102, 228–29, 290–92. See also Johnson, *The Vantage Point*, pp. 149, 317–19, 406–7.

[73] See, on this point, Gallucci, *Neither Peace Nor War*, pp. 128–30.

*"The idea that we are here simply because the Vietnamese want us to be here . . . ; that we have no national interest in being here ourselves; and that if some of them don't

narrow, often unconsciously, with the result that means employed can become inappropriate to, even destructive of, ends envisaged. This narrowing of perspective, this loss of proportion, this failure to detect the extent to which short-term means can corrupt long-term ends, was the fourth and perhaps most lasting deficiency of "flexible response" as applied in Vietnam.

The tendency appeared vividly in South Vietnam itself, where the administration failed to anticipate the sheer strain several hundred thousand U.S. troops would place on the social and economic structure of that country. Despite American efforts to keep it down, the cost of living in the cities rose by at least 170 percent between 1965 and 1967, just as Westmoreland's "search and destroy" operations were swelling their populations with refugees. Corruption, of course, had always been present in Vietnam, but the proliferation of television sets, motorcycles, watches, refrigerators, and loose cash that accompanied the Americans greatly intensified it. "[T]he vast influx of American dollars," one observer recalls, "had almost as much influence . . . as the bombing had on the countryside":

> It turned the society of Saigon inside out. . . . In the new economy a prostitute earned more than a GVN minister, a secretary working for USAID more than a full colonel, a taxi owner who spoke a few words of English more than a university professor. . . . The old rich of Saigon had opposed the Communists as a threat to their position in society; they found that the Americans took away that position in a much quicker and more decisive fashion—and with it, what was left of the underpinning of Vietnamese values.

A similar phenomenon spread to rural areas as well: "Around the American bases from An Khe to Nha Trang, Cu Chi, and Chu Lai, there had grown up entire towns made of packing cases and waste tin . . . entire towns advertising Schlitz, Coca-Cola, or Pepsi Cola . . . towns with exactly three kinds of industry—the taking in of American laundry, the selling of American cold drinks to American soldiers, and prostitution for the benefit of the Americans."[74]

---

want us to stay, we ought to get out is to me fallacious," Ambassador Henry Cabot Lodge cabled from Saigon in 1966. "In fact, I doubt whether we would have the moral right to make the commitment we have made here solely as a matter of charity towards the Vietnamese and without the existence of a strong United States interest. . . . Some day we may have to decide how much it is worth to us to deny Viet-Nam to Hanoi and Peking—regardless of what the Vietnamese may think." (Lodge to State Department, May 23, 1966, *Pentagon Papers*, IV, 99–100.)

[74] FitzGerald, *Fire in the Lake*, pp. 315–16, 349, 352–53.

The effect of this overbearing presence was to erode South Vietnam's capacity for self-reliance, the very quality the Americans had sought to strengthen in the first place. To be sure, Washington never succeeded in controlling its clients in all respects: the very profligacy of the U.S. investment in South Vietnam made occasional threats to cut it off less than credible. "The harsh truth is," one report noted early in 1968, "that given a showdown situation or an intolerable divergence between GVN and US methods, the US advisor will lose." But recalcitrance is not the same thing as independence. The same report noted that "[t]he Vietnamese in the street is firmly convinced that the US totally dominates the GVN and dictates exactly what course shall be followed."[75] And Vietnamese at the military or governmental level, while certainly not puppets, while clearly resentful at the extent to which the Americans had come to dominate their culture, were at the same time terrified at the prospect that the Americans might one day leave.[76] The result was an ambiguous but deep dependency, the extent of which became clear only after the United States did at last withdraw from the war, in 1973.

It is hard to say, in retrospect, what the cross-over point would have been between the level of outside aid necessary to sustain South Vietnam against its enemies and the amount beyond which self-reliance would have been impaired. Perhaps there was no such point; perhaps South Vietnam never had the capacity to stand on its own. What is clear, though, is that Washington made few efforts to find out. The American buildup took place almost totally without regard to the destructive impact it was having on the society it was supposed to defend. "It became necessary to destroy the town, to save it," an Air Force major explained, following the bombing of a Mekong delta village occupied by Viet Cong after the Tet offensive in 1968."[77] The comment could be applied to the whole American experience in Vietnam, and to the dilemma of disproportionate means which the strategy of "flexible response," despite its original emphasis on matching response to offense, never seemed able to resolve.

Securing South Vietnam's independence had not been the only reason for the American presence in that country, though: there had also been a determination to show potential aggressors elsewhere that aggression would not pay. "To withdraw from one battlefield means only to prepare for the next," Johnson argued. "We must say in southeast Asia—as we did in Europe—. . . . 'Hitherto shalt thou

[75] MACCORDS report on Bien Hoa province for period ending December 31, 1967, *Pentagon Papers,* II, 406.

[76] FitzGerald, *Fire in the Lake,* p. 357.

[77] Quoted in Alexander Kendrick, *The Wound Within: America in the Vietnam Years, 1945-1974* (Boston: 1974), p. 251.

come, but no further.' ''[78] Interestingly, administration officials did not consider success in South Vietnam as necessarily a requirement in communicating that message. However things turned out there, John McNaughton reflected in 1964, it was "essential . . . that [the] US emerge as a 'good doctor.' We must have kept promises, been tough, taken risks, gotten bloodied, and hurt the enemy very badly." Sustained reprisals against the north might not work, McGeorge Bundy acknowledged early in 1965—the chances of success, he thought, were between 25 and 75 percent. But "even if it fails, the policy will be worth it. At a minimum it will damp down the charge that we did not ,do all we could. . . . Beyond that, a reprisal policy . . . will set a higher price for the future upon all adventures of guerrilla warfare."[79] The important thing, in projecting resolve, was to make a commitment; failure, while both possible and undesirable, would not be as bad as not having acted in the first place.

And yet, the signal actually communicated was very different. The inability of the steadily growing American commitment to halt North Vietnamese infiltration or Viet Cong attacks—a pattern made painfully evident by the 1968 Tet offensive—seemed only to demonstrate the irrelevancy of the kind of power the United States could bring to bear in such situations: technology, in this respect, may well have been more of a hindrance than a help in Vietnam.[80] The war also confirmed Mao Tse-tung's theory that relatively primitive forces could prevail against more sophisticated adversaries if they had both patience and will, qualities Ho Chi Minh perceived more accurately than Johnson to be lacking in the American attitude toward Vietnam.[81] Finally, Washington's commitment in that country had grown to the point, by 1968, that the United States would have been hard-pressed to respond anywhere else in the world had a comparable crisis developed.[82] What was demonstrated in Vietnam, then, was not so much the costs of committing aggression as of resisting it. . . .

[78] Johnson address at Johns Hopkins University, April 7, 1965, *JPP: 1965*, p. 395.

[79] McNaughton draft memorandum, "Aims and Options in Southeast Asia," October 13, 1964, *Pentagon Papers*, III, 582; Bundy memorandum, "A Policy of Sustained Reprisal," February 7, 1965, *ibid.*, p. 314.

[80] See, on this point, Lewy, *America in Vietnam*, pp. 60, 96, 175, 181–82, 207, 306, 437–38.

[81] See especially "On Protracted War," in the *Selected Military Writings of Mao Tse-tung* (Peking: 1967), pp. 210–19.

[82] Johnson, *The Vantage Point*, p. 389. See also Schandler, *The Unmaking of a President*, pp. 109, 171.

Nuclear Weapons and The 1973 Middle
East Crisis

BARRY M. BLECHMAN and
DOUGLAS M. HART

Ever since the Eisenhower Administration's policy of massive retaliation failed to stem either the tide of left-leaning nationalist revolutions in the third world or continuing Soviet pressures on Central
Europe, mainstream American opinion has tended to view the
potential of nuclear weapons to support U.S. foreign policy rather
skeptically. Because of the tremendous risks associated with the
use of nuclear weapons, most observers agree, a threat of nuclear
war is credible only in certain situations—those in which the nation's most important interests are evidently at stake. As such,
nuclear weapons can serve only narrow and distinct purposes. The
threat of nuclear retaliation, of course, serves to deter attacks on,
or coercion of, the United States itself. Also, it is widely believed
that this nuclear umbrella can be extended to those few nations,
primarily the industrialized democracies, for which—for reasons of
history and ethnic, cultural, economic, and political affinities—an
American threat to risk nuclear holocaust on their behalf may be
credible. Beyond that, however, since the late 1950s few have been
willing to argue publicly that other important political or military
purposes can or should be served by the nation's nuclear arsenal.

There is reason to question whether this common perspective on
the utility of nuclear weapons is complete, however. There is a
minority view which maintains that nuclear weapons (that is, the
threat of nuclear war which they imply) actually have served the
nation's policymakers more often and in more ways than are generally recognized. (Interestingly, this view is held by some on both
the extreme right and the extreme left of the American political
spectrum.) Indeed, there is at least some reason to believe that U.S.
decisionmakers have turned to nuclear threats in support of policy

From "The Political Utility of Nuclear Weapons" by Barry M. Blechman and
Douglas M. Hart, *International Security*, Summer 1982 (Vol. 7, No. 1) pp. 132–156.
© 1982 by the President and Fellows of Harvard College and of the Massachusetts
Institute of Technology. Reprinted by permission of MIT Press, Cambridge, Massachusetts and the copyright holders. Portions of the text have been omitted; all
referential and some explanatory footnotes have also been omitted.

in more than 20 specific incidents. Upon closer investigation, many of these incidents prove to be inadvertent, or misunderstood, or simply false; yet, there is some core number of cases—roughly one-half dozen—for which it can be documented that the nation's leaders consciously employed nuclear threats, or at least deliberately drew attention to the risk of nuclear war, as a means of bolstering American policy.

Most of these incidents took place in the 1950s, but the 1960s and 1970s have not been devoid of them. The most recent took place early in 1980, when the credibility of President Carter's commitment to defend the Persian Gulf came into question, and there was reason to believe that the Soviet Union was preparing to move into Iran. Within ten days of the President's statement, U.S. officials made clear nuclear threats on three separate occasions in a desperate attempt to put a real sanction behind the President's words. . . .

Perhaps the most relevant of the past nuclear threats took place during the Arab-Israeli War in October 1973. For the first time when both had mature and robust strategic nuclear forces, there was a serious threat of military conflict between the United States and the Soviet Union. By 1973, both superpowers had deployed nuclear forces that, on paper at least, seemed likely to be able to survive a first strike and retaliate with devastating force against the attacker. According to Western theories of nuclear deterrence, theories upon which we have staked our survival, such a balance of strategic capabilities should have inclined both sides to avoid any move that might have precipitated escalation and led to a greater risk of confrontation and nuclear war. In short, the balance of strategic nuclear forces should have led to stable political relations. This did not prove to be the case, however; in October 1973 both the United States and the Soviet Union took military steps in the Middle East of some significance. Moreover, for the first time since the Cuban missile crisis in October 1962, U.S. policymakers perceived a need to manipulate the risk of nuclear war overtly with the objective of influencing Soviet behavior.

Why was this done? What was expected to be accomplished? And how? To answer these questions, we interviewed several of the five principal participants in the Washington Special Action Group (WSAG)—the forum for crisis management during the Nixon Administration—and additional members of their senior staffs.[1] These

---

[1] Participants in the WSAG included Secretary of State Henry A. Kissinger, Secretary of Defense James R. Schlesinger, Director of Central Intelligence William E. Colby, the President's Deputy National Security Advisor General Brent Scowcroft, and Chairman of the Joint Chiefs of Staff Admiral Thomas Moorer; President Nixon took no part in the WSAG's deliberations. The ground rules governing our interviews preclude direct quotations.

interviews, and supplementary material found in published sources, can make an important contribution to the current debate on the utility of nuclear weapons in the conduct of American foreign policy.

THE CRISIS

The superpower confrontation in 1973 lasted less than 48 hours, beginning early in the morning of October 24th. There was no time for extensive deliberations, for the formulation of sophisticated policy options, for debate. Decision-makers were occupied almost entirely with keeping abreast of a rapidly changing situation and formulating necessarily *ad hoc* reactions to unfolding events. Given the capabilities of modern communications and control systems, this compression of decision-making time is likely to characterize most future crises and will have to be a fundamental consideration in crisis management.

As the Washington Special Action Group met on the morning of October 24th, fighting between Israel and Egypt continued in the Middle East, despite two UN Security Council cease-fire resolutions in as many days. By this time Israel had repulsed the Syrian and Egyptian incursions which started the war and at considerable cost had begun to move deep into Arab territory. A cease-fire had been declared and was holding on the Syrian front, but fighting continued on the west bank of the Suez Canal, where Israeli forces had trapped an entire Egyptian army. Although the United States put considerable pressure on Israel to abide by the cease-fire, it was clear that American concerns were not decisive. At a minimum, the Israelis seemed determined to retain the encircled Egyptian Third Army as a bargaining chip in any future disengagement talks. Israeli policymakers might also have contemplated destroying the Third Army as a "lesson" to any future would-be aggressors. Despite contrary orders from Cairo, the commander of the Third Army persisted in attempts to break out of the trap his forces were in, but succeeded only in giving Israel an excuse for continuing operations against the beleaguered units. Israeli troops refused to allow UN observers to reach the surrounded Egyptian divisions. And in Tel Aviv, General Chaim Herzog stated that the Third Army's only option was "surrender with honor."

KISSINGER AND THE DOUBLE-CROSS RISK

The extent to which Israel's belligerent attitude may have resulted from deliberate or inadvertent signals from Henry Kissinger is uncertain. Kissinger flew to Moscow and agreed with the Russians to seek a cease-fire on October 20th. Two days later he was in Israel. He spent three and a half hours closeted with Prime Minister Golda

Meir and members of her cabinet trying to persuade them to accept the cease-fire terms he had negotiated with the Soviets. Mrs. Meir and her "kitchen cabinet" were quite unhappy, to say the least, with the deal. In effect, the Israelis were being asked to forgo destruction of the Third Army in return for the promise of face-to-face talks with the Egyptians "aimed at establishing a just and durable peace in the Middle East." To add insult to injury, the terms of the deal had been delivered with the instructions that no changes, substantive or semantic, could be made in the language of the agreement.

Accounts of Kissinger's performance in Israel vary. Some observers claim that the Secretary encouraged Israel to believe that the twelve-hour deadline for implementation of the cease-fire, stated in the agreement, was actually flexible. The Israelis reportedly interpreted this statement as a sign that Washington was prepared to allow them to complete the encirclement of the Third Army. Another version holds that Kissinger pressed Mrs. Meir and her advisers for an immediate cease-fire and strict adherence to the terms of the agreement. According to this view, Kissinger repeatedly stressed that both the United States and the Soviet Union opposed the destruction of the Egyptian Third Army.

Exactly what the Secretary of State told Mrs. Meir on the 22nd, however, is not nearly as important as the results of the meeting. Kissinger left Israel believing that the end of the war was near and that with careful diplomacy in the weeks ahead the situation could be defused. The Israelis, on the other hand, thought that they had some time left to fulfill their military objectives. And the Soviets thought that Kissinger had taken them to the cleaners. By the time the Secretary's plane had returned to Washington on the 23rd, the tactical situation had deteriorated; Israel seemed to be ignoring the cease-fire. A hotline message from Brezhnev to Nixon late on October 23rd, the eve of the crisis, confirmed that Moscow felt betrayed:

> . . . the words were hard and cold, he urged that the U.S. move decisively to stop the violations. He curtly implied that we might even have colluded in Israel's action.

This feeling of betrayal seems to have been central in determining Moscow's subsequent behavior. Kissinger himself apparently empathized. Upon learning that Israel had completed surrounding the Third Army after the cease-fire deadline, he is reported to have exclaimed, "My God, the Russians will think I double-crossed them. And in their shoes, who wouldn't?"

SOVIET PREPARATIONS FOR INTERVENTION

The Soviets moved decisively to rectify the situation. By October 24th, signs of Soviet preparations for military intervention in Egypt had become a source of serious concern. All seven Soviet airborne divisions were then on alert; three had been placed on alert as early as October 11, the rest in the early morning hours of the 24th. An airborne command post had been established in Southern Russia and Soviet Air Force units were also on alert. Together these forces represented some 40,000 combat troops. According to some reports, preparations for imminent departures were visible at several bases used by the airborne divisions. Indeed, one source reports that one of the seven divisions had been moved from its base outside Moscow to an airfield near Belgrade the week before. On the 17th of October, a unit of 30 *Antonov* transports (the same squadron that spearheaded the invasion of Czechoslovakia in 1968) was said also to have been moved to Belgrade.

In addition, seven Soviet amphibious assault vessels, some possibly with naval infantrymen on board, and two helicopter carriers were deployed in the Mediterranean. The Soviet Mediterranean fleet itself numbered some 85 ships, a figure that Bernard and Marvin Kalb refer to as "unprecedented."

There was also a nuclear specter in the midst of the Soviet naval activity. U.S. intelligence had been tracking a Russian ship carrying radioactive materials since it had entered the Mediterranean via the Bosporus on the 22nd. Our interviewees confirmed that the U.S. intelligence community was quite positive that there was nuclear material aboard the ship, even though the reason for the radioactivity could not be defined. When the ship docked at Port Said on the 25th, there was some speculation that it was transporting warheads for a brigade of Soviet SCUD missiles previously deployed near Cairo. This rumor was never confirmed, and the radioactive emissions could have come from naval weapons with nuclear warheads or from something else. Still, these reports about the movement of nuclear materials on the Soviet ship heightened concern among the members of the WSAG that a Soviet intervention was imminent and introduced a new dimension to the crisis.

Early in the morning of the 24th, an apparent standdown in Soviet airlift of weapons and supplies to Egypt and Syria had been welcomed as a sign that Moscow was prepared to move in concert with the United States to limit arms transfers to the belligerents. But by noon, this pause appeared more ominous. A large portion of the Soviet airlift fleet could not be located by U.S. intelligence systems, electronic intercepts indicated that Soviet flight plans for the next day were being changed, and certain "communications nets" showed a surge in activity, indicating that a major change in Soviet operations would be expected soon.

THE UN RESOLUTION AND THE SUPERPOWER TANGLE

In the afternoon of the 24th, events began to accelerate even more dangerously. At 3:00 p.m., amid signs of increasing panic in Cairo, President Sadat appealed to the United States and the Soviet Union to impose a joint peacekeeping force between Egyptian and Israeli units. At the UN, a group of nonaligned countries began to circulate informally a draft Security Council resolution calling on the superpowers to separate the combatants. Around 7:00 p.m., Soviet Ambassador Dobrynin informed Kissinger that their UN Ambassador had orders to support such a proposal. About this same time, President Nixon's reply to Sadat's public appeal for joint intervention was received in Cairo. The note, drafted by Kissinger, rejected the proposed joint intervention and stressed the risks of superpower involvement.

> Should the two great nuclear powers be called upon to provide forces, it would introduce an extremely dangerous potential for great-power rivalry in the area.

Perhaps Kissinger hoped that this blunt refusal would reach the Politburo in time to head off the coming showdown. But a phone call to Dobrynin about fifteen minutes later dashed whatever hopes might have existed for containing events at this juncture. The Soviet Ambassador informed the Secretary that the USSR might not wait for the nonaligned proposal in the UN; it might introduce a similar motion itself. Kissinger warned Dobrynin that the situation was becoming very dangerous: "I urged him not to push us to the extreme. We would not accept Soviet troops in any guise. Dobrynin replied that in Moscow, 'they have become so angry, they want troops.' "

Around 9:00 p.m., a message from Brezhnev arrived blaming the Israelis for continued fighting on the west bank of the Suez Canal. This note, however, appears to have been only a preamble to a second Brezhnev message, delivered over the telephone by Dobrynin to Kissinger a half-hour later. The second note is the key to the crisis. . . . Henry Kissinger recently claimed it constituted "one of the most serious challenges to an American President." Senator Fulbright referred to the text as "urgent." Senator Jackson called it "brutal, rough." Publicly, the President described the message as "very firm," and added that it left very little to the imagination. The British Ambassador to the United States at the time was also impressed with the toughness of the language. The note reportedly blamed Israel once again for violating the cease-fire resolutions and called on the United States to send forces in conjunction with the Soviet Union to Egypt. In the crucial passage, Brezhnev warned that if the U.S. was unwilling to participate in such a joint undertaking, the Soviets would be forced to consider unilateral action. Kissinger assembled a team of Kremlinologists to examine the two Soviet messages. These experts found the second communication "totally different" and more threatening than the first.

At 11:00 p.m. on October 24th, the Secretary of State again convened the Washington Special Action Group. All the individuals interviewed for this article agree as to the essence of the situation they faced at that time. All evidence pointed to serious preparations by the Soviets for an intervention in Egypt in the very near future—within 24 hours. Brezhnev's second note, a continuing increase in traffic on relevant communications nets, the nuclear specter alluded to previously, and growing evidence of the actual loading of transport aircraft at Soviet airborne division bases led the group to request presidential authority to place U.S. forces on a higher level of alert. As one participant put it, "They [the Soviets] had the capability, they had the motive, and the assets (i.e., transport aircraft) had disappeared from our screens." If the United States had not reacted to these military preparations, all participants agree, it would have been imprudent in the extreme. The only question concerns the form that the reaction took.

THE UNSPOKEN MESSAGE: THE AMERICAN MILITARY ALERT

Nixon gave his concurrence to the alert and the Chairman of the Joint Chiefs of Staff ordered the alert status of U.S. forces advanced to DEFCON III[2] around midnight. By 2:00 a.m., the alert status of all major U.S. commands had been advanced, including the Strategic Air Command—the component charged with nuclear missions. In a key action, fifty to sixty B-52 strategic bombers—a long-standing symbol and central component of U.S. nuclear capabilities—were moved from their base on Guam to the United States. Aerial refueling tankers assigned to the Strategic Air Command were dispersed to a larger number of bases and began non-routine operations. Marginal changes also were made in the status of U.S. strategic submarines and land-based intercontinental missiles. Finally, the aircraft carrier *John F. Kennedy* was dispatched toward the Mediterranean from just west of the Straits of Gibraltar, and the

---

[2] There are five defense readiness conditions (DEFCONs), of which DEFCON 1 indicates a state of war. Although parts of the strategic forces, such as the Strategic Air Command and parts of the Polaris and Poseidon fleets are regularly kept at DEFCON III, the measures taken in the early morning hours of October 25th moved all forces up one level of readiness.

82nd Airborne Division (about 15,000 troops) was told to be ready to move by 6:00 a.m.

The intent was that these military actions themselves would carry the message to the Soviets. There was no public announcement of the alert and, despite Dobrynin's request for an "immediate" reply to Brezhnev's second note, there were no private communications with the Soviets until 5:00 a.m. In a move calculated to show the Administration's displeasure with the Soviets' implied threat and to raise their apprehension about U.S. plans, Kissinger refused any contact with Dobrynin despite the latter's repeated requests, by telephone, for a response. Kissinger and others believed that it would be helpful if the initial signals of the American response picked up by the Kremlin were the indicators of U.S. military activity intercepted by Soviet intelligence systems. The unusual coolness in the Kissinger-Dobrynin relationship also was deliberate and was meant to show the Administration's displeasure with Brezhnev's last message. When a written response finally was given to Dobrynin at 5:40 a.m. on the 25th, it was passed to the Ambassador by Brent Scowcroft, Kissinger's deputy—again, an unusual and deliberate move. The whole manner with which these early morning exchanges were held were meant to show that, even so far as personal relationships were concerned, as long as the Soviets' threat of intervention remained valid, it could no longer be "business-as-usual."

The text of the message delivered to Dobrynin reflected the Administration's concern and contained hints of the potentially serious military confrontation threatened by U.S. military forces:

Mr. General Secretary:

I have carefully studied your important message of this evening. I agree with you that our understanding to act jointly for peace is one of the highest value and that we should implement that understanding in this complex situation.

I must tell you, however, that your proposal for a particular kind of joint action, that of sending Soviet and American military contingents to Egypt, is not appropriate in the present circumstances.

We have no information which would indicate that the cease-fire is now being violated on any significant scale. . . .

In these circumstances, *we must view your suggestion of unilateral action as a matter of gravest concern, involving incalculable consequences.*

It is clear that the forces necessary to impose the cease-fire terms on the two sides would be massive and would require closest coordination so as to avoid bloodshed. This is not clearly infeasible, but it is not appropriate to the situation.

It would be understood that this is an extraordinary and temporary step, solely for the purpose of providing adequate information concerning compliance by both sides with the terms of the cease-fire. If this is what you mean by contingents, we will consider it.

Mr. General Secretary, in the spirit of our agreements [i.e., the 1973 Agreement on the Prevention of Nuclear War] this is the time for acting not unilaterally, but in harmony and with cool heads. *I believe my proposal is consonant with the letter and spirit of our understandings* and would ensure a prompt implementation of the cease-fire. . . .

You must know, however, that we could in no event accept unilateral action. . . . As I stated above, such action would produce *incalculable consequences* which would be in the interest of neither of our countries and which would end all we have striven so hard to achieve.

Nuclear threats or even allusions to nuclear weapons were absent from the note, save for the oblique reference to the 1973 agreement on preventing nuclear war in the penultimate paragraph. References to matters "of the gravest concern" and repeated use of the phrase "incalculable consequences," however, could only be taken as hints of the possibility of nuclear war if the situation were not contained quickly.

Cleverly, the note also contained a face-saving gesture for Moscow, by permitting the introduction of a small number of observers. This gave Brezhnev a way out of the crisis and eventually resulted in the dispatch of 70 Soviet "representatives" to monitor the cease-fire.

More importantly, the United States sought to placate Soviet concerns by simultaneously reining in its recalcitrant ally. Shortly after the alert was in place, Kissinger informed Israeli Ambassador Simcha Dinitz of Soviet preparations for an intervention and of the U.S. response. His purpose was to impress Jerusalem with the gravity of the situation and the imminent danger of catastrophe should Israel force the Soviets' hand by annihilating the Third Army. Clearly, the Secretary of State hoped to convince Israel to spare the Egyptian unit by demonstrating that further hostilities would have far more than a regional impact. In short, the U.S. adopted a dual approach. On the one hand, it stood tough in the face of the threatened Soviet intervention. On the other hand, more privately, it tried to alter the conditions that had led to the Soviet threat to begin with.

Among the reasons why the Washington Special Action Group selected the alert as the most appropriate response to the threat of Soviet intervention was the group's belief that this type of move would send a clear and immediate signal to the Soviets without engendering a serious public debate in the United States, at least during the crisis itself. This expectation proved to be naive, however, and eventually harmed the Administration's political position at home.

By the 7:00 a.m. news on the 25th, the alert was the lead story in all national media. Most Americans awoke on that Saturday to TV footage of U.S. preparations for war—soldiers returning from leave, B-52s taking off and landing, war ships preparing to go to sea. As the public had gone to sleep unaware of the Soviet preparations for intervention in the Middle East, the reasons for this U.S. military activity were unclear. In the political atmosphere that had resulted from, first, years of increasingly strained efforts to present a favorable picture of the war in Vietnam and, second, the revelations of Presidential misdeeds associated with Watergate, the U.S. military activity was viewed, if not cynically, at least skeptically. Indeed, by the time the Special Action Group reconvened in the morning of October 25th, its primary task was to prove that the crisis was real and not an outrageous attempt to distract attention from Watergate.

The burden of proof then fell on Secretary Kissinger, who had previously scheduled a press conference for noon of the 25th. Perhaps for this reason—to emphasize the gravity of the situation for domestic purposes—but also perhaps to reinforce the message of nuclear danger which already had been communicated to the Soviets by word and deed—the Secretary chose to stress the nuclear aspects of the crisis. In an opening statement during which he departed from a prepared text, glared at the cameras, and intoned in his most ominous voice, Dr. Kissinger dealt extensively with the dangers of superpower confrontations:

> The United States and the Soviet Union are, of course, ideological and to some extent political adversaries. But the United States and the Soviet Union also have a very special responsibility.
>
> We possess, each of us, nuclear arsenals capable of annihilating humanity. We, both of us, have a special duty to see to it that confrontations are kept within bounds that do not threaten civilized life.
>
> Both of us, sooner or later, will have to come to realize that the issues that divide the world today, and foreseeable issues, do not justify the unparalleled catastrophe that a nuclear war would represent.

The Secretary returned to the theme of the horrendous consequences of nuclear conflict at several points during the question period (". . . humanity cannot stand the eternal conflicts of those who have the capacity to destroy."). The performance was quite impressive and—regardless of its effect on the American press—delivered a clear message to the Soviet Union.

The crisis ended within hours. In the early afternoon of the 25th, the Soviet Ambassador to the UN, acting on new instructions, stopped his efforts to secure the inclusion of U.S. and Soviet troops in the UN peacekeeping force. The dispatch of an international force excluding both Soviet and U.S. troops was ratified by the

Security Council soon afterwards. Coincidentally, Israeli military activity also ceased. . . . Also around this time, a message arrived from Brezhnev taking advantage of the conciliatory gesture contained in the U.S. note, informing the United States that the Soviet Union was sending a small number of observers to monitor Israeli compliance with the cease-fire.

Participants' memories of when the crisis ended in fact, if not formally, differ, however. Some maintain that it was clear early in the morning of the 25th that the U.S. had achieved its objective. One Soviet aircraft touched down at the Cairo West airfield in the early morning hours, but returned home almost immediately. It was as if this aircraft, containing the lead element of the interventionary force, had been caught en route when the Kremlin decided the risk was too great and reversed course. Other signs that Soviet military forces were returning to normal activities soon followed. If this analysis is accurate, Kissinger's statements at the press conference alluding to nuclear risks could only have been intended to be sure these favorable developments were continued and to emphasize how grave the situation had been for domestic purposes. Others, however, maintain that it was not clear at the time of the press conference that the crisis had been resolved successfully. If so, then Kissinger's remarks were intended primarily to draw a line for the Kremlin, to indicate in the strongest terms that the U.S. was not prepared to tolerate unilateral Soviet intervention in the Middle East and that it was prepared to undertake very grave risks to prevent it.

Communications, or signals, intelligence not only provided the most important warnings that the Soviet Union was preparing to intervene in Egypt in October 1973, but also was the major medium chosen by the United States to transmit the threat designed to thwart the possibility of such a move. Yet the inability of even key participants to identify a distinct end to the crisis illustrates the vagaries of confrontations in which nations communicate primarily through this netherworld of the technology of eavesdropping. As Secretary of Defense Schlesinger stated on October 26th, it was easier to determine when the Soviets had gone on alert than when they had reduced their level of readiness.

ANALYSIS

If the 1973 crisis is to help analysts to understand the potential future role of nuclear weapons, or nuclear threats, in American policy, it is essential to deduce the answers to two crucial questions: Why did American decision-makers decide to stress the nuclear dimension of the crisis? And what were the consequences of this decision?

Reasons for the decision to advance the state of alert of American military forces itself are fairly clear. There was sufficient evidence to believe that a Soviet intervention was likely. There was agreement that such a move left unopposed would have had a major adverse impact, not only on the American position in the Middle East but, given then-recent history (particularly in Southeast Asia), on the U.S. position worldwide. Individuals present at the WSAG meetings agree that the shift to DEFCON III was seen as a clear, unambiguous, and prompt way to convey the gravity with which the United States viewed the situation and of its intent to combat any Soviet move, if necessary, with military force. Most to the point, the alert had the benefit that it would be detected virtually immediately by Soviet intelligence systems through the changes it would cause in U.S. military communications patterns, while it was expected these signals would be relatively invisible to most of the world for some period of time.

At the same time, the alert had the added benefit that, as one participant put it, ". . . [it was] not so desperate a signal as to get the two nations past the point of no return." As such, particularly when combined with the "out" left to the Soviets in the telegraphed response to Brezhnev's message, it allowed both nations sufficient maneuvering room so that they would be able to defuse the situation before things got too far out of hand.

Another participant explained that the alert fit closely with Kissinger's approach to crisis management. Rather than matching Soviet actions "tit for tat," the Secretary believed, it was necessary to do something more dramatic, something which would get the attention of Soviet decision-makers because it was several times more alarming than their own action. The point, he stressed, was to do something unmistakably above the noise level, something that would make unambiguously plain how seriously the United States viewed the situation and, thus, how grave were the risks of not reaching accommodation.

It was this reasoning which led to inclusion of the nuclear dimension in the American response. A conventional response would not have been sufficient to quickly and forcefully make clear the U.S. position. The war in the Middle East had been going on for several weeks and, as a result, U.S. and Soviet conventional military capabilities had already been enhanced. The U.S. Sixth Fleet in the Mediterranean had already been beefed up, U.S. airlift aircraft were already heavily engaged, U.S. equipment in Europe had already been tapped for use in the Middle East. Given the perceived imminence of the Soviet intervention, and given these previous military preparations, only escalation to the nuclear level, symbolically of course, was seen as dramatic and threatening enough to make absolutely clear the gravity with which the United States perceived the situation and its determination to do whatever was necessary to stop it.

It should be noted that this view is not unanimous. Others, even among the participants, believe that the nuclear aspects of the crisis were unimportant. Much of the activity involving strategic forces, they argue, occurred inadvertently; the orders were given for the alert and, virtually automatically, all components of the armed forces advanced their readiness for war, including SAC. As for the shift of B-52s from Guam to the United States, the most visible and clearly deliberate move involving nuclear forces, this, it is argued, was simply the Defense Department's taking advantage of the crisis to carry out a long-sought shift of military assets for reasons of economy. Secretary of Defense Schlesinger had sought permission to make such a move for some time, it is noted, but was denied authorization because the State Department feared the political consequences of further reductions in U.S. military forces in the Pacific. When the crisis erupted, it is said, the Defense Department saw a new opportunity to justify a move.

Those who hold to this view assert that none of the key participants in the crisis took the possibility of nuclear war seriously. That is likely to be the case; nonetheless, it does not detract from the role played by the *risk of* nuclear war in resolving the crisis, nor the perception by at least some American decision-makers that emphasizing these dangers could help to achieve the U.S. objective. To appreciate this, it is important to understand the character of the threat made by the United States. American decisionmakers were not threatening to unleash nuclear war, to launch its nuclear-armed missiles and bombers at the USSR if Soviet troops landed in Egypt; something much more subtle was involved.

Changes in the alert status, disposition, and activity patterns of U.S. nuclear forces, as well as the hints in Nixon's response to Brezhnev and the much clearer statements in Kissinger's press conference, served both to stress the dangers of confrontation and to emphasize the stake which the United States perceived in the situation. In effect, these actions constituted manipulation of the risk of nuclear war; they both drew attention to the ultimate dangers of confrontation and advanced U.S. preparations to fight a nuclear conflict. As such, they carried a clear message. In effect, the U.S. actions said to Soviet decision-makers: "If you persist in your current activity, if you actually go ahead and land forces in Egypt, you will initiate an interactive process between our armed forces whose end results are not clear, but which could be devastating. Moreover, the United States feels so strongly about this issue that it is prepared to participate in this escalatory process until our objectives are achieved. The United States is prepared to continue escalating the confrontation up to and including a central nuclear exchange between us, even though we understand that the consequences of such an interaction potentially are 'incalculable.' " In short, in its nuclear moves and statements, the United States was demonstrating and making credible the vital stake it perceived in the situation. It indicated that it understood what might result from confrontation, but that it was prepared to carry on in any event. And it posed the choice to the Soviets of cutting short the crisis before the escalatory process went too far, or continuing in awareness that the risks could grow to terrifying proportions.

INFLUENCING FRIENDS AND DETERRING ADVERSARIES

The U.S. actions served one additional purpose as well. They camouflaged the fact, and thus made it politically acceptable, that although the United States had achieved its objective—halting the threatened Soviet intervention—the ostensible Soviet objective in contemplating the intervention also had been achieved: Israeli actions against the encircled Egyptian Third Army were halted. The central difficulty throughout the crisis was the need to influence the behavior of an adversary and the behavior of an ally at the same time. If the United States simply had countered the Soviet threat, and done nothing about Israeli efforts to dismember the Egyptian army, Sadat's regime would have been imperiled and the chances for a negotiated settlement in the Middle East destroyed. Moreover, had Washington put its forces on alert without pressing Israel to comply with the cease-fire, Russian suspicions of a double-cross would have been confirmed and the situation could easily have gotten out of control. On the other hand, the United States could have attempted to halt the Israelis while ignoring the Soviet threat, on the assumption that such a course of action would remove the cause of Moscow's displeasure. However, this would have set a dangerous precedent for future crisis by signalling to the Soviets that coercive threats could be invoked without fear of reciprocal counter-threats.

DOMESTIC AND THIRD PARTY AUDIENCES

It is irrelevant that the survival of the Third Army (and thereby Sadat's regime) was also in the United States' and Israel's long-term interests. . . . Politically, the U.S. could not be seen to be stopping the Israelis in response to Soviet pressures. Use of the word "politically" here refers to both domestic politics and to the consequences of such an action for political relations between the United States and a number of nations. For example, the 1973 War marked one of the most divisive moments in the history of NATO. The oil embargo, which began on October 18, created an atmosphere of panic and disunity in Western Europe. Deliveries of arms purchases made by Israel in several European countries months before the outbreak of hostilities were held up, and the U.S. resupply effort was denied various forms of support by many NATO allies. Emotions were running high. Any sign of U.S. weakness *vis à vis* the Soviet Union during this tense period, Kissinger and others feared, could have permanently crippled the alliance. . . .

THE AFTERMATH OF CRISIS

Finally, the alert gave the United States added leverage in its relations with Israel immediately following the crisis. Although they halted offensive military operations against the Third Army on October 25, the Israelis were reluctant to grant passage to convoys carrying food, water, and medical supplies to the trapped unit. On the afternoon of the 26th, Kissinger made another *démarche* to Dinitz. The crisis had demonstrated quite dramatically how seriously both superpowers viewed the current situation, he said, and it could be a harbinger of future disaster if "humanitarian convoys" were not allowed to reach the Third Army. Kissinger skillfully portrayed the Israelis as holding the key to regional and world stability. The following day Jerusalem bowed to American pressure and agreed to allow the convoys to reach the Egyptian troops.

The import of the U.S. manipulation of the risk of nuclear war was not lost on the Russians. Initially, the Soviets were taciturn about the crisis. Following Kissinger's press conference, *Tass* merely noted the new cease-fire and the dispatch of 7,000 peace-keeping troops to the battle zone. On the following day, however, Brezhnev delivered a polemical address in which he accused "some NATO countries" of formulating an "absurd" response in the wake of "fantastic speculation" as to Soviet intentions. This line became the standard Soviet public interpretation of the events of October 24th and 25th.

According to one member of Kissinger's senior staff, however, the Soviets took a very different tack in private conversations. He noted that the Soviets never tried to belabor their American interlocutor with protests that the United States had misinterpreted their actions, or that it had overreacted. Such contrasting behavior, our interviewee believes, confirms that the Soviets were seriously contemplating an intervention and that they understood the seriousness of the American signals sent by the nuclear threat.

Given, then, that the United States did deliberately draw attention to the risk of nuclear war in October 1973 and that this message was received clearly by the Soviets, what was its effect? How important was the nuclear alert? The answer to this question, of course, is unknown and unknowable short of public testimony by Leonid Brezhnev and other Soviet decision-makers. And even then, one could not be certain that their answers were honest nor their memories clear. Moreover, as was the case with the American participants in the crisis, it may be that the perceptions of those Soviets that were involved would differ—that different individuals would stress different aspects of the U.S. response as decisive.

1962/1973: ANALOGIES TO THE CUBAN MISSILE CRISIS

This question mirrors a more well-known debate over the importance of nuclear forces to the U.S. success in the 1962 Cuban missile crisis. Many observers of that earlier confrontation, perhaps most, conclude that the Soviet Union withdrew its missiles from Cuba in that incident because the United States had overwhelming nuclear superiority. Faced with the certainty that they would "lose," if the situation escalated to a central nuclear exchange, those holding to this viewpoint argue, the USSR decided to terminate the confrontation early. Many others, however, including each of President Kennedy's three senior advisors during the crisis (Secretary of State Dean Rusk, Secretary of Defense Robert McNamara, and National Security Advisor McGeorge Bundy), argue that the decisive factor was U.S. naval superiority in the Atlantic and Caribbean and the huge buildup of conventional forces in the Southeastern United States in preparation for an invasion. According to these individuals, even though the United States had a clear-cut advantage in long-range nuclear forces, a threat to go to nuclear war if the missiles were not removed would not have been credible because no president could have deliberately taken a move that would have resulted in even the few million casualties that would have been expected in 1962. While a threat of nuclear retaliation against the Soviet Union if missiles were launched from Cuba *was* made, this was a deterrent threat, aimed at forestalling the Soviets from shifting the focus of the confrontation elsewhere, particularly to Berlin. The effective compellent mechanism—that which brought about the withdrawal of Soviet missiles—it is argued, was the demonstration of conventional military capabilities.

Our analysis of the 1973 confrontation sheds some light on this debate; it demonstrates that both views are incorrect, or perhaps that both are partially correct.

It is clear that, on October 24, 1973, the Soviets had made all the preparations necessary for them to intervene in Egypt within 24 hours. All of the members of the WSAG believed that the possibility of intervention was serious enough to require a decisive American response. Yet the Soviets chose not to, finding a way, instead, of ending the confrontation and, thus, of appearing to yield to American pressures.[3] Why? The Soviet Union clearly did not back down because the United States had an edge in strategic weaponry and could "win" a nuclear exchange. There was a rough balance of strategic forces between the superpowers in the early 1970s. Neither side possessed the capability for a disarming first strike, and each would have expected to suffer devastating retaliation if it launched nuclear war. On the other hand, it is hard to believe that the alert of U.S. conventional forces, at least in terms of the specific military threat implied by that move, was decisive either. It was probably unclear to both sides which nation would have come out ahead in a naval battle in the Mediterranean or in a contest between their respective interventionary forces in Egypt itself. Indeed, our interviewees noted that there was no time to even contemplate what military steps would have been taken if the alert had failed to dissuade the Soviets from their proposed course.

DEMONSTRATING INTEREST, CAPABILITY, AND WILL

The Soviets chose not to land troops in Egypt because of more fundamental considerations. The United States was able to convince Soviet leaders that strategic parity, an uncertain conventional balance, and domestic problems notwithstanding, the President was willing to risk war with the USSR to block the contemplated Soviet action. This resolve was made credible by three related and mutually reinforcing components of the American response.

First, there was the historical context in which the October 1973 crisis took place. This component is at once the most important and least tangible. For more than 20 years, statements by U.S. decision-makers had made clear the importance which they attached to stability in the Middle East. Moreover, on literally dozens of occasions, the United States had acted in specific situations to ensure that the *status quo* in the Middle East was not changed by force. At times these actions included the deployment of American military forces. Some of these actions stemmed from the long-standing commitment to Israel, but it went well beyond that. Throughout the 1950s, 1960s, and into the 1970s, U.S. armed forces and diplomacy had been used to counter threats to Middle Eastern stability, whether in an Arab-Israeli or intra-Arab context, and whether the threat was posed by local powers, the Soviet Union, or even—on one occasion—by NATO allies. Given this history, the U.S. threat to risk war in order to prevent Soviet intervention in the Middle East sounded genuine; it fit the historic pattern of U.S. behavior

---

[3] Soviet achievement of their tactical objective—final Israeli acceptance of the cease-fire—was a factor, but irrelevant to considerations of the political consequences of the superpower confrontation.

and reflected long-standing American perceptions of its vital interests.

Second, there were the actions taken involving conventional U.S. forces. Apart from their direct effects on U.S. military preparedness, indicators of preparations for the use of conventional forces, such as the alert of the 82nd airborne division, communicated American resolve and seriousness to Soviet decision-makers. It signalled that the United States was contemplating realistic and feasible moves in this early stage of the crisis, and that a number of credible options would be available to the American president if the Soviet intervention took place. Moreover, the conventional alert added credibility to the nuclear threat. It indicated that steps would be taken that would begin and facilitate the escalatory process. It showed that the United States would not have to choose between accepting the Soviet *fait accompli* and initiating nuclear war, in which case, Soviet leaders would reason, the nuclear decision would be unlikely. Rather, American decision-makers would have to choose only between accepting the Soviet intervention and a military action whose worst immediate consequences were calculable. It made the U.S. position and the risk to escalation to nuclear war seem credible.

Third, there was the nuclear threat itself. But it is essential to keep in mind the character of the threat. It was not to unleash nuclear war, but to get involved in the situation militarily and to pursue an escalatory process despite awareness that its potential consequences were incalculable. The nuclear threat, in short, served to make clear just how importantly the United States viewed the stakes in the situation and the ultimate cost which could be suffered by the Soviet Union if it initiated a process of military interaction. . . .

LESSONS

It is always difficult and sometimes misleading to derive lessons from the past. Yet, it has been demonstrated on numerous occasions that statesmen can ignore history only at their peril. Nuclear weapons and the threats they imply can be used, at times, to help protect American interests in difficult situations. Raising the risk of nuclear war obviously is not without its dangers, however. The 1973 crisis can tell us something about both the ways in which nuclear threats can be used to support policy, and the dangers of turning to such desperate tactics.

Today and into the foreseeable future, as in 1973, both the United States and the Soviet Union maintain sizable forces of nuclear-armed missiles and bombers capable of withstanding an attack and retaliating with tremendous destruction against the military forces,

economy, and population of the attacker. Under such circumstances, a statesman cannot actually threaten nuclear war more
credibly than to draw attention to the fact that a process has been
set in motion which, unless stopped, could lead to nuclear war.
Such deliberate manipulation of the opponent's assessment of the
likelihood of a nuclear exchange can be used to define, and to make
clear to the opponent, that one perceives a vital stake in the
situation. For such an attempt to define a vital stake in a situation
to be credible, however, circumstances must be appropriate. The
nation making the nuclear statement must have an evidently vital
interest in the situation, such as its geostrategic location or its
economic value. And there must be some historical continuity to its
interest there. For the United States to manipulate the risk of
nuclear war to compel the withdrawal of Cuban forces from Angola
would be as inappropriate and ineffective as would Soviet nuclear
threats in defense of the Sandinista regime in Nicaragua. Only in
certain places and very special circumstances might attempts to
manipulate the risk of nuclear war be credible. For the United
States, these probably include military contingencies involving Europe, Japan, and Korea, for which a willingness to make first use of
nuclear weapons has long been articulated policy. Elsewhere, such
U.S. threats probably would only be credible in the Middle East
(including the Persian Gulf), and only when taken in response to
Soviet, not local, actions. For the Soviet Union, military challenges
to its position in Eastern Europe would no doubt trigger credible
threats of nuclear war, as would a serious military confrontation
with China in Central Asia. In all other places, Soviet nuclear
threats would only be credible in the context of direct military
confrontation with the United States and, even then, would depend
on the circumstances which had precipitated the conflict to begin
with.

   This view of the character of nuclear threats in an age of substantial nuclear retaliatory capabilities on both sides also suggests that
within fairly permissive boundaries, the effectiveness of nuclear
threats may not be influenced by the *aggregate* strategic balance.
The threat is not so much to go deliberately to nuclear war as it is
to participate and persevere in an escalatory process, even though
it might *result* in nuclear war. Accordingly, the credibility of the
threat would not, from a first approximation, be influenced by
calculations of just how badly off each side would be if the escalation
ran its course, presuming, of course, that both sides had maintained
substantial forces. Its credibility would depend on the ability of the
nation making the threat to demonstrate convincingly that it perceived such vital interests at stake that it was even prepared to fight
a nuclear war, if that became necessary.

On the other hand, this analysis emphasizes the vital importance of maintaining adequate conventional military forces. For one, in those situations in which the nation's non-nuclear military capabilities are obviously dominant, there is no need for nuclear threats, and thus no need either to run the risks implied by such actions. It would, moreover, be unwise to tarnish this potentially crucial instrument of foreign policy by overuse. But even in more ambiguous situations, adequate conventional forces are necessary to make credible the message contained in nuclear threats. The risk of nuclear war can only be emphasized credibly when one can demonstrate how the initial stages of the escalatory process might take place.

What would have happened if Soviet forces had attempted to land in Egypt despite the U.S. nuclear alert is difficult to say; the risks, though, were tremendous. Say, for example, that coincident with its alert, the United States had not been able to persuade Israel to refrain from attacking the beleaguered Egyptian Third Army—and, as a result, that the Soviet Union had felt compelled, despite its awareness of the dangers, to intervene. What then?

In an optimistic scenario, Soviet airborne forces would have been deployed so as to defend Cairo and the Egyptian heartland in a gesture of greater political than military import, thus avoiding actual conflict with Israeli forces. In response, the United States could have made a comparable deployment of American troops in Israel, well away from the battle area, and the crisis could have been resolved at that point.

But what if the Soviets had decided to intervene in a more direct way in the war? Or what if the Israelis, fearing that such a direct intervention might occur, chose to attack Soviet transports as they entered the war zone? (Note that Israeli aircraft deliberately provoked a battle with Soviet aircraft in 1970, when Soviet air defense units were deployed in Egypt.) Or what if the Soviets, believing that the United States would interfere with Soviet transports during their vulnerable landing period, chose to attack the U.S. Sixth Fleet preemptively, perhaps along with Israeli Air Force facilities? What then? Where would the conflict have ended? Moreover, given that the United States already had introduced the possibility, perhaps likelihood, that the confrontation would escalate to the nuclear level, would not the Soviets have chosen to initiate the use of nuclear weapons, thus gaining whatever advantage might reside in the side that strikes first?

Speculation like this is open-ended. But it serves to illustrate that once the threshold of active military involvement is crossed, finding a stopping point becomes far from easy. By raising the specter of nuclear war at the onset of the confrontation, the United States made more difficult the termination of any escalatory process which might have ensued short of the use of nuclear weapons. Of course, this is precisely what made the nuclear threat so effective. The two go hand in hand; one cannot have the ostensible benefit of a nuclear threat without running its risks. Good reason to turn to nuclear threats only in the most desperate situations.

Finally, we might view the October 1973 crisis in the broader perspective of relations between each of the superpowers and their clients in the third world, and the consequences of those ties for U.S.-Soviet relations. In the 1973 incident, first Egypt and then Israel, through actions of their own, actions which their patrons were powerless to prevent, brought the United States and the Soviet Union to the edge of catastrophe. Evidence that the Soviet Union did not support President Sadat's decision to go to war is persuasive. Similarly, there is no question that the United States sought to prevent an all-out Israeli military victory so as to facilitate a longer-lasting political settlement and to enhance the U.S. position in the Middle East. Yet, the two ostensibly dependent nations dominated the situation. Egypt began the war; Israel continued to act against the Third Army in the face of U.S. protests. The result was the Soviet-American confrontation. . . .

How Kuwait Was Won: Strategy in the Gulf War

LAWRENCE FREEDMAN AND EFRAIM KARSH

The dust has yet to settle after the 1991 Gulf War and it may not settle for some time. After the grand finale of the 100-hour land campaign came the confusion of the Shi'ite and Kurdish insurrection and the torrent of refugees into Turkey and Iran. The accumulation of human suffering, material decline, and environmental damage did not stop with the fighting. Nor were the political futures of either Iraq or Kuwait settled; nor the responsibilities of the victorious powers for the peace and security of the area concluded.

Whatever the political outcome, the most important feature of the Gulf War in military terms was its decisive, overwhelming character. At no point did Iraq offer any serious resistance. Its air force retreated in the face of combat; its small navy, which had nowhere to hide, was decimated in a side-show; the army crumbled in the face of the coalition advance.

The strategy that led to the victory—a relatively protracted and systematic air campaign followed by a land campaign based on envelopment and maneuver—was fully advertised beforehand. So was the Iraqi strategy based on threatening the United States with a "second Vietnam" and absorbing the air offensive.

In this article we demonstrate how the strategies of both sides in the Gulf War were governed by a sensitivity to its political context, both domestically and internationally. It was widely expected that Iraqi forces would only be expelled from Kuwait following a ferocious land battle. This created a severe risk of extremely high American casualties, given that the United States was providing the bulk of the coalition forces ranged against Iraq. This put the Bush administration under intense pressure to adopt a strategy that would minimize coalition casualties. It was also widely expected that the disparate coalition of Western and Arab states would split under the stresses and strains of war: American military strategy therefore had to be reinforced by a careful leadership of the alliance.

Reprinted from *International Security*, Fall 1991 (Vol. 16, No. 2), pp. 5–42, "How Kuwait Was Won," by permission of The MIT Press, Cambridge, Massachusetts. © 1991 by the President and Fellows of Harvard College and of the Massachusetts Institute of Technology. Footnotes and portions of the text have been omitted.

These demands on the Bush administration suggested the opportunities for Iraq. President Saddam Hussein's strategy had to be based on increasing American casualties and sowing division within the coalition. This led to a war in which Iraq was on the military defensive but on the political offensive. For either side, the political and military strands of strategy could not work independently. Success would depend on mutual reinforcement. In the end the United States was successful because the strength of its military offensive eased the pressure on its political defenses.

IRAQI STRATEGY

Saddam Hussein should have had serious misgivings regarding Iraq's capacity to sustain a prolonged and ferocious conflict. The persistence of the Iran-Iraq War had not been of his own choice: it had been imposed on him by a fanatical foe who openly demanded his downfall. He survived the war largely by shielding the Iraqi public from its effects. Iraq's much-celebrated defensive prowess was overstated. Iraqi military operations during the Iran-Iraq War had been conducted under ideal circumstances, with superior firepower and complete mastery of the air. Still, Iraq's formidable defenses had been repeatedly breached by the ill-equipped Iranian teenagers, whose advance had been contained with great difficulty, at times through the use of chemical weapons.

Perhaps in light of all of this, Saddam's strategy from the beginning of the Gulf crisis has been geared toward preventing an armed confrontation and, should hostilities break out, toward quick termination. But if it made such sense for Saddam to avoid war, why did he fail to seize the various face-saving formulas offered to him during the crisis to withdraw from Kuwait, let alone fail to launch a serious diplomatic initiative of his own? An unconditional withdrawal from Kuwait, or one with a cosmetic face-saving formula added, was totally unacceptable to Saddam from the outset, since it did not address the fundamental predicament underlying the invasion of Kuwait. He had not occupied Kuwait for reasons of power-seeking or political aggrandizement, although certainly his prestige across the Arab world and among his own subjects would have grown enormously with a successful takeover of Kuwait. Rather, the invasion had been a desperate attempt to shore up his regime in the face of dire economic straits created by the Iran-Iraq War. This economic plight had not only remained after the invasion of Kuwait but had been significantly aggravated by the sanctions, and Saddam therefore felt that any turn-about on his part would damage his position beyond repair.

By the start of 1991 Saddam should have been aware that the coalition was more cohesive than he had expected: his calls for popular insurrections against Arab members of the coalition had produced a minimal response; his attempt to wean France away through preferential release of hostages had failed; the Soviet Union had supported a series of tough anti-Iraq resolutions in the UN, including Resolution 678. Nonetheless Saddam still apparently hoped that the vociferous peace camp in the West, and the variety of would-be intermediaries visiting him in Baghdad, would help him avert war. He interpreted President Bush's November 30 offer of direct talks as readiness to reach a compromise. "Bush's initiative is a submission to Iraq's demand, [on] which it has insisted and is still insisting," gloated the Iraqi media, "namely, the need to open a serious dialogue on the region's issues."

During this period Saddam made two decisions that undermined his military position and must have reflected some optimism that a settlement could be reached or, at least, that war could be delayed. The first was to release all Western hostages on December 6. Saddam appears to have been persuaded by Arab supporters, such as PLO leader Yasser Arafat and visiting elder statesmen from the West (such as the former British Premier Edward Heath and the former German Chancellor Willy Brandt) that holding the hostages was detrimental to his image, and that their release would be taken as a serious gesture of reconciliation and would generate a momentum towards a negotiated settlement that President Bush would find difficult to contain. He might also have judged that, rather than encouraging the United States to stay its hand, the holding of foreign nationals might stimulate outrage and a more ferocious reaction. On balance, the release of the hostages turned out to be a strategic mistake, as Saddam himself was about to admit later with uncharacteristic frankness. It did not weaken the coalition's resolve to dislodge Iraq from Kuwait, and it facilitated its military planning. Despite Western statements that the location of the hostages at "strategic sites" did not affect operational plans, clearly this could not be wholly true. Once the hostages were out, the U.S. Air Force added many facilities to its target list that had been excluded before.

The second indication of Saddam's disbelief in war was his decision not to preempt by attacking coalition forces in Saudi Arabia, a move which could have disrupted and confused the coalition's own military preparation. From the beginning of the crisis he vehemently denied the American allegations of Iraqi intentions to attack Saudi Arabia, and took great pains not to threaten the coalition with preemption. Preemption would be unlikely to change the eventual outcome of the crisis and would have made inevitable a conflict that might still have been avoided. If this latter factor was influential, then it too would indicate Saddam's hope that the start of war might be delayed.

In essence Saddam's strategy was to rely on his defenses around Kuwait and the cost that could be imposed on coalition forces if they could be drawn into killing zones, as had been Iranian forces during the Iran-Iraq War. His initial worry was an amphibious assault, which led him to order extensive coastal defenses and mining of the adjacent waters. The size of the U.S. ground forces moving into Saudi Arabia then encouraged the construction of extensive fortifications along the Saudi-Kuwait border. These followed the pattern of those developed during the Iran-Iraq War, but could not be quite the same. There, the swampy conditions allowed for areas to be flooded, thus forcing attacking forces into a killing ground. Here, berms or ridges of bulldozed sand were constructed and combined with ditches, some filled with oil, barbed wire, and a variety of other anti-tank obstacles. These were backed up by tanks and artillery (believed in the West to be an Iraqi specialty) and numerous troops. But the stark desert provided less opportunity for natural obstacles than the waters around Basra. Furthermore, these fortifications did not extend much beyond the Kuwaiti-Saudi border. Belatedly the Iraqis realized that their fortifications could be outflanked by a desert attack through Iraq, so suffering the same fate as the Maginot Line. Although some attempt was made to extend the line to cover the whole of the border with Saudi Arabia, only limited results were achieved and the resultant gap was later exploited mercilessly.

Saddam was able to call upon large number of reserves. Iraq's overall population was not large at 19 million, but he could put together an army of some million men because the country had been on a war footing for nearly a decade. The expedient if disadvantageous settlement with Iran made it possible to shift a number of divisions from that border. As the crisis developed, and in particular after Bush's November 8 announcement of the U.S. buildup, the number of divisions was boosted; all young men were called up and then the middle-aged. There does seem to have been some belief that large numbers of defenders would have a deterrent effect. This may have reflected a belief in the famous 3-to-1 ratio, held to be necessary for an attacking force against an entrenched defense.

However, this buildup was geared to the protection of Iraq as a whole and not just the new Kuwaiti acquisition, and the threats involved did not come simply from the United States. Significant forces had to remain deployed along Iraq's borders with its Iranian, Turkish, and Syrian neighbors. The elite Republican Guards, Iraq's best-equipped units of some eight divisions strong, were similarly not pushed far over the border into Kuwait, for Saddam was anxious not to hazard the praetorian protectors of his personal rule. Consequently, there were not enough forces for a wide front and so the border defenses would be manned by less capable troops while the Republican Guards were kept back as, at best, a strategic armored reserve.

The large numbers claimed by Iraq did not arrive in the Kuwait theater. After the end of the war, estimates suggested that there may have been as few as 350,000 Iraqi troops available prior to hostilities, despite Western estimates at the time (reinforced by Iraqi statements) of at least 540,000 Iraqi troops. The numbers that were deployed created major logistical difficulties; the stretched supply lines from Iraq were easily disrupted by the coalition's air strikes. Such vulnerabilities would have been magnified if Iraq had sent more troops to Kuwait.

The most obvious weakness in the Iraqi military structure was the lack of air support. On the face of it, Iraq's air force was substantial, with some high-quality aircraft. The key role it played during the war with Iran, breaking enemy morale through sustained campaigns against strategic targets and population centers, underscored the significance of air power in modern war. The hardened bunkers prepared for the most valuable aircraft, the enormous airfields, and the redundant command and control system all indicated Iraqi sensitivity to the dangers of preemptive air attack, and presumably the central importance of air power in Israeli strategy. And yet, even during the Iran-Iraq War, Saddam displayed considerable restraint in the employment of air power, refraining for a long time from carrying Iraq's overwhelming aerial superiority to its logical end. This timidity reflected Saddam's reluctance to put at risk his most effective reserve of military force. This insecure operational conception was extended into the Kuwaiti crisis.

Another key Iraqi underestimation was in the area of precision-guided weapons, with which Iraqi defenses proved unable to cope. This may not have been wholly unreasonable, given that many of the most modern weapons were unproven and their effectiveness was widely questioned even in the West. In addition, the full significance of electronic warfare was imperfectly understood.

Saddam saw missiles as his most reliable means of inflicting a painful blow on the enemy. The Iraqi stocks of ballistic missiles were extensive and, with the benefit of European technology, their ranges had been extended. According to Iraqi disclosures to the United Nations after the war, Iraq had thirty chemical warheads for its Scuds. Saddam had long spoken of his missile force as an "anti-Israel" capability and reemphasized this on the eve of the war. Designed to divide the coalition by giving the crisis an Arab-Israeli dimension, these threats followed a diplomatic campaign that sought to link the occupation of Kuwait with the Palestinian problem. The missiles could also be used against Saudi population centers, and to a lesser extent as a threat to the Saudi oil installations. They represented Saddam's best prospects of taking the war into the enemy camp.

The Iraqi strategy therefore was based on deterring and if necessary rebuffing the central thrust of the enemy campaign, by exacerbating the prospective war's stresses and strains on the political cohesion of the coalition while absorbing the enemy air assault. There was no obvious strategy for war termination other than inflicting such discomfort that the coalition would develop an interest in a cease-fire on terms other than the full implementation of all UN resolutions. Saddam strongly believed that the United States Achilles' heel was its extreme sensitivity to casualties, and he was determined to exploit this weakness to the full. He told the American ambassador to Baghdad, April Glaspie, shortly before the invasion of Kuwait: "Yours is a society which cannot accept 10,000 dead in one battle."

In a speech a few days before the war began, Saddam told an Islamic gathering in Baghdad that "thousands of men" at the front were "underground in strong reinforced positions," ready to "rise against" the enemy as soon as it attacked. He acknowledged that the coming war would be a testing ground for advanced technology but stressed Iraqi numerical superiority and its experience of war. The Americans would "carry out acrobatics just like a Rambo movie. . . . They tell you that the Americans have advanced missiles and warplanes, but they ought to rely on their soldiers armed with rifles and grenades."

COALITION STRATEGY

The Vietnam War had as profound an influence on American calculations as the war with Iran had on Iraq. Key actors in the American political process were determined not to repeat the mistakes of the 1960s: the administration was resolved not to get trapped in an unwinnable war; the military would not allow civilians to impose artificial restrictions that would deny them the possibility of a decisive victory; Congress refused to be railroaded into giving the executive *carte blanche* to wage war; and the diplomats did not wish to find themselves supporting a military campaign in isolation from natural allies.

For the administration there was no doubting the unwisdom of getting drawn into a messy ground war with a Third World country. One view—the quagmire thesis—was that this was an inevitable feature of any such conflict. This view had been reinforced with the more recent relevant experience in Lebanon in 1983. Another—the escalation thesis—held that a quagmire was unnecessary, the result of attempting to employ force in a graduated, incremental manner.

President Bush demanded of the military that they avoid at all costs another Vietnam. On November 30 he promised the U.S. people that any military action would not "be another Vietnam," while one of his first comments after the war concluded was to claim that the United States had "kicked the Vietnam syndrome." This focus had an impact on coalition strategy in both the setting of objectives and the choice of strategy designed to achieve these objectives.

The administration insisted that its primary objective was to liberate Kuwait and not to change the Iraqi regime, despite continuing public allegations to the contrary, reinforced by the "demonizing" of Saddam Hussein. This objective would obviously require attacking targets in Iraq; the administration evidently saw an opportunity in this to destroy the most threatening aspects of Iraqi military power. However, the administration also determined that it would be extremely unwise to be seen to try to change the regime in Baghdad. This would alarm the Arab members of coalition and also Iran, which had expressed its fear of a permanent, intrusive American presence. It would involve taking over responsibility for Iraq, which could be a long-term liability especially if there was popular opposition. Even getting to Baghdad and taking it would involve more difficult and painful fighting than the liberation of Kuwait.

Restricting the objectives to the liberation of Kuwait did not involve the risk of a Vietnam-type quagmire, which was the consequence of fighting a largely guerrilla war in difficult terrain and under unfavorable political conditions. It is of note that when the United States began to get sucked into the postwar civil war in Iraq, it was this fear of a quagmire that was most often mentioned.

However, even if the United States could fight the war on terms for which it was best prepared, a presumed lesson of Vietnam was that the public would be intolerant of high casualties. As with many other such lessons, the evidence was ambiguous. Both Vietnam and the British experience in the Falklands suggested the countervailing importance of the "rally round the flag" factor once war begins, and this factor became evident during the Gulf War as well.

Nonetheless, prior to the war all the indications were that U.S. public opinion was most brittle on the question of casualties. An opinion poll in early January 1991 showed a strengthening of support for war—63 percent, compared to 55 percent in early December— but also continuing optimism over the possibility of a diplomatic solution. Support was less if the assumption was 1000 American troops killed—to 44 percent in favor of war and 53 percent opposed—and it further declined to only 35 percent in favor, with 61 percent opposed, if the cost were to be 10,000 troops killed.

This, as we have seen, was Saddam Hussein's main hope. Just as his strategy depended on convincing—if necessary with proof— American public opinion that the level of casualties would be unacceptably high, President Bush had to demonstrate the opposite. Few in the United States doubted that the coalition could inflict a crippling military defeat on Iraq and eject it from Kuwait. The severity of the sacrifice depended to some extent on the quality of the coalition strategy. An all-out assault on entrenched Iraqi positions could put casualties up to several tens of thousands; skillful use of air power, mobility, and night-fighting capability could reduce this to a fraction. However, it was feared that there was still an irreducible minimum. For example, Edward Luttwak, one of the most visible and vocal opponents of a land campaign, argued that high casualties were "almost mathematically certain" even given what he deemed to be extremely optimistic assumptions (which in fact approximated to the actual state of affairs when the land campaign came). High casualties, he argued, would result from "the incidentals of war: troops stepping on unmarked mines, short fire-fights with stragglers and hold-outs, mechanical accidents, and the ragged fire of some surviving fraction of the huge number of Iraqi artillery tubes."

Luttwak argued that the way to avoid such casualties was to avoid a ground war and rely instead on an intensive air campaign. In this view he was not alone. However, it is important to note that there were a number of distinct air power strategies, each one reflecting a different assessment of the political character of the conflict and the role of military force in its resolution, as well as the particular attributes of this sort of warfare. In terms of air power theory it was of interest that there were no serious proposals to attack the regime through direct assaults on the civilian population and its morale, even though, as argued below, the eventual attacks on civilian infrastructure do appear to have undermined Iraqi reso-lution.

All of the air power proposals assumed relatively accurate strikes against military targets, but beyond that there were significant variations. Luttwak's objective was to denude Iraq of its military capacity, thus limiting the potential damage it could do in the future. He claimed that an air offensive directed not against ground forces but against the basis of Saddam's long-term strategic power "could literally demolish Saddam Hussein's military ambitions within a week or so, and with the loss of not more than a few dozen aircrew at most." Richard Perle, by contrast, was more concerned with getting Iraq out of Kuwait and so he proposed the use of air power to support a war of attrition, exploiting Iraq's problem of resupply-ing its forces of occupation. Henry Kissinger also wanted to force Iraq out of Kuwait, but he conceived of the use of airpower more along the lines of traditional coercive diplomacy. It would serve as an adjunct to sanctions, raising "the cost of occupying Kuwait to unacceptable levels while reducing Iraq's capacity to threaten its neighbors." Kissinger, declaring himself "extremely skeptical about a full-scale ground assault," believed that the reduction of Iraq's military power would mean the erosion of the dictatorship's base, thereby encouraging a "negotiation more compatible with stated U.S. objectives."

The most forceful case for primary reliance on airpower from within the administration came in a September interview with Air Force Chief of Staff General Michael Dugan, which led to his firing. He reported what he claimed to be the conclusion of the Joint Chiefs of Staff that U.S. air power could force Iraq out of Kuwait without a bloody land war. There would be a role for ground forces, intimidating Iraqi forces and channelling them into killing zones for aircraft. However, the "cutting edge would be downtown Baghdad." The enemy had to be targeted where it hurts, "at home, not out in the woods someplace." He had been advised, by the Israelis amongst others, that "the best way to hurt Saddam" was to target his family, his personal guard, and his mistress. Because Saddam was a "one-man show" in Iraq, Dugan said, "if and when we choose violence he ought to be at the focus of our efforts." Without him, Iraqi troops "would all of a sudden lose their legitimacy and they would be back in Iraq in a matter of hours, in disarray."

General Colin Powell, chairman of the Joint Chiefs of Staff, challenged proposals for "surgical air strikes or perhaps a sustained air strike" and other "nice, tidy, alleged low-cost incremental, may-work options." Their "fundamental flaw" was to leave the initiative with the Iraqi president: "He makes the decision as to whether or not he will or will not withdraw. He decides whether he has been punished enough so that it is now necessary for him to reverse his direction and take a new political tack." A second problem was that such strategies were indecisive and "not success oriented." They took no account of Saddam's demonstrable willingness and ability "to absorb punishment, to callously expend Iraqi lives and to care not a whit about what happens to the citizens of his country." Third, such strategies would allow Iraq to concentrate on one threat. Powell did not doubt "the competence and ability of our United States Air Force to inflict terrible punishment." However, he said, "One can hunker down. One can dig in. One can disperse to try to ride out such a single-dimensioned attack. Recognizing that such attack will do grievous damage to the defenders after such strategy has been executed, the decision is still in the hands of the defender to decide whether or not he has had enough punishment."

He also dismissed any interest in a strategy of "cannon fodder," in which "we are just going to run into fortifications without thinking our way through this." In practice the real question was not whether a ground campaign would be required, but the speed with which it should be entered into. Powell indicated in advance that the conflict would begin with a decisive air campaign and that the ground war would not be simultaneous but would follow the air campaign. His basic view was that there was no need for the coalition to restrict its military options.

The Bush administration had a number of advantages that made possible a decisive application of Western military power. It was possible to bring in all types of military capabilities to high levels. This was an enormous logistical effort that would not have been easy to reproduce in other locations that did not have existing garrisons of Western forces. It was possible in the Gulf, initially because of the existence of pre-positioned stocks, but more importantly because of first-class ports and military airfields. Saudi Arabia was, in effect, one large petrol station, which dramatically eased one of the most critical logistical problems. The United States was further helped by the complete lack of interference and harassment from Iraq. The difficulties imposed on Iraq as a result of the arms embargo were considerable. Even though the Iraqi military was given priority, it was still required to husband resources and limit training and exercises. Resupply from the Soviet Union was not a possibility.

There was time to gather full intelligence and prepare plans. By the time Desert Storm began, the basic elements of the Iraqi order of battle as well as the essential elements of its communications and supply networks were well known to its opponents. By comparison Iraqi intelligence was minimal. The coalition had no need to consider a "second front." Neither Jordan nor Iran had any interest in taking military action in support of Iraq. Terrorism was a serious risk, but some fears were alleviated by Syria's membership in the coalition and by the attention of the security services to Iraq's diplomatic missions.

The primary political objective—expelling Iraqi forces from Kuwait—was clear and had been clarified during the buildup to direct military action. It provided obvious guidelines. All of this meant that coalition planning could follow staff college principles in an almost classic manner. The strategy was dictated by the logic of Western air superiority, a determination to minimize Western casualties and the objective of expelling Iraq from Kuwait.

The coalition also had good reasons not to be overawed by Iraq's military capability. The major uncertainties surrounded its readiness and ability to use chemical weapons, and the potential effects of its ballistic missile force. Although fear of an eventual Iraqi nuclear capability was one of the reasons for defeating Saddam, no one thought that such a capability was then already available. Only a limited number of Iraqi divisions were considered competent, and only the elite Republican Guard had modern Soviet T-72 tanks. Nearly half of the troops were mobilized reservists who had shown a readiness to surrender during the war with Iran when the opportunity arose. There was also evidence that Iraq's less capable and youngest troops were being put in the lightly defended forward positions. The air force had been ineffective in close air support and the pilots were judged to be poor. The chain of command was heavily centralized and unresponsive. Generals who had made their names in the war with Iran were retired, dead, or under arrest. The defensive methods developed during the war with Iran had been based on massive earthworks combined with flooding to channel any offensive onto a killing ground. The Kuwaiti border did not offer the same potential for water barriers, nor were there any natural barriers such as the Shatt-al-Arab waterway. It was also apparent that the Iraqi force on the border to the west was more thinly spread.

From early on it was recognized that the American priorities would be to achieve air superiority, eliminate missiles and Iraq's small fleet of fast patrol boats, interdict supply lines, and then engage in a fast and mobile desert campaign based on maneuver rather than attrition. In a variety of unofficial publications, the most likely targets for the air campaign were outlined and the most likely instruments of attack were indicated. The preference for flanking maneuvers rather than direct assaults on Iraqi fortifications were made clear. The military options were so fully explored in the weeks before the start of hostilities in hearings held by the Armed Services Committees of the U.S. Senate and the House of Representatives that it was possible for the chairman of the House Committee, Representative Les Aspin, to produce a detailed and largely accurate forecast of the course of the war.

SADDAM'S OBJECTIVES AND MISCALCULATIONS

From the outset of the Kuwaiti crisis in the summer of 1990, there was an absolute certainty in Saddam's mind of what could not be sacrificed—his political survival. Kuwait, the Palestinian cause, Iraqi lives: all were important only so long as they served the perpetuation of Saddam. So was his military strategy and deployment: key units had been held back from the start for this purpose and he was clearly anxious that as many units as possible who had been caught in the Kuwait/Southern Iraq theater would get back to save the regime rather than make a gallant last stand.

A less obvious objective was Saddam's desire to ensure that the ruling al-Sabah family would not get Kuwait back intact but that their country would be left permanently damaged; thus, the mining of the oil wells and the campaign of vandalism and murder which began even before the Moscow peace initiative had run its course. Another objective, in which he was far less successful, was to attack Israel's nuclear capability, possibly in retaliation for the Israeli destruction of Iraq's nuclear capability. These represented an attempt to recoup something from the war in terms of hurt to opponents, even though, at least in the case of the action against Kuwait, this gave the United States a helpful argument to reject negotiations and accelerate the ground war.

The Gulf War is viewed as the first real "electronics war." The sight of cruise missiles and smart bombs roaming to their destination with pin-point accuracy has created a widespread impression of an uneven match between a high-tech power and a hapless, ill-equipped, and backward Third World army. However intriguing, this notion is largely misconceived. While the war clearly represents a military victory of a technological society over a non-industrialized one, such an astounding outcome was by no means a foregone conclusion. The Iraqi army, it is true, proved to be a far cry from the formidable power portrayed in the West prior to the war, and it was inferior to the coalition forces in crucial technological respects, but the fact that it fought so badly was mainly the outcome of more "traditional" factors, such as a poor combat performance along with incompetent politico-military leadership and war strategy.

The main cause of Iraq's military debacle lies in Saddam's personality and the nature of his regime. As aptly noted by General Schwarzkopf, Saddam is no strategist, nor a soldier. His poor understanding of military affairs, and his complete subordination of military strategy to the ultimate goal of political survival, drove him to fight a political war with one eye set on his postwar survival. He was cautious when it came to initiatives, reluctant to hazard his air force, and did not want to commit the Republican Guards to an offensive move that could decimate them, because he needed them for the postwar situation, as illustrated by their brutal repression of the later Shi'ite uprising in southern Iraq.

This flawed strategy reflected a fundamental misunderstanding of the lessons of the Iran-Iraq War. Saddam's failure to distinguish between the coalition forces confronting him and the poorly equipped and ill-trained Iranian army led him to the mistaken belief that Iraq's defensive posture would suffice to inflict unacceptable pain on the enemy. Secondly, he failed to appreciate the decisive role of air power on the modern battlefield. Thirdly, the substantial desertions in the first months of the Iran-Iraq War, after Saddam had voluntarily surrendered the initiative, should have warned him of the consequences of a collapse of morale.

Saddam's vicious success in putting down the postwar insurrection in Iraq took the shine off Bush's victory, but the American military strategy was largely vindicated. Casualties on the coalition side were extraordinarily light. Early analysis suggested that 8 to 10 percent casualty rates could be anticipated. On the eve of the ground war President Bush was warned to expect some 5000 casualties. In the event, U.S. battle deaths were under 150. As many American lives were lost in the air campaign as in the land campaign.

STILL GRADUATED RESPONSE

The Gulf War offered a unique opportunity for the exercise of military force on a decisive scale. The strategic options available to the Bush administration were quite different in kind to those confronting the Johnson administration in Vietnam. In this sense, the claim that the Gulf War represented a break with the old concepts of graduated response has to be treated with care. According to this view, the failure in Vietnam could be attributed in part to the policy of graduated response, understood as a strategy of incremental pressure, with a series of restrictions on targets that were imposed by the politicians. At each stage, the opponent was to face a choice between compliance and further pressure until eventually its breaking point was reached. The critique of this strategy argues that these small steps merely provide the opponent with time to adjust and develop forms of counter-pressure.

From the early decision to introduce ground forces into Saudi Arabia, Powell urged Bush not to go for a minimum force but to ensure sufficient numbers to cope with all eventualities, and also to refrain from engaging in political micro-management. The administration accepted both these arguments.

To avoid charges of micro-management, civilian officials avoided amending the target list for the air campaign (which practice had been judged to be a particular fault of the Johnson administration), although the commanders were expected to show political sensitivity. It was reported that Bush was not informed of the detailed target set. However, after the raid on the Amiriyah bunker, Secretary of Defense Dick Cheney ordered Powell to review all subsequent missions over Baghdad, and a number of the "softer" targets that might have contained large numbers of civilians were removed from the list.

While Bush may have felt that his strategy represented a sharp break with that adopted in Vietnam, the real difference lay in the political and military context, which was altogether simpler in the Gulf. The debate over escalation in Vietnam had largely developed in connection with the Rolling Thunder bombing campaign, which began in February 1965. This was adopted initially as a means of boosting the morale of the South Vietnamese government, as an alternative to dealing with the government's main problems, its weakness and corruption and its inability to counter communist strength. Those who believed that the bombing campaign would help differed as to whether this would be done by persuading the North Vietnamese government to cease this support for the infiltration routes. In the attempt to coerce the North, the Johnson administration still did not want to provoke China or the Soviet Union into direct intervention. No serious negotiating track was available to take advantage of any move from Hanoi toward concessions. Not surprisingly, the bombing campaign was soon recognized to be inadequate by itself and attention turned to the introduction of substantial ground forces, although here the process was shaped by Johnson's anxiety to play down the significance of the move.

The political situation in the Gulf was in all respects easier; the Kuwaiti people were all clearly opposed to the Iraqi occupation. The military basis of the Iraqi occupation was evident, including the supply lines through which it was sustained. So long as U.S. objectives did not extend to a change of regime in Iraq, the Soviet Union and China were generally supportive, and at least in the Soviet case were willing to supply intelligence information on their former client.

In the Gulf, the administration was still obliged to follow a version of graduated response in order to develop a domestic and international consensus supporting direct military action. The pressure on Iraq was built up in stages, first with economic sanctions; then with a naval blockade, air blockade, and the threat of direct military action; followed by the offer of negotiations. Even once the war began, there was a clear break between the air and the land campaigns during which time there was a flurry of diplomatic activity. In strict terms the key threshold in terms of violence was passed by the imposition of a blockade, for this is an act of war. The only reason it did not become serious was because of Iraqi reluctance to try to break it. Most of the controversial decisions surrounded moving from one stage to the next, especially the move to direct military action. The challenge to President Bush was in developing the political support to transcend this threshold.

CONCLUSION

The ferocious and comprehensive nature of the eventual employment of force raised the question whether the coalition could have achieved its objectives with a greater economy, and whether the air campaign on its own could have decided the war. It is arguable that Iraq was already on the ropes when the land war began and that it merely provided Saddam with his main opportunity to inflict pain on American forces to counter the pain the U.S. Air Force could undoubtedly inflict on Iraq. Against this argument, three points can be made. First, if the Western presence in Saudi Arabia had been smaller, then Saddam's opportunities to extend the war would have been greater. Second, an air offensive directed solely at purely military targets might not have moved Iraq, especially if it could counter with missile attacks against Israel and Saudi Arabia, however ineffectual they might be in strict military terms. To put pressure on Saddam required imposing real distress on the civilian population, and there could have been no guarantee that Saddam could not turn the consequential unease in the West to his political advantage. Third, it was the ground campaign that ensured rapid Iraqi agreement to all UN resolutions. The argument over air power will therefore rumble on, but it does so after a convincing demonstration that chronic inferiority in this area is a strategic liability for which it is almost impossible to compensate in regular conventional warfare.

Simply because he was leading a disparate coalition rather than a unitary state, President Bush was on the political defensive. This provided Saddam with his main strategic opportunity. The pattern of employment of U.S. air power was shaped by this political context. Direct military action was required because Bush could not be sure that the cohesion of the coalition could withstand a long wait for sanctions to bite, and then it had to be swift because the coalition, and Bush's support at home, would have been strained by a prolonged conflict. When it came to using air power to undermine

Saddam's ability to resist a ground offensive, Bush had to depend upon international tolerance of the spectacle of a largely unopposed air bombardment continuing day after day. When he called for a ceasefire, it was because he was aware of a growing unease at the carnage inflicted upon Iraqi troops, and because his basic objectives had now been achieved, even if the future of Saddam himself was left unresolved.

Saddam by this time had been deprived of a strategy other than one of political survival. The blunting of his political offensive had exposed the weaknesses of his wholly inadequate military defense.

Part III
The Nuclear Revolution

Traditionally, the modern state system is dated from the Treaty of Westphalia, concluded in 1648. For the next three centuries, five or more states strove to coexist or contended for mastery. The Second World War revolutionized the state system by turning it into a bipolar one. The Second World War produced a second revolution, as important as the first one, through the invention and use of atomic bombs. In a 1946 essay, Bernard Brodie argued that nuclear weapons radically changed the problem that statesmen and soldiers face. The problem became, not how to use one's best weapons to prevail in war, but how to prevent wars from being fought.

The bipolar world has all but vanished; nuclear weapons remain. Although we have lived in the nuclear revolution for four decades, its meaning and implications are still matters of controversy. The stark confrontation of Soviet and American power no longer defines great power politics.

With nuclear weapons now in the hands of nine or more states, to understand the nuclear revolution is more urgent than ever. The selections of Part III offer a variety of views about the effects of nuclear weapons.

In his essay, Kenneth N. Waltz argues that nuclear weapons deter their possessors not only from fighting nuclear wars but also from fighting major conventional ones. Glenn Snyder distinguishes pre-attack deterrence from post-attack defense and argues that nuclear weapons produce a conflict between them. The selections under "Nuclear Strategies: The Record" deal with choices statesmen have made in planning for the use of nuclear weapons. Robert S. McNamara contends that a country's nuclear weapons serve only the purpose of deterring other countries from using them and that NATO strategy therefore had to be one of "flexible response," relying on conventional weapons to dissuade the Soviet Union from attacking western Europe. John Mueller argues that war among modern industrial states is fast becoming obsolete and that nuclear weapons have little, if anything, to do with this. McGeorge Bundy believes, with McNamara, that nuclear weapons give one advantage only to countries that have them—to prevent others from using theirs; no other political, diplomatic or military advantage is gained. Robert Jervis, contrary to McNamara, Mueller and Bundy, argues that the effects of nuclear weapons on international politics are powerful and pervasive. Finally, Jean-Louis Gergorin speculates on the role of nuclear weapons in the world after the Cold War.

Nuclear Myths and Political Realities

KENNETH N. WALTZ

Nuclear weapons have been given a bad name not just by the left, as one might have expected, but by the center and right as well. Throughout the long life of NATO, calls for strengthening conventional forces have been recurrently heard, reflecting and furthering debate about the wisdom of relying on nuclear deterrence. Doubts were spread more widely when McGeorge Bundy, George Kennan, Robert McNamara, and Gerard Smith published their argument for adopting a NATO policy of "no first use" in the spring, 1982, issue of *Foreign Affairs*. From the right came glib talk about the need to be prepared to fight a protracted nuclear war in order to "deter" the Soviet Union and proclaiming the possibility of doing so. Brigadier General Louis Guifridda, when he was Director of the Federal Emergency Management Agency, well described the Reagan administration's intended nuclear stance. "The administration," he said, "categorically rejected the short war. We're trying to inject a long-war mentality." Such statements, having scared people at home and abroad out of their wits, quickly disappeared from public discourse. Preparation to carry the policy through nevertheless proceeded apace. In 1982, Secretary of Defense Caspar Weinberger signed the five-year Defense Guidance Plan, which was to provide the means of sustaining a nuclear war, and in March of that year, an elaborate war game, dubbed Ivy League, "showed" that it could be done. Finally, in March of 1983, President Reagan offered his vision of a world in which defensive systems would render nuclear weapons obsolete.

With their immense destructive power, nuclear weapons are bound to make people uneasy. Decades of fuzzy thinking in high places about what deterrence is, how it works, and what it can and cannot do have deepened the nuclear malaise. Forty-some years after the first atomic bombs fell on Japan, we have yet to come to grips with the strategic implications of nuclear weapons. This essay applies nuclear reasoning to military policy and, in doing so, contrasts the logic of conventional and nuclear weapons.

Uneasiness over nuclear weapons, and the search for alternative means of security, stem in large measure from widespread failure to

From *American Political Science Review*, September 1990, Vol. 84, no. 3. Published by the American Political Science Association. Reprinted by permission.

understand the nature and requirements of deterrence. Not unexpectedly, the language of strategic discourse has deteriorated over
the decades. This happens whenever discussion enters the political
arena, where words take on the meanings and colorations that
reflect the preferences of their users. Early in the nuclear era,
"deterrence" carried its dictionary definition—dissuading some-
body from doing something by frightening him with the consequences that his action may produce. To deter an adversary from
attacking one need have only a force that can survive a first strike
and strike back hard enough to outweigh any gain the aggressor had
hoped to realize. Deterrence in its pure form entails no ability to
defend; a deterrent strategy promises not to fend off an aggressor
but to damage or destroy things the aggressor holds dear. Both
defense and deterrence are strategies that a status-quo country may
follow, hoping to dissuade a state from attacking. They are different
strategies designed to accomplish a common end in different ways,
using different weapons differently deployed. Wars can be prevented, as they can be caused, in various ways.

Deterrence antedates nuclear weapons, but in a conventional
world deterrent threats are problematic. Stanley Baldwin warned in
the middle 1930s when he was Prime Minister of England that the
bomber would always get through, a thought that helped to demor-
alize England. It proved seriously misleading in the war that soon
followed. Bombers have to make their way past fighter planes and
through ground fire before finding their targets and hitting them
quite squarely. Nuclear weapons purify deterrent strategies by
removing elements of defense and war fighting from them. Nuclear
warheads eliminate the necessity of fighting and remove the possibility of defending, because only a small number of warheads need
to reach their targets.

Ironically, as multiplication of missiles increased the ease with
which destructive blows can be delivered, the distinction between
deterrence and defense began to blur. Early in President Kennedy's
administration, Secretary McNamara began to promote a strategy
of Flexible Response, which was half-heartedly adopted by NATO
in 1967. Flexible Response calls for the ability to meet threats at all
levels from irregular warfare through the conventional and to the
nuclear level. In the 1970s and '80s, more and more emphasis was
placed on the need to fight and defend at all levels in order to
"deter." The melding of defense, war fighting, and deterrence
overlooks a simple truth, proclaimed in the title of a book of essays
Bernard Brodie coauthored and edited in 1946: nuclear weapons are
absolute. Nuclear weapons can carry out their deterrent task no
matter what other countries do. If one nuclear power should gain
the ability to destroy almost all of another's strategic warheads with
practical certainty, or to defend against all but a few strategic
warheads coming in, nuclear weapons would lose their absolute

quality. Because so much explosive power comes in such small packages, the invulnerability of a sufficient number of warheads is easy to achieve and the delivery of fairly large numbers of warheads impossible to thwart. These statements will hold as far into the future as one can see. The absolute quality of nuclear weapons sharply sets a nuclear world off from a conventional one.

WHAT DETERS?

Most discussions of deterrence are based on the belief that deterrence is difficult to achieve. In the Eisenhower years, "massive retaliation" was the phrase popularly used to describe the response we would supposedly make should the Soviet Union attack. Deterrence must be difficult if the threat of massive retaliation is required to achieve it. As the Soviet Union's arsenal grew, MAD (mutual assured destruction) became the acronym of choice, thus preserving the notion that deterrence depends on being willing and able to destroy much if not most of a country.

That one must be able to destroy a country in order to deter it is an odd notion, but one of distinguished lineage. During the 1950s, emphasis was put on the "massive" in massive retaliation. Beginning in the 1960s, the emphasis was put on the "assured destruction" in the doctrine of MAD. Thus viewed, deterrence becomes a monstrous policy, as innumerable critics have charged. One quotation can stand for many others. In a warning to NATO defense ministers that became famous, Henry Kissinger counselled the European allies not to keep "asking us to multiply strategic assurances that we cannot possibly mean or if we do mean, we should not want to execute because if we execute, we risk the destruction of civilization." The notion that the failure of deterrence would lead to national suicide or to mutual annihilation betrays a misunderstanding of both political behavior and nuclear realities.

Introducing the Eisenhower administration's New Look policy in January of 1954, John Foster Dulles gave the impression that aggression anywhere would elicit heavy nuclear retaliation. Just three months later, he sensibly amended the policy. Nuclear deterrence, Dulles and many others quickly came to realize, works not against minor aggression at the periphery but only against major aggression at the center of international politics. Moreover, to deter major aggression, Dulles now said, "the probable hurt" need only "outbalance the probable gain." Like Brodie before him, Dulles based deterrence on the principle of proportionality—let the punishment fit the crime.

What would we expect the United States to do if the Soviet Union should launch a major conventional attack against vital American interests, say, in Western Europe? Military actions have to be related to an objective. Because of the awesome power of nuclear weapons, the pressure to use them in ways that achieve the objective

at hand while doing and suffering a minimum of destruction would
be immense. It is preposterous to think that if a Soviet attack should
break through NATO's defenses, the United States would strike
thousands of Soviet military targets or hundreds of Soviet cities.
Doing so would serve no purpose. Who would want to make a bad
situation worse by launching wantonly destructive attacks on a
country that can strike back with comparable force, or, for that
matter, on a country that could not do so? We might strike a target
or two, military or industrial, chosen to keep casualties low. If the
Soviet Union had run the preposterous risk of attacking the center
of Europe, believing it could escape retaliation, we would thus show
them that they were wrong, while conveying the idea that more will
follow if they persist. Among countries having abundant nuclear
weapons, none can gain an advantage by striking first. The purpose
of demonstration shots is simply to remind everyone—should anyone forget—that catastrophe threatens. Some people purport to
believe that if a few warheads go off, many will follow. This would
seem to be the least likely of all the unlikely possibilities. That no
country gains by destroying another's cities and then seeing a
comparable number of its own destroyed in return is obvious to
everyone.

Despite widespread beliefs to the contrary, deterrence does not
depend on destroying cities. Deterrence depends on what one *can*
do, not on what one *will* do. What deters is the fact that we can do
as much damage to them as we choose, and they to us. The country
suffering the retaliatory attack cannot limit the damage done. Only
the retaliator can do that.

With nuclear weapons, countries need threaten to use only a
small amount of force. This is so because once the willingness to
use a little force is shown, so much more can so easily be added.
This is not true with conventional weapons, and therefore it is often
useful for a country to threaten to use a lot of force if conflict should
lead to war. The stance may be intended as a deterrent one, but the
ability to carry the threat through is problematic. With conventional
weapons, countries tend to emphasize the first phase of war. Striking hard to achieve a quick victory may decrease the cost of war.
With nuclear weapons, political leaders worry not about what may
happen in the first phase of fighting but about what may happen in
the end. As Clausewitz wrote, if war should ever approach the
absolute, it would become "imperative . . . not to take the first step
without considering what may be the last."

Since war now approaches the absolute, it is hardly surprising
that President Kennedy echoed Clausewitz's words during the Cuban Missile Crisis of 1962. "It isn't the first step that concerns me,"
he said, "but both sides escalating to the fourth and fifth step—and
we don't go to the sixth because there is no one around to do so."
In conventional crises, leaders may sensibly seek one advantage or

another. They may bluff by threatening escalatory steps they are in fact unwilling to take. They may try one stratagem or another and run considerable risks. Since none of the parties to the struggle can predict what the outcome will be, they may have good reason to prolong crises, even crises entailing the risk of war. A conventional country enjoying military superiority is tempted to use it before other countries right the military balance. A nuclear country enjoying superiority is reluctant to use it because no one can promise the full success of a disarming first strike. As Henry Kissinger retrospectively said of the Cuban missile crisis, the Soviet Union had only "60–70 truly strategic weapons while we had something like 2000 in missiles and bombs." But, he added, "with some proportion of Soviet delivery vehicles surviving, the Soviet Union could do horrendous damage to the United States." We could not be sure that our 2000 weapons would destroy almost all of their 60 or 70. Even with numbers immensely disproportionate, a small force strongly inhibits the use of a large one.

The catastrophe promised by nuclear war contrasts sharply with the extreme difficulty of predicting outcomes among conventional competitors. This makes one wonder about the claimed dependence of deterrence on perceptions and the alleged problem of credibility. In conventional competitions, the comparative qualities of troops, weaponry, strategies, and leaders are difficult to gauge. So complex is the fighting of wars with conventional weapons that their outcomes have been extremely difficult to predict. Wars start more easily because the uncertainties of their outcome make it easier for the leaders of states to entertain illusions of victory at supportable cost. In contrast, contemplating war when the use of nuclear weapons is possible focuses one's attention not on the probability of victory but on the possibility of annihilation. Because catastrophic outcomes of nuclear exchanges are easy to imagine, leaders of states will shrink in horror from initiating them. With nuclear weapons, stability and peace rest on easy calculations of what one country can do to another. Anyone—political leader or man in the street—can see that catastrophe lurks if events spiral out of control and nuclear warheads begin to fly. The problem of the credibility of deterrence, a big worry in a conventional world, disappears in a nuclear one.

Yet the credibility of deterrence has been a constant American worry. The worry is a hangover from the 1930s. Concern over credibility, and the related efforts to show resolve in crises or wars where only peripheral interests are at stake, were reinforced because the formative experiences of most of the policymakers of the 1950s and '60s took place in the 1930s. In rearming Germany, in reoccupying the Rhineland, in annexing Austria, in dismantling Czechoslovakia, Hitler went to the brink and won. "We must not let that happen again" was the lesson learned, but in a nuclear world the lesson no longer applies. Despite rhetoric to the contrary, practice accords with nuclear logic because its persuasive force is so strong and the possible consequences of ignoring it so grave. Thus, John Foster Dulles, who proclaimed that maintaining peace requires the courage to go to the brink of war, shrank from the precipice during the Hungarian uprising of 1956. And so it has been every time that events even remotely threatened to get out of hand at the center of international politics.

Still, strategists' and commentators' minds prove to be impressively fertile. The imagined difficulties of deterrence multiply apace. One example will do. Paul Nitze argued in the late 1970s that, given a certain balance of strategic forces, given the Soviet Union's supposed goal of world domination, and given its presumed willingness to run great risks, the Soviet Union might launch a first-strike against our land-based missiles, our bombers on the ground, and our strategic submarines in port. The Soviet Union's strike would tilt the balance of strategic forces sharply against us. Rather than retaliate, our president might decide to acquiesce. That is, we might be "self deterred." Nitze's scenario is based on faulty assumptions, unfounded distinctions, and preposterous notions about how governments behave. Soviet leaders, according to him, may have concluded from the trend in the balance of nuclear forces in the middle 1970s that our relatively small warheads and their civil defense would enable the Soviet Union to limit the casualties resulting from our retaliation to 3 or 4 percent of their population. Their hope for such a "happy" outcome would presumably rest on confidence that their first strike would be well timed and accurate and that their intelligence agencies would have revealed the exact location of almost all of their intended targets. In short, their leaders would have to believe that all would go well in a huge, unrehearsed missile barrage, that the United States would fail to launch on warning, and that if by chance they had failed to "deter our deterrent," they would still be able to limit casualties to only ten million people or so.[1] How could they entertain such a hope when, by Nitze's estimate, their first strike would have left us with 2,000 warheads in our submarine force in addition to warheads carried by surviving bombers?

Nitze's fear rested on the distinction between counterforce and countervalue strikes—between strikes aimed at weapons and strikes aimed at cities. Because the Soviet Union's first strike would be counterforce, any American president would seemingly have good reason to refrain from retaliation, thus avoiding the loss of cities still held hostage by the Soviet Union's remaining strategic forces. But this thought overlooks the fact that, once strategic missiles

---

[1] Nitze blandly adds that, if we do launch on warning, "the estimates in the Soviet civil defense manuals are overoptimistic from the Soviet viewpoint."

numbered in the low hundreds are fired, the counterforce/counter-value distinction blurs. One would no longer know what the attackers' intended targets might be. The Soviet Union's counterforce strike would require that thousands, not hundreds, of warheads be fired. Moreover, the extent of their casualties, should we decide to retaliate, would depend on how many of our warheads we chose to fire, on what targets we aimed at, and on whether we used ground bursts to increase fallout. Several hundred warheads can destroy the United States or the Soviet Union as going societies. The assumptions made in the effort to make a Soviet first strike appear possible are ridiculous. How could the Soviet Union, or any country, somehow bring itself to run stupendous risks in the presence of nuclear weapons? What objectives might its leaders seek that could justify the risks entailed? Answering these questions sensibly leads one to conclude that deterrence is deeply stable. Those who favor increasing the strength of our strategic forces, however, shift to a different question. "The crucial question," according to Nitze, "is whether a future U.S. president should be left with only the option of deciding within minutes, or at most within two or three hours, to retaliate after a counterforce attack in a manner certain to result not only in military defeat for the United States but in wholly disproportionate and truly irremediable destruction to the American people." One of the marvels of the nuclear age is how easily those who write about the unreliability of deterrence focus on the retaliator's possible inhibitions and play down the attacker's obvious risks. Doing so makes deterrence seem hard and leads to arguments for increasing our military spending in order "to deny the Soviet Union the possibility of a successful war-fighting capability," a strategic capability that the Soviet Union has never remotely approached.

We do not need ever-larger forces to deter. Smaller forces, so long as they are invulnerable, would be quite sufficient. Yet the vulnerability of fixed, land-based missiles has proved worrisome. Those who do the worrying dwell on the vulnerability of one class of weapons. The militarily important question, however, is not about the vulnerability of one class of weapons but about the vulnerability of a whole strategic-weapons system. Submarine-launched missiles make land-based missiles invulnerable since destroying only the latter would leave thousands of strategic warheads intact. To overlook this again reflects conventional thinking. In the absence of a dominant weapon, the vulnerability of one weapon or another may be a big problem. If the means of protecting sealanes of communications were destroyed, for example, we would be unable to deploy and support troops abroad. The problem disappears in a nuclear world. Destroying a portion of one's strategic force means little if sufficient weapons for deterrence survive.

Thinking about deterrence is often faulted for being abstract and deductive, for not being grounded in experience. The criticism is an odd one since all statements about the military implications of nuclear weapons are inferred from their characteristics. Deterrers from Brodie onward have drawn conclusions from the all but unimaginable increase in easily delivered firepower that nuclear warheads embody. Those who in the nuclear era apply lessons learned in conventional warfare make the more problematic claim that despite profound changes in military technology the classic principles of warfare endure. We all, happily, lack the benefit of experience. Moreover, just as deterrent logic is abstract and deductive, so too are the weaknesses attributed to it. Scenarios showing how deterrence might fail are not only abstract but also farfetched. Deterrence rests on simple propositions and relies on forces obviously sufficient for their purpose.

DETERRING THE SOVIET UNION

Underlying much of the concern about the reliability of nuclear deterrence is the conviction that the Soviet Union is especially hard to deter. Three main reasons are given for believing this. First, the Soviet Union's ambitions are said to be unlimited. In 1984, Secretary of Defense Caspar Weinberger, when asked why the Soviet Union armed itself so heavily, answered the question bluntly: "World domination, it's that simple." Second, her military doctrine seemed to contemplate the possibility of fighting and winning combined conventional and nuclear wars, while rejecting the doctrine of deterrence. Third, the Soviet Union has appeared to many people in the West to be striving for military superiority.

These three points make a surprisingly weak case, even though it has been widely accepted. Ambitions aside, looking at the Soviet Union's behavior one is impressed with its caution when acting where conflict might lead to the use of major force. Leaders of the Soviet Union may hope that they can one day turn the world to Communism. Although the Soviet Union's intentions may be extraordinary, her behavior has not been. Everyone agrees that, except in the military sector, the Soviet Union is the lagging competitor in a two-party race. The Soviet Union has been opportunistic and disruptive, but one expects the lagging party to score a point or two whenever it can. The Soviet Union has not scored many. Her limited international successes should not obscure the fact that what the Soviet Union has done mostly since 1948 is lose.

The second point rests on basic misunderstandings about deterrence. It has often been argued that we could not rely on deterrence when the Soviet Union was rejecting the doctrine. One of the drawbacks of the "theory" of assured destruction, according to Henry Kissinger, was that "the Soviets did not believe it." The efficacy of nuclear deterrence, however, does not depend on anyone's accepting it. Secretaries of Defense nevertheless continue to worry that Soviet values, perceptions, and calculations may be different from ours. Thus Secretary of Defense Harold Brown, worried by the Soviets' emphasis "on the acquisition of war-winning capabilities," concluded that we must "continue to adapt and update our countervailing capabilities so that the Soviets will clearly understand that we will never allow them to use their nuclear forces to achieve any aggressive aim at an acceptable cost."

The belief that the Soviet Union's having an aggressive military doctrine makes her especially hard to deter is another hangover from conventional days. Germany and Japan in the 1930s were hard to deter, but then the instruments for deterrence were not available. We can fairly say that their leaders were less averse to running risks than most political leaders are. But that is no warrant for believing that had they been confronted with second-strike nuclear forces, they would have been so foolhardy as to risk the sudden destruction of their countries. The decision to challenge the vital interests of a nuclear state, whether by major conventional assault or by nuclear first strike, would be a collective decision involving a number of political and military leaders. One would have to believe that a whole set of leaders might suddenly go mad. Rulers like to continue to rule. Except in the relatively few countries of settled democratic institutions, one is struck by how tenaciously rulers cling to power. We have no reason to expect Russian leaders to be any different. The notion that Russian leaders might risk losing even a small number of cities by questing militarily for uncertain gains is fanciful. Malenkov and Khrushchev lost their positions for lesser failures.

With conventional weapons a status quo country must ask itself how much power it must harness to its policy in order to dissuade an especially aggressive state from striking. Countries willing to run high risks are hard to dissuade. The varied qualities of governments and the temperaments of leaders have to be carefully weighed. In a nuclear world, any state will be deterred by another state's second-strike forces. One need not become preoccupied with the characteristics of the state that is to be deterred or scrutinize its leaders.

The third worry remains: the Soviet Union's seeming aspiration for military superiority. One might think that the worry should have run the other way through most of the years of the Cold War. In the nuclear business, the United States moved from monopoly to superiority. In the late fifties, Khrushchev deeply cut conventional arms, and the Soviet Union failed to produce strategic warheads and missiles as rapidly as we had expected. Nevertheless, the Kennedy administration undertook the largest peacetime military buildup the world had yet seen, in both nuclear and conventional weaponry. So far did we forge ahead strategically that McNamara thought the Soviet Union would not even try to catch up. "There is," he said, "no indication that the Soviets are seeking to develop a strategic nuclear force as large as ours." To expect that the Soviet Union would give up one had to believe that it would behave in a historically unprecedented manner. Instead, the Soviet Union tried to compete. Yet to catch up with the United States was difficult. In the 1970s, the decade in which we are told the Soviet Union moved toward superiority—or, according to President Reagan, achieved it—the United States in fact added more nuclear warheads to its arsenal than the Soviet Union did.

We have exaggerated the strength of the Soviet Union, and they, no doubt, have exaggerated ours. One may wonder whether the Soviet Union ever thought itself superior, or believed it could become so. Americans easily forget that the Soviet Union has the strategic weapons of four countries pointed at it and sees itself threatened from the East as well as the West. More fundamentally, continued preoccupation with denying "superiority" to the Soviet Union, if not seeking it ourselves, suggests that a basic strategic implication of nuclear weapons is yet to be appreciated. So long as two or more countries have second-strike forces, to compare them is pointless. If no state can launch a disarming attack with high confidence, force comparisons become irrelevant. For deterrence one asks how much is enough, and enough is defined as having a second-strike capability. This does not imply that a deterrent force deters everything, but rather that beyond a certain level of capability, additional forces provide no additional coverage for one party and pose no additional threat to others. The United States and the Soviet Union have long had second-strike forces, with neither able to launch a disarming first strike against the other. Two countries with second-strike forces have the same amount of strategic power, since short of attaining a first-strike capability, adding more weapons does not change the effective military balance.

WHY NUCLEAR WEAPONS DOMINATE STRATEGY

Deterrence is easier to contrive than most strategists have believed. With conventional weapons, weapons that are relative and not absolute, a number of strategies are available, strategies combining and deploying forces in different ways. Strategies may do more than weapons to determine the outcomes of wars. Nuclear weapons are different; they dominate strategies. As Brodie clearly saw, the effects of nuclear weapons derive not from any particular design for their employment in war, but simply from their presence. Indeed, in an important sense, nuclear weapons eliminate strategy. If one thinks of strategies as being designed for the defense of national objectives or for the gaining of them by military force, and if one thinks of strategies as implying a choice about how major wars will be fought, then nuclear weapons make strategy obsolete. Nevertheless, the conviction that the only reliable deterrent force is one able to win a war, or fight one in a way that leaves us in a better position than the Soviet Union, is widespread. Linton F. Brooks, while a

Captain in the United States Navy, wrote that "War is the ultimate test of any strategy; a strategy useless in war cannot deter."

NATO policy well illustrates the futility of trying to transcend deterrence by fashioning war-fighting strategies. The supposed difficulties of extending deterrence to cover major allies has led some to argue that we require nuclear superiority, that we need nuclear war-fighting capabilities, and that we must build up our conventional forces. Once the Soviet Union achieved nuclear parity, confidence in our extended deterrent declined in the West. One wonders whether it did in the East. Denis Healey once said that one chance in a hundred that a country will retaliate is enough to deter an adversary, although not enough to reassure an ally. Many have repeated his statement, but none, I believe, has added that reassuring allies is unnecessary militarily and unwise politically. Politically, allies who are unsure of one another's support have reason to work harder for the sake of their own security. Militarily, deterrence requires only that conventional forces be able to defend long enough to determine that an attack is a major one and not merely a foray. For this a trip-wire force as envisioned in the 1950s, with perhaps 50,000 American troops in Europe, would be sufficient. Beyond that, deterrence requires only that forces be invulnerable and that the area protected be of manifestly vital interest. Western European countries can be counted on to maintain forces of trip-wire capability.

Nuclear weapons strip conventional forces of most of their functions. Bernard Brodie pointed out that in "a total war" the army "might have no function at all." Herman Kahn cited "the claim that in a thermonuclear war it is important to keep the sealanes open" as an example of the "quaint ideas" still held by the military.[2] Conventional forces have only a narrow role in any confrontation between nuclear states over vital interests, since fighting beyond the trip-wire level serves no useful purpose. Enlarging conventional capabilities does nothing to strengthen deterrence. Strategic stalemate does shift military competition to the tactical level. But one must add what is usually omitted: Nuclear stalemate limits the use of conventional forces and reduces the extent of the gains one can seek without risking devastation. For decades American policy has nevertheless aimed at raising the nuclear threshold in Europe. Stronger conventional forces would presumably enable NATO to sustain a longer war in Europe at higher levels of violence. At some moment in a major war, however, one side or the other—or perhaps both—would believe itself to be losing. The temptation to introduce nuclear weapons may then prove irresistible, and they would be

[2] Quaint ideas die hard. In the fall of 1989, NATO resisted discussing naval disarmament with the Soviet Union because of the need for forces to guard the sealanes to Europe.

fired in the chaos of defeat with little chance of limited and discrim-
inant use. Early use would promise surer control and closer limitation of damage. In a nuclear world, a conventional war-fighting
strategy would appear to be the worst possible one, more dangerous
than a strategy of relying on deterrence.

Attempts to gain escalation dominance, like efforts to raise the
nuclear threshold, betray a failure to appreciate the strategic implications of nuclear weapons. Escalation dominance, so it is said,
requires "a seamless web of capabilities" up and down "the escalation ladder." Earlier it had been thought that the credibility of
deterrence would be greater if some rungs of the escalation ladder
were missing. The inability to fight at some levels would make the
threat to use higher levels of force easy to credit. But, again, since
credibility is not a problem, this scarcely matters militarily. Filling
in the missing rungs neither helps nor hurts. Escalation dominance
is useful for countries contending with conventional weapons only.
Dominance, however, is difficult to achieve in the absence of a
decisive weapon. Among nuclear adversaries the question of dominance is pointless because one second-strike force cannot dominate
another. Since strategic nuclear weapons will always prevail, the
game of escalation dominance cannot be played. Everyone knows
that anyone can quickly move to the top rung of the ladder. Because
anyone can do so, all of the parties in a serious crisis have an
overriding incentive to ask themselves one question: How can we
get out of this mess without nuclear warheads exploding? Deescalation, not escalation, becomes the problem that the presence of
nuclear weapons forces them to solve.

To gain escalation dominance, were it imaginable, would require
the ability to fight nuclear wars. War-fighting strategies take nuclear
weapons to be relative, with the country having more and better
ones able in some unspecified way to prevail. No one, however, has
shown how such a war could be fought. Indeed, Desmond Ball has
argued that a nuclear war could not be sustained beyond the
exchange of strategic warheads numbered not in the hundreds but
in the tens. After a small number of exchanges no one would know
what was going on or be able to maintain control. Yet, as ever,
nuclear weapons save us from our folly. Fanciful strategies are
irrelevant because no one will run the appalling risk of testing them.

Deterrence has been faulted for its lack of credibility, its dependence on perceptions, its destructive implications, and its inability
to cover interests abroad. The trouble with deterrence, however,
lies elsewhere. The trouble with deterrence is that it can be implemented cheaply. The claim that we need a seamless web of capabilities in order to deter does serve one purpose: It keeps military
budgets wondrously high. Efforts to fashion a defensive and war-
fighting strategy for NATO are pointless because deterrence prevails, and futile because strategy cannot transcend the military
conditions that nuclear weapons create.

NUCLEAR ARMS AND DISARMAMENT

The probability of major war among states having nuclear weapons approaches zero. But the "real war" may, as William James claimed, lie in the preparation for waging it. The logic of deterrence, if followed, circumscribes the causes of "real wars." Nuclear weapons make it possible for a state to limit the size of its strategic forces as long as other states are unable to achieve disarming first-strike capabilities by improving their forces.

Within very wide ranges, a nuclear balance is insensitive to variation in numbers and size of warheads. This has occasionally been seen by responsible officials. Harold Brown said, when he was Secretary of Defense, purely deterrent forces "can be relatively modest, and their size can perhaps be made substantially, though not completely, insensitive to changes in the posture of an opponent." Somehow he nevertheless managed to argue that we need "to design our forces on the basis of essential equivalents." Typically over the past three decades, Secretaries of Defense have sought, albeit vainly, the superiority that would supposedly give us a war-fighting capability. But they have failed to explain what we can do with 12,000 strategic nuclear warheads that we could not do with 2,000, or with a still smaller number. What difference does it make if we have 2,000 strategic weapons and the Soviet Union has 4,000? We thought our deterrent did not deter very much, and did not work with sufficient reliability, just as we were reaching a peak of numerical superiority in the mid-1960s. Flexible response, with emphasis on conventional arms, was a policy produced in our era of nuclear plenty. "Superiority" and "parity" have had the same effect on our policy.

Many who urge us to build ever more strategic weapons in effect admit the military irrelevance of additional forces when, as so often, they give political rather than military reasons for doing so. Spending less, it is said, would signal weakness of will. Yet militarily only one perception counts, and that is the perception that a country has second-strike forces. Nuclear weapons make it possible for states to escape the dynamics of arms racing, yet the United States and the Soviet Union have multiplied their weaponry far beyond the requirements of deterrence. Each has obsessively measured its strategic forces against the other's. The arms competition between them has arisen from failure to appreciate the implications of nuclear weapons for military strategy and, no doubt, from internal military and political pressures in both countries.

Many of the obstacles to arms reduction among conventional powers disappear or dwindle among nuclear nations. For the former, the careful comparison of the quantities and qualities of forces is important. Because this is not so with nuclear weapons, the problem of verifying agreements largely disappears. Provisions for verification may be necessary in order to persuade the Senate to ratify an agreement, but the possibility of non-compliance is not very worrisome. Agreements that reduce one category of conventional weapons may shift competition to other types of weapons and lead to increases in their numbers and capabilities. Because with nuclear weapons sufficiency is easily defined, there is no military reason for reductions in some weapons to result in increases in others. Conventionally, multiparty agreements are hard to arrive at because each party has to consider how shifting alignments may alter the balance of forces if agreements are reached to reduce them. In a world of second-strike nuclear forces, alliances have little effect on the strategic balance. The Soviet Union's failure to insist that British, French, and Chinese forces be counted in strategic arms negotiations may reflect its appreciation of this point. Finally, conventional powers have to compare weapons of uncertain effectiveness. Arms agreements are difficult to reach because their provisions may bear directly on the prospects for victory or defeat. Because in a nuclear world peace is maintained by the presence of deterrent forces, strategic arms agreements have not military but economic and political significance. They can benefit countries economically and help to improve their relations.

A minority of American military analysts have understood the folly of maintaining more nuclear weapons than deterrence requires. In the Soviet Union, Mikhail Gorbachev and some others have put forth the notion of "reasonable sufficiency," defined as having a strategic force roughly equal to ours and able, in retaliation, to inflict unacceptable damage. Edward Warner points out that some civilian analysts have gone further, "suggesting that as long as the USSR had a secure second-strike capability that could inflict unacceptable damage, it would not have to be concerned about maintaining approximate numerical parity with U.S. strategic nuclear forces." If leaders in both countries come to accept the minority view—and also realize that a deterrent force greatly reduces conventional requirements on central fronts—both countries can enjoy security at much lower cost.

STRATEGIC DEFENSE

Strategic defenses would radically change the propositions advanced in this essay. The Strategic Defense Initiative, in Reagan's vision, was to provide an area defense that would protect the entire population of the United States. Strategic defenses were to pose an absolute defense against what have been absolute weapons, thus rendering them obsolete. The consequences that would follow from mounting such a defense boggle the mind. That a perfect defense against nuclear weapons could be deployed and sustained is inconceivable. This is so for two reasons. First, nuclear weapons are small and light; they are easy to move, easy to hide, and easy to deliver in a variety of ways. Even an unimaginably perfect defense against ballistic missiles would fail to negate nuclear weapons. Such a defense would instead put a premium on the other side's ability to deliver nuclear weapons in different ways: firing missiles on depressed trajectories, carrying bombs in suitcases, placing nuclear warheads on freighters to be anchored in American harbors. Indeed, someone has suggested that the Soviet Union can always hide warheads in bales of marijuana, knowing we cannot keep them from crossing our borders. To have even modestly effective defenses we would, among other things, have to become a police state. We would have to go to extraordinary lengths to police our borders and exercise control within them. Presumably, the Soviet Union does these things better than we do. It is impossible to imagine that an area defense can be a success because there are so many ways to thwart it. In no way can we prevent the Soviet Union from exploding nuclear warheads on or in the United States if it is determined to do so.

Second, let us imagine for a moment that an airtight defense, however defined, is about to be deployed by one country or the other. The closer one country came to deploying such a defense, the harder the other would work to overcome it. When he was Secretary of Defense, Robert McNamara argued that the appropriate response to a Soviet defensive deployment would be to expand our deterrent force. More recently, Caspar Weinberger and Mikhail Gorbachev have made similar statements. Any country deploying a defense effective for a moment cannot expect it to remain so. The ease of delivering nuclear warheads, and the destructiveness of small numbers of them, make the durability of defenses highly suspect.

The logic of strategic defense is the logic of conventional weaponry. Conventional strategies pit weapons against weapons. That is exactly what a strategic defense would do, thereby recreating the temptations and instabilities that have plagued countries armed only with conventional weapons. If the United States and the Soviet Union deploy defensive systems, each will worry, no doubt excessively, about the balance of offensive and defensive capabilities. Each will fear that the other may score an offensive or defensive breakthrough. If one side should do so, it might be tempted to strike in order to exploit its temporary advantage. The dreaded specter of the hair-trigger would reappear. Under such circumstances, a defensive system would serve as the shield that makes the sword useful. An offensive/defensive race would introduce many uncertainties. A country enjoying a momentary defensive advantage would be tempted to strike in the forlorn hope that its defenses would be able to handle a ragged and reduced response to its first strike. Both countries would prepare to launch on warning, while obsessively weighing the balance between offensive and defensive forces.

Finally, let us imagine what is most unimaginable of all—that both sides deploy defenses that are impregnable and durable. Such defenses would make the world safe for World War III, fought presumably in the manner of World War II but with conventional weapons of much greater destructive power. Still, some have argued that, even if some American cities remain vulnerable, defenses are very good for the cities they do cover. The claim is spurious. In response to the Soviet Union's deploying antiballistic missiles to protect Moscow, we multiplied the number of missiles aimed at that city. We expect to overcome their defenses and still deliver the "required" number of warheads. The result of defending cities may be that more warheads strike them. This is especially so since we and they, working on worst-case assumptions, are likely to overestimate the number of missiles the other country's system will be able to shoot down. Strategic defenses are likely to increase the damage done.

Most knowledgeable people believe that an almost leak-proof defense cannot be built. Many, however, believe that if improved hard-point defenses result from the SDI program, they will have justified its price. Defense of missiles and of command, control, and communications installations will strengthen deterrence, so the argument goes. That would be a solution all right, but we lack a problem to go with it. Deterrence is vibrantly healthy. If the Soviet Union believes that even one Trident submarine would survive its first strike, surely it will be deterred.[3] Since we do not need hardpoint defenses, we should not buy them. The deployment of such defenses by one side would be seen by the other as the first step in deploying an area defense. Strategic considerations should dominate technical ones. In a nuclear world, defensive systems are predictably destabilizing. It would be folly to move from a condition of stable deterrence to one of unstable defense.

CONCLUSION

Nuclear weapons dissuade states from going to war more surely than conventional weapons do. In a conventional world, states going to war can at once believe that they may win and that, should they lose, the price of defeat will be bearable. World Wars I and II called the latter belief into question before atomic bombs were ever dropped. Were the United States and the Soviet Union now armed only with conventional weapons, the lesson of those wars would be strongly remembered, especially by Russia since she has suffered more in war than we have. Had the atom never been split, the United States and the Soviet Union would still have much to fear from each other. The stark opposition of countries of continental size, armed

---

[3] An Ohio-class Trident submarine carries 24 missiles, each having eight warheads.

with ever more destructive conventional weapons, would strongly constrain them. Yet in a conventional world, even strong and sad lessons have proved to be exceedingly difficult for states to learn. Recurrently in modern history, one great power or another has looked as though it might become dangerously strong: Louis XIV's and Napoleon's France, Wilhelm II's and Hitler's Germany. Each time an opposing coalition formed, if belatedly, and turned the expansive state back. The lesson would seem to be clear: In international politics, success leads to failure. The excessive accumulation of power by one state or coalition of states elicits the opposition of others. The leaders of expansionist states have nevertheless been able to persuade themselves that skillful diplomacy and clever strategy would enable them to transcend the normal processes of balance-of-power politics. The Schlieffen Plan, for example, seemed to offer a strategy that would enable Germany to engage enemies on two fronts but to do so serially. Germany would defeat France before Russia could mobilize fully and move westward in force. Later Hitler, while denouncing the "boobs" of Wilhelmine Germany for getting themselves into a war on two fronts, reenacted their errors.

How can we perpetuate peace without solving the problem of war? This is the question that states having nuclear weapons must constantly answer. Nuclear states continue to compete militarily. With each state tending to its security interests as best it can, war is constantly possible. Although the possibility of war remains, nuclear weapons have drastically reduced the probability of its being fought by states having them. Wars that might bring nuclear weapons into play have become extraordinarily hard to start. Over the centuries great powers have fought more wars and lesser states have fought fewer. The frequency of war has correlated less closely with the attributes of states than with their international standing. Yet, because of a profound change in military technology, waging war has more and more become the privilege of poor and weak states. Nuclear weapons have reversed the fates of strong and weak states. Never since the Treaty of Westphalia in 1648, which conventionally marks the beginning of modern history, have great powers enjoyed a longer period of peace than we have known since the Second World War. One can scarcely believe that the presence of nuclear weapons does not greatly help to explain this happy condition.

Deterrence and Defense

GLENN H. SNYDER

National security still remains an "ambiguous symbol," as one scholar described it almost a decade ago.[1] Certainly it has grown more ambiguous as a result of the startling advances since then in nuclear and weapons technology, and the advent of nuclear parity between the United States and the Soviet Union. Besides such technological complications, doctrine and thought about the role of force in international politics have introduced additional complexities. We now have, at least in embryonic form, theories of limited war, of deterrence, of "tactical" vs. "strategic" uses of nuclear weapons, of "retaliatory" vs. "counterforce" strategies in all-out war, of "limited retaliation," of the mechanics of threat and commitment-making, of "internal war," "protracted conflict," and the like. Above all, the idea of the "balance of terror" has begun to mature, but its relation to the older concept of the "balance of power" is still not clear. We have had a great intellectual ferment in the strategic realm, which of course is all to the good. What urgently remains to be done is to tie together all of these concepts into a coherent framework of theory so that the end-goal of national security may become less ambiguous, and so that the military means available for pursuance of this goal may be accumulated, organized, and used more efficiently. This book can claim to make only a start in this direction.

The central theoretical problem in the field of national security policy is to clarify and distinguish between the two central concepts of *deterrence* and *defense*. Essentially, deterrence means discouraging the enemy from taking military action by posing for him a prospect of cost and risk outweighing his prospective gain. Defense means reducing our own prospective costs and risks in the event that deterrence fails. Deterrence works on the enemy's *intentions*; the *deterrent value*

From *Deterrence and Defense: Toward a Theory of National Security* by Glenn H. Snyder, pp. 3–16, 31, 33–40, 50, 97–109. Copyright © 1961 by Princeton University Press. Reprinted by permission of Princeton University Press. Portions of the text and some footnotes have been omitted.

[1] Arnold Wolfers, " 'National Security' as an Ambiguous Symbol," *Political Science Quarterly*, Vol. LXVII, No. 4 (December 1952), pp. 481ff.

of military forces is their effect in reducing the likelihood of enemy military moves. Defense reduces the enemy's *capability* to damage or deprive us; the *defense value* of military forces is their effect in mitigating the adverse consequences for us of possible enemy moves, whether such consequences are counted as losses of territory or war damage. The concept of "defense value," therefore, is broader than the mere capacity to hold territory, which might be called "denial capability." Defense value is denial capability plus capacity to alleviate war damage.

It is commonplace, of course, to say that the primary objectives of national security policy are to deter enemy attacks and to defend successfully, at minimum cost, against those attacks which occur. It is less widely recognized that different types of military force contribute in differing proportions to these two objectives. Deterrence does not vary directly with our capacity for fighting wars effectively and cheaply; a particular set of forces might produce strong deterrent effects and not provide a very effective denial and damage-alleviating capability. Conversely, forces effective for defense might be less potent deterrents than other forces which were less efficient for holding territory and which might involve extremely high war costs if used.

One reason why the periodic "great debates" about national security policy have been so inconclusive is that the participants often argue from different premises—one side from the point of view of deterrence, and the other side from the point of view of defense. For instance, in the famous "massive retaliation" debate of 1954, the late Secretary of State Dulles and his supporters argued mainly that a capacity for massive retaliation would deter potential Communist mischief, but they tended to ignore the consequences should deterrence fail. The critics, on the other hand, stressed the dire consequences should the threat of massive retaliation fail to deter and tended to ignore the possibility that it might work. The opposing arguments never really made contact because no one explicitly recognized that considerations of reducing the probability of war and mitigating its consequences must be evaluated simultaneously, that the possible consequences of a failure of deterrence are more or less important depending on the presumed likelihood of deterrence. Many other examples could be cited.

Perhaps the crucial difference between deterrence and defense is that deterrence is primarily a peacetime objective, while defense is a wartime value. Deterrent value and defense value are directly enjoyed in different time periods. We enjoy the deterrent value of our military forces prior to the enemy's aggressive move; we enjoy defense value after the enemy move has already been made, although we indirectly profit from defense capabilities in advance of war through our knowledge that if the enemy attack occurs we have the means of mitigating its consequences. The crucial point is that *after* the enemy's attack takes place, our military forces perform different functions and yield wholly different values than they did as deterrents prior to the attack. As deterrents they engaged in a psychological battle—dissuading the enemy from attacking by attempting to confront him with a prospect of costs greater than his prospective gain. After the enemy begins his attack, while the psychological or deterrent aspect does not entirely disappear, it is partly supplanted by another purpose: to resist the enemy's onslaught in order to minimize *our* losses or perhaps maximize *our* gains, not only with regard to the future balance of power, but also in terms of intrinsic or non-power values. That combination of forces which appeared to be the optimum one from the point of view of deterrence might turn out to be far inferior to some other combination from the point of view of defense should deterrence fail. In short, maximizing the enemy's cost expectancy may not always be consistent with minimizing our own. Thus we must measure the value of our military forces on two yardsticks, and we must find some way of combining their value on *both* yardsticks, in order accurately to gauge their aggregate worth or "utility" and to make intelligent choices among the various types of forces available.

Before launching into a theoretical analysis of the concepts of deterrence and defense, it may be useful to present a sampling of policy issues involving a need to choose between deterrence and defense; the examples will be treated in more detail in subsequent chapters.

EXAMPLES OF CHOICES AND CONFLICTS BETWEEN
DETERRENCE AND DEFENSE

A strategic retaliatory air force sufficient only to wreak minimum "unacceptable" damage on Soviet cities—to destroy, say, 20 cities—after this force has been decimated by a surprise Soviet nuclear attack, would have great value for deterring such a surprise attack and might be an adequate deterrent against that contingency. But if deterrence were to fail and the Soviet attack took place, it would then not be rational to *use* such a minimum force in massive retaliation against Soviet cities, since this would only stimulate the Soviets to inflict further damage upon us and would contribute nothing to our "winning the war." If we are interested in defense—i.e., in winning the war and in minimizing the damage to us—as well as in deterrence, we may wish to have (if technically feasible) a much larger force and probably one of different composition—a force which can strike effectively at the enemy's remaining forces (thus reducing our own costs) and, further, either by actual attacks or the threat of attacks, force the enemy to surrender or at least to give up his territorial gains.

The threat of massive nuclear retaliation against a Soviet major ground attack in Western Europe may continue to provide considerable deterrence against such an attack, even if actually to carry out the threat would be irrational because of the enormous costs we would suffer from Soviet counterretaliation. Strategic nuclear weapons do not provide a rational means of defense in Western Europe unless they not only can stop the Russian ground advance but also, by "counterforce" strikes, can reduce to an acceptable level the damage we would suffer in return. We may not have this capability now and it may become altogether infeasible as the Soviets develop their missile technology. For a means of rational defense, therefore, NATO may need enough ground forces to hold Europe against a full-scale attack by Soviet ground forces. This does not mean, however, that we necessarily must maintain ground forces of this size. If we think the probability of attack is low enough, we may decide to continue relying on nuclear deterrence primarily, even though it does not provide a rational means of defense. In other words, we might count on the Soviet uncertainties about whether or not nuclear retaliation is rational for us, and about how rational we are, to inhibit the Soviets from attacking in the face of the terrible damage they *know* they would suffer if they guessed wrong.

An attempt to build an effective counterforce capability, in order to have both a rational nuclear defense and a more credible nuclear deterrent against ground attack in Europe, might work against the *deterrence* of direct nuclear attack on the United States. Since such a force, by definition, would be able to eliminate all but a small fraction of the Soviet strategic nuclear forces if it struck first, the Soviets might, in some circumstances, fear a surprise attack and be led to strike first themselves in order to forestall it.

Tactical nuclear weapons in the hands of NATO forces in Europe have considerable deterrent value because they increase the enemy's cost expectation beyond what it would be if these forces were equipped only with conventional weapons. This is true not only because the tactical weapons themselves can inflict high costs on the enemy's forces, but also because their use (or an enemy "preemptive" strike against them) would sharply raise the probability that the war would spiral to all-out dimensions. But the defense value of tactical nuclear weapons against conventional attack is comparatively low against an enemy who also possesses them, because their use presumably would be offset by the enemy's use of them against our forces, and because in using such weapons we would be incurring much greater costs and risks than if we had responded conventionally.

For deterrence, it might be desirable to render automatic a response which the enemy recognizes as being costly for us, and communicate the fact of such automation to the enemy, thus reducing his doubts that we would actually choose to make this response when the occasion for it arose. For example, a tactical nuclear response to conventional aggression in Europe may be made semi-automatic by thoroughly orienting NATO plans, organization, and strategy around this response, thus increasing the difficulty of following a non-nuclear strategy in case of a Soviet challenge. But such automation would not be desirable for defense, which would require flexibility and freedom to choose the least costly action in the light of circumstances at the time of the attack.

The Continental European attitude toward NATO strategy is generally ambivalent on the question of deterrence vs. defense; there is fear that with the Soviet acquisition of a substantial nuclear and missile capability, the willingness of the United States to invoke massive retaliation is declining, and that therefore the deterrent to aggression has weakened. Yet the Europeans do not embrace the logical consequence of this fear: the need to build up an adequate capacity to defend Europe on the ground. A more favored alternative, at least in France, is the acquisition of an independent strategic nuclear capability. But when European governments project their imaginations forward to the day when the enemy's divisions cross their borders, do they really envisage themselves shooting off their few missiles against an enemy who would surely obliterate them in return? One doubts that they do, but this is not to say that it is irrational for them to acquire such weapons; they might be successful as a deterrent because of Soviet uncertainty as to whether they would be used, and Soviet unwillingness to incur the risk of their being used.

Further examples easily come to mind. For the sake of deterrence in Europe, we might wish to deploy the forces there as if they intended to respond to an attack with nuclear weapons; but this might not be the optimum deployment for defense once the attack has occurred, if the least-cost defense is a conventional one. For deterrence of limited aggressions in Asia, it might be best to deploy troops on the spot as a "plate-glass window." But for the most efficient and flexible defense against such contingencies, troops might better be concentrated in a central reserve, with transport facilities for moving them quickly to a threatened area.

As Bernard Brodie has written,[2] if the object of our strategic air forces is only deterrence, there is little point in developing "clean" bombs; since deterrence is to be effected by the threat of dire punishment, the dirtier the better. But if we also wish to minimize our own costs once the war has begun, we might wish to use bombs producing minimum fall-out, to encourage similar restraint in the enemy.

[2] Bernard Brodie, *Strategy in the Missile Age*, Princeton: Princeton University Press, 1959, p. 295.

For deterrence, it might be desirable to disperse elements of the Strategic Air Command to civilian airfields, thus increasing the number of targets which the enemy must hit if he is to achieve the necessary attrition of our retaliatory power by his first strike. However, this expedient might greatly increase the population damage we would suffer in the enemy's first strike, since most civilian airfields are located near large cities, assuming that the enemy would otherwise avoid hitting cities.

THE TECHNOLOGICAL REVOLUTION

The need to *choose* between deterrence and defense is largely the result of the development of nuclear and thermonuclear weapons and long-range airpower. Prior to these developments, the three primary functions of military force—to *punish* the enemy, to *deny* him territory (or to take it from him), and to *mitigate damage* to oneself— were embodied, more or less, in the same weapons. Deterrence was accomplished (to the extent that military capabilities were the instruments of deterrence) either by convincing the prospective aggressor that his territorial aim was likely to be frustrated, or by posing for him a prospect of intolerable cost, or both, but both of these deterrent functions were performed by the *same* forces. Moreover, these same forces were also the instruments of defense if deterrence failed.

Long-range airpower partially separated the function of punishment from the function of contesting the control of territory, by making possible the assault of targets far to the rear whose relation to the land battle might be quite tenuous. Nuclear weapons vastly increased the relative importance of prospective *cost* in deterring the enemy and reduced (relatively) the importance of frustrating his aggressive enterprise. It is still true, of course, that a capacity to deny territory to the enemy, or otherwise to block his aims, may be a very efficient deterrent. And such denial *may* be accomplished by strategic nuclear means, though at high cost to the defender. But it is now conceivable that a prospective aggressor may be deterred, in some circumstances at least, solely or primarily by threatening and possessing the capability to inflict extreme punishment on his homeland assets and population, even though he may be superior in capabilities for contesting the control of territory. Nuclear powers must, therefore, exercise a conscious choice between the objectives of deterrence and defense, since the relative proportion of "punishment capacity" to "denial capacity" in their military establishments has become a matter of choice.

This is the most striking difference between nuclear and prenuclear strategy: the partial separation of the functions of pre-attack deterrence and post-attack defense, and the possibility that deterrence may now be accomplished by weapons which might have no rational use for defense should deterrence fail.

DETERRENCE

Deterrence, in one sense, is simply the negative aspect of political power; it is the power to dissuade as opposed to the power to coerce or compel. One deters another party from doing something by the implicit or explicit threat of applying some sanction if the forbidden act is performed, or by the promise of a reward if the act is not performed. Thus conceived, deterrence does not have to depend on military force. We might speak of deterrence by the threat of trade restrictions, for example. The promise of economic aid might deter a country from military action (or any action) contrary to one's own interests. Or we might speak of the deterrence of allies and neutrals as well as potential enemies—as Italy, for example, was deterred from fighting on the side of the Dual Alliance in World War I by the promise of substantial territorial gains. In short, deterrence may follow, first, from any form of control which one has over an opponent's present and prospective "value inventory"; secondly, from the communication of a credible threat or promise to decrease or increase that inventory; and, thirdly, from the opponent's degree of confidence that one intends to fulfill the threat or promise.

In an even broader sense, however, deterrence is a function of the *total* cost-gain expectations of the party to be deterred, and these may be affected by factors other than the apparent capability and intention of the deterrer to apply punishments or confer rewards. For example, an incipient aggressor may be inhibited by his own conscience, or, more likely, by the prospect of losing moral standing, and hence political standing, with uncommitted countries. Or, in the specific case of the Soviet Union, he may fear that war will encourage unrest in, and possibly dissolution of, his satellite empire, and perhaps disaffection among his own population. He may anticipate that his aggression would bring about a tighter welding of the Western alliance or stimulate a degree of mobilization in the West which would either reduce his own security or greatly increase the cost of maintaining his position in the arms race. It is also worth noting that the benchmark or starting point for the potential aggressor's calculation of costs and gains from military action is not his *existing* value inventory, but the extent to which he expects that inventory to be changed if he refrains from initiating military action. Hence, the common observation that the Russians are unlikely to undertake overt military aggression because their chances are so good for making gains by "indirect" peaceful means. Conceivably the Soviets might attack the United States, even though they foresaw greater costs than gains, if the alternative of not attacking seemed to carry within it a strong possibility that the United States would strike them first and, in doing so, inflict greater costs on the Soviet Union than it could by means of retaliation after the Soviets had struck first. In a (very abstract) nutshell, the potential aggressor presumably is deterred from a military move not simply when his expected cost exceeds his expected gain, but when the net gain is less or the net loss is more than he can expect if he refrains from the move. But this formulation must be qualified by the simple fact of inertia: deliberately to shift from a condition of peace to a condition of war is an extremely momentous decision, involving incalculable consequences, and a government is not likely to make this decision unless it foresees a very large advantage in doing so. The great importance of *uncertainty* in this context will be discussed below.

In a broad sense, deterrence operates during war as well as prior to war. It could be defined as a process of influencing the enemy's *intentions*, whatever the circumstances, violent or non-violent. Typically, the outcome of wars has not depended simply on the clash of physical capabilities. The losing side usually accepts defeat somewhat before it has lost its physical ability to continue fighting. It is deterred from continuing the war by a realization that continued fighting can only generate additional costs without hope of compensating gains, this expectation being largely the consequence of the previous application of force by the dominant side. In past wars, such deterrence usually has been characteristic of the terminal stages. However, in the modern concept of limited war, the intentions factor is more prominent and pervasive; force may be threatened and used partly or even primarily, as a bargaining instrument to persuade the opponent to accept terms of settlement or to observe certain limitations. Deterrence in war is most sharply illustrated in proposals for a strategy of limited retaliation, in which initial strikes, in effect, would be *threats* of further strikes to come, designed to deter the enemy from further fighting. In warfare limited to conventional weapons or tactical nuclear weapons, the strategic nuclear forces held in reserve by either side may constitute a deterrent against the other side's expanding the intensity of its war effort. Also, limited wars may be fought in part with an eye to deterring future enemy attacks by convincing the enemy of one's general willingness to fight.

The above observations were intended to suggest the broad scope of the concept of deterrence, its non-limitation to military factors, and its fundamental affinity to the idea of political power. In the discussion following, we shall use the term in a narrower sense, to mean the discouragement of the *initiation* of military aggression by the threat (implicit or explicit) of applying military force in response to the aggression. We shall assume that when deterrence fails and war begins, the attacked party is no longer "deterring" but rather "defending." Deterrence in war and deterrence, by military action, of subsequent aggressions will be considered as aspects of defense and will be treated later in this chapter.

The logic of deterrence. The object of military deterrence is to reduce the probability of enemy military attacks, by posing for the enemy a sufficiently likely prospect that he will suffer a net loss as a result of the attack, or at least a higher net loss or lower net gain than would follow from his not attacking. If we postulate two contending states, an "aggressor" (meaning potential aggressor) and a "deterrer," with other states which are objects of conflict between these two, the probability of any particular attack by the aggressor is the resultant of essentially four factors which exist in his "mind." All four taken together might be termed the aggressor's "risk calculus." They are (1) his valuation of his war objectives; (2) the cost which he expects to suffer as a result of various possible responses by the deterrer; (3) the probability of various responses, including "no response"; and (4) the probability of winning the objectives with each possible response. We shall assume, for simplicity's sake, that the deterrer's "response" refers to the deterrer's entire strategy of action throughout the war precipitated by the aggressor's move—i.e., not only the response to the initial aggressive move, but also to all subsequent moves by the aggressor. Thus the aggressor's estimate of costs and gains is a "whole war" estimate, depending on his image of the deterrer's entire sequence of moves up to the termination of the war, as well as on his own strategic plans for conducting the war, plans which may be contingent on what moves are made by the deterrer during the war.

Obviously, we are dealing here with factors which are highly subjective and uncertain, not subject to exact measurement, and not commensurate except in an intuitive way. Nevertheless, these are the basic factors which the potential aggressor must weigh in determining the probable costs and gains of his contemplated venture.

Certain generalizations can be made about the relationship among these factors. Factor 3 in the aggressor's calculus represents the "credibility" of various possible responses by the deterrer. But credibility is only one factor: it should not be equated with the deterrent *effectiveness* of a possible or threatened response, which is a function of all four factors—i.e., the net cost or gain which a response promises, discounted by the probability (credibility) of its being applied. An available response which is very low in credibility might be sufficient to deter if it poses a very severe sanction (e.g., massive retaliation) or if the aggressor's prospective gain carries very little value for him. Or a threatened response that carries a rather high credibility but poses only moderate costs for the aggressor—e.g., a conventional response, or nuclear retaliation after the aggressor has had the advantage of the first strategic strike—may not deter if the aggressor places a high value on his objective and anticipates a good chance of attaining it.

The credibility factor deserves special attention because it is in terms of this component that the risk calculus of the aggressor "interlocks" with that of the deterrer. The deterrer's risk calculus is similar to that of the aggressor. If the deterrer is rational, his response to aggression will be determined (within the limits, of course, of the military forces he disposes) largely by four factors: (1) his valuation of the territorial objective and of the other intangible gains (e.g., moral satisfaction) which he associates with a given response; (2) the estimated costs of fighting; (3) the probability of successfully holding the territorial objective and other values at stake; and (4) the change in the probability of future enemy attacks on other objectives which would follow from various responses. Variations on, and marginal additions to, these factors may be imagined, but these four are the essential ones. The deterrer will select the response which minimizes his expectation of cost or maximizes his expectation of gain. (As in the case of the aggressor's calculus, we assume that the deterrer's estimates of cost and gain are "whole war" estimates—i.e., the aggregate effects not only of the deterrer's initial response, but also of all the aggressor's countermoves, combined with the deterrer's counter-countermoves, over the entire progress of the war.) The credibility of various possible responses by the deterrer depends on the aggressor's image of the deterrer's risk calculus—i.e., of the latter's net costs and gains from each response—as well as on the aggressor's assessment of the deterrer's capacity to act rationally.

The aggressor, of course, is not omniscient with respect to the deterrer's estimates of cost and gain. Even the deterrer will be unable to predict in advance of the attack how he will visualize his cost-gain prospects and, hence, exactly what response he will choose once the aggression is under way. (Witness the United States response to the North Korean attack in 1950, which was motivated by values which apparently did not become clear to the decision-makers until the actual crisis was upon them.) Nor can the aggressor be sure the deterrer will act rationally according to his own cost-gain predictions. Because of these uncertainties, the aggressor's estimate of credibility cannot be precise. More than one response will be possible, and the best the aggressor can do is attempt to guess how the deterrer will visualize his gains and losses consequent upon each response, and from this guess arrive at a judgment about the likelihood or probability of each possible response.

The deterrer evaluates the *effectiveness* of his deterrent posture by attempting to guess the values of the four factors in the aggressor's risk calculus. In estimating the credibility factor, he attempts to guess how the aggressor is estimating the factors in *his* (the deterrer's) calculus. He arrives at some judgment as to whether the aggresor is likely to expect a net cost or net gain from the aggressive move and, using this judgment and his degree of confidence in it as a basis, he determines the probability of aggression. Happily, the spiral of "guesses about the other's guesses" seems to stop here. In other words, the aggressor's decision whether or not to attack is not in turn affected by his image of the deterrer's estimate of the likelihood of attack. He knows that once the attack is launched the deterrer will select the response which promises him the least cost or greatest gain—at that point, the deterrer's previous calculations about "deterrence" of that attack become irrelevant.

Denial vs. punishment. It is useful to distinguish between deterrence which results from capacity to deny territorial gains to the enemy, and deterrence by the threat and capacity to inflict nuclear punishment. Denial capabilites—typically, conventional ground, sea, and tactical air forces—deter chiefly by their effect on the fourth factor in the aggressor's calculus: his estimate of the probability of gaining his objective. Punishment capabilities—typically, strategic nuclear power for either massive or limited retaliation—act primarily on the second factor, the aggressor's estimate of possible costs, and may have little effect on his chances for territorial gain. Of course, this distinction is not sharp or absolute; a "denial" response, especially if it involves the use of nuclear weapons tactically, can mean high direct costs, plus the risk that the war may get out of hand and ultimately involve severe nuclear punishment for both sides. This prospect of cost and risk may exert a significant deterring effect. A "punishment" response, if powerful enough, may foreclose territorial gains, and limited reprisals may be able to force a settlement short of complete conquest of the territorial objective. However, there are some differences worth noting between these two types or strategies of deterrence.

Apart from their differential impact on the cost and gain elements of the aggressor's calculations, the two types of response are likely to differ also in their credibility or probability of application. As a response to all-out nuclear attack on the deterrer, the application of punishment will be highly credible. But for lesser challenges, such as a conventional attack on an ally, a threat to inflict nuclear punishment normally will be less credible than a threat to fight a "denial" action —assuming, of course, that denial capabilities are available. While the making of a *threat* of nuclear punishment may be desirable and rational, its *fulfillment* is likely to seem irrational after the aggressor has committed his forces, since punishment alone may not be able to hold the territorial objective and will stimulate the aggressor to make counterreprisals. The deterrer therefore has a strong incentive to renege on his threat. Realizing this in advance, the aggressor may not think the threat a very credible one. A threat of denial action will seem more credible on two counts: it is less costly for the deterrer and it may be effective in frustrating the aggressor's aims, or at least in reducing his gains. A denial response is more likely than resprisal action to promise a rational means of *defense* in case deterrence fails; this consideration supports its credibility as a deterrent.

A related difference is that the threat of denial action is likely to be appraised by the aggressor in terms of the deterrer's *capabilities*; threats of nuclear punishment require primarily a judgment of *intent*. It is fairly certain that the deterrer will fight a threatened denial action if he has appropriate forces;[3] the essential question for the aggressor, therefore, is whether these forces are strong enough to prevent him from making gains. In the case of nuclear reprisals, however, the capability to inflict unacceptable punishment is likely to be unquestioned, at least for large nuclear powers; here the aggressor must attempt to look into the mind of the deterrer and guess whether the will to apply punishment exists. Thus a denial threat is much more calculable for the aggressor than a reprisal threat—assuming that a comparison of military capabilities is easier than mind-reading. This may make a denial strategy the more powerful deterrent of the two if the deterrer has strong denial forces; but if he obviously does not have enough ground and tactical forces to block conquest, the threat may be weaker than a nuclear reprisal threat. Even if there is doubt in the aggressor's mind that the reprisals will be carried out, these doubts may be offset by the possible severity of his punishment if he miscalculates and the threat is fulfilled. . . .

DEFENSE[4]

The deterrer, in choosing his optimum military and threat posture in advance of war, must estimate not only the effectiveness of that posture for deterrence, but also the consequences for himself should deterrence fail. In short, he is interested in defense as well as in deterrence; his security is a function of both of these elements. Capabilities and threats which produce a high level of deterrence may not yield a high degree of security because they promise very high costs and losses for the deterrer should war occur. . . .

Strategic value and deterrent value. Much of the inconclusiveness of the recurring "great debates" about military policy might be avoided if the concept of "strategic value" could be clarified and clearly separated from the deterrent effects of military action. The strategic

---

[3] It is possible that the aggressor may be able to deter "denial" resistance by threatening to take punitive action if resistance occurs. This is perhaps most feasible with respect to allies of the country attacked whose troops are not deployed on the territory of the victim.

[4] The reader is reminded that I am using the word "defense" in a rather special sense, which is narrower than one ordinary usage of the term and broader than another. Obviously it is narrower than the usage which makes "defense" synonymous with all military preparedness. It is broader, however, than "capacity to hold territory in case of attack," which I would prefer to call "denial capability."

value of a particular piece of territory is the effect which its loss would have on increasing the enemy's *capability* to make various future moves, and on decreasing our own capacity to resist further attacks. The deterrent value of defending or attempting to defend that piece of territory is the effect of the defense on the enemy's *intention* to make future moves. The failure to recognize this distinction contributed to the apparent about-face in United States policy toward South Korea, when we decided to intervene after the North Korean attack in June 1950. Earlier, the Joint Chiefs of Staff had declared that South Korea had no strategic value—apparently meaning that its loss would have no significant effect on the U.S. capacity to fight a general war with the Soviet Union. This determination was thought to justify—or at least was used as a rationalization for—the withdrawal of U.S. combat forces from the Korean peninsula in 1948 and 1949. Secretary of State Dean Acheson strengthened the impression that "no strategic value" meant "no value" when, in a speech early in 1950, he outlined a U.S. "defense perimeter" in the Far East which excluded Korea. Then when the North Koreans, perhaps encouraged by these high-level U.S. statements, attacked in June 1950, the United States government suddenly discovered that it had a deterrent interest, as well as strong political and intrinsic interests, in coming to the rescue of South Korea. The dominant theme in the discussions leading up to the decision to intervene was that if the Communists were "appeased" this time, they would be encouraged to make further attacks on other areas.[5] The chief motive behind the intervention was to prevent such encouragement from taking place, and positively to deter similar attempts in the future.

[5] As former President Truman has stated: "Our allies and friends abroad were informed through our diplomatic representatives that it was our feeling that it was essential to the maintenance of peace that this armed aggression against a free nation be met firmly. We let it be known that we considered the Korean situation vital as a symbol of the strength and determination of the West. Firmness now would be the only way to deter new actions in other portions of the world. Not only in Asia but in Europe, the Middle East, and elsewhere the confidence of peoples in countries adjacent to the Soviet Union would be very adversely affected, in our judgment, if we failed to take action to protect a country established under our auspices and confirmed in its freedom by action of the United Nations. If, however, the threat to South Korea was met firmly and successfully, it would add to our successes in Iran, Berlin and Greece a fourth success in opposition to the aggressive moves of the Communists. And each success, we suggested to our allies, was likely to add to the caution of the Soviets in undertaking new efforts of this kind. Thus the safety and prospects for peace of the free world would be increased." Harry S. Truman, *Years of Trial and Hope*, New York: Doubleday and Co., 1956, pp. 339–40.

The primary political value of the intervention, as U.S. decisionmakers saw it, was that it would give other free nations confidence that they could count on U.S. aid in resisting aggression. The most salient intrinsic values were moral value in opposing the aggressive use of force, support for the "rule of law" in international affairs, support for the collective security system embodied in the United Nations Charter, and the special responsibility the United States felt for the Republic of Korea, whose government it had played a major role in establishing. "Support for the collective security system" of course had deterrent and political as well as moral overtones.

Another case in point was the debate about the desirability of a United States commitment to defend the Chinese offshore islands of Quemoy and Matsu. Those who took the negative in this debate stressed that these two small islands held no "strategic value" for the United States, that they were not "vital" to the defense of Formosa, etc. Former Secretary of State Dean Acheson declared that the islands were not worth a single American life.[6] Administration spokesmen, on the other hand, emphasized the political and deterrent value of defending Quemoy and Matsu. President Eisenhower, for example, said that this country's allies "would be appalled if the United States were spinelessly to retreat before the threat of Sino-Soviet armed aggression."[7] Secretary of State Dulles asserted that the stakes were not "just some square miles of real estate," but the preservation of confidence in other countries—both allies and enemies—that the United States would resist aggression. It was better to meet the challenge at the beginning, Mr. Dulles said, than after "our friends become disheartened and our enemies overconfident and miscalculating."[8]

Power values are sometimes discussed in terms of the "falling domino" theory. According to this reasoning, if one objective is lost to the enemy, other areas contiguous to the first one inevitably will be lost as well, then still additional areas contiguous to these, etc., as a whole row of dominoes will fall when the first one is knocked over.[9] In its extreme form, the domino thesis would value any objective, no matter how small, as dearly as the value which the United States placed on the continued independence of all other non-Communist countries. Thus we should be as willing to fight for one place as another, since a failure to resist once inevitably means future losses. The important thing is to "draw a line" and resist violations of the line, whatever their dimensions and wherever and whenever they may occur.

The domino theory tends to overstate power values: since the enemy may have limited aims and may be satisfied with a small gain, his increase in capability from a single small conquest may not significantly shift the balance of capabilities in his favor, and the loss of single small areas may not have adverse political effects among

[6] *New York Times,* October 3, 1958, p. 3.
[7] *Ibid.,* October 5, 1958, p. 1.
[8] *Ibid.,* September 26, 1958, p. 1.
[9] Apparently the domino theory was first given public expression by President Eisenhower on April 7, 1954, when he said, in reply to a request that he explain the strategic value of Indo-China to the United States: "You had a row of dominoes set up, and you knocked over the first one, and what would happen to the last one was the certainty that it would go over very quickly. So you could have a beginning of a disintegration that would have the most profound influences." The President then referred to "the possible sequence of events, the loss of Indo-China, of Burma, of Thailand, of the peninsula, and Indonesia following." *Ibid.,* April 8, 1954, p. 18.

neutrals and allies.[10] Nevertheless, the domino image does highlight an important truth: the strategic and intrinsic value of the immediate territorial prize is not a sufficient criterion for evaluating the wisdom of resisting aggression, or for estimating the forces necessary for successful resistance. The enemy's possible ultimate objective must also be considered, as well as the effect of resistance in discouraging him from attempting further progress toward that objective, and in forestalling political changes among other countries which would tend to further that ultimate objective.

There is a relationship between the strategic, political, and intrinsic value which the enemy believes one attaches to a given objective, and the deterrent value which can be realized by responding to an attack on that objective. For example, a failure to resist effectively a Communist attack on the offshore islands of Quemoy and Matsu might not increase perceptibly the chances of Chinese Communist attacks on other non-Communist countries in Asia, if the Communists did not believe we placed a high intrinsic and strategic value on these islands. On the other hand, it could be argued that a determined and costly response to an attack on an objective which the enemy thinks means little to us in strategic and intrinsic terms is likely to give him greater pause with respect to his future aggressive intentions. Thus, if the objective is to "draw a line" to deter future aggression, perhaps the best place to draw it is precisely at places like Quemoy and Matsu. The enemy would reason that if the United States were willing to fight for a place of such trivial intrinsic and strategic value to itself, it must surely be willing to fight for other places of greater value. Thus, the deterrent value of defending any objective varies inversely with the enemy's perception of its value to us on other accounts. There is a further consideration: if it is thought necessary to fight a certain amount of war, or risk a certain amount of war, to convince the other side of our willingness to fight generally, what better place to do it than at places like Quemoy and Matsu, where it is least likely that the war will spiral to all-out dimensions?

Mutually shared expectations are extremely important in determining the deterrent value of military actions. The United States did not lose much in deterrent utility by failing to intervene in Hungary in 1956, because both sides regarded Hungary as part of the Communist camp. But a failure to defend Berlin would severely undermine the U.S. capability to deter future Communist incursions in Europe or elsewhere.

---

[10] It is hard to believe, for example, that a Communist Chinese conquest of Quemoy and Matsu would have reduced the confidence of the European allies in the willingness of the United States to defend Europe. The solidarity of NATO might have been weakened by a U.S. attempt to defend the islands.

The consequences of enemy moves, and the defense value of forces for resisting them, are subject to modification by policy declarations. Threats and commitments may involve one's honor and prestige in a particular area or objective, and this involvement increases the deterrent, political, and intrinsic value of defending such places and the value of forces which are able to defend. Thus the adverse consequences of an unresisted Communist attack on Quemoy and Matsu were increased by the various official statements, including the Formosa Resolution passed by Congress, to the effect that these offshore islands were "related" to the defense of Formosa. But these consequences were not increased as much as they might have been, had the United States made an unequivocal commitment to defend the islands.

Of course, losses of power values through the loss of an ally or neutral to the enemy may be offset by increased mobilization of domestic resources. The cost of the additional mobilization required might be taken as a measure of the power value of the territory in question. Thus the defending power might ask itself: "If I let this piece of territory or this ally be taken over by the enemy, how many additional resources will I have to spend for military weapons to have the same degree of security I have been enjoying?"

Once war is entered into, consideration of deterrent possibilities may call for a different strategy than would be the case if we were interested only in the strategic and intrinsic values of the particular area attacked. If the latter were our only interest, our war aims might be limited to restoration of the *status quo ante*; deterrence of future aggressions, however, might dictate more ambitious aims. In the Korean War, for example, it is possible that if closer consideration had been given to deterrent benefits, the U.N. armies might have pushed on farther than they did—if not to the Yalu, then perhaps at least to the "narrow neck" of the Korean peninsula. The opportunity was not taken to show the Communists that their aggressions were likely to result in losses not only of manpower but also of territory; that in future limited wars they could not hope to end up at least where they started.

In general, we will be willing to suffer higher costs in fighting a limited war if deterrence is an objective than if it is not. In other words, it may be desirable to fight on longer and in the face of a higher cost expectancy if an important objective is to assure the enemy of our willingness to suffer costs in future contingencies.

The objective of deterrence may call for the use of different weapons than would the simple objective of blocking enemy conquest of an area at least cost. Our use of nuclear weapons probably would support the Communist estimate of our willingness to use them in the future; and, conversely, to refrain from using them when such use would be militarily advantageous would weaken that estimate.

However, as in the decision whether or not to fight at all, the strategic and intrinsic value of the immediate objective is relevant to the deterrent effects: the use of nuclear weapons to defend highly valued objectives might support but little the probability that they would be used to meet lesser challenges;[11] the failure to use them when the prize was small would not necessarily signal a reluctance to do so when the object of the conflict was vital.

Finally, for deterrent reasons it might be desirable to *attempt* resistance against a particular limited enemy attack even though we knew in advance that our resistance would fail. The purpose would be to inform the enemy, for future reference, that although he could expect to make gains from limited aggression in the future, these gains could be had only at a price which (we hoped) the enemy would not want to pay. Proposals for limited nuclear retaliation against one or a few enemy cities in response to limited ground aggression may draw on this kind of reasoning.

Of course, the concept of "deterrence by action" has no relevance in determining the appropriate response to a direct thermonuclear attack on the United States, or in valuing the forces for the response. In that event there would be no future contingencies which would seem worth deterring or worrying about at all, compared with the magnitude of the catastrophe which had already taken place. The primary values would be intrinsic values associated with reducing war damage, perhaps limiting the enemy's territorial gains in Eurasia, and preserving the independence of the United States itself.[12]

Power values lost by the defender represent power values gained by the attacker, although the values may not be equally important to each side. For example, the Middle East has strategic value for the United States because its geographic location and resources add significantly to the West's capacity to fight limited war in Europe and elsewhere, and because the area, in the hands of the Soviets, would increase the Soviets' capacity to fight such wars—because of its position athwart vital transportation routes if not because of its oil resources. Our strategic loss if the Middle East should fall under Communist control would be the sum of the deprivation to the West's future military capabilities and the increment to the Soviet capabilities. Similarly, the strategic gain to the Soviets would be the sum of their own direct gain in military resources plus the losses for the West.

---

[11] On the other hand, any use of nuclear weapons would set a precedent. The symbolic or psychological barrier to their use which had rested on their previous non-use would be eroded. The Russians might believe, after they had been used once, that the probability of their use in *any* future conflict had increased.

[12] We might, of course, attempt to "deter" the enemy from continuing his attacks, thus reducing our war costs and perhaps preserving our independence and the essential fabric of our society, by a discriminating use of the weapons we had left after absorbing a surprise attack, accompanied by appropriate bargaining tactics. . . .

It is less obvious that deterrent values also have this reciprocal character. When, by fighting in Korea, we demonstrated our willingness to defend free institutions in Asia, not only did we gain "deterrent value" with respect to other possible Communist moves in Asia; the Communists lost something analogous to it in their own value system. Presumably they became less confident that overt aggression could be attempted again without U.S. intervention. Their "expected value" from future aggressive moves declined perhaps below what it was before Korea, and certainly below what it would have been if the North Korean aggression had been unopposed by the United States.

When an aggressor state successfully completes a conquest, or has its demands satisfied short of war, its willingness in the future to make war, or to make demands at the risk of war, presumably is strengthened by the reduction of expected cost or risk which it perceives in such future moves. This reduction in the perceived chances of being opposed in the future we might label "expectation value," to differentiate it from "deterrent value," which is peculiarly associated with *status quo* powers. Deterrent and expectational values are in obverse relationship—i.e., when the defender loses deterrent value by failing to fight or to carry out a threat, the aggressor gains expectational value, and vice versa—although again the gain or loss may have a stronger psychological impact on one side than on the other, since the value in question is highly subjective.

This distinction is similar to Thomas Schelling's distinction between "compellent" and "deterrent" threats.[13] A compellent threat is used in an aggressive way; it is designed to persuade the opponent to give up some value. A deterrent threat, on the other hand, is intended to dissuade the opponent from initiating some positive action. A successful conquest would increase an aggressor's compellent power with respect to other possible victims, especially if the fighting had included the use of nuclear weapons; other countries would lose deterrent power, since their psychological capacity to resist demands would be weakened by the aggressor's demonstration of willingness to risk or to undertake nuclear war.

Strategic gains by the Soviets might appear in their risk calculus as an increased probability that future attacks on other areas would be successful, or perhaps as a decreased expectation of cost in making future conquests. Gains in expectational value would appear as a decreased probability of resistance to future attacks, or perhaps as a reduced probability of a high-cost response by the defender or its allies. The aggregate of strategic gains and expectational gains pro-

[13] Thomas C. Schelling, *The Strategy of Conflict*, Cambridge: Harvard University Press, 1960, pp. 195-196.

duces an increase in "expected value" to be gained from future moves (or a reduction in "expected cost").

This might not always be the case if the consequence of a successful aggression were to stimulate an increased level of military mobilization by the United States and its allies and/or an increased determination to resist future attacks. Thus a successful limited attack might backfire and *reduce* the Soviets' strategic position as well as their expectational value, although of course they would retain whatever intrinsic values they had gained by their conquest. . . .

THE NEW BALANCE OF POWER

. . . The existence of a balance of power, or the capabilities requirements for balancing, can hardly be determined without attempting to look into the "mind" of the enemy. One might say that a subjective "balance of intentions" has become at least as important as the more objectively calculable "balance of capabilities."

A corollary of the increased relative importance of intentions is that methods of communicating intent have become more important *means* in the balancing process than they have been in the past. First, nations are becoming more sensitive to what they say to each other about their intentions; the psychological importance of threats and other declarations is on the increase. Secondly, the function of military forces themselves may be shifting in the direction of a demonstrative role: the signaling of future intentions to use force in order to influence the enemy's intentions, as opposed to being ready to use, or using force simply as a physical means of conquest or denial. Hence the enhanced importance of *deterrence* in the modern balance of power as compared with *defense*. We are likely to see more imaginative and subtle uses of "force demonstration" in time of peace.

. . . Warfare itself may in the future become less a raw physical collision of military forces and more a contest of wills, or a bargaining process, with military force being used largely to demonstrate one's willingness to raise the intensity of fighting, with the object of inducing the enemy to accept one's terms of settlement. While direct conflict or competition is going on at a low level of the spectrum of violence, selective force demonstrations using means appropriate to higher levels may take place as threats to "up the ante." . . .

Massive Retaliation

JOHN FOSTER DULLES

. . . As a loyal member of the United Nations, we had responded with force to repel the Communist aggression in Korea. And when that effort exposed our military weakness, we rebuilt rapidly our military establishment, and we helped to build quickly new strength in Western Europe.

KOREA

These were the acts of a nation which saw the danger of Soviet communism; which realized that its own safety was tied up with that of others; and which was capable of responding boldly and promptly to emergencies. These are precious values to be acclaimed. And also, we can pay tribute to the congressional bipartisanship which puts politics second and the nation first.

But we need to recall that what we did was in the main emergency action, imposed on us by our enemies.

Let me illustrate.

We did not send our Army into Korea because we judged, in advance, that it was sound military strategy to commit our Army to fight land battles in Asia. Our decision had been to pull out of Korea. It was a Soviet-inspired decision that pulled us back.

We did not decide in advance that it was wise to grant billions annually as foreign economic aid. We adopted that policy in response to the Communist efforts to sabotage the free economies of Western Europe.

We did not build up our military establishments at a rate which involved huge budget deficits, a depreciating currency and a feverish economy because this seemed, in advance, to be good policy. Indeed, we decided otherwise until the Soviet military threat was clearly revealed. . . .

. . . It is necessary also to say that emergency measures—however good for the emergency—do not necessarily make good permanent policies. Emergency policies are costly, they are superficial and they

Excerpts from a speech delivered before the Council on Foreign Relations, New York City, January 12, 1954.

imply that the enemy has the initiative. They cannot be depended upon to serve our long-time interests.

Now this "long time" factor is of critical importance.

SOVIET PLANS

The Soviet Communists are planning for what they call "an entire historical era," and we should do the same. They seek through many types of maneuvers gradually to divide and weaken the free nations by over-extending them in efforts which, as Lenin put it, are "beyond their strength, so that they come to practical bankruptcy." Then, said Lenin, "our victory is assured." Then, said Stalin, will be "the moment for the decisive blow."

In the face of such a strategy, our own measures cannot be judged adequate merely because they ward off an immediate danger. That, of course, needs to be done. But it is also essential to do this without exhausting ourselves.

And when the Eisenhower Administration applied this test, we felt that some transformations were needed.

It is not sound military strategy permanently to commit United States land forces to Asia to a degree that gives us no strategic reserves.

It is not sound economics to support permanently other countries; nor is it good foreign policy, for in the long run, that creates as much ill will as good.

It is not sound to become permanently committed to military expenditures so vast that they lead to what Lenin called "practical bankruptcy."

Change was imperative to assure the stamina needed for permanent security. But also it was imperative that change should be accompanied by understanding of what were our true purposes. There are some who wanted and expected sudden and spectacular change. That could not be. That kind of change would have created a panic among our friends, and our enemies might have miscalculated and misunderstood our real purposes and have assumed that we were prepared to tolerate their aggression.

So while we had to change also we had to change carefully.

We can, I believe, make a good report in these respects.

NATIONAL SECURITY

Take first the matter of national security. We need allies and we need collective security. And our purpose is to have them, but to have them on a basis which is more effective and on a basis which is less costly. How do we do this? The way to do this is to place more reliance upon community deterrent power, and less dependence upon local defensive power.

This is accepted practice so far as our local communities are concerned. We keep locks on the doors of our homes; but we do not have armed guards in every home. We rely principally on a community security system so well equipped to catch and punish any who break in and steal that, in fact, would-be aggressors are generally deterred. That is the modern way of getting maximum protection at bearable cost.

INTERNATIONAL SECURITY

What the Eisenhower Administration seeks is a similar international security system. We want for ourselves and for others a maximum deterrent at bearable cost.

Local defense will always be important. But there is no local defense which alone will contain the mighty land power of the Communist world. Local defense must be reinforced by the further deterrent of massive retaliatory power.

A potential aggressor must know that he cannot always prescribe the battle conditions that suit him. Otherwise, for example, a potential aggressor who is glutted with manpower might be tempted to attack in confidence that resistance would be confined to manpower. He might be tempted to attack in places where his superiority was decisive.

The way to deter aggression is . . .

MORE SECURITY, LESS COST

. . . To depend primarily upon a great capacity to retaliate instantly by means and at places of our choosing. . . . Now the Department of Defense and the Joint Chiefs of Staff can shape our military establishment to fit what is our policy instead of having to try to be ready to meet the enemy's many choices. And that permits of a selection of military means instead of a multiplication of means. And as a result it is now possible to get, and to share, more security at less cost.

Now let us see how this concept has been practically applied to foreign policy, taking first the Far East. In Korea this Administration effected a major transformation. The fighting has been stopped on honorable terms.

That was possible because the aggressor, already thrown back to and behind his place of beginning, was faced with the possibility that the fighting might, to his own great peril, soon spread beyond the limits and the methods which he had selected.

The cruel toll of American youth, and the nonproductive expenditure of many billions has been stopped. Also our armed forces are no longer committed to the Asian mainland. We can begin to create a strategic reserve which greatly improves our defensive posture.

This change gives added authority to the warning of the members of the United Nations which fought in Korea that if the Communists renewed the aggression, the United Nations' response would not necessarily be confined to Korea.

I have said, in relation to Indo-China, that if there were open Red Chinese aggression there, that would have "grave consequences which might not be confined to Indo-China."

I expressed last month the intention of the United States to maintain its position in Okinawa. This is needed to ensure adequate striking power to implement our new collective security concept.

All this is summed up in President Eisenhower's important statement of Dec. 26. He announced the progressive reduction of the United States ground forces in Korea. And in doing so, he pointed out that United States military forces in the Far East will now feature "highly mobile naval, air and amphibious units"; and he said that in this way, despite some withdrawal of land forces, the United States will have a capacity to oppose aggression "with even greater effect than heretofore."

The bringing home of our land forces also provides a most eloquent rebuttal to the Communist charges of "Western imperialism" in Asia.

EUROPEAN SECURITY

Let us turn now to Europe. . . .

Last April, when we went to the meeting of the NATO Council, the United States put forward a new concept which is now known as that of the "long haul." That meant a steady development of defensive strength at a rate that will preserve and not exhaust the economic strength of our allies and ourselves. This defensive strength would be reinforced by the striking power of strategic air based upon internationally agreed positions.

At this April meeting our ideas met with some skepticism. But when we went back as we did last month, December, we found that there had come about general acceptance of this "long haul" concept, and recognition that it better served the probable needs than an effort to create full defensive land strength at a ruinous price. . . .

FOREIGN AID

Turning now to foreign aid we see that new collective security concepts reduce nonproductive military expenses of our allies to a point where it is desirable and practicable also to reduce economic aid. There was need of a more self-respecting relationship, and that, indeed, is what our allies wanted. Trade, broader markets and a flow of investments are far more healthy than intergovernmental grants-in-aid.

There are still some strategic spots where local governments cannot maintain adequate armed forces without some financial help from us. In these cases we take the judgment of our military advisers as to how to proceed in the common interest. For example, we have contributed largely, ungrudgingly, and I hope constructively, to help to end aggression and advance freedom in Indo-China.

We do not, of course, claim to have found some magic formula that insures against all forms of Communist successes. It is normal that at some times at some places there may be setbacks to the cause of freedom. What we do expect to insure is that any setbacks will only be temporary and local because they will leave unimpaired those free world assets which in the long run will prevail.

If we can deter such aggression as would mean general war, and that is our confident resolve, then we can let time and fundamentals work for us. Under these conditions we do not need self-imposed policies which sap our strength.

Mutual Deterrence

NIKITA S. KHRUSHCHEV

While visiting the USA we became convinced that the most farsighted statesmen, businessmen, representatives of the American intelligentsia —not to speak of workers and farmers—desire not a continuation of the armament race, not a further increase in nervous tension, but calm and peace.

After the launching of the Soviet artificial satellites and cosmic rockets which demonstrated the possibilities of modern technology, the fact that the USA is now by no means less vulnerable in the military sense than any other country has firmly entered the mind of the American people.

I believe that nobody will suspect me of the intention of intimidating anybody by such words. No, this is the actual state of affairs, and

Excerpt of an address to the Supreme Soviet, January 14, 1960

it is evaluated in this way not only by us but also by Western statesmen of the USA herself. . . .

We cannot as yet give up completely the production of nuclear arms. Such decisions must be the result of an agreement among countries possessing nuclear arms.

Our state has at its disposal powerful rocket equipment. The air force and navy have lost their previous importance in view of the modern development of military equipment. This type of arms is not being reduced but replaced.

Almost the whole of the air force is being replaced by rocket equipment. We have by now cut down sharply and it seems will continue to cut down and even discontinue the manufacture of bombers and other obsolete machinery.

In the navy, the submarine fleet assumes great importance, whilst abovewater ships can no longer play the part they did in the past.

In our country, the armed forces have been to a considerable extent transferred to rocket and nuclear arms. These arms are being perfected and will continue to be perfected until the time they are banned.

The proposed reduction will in no way reduce the firepower of our armed forces, and this is the main point.

I am emphasizing once more that we already possess so many nuclear weapons, both atomic and hydrogen, and the necessary rockets for sending these weapons to the territory of a potential aggressor, that should any madman launch an attack on our state or on other Socialist states we would be able literally to wipe the country or countries which attack us off the face of the earth.

The Central Committee of the Communist Party and the Soviet Government can inform you, Comrade Deputies, that, though the weapons we have now are formidable weapons indeed, the weapon we have today in the hatching stage is even more perfect and more formidable.

The weapon, which is being developed and is, as they say, in the portfolio of our scientists and designers, is a fantastic weapon.

The following question arises, however, inevitably: if the possibility is not excluded that some capitalist countries will draw level with us in the field of contemporary armament, will they not, possibly, show perfidy and attack us first in order to make use of the factor of the unexpectedness of attack with such a formidable weapon as the rocket-atomic one and thus have an advantage to achieve victory?

No. Contemporary means of waging war do not give any country such advantage.

The "No-Cities" Doctrine

ROBERT S. MC NAMARA

... What I want to talk to you about here today are some of the concrete problems of maintaining a free community in the world today. I want to talk to you particularly about the problems of the community that bind together the United States and the countries of Western Europe. . . .

Today, NATO is involved in a number of controversies, which must be resolved by achieving a consensus within the organization in order to preserve its strength and unity. . . .

It has been argued that the very success of Western European economic development reduces Europe's need to rely on the U.S. to share in its defenses.

It has been argued that the increasing vulnerability of the U.S. to nuclear attack makes us less willing as a partner in the defense of Europe, and hence less effective in deterring such an attack.

It has been argued that nuclear capabilities are alone relevant in the face of the growing nuclear threat, and that independent national nuclear forces are sufficient to protect the nations of Europe.

I believe that all of these arguments are mistaken. . . . In our view, the effect of the new factors in the situation, both economic and military, has been to increase the interdependence of national security interests on both sides of the Atlantic, and to enhance the need for the closest coordination of our efforts.

A central military issue facing NATO today is the role of nuclear strategy. Four facts seem to us to dominate consideration of that role. All of them point in the direction of increased integration to achieve our common defense. First, the Alliance has over-all nuclear strength adequate to any challenge confronting it. Second, this strength not only minimizes the likelihood of major nuclear war, but it makes possible a strategy designed to preserve the fabric of our societies if war should occur. Third, damage to the civil societies of the Alliance resulting from nuclear warfare could be very grave. Fourth, improved non-nuclear forces, well within Alliance resources, could enhance deterrence of any aggressive moves short of direct, all-out attack on Western Europe.

Excerpts from a speech delivered at the Commencement Exercises, University of Michigan, Ann Arbor, Michigan, June 16, 1962.

Let us look at the situation today. First, given the current balance of nuclear power, which we confidently expect to maintain in the years ahead, a surprise nuclear attack is simply not a rational act for any enemy. Nor would it be rational for an enemy to take the initiative in the use of nuclear weapons as an outgrowth of a limited engagement in Europe or elsewhere. I think we are entitled to conclude that either of these actions has been made highly unlikely.

Second, and equally important, the mere fact that no nation could rationally take steps leading to a nuclear war does not guarantee that a nuclear war cannot take place. Not only do nations sometimes act in ways that are hard to explain on a rational basis, but even when acting in a "rational" way they sometimes, indeed disturbingly often, act on the basis of misunderstandings of the true facts of a situation. They misjudge the way others will react, and the way others will interpret what they are doing. We must hope, indeed I think we have good reason to hope, that all sides will understand this danger, and will refrain from steps that even raise the possibility of such a mutually disastrous misunderstanding. We have taken unilateral steps to reduce the likelihood of such an occurrence. . . .

For our part, we feel and our NATO allies must frame our strategy with this terrible contingency, however remote, in mind. Simply ignoring the problem is not going to make it go away.

The U.S. has come to the conclusion that to the extent feasible, basic military strategy in a possible general nuclear war should be approached in much the same way that more conventional military operations have been regarded in the past. That is to say, principal military objectives, in the event of a nuclear war stemming from a major attack on the Alliance, should be the destruction of the enemy's military forces, not of his civilian population.

The very strength and nature of the Alliance forces make it possible for us to retain, even in the face of a massive surprise attack, sufficient reserve striking power to destroy an enemy society if driven to it. In other words, we are giving a possible opponent the strongest imaginable incentive to refrain from striking our own cities.

The strength that makes these contributions to deterrence and to the hope of deterring attack upon civil societies even in wartime does not come cheap. . . .

. . . Relatively weak national nuclear forces with enemy cities as their targets are not likely to be sufficient to perform even the function of deterrence. If they are small, and perhaps vulnerable on the ground or in the air, or inaccurate, a major antagonist can take a variety of measures to counter them. Indeed, if a major antagonist came to believe there was a substantial likelihood of it being used independently, this force would be inviting a pre-emptive first strike against it. In the event of war, the use of such a force against the cities of a major nuclear power would be tantamount to suicide, whereas its employment against significant military targets would have a negligible effect on the outcome of the conflict. Meanwhile, the creation of a single additional national nuclear force encourages the proliferation of nuclear power with all of its attendant dangers.

In short, then, limited nuclear capabilities, operating independently, are dangerous, expensive, prone to obsolescence, and lacking in credibility as a deterrent. Clearly, the United States nuclear contribution to the Alliance is neither obsolete nor dispensable.

At the same time, the general strategy I have summarized magnifies the importance of unity of planning, concentration of executive authority, and central direction. There must not be competing and conflicting strategies to meet the contingency of nuclear war. We are convinced that a general nuclear war target system is indivisible, and if, despite all our efforts, nuclear war should occur, our best hope lies in conducting a centrally controlled campaign against all of the enemy's vital nuclear capabilities, while retaining reserve forces, all centrally controlled.

We know that the same forces which are targeted on ourselves are also targeted on our allies. Our own strategic retaliatory forces are prepared to respond against these forces, wherever they are and whatever their targets. This mission is assigned not only in fulfillment of our treaty commitments but also because the character of nuclear war compels it. More specifically, the U.S. is as much concerned with that portion of Soviet nuclear striking power that can reach Western Europe as with the portion that also can reach the United States. In short, we have undertaken the nuclear defense of NATO on a global basis. . . .

Limited Nuclear Options

JAMES SCHLESINGER

THE NEED FOR OPTIONS

President Nixon underlined the drawbacks to sole reliance on assured destruction in 1970 when he asked:

From Report of the Secretary of Defense to Congress on the FY 1975 budget and the FY 1975-79 defense program, March 4, 1974, pp. 35-41.

"Should a President, in the event of a nuclear attack, be left with the single option of ordering the mass destruction of enemy civilians, in the face of the certainty that it would be followed by the mass slaughter of Americans? Should the concept of assured destruction be narrowly defined and should it be the only measure of our ability to deter the variety of threats we may face?"

The questions are not new. They have arisen many times during the nuclear era, and a number of efforts have been made to answer them. We actually added several response options to our contingency plans in 1961 and undertook the retargeting necessary for them. However, they all involved large numbers of weapons. In addition, we publicly adopted to some degree the philosophies of counterforce and damage-limiting. Although differences existed between those two concepts as then formulated, particularly in their diverging assumptions about cities as likely targets of attack, both had a number of features in common.

—Each required the maintenance of a capability to destroy urban-industrial targets, but as a reserve to deter attacks on U.S. and allied cities rather than as the main instrument of retaliation.

—Both recognized that contingencies other than a massive surprise attack on the United States might arise and should be deterred; both argued that the ability and willingness to attack military targets were prerequisites to deterrence.

—Each stressed that a major objective, in the event that deterrence should fail, would be to avoid to the extent possible causing collateral damage in the USSR, and to limit damage to the societies of the United States and its allies.

—Neither contained a clear-cut vision of how a nuclear war might end, or what role the strategic forces would play in their termination.

—Both were considered by critics to be open-ended in their requirement for forces, very threatening to the retaliatory capabilities of the USSR, and therefore dangerously stimulating to the arms race and the chances of pre-emptive war.

—The military tasks that each involved, whether offensive counterforce or defensive damage-limiting, became increasingly costly, complex, and difficult as Soviet strategic forces grew in size, diversity, and survivability.

Of the two concepts, damage-limiting was the more demanding and costly because it required both active and passive defenses as well as a counterforce capability to attack hard targets and other strategic delivery systems. Added to this was the assumption (at least for planning purposes) that an enemy would divide his initial attack between our cities and our retaliatory forces, or switch his fire to our cities at some later stage in the attack. Whatever the realism of that assumption, it placed an enormous burden on our active and passive defenses—and particularly on anti-ballistic missile (ABM) systems—for the limitation of damage.

With the ratification of the ABM treaty in 1972, and the limitation it imposes on both the United States and the Soviet Union to construct no more than two widely separated ABM sites (with no more than 100 interceptors at each), an essential building-block in the entire damage-limiting concept has now been removed. As I shall discuss later, the treaty has also brought into question the utility of large, dedicated anti-bomber defenses, since without a defense against missiles, it is clear that an active defense against bombers has little value in protecting our cities. The salient point, however, is that the ABM treaty has effectively removed the concept of defensive damage limitation (at least as it was defined in the 1960s) from the contention as a major strategic option.

Does all of this mean that we have no choice but to rely solely on the threat of destroying cities? Does it even matter if we do? What is wrong, in the final analysis, with staking everything on this massive deterrent and pressing ahead with a further limitation of these devastating arsenals?

No one who has thought much about these questions disagrees with the need, as a minimum, to maintain a conservatively designed reserve for the ultimate threat of large-scale destruction. Even more, if we could all be guaranteed that this threat would prove fully credible (to friend and foe alike) across the relevant range of contingencies—and that deterrence would never be severely tested or fail—we might also agree that nothing more in the way of options would ever be needed. The difficulty is that no such guarantee can be given. There are several reasons why any assurance on this score is impossible.

Since we ourselves find it difficult to believe that we would actually implement the threat of assured destruction in response to a limited attack on military targets that caused relatively few civilian casualties, there can be no certainty that, in a crisis, prospective opponents would be deterred from testing our resolve. Allied concern about the credibility of this particular threat has been evident for more than a decade. In any event, the actuality of such a response would be utter folly except where our own or allied cities were attacked.

Today, such a massive retaliation against cities, in response to anything less than an all-out attack on the U.S. and its cities, appears less and less credible. Yet . . . deterrence can fail in many ways. What we need is a series of measured responses to aggression which bear some relation to the provocation, have prospects of terminating hostilities before general nuclear war breaks out, and leave some possibility for restoring deterrence. It has been this problem of not having sufficient options between massive response and doing nothing, as the Soviets built up their strategic forces, that has prompted the President's concerns and those of our Allies.

Threats against allied forces, to the extent that they could be deterred by the prospect of nuclear retaliation, demand both more limited responses than destroying cities and advanced planning tailored to such lesser responses. Nuclear threats to our strategic forces, whether limited or large-scale, might well call for an option to respond in kind against the attacker's military forces. In other words, to be credible, and hence effective over the range of possible contingencies, deterrence must rest on many options and on a spectrum of capabilities (within the constraints of SALT) to support these options. Certainly such complex matters as response options cannot be left hanging until a crisis. They must be thought through beforehand. Moreover, appropriate sensors to assist in determining the nature of the attack, and adequately responsive command-control arrangements, must also be available. And a venturesome opponent must know that we have all of these capabilities.

Flexibility of response is also essential because, despite our best efforts, we cannot guarantee that deterrence will never fail; nor can we forecast the situations that would cause it to fail. Accidents and unauthorized acts could occur, especially if nuclear proliferation should increase. Conventional conflicts could escalate into nuclear exchanges; indeed, some observers believe that this is precisely what would happen should a major war break out in Europe. Ill-informed or cornered and desperate leaders might challenge us to a nuclear test of wills. We cannot even totally preclude the massive surprise attack on our forces which we use to test the design of our second-strike forces, although I regard the probability of such an attack as close to zero under existing conditions. To the extent that we have selective response options—smaller and more precisely focused than in the past—we should be able to deter such challenges. But if deterrence fails, we may be able to bring all but the largest nuclear conflicts to a rapid conclusion before cities are struck. Damage may thus be limited and further escalation avoided.

I should point out in this connection that the critics of options cannot have the argument both ways. If the nuclear balance is no longer delicate and if substantial force asymmetries are quite tolerable, then the kinds of changes I have been discussing here will neither perturb the balance nor stimulate an arms race. If, on the other hand, asymmetries do matter (despite the existence of some highly survivable forces), then the critics themselves should consider seriously what responses we should make to the major programs that the Soviets currently have underway to exploit their advantages in numbers of missiles and payload. Whichever argument the critics prefer, they should recognize that:

—inertia is hardly an appropriate policy for the United States in these vital areas;

—we have had some large-scale pre-planned options other than attacking cities for many years, despite the rhetoric of assured destruction;

—adding more selective, relatively small-scale options is not necessarily synonymous with adding forces, even though we may wish to change their mix and improve our command, control, and communications.

It is worth stressing at this point . . . that targets for nuclear weapons may include not only cities and silos, but also airfields, many other types of military installations, and a variety of other important assets that are not necessarily collocated with urban populations. We already have a long list of such possible targets; now we are grouping them into operational plans which would be more responsive to the range of challenges that might face us. To the extent necessary, we are retargeting our forces accordingly.

Which among these options we might choose in a crisis would depend on the nature of any enemy's attack and on his objectives. Many types of targets can be pre-programmed as options—cities, other targets of value, military installations of many different kinds, soft strategic targets, hard strategic targets. A number of so-called counterforce targets, such as airfields, are quite soft and can be destroyed without pinpoint accuracy. The fact that we are able to knock out these targets—counterforce though it may be—does not appear to be the subject of much concern.

In some circumstances, however, a set of hard targets might be the most appropriate objective for our retaliation, and this I realize is a subject fraught with great emotion. Even so, several points about it need to be made.

—The destruction of a hardened target is not simply a function of accuracy; it results from the combined effects of accuracy, nuclear yield, and the number of warheads applied to the target.

—Both the United States and the Soviet Union already have the necessary combinations of accuracy, yield, and numbers in their missile forces to provide them with some hard-target-kill capability, but it is not a particularly efficient capability.

—Neither the United States nor the Soviet Union now has a disarming first strike capability, nor are they in any position to acquire such a capability in the foreseeable future, since each side has large numbers of strategic offensive systems that remain untargetable by the other side. Moreover, the ABM Treaty forecloses a defense against missiles. As I have already noted in public: "The

Soviets, under the Interim Offensive Agreement, are allowed 62 submarines and 950 SLBM launchers. In addition, they have many other nuclear forces. Any reasonable calculation would demonstrate, I believe, that it is not possible for us even to begin to eliminate the city-destruction potential embodied in their ICBMs, let alone their SLBM force."

The moral of all this is that we should not single out accuracy as some sort of unilateral or key culprit in the hard-target-kill controversy. To the extent that we want to minimize unintended civilian damage from attacks on even soft targets, as I believe we should, we will want to emphasize high accuracy, low yields, and airburst weapons.

To enhance deterrence, we may also want a more efficient hard-target-kill capability than we now possess: both to threaten specialized sets of targets (possibly of concern to allies) with a greater economy of force, and to make it clear to a potential enemy that he cannot proceed with impunity to jeoparize our own system of hard targets.

Thus, the real issue is how much hard-target-kill capability we need, rather than the development of new combinations of accuracy and yield per se. Resolution of the quantitative issue, as I will discuss later, depends directly on the further evolution of the Soviet strategic offensive forces and on progress in the current phase of the Strategic Arms Limitation Talks. . . .

With a reserve capability for threatening urban-industrial targets, with offensive systems capable of increased flexibility and discrimination in targeting, and with concomitant improvements in sensors, surveillance, and command-control, we could implement response options that cause far less civilian damage than would now be the case. For those who consider such changes potentially destabilizing because of their fear that the options might be used, let me emphasize that without substantially more of an effort in other directions than we have any intention of proposing, there is simply no possibility of reducing civilian damage from a large-scale nuclear exchange sufficiently to make it a tempting prospect for any sane leader. But that is not what we are talking about here. At the present time, we are acquiring selective and discriminating options that are intended to deter another power from exercising any form of nuclear pressure. Simultaneously . . . we and our allies are improving our general purpose forces precisely so as to raise the threshold against the use of any nuclear forces.

The Countervailing Strategy

HAROLD BROWN

A significant achievement in 1980 was the codification of our evolving strategic doctrine, in the form of Presidential Directive No. 59. In my Report last year, I discussed the objectives and the principal elements of this countervailing strategy, and in August 1980, after P.D. 59 had been signed by President Carter, I elaborated it in some detail in a major policy address. Because of its importance, however, the countervailing strategy warrants special attention in this Report as well.

Two basic points should underlie any discussion of the countervailing strategy. *The first is that, because it is a strategy of deterrence, the countervailing strategy is designed with the Soviets in mind.* Not only must we have the forces, doctrine, and will to retaliate if attacked, we must convince the Soviets, *in advance,* that we do. Because it is designed to deter the Soviets, our strategic doctrine must take account of what we know about Soviet perspectives on these issues, for, by definition, deterrence requires shaping Soviet assessments about the risks of war—assessments they will make using their models, not ours. We must confront these views and take them into account in our planning. We may, and we do, think our models are more accurate, but theirs are the reality deterrence drives us to consider.

Several Soviet perspectives are relevant to the formulation of our deterrent strategy. First, Soviet military doctrine appears to contemplate the possibility of a relatively prolonged nuclear war. Second, there is evidence that they regard military forces as the obvious first targets in a nuclear exchange, not general industrial and economic capacity. Third, the Soviet leadership clearly places a high value on preservation of the regime and on the survival and continued effectiveness of the instruments of state power and control—a value at least as high as that they place on any losses to the general population, short of those involved in a general nuclear war. Fourth, in some contexts, certain elements of Soviet leadership seem to consider Soviet victory in a nuclear war to be at least a theoretical possibility.

From Report of the Secretary of Defense to the Congress on the FY 1982 Budget, FY 1983 Authorization Request and FY 1982–1986 Defense Programs, pp. 38–43. January 19, 1981.

All this does not mean that the Soviets are unaware of the destruction a nuclear war would bring to the Soviet Union; in fact, they are explicit on that point. Nor does this mean that we cannot deter, for clearly we can and we do.

The second basic point is that, because the world is constantly changing, our strategy evolves slowly, almost continually, over time to adapt to changes in U.S. technology and military capabilites, as well as Soviet technology, military capabilities, and strategic doctrine. A strategic doctrine that served well when the United States had only a few dozen nuclear weapons and the Soviets none would hardly serve as well unchanged in a world in which we have about 9,000 strategic warheads and they have about 7,000. As the strategic balance has shifted from overhwhelming U.S. superiority to essential equivalence, and as ICBM accuracies have steadily improved to the point that hard target kill probabilities are quite high, our doctrine must adapt itself to these new realities.

This does not mean that the objective of our doctrine changes; on the contrary, deterrence remains, as it always has been, our basic goal. Our countervailing strategy today is a natural evolution of the conceptual foundations built over a generation by men like Robert McNamara and James Schlesinger.

The United States has never—at least since nuclear weapons were available in significant numbers—had a strategic doctrine based simply and solely on reflexive, massive attacks on Soviet cities and populations. Previous administrations, going back almost 20 years, recognized the inadequacy as a deterrent of a targeting doctrine that would give us too narrow a range of options. Although for programming purposes, strategic forces were sometimes measured in terms of ability to strike a set of industrial targets, we have always planned both more selectively (for options limiting urban-industrial damage) and more comprehensively (for a wide range of civilian and military targets). The unquestioned Soviet attainment of strategic parity has put the final nail in the coffin of what we long knew was dead—the notion that we could adequately deter the Soviets solely by threatening massive retaliaton against their cities. . . .

Our countervailing strategy—designed to provide effective deterrence—tells the world that no potential adversary of the United States could ever conclude that the fruits of his aggression would be worth his own costs. This is true whatever the level of conflict contemplated. To the Soviet Union, our strategy makes clear that no course of aggression by them that led to use of nuclear weapons, on any scale of attack and at any stage of conflict, could lead to victory, however they may define victory. Besides our power to devastate the full target system of the USSR, the United States would have the option for more selective, lesser retaliatory attacks that would exact a prohibitively high price from the things the Soviet leadership prizes most—political and military control, nuclear and conventional military force, and the economic base needed to sustain a war.

Thus, the countervailing strategy is designed to be fully consistent with NATO's strategy of flexible response by providing options for appropriate response to aggression at whatever level it might occur. The essence of the countervailing strategy is to convince the Soviets that they will be successfully opposed at any level of aggression they choose, and that no plausible outcome at any level of conflict could represent "success" for them by any reasonable definition of success.

Five basic elements of our force employment policy serve to achieve the objectives of the countervailing strategy.

A. *Flexibility*

Our planning must provide a continuum of options, ranging from use of small numbers of strategic and/or theater nuclear weapons aimed at narrowly defined targets, to employment of large portions of our nuclear forces against a broad spectrum of targets. In addition to pre-planned targeting options, we are developing an ability to design other employment plans—in particular, smaller scale plans—on short notice in response to changing circumstances.

In theory, such flexibility also enhances the possibility of being able to control escalation of what begins as a limited nuclear exchange. I want to emphasize once again two points I have made repeatedly and publicly. First, I remain highly skeptical that escalation of a limited nuclear exchange can be controlled, or that it can be stopped short of an all-out, massive exchange. Second, even given that belief, I am convinced that we must do everything we can to make such escalation control possible, that opting out of this effort and consciously resigning ourselves to the inevitability of such escalation is a serious abdication of the awesome responsibilities nuclear weapons, and the unbelievable damage their uncontrolled use would create, thrust upon us. Having said that, let me proceed to the second element, which is escalation control.

B. *Escalation Control*

Plans for the controlled use of nuclear weapons, along with other appropriate military and political actions, should enable us to provide leverage for a negotiated termination of the fighting. At an early stage in the conflict, we must convince the enemy that further escalation will not result in achievement of his objectives, that it will not mean "success," but rather additional costs. To do this, we must leave the enemy with sufficient highly valued military, economic, and political resources still surviving but still clearly at risk, so that he has a strong incentive to seek an end to the conflict.

C. *Survivability and Endurance*

The key to escalation control is the survivability and endurance of our nuclear forces and the supporting communications, command and control, and intelligence (C^3I) capabilities. The supporting C^3I is critical to effective deterrence, and we have begun to pay considerably more attention to these issues than in the past. We must ensure that the United States is not placed in a "use or lose" situation, one that might lead to unwarranted escalation of the conflict. That is a central reason why, while the Soviets cannot ignore our *capability* to launch our retaliatory forces before an attack reaches its targets, we cannot afford to rely on "launch on warning" as the long-term solution to ICBM vulnerability. . . . Survivability and endurance are essential prerequisites to an ability to adapt the employment of nuclear forces to the entire range of potentially rapidly changing and perhaps unanticipated situations and to tailor them for the appropriate responses in those situations. And, without adequate survivability and endurance, it would be impossible for us to keep substantial forces in reserve.

D. *Targeting Objectives*

In order to meet our requirements for flexibility and escalation control, we must have the ability to destroy elements of four general categories of Soviet targets.

1. *Strategic Nuclear Forces*

The Soviet Union should entertain no illusion that by attacking our strategic nuclear forces, it could significantly reduce the damage it would suffer. Nonetheless, the state of the strategic balance after an initial exchange—measured both in absolute terms and in relation to the balance prior to the exchange—could be an important factor in the decision by one side to initiate a nuclear exchange. Thus, it is important—for the sake of deterrence—to be able to deny to the potential aggressor a fundamental and favorable shift in the strategic balance as a result of a nuclear exchange.

2. *Other Military Forces*

"Counterforce" covers much more than central strategic systems. We have for many years planned options to destroy the full range of Soviet (and, as appropriate, non-Soviet Warsaw Pact) military power, conventional as well as nuclear. Because the Soviets may define victory in part in terms of the overall post-war military balance, we will give special attention, in implementing the countervailing strategy, to more effective and more flexible targeting of the full range of military capabilities, so as to strengthen deterrence.

3. *Leadership and Control*

We must, and we do, include options to target organs of Soviet political and military leadership and control. As I indicated earlier, the regime constituted by these centers is valued highly by the Soviet leadership. A clear U.S. ability to destroy them poses a marked challenge to the essence of the Soviet system and thus contributes to deterrence. At the same time, of course, we recognize the role that a surviving supreme command could and would play in the termination of hostilities, and can envisage many scenarios in which destruction of them would be inadvisable and contrary to our own best interests. Perhaps the obvious is worth emphasizing: possession of a capability is not tantamount to exercising it.

4. *Industrial and Economic Base*

The countervailing strategy by no means implies that we do not—or no longer—recognize the ultimate deterrent effect of being able to threaten the full Soviet target structure, including the industrial and economic base. These targets are highly valued by the Soviets, and we must ensure that the potential loss of them is an ever-present factor in the Soviet calculus regarding nuclear war. Let me also emphasize that while, as a matter of policy, we do not target civilian population *per se*, heavy civilian fatalities and other casualties would inevitably occur in attacking the Soviet industrial and economic base, which is collocated with the Soviet urban population. I should add that Soviet civilian casualties would also be large in more focused attacks (not unlike the U.S. civilian casualty estimates cited earlier for Soviet attacks on our ICBM silos); indeed, they could be described as limited only in the sense that they would be significantly less than those resulting from an all-out attack.

E. *Reserve Forces*

Our planning must provide for the designation and employment of adequate, survivable, and enduring reserve forces and the supporting C³I systems both during and after a protracted conflict. At a minimum, we will preserve such a dedicated force of strategic weapon systems.

Because there has been considerable misunderstanding and misinterpretation of the countervailing strategy and of P.D. 59, it is worth restating what the countervailing strategy is *not*.

—It is *not* a new strategic doctrine; it is *not* a radical departure from U.S. strategic policy over the past decade or so. It *is* a refinement, a re-codification of previous statements of our strategic policy. It *is* the same essential strategic doctrine, restated more clearly and related more directly to current and prospective conditions and capabilities—U.S. and Soviet.

—It does *not* assume, or assert, that we can "win" a limited nuclear war, nor does it pretend or intend to enable us to do so. It *does* seek to convince the Soviets that they could not win such a war, and thus to deter them from starting one.

—It does *not* even assume, or assert, that a nuclear war could remain limited. I have made clear my view that such a prospect is highly unlikely. It *does*, however, prepare us to respond to a limited Soviet nuclear attack in ways other than automatic, immediate, massive retaliation.

—It does *not* assume that a nuclear war will in fact be protracted over many weeks or even months. It *does*, however, take into account evidence of Soviet thinking along those lines, in order to convince them that such a course, whatever its probability, could not lead to Soviet victory.

—It does *not* call for substituting primarily military for primarily civilian targets. It *does* recognize the importance of military and civilian targets. It does provide for increasing the number and variety of options available to the President, covering the full range of military and civilian targets, so that he can respond appropriately and effectively to any kind of an attack, at any level.

—It is *not* inconsistent with future progress in arms control. In fact, it *does* emphasize many features—survivability, crisis stability, deterrence—that are among the core objectives of arms control. It does *not* require larger strategic arsenals; it *does* demand more flexibility and better control over strategic nuclear forces, whatever their size.

—Lastly, it is *not* a first strike strategy. Nothing in the policy contemplates that nuclear war can be a deliberate instrument for achieving our national security goals, because it cannot be. The premise, the objective, the core of our strategic doctrine remains unchanged—deterrence. The countervailing strategy, by specifying what we would do in response to any level of Soviet attack, serves to deter any such attack in the first place.

The Interrelationships between Major Components of Defense Policy

DR. ANDREI KOKOSHIN

A substantial reevaluation of all of the major components of the national security policy of the USSR and its major allies is under way. The following are the major sources of this reevaluation:

—A new look at the nature of conflict in international politics and a growing interest in the subject of the future of the international system.

—A full and widely-shared recognition (including by the military establishment) that there can be no victory or winners in a nuclear war, and that a large-scale conventional war in Europe could lead to catastrophic destruction, similar to that which would result from a nuclear war.

—A growing appreciation of existing economic constraints, and of the necessity of redirecting more resources towards domestic economic and social development and, in particular, civilian science and technology.

With these new pressures as a major catalyst, the doctrine of the Soviet Armed Forces has undergone a fundamental change. The central concept in the strategy, operational art, force structure, procurement, and the Research and Development (R & D) policy of the Soviet Armed Forces is now *reasonable sufficiency*. It has taken some time for reasonable sufficiency (or reasonable defense sufficiency), announced by General Secretary M. S. Gorbachev at the XXVII CPSU Congress in 1986, to be defined in more precise terms, at the strategic-operational level.

According to the February 8, 1989 Statement of Soviet Minister of Defense General D. T. Yazov, reasonable sufficiency means:

> "For strategic nuclear forces sufficiency today is defined by the ability of not permitting a nuclear attack on our country to go unpunished in any, even the most unfavourable circumstances. For conventional arms, sufficiency envisages a minimal necessary quantity of high quality armed forces and arms that are capable of providing a reliable defense for the country."

From *Review of International Affairs,* Vol. 40, Nov. 20, 1989, pp. 9–12. Reprinted by permission. Portions of the text and footnotes have been omitted.

A similar definition of reasonable defense sufficiency was given by Chief of the General Staff of the Soviet Armed Forces Army General M. A. Moiseev on March 13, 1989: the creation of a non-offensive structure for the Soviet Armed Forces; the maximum possible limitations on "strike" weapon systems (i.e., those most useful for an offensive); changes in the dislocation of troop formations in order to enable them to fulfill defensive tasks; the decrease of the mobilization capacity of the Soviet Armed Forces and the production capacity of the Soviet Union's defense industries.

At the strategic nuclear level one of the practical steps for implementing the concept of reasonable sufficiency was the formulation of the policy of an asymmetrical response by the Soviet Armed Forces and defense industry to the implementation of the research and development results of the U.S. Strategic Defense Initiative. Intensive studies of the subject, critical analysis of Soviet experience in attempts to develop a ballistic missile defense for the country's entire territory, a new understanding of the parameters of strategic stability, and economic and budgetary considerations led to the conclusion that, instead of building a similar system in response, the Soviet Union should concentrate on a much cheaper (but equally effective) set of countermeasures, should the United States begin to develop a new BMD system and withdraw from the 1972 ABM Treaty. (Again, one of the major factors in the Soviet Union adopting this approach was the fact that some studies show that the cost of this counter-SDI Program would be about only 10% of that of a BMD system resulting from SDI.)

The idea of having the major emphasis on defensive operations and actions, instead of on the offensive, has been transformed into substantial changes in the size and structure of the Soviet Armed Forces. For example:

In 1989–1990 the number of personnel in the Soviet Armed Forces will be cut by 500,000 men, 50,000 of whom will be drawn from the Soviet forces stationed on the territory of allied countries of the WTO. There will be 190,000 less uniformed members of the military in the European part of the Soviet Union, 60,000 less in the South and a 200,000 reduction in the East.

Substantial cuts in Soviet defense spending are also being implemented by the Soviet government, with the transfer of savings to civilian use. As a result, in 1989–1990 the USSR's defense budget will be 10 billion roubles (14.2%) less than in 1988. In addition, in 1988 about 40% of the enterprises in the USSR defense industry produced civilian goods. The goal is to increase this from 40 to 46% in 1990, and to 60% in 1995.

The comprehensive implementation of the idea of reasonable sufficiency is not possible without similar actions by the West. Reciprocity could be achieved either through negotiated agreements or through similar unilateral actions, which will be noticed by the

USSR and its allies and will not be left, I am sure, without a positive response from the Eastern side.

Unfortunately, there are not enough signs from the West that it is changing its military posture, operational-strategic doctrines, long-range plans for defense research and development, and so on. In the view of many Soviet experts there is a gap between the political-military declarations of American and other NATO leaders and the military activities of the United States and several NATO countries. There is still an emphasis on increasing the counterforce capabilities of U.S. strategic nuclear forces; on offensive operations for the U.S. Army and its tactical air force, based on the "Air-Land Battle" concept and the "Basic Aerospace Doctrine"; on the U.S. Navy's "Maritime Strategy" offensive operations, among others. All of these elements are the subject of serious concern to WTO countries; they create among public opinion in the East doubts about the sincerity of Western leaders regarding arms control and better East-West relations.

In its most compact form, mutual reasonable sufficiency in the medium-term future for the United States and the USSR, NATO and WTO, could be expressed in the following way: a combination of minimum (finite) deterrence for strategic nuclear and theater nuclear forces, along with a defensive defense posture for conventional forces. Naval forces should not be excluded from this formula.

A mixture of minimum nuclear deterrence and conventional defensive defense would help to optimize military forces and postures on both sides and also establish a more logical relationship between political-military goals, operational-strategic concepts and operational plans, and weapons systems and military technologies.

There is a quite good historical chance at present, in my view, to obtain substantive results in this field, to achieve much more stable political-military relations not only between the USSR and the United States, the WTO and NATO, but also in many other areas and regions, especially Asia. But history also tells us that such favourable situations do not unfortunately last for long. There is no guarantee that the process of the reevaluation of the direct role of military power in international relations has already become irreversible. When we look at the situation in the Third World, for example, we find that the level of violence (both international and intranational) is hardly decreasing. The growth of Third-World military capabilities, including military industries, is much faster than that of the developed North, and many countries in the North share a great deal of the responsibility for this. The growing interdependence of the international system does not guarantee that developed countries will not be increasingly affected by this trend in the Third World.

The Military Role of Nuclear Weapons: Perceptions and Misperceptions

ROBERT S. McNAMARA

I would ask the reader momentarily to guess whether the following three statements come from leaders in peace movements:

> At the theatre or tactical level any nuclear exchange, however limited it might be, is bound to leave NATO worse off in comparison to the Warsaw Pact, in terms both of military and civilian casualties and destruction. . . . To initiate use of nuclear weapons . . . seems to me to be criminally irresponsible.

> I am in favor of retaining nuclear weapons as potential tools, but not permitting them to become battlefield weapons. I am not opposed to the strategic employment of these weapons; however, I am firmly opposed to their tactical use on our soil.

> The European allies should not keep asking us to multiply strategic assurances that we cannot possibly mean, or if we do mean, we should not want to execute because if we execute, we risk the destruction of civilization.

The answer is that none do. The first is by Field Marshall Lord Carver, Chief of the British Defence Staff from 1973 to 1976; the second by General Johannes Steinhoff, former Chief of Staff of the Federal German Air Force; and the third by former Secretary of State Henry A. Kissinger.

And, if one were to accept all three propositions, there follows logically the statement of Admiral Noel A. Gayler, former Commander in Chief of U.S. forces in the Pacific: "There is no sensible military use of any of our nuclear forces. Their only reasonable use is to *deter* our opponent from using his nuclear forces."

On the other hand, a number of statements by senior officials in the Reagan Administration have suggested that a nuclear war could be limited. Secretary of Defense Caspar Weinberger contends that: "The nuclear option [i.e., early first use of nuclear weapons] remains an important element in deterring Soviet [conventional] attack." And in the same vein, former Secretary of State Alexander Haig, also a former NATO Supreme Commander, concedes that it is

From *Foreign Affairs*, Fall 1983, pp. 59–80. © 1983 by Robert S. McNamara. Reprinted by permission of the author. Most footnotes have been omitted.

unlikely nuclear war could be limited, but argues that "adoption of a policy of no first use would remove a threat which deters Soviet aggression and, therefore, would increase the danger of war."

More broadly, President Reagan—in proposing a program to develop an anti-ballistic missile defense in March 1983—said that "our objective should be to move to an impenetrable defense against Soviet nuclear strikes, thereby totally neutralizing their offensive nuclear forces." He added that it would be in our interest for the Soviets to possess a similar defense, thus stating in effect that the Soviet Union and the United States would both be better off if nuclear weapons were totally eliminated. (Under such circumstances, NATO would depend, of course, solely on conventional forces for deterrence of Soviet aggression.) And on June 16, 1983, the President made an even more categorical statement in favor of a non-nuclear world: "I pray for the day when nuclear weapons will no longer exist anywhere on earth."

A similar thought has been expressed by Melvin Laird, Secretary of Defense in the Nixon Administration: "A worldwide zero nuclear option with adequate verification should now be our goal. . . . These weapons . . . are useless for military purposes."

These quotations from European and American political and military leaders show the depth of doubt and division that exist today. It is clear that there are three quite contradictory and mutually exclusive views of the military role of nuclear weapons:

—Such weapons can be used in a controlled or selective way, i.e., they have a war-fighting role in defense of the NATO nations. Therefore, a strategy of "flexible response," which has been the foundation of NATO's war plans since 1967, including possible "early first use of nuclear weapons," should be continued. Underlying this policy is the belief that NATO can achieve "escalation dominance"—i.e., NATO can prevent the Warsaw Pact from extending the use of nuclear weapons beyond the level NATO chooses, with the implication that a nuclear war once started can remain limited.

—Any use of nuclear weapons by the United States or the Soviet Union is likely to lead to uncontrolled escalation with unacceptable damage to both sides. Therefore, nuclear weapons have no military use other than to *deter* first use of such weapons by one's adversary.

—Although initiating the use of nuclear weapons is likely to lead to uncontrolled escalation, with devastation of both societies, the threat of such use by NATO acts as a deterrent to both Soviet conventional and nuclear aggression. It is not practical to build up an equivalent deterrent in the form of conventional forces; therefore the threat of early use of nuclear weapons should never be withdrawn.

I propose to examine these views by exploring four questions:

—What is NATO's present nuclear strategy and how did it evolve?
—Can NATO initiate the use of nuclear weapons, in response to a Soviet attack, with benefit to the Alliance?
—Even if the "first use" of nuclear weapons is not to NATO's advantage, does not the threat of such use add to the deterrent and would not the removal of the threat increase the risk of war?
—If it is not to NATO's advantage to respond to a Soviet conventional attack by the use of nuclear weapons, can NATO's conventional forces, within realistic political and financial constraints, be strengthened sufficiently to substitute for the nuclear threat as a deterrent to Soviet aggression?

II

Questions of the military utility of nuclear weapons are addressed most realistically in the context of the possibility of warfare in Europe. Throughout the postwar period the security of Europe has been the centerpiece of U.S. foreign policy; it is likely to remain so indefinitely. In no other region have the two great powers deployed so many nuclear weapons. In no other part of the world are military doctrines which specify the use of nuclear weapons granted such wide-ranging credibility.

The use of nuclear weapons has been an integral part of NATO's military strategy since virtually the inception of the Alliance.

Shortly after the North Atlantic Treaty was ratified in 1949, estimates were made of the size of the Soviet military threat as a basis for developing NATO's military strategy and force structure. Believing that the U.S.S.R. could muster as many as 175 divisions against Western Europe, NATO military planners concluded that the Alliance would require 96 of its own divisions—which were larger than those of the Soviet Union—in order to mount an adequate defense. This estimate was accepted by the NATO ministers in February 1952 at their annual meeting in Lisbon.

It soon became clear, however, that the member nations were not willing to meet these so-called Lisbon force goals. Instead, the Alliance turned consciously to nuclear weapons as a substitute for the financial and manpower sacrifices which would have been necessary to mount an adequate conventional defense.

That budgetary considerations were a key factor in NATO's decision to rely on nuclear weapons is evident from the following statement by then Secretary of State John Foster Dulles:

> The total cost of our security efforts (and those of our Allies) . . . could not be continued long without grave budgetary, economic, and social consequences. But before military planning could be changed the President and his advisers . . . had to make some basic policy decisions. This

has been done. The basic decision was to depend primarily upon a greater [nuclear] capacity to retaliate instantly by means and at places of our own choosing. As a result it is now possible to get and to share more basic security at less cost.

Nor was this new emphasis only rhetorical. A Presidential Directive (NSC-162/2) ordered the Joint Chiefs of Staff to plan on using nuclear armaments whenever it would be to the U.S. advantage to do so. Changes were made in the organization and plans for the U.S. Army so that it would be better able to fight on nuclear battlefields. By late 1953, substantial numbers of tactical nuclear weapons—artillery shells, bombs, short-range missiles, nuclear mines, and others— were beginning to be deployed in Europe. The buildup of NATO tactical nuclear weapons continued steadily, peaking in the mid-1960s at around 7,000. Although large numbers of conventional forces were retained on the continent, until the early 1960s their only purpose was seen to be to contain an attack long enough for nuclear strikes to defeat the aggressor.

If there were any doubts about the seriousness of NATO's nuclear threats in the 1950s, they should have been dispelled by the following statement by General Bernard Montgomery, the Deputy Supreme Allied Commander in Europe, who said in late 1954:

I want to make it absolutely clear that we at SHAPE are basing all our operational planning on using atomic and thermonuclear weapons in our own defense. With us it is no longer: "They may possibly be used." It is very definitely: "They will be used, if we are attacked."

By December 1954, the NATO ministers felt comfortable enough with the nuclear strategy to reduce the force level objective from 96 to 30 active divisions. Two years later, the Alliance formally adopted the policy of "massive retaliation" in a document known as MC 14/2.

Whether the balance of nuclear forces between the Warsaw Pact and NATO, as it was developing during the mid-1950s, justified adoption of NATO's nuclear strategy is arguable. But its merit had become questionable to many by the early 1960s. Soon after taking office in January 1961, the Kennedy Administration began a detailed analysis of the policy's strengths and weaknesses.

These studies revealed two major deficiencies in the reasoning that had led to the adoption of MC 14/2: first, the relative balance of NATO and Warsaw Pact conventional forces was far less unfavorable from a Western perspective than had been assumed (the power of Soviet forces had been overestimated and that of NATO forces underestimated); and second, there was a great uncertainty as to whether and, if so, how nuclear weapons could be used to NATO's advantage.

President Kennedy, therefore, authorized me as Secretary of

Defense to propose, at a meeting of the NATO ministers in Athens in May 1962, to substitute a strategy of "flexible response" for the existing doctrine of "massive retaliation."

The new strategy required a buildup of NATO's conventional forces, but on a scale that we believed to be practical on both financial and political grounds. Instead of the early massive use of nuclear weapons, it permitted a substantial raising of the nuclear threshold by planning for the critical initial responses to Soviet aggression to be made by conventional forces alone. The strategy was based on the expectation that NATO's conventional capabilities could be improved sufficiently so that the use of nuclear weapons would be unnecessary. But, under the new doctrine, even if this expectation turned out to be false, any use of nuclear weapons would be "late and limited."

Our proposal of the new strategy was the result of the recognition by U.S. civilian and military officials that NATO's vastly superior nuclear capabilities, measured in terms of numbers of weapons, did not translate into usable military power. Moreover, we understand that the initial use of even a small number of strategic or tactical nuclear weapons implied risks which could threaten the very survival of the nation. Consequently, we, in effect, proposed confining nuclear weapons to only two roles in the NATO context:

—deterring the Soviets' initiation of nuclear war;
—as a weapon of last resort, if conventional defense failed, to persuade the aggressor to terminate the conflict on acceptable terms.

The proposed change in NATO's strategy met with strong opposition.

Some opponents argued that the United States was seeking to "decouple" itself from the defense of Europe. These critics shared our view that a "tactical" nuclear war in Europe would quickly escalate to a strategic exchange involving the U.S. and Soviet homelands, but they saw this danger as the primary factor which deterred Soviet aggression. Any reduction in this prospect, they argued, might cause the Soviets to believe that hostilities could be confined to Central Europe, and thus tempt them into adventures.

Other critics maintained that the proposed buildup of NATO's conventional forces was totally beyond what the Alliance would be willing to support. Still others argued that we had greatly exaggerated the dangers of limited uses of nuclear weapons.

The argument raged for five years. It was not until 1967 that NATO adopted the strategy of "flexible reponse," inscribing it in a document known as MC 14/3.

The revised strategy proposed to deter aggression by maintaining forces adequate to counter an attack at whatever level the aggressor

chose to fight. Should such a direct confrontation not prove successful, the strategy proposed to escalate as necessary, including the
initial use of nuclear weapons, forcing the aggressor to confront
costs and risks disproportionate to his initial objectives. At all times,
however, the flexible response strategy specified that efforts should
be made to control the scope and intensity of combat. Thus, for
example, initial nuclear attacks presumably would be made by
short-range tactical systems in an attempt to confine the effects of
nuclear warfare to the battlefield. Even so, the strategy retained the
ultimate escalatory threat of a strategic exchange between U.S. and
Soviet homelands to make clear the final magnitude of the dangers
being contemplated.

"Flexible response" has remained NATO's official doctrine for
more than 15 years. Its essential element, however—building sufficient conventional capabilities to offset those of the Warsaw Pact—
has never been achieved. Indeed, during the late 1960s and early
1970s, the Alliance may have fallen farther behind its opponent.
Although NATO has made considerable strides in improving its
conventional posture in more recent years, most military experts
believe that the conventional balance continues to favor the Warsaw
Pact; they thus conclude that an attack by Soviet conventional
forces would require the use of nuclear weapons, most likely within
a matter of hours. NATO's operational war plans reflect this belief.
The substantial raising of the "nuclear threshold," as was envisioned when "flexible response" was first conceived, has not become a reality.

Before turning to the question whether NATO can initiate the use
of nuclear weapons—in response to a Soviet attack—with benefit to
the Alliance, I should perhaps comment on the evolution of Soviet
nuclear strategy over the past three decades.

For much of the postwar period, Soviet military doctrine appears
to have assumed that war between the great powers would include
the use of nuclear weapons. Soviet publications stressed the use of
both long- and intermediate-range nuclear weapons in the initial
hours of a conflict, to destroy concentrations of enemy forces and
the ports, airfields, and other facilities necessary to support military
operations. And these publications emphasized as well the use of
tactical nuclear weapons on the battlefield.

The way that Soviet soldiers trained, the protective clothing and
decontamination equipment with which they were equipped, and
the nature of their military exercises—which for years always included a nuclear phase—suggested that the written expressions of
Soviet military doctrine constituted deadly serious descriptions of
the way the U.S.S.R. planned to fight the next war.

In fact, until the mid-1960s, writings of Soviet military officials
consistently maintained that the only conflict possible between the
great powers was an all-out nuclear war. They asserted, moreover,

that it was possible to prevail in such a conflict, and they urged the military and social preparations necessary to ensure that the U.S.S.R. emerged triumphant from any nuclear conflict. It was these writings which, in the late 1970s, were used so devastatingly by opponents of nuclear arms control in the debate on the SALT II Treaty.

By that time, however, this portrayal of Soviet military doctrine was becoming badly out of date.

Official Soviet doctrine changed slightly in the mid-1960s as Soviet writers began to admit the possibility of a "war by stages" in Europe, in which the first phase would be a conventional one. Although they asserted that this initial stage would be very short, and further noted that the conflict "inevitably" would escalate to all-out nuclear war, the previous doctrinal rigidity had been broken.

Soviet experts and military officials debated the inevitability of nuclear escalation throughout the 1960s and much of the 1970s. By the time of a famous speech of Leonid Brezhnev at Tula in 1977, the question seems to have been settled: Soviet theorists then admitted the possibility of a major protracted war between East and West in which nuclear weapons would not be used.

Indeed, the Soviets now officially maintain that they would not be the first to make use of nuclear weapons. As stated by Defense Minister Ustinov in 1982: "Only extraordinary circumstances—a direct nuclear aggression against the Soviet state or its allies—can compel us to resort to a retaliatory nuclear strike as a last means of self-defense."

This is a new position for the U.S.S.R. It was first articulated by Brezhnev at the U.N. Special Session on Disarmament in June 1982. Previously, Soviet spokesmen had only been willing to say that they would not use nuclear weapons against non-nuclear powers.

Along with this shift has come the explicit and repeated renunciation of what Soviet spokesmen had declared for more than two decades: that it was possible to fight and win a nuclear war. All Soviet writers and political leaders addressing this question now solemnly declare that "there will be no victors in a nuclear war."

Does this doctrinal shift suggest that the U.S.S.R. is no longer prepared for nuclear war in Europe? Certainly not. In addition to the deployment of intermediate-range SS-20 missiles, the Soviets are busily modernizing their shorter-range nuclear-armed missiles in Europe (SS-21s, SS-22s and SS-23s). Two types of artillery tubes capable of firing nuclear charges have been seen with Soviet units in Eastern Europe in larger numbers in recent years. And there are now many more aircraft capable of delivering nuclear bombs deployed with Soviet forces in Europe than was the case not many years ago.

The U.S.S.R. is obviously prepared to respond if NATO chooses to initiate nuclear war. I turn, then, to the question of whether NATO can initiate the use of nuclear weapons, in response to a Soviet conventional attack, with benefit to the Alliance.

III

Doubts about the wisdom of NATO's strategy of flexible response, never far from the surface, emerged as a major issue in the late 1970s; debate has intensified in the ensuing years. The debate hinges on assessments of the military value of nuclear weapons.

The nuclear balance has changed substantially since the Kennedy Administration first proposed a strategy of flexible response. Both sides have virtually completely refurbished their inventories, increasing the number of weapons of all three different types—battlefield, intermediate-range and strategic—and vastly improving the performance characteristics of both the weapons themselves and their delivery systems. Because the Soviet Union was so far behind the United States in the early 1960s, the quantitative changes, at least, appear to have been more favorable for the U.S.S.R. The ratio of warheads on strategic intermediate-range launchers, for example, has shifted from a very great U.S. advantage in 1962 to a far more modest advantage at present.

As the Soviet Union moved toward and then achieved rough parity in strategic and intermediate-range forces, a crucial element of the flexible response strategy became less and less credible.

It will be recalled that the strategy calls for the Alliance to initiate nuclear war with battlefield weapons if conventional defenses fail, and to escalate the type of nuclear weapons used (and therefore the targets of those weapons), as necessary, up to and including the use of strategic forces against targets in the U.S.S.R. itself. Given the tremendous devastation which those Soviet strategic forces that survived a U.S. first strike would now be able to inflict on this country, it is difficult to imagine any U.S. President, under any circumstances, initiating a strategic strike except in retaliation against a Soviet nuclear strike. It is this reasoning which led to the much criticized statement by Henry Kissinger in Brussels in 1979, quoted earlier. Kissinger's speech was criticized not for its logic, however, only for its frankness.

In short, a key element of the flexible response strategy has been overtaken by a change in the physical realities of the nuclear balance. With huge survivable arsenals on both sides, strategic nuclear weapons have lost whatever military utility may once have been attributed to them. Their sole purpose, at present, is to deter the other side's first use of its strategic forces.

Thus, given that NATO would not be the first to use strategic nuclear weapons, is it conceivable that the first use of tactical weapons would be to its military advantage?

The roughly 6,000 NATO nuclear weapons now deployed in Europe consist of warheads for air-defense missiles, nuclear mines (known as atomic demolition munitions), warheads for shorter-range missiles, nuclear bombs, and nuclear-armed artillery shells. The North Atlantic Assembly recently published a rough estimate of the distribution of these weapons. It is shown in the table below.

U.S. NUCLEAR WARHEADS
LOCATED IN EUROPE IN 1981

Bombs to be delivered by aircraft	1069
Artillery Shells (203mm and 155mm)	2000
Missiles: Pershing 1A	270
Lance and Honest John	910
Air Defense and Atomic Demolition Charges	1750
Total	5999

According to these figures, nuclear artillery shells comprise the largest portion of the stockpile, about one-third of the total. They are also the weapons which cause the greatest worry.

There are two types of nuclear artillery shells in the NATO inventory: those for 155mm howitzers and those for 203mm cannons. Both the howitzers and cannons are dual-capable: they can be used to fire shells containing conventional explosives as well as nuclear weapons. The precise ranges of these systems are classified, but most put them at around ten miles. Because of the short range of nuclear artillery, the guns and their nuclear shells tend to be deployed close to the potential front lines of any conflict in Europe—there are, in effect, approximately 2,000 short-range nuclear warheads concentrated at a few sites close to the German border.

Atomic demolition munitions (ADMs) also raise particular concerns. These weapons are about 25 years old and probably no longer reliable. Intended to block mountain passes and other "choke points" on potential Soviet invasion routes, their effects would be felt on NATO territory. Moreover, to be effective they would have to be emplaced before a war actually began. Such an action could aggravate a crisis and would probably contribute to the likelihood of the war starting. At the same time, because ADMs would have to be used at the very onset of the conflict, their use would mean that NATO had not tested the ability of its conventional forces to contain a Warsaw Pact invasion.

Similar problems beset nuclear-armed air defense systems. They are old and probably unreliable. And they are intended for use at the onset of a conflict—to disrupt the large-scale air attacks that would accompany a Warsaw Pact invasion—thus negating the strategy of "flexibility response."

In an acute crisis in which the risk of war seemed to be rising, these characteristics of nuclear artillery, mines, and air defense systems would be likely to lead to pressures on NATO's political leaders, particularly the U.S. President, to delegate the authority to release these weapons to the military commanders on the scene. Whether such authority were delegated or not, it is these characteristics—most importantly the vulnerability of NATO's nuclear artillery—which lead many observers to predict that the Alliance would use tactical nuclear weapons within hours of the start of a war in Europe. In effect, whether its military or civilian leaders retained decision authority, NATO would be likely to face the choice of either using its battlefield nuclear weapons or seeing them overrun or destroyed by the enemy.

In terms of their military utility, NATO has not found it possible to develop plans for the use of nuclear artillery which would both assure a clear advantage to the Alliance and at the same time avoid the very high risk of escalating to all-out nuclear war.

Current guidelines on the initial use of nuclear weapons date from the early 1970s. A former member of the High Level Group, a special official committee established by NATO in 1978 to examine the Alliance's nuclear posture, stated recently that despite discussions lasting for years, "NATO has not yet managed to agree on guidelines for the follow-on use of nuclear weapons if a first attempt to communicate NATO's intentions through a controlled demonstrative use did not succeed in persuading the adversary to halt hostilities."

Two problems stand in the way.

First, since the assumption is made that NATO will be responding to a Warsaw Pact invasion of Western Europe, and since the artillery has short range, the nuclear explosions would occur on NATO's own territory. If a substantial portion of the 2,000 nuclear artillery shells were fired, not only would the Warsaw Pact likely suffer heavy casualties among its military personnel, but large numbers of NATO's civilian and military personnel also would likely be killed and injured. There also would be considerable damage to property, farmland and urbanized areas.*

Moreover, there is no reason to believe that the Warsaw Pact, now possessing tactical and intermediate-range nuclear forces at least comparable to those of NATO, would not respond to NATO's initiation of nuclear war with major nuclear attacks of its own. These attacks would probably seek most importantly to reduce

* A 100-kiloton tactical nuclear weapon would be needed to destroy approximately 50 to 100 armored fighting vehicles (e.g., tanks) in dispersed formation, the equivalent of a regiment. Such a weapon would create general destruction (of structures and people) in a circle with a diameter of 4.5 miles (an area of 15 square miles). A blast circle of this size, in typical Western European countries, would be likely to include two or three villages or towns of several thousand persons. In addition, depending on the nature of the weapon and height of burst, a much larger area could be affected by fallout. Several hundred of such tactical nuclear weapons would be required to counter an armored development in Europe. See Seymour J. Deitchman, *New Technology and Military Power*, Boulder (Colo.): Westview Press, 1979, p. 12.

NATO's ability to fight a nuclear war by destroying command and control facilities, nuclear weapon storage sites, and the aircraft, missiles, and artillery which would deliver NATO's nuclear weapons. Direct support facilities like ports and airfields would likely also be attacked in the initial Warsaw Pact nuclear offensive. Thus the war would escalate from the battlefield to the rest of Western Europe (and probably to Eastern Europe as well, as NATO retaliated).

What would be the consequences of such a conflict? In 1955 an exercise called "Carte Blanche" simulated the use of 335 nuclear weapons, 80 percent of which were assumed to detonate on German territory. In terms of immediate casualties (ignoring the victims of radiation, disease, and so forth), it was estimated that between 1.5 and 1.7 million people would die and another 3.5 million would be wounded—more than five times the German civilian casualties in World War II—in the first two days. This exercise prompted Helmut Schmidt to remark that the use of tactical nuclear weapons "will not defend Europe, but destroy it."

Additional studies throughout the 1960s confirmed these results. They prompted two of my former aides in the Pentagon to write in 1971:

> Even under the most favorable assumptions, it appeared that between 2 and 20 million Europeans would be killed, with widespread damage to the economy of the affected area and a high risk of 100 million dead if the war escalated to attacks on cities.

Have the more modern weapons deployed on both sides in the 1970s changed the likely results of nuclear war in Europe? Not at all! A group of experts was assembled recently by the U.N. Secretary General to study nuclear war. They simulated a conflict in which 1,500 nuclear artillery shells and 200 nuclear bombs were used by the two sides against each other's military targets. The experts concluded that as a result of such a conflict there would be a minimum of five to six million immediate civilian casualties and 400,000 military casualties, and that at least an additional 1.1 million civilians would suffer from radiation disease.

It should be remembered that all these scenarios, as horrible as they would be, involve the use of only a small portion of the tactical nuclear weapons deployed in Europe, and assume further that none of the roughly 20,000 nuclear warheads in the U.S. and U.S.S.R.'s central strategic arsenals would be used. Yet portions of those central forces are intended for European contingencies: the United States has allocated 400 of its submarine-based Poseidon warheads for use by NATO; the Soviet Union, it is believed, envisions as many as several hundred of its ICBMs being used against targets in Europe.

Is it realistic to expect that a nuclear war could be limited to the detonation of tens or even hundreds of nuclear weapons, even though each side would have tens of thousands of weapons remaining available for use? The answer is clearly no. Such an expectation requires the assumption that even though the initial strikes would have inflicted large-scale casualties and damage to both sides, one or the other—feeling disadvantaged—would give in. But under such circumstances, leaders on both sides would be under unimaginable pressure to avenge their losses and secure the interests being challenged. And each would fear that the opponent might launch a larger attack at any moment. Moreover, they would both be operating with only partial information because of the disruption to communications caused by the chaos on the battlefield (to say nothing of possible strikes against communications facilities). Under such conditions, it is highly likely that rather than surrender, each side would launch a larger attack, hoping that this step would bring the action to a halt by causing the opponent to capitulate.

It was assessments like these which led not only Field Marshall Lord Carver, but Lord Louis Mountbatten and several other of the eight retired Chiefs of the British Defence Staff as well, to indicate that under no circumstances would they have recommended that NATO initiate the use of nuclear weapons.

And it was similar considerations which led me to the same conclusions in 1961 and 1962.

It is inconceivable to me, as it has been to others who have studied the matter, that "limited" nuclear wars would remain limited—any decision to use nuclear weapons would imply a high probability of the same cataclysmic consequences as a total nuclear exchange. In sum, I know of no plan which gives reasonable assurance that nuclear weapons can be used beneficially in NATO's defense.

I do not believe the Soviet Union wishes war with the West. And certainly the West will not attack the U.S.S.R. or its allies. But dangerous frictions between the Warsaw Pact and NATO have developed in the past and are likely to do so in the future. If deterrence fails and conflict develops, the present NATO strategy carries with it a high risk that Western civilization, as we know it, will be destroyed.

If there is a case for NATO retaining its present strategy, that case must rest on the strategy's contribution to the deterrence of Soviet aggression being worth the risk of nuclear war in the event deterrence fails.

IV

The question of what deters Soviet aggression is an extremely difficult one. To answer it, we must put ourselves in the minds of several individuals who would make the decision to initiate war. We must ask what their objectives are for themselves and their nation, what they value and what they fear. We must assess their proclivity to take risks, to bluff, or to be bluffed. We must guess at how they see us—our will and our capabilities—and determine what we can do to strengthen their belief in the sincerity of our threats and our promises.

But most difficult of all, we must evaluate all these factors in the context of an acute international crisis. Our problem is not to persuade the Soviets not to initiate war today. It is to cause them to reach the same decision at some future time when, for whatever reason—for example, an uprising in Eastern Europe that is getting out of control, or a U.S.-Soviet clash in Iran, or conflict in the Middle East—they may be tempted to gamble and try to end what they see as a great threat to their own security.

In such a crisis, perceptions of risks and stakes may change substantially. What may look like a reckless gamble in more tranquil times might then be seen merely as a reasonable risk. This will be the case particularly if the crisis deteriorates so that war begins to appear more and more likely. In such a situation, the advantages of achieving tactical surprise by going first can appear to be more and more important.

As I have indicated, the launch of strategic nuclear weapons against the Soviet homeland would lead almost certainly to a response in kind which would inflict unacceptable damage on Europe and the United States—it would be an act of suicide. The threat of such an action, therefore, has lost all credibility as a deterrent to Soviet conventional aggression. The ultimate sanction in the flexible response strategy is thus no longer operative. One cannot build a credible deterrent on an incredible action.

Many sophisticated observers in both the United States and Europe, however, believe that the threat to use tactical nuclear weapons in response to Warsaw Pact aggression increases the perceived likelihood of such an action, despite its absolute irrationality. They believe that by maintaining battlefield weapons near the front lines, along with the requisite plans and doctrines to implement the strategy that calls for their use, NATO confronts the Warsaw Pact with a dangerous possibility which cannot be ignored.

In contemplating the prospect of war, they argue, Soviet leaders must perceive a risk that NATO would implement its doctrine and use nuclear weapons on the battlefield, thus initiating an escalatory process which could easily get out of control, leading ultimately to a devastating strategic exchange between the two homelands. It is not that NATO would coolly and deliberately calculate that a strategic exchange made sense, they explain, but rather that the dynamics of the crisis would literally force such an action—or so Soviet leaders would have to fear.

Each step of the escalation would create a new reality, altering each side's calculation of the risks and benefits of alternative courses of action. Once U.S. and Soviet military units clashed, perceptions of the likelihood of more intense conflicts would be changed radically. Once any nuclear weapons had been used operationally, assessments of other potential nuclear attacks would be radically altered.

In short, those who assert that the nuclear first use threat serves to strengthen NATO's deterrent believe that, regardless of objective assessments of the irrationality of any such action, Soviet decision-makers must pay attention to the realities of the battlefield and the dangers of the escalatory process. And, in so doing, they maintain, the Soviets will perceive a considerable risk that conventional conflict will lead to the use of battlefield weapons, which will lead in turn to theater-wide nuclear conflict, which will inevitably spread to the homelands of the superpowers.

In fact, it was a desire to strengthen the perception of such a likely escalation that led NATO to its December 1979 decision to deploy the new intermediate-range Pershing II and the nuclear-armed cruise missiles in Europe. The key element in that decision was that the new missiles would be capable of striking Soviet territory, thus presumably precipitating a Soviet attack on U.S. territory and a U.S. retaliation against the whole of the Soviet homeland. The new weapons thus "couple" U.S. strategic forces with the forces deployed in Europe, easing concerns that the Soviets might perceive a firebreak in the escalatory process. So long as the escalation is perceived to be likely to proceed smoothly, the logic continues, then the Warsaw Pact will be deterred from taking the first step—the conventional aggression—which might start the process.

But for the same reason that led Henry Kissinger to recognize that a U.S. President is unlikely to initiate the use of U.S.-based strategic nuclear weapons against the U.S.S.R., so a President would be unlikely to launch missiles from European soil against Soviet territory.

And, as I have indicated, more and more Western political and military leaders are coming to recognize, and publicly avowing, that even the use of battlefield nuclear weapons in Europe would bring greater destruction to NATO than any conceivable contribution they might make to NATO's defense.

There is less and less likelihood, therefore, that NATO would authorize the use of any nuclear weapons except in response to a Soviet nuclear attack. As this diminishing prospect becomes more and more widely perceived—and it will—whatever deterrent value still resides in NATO's nuclear strategy will diminish still further.

There are additional factors to be considered. Whether it contributes to deterrence or not, NATO's threat of "first use" is not without its costs: it is a most contentious policy, leading to divisive debates both within individual nations and between the members of the

Alliance; it reduces NATO's preparedness for conventional war; and, as I have indicated, it increases the risk of nuclear war.

Preparing for tactical nuclear war limits NATO's ability to defend itself conventionally in several ways. Nuclear weapons are indeed "special" munitions. They require special command, control and communications arrangements. They require special security precautions. They limit the flexibility with which units can be deployed and military plans altered. Operations on a nuclear battlefield would be very different than those in a conventional conflict; NATO planning must take these differences into account.

Moreover, since most of the systems that would deliver NATO's nuclear munitions are dual-purpose, some number of aircraft and artillery must be reserved to be available for nuclear attacks early in a battle, if that became necessary, and are thus not available for delivering conventional munitions.

Most important, though, the reliance on NATO's nuclear threats for deterrence makes it more difficult to muster the political and financial support necessary to sustain an adequate conventional military force. Both publics and governments point to the nuclear force as the "real deterrent," thus explaining their reluctance to allocate even modest sums for greater conventional capabilities.

To the extent that the nuclear threat has deterrent value, it is because it in fact increases the risk of nuclear war. The location of nuclear weapons in what would be forward parts of the battlefield; the associated development of operational plans assuming the early use of nuclear weapons; the possibility that release authority would be delegated to field commanders prior to the outset of war—these factors and many others would lead to a higher probability that if war actually began in Europe, it would soon turn into a nuclear conflagration.

Soviet predictions of such a risk, in fact, could lead them to initiate nuclear war themselves. For one thing, preparing themselves for the possibility of NATO nuclear attacks means that they must avoid massing their offensive units. This would make it more difficult to mount a successful conventional attack, raising the incentives to initiate the war with a nuclear offensive. Moreover, if the Soviets believe that NATO would indeed carry out its nuclear threat once they decided to go to war—whether as a matter of deliberate choice or because the realities of the battlefield would give the Alliance no choice—the Soviets would have virtually no incentive not to initiate nuclear war themselves.

I repeat, this would only be the case if they had decided that war was imminent and believed there would be high risk that NATO's threats would be fulfilled. But if those two conditions were valid, the military advantages to the Warsaw Pact of preemptive nuclear strikes on NATO's nuclear storage sites, delivery systems, and support facilities could be compelling.

The costs of whatever deterrent value remains in NATO's nuclear strategy are, therefore, substantial. Could not equivalent deterrence be achieved at lesser "cost"? I believe the answer is yes. Compared to the huge risks which the Alliance now runs by relying on increasingly less credible nuclear threats, recent studies have pointed to ways by which the conventional forces may be strengthened at modest cost.

V

Writing in these pages only 15 months ago, General Bernard Rogers, the present Supreme Allied Commander in Europe, stated that major improvements in NATO's conventional forces were feasible at a modest price. These improvements, he said, would permit a shift from the present strategy requiring the early use of nuclear weapons to a strategy of "no early use of nuclear weapons." General Rogers estimated the cost to be approximately one percent per year greater than the three percent annual increase (in real terms) which the members of NATO, meeting in Washington, had agreed to in 1978.

An experienced Pentagon consultant, MIT Professor William W. Kaufmann, has taken General Rogers' suggestions of four percent annual increases in NATO defense budgets and analyzed how those funds could best be allocated to improve the Alliance's conventional defenses. After an exhaustive analysis, he concluded that a conventional force could be acquired which would be sufficiently strong to give a high probability of deterring Soviet aggression without threatening the use of nuclear weapons.

Recently, an international study group also analyzed the possibilities for moving away from NATO's present nuclear reliance. The steering committee of this "European Security Study" included among its members General Andrew Goodpaster, who once served as the Supreme Allied Commander in Europe; General Franz-Josef Schulze, a German officer, formerly Commander in Chief of Allied Forces in Central Europe; and Air Marshall Sir Alasdair Steedman, formerly the United Kingdom's military representative to NATO.

Their report concludes that NATO's conventional forces could be strengthened substantially at very modest cost—a total of approximately $20 billion which would be spent over a period of five or six years. For comparative purposes, note that the MX missile program is expected to cost $18 billion over the next five years.

The European Security Study stated that to constitute an effective deterrent, NATO's conventional forces did not have to match specific Soviet capabilities. Rather, these forces need only be strong enough to create serious concerns for Warsaw Pact planners whether or not their attack could succeed.

To accomplish this, the study concluded, NATO's conventional forces would have to be able to:

—stop the initial Warsaw Pact attack;
—erode the enemy's air power;
—interdict the follow-on and reinforcing armored formations which the Pact would attempt to bring up to the front lines;
—disrupt the Pact's command, control, and communications network; and
—ensure its own secure, reliable, and effective communications.

The report outlines in detail how NATO could achieve these five objectives utilizing newly available technologies, and accomplishing with conventional weapons what previously had required nuclear munitions. These technological advances would permit the very accurate delivery of large numbers of conventional weapons, along with dramatic improvements in the ability to handle massive quantities of military information.

The effectiveness of the new technologies was testified to most recently by Senator Sam Nunn, a leading congressional expert on European defense issues:

> We now have at hand new conventional technologies capable of destroying the momentum of a Soviet invasion by means of isolating the first echelon of attacking forces from reinforcing follow-on echelons. These technologies . . . capitalize on three major advances. The first is the substantially improved lethality of improved conventional munitions. . . . The second is the . . . growing capability of microelectronics to enhance the rapid collection, processing, distribution, and ability to act upon information about the size, character, location, and movement of enemy units. . . . The third is improved ability to move and target quickly large quantities of improved conventional firepower against enemy force concentrations.

The potential of these new conventional technologies is great. Unfortunately, they have not yet been accepted by any NATO nation for incorporation in its force structure and defense budget.

Moving from the present situation to revised strategic doctrines, war plans, and force structures to implement a conventional deterrent strategy could not be accomplished overnight. Still, over time, NATO's basic strategy could be modified within realistic political and financial constraints.

The process should probably begin with a statement by the Alliance, at a summit meeting of its heads of government, of its intention to move to a policy of deterrence of Soviet conventional-force aggression solely through the use of non-nuclear forces.

This statement of intention could then be followed by the drafting of detailed plans and programs. Conventional defense improvements would be set in motion; new doctrines debated and approved; parliaments tested as to their willingness to support the modestly larger expenditures necessary for strengthening the conventional forces.

In the meantime, immediate steps could be taken to reduce the risk of nuclear war. For example:

—Weapons modernization programs designed to support a strategy of early use of nuclear weapons—such as those to produce and deploy new generations of nuclear artillery shells—could be halted.

—The Alliance's tactical nuclear posture could be thoroughly overhauled, with an eye toward shifting to a posture intended solely to deter the first use of nuclear weapons by the Warsaw Pact. Such a shift would permit major reductions in the number of nuclear weapons now deployed with NATO's forces in Europe; no more, and probably less, than 3,000 weapons would be sufficient. Those weapons which raise the most serious problems of release authority and pressures for early use—atomic demolition munitions and nuclear air defense systems—could be withdrawn immediately. Nuclear artillery could be withdrawn as the program to improve the conventional posture was implemented.

—The creation of a zone on both sides of the border in Europe, beginning in the Central Region, within which no nuclear munitions could be deployed, could be proposed to the Soviets. The agreement to create such a zone could be verified by on-site inspections on a challenge basis. The Soviet Union has stated officially that it supports a nuclear-free zone, although it proposed that the width of the zone be far greater than is likely to be acceptable to NATO. If agreement could be reached on the size of the zone and adequate methods established to verify compliance with the agreement, such an agreement could build confidence on both sides that pressures for early use of nuclear weapons could be controlled. The January 1984 international conference in Stockholm on confidence-building measures in Europe would be a logical forum in which to discuss such an idea.

VI

I now want to conclude this article by stating unequivocally my own views on the military role of nuclear weapons.

Having spent seven years as Secretary of Defense dealing with the problems unleashed by the initial nuclear chain reaction 40 years ago, I do not believe we can avoid serious and unacceptable risk of nuclear war until we recognize—and until we base all our military plans, defense budgets, weapon deployments, and arms negotiations on the recognition—that *nuclear weapons serve no military purpose whatsoever. They are totally useless—except only to deter one's opponent from using them.*

This is my view today. It was my view in the early 1960s.

At that time, in long private conversations with successive Presidents—Kennedy and Johnson—I recommended, without qualification, that they never initiate, under any circumstances, the use of nuclear weapons. I believe they accepted my recommendation.

I am not suggesting that all U.S. Presidents would behave as I believe Presidents Kennedy and Johnson would have, although I hope they would. But I do wish to suggest that if we are to reach a consensus within the Alliance on the military role of nuclear weapons—an issue that is fundamental to the peace and security of both the West and the East—we must face squarely and answer the following questions.

—Can we conceive of ways to utilize nuclear weapons, in response to Soviet aggression with conventional forces, which would be beneficial to NATO?

—Would any U.S. President be likely to authorize such use of nuclear weapons?

—If we cannot conceive of a beneficial use of nuclear weapons, and if we believe it unlikely that a U.S. President would authorize their use in such a situation, should we continue to accept the risks associated with basing NATO's strategy, war plans and nuclear warhead deployment on the assumption that the weapons would be used in the early hours of an East-West conflict?

—Would the types of conventional forces recommended by General Rogers, Professor William Kaufmann and the European Security Study, serve as an adequate deterrent to non-nuclear aggression by the U.S.S.R.? If so, are we not acting irresponsibly by continuing to accept the increased risks of nuclear war associated with present NATO strategy in place of the modest expenditures necessary to acquire and sustain such forces?

—Do we favor a world free of nuclear weapons? If so, should we not recognize that such a world would not provide a "nuclear deterrent" to Soviet conventional aggression? If we could live without such a deterrent then, why can't we do so now—thereby moving a step toward a non-nuclear world?

The Obsolescence of War in the Modern Industrialized World

JOHN MUELLER

It is widely assumed that, for better or worse, the existence of nuclear weapons has profoundly shaped our lives and destinies. Some find the weapons supremely beneficial. Defense analyst Edward Luttwak says, "we have lived since 1945 without another world war precisely because rational minds . . . extracted a durable peace from the very terror of nuclear weapons."[1] And Robert Art and Kenneth Waltz conclude, "the probability of war between America and Russia or between NATO and the Warsaw Pact is practically nil precisely because the military planning and deployments of each, together with the fear of escalation to general nuclear war, keep it that way."[2] Others argue that, while we may have been lucky so far, the continued existence of the weapons promises eventual calamity: The doomsday clock on the cover of the *Bulletin of the Atomic Scientists* has been pointedly hovering near midnight for over 40 years now, and in his influential bestseller, *The Fate of the Earth,* Jonathan Schell dramatically concludes that if we do not "rise up and cleanse the earth of nuclear weapons," we will "sink into the final coma and end it all."[3]

This article takes issue with both of these points of view and concludes that nuclear weapons neither crucially define a fundamental stability nor threaten severely to disturb it.

The paper is in two parts. In the first it is argued that, while nuclear weapons may have substantially influenced political rhetoric, public discourse, and defense budgets and planning, it is not at all clear that they have had a significant impact on the history of

From *International Security,* Fall 1988 (Vol. 13, No. 2). Reprinted by permission of MIT Press, Cambridge, Massachusetts. © 1988 by the President and Fellows of Harvard College and of the Massachusetts Institute of Technology. Portions of the text and some footnotes have been omitted.

[1] Edward N. Luttwak, "Of Bombs and Men," *Commentary,* August 1983, 82.

[2] Robert J. Art and Kenneth N. Waltz, "Technology, Strategy, and the Uses of Force," in Robert J. Art and Kenneth N. Waltz, eds., *The Use of Force* (Lanham, Md.: University Press of America, 1983), 28. See also Klaus Knorr, "Controlling Nuclear War," *International Security,* 9, no. 4 (Spring 1985): 79; John J. Mearsheimer, "Nuclear Weapons and Deterrence in Europe," *International Security,* 9, no. 3 (Winter 1984/85): 25–26; Robert Gilpin, *War and Change in World Politics* (Cambridge: Cambridge University Press, 1981), 213–19.

[3] Jonathan Schell, *The Fate of the Earth* (New York: Knopf, 1982), 231.

world affairs since World War II. They do not seem to have been necessary to deter World War III, to determine alliance patterns, or to cause the United States and the Soviet Union to behave cautiously.

In the second part, these notions are broadened to a discussion of stability in the postwar world. It is concluded that there may be a long-term trend away from war among developed countries and that the long peace since World War II is less a peculiarity of the nuclear age than the logical conclusion of a substantial historical process. Seen broadly, deterrence seems to be remarkably firm; major war— a war among developed countries, like World War II or worse—is so improbable as to be obsolescent; imbalances in weapons systems are unlikely to have much impact on anything except budgets; and the nuclear arms competition may eventually come under control not so much out of conscious design as out of atrophy born of boredom.

THE IMPACT OF NUCLEAR WEAPONS

The postwar world might well have turned out much the same even in the absence of nuclear weapons. Without them, world war would have been discouraged by the memory of World War II, by superpower contentment with the postwar status quo, by the nature of Soviet ideology, and by the fear of escalation. Nor do the weapons seem to have been the crucial determinants of Cold War developments, of alliance patterns, or of the way the major powers have behaved in crises.

Deterrence of World War

It is true that there has been no world war since 1945 and it is also true that nuclear weapons have been developed and deployed in part to deter such a conflict. It does not follow, however, that it is the weapons that have prevented the war—the peace has been, in Winston Churchill's memorable construction, "the sturdy child of [nuclear] terror." To assert that the ominous presence of nuclear weapons has prevented a war between the two power blocs, one must assume that there would have been a war had these weapons not existed. This assumption ignores several other important war-discouraging factors in the postwar world.

The Memory of World War II   A nuclear war would certainly be vastly destructive, but for the most part nuclear weapons simply compound and dramatize a military reality that by 1945 had already become appalling. Few with the experience of World War II behind them would contemplate its repetition with anything other than horror. Even before the bomb had been perfected, world war had become spectacularly costly and destructive, killing some 50 million worldwide. . . .

Postwar Contentment   For many of the combatants, World War I was as destructive as World War II, but its memory did not prevent another world war. Of course, as will be discussed more fully in the second half of this article, most nations *did* conclude from the horrors of World War I that such an event must never be repeated. If the only nations capable of starting World War II had been Britain, France, the Soviet Union, and the United States, the war would probably never have occurred. Unfortunately other major nations sought direct territorial expansion, and conflicts over these desires finally led to war.

Unlike the situation after World War I, however, the only powers capable of creating another world war since 1945 have been the big victors, the United States and the Soviet Union, each of which has emerged comfortably dominant in its respective sphere. As Waltz has observed, "the United States, and the Soviet Union as well, have more reason to be satisfied with the status quo than most earlier great powers had."[4] (Indeed, except for the dismemberment of Germany, even Hitler might have been content with the empire his arch-enemy Stalin controlled at the end of the war.) While there have been many disputes since the war, neither power has had a grievance so essential as to make a world war—whether nuclear or not—an attractive means for removing the grievance.

Soviet Ideology   Although the Soviet Union and international communism have visions of changing the world in a direction they prefer, their ideology stresses revolutionary procedures over major war. The Soviet Union may have hegemonic desires as many have argued but, with a few exceptions (especially the Korean War) to be discussed below, its tactics, inspired by the cautiously pragmatic Lenin, have stressed subversion, revolution, diplomatic and economic pressure, seduction, guerrilla warfare, local uprising, and civil war—levels at which nuclear weapons have little relevance. The communist powers have never—before or after the invention of nuclear weapons—subscribed to a Hitler-style theory of direct, Armageddon-risking conquest, and they have been extremely wary of provoking Western powers into large-scale war. Moreover, if the memory of World War II deters anyone, it probably does so to an extreme degree for the Soviets. Officially and unofficially they seem obsessed by the memory of the destruction they suffered. . . .

The Belief in Escalation   Those who started World Wars I and II did so not because they felt that costly wars of attrition were desirable, but because they felt that escalation to wars of attrition could be avoided. In World War I the offensive was believed to be dominant, and it was widely assumed that conflict would be short and decisive.[5]

---

[4] Kenneth N. Waltz, *Theory of International Politics* (Reading, Mass.: Addison-Wesley, 1979), 190. See also Joseph S. Nye, Jr., "Nuclear Learning and U.S.-Soviet Security Regimes," *International Organization*, 41, no. 3 (Summer 1987): 377.

[5] Jack Snyder, *The Ideology of the Offensive* (Ithaca: Cornell University Press,

In World War II, both Germany and Japan experienced repeated success with bluster, short wars in peripheral areas, and blitzkrieg, aided by the counterproductive effects of their opponents' appeasement and inaction.

World war in the post-1945 era has been prevented not so much by visions of nuclear horror as by the generally accepted belief that conflict can easily escalate to a level, nuclear or not, that the essentially satisfied major powers would find intolerably costly.

To deal with the crucial issue of escalation, it is useful to assess two important phenomena of the early postwar years: the Soviet preponderance in conventional arms and the Korean War.

First, it has been argued that the Soviets would have been tempted to take advantage of their conventional strength after World War II to snap up a prize like Western Europe if its chief defender, the United States, had not possessed nuclear weapons. As Winston Churchill put it in 1950, "nothing preserves Europe from an overwhelming military attack except the devastating resources of the United States in this awful weapon."[6]

This argument requires at least three questionable assumptions: (1) that the Soviets really think of Western Europe as a prize worth taking risks for; (2) that, even without the atomic bomb to rely on, the United States would have disarmed after 1945 as substantially as it did; and (3) that the Soviets have actually ever had the strength to be quickly and overwhelmingly successful in a conventional attack in Western Europe.[7]

However, even if one accepts these assumptions, the Soviet Union would in all probability still have been deterred from attacking Western Europe by the enormous potential of the American war machine. Even if the USSR had the ability to blitz Western Europe, it could not have stopped the United States from repeating what it did after 1941: mobilizing with deliberate speed, putting its economy onto a wartime footing, and wearing the enemy down in a protracted conventional major war of attrition massively supplied from its unapproachable rear base.

The economic achievement of the United States during the war was astounding. While holding off one major enemy, it concentrated with its allies on defeating another, then turned back to the first. Meanwhile, it supplied everybody. With 8 million of its ablest men out of the labor market, it increased industrial production 15 percent per year and agricultural production 30 percent overall. Before the

1984); Stephen Van Evera, "Why Cooperation Failed in 1914," *World Politics*, 38, no. 1 (October 1985): 80–117. See also the essays on "The Great War and the Nuclear Age" in *International Security*, 9, no. 1 (Summer 1984): 7–186.

[6] Matthew A. Evangelista, "Stalin's Postwar Army Reappraised." *International Security*, 7, no. 3 (Winter 1982/83), 110.

[7] This assumption is strongly questioned in ibid., 110–38.

end of 1943 it was producing so much that some munitions plants were closed down, and even so it ended the war with a substantial surplus of wheat and over $90 billion in surplus war goods. (National governmental expenditures in the first peacetime year, 1946, were only about $60 billion.) As Denis Brogan observed at the time, "to the Americans war is a business, not an art."[8]

If anyone was in a position to appreciate this, it was the Soviets. By various circuitous routes the United States supplied the Soviet Union with, among other things, 409,526 trucks; 12,161 combat vehicles (more than the Germans had in 1939); 32,200 motorcycles; 1,966 locomotives; 16,000,000 pairs of boots (in two sizes); and over one-half pound of food for every Soviet soldier for every day of the war (much of it Spam).[9] It is the kind of feat that concentrates the mind, and it is extremely difficult to imagine the Soviets willingly taking on this somewhat lethargic, but ultimately hugely effective juggernaut. That Stalin was fully aware of the American achievement—and deeply impressed by it—is clear. Adam Ulam has observed that Stalin had "great respect for the United States' vast economic and hence military potential, quite apart from the bomb," and that his "whole career as dictator had been a testimony to his belief that production figures were a direct indicator of a given country's power."[10] As a member of the Joint Chiefs of Staff put it in 1949, "if there is any single factor today which would deter a nation seeking world domination, it would be the great industrial capacity of this country rather than its armed strength."[11] Or, as Hugh Thomas has concluded, "if the atomic bomb had not existed, Stalin would still have feared the success of the U.S. wartime economy."[12]

After a successful attack on Western Europe the Soviets would have been in a position similar to that of Japan after Pearl Harbor: They might have gains aplenty, but they would have no way to stop the United States (and its major unapproachable allies, Canada and

[8] Despite shortages, rationing, and tax surcharges, American consumer spending increased by 12 percent between 1939 and 1944. Richard R. Lingeman, *Don't You Know There's a War On?* (New York: Putnam, 1970), 133, 357, and ch. 4; Alan S. Milward, *War, Economy and Society 1939–1945* (Berkeley and Los Angeles: University of California Press, 1977), 63–74, 271–75; Mercedes Rosebery, *This Day's Madness* (New York: Macmillan, 1944), xii.

[9] John R. Deane, *The Strange Alliance* (New York: Viking, 1947), 92–95; Robert Huhn Jones, *The Roads to Russia* (Norman: University of Oklahoma Press, 1969), Appendix A. Additional information from Harvey DeWeerd.

[10] Adam Ulam, *The Rivals: America and Russia Since World War II* (New York: Penguin, 1971), 95 and 5. In essence, Stalin seems to have understood that in Great Power wars, as Paul Kennedy put it, "victory has always gone to the side with the greatest material resources." Paul Kennedy, *The Rise and Fall of the Great Powers* (New York: Random House, 1987), 439.

[11] Samuel P. Huntington, *The Common Defense* (New York: Columbia University Press, 1961), 46. See also Walter Mills, ed., *The Forrestal Diaries* (New York: Viking, 1951), 350–51.

[12] Thomas, *Armed Truce*, 548.

Japan) from eventually gearing up for, and then launching, a war of attrition. All they could hope for, like the Japanese in 1941, would be that their victories would cause the Americans to lose their fighting spirit. But if Japan's Asian and Pacific gains in 1941 propelled the United States into war, it is to be expected that the United States would find a Soviet military takeover of an area of far greater importance to it—Western Europe—to be alarming in the extreme. Not only would the United States be outraged at the American casualties in such an attack and at the loss of an important geographic area, but it would very likely conclude (as many Americans did conclude in the late 1940s even without a Soviet attack) that an eventual attack on the United States itself was inevitable. . . .

Second, there is the important issue of the Korean War. Despite the vast American superiority in atomic weapons in 1950, Stalin was willing to order, approve, or at least acquiesce in an outright attack by a communist state on a noncommunist one, and it must be assumed that he would have done so at least as readily had nuclear weapons not existed. The American response was essentially the result of the lessons learned from the experiences of the 1930s: Comparing this to similar incursions in Manchuria, Ethiopia, and Czechoslovakia (and partly also to previous Soviet incursions into neighboring states in East Europe and the Baltic area), Western leaders resolved that such provocations must be nipped in the bud. If they were allowed to succeed, they would only encourage more aggression in more important locales later. Consequently it seems likely that the Korean War would have occurred in much the same way had nuclear weapons not existed.

For the Soviets the lessons of the Korean War must have enhanced those of World War II: Once again the United States was caught surprised and underarmed, once again it rushed hastily into action, once again it soon applied itself in a forceful way to combat— in this case for an area that it had previously declared to be of only peripheral concern. If the Korean War was a limited probe of Western resolve, it seems the Soviets drew the lessons the Truman administration intended. . . .

The Korean experience may have posed a somewhat similar lesson for the United States. In 1950, amid talk of "rolling back" communism and sometimes even of liberating China, American-led forces invaded North Korea. This venture led to a costly and demoralizing, if limited, war with China, and resulted in a considerable reduction in American enthusiasm for such maneuvers. Had the United States been successful in taking over North Korea, there might well have been noisy calls for similar ventures elsewhere— though, of course, these calls might well have gone unheeded by the leadership.

It is not at all clear that the United States and the Soviet Union needed the Korean War to become viscerally convinced that escalation was dangerously easy. But the war probably reinforced that belief for both of them and, to the degree that it did, Korea was an important stabilizing event.

Cold War and Crisis

If nuclear weapons have been unnecessary to prevent world war, they also do not seem to have crucially affected other important developments, including development of the Cold War and patterns of alliance, as well as behavior of the superpowers in crisis.

The Cold War and Alliance Patterns The Cold War was an outgrowth of various disagreements between the United States and the USSR over ideology and over the destinies of Eastern, Central, and Southern Europe. The American reaction to the perceived Soviet threat in this period mainly reflects prenuclear thinking, especially the lessons of Munich.

For example, the formation of the North Atlantic Treaty Organization and the division of the world into alliances centered on Washington and Moscow suggests that the participants were chiefly influenced by the experience of World War II. If the major determinant of these alliance patterns had been nuclear strategy, one might expect the United States and, to a lesser extent, the Soviet Union, to be only lukewarm members, for in general the alliances include nations that contribute little to nuclear defense but possess the capability unilaterally of getting the core powers into trouble. And one would expect the small countries in each alliance to tie themselves as tightly as possible to the core nuclear power in order to have maximum protection from its nuclear weapons. However, the weakening of the alliance which has taken place over the last three decades has not come from the major partners.

The structure of the alliances therefore better reflects political and ideological bipolarity than sound nuclear strategy. As military economist (and later Defense Secretary) James Schlesinger has noted, the Western alliance "was based on some rather obsolescent notions regarding the strength and importance of the European nations and the direct contribution that they could make to the security of the United States. There was a striking failure to recognize the revolutionary impact that nuclear forces would make with respect to the earlier beliefs regarding European defense."[13] Or, as Warner Schilling has observed, American policies in Europe were "essentially pre-nuclear in their rationale. The advent of nuclear weapons has not influenced the American determination to restore the European balance of power. It was, in fact, an objective which the United States would have had an even greater incentive to undertake if the fission bomb had not been developed."[14]

---

[13] James Schlesinger, *On Reading Non-technical Elements to Systems Studies,* P-3545 (Santa Monica, Cal.: RAND, February 1967), 6.
[14] Warner R. Schilling, "The H-Bomb Decision," *Political Science Quarterly,* 76,

Crisis Behavior   Because of the harrowing image of nuclear war, it is sometimes argued, the United States and the Soviet Union have been notably more restrained than they might otherwise have been, and thus crises that might have escalated to dangerous levels have been resolved safely at low levels.[15]

There is, of course, no definitive way to refute this notion since we are unable to run the events of the last forty years over, this time without nuclear weapons. And it is certainly the case that decision makers are well aware of the horrors of nuclear war and cannot be expected to ignore the possibility that a crisis could lead to such devastation.

However, this idea—that it is the fear of nuclear war that has kept behavior restrained—looks far less convincing when its underlying assumption is directly confronted: that the major powers would have allowed their various crises to escalate if all they had to fear at the end of the escalatory ladder was something like a repetition of World War II. Whatever the rhetoric in these crises, it is difficult to see why the unaugmented horror of repeating World War II, combined with considerable comfort with the status quo, wouldn't have been enough to inspire restraint.

Once again, escalation is the key: What deters is the belief that escalation to something intolerable will occur, not so much what the details of the ultimate unbearable punishment are believed to be. Where the belief that the conflict will escalate is absent, nuclear countries *have* been militarily challenged with war—as in Korea, Vietnam, Afghanistan, Algeria, and the Falklands.

To be clear: None of this is meant to deny that the sheer horror of nuclear war is impressive and mind-concentratingly dramatic, particularly in the speed with which it could bring about massive destruction. Nor is it meant to deny that decision makers, both in times of crisis and otherwise, are fully conscious of how horribly destructive a nuclear war could be. It is simply to stress that the sheer horror of repeating World War II is not all that much *less* impressive or dramatic, and that powers essentially satisfied with the status quo will strive to avoid anything that they feel could lead to *either* calamity. World War II did not cause total destruction in the world, but it did utterly annihilate the three national regimes that brought it about. It is probably quite a bit more terrifying to

---

no. 1 (March 1961): 26. See also Waltz: "Nuclear weapons did not cause the condition of bipolarity. . . . Had the atom never been split, [the US and the USSR] would far surpass others in military strength, and each would remain the greatest threat and source of potential damage to the other." Waltz, *Theory of International Politics,* 180–81.

[15] John Lewis Gaddis, *The Long Peace* (New York: Oxford University Press, 1987), 229–232; Gilpin, *War and Change in World Politics,* 218; Coit D. Blacker, *Reluctant Warriors* (New York: Freeman, 1987), 46.

think about a jump from the 50th floor than about a jump from the 5th floor, but anyone who finds life even minimally satisfying is extremely unlikely to do either.

Did the existence of nuclear weapons keep the Korean conflict restrained? As noted, the communist venture there seems to have been a limited probe—though somewhat more adventurous than usual and one that got out of hand with the massive American and Chinese involvement. As such, there was no particular reason—or meaningful military opportunity—for the Soviets to escalate the war further. In justifying *their* restraint, the Americans continually stressed the danger of escalating to a war with the Soviet Union—something of major concern whether or not the Soviets possessed nuclear weapons. . . .

Much the same could be said about other instances in which there was a real or implied threat that nuclear weapons might be brought into play: the Taiwan Straits crises of 1954–55 and 1958, the Berlin blockade of 1948–49, the Soviet-Chinese confrontation of 1969, the Six-Day War in 1967, the Yom Kippur War of 1973, Cold War disagreements over Lebanon in 1958, Berlin in 1958 and 1961, offensive weapons in Cuba in 1962. All were resolved, or allowed to dissipate, at rather low rungs on the escalatory ladder. While the horror of a possible nuclear war was doubtless clear to the participants, it is certainly not apparent that they would have been much more casual about escalation if the worst they had to visualize was a repetition of World War II.

Of course nuclear weapons add new elements to international politics: new pieces for the players to move around the board (missiles in and out of Cuba, for example), new terrors to contemplate. But in counter to the remark attributed to Albert Einstein that nuclear weapons have changed everything except our way of thinking, it might be suggested that nuclear weapons have changed little except our way of talking, gesturing, and spending money.

STABILITY

The argument thus far leads to the conclusion that stability is overdetermined—that the postwar situation contains redundant sources of stability. The United States and the Soviet Union have been essentially satisfied with their lot and, fearing escalation to another costly war, have been quite willing to keep their conflicts limited. Nuclear weapons may well have enhanced this stability—they are certainly dramatic reminders of how horrible a big war could be. But it seems highly unlikely that, in their absence, the leaders of the major powers would be so unimaginative as to need such reminding. Wars are not begun out of casual caprice or idle fancy, but because one country or another decides that it can profit from (not simply win) the war—the combination of risk, gain, and cost appears preferable to peace. Even allowing considerably for stupidity, ineptness, miscalculation, and self-deception in these considerations, it does not appear that a large war, nuclear or otherwise, has been remotely in the interest of the essentially contented, risk-averse, escalation-anticipating powers that have dominated world affairs since 1945.

It is *conceivable* of course that the leadership of a major power could be seized by a lucky, clever, risk-acceptant, aggressive fanatic like Hitler; or that an unprecedentedly monumental crisis could break out in an area, like Central Europe, that is of vital importance to both sides; or that a major power could be compelled toward war because it is consumed by desperate fears that it is on the verge of catastrophically losing the arms race. It is not obvious that any of these circumstances would necessarily escalate to a major war, but the existence of nuclear weapons probably does make such an escalation less likely; thus there are imaginable circumstances under which it might be useful to have nuclear weapons around. In the world we've actually lived in, however, those extreme conditions haven't come about, and they haven't ever really even been in the cards. This enhancement of stability is, therefore, purely theoretical—extra insurance against unlikely calamity.

Crisis Stability, General Stability, and Deterrence

In further assessing these issues, it seems useful to distinguish crisis stability from a more general form of stability. Much of the literature on defense policy has concentrated on crisis stability, the notion that it is desirable for both sides in a crisis to be so secure that each is able to wait out a surprise attack fully confident that it would be able to respond with a punishing counterattack. In an ideal world, because of its fear of punishing retaliation, neither side would have an incentive to start a war no matter how large or desperate the disagreement, no matter how intense the crisis. Many have argued that crisis stability is "delicate": easily upset by technological or economic shifts.[16]

There is a more general form of stability, on the other hand, that is concerned with balance derived from broader needs, desires, and concerns. It prevails when two powers, taking all potential benefits, costs, and risks into account, greatly prefer peace to war—in the extreme, even to victorious war—whether crisis stability exists or not. For example, it can be said that general stability prevails in the relationship between the United States and Canada. The United States enjoys a massive military advantage over its northern neighbor since it could attack at any time with little concern about

[16] The classic statement of this position is, of course, Albert Wohlstetter, "The Delicate Balance of Terror," *Foreign Affairs*, 27, no. 2 (January 1959): 211–34. See also Glenn H. Snyder, *Deterrence and Defense* (Princeton: Princeton University Press, 1961), 97–109.

punishing military retaliation or about the possibility of losing the war (that is, it has a full "first strike capability"), yet the danger that the United States will attack Canada is nil. General stability prevails.

Although the deterrence literature is preoccupied with military considerations, the deterrence concept may be more useful if it is broadened to include nonmilitary incentives and disincentives. For example, it seems meaningful to suggest that the United States is "deterred" from attacking Canada, but not, obviously, by the Canadians' military might. If anyone in Washington currently were even to contemplate a war against Canada (a country, it might be noted, with which the United States has been at war in the past and where, not too long ago, many Americans felt their "manifest destiny" lay), the planner would doubtless be dissuaded by nonmilitary factors. For example, the war would disrupt a beneficial economic relationship; the United States would have the task of occupying a vast new area with sullen and uncooperative inhabitants; the venture would produce political turmoil in the United States. Similar cases can be found in the Soviet sphere. Despite an overwhelming military superiority, the USSR has been far from anxious to attack such troublesome neighboring states as Poland and Romania. It seems likely that the vast majority of wars that never take place are caused by factors that have little to do with military considerations. . . .

If a kind of overwhelming general stability really prevails, it may well be that the concerns about arms and the arms race are substantially overdone. That is, the often-exquisite numerology of the nuclear arms race has probably had little to do with the important dynamics of the Cold War era, most of which have taken place at militarily subtle levels such as subversion, guerrilla war, local uprising, civil war, and diplomatic posturing. As Benjamin Lambeth has observed, "it is perhaps one of the notable ironies of the nuclear age that while both Washington and Moscow have often lauded superiority as a military force-posture goal, neither has ever behaved as though it really believed superiority significantly mattered in the resolution of international conflicts.[17] In their extensive study of the use of the threat and force since World War II, Blechman and Kaplan conclude that, "especially noteworthy is the fact that our data do not support a hypothesis that the strategic weapons balance between the United States and the USSR influences outcomes."[18]

A special danger of weapons imbalance is often cited: A dominant

[17] Benjamin S. Lambeth, "Deterrence in the MIRV Era," *World Politics*, 24, no. 2 (January 1972): 234n.

[18] Barry M. Blechman and Stephen S. Kaplan, *Force Without War* (Washington, D.C.: Brookings, 1978), 132. See also Jacek Kugler, "Terror Without Deterrence: Reassessing the Role of Nuclear Weapons," *Journal of Conflict Resolution*, 28, no. 3 (September 1984): 470–506.

country might be emboldened to use its superiority for purposes of pressure and intimidation. But unless its satisfaction with the status quo falls enormously and unless its opponent's ability to respond becomes very low as well, the superior power is unlikely to push its advantage very far, and certainly not anywhere near the point of major war. Even if the war could be kept nonnuclear and even if that power had a high probability of winning, the gains are likely to be far too low, the costs far too high.

Stability: Trends

Curiously, in the last twenty-five years crisis stability between the United States and the USSR has probably gotten worse while general stability has probably improved.

With the development of highly accurate multiple warhead missiles, there is a danger that one side might be able to obtain a first-strike counterforce capability, at least against the other side's land-based missiles and bombers, or that it might become able to cripple the other's command and control operations. At the same time, however, it almost seems—to put it very baldly—that the two major powers have forgotten how to get into a war. Although on occasion they still remember how to say nasty things about each other, there hasn't been a true, bone-crunching confrontational crisis for over a quarter-century. Furthermore, as Bernard Brodie notes, even the last crisis, over missiles in Cuba, was "remarkably different . . . from any previous one in history" in its "unprecedented candor, direct personal contact, and at the same time mutual respect between the chief actors."[19] Events since then that seem to have had some warlike potential, such as the military alert that attended the Yom Kippur War of 1973, fizzled while still at extremely low levels. . . .

It seems reasonable, though perhaps risky, to extrapolate from this trend and to suggest that, whatever happens with crisis stability in the future, general stability is here to stay for quite some time. That is, major war—war among developed countries—seems so unlikely that it may well be appropriate to consider it obsolescent. Perhaps World War II was indeed the war to end war—at least war of that scale and type.

The Hollandization Phenomenon   There are, of course, other possibilities. Contentment with the status quo could diminish in time and, whatever the traumas of World War II, its lessons could eventually wear off, especially as postwar generations come to power. Somehow the fear of escalation could diminish, and small, cheap wars among major countries could again seem viable and attractive. We could get so used to living with the bomb that its use

[19] Bernard Brodie, *War and Politics* (New York: Macmillan, 1973), 426.

becomes almost casual. Some sort of conventional war could re-
emerge as a viable possibility under nuclear stalemate. But, as
noted, the trends seem to be substantially in the opposite direction:
Discontent does not seem to be on the rise, and visceral hostility
seems to be on the decline.

Moreover, it might be instructive to look at some broad historical
patterns. For centuries now, various countries, once warlike and
militaristic, have been quietly dropping out of the war system to
pursue neutrality and, insofar as they are allowed to do so, perpetual
peace. Their existence tends to go unremarked because chroniclers
have preferred to concentrate on the antics of the "Great Powers."
"The story of international politics," observes Waltz, "is written in
terms of the great powers of an era."[20] But it may be instructive for
the story to include Holland, a country which chose in 1713,
centuries before the invention of nuclear weapons, to abandon the
fabled "struggle for power," or Sweden, which followed Holland's
lead in 1721. Spain and Denmark dropped out too, as did Switzerland, a country which fought its last battle in 1798 and has shown a
"curious indifference" to "political or territorial aggrandizement,"
as one historian has put it.[21]

While Holland's bandwagon was quietly gathering riders, an
organized movement in opposition to war was arising. The first
significant peace organizations in Western history emerged in the
wake of the Napoleonic Wars in 1815, and during the next century
they sought to promote the idea that war was immoral, repugnant,
inefficient, uncivilized, and futile. They also proposed remedies like
disarmament, arbitration, and international law and organization,
and began to give out prizes for prominent peaceable behavior.
They had become a noticeable force by 1914 but, as one of their
number, Norman Angell, has recalled, they tended to be dismissed
as "cranks and faddists . . . who go about in sandals and long
beards, live on nuts."[22] Their problem was that most people living
within the great power system were inclined to disagree with their
central premise: that war was bad. As Michael Howard has observed, "before 1914 war was almost universally considered an
acceptable, perhaps an inevitable and for many people a desirable
way of settling international differences."[23] One could easily find
many prominent thinkers declaring that war was progressive, beneficial, and necessary; or that war was a thrilling test of manhood and

[20] Waltz, *Theory of International Politics*, 72.
[21] Lynn Montross, quoted in Jack S. Levy, *War in the Modern Great Power System* (Lexington: University Press of Kentucky), 45. On this issue, see also Brodie, *War and Politics*, 314.
[22] Norman Angell, *After All* (New York: Farrar, Straus, and Young, 1951), 147. See also A. C. F. Beales, *The History of Peace* (New York: Dial, 1931); Roger Chickering, *Imperial Germany and a World Without War* (Princeton: Princeton University Press, 1975).
[23] Howard, "The Causes of Wars," 92.

a means of moral purification and spiritual enlargement, a promoter of such virtues as orderliness, cleanliness, and personal valor.

It should be remembered that a most powerful effect of World War I on the countries that fought it was to replace that sort of thinking with a revulsion against wars and with an overwhelming, and so far permanent, if not wholly successful, desire to prevent similar wars from taking place. Suddenly, after World War I, peace advocates were a decided majority. As A. A. Milne put it in 1935, "in 1913, with a few exceptions we all thought war was a natural and fine thing to happen, so long as we were well prepared for it and had no doubt about coming out the victor. Now, with a few exceptions, we have lost our illusions; we are agreed that war is neither natural nor fine, and that the victor suffers from it equally with the vanquished."[24]

For the few who didn't get the point, the lesson was substantially reinforced by World War II. In fact, it almost seems that after World War I the only person left in Europe who was willing to risk another total war was Adolf Hitler. He had a vision of expansion and carried it out with ruthless and single-minded determination. Many Germans found his vision appealing, but unlike the situation in 1914 where enthusiasm for war was common, Hitler found enormous reluctance at all levels within Germany to use war to quest after the vision. As Gerhard Weinberg has concluded, "whether any other German leader would indeed have taken the plunge is surely doubtful, and the very warnings Hitler received from some of his generals can only have reinforced his belief in his personal role as the one man able, willing, and even eager to lead Germany and drag the world into war."[25] Hitler himself told his generals in 1939 "in all modesty" that he alone possessed the nerve required to lead Germany to fulfill what he took to be its mission. In Italy, Benito Mussolini also sought war, but only a small one, and he had to deceive his own generals to get that.[26] Only in Japan, barely touched by World War I, was the willingness to risk major war fairly widespread.

Since 1945 the major nuclear powers have stayed out of war with each other, but equally interesting is the fact that warfare of *all* sorts seems to have lost its appeal within the developed world. With only minor and fleeting exceptions (the Falklands War of 1982, the Soviet invasions of Hungary and Czechoslovakia), there have been

---

[24] A. A. Milne, *Peace With Honour* (New York: Dutton, 1935), 9–10. See also Paul Fussell, *The Great War and Modern Memory* (New York: Oxford University Press, 1975); I. F. Clarke, *Voices Prophesying War 1763–1984* (London: Oxford University Press, 1966), chap. 5.

[25] Gerhard Weinberg, *The Foreign Policy of Hitler's Germany* (Chicago: University of Chicago Press, 1982), 664.

[26] MacGregor Knox, *Mussolini Unleashed 1939–1941* (Cambridge: Cambridge University Press, 1982), chap. 3.

no wars among the 48 wealthiest countries in all that time. Never before have so many well-armed countries spent so much time not using their arms against each other. This phenomenon surely goes well beyond the issue of nuclear weapons; they have probably been no more crucial to the non-war between, say, Spain and Italy than they have been to the near-war between Greece and Turkey or to the small war between Britain and Argentina.

Consider the remarkable cases of France and Germany, important countries which spent decades and centuries either fighting each other or planning to do so. For this age-old antagonism, World War II was indeed the war to end war. Like Greece and Turkey, they certainly retained the creativity to discover a motivation for war if they had really wanted to, even under an over-arching superpower balance; yet they have now lived side-by-side for nearly half a century, perhaps with some bitterness and recrimination, but without even a glimmer of war fever. They have become Hollandized with respect to one another. The case of Japan is also instructive: Another formerly aggressive major power seems now to have embraced fully the virtues and profits of peace.

The existence of nuclear weapons also does not help very much to explain the complete absence since 1945 of civil war in the developed world (with the possible exception of the 1944–49 Greek civil war, which could be viewed instead as an unsettled carryover of World War II). The sporadic violence in Northern Ireland or the Basque region of Spain has not really been sustained enough to be considered civil war, nor have the spurts of terrorism carried out by tiny bands of self-styled revolutionaries elsewhere in Western Europe. Except for the case of Hungary in 1956, Europeans under Soviet domination have not (so far) resorted to major violence, no matter how desperate their disaffection. . . .

As a form of activity, war in the developed world may be following once-fashionable dueling into obsolescence: The perceived wisdom, value, and efficacy of war may have moved gradually toward terminal disrepute. Where war was often casually seen as beneficial, virtuous, progressive, and glorious, or at least as necessary or inevitable, the conviction has now become widespread that war in the developed world would be intolerably costly, unwise, futile, and debased.

World war would be catastrophic, of course, and so it is sensible to be concerned about it even if its probability is microscopic. Yet general stability seems so firm and the trends so comforting that the concerns of Schell and others about our eventual "final coma" seem substantially overwrought. By themselves, weapons do not start wars, and if nuclear weapons haven't had much difference, reducing their numbers probably won't either. They may be menacing, but a major war seems so spectacularly unlikely that for those who seek to save lives it may make sense to spend less time worrying about something so improbable as major war and more time dealing with limited conventional wars outside the developed world, where war still can seem cheap and tempting, where romantic notions about holy war and purifying revolution still persist and sometimes prevail, and where developed countries sometimes still fight carefully delimited surrogate wars. Wars of that sort are still far from obsolete and have killed millions since 1945.

Over a quarter century ago, strategist Herman Kahn declared that "it is most unlikely that the world can live with an uncontrolled arms race lasting for several decades." He expressed his "firm belief" that "we are not going to reach the year 2000—and maybe not even the year 1965—without a cataclysm" unless we have "much better mechanisms than we have had for forward thinking."[27] Reflecting again on the cases of the United States and Canada, of Sweden and Denmark, of Holland, of Spain and Switzerland, of France and Germany, and of Japan, it might be suggested that there is a long-term solution to the arms competition between the United States and the Soviet Union, and that it doesn't have much to do with "mechanisms." Should political tensions decline, as to a considerable degree they have since the classic Cold War era of 1945–63, it may be that the arms race will gradually dissipate. And it seems possible that this condition might be brought about not principally by ingenious agreements over arms control, but by atrophy stemming from a dawning realization that, since preparations for major war are essentially irrelevant, they are profoundly foolish.

[27] Herman Kahn, *On Thermonuclear War* (Princeton: Princeton University Press, 1961), 574, x, 576.

The Unimpressive Record of Atomic Diplomacy

MCGEORGE BUNDY

In addressing the question of the role of nuclear weapons in diplomacy, it is well to begin with an expression of one's own general position on the nuclear problem. My view of these weapons is that for my own country they are a necessary evil. I do not think it acceptable for the United States to renounce the possession of nuclear capabilities while they are maintained in the Soviet Union. In that most basic sense I accept the need for nuclear deterrence and am unimpressed by arguments that neglect this requirement. . . .

I also believe that not all the consequences of the nuclear arsenals are bad. The very existence of nuclear stockpiles has created and enforced a considerable caution in the relations among nuclear-weapon states, so that where the interests of those states are clear and their political and military engagement manifest, as with the Soviet Union and the United States in Eastern and Western Europe respectively, there is an intrinsic inhibition on adventure which is none the less real for being essentially independent of doctrines—and even of nuclear deployments—on either side. I have elsewhere called this phenomenon "existential deterrence,"[1] and I think it has more to do with the persisting peace—and division—of Europe than all the particular nuclear doctrines and deployments that have so often bedeviled the European scene. . . .

Indeed the acceptance of nuclear deterrence, for me as for the American Catholic bishops, is "strictly conditioned," not only on a constant readiness to move to agreed arms reductions as drastic as the most skillful and dedicated negotiations permit, but also on a reluctance to depend on nuclear weapons for purposes beyond that of preventing nuclear war. On the historical record since Nagasaki, I think that these weapons have not been of great use to any government for such wider purposes, and I also think a misreading of that record has led to grossly mistaken judgments and to unnecessary, costly, and sometimes dangerous nuclear deployments by

"The Unimpressive Record of Atomic Diplomacy" by McGeorge Bundy from *The Choice: Nuclear Weapons vs. Security,* edited by Gwyn Prins. Reprinted by permission of Chatto & Windus, one of the publishers in The Random Century Group Ltd. Portions of the text and some footnotes have been omitted.

[1] McGeorge Bundy, "The bishops and the bomb," *New York Review of Books,* June 16, 1983.

both superpowers, and perhaps by others. Let us begin by considering what good these weapons have done the United States, which was their first and for a short four years their only possessor. I am willing to concede, though it cannot be proven, that in the years of American monopoly, and perhaps for a short time thereafter (in my view, not beyond 1955, at the latest) American nuclear superiority had some military and political value in Europe. We must recognize that fear of what the Russians would otherwise do with what was then an enormous advantage in conventional strength was not limited to Winston Churchill. Niels Bohr too believed that the American atomic bomb was a necessary balancing force, and so did many other highly peaceable men. But the time has long since passed when either side could hope to enjoy either monopoly or overwhelming superiority, so from the standpoint of the present and the future it is not necessary to challenge this particular bit of conventional wisdom. We do not really know that the American monopoly saved Europe in the early postwar years, but we do not know it did not, and we need not decide.

What is more interesting is to examine these years of evident American nuclear advantage from another angle, to try to see what usefulness that advantage may have had in supporting American diplomacy or in restraining specific adventures of others outside Western Europe. Aside from this debatable European case, there is very little evidence that American atomic supremacy was helpful in American diplomacy. Broadly speaking, the years from 1945 to 1949 were a time in which Soviet power and the power of such major Soviet allies as the Chinese communists was expanding and consolidating itself at a rate not remotely equaled since then, and there is no evidence whatever that fear of the American bomb had any restraining effect on this enormous process. It is true that for a short time in the autumn of 1945 Secretary of State James Byrnes believed that the silent presence of the bomb might constructively affect Soviet behavior at the negotiating table, but in fact it had no such impact, and before the end of the year Byrnes himself had changed his tactics. The importance of this brief and foolish flirtation with atomic diplomacy has been grossly exaggerated by students misreading a marginal and passing state of mind into a calculated effort in which Hiroshima itself is read largely as an effort to impress the Russians.[2] But this misreading is less important than the deeper point that to whatever degree atomic diplomacy may have tempted this or that American leader at this or that moment in those years, it did not work.

[2] The case for the prosecution was presented by Gar Alperowitz in *Atomic Diplomacy: Hiroshima and Potsdam* (New York, 1956). His thesis has not fared well under analysis by more careful historians, many themselves revisionists—see, e.g., Barton J. Bernstein, ed., *The Atomic Bomb: The Critical Issues* (Boston, 1976), 69–71.

The point becomes still more evident when we look at moments which American presidents themselves, in later years, came to see as evidence of the power of the atomic possibility. The two most notable cases are the Soviet withdrawal from Iran in 1946 and the armistice agreement that ended the Korean War in 1953.

In April 1952 President Harry Truman told an astonished press conference that not long after the end of World War II he had given Joseph Stalin "an ultimatum"—to get his troops out of Iran—and "they got out." Truman was referring to events in March 1946, when the Soviet Union kept troops in northern Iran after the expiration of an agreed date for British and Russian withdrawal that had been honored by the British. The Soviet stance stirred a vigorous international reaction, and after three weeks of increasing tension there came a Soviet announcement of a decision to withdraw that was executed over the following weeks. Truman never doubted that his messages had been decisive. Out of office, in 1957, he described his action still more vividly: "The Soviet Union persisted in its occupation until I personally saw to it that Stalin was informed that I had given orders to our military chiefs to prepare for the movement of our ground, sea and air forces. Stalin then did what I knew he would do. He moved his troops out." If this statement were accurate, it would be an extraordinary confirmation of the effectiveness of American threats in the age of atomic monopoly, because a troop movement of this sort, in 1946, into an area so near the Soviet Union and so far from the United States could only have been ventured, or feared, because of the nuclear monopoly.[3]

The only trouble with this picture is that no such message ever went to Stalin and no such orders to American officers. What actually happened is wholly different. Stalin did indeed attempt to gain a special position in Iran by keeping his troops beyond the deadline, but what made his effort a failure was not an ultimatum from Truman but primarily the resourceful resistance of the Iranian government, supported indeed by American diplomacy (especially at the United Nations) and still more by a wide and general international reaction. Stalin's was a low-stake venture in an area of persistent Soviet hope. He pulled back when he found the Iranian government firm but not belligerent, his Iranian supporters weak, and the rest of the watching world critical. One of the critics was Harry Truman, and we need not doubt the strength of his feelings. But the messages he actually sent (all now published) were careful and genuinely diplomatic. The United States Government "cannot remain indifferent," and "expresses the earnest hope" of immediate

[3] Truman's press conference is in the *Public Papers of the Presidents* (1952), at pages 290–96. His 1957 remarks appeared in the *New York Times*, August 25, 1957, and are quoted in Stephen S. Kaplan, *Diplomacy of Power* (Washington, D.C., 1981), 70–71.

Soviet withdrawal, all "in the spirit of friendly association." There
is no deadline and no threat. What we have here is no more than an
understandable bit of retrospective braggadocio. As George Kennan
later remarked—he had been *chargé d'affaires* in Moscow at the
time and was the man who would have had to deliver any ultimatum—Truman "had an unfortunate tendency to exaggerate, in later
years, certain aspects of the role that he played" in relations with
Stalin.[4]

Regrettably, Truman's retrospective version of events was not
harmless. Among stouthearted and uncomplicated anticommunists
it became a part of the folklore showing that Harry Truman knew
how to stop aggression by toughness, when in fact what he and his
colleagues knew, in this case, was something much more important:
that their task was to help keep up Iranian courage, but precisely
not to confront Stalin directly. American diplomacy was adroit but
not menacing, and Kennan is right again in describing the result: "It
was enough for Stalin to learn that a further effort by the Soviet
Union to retain its forces in Persia would create serious international
complications. He had enough problems at the moment without
that." Truman's messages had certainly helped in this learning
process, and not least because they had expressly avoided the kind
of threat he later came to believe he made. So his faulty memory
led others to learn the wrong lesson.

Dwight Eisenhower contributed even more than Harry Truman to
the folklore of atomic diplomacy. He believed that it was the threat
of atomic war that brought an armistice in Korea in 1953. In his
memoirs he cited a number of warnings and signals to make his
case, and his Secretary of State, John Foster Dulles, told allied
statesmen in private a lurid tale of nuclear deployments made known
to the Chinese. But here again the historical record raises questions.
The decisive shift in the position of the communists, a shift away
from insistence on the forced repatriation of prisoners, occurred
before any of these signals was given, shortly after the death of
Stalin in March. While Eisenhower certainly intended the whiff of
nuclear danger to reach Peking, the records now available make it
clear that he in fact held back from any audible threat because of
his recognition that it would be as divisive in 1953 as it had been in
1950, when Harry Truman, by a casual press conference response
to a question on the possibility of using nuclear weapons, had

[4] Truman's message of March 6 is printed in part in his own *Memoirs, II, Years of
Trial and Hope* (Garden City, New York, 1956), 94–95, and is available also now in
Foreign Relations of the United States (1946), 7: 340–43. The whole episode is
covered with great clarity in Bruce R. Kuniholm, *The Origins of the Cold War in the
Near East: Great Power Conflict and Diplomacy in Iran, Turkey and Greece* (Princeton, N.J., 1980), 304–37. Kennan's later remark and the one quoted below are in a
letter to Kuniholm printed at 321.

brought Prime Minister Attlee across the Atlantic to receive assurance that no such step was in prospect. Quite aside from any nuclear threat, there were other and excellent reasons in 1953 for the communist side to want to end the war: their own heavy losses, the absence of any prospect for further gains, and the continuing high cost of unsuccessful probes of United Nations forces on the ground. At the most the springtime signals of a nuclear possibility were a reinforcement to Chinese preferences already established before those signals were conveyed.

Yet Eisenhower clearly did believe that the Korean case showed the value of nuclear threats, and indeed he and Dulles made the threat permanent in the language of a public declaration after the armistice that those who had supported South Korea would respond to any renewed aggression in ways that might not be limited. In two later crises, over the offshore islands of Quemoy and Matsu in 1955 and 1958, Eisenhower used both open references to nuclear weapons and visible deployments of nuclear-armed forces to underline the risks Mao was running. What actually held off the attacking Chinese forces, in both crises, was not these threats but the effective use of local air and naval superiority, but it cannot be denied that the nuclear possibility may have contributed to Chinese unwillingness to raise the stakes. It is also possible that the readiness of the United States to help defend these small and unimportant islands was increased by the fact that against China the United States then held a nuclear monopoly.

In this case too the threat was almost as alarming to friends as to opponents. Fully aware of the fiercely divisive consequences of any actual use of a nuclear weapon, Eisenhower devoted himself in these crises to the energetic and skillful support of the conventional forces and tactics which fended off the Chinese attacks. He was very careful indeed not to lose his control over the nuclear choice, either by any unconditional public threat or by a delegation of authority. The nuclear reply remained a possibility, not a policy. As he told Nixon in 1958, "You should never let the enemy know what you will not do." In the offshore islands affair as in Korea, Eisenhower kept the use of nuclear weapons as something the enemy could not know he would not do, and believed he gained from this stance.[5]

But the President was teaching his Vice President a lesson that was going out of date even as he explained it. The offshore islands crisis of 1958, so far from being a model for the future, turns out to be the last case we have of a crisis between the United States and a nation not the Soviet Union in which nuclear weapons or threats of their use play any role whatever. Consider the war in Vietnam. Here the president whose inaction proves the point conclusively is the same Richard Nixon who had been Eisenhower's eager student.

[5] Eisenhower to Nixon is in Richard Nixon, *The Real War* (New York, 1980), 255.

Nixon came to the White House in 1969 determined to apply to Hanoi the same techniques of credible threat that he thought he had seen used successfully in Korea. If he had continued to believe a nuclear threat would be credible, he would surely have conveyed it. But once he considered the matter carefully he was forced to recognize that there was in reality no way of making a credible nuclear threat because the men in Hanoi knew as well as he did that no American president, by 1969, could in fact have used nuclear weapons in Indochina. To do so would plainly outrage allies and split his own country in half. What you cannot conceivably execute, you cannot plausibly threaten.[6]

The evolution from what Eisenhower believed in 1958 to what Nixon was forced to recognize in 1969 is extraordinarily important, and not all the reasons for it are clear. One of them certainly is the spreading awareness of the danger inherent in the thermonuclear age. The end of the 1950s saw the first large-scale popular reactions to nuclear danger, and the searing experience of the Cuban Missile Crisis gave the threat of nuclear warfare new meaning. More broadly, if less consciously, men had come to believe more and more strongly in the value and importance of respecting the "firebreak" between conventional and nuclear weapons. In September 1964, President Lyndon Johnson had stated the case with characteristic passion and force during his campaign against Barry Goldwater:

> Make no mistake. There is no such thing as a conventional nuclear weapon. For nineteen peril-filled years no nation has loosed the atom against another. To do so now is a political decision of the highest order. And it would lead us down an uncertain path of blows and counterblows whose outcome none may know.[7]

To all these general considerations one must add that by 1969 the morality of the Vietnam War was a profoundly divisive question in the United States. To resort to nuclear weapons in such a war would be to outrage still further the angry opponents of the war and probably to multiply their numbers.

So what Richard Nixon thought he had learned turned out only ten years later not to be so, and by his own wise refusal to present a nuclear threat to Hanoi he reinforced the very tradition whose strength he had not at first understood. If the United States could not threaten the use of nuclear weapons even in such a long and painful contest as Vietnam, in what case was such a threat possible? The answer, today, on all the evidence, is that the only places where a nuclear threat remains remotely plausible are those where it has

---

[6] Nixon's recognition that he could not use nuclear weapons in Vietnam is described in his *Memoirs* at 347.

[7] *Public Papers of the Presidents, 1963–4*, 2: 1051.

been present for decades—in Western Europe and in Korea, because of the special historical connections noted above, and much more diffusely and existentially in the general reality that any prospect of direct confrontation between the United States and the Soviet Union presents nuclear risks which enforce caution.

A stronger proposition may be asserted. International support for the maintenance of the nuclear firebreak now operates not only to make nuclear threats largely ineffective, but also to penalize any government that resorts to them. This rule applies as much to the Soviet Union as to the United States. The Soviet government, in the heyday of Nikita Khrushchev, set international records for nuclear bluster. The favorite target was the United Kingdom, not only in the Suez crisis but more generally. Khrushchev clearly believed that his rockets gave him a politically usable superiority and talked accordingly. Yet in fact Soviet threats were not decisive at Suez; they were not even issued until what really was decisive—American opposition to the adventure—had been clear for several days. By 1957 Soviet reminders of British vulnerability, so logical from the point of view of believers in the political value of atomic superiority, were serving only to strengthen the Macmillan government in its determination to maintain and improve its own deterrent. The Soviet triumph in launching Sputnik did indeed help Soviet prestige, but attempts to capitalize on it by crude threats were unproductive.

Still more striking is the failure of Soviet atomic diplomacy in relation to China. Having first made the enormous mistake of helping the Chinese toward nuclear weapons, the Soviets reversed their field at the end of the 1950s and addressed themselves assiduously, but with no success whatever, to an effort to persuade the Chinese that they would be happier without any nuclear weapons of their own. Neither cajolery nor the withdrawal of assistance was effective. Probably nothing could have changed the Chinese purpose, but Soviet unreliability only intensified it, and at no time before the first Chinese explosion in 1964 was the Kremlin prepared to make the matter one of war or peace. By the time that possibility was actively considered, in 1969, the Chinese bomb was a reality requiring caution. In a limited but crucial way the Chinese themselves now had an existential deterrent.

But of course Khrushchev's greatest adventure in atomic diplomacy was also his worst fiasco: the deployment of missiles to Cuba in 1962. It is not clear yet how he hoped to gain from the adventure, but he must have believed that placing these weapons in Cuba would produce advantages of some sort. Whether they were there to be bargained against concessions in Europe, or to demonstrate Soviet will and American impotence, or to establish a less uneven strategic balance, we cannot know. That they were there merely to be traded for a pledge against a U.S. invasion of Cuba we must doubt. Nor need we linger on the fact of the failure.

What deserves attention is rather that in this most important crisis of all we can see clearly three persistent realities. First, it was not what the weapons could actually do but the political impact of the deployment that counted most to both sides; second, both leaders understood that any nuclear exchange would be a personal, political, and national catastrophe; third, as a consequence the determinant of the crisis must be in the level of will and ability to act by less than nuclear means. While this set of propositions does not of itself justify President Kennedy's course, it does make clear the folly of Khrushchev's: He left himself open to the use of conventional superiority by an opponent for whom the choice of inaction was politically impossible. I recognize that many students have asserted the commanding importance of U.S. nuclear superiority in the Cuban Missile Crisis, but I am deeply convinced that they are wrong. Along with five other senior members of the Kennedy Administration, including Dean Rusk and Robert McNamara, I am convinced that the missile crisis illustrates "not the significance but the insignificance of nuclear superiority in the face of survivable thermonuclear retaliatory forces."[8]

The missile crisis had powerful and lasting consequences for the notion of atomic diplomacy. It showed the world that both great governments had a profound lack of enthusiasm for nuclear war, and in so doing it reduced the plausibility of nuclear threats of any kind. It also increased the political costs of such posturing. Even before 1962 Khrushchev had learned to try to couch his threats in relatively civil terms—of course I don't want to crush you, but it's only sensible to note that I can.[9] In October 1962, it was precisely nuclear war that both sides plainly chose to stay clear of, and the world took note. Since that time there has been no open nuclear threat by any government. I think it is not too much to say that this particular type of atomic diplomacy has been permanently discredited.

Even the very occasional use of nuclear signals in a crisis has had low importance in recent decades. The most notable case available is the short alert called in President Nixon's name on October 24, 1973, at the height of Yom Kippur war for the purpose of deterring unilateral Soviet action. This alert, by Henry Kissinger's authoritative account, was intended as a general show of resolution and in no way as a specifically thermonuclear threat. More significantly still, Kissinger's account makes it clear that the alert was unnecessary. The possibility of a unilateral Soviet troop movement to Egypt was effectively blocked by Sadat's overnight decision, before he ever heard of the U.S. alert, to back away from the Soviet proposals.

---

[8] See "The lessons of the Cuban Missile Crisis," *Time,* September 27, 1982, 85.
[9] For a good example of this sort of thing, see Adam Ulam, *Expansion and Coexistence,* 2nd ed. (New York, 1974), 612.

In recent years there has been one remarkable revival of the notion of atomic diplomacy, together with an equally remarkable demonstration of its lack of content. The revival occurred among frightened American hawks eager to demonstrate that the Soviet nuclear build-up of the 1970s was conferring on Moscow a level of superiority that would inescapably translate into usable political leverage. In its most dramatic form the argument was that the Russians were getting a superiority in large, accurate ICBMs that would soon allow them to knock out our own ICBMs and defy us to reply for fear of annihilation. This was the famous "window of vulnerability," and the argument was that this kind of strategic superiority, because both sides would be aware of it, would make the Soviet Union's political pressures irresistible around the world. It was all supposed to happen before now—in the early 1980s. The argument was riddled with analytical errors, ranging from the over-simplification of the problems of such an attack through the much too facile assumption that no credible reply could be offered, and on to the quite untested notion that a threat of this kind would have useful results for the threat-maker. It is not at all surprising that history has shown the notion empty. There has been no Soviet action anywhere that can be plausibly attributed to the so-called window of vulnerability, and indeed after riding this wave of fear—and others—into the White House, the Reagan Administration eventually managed to discover that the window did not exist. First, in the spring of 1983, the Scowcroft Commission concluded that the existing capabilities of American forces, taken as a whole, made such a scenario implausible, and in early 1984 Ronald Reagan himself concluded that we are all safer now because "America is back—standing tall," though out there in the real world the strategic balance remains almost exactly the one which led to the foolish fears in the first place. The notion of a new vulnerability to nuclear diplomacy was unreal; perhaps we were dealing instead with a little atomic politics. . . .

My general moral is a simple one. The more we learn about living with nuclear arsenals, the less we are able to find any good use for them but one—the deterrence of nuclear aggression by others—and the more we are led to the conclusion that this one valid and necessary role is not nearly as demanding as the theorists of countervailing strategy assert. No sane government wants nuclear war, and the men in the Kremlin, brutal and cynical tyrants to be sure, are eminently sane. There are two places still—Western Europe and South Korea—where we Americans do have outstanding undertakings to go first with nuclear weapons if necessary. I believe those commitments are increasingly implausible and ripe for revision. They may also create pressure for, though they do not in fact require, special and politically neuralgic deployments.

Such deployments are a subset of the competition in weapons

systems that is now itself becoming the largest single threat to peace. The systems now coming in sight, especially those that might seem to offer effective prospects for defense, do indeed raise the specter of a world in which at some moment of great tension in the future one side or the other might feel that its only hope was to "preempt"—to go first—to aim at a simultaneous offensive and defensive knockout. That would be another and much nastier world than the one we now have, and it is worth great efforts to see to it that it does not come into being.

Meanwhile what remains remarkable about the enormous arsenals of the superpowers is how little political advantage they have conferred. It is a question for another essay whether other nuclear powers have gained more.

The Utility of Nuclear Deterrence

ROBERT JERVIS

Perhaps the most striking characteristic of the postwar world is just that—it can be called "postwar" because the major powers have not fought each other since 1945. Such a lengthy period of peace among the most powerful states is unprecedented.[1] Almost as unusual is the caution with which each superpower has treated the other. Although we often model superpower relations as a game of chicken, in fact the United States and USSR have not behaved like reckless teenagers. Indeed, superpower crises are becoming at least as rare as wars were in the past. Unless one strains and counts 1973, we have gone over a quarter of a century without a severe crisis. Furthermore, in those that have occurred, each side has been willing to make concessions to avoid venturing too near the brink of war. Thus the more we see of the Cuban missile crisis, the more it appears as compromise rather than an American victory. Kennedy was not willing to withhold all inducements and push the Russians as hard as he could if this required using force or even continuing the volatile confrontation.[2]

It has been common to attribute these effects to the existence of nuclear weapons. Because neither side could successfully protect itself in an all-out war, no one could win—or, to use John Mueller's phrase, profit from it.[3] Of course this does not mean that wars will

From *International Security*, Fall 1988 (Vol. 13, no. 2). Reprinted by permission of The MIT Press, Cambridge, Massachusetts. © 1988 by the President and Fellows of Harvard College and of the Massachusetts Institute of Technology. Portions of the text and some footnotes have been omitted.

[1] Paul Schroeder, "Does Murphy's Law Apply to History?" *Wilson Quarterly*, 9, no. 1 (New Year's 1985): 88; Joseph S. Nye, Jr., "The Long-Term Future of Nuclear Deterrence," in Roman Kolkowicz, *The Logic of Nuclear Terror* (Boston: Allen & Unwin, 1987), 234.

[2] See the recent information in McGeorge Bundy, transcriber, and James G. Blight, ed., "October 27, 1962: Transcripts of the Meetings of the ExComm," *International Security*, 12, no. 3 (Winter 1987/88): 30–92, and James G. Blight, Joseph S. Nye, Jr., and David A. Welch, "The Cuban Missile Crisis Revisited," *Foreign Affairs*, 66 (Fall 1987): 178–79. Long before this evidence became available, Alexander George stressed Kennedy's moderation; see Alexander L. George, David K. Hall, and William E. Simons, *The Limits of Coercive Diplomacy: Laos, Cuba, Vietnam* (Boston: Little Brown, 1971), 86–143.

[3] "The Essential Irrelevance of Nuclear Weapons: Stability in the Postwar World." But as we will discuss below, it can be rational for states to fight even when profit is not expected.

not occur. It is rational to start a war one does not expect to win (to be more technical, whose expected utility is negative), if it is believed that the likely consequences of not fighting are even worse.[4] War could also come through inadvertence, loss of control, or irrationality. But if decision makers are "sensible,"[5] peace is the most likely outcome. Furthermore, nuclear weapons can explain superpower caution. When the cost of seeking excessive gains is an increased probability of total destruction, moderation makes sense.

Some analysts have argued that these effects either have not occurred or are not likely to be sustained in the future. Thus Fred Iklé is not alone in asking whether nuclear deterrence can last out the century.[6] It is often claimed that the threat of all-out retaliation is credible only as a response to the other side's all-out attack: Thus Robert McNamara agrees with more conservative analysts whose views he usually does not share that the "sole purpose" of strategic nuclear force "is to deter the other side's first use of its strategic forces."[7] At best, then, nuclear weapons will keep the nuclear peace, they will not prevent—and, indeed, may even facilitate—the use of lower levels of violence.[8] It is then not surprising that some observers attribute Soviet adventurism, particularly in Africa, to the Russians' ability to use the nuclear stalemate as a shield behind which they can deploy pressure, military aid, surrogate troops, and even their own forces in areas they had not previously controlled. The moderation mentioned earlier seems, to some, to be only one-sided. Indeed, American defense policy in the past decade has been driven by the felt need to create limited nuclear options to deter Soviet incursions that, while deeply menacing to our values, fall short of threatening immediate destruction of the United States.

Furthermore, while nuclear weapons may have helped keep the peace between the United States and USSR, ominous possibilities for the future are hinted at by other states' experiences. Allies of nuclear-armed states have been attacked: Vietnam conquered Cambodia and China attacked Vietnam. Two nuclear powers have fought each other, albeit on a very small scale: Russia and China skir-

---

[4] Alternatively, to be even more technical, a decision maker could expect to lose a war and at the same time could see its expected utility as positive if the slight chance of victory was justified by the size of the gains that victory would bring. But the analysis here requires only the simpler formulation.

[5] See the discussion in Patrick M. Morgan, *Deterrence: A Conceptual Analysis* (Beverly Hills, Calif: Sage, 1977), 101–24.

[6] Fred Iklé. "Can Nuclear Deterrence Last Out the Century?" *Foreign Affairs*, 51, no. 2 (January 1973): 267–85.

[7] Robert McNamara, "The Military Role of Nuclear Weapons," *Foreign Affairs*, 62, no. 4 (Fall 1983): 68. For his comments on how he came to this view, see his interview in Michael Charlton, *From Deterrence to Defense* (Cambridge: Harvard University Press, 1987), 18.

[8] See Glenn Snyder's discussion of the "stability-instability paradox" in "The Balance of Power and the Balance of Terror," in Paul Seabury, ed., *The Balance of Power* (San Francisco: Chandler, 1965), 184–201.

mished on their common border. A nonnuclear power has even threatened the heartland of a nuclear power: Syria nearly pushed Israel off the Golan Heights in 1973 and there was no reason for Israel to be confident that Syria was not trying to move into Israel proper. Some of those who do not expect the United States to face such a menace have predicted that continued reliance on the threat of mutual destruction "would lead eventually to the demoralization of the West. It is not possible indefinitely to tell democratic republics that their security depends on the mass extermination of civilians . . . without sooner or later producing pacifism and unilateral disarmament."[9]

John Mueller has posed a different kind of challenge to claims for a "nuclear revolution." He disputes, not the existence of a pattern of peace and stability, but the attributed cause. Nuclear weapons are "essentially irrelevant" to this effect; modernity and highly destructive nonnuclear weapons would have brought us pretty much to the same situation had it not been possible to split the atom.[10] Such intelligent revisionism makes us think about questions whose answers had seemed self-evident. But I think that, on closer inspection, the conventional wisdom turns out to be correct. Nevertheless, there is much force in Mueller's arguments, particularly in the importance of what he calls "general stability" and the reminder that the fact that nuclear war would be so disastrous does not mean that conventional wars would be cheap.

Mueller is certainly right that the atom does not have magical properties. There is nothing crucial about the fact that people, weapons, industry, and agriculture may be destroyed as a result of a particular kind of explosion, although fission and fusion do produce special byproducts like fallout and electromagnetic pulse. What is important are the political effects that nuclear weapons produce, not the physics and chemistry of the explosion. We need to determine what these effects are, how they are produced, and whether modern conventional weapons would replicate them.

POLITICAL EFFECTS OF NUCLEAR WEAPONS

The existence of large nuclear stockpiles influences superpower politics from three directions. Two perspectives are familiar: First,

[9] Henry Kissinger, "After Reykjavik: Current East-West Negotiations." *The San Francisco Meeting of the Tri-Lateral Commission, March 1987* (New York: The Trilateral Commission, 1987). 4; see also ibid., 7, and his interview in Charlton. *From Deterrence to Defense*, 34.

[10] Mueller, "The Essential Irrelevance." Waltz offers yet a third explanation for peace and stability—the bipolar nature of the international system, which, he argues, is not merely a product of nuclear weapons. See Kenneth Waltz, *Theory of International Politics* (Reading, Mass.: Addison-Wesley, 1979). But in a later publication he places more weight on the stabilizing effect of nuclear weapons: *The Spread of Nuclear Weapons: More May be Better*, Adelphi, Paper No. 171 (London: International Institute for Strategic Studies, 1981).

the devastation of an all-out war would be unimaginably enormous. Second, neither side—nor, indeed, third parties—would be spared this devastation. As Bernard Brodie, Thomas Schelling, and many others have noted, what is significant about nuclear weapons is not "overkill" but "mutual kill."[11] That is, no country could win an all-out nuclear war, not only in the sense of coming out of the war better than it went in, but in the sense of being better off fighting than making the concessions needed to avoid the conflict. It should be noted that although many past wars, such as World War II for all the Allies except the United States (and, perhaps, the USSR), would not pass the first test, they would pass the second. For example: Although Britain and France did not improve their positions by fighting, they were better off than they would have been had the Nazis succeeded. Thus it made sense for them to fight even though, as they feared at the outset, they would not profit from the conflict. Furthermore, had the Allies lost the war, the Germans—or at least the Nazis—would have won in a very meaningful sense, even if the cost had been extremely high. But "a nuclear war," as Reagan and Gorbachev affirmed in their joint statement after the November 1985 summit, "cannot be won and must never be fought."[12]

A third effect of nuclear weapons on superpower politics springs from the fact that the devastation could occur extremely quickly, within a matter of days or even hours. This is not to argue that a severe crisis or the limited use of force—even nuclear force—would inevitably trigger total destruction, but only that this is a possibility that cannot be dismissed. At any point, even in calm times, one side or the other could decide to launch an unprovoked all-out strike. More likely, a crisis could lead to limited uses of force which in turn, through a variety of mechanisms, could produce an all-out war. Even if neither side initially wanted this result, there is a significant, although impossible to quantify, possibility of quick and deadly escalation.

Mueller overstates the extent to which conventional explosives could substitute for nuclear ones in these characteristics of destructiveness, evenhandedness, and speed. One does not have to underestimate the horrors of previous wars to stress that the level of destruction we are now contemplating is much greater. Here, as in other areas, there comes a point at which a quantitative difference becomes a qualitative one. Charles De Gaulle put it eloquently: After a nuclear war, "two sides would have neither powers, nor laws, nor cities, nor cultures, nor cradles, nor tombs."[13] While a

[11] Bernard Brodie, ed., *The Absolute Weapon: Atomic Power and World Order* (New York: Harcourt Brace, 1946); Thomas Schelling, *Arms and Influence* (New Haven: Yale University Press, 1966).

[12] *New York Times*, November 22, 1985, A12.

[13] Speech of May 31, 1960, in Charles De Gaulle, *Discours Et Messages*, 3 (Paris: Plon, 1970): 218. I am grateful to McGeorge Bundy for the reference and translation.

total "nuclear winter" and the extermination of human life would
not follow a nuclear war, the worldwide effects would be an order
of magnitude greater than those of any previous war.[14] Mueller
understates the differences in the scale of potential destruction:
"World War II did not cause total destruction in the world, but it
did utterly annihilate the three national regimes that brought it
about. It is probably quite a bit more terrifying to think about a
jump from the 50th floor than about a jump from the 5th floor, but
anyone who finds life even minimally satisfying is extremely unlikely
to do either."[15] The war did indeed destroy these national regimes,
but it did not utterly destroy the country itself or even all the values
the previous regimes supported. Most people in the Axis countries
survived World War II; many went on to prosper. Their children,
by and large, have done well. There is an enormous gulf between
this outcome—even for the states that lost the war—and a nuclear
holocaust. It is far from clear whether societies could ever be
reconstituted after a nuclear war or whether economies would ever
recover.[16] Furthermore, we should not neglect the impact of the
prospect of destruction of culture, art, and national heritage: even a
decision maker who was willing to risk the lives of half his population might hesitate at the thought of destroying what has been
treasured throughout history.

Mueller's argument just quoted is misleading on a second count
as well: The countries that started World War II were destroyed,
but the Allies were not. It was more than an accident but less than
predetermined that the countries that were destroyed were those
that sought to overturn the status quo; what is crucial in this context
is that with conventional weapons at least one side can hope, if not
expect, to profit from war. Mueller is quite correct to argue that
near-absolute levels of punishment are rarely required for deterrence, even when the conflict of interest between the two sides is
great—i.e., when states believe that the gross gains (as contrasted
with the net gains) from war would be quite high. The United States,
after all, could have defeated North Vietnam. Similarly, as Mueller
notes, the United States was deterred from trying to liberate East
Europe even in the era of American nuclear monopoly.

But, again, one should not lose sight of the change in scale that
nuclear explosives produce. In a nuclear war the "winner" might
end up distinguishably less worse off than the "loser," but we
should not make too much of this difference. Some have. As Harold

[14] Starley Thompson and Stephen Schneider, "Nuclear Winter Reappraised,"
Foreign Affairs, 64, no. 5 (Summer 1986): 981–1005.
[15] "The Essential Irrelevance," 66–67.
[16] For a discussion of economic recovery models, see Michael Kennedy and Kevin
Lewis, "On Keeping Them Down: Or, Why Do Recovery Models Recover So Fast?"
in Desmond Ball and Jeffrey Richelson, *Strategic Nuclear Targeting* (Itahaca, N.Y.:
Cornell University Press, 1986), 194–208.

Brown put it when he was Secretary of the Air Force, "if the Soviets thought they may be able to recover in some period of time while the U.S. would take three or four times as long, or would never recover, then the Soviets might not be deterred."[17] Similarly, one of the criteria that Secretary of Defense Melvin Laird held necessary for the essential equivalence of Soviet and American forces was: "preventing the Soviet Union from gaining the ability to cause considerably greater urban/industrial destruction than the United States would in a nuclear war."[18] A secret White House memorandum in 1972 used a similar formulation when it defined "strategic sufficiency" as the forces necessary "to ensure that the United States would emerge from a nuclear war in discernably better shape than the Soviet Union."[19]

But this view is a remarkably apolitical one. It does not relate the costs of the war to the objectives and ask whether the destruction would be so great that the "winner," as well as the loser, would regret having fought it. Mueller avoids this trap, but does not sufficiently consider the possibility that, absent nuclear explosives, the kinds of analyses quoted above would in fact be appropriate. Even very high levels of destruction can rationally be compatible with a focus on who will come out ahead in an armed conflict. A state strongly motivated to change the status quo could believe that the advantages of domination were sufficiently great to justify enormous blood-letting. For example, the Russians may feel that World War II was worth the cost not only when compared with being conquered by Hitler, but also when compared with the enormous increase in Soviet prestige, influence, and relative power.

Furthermore, without nuclear weapons, states almost surely would devote great energies to seeking ways of reducing the costs of victory. The two world wars were enormously destructive because they lasted so long. Modern technology, especially when combined with nationalism and with alliances that can bring others to the rescue of a defeated state, makes it likely that wars will last long: Defense is generally more efficacious than offense. But this is not automatically true; conventional wars are not necessarily wars of attrition, as the successes of Germany in 1939–40 and Israel in 1967 remind us. Blitzkrieg can work under special circumstances, and when these are believed to apply, conventional deterrence will no longer be strong.[20] Over an extended period of time, one side or

[17] U.S. Senate, Preparedness Investigating Subcommittee of the Committee on Armed Services, *Hearings on Status of U.S. Strategic Power*, 90th Cong., 2d sess., April 30, 1968 (Washington, D.C.: U.S. Government Printing Office, 1968), 186.

[18] U.S. House of Representatives, Subcommittee on Department of Defense, *Appropriations for the FY 1973 Defense Budget and FY 1973–1977 Program*, 92nd Cong., 2d sess., February 22, 1972, 65.

[19] Quoted in Gregg Herken, *Counsels of War* (New York: Knopf, 1985), 266.

[20] John J. Mearsheimer, *Conventional Deterrence* (Ithaca, N.Y.: Cornell University Press, 1983). It should be noted, however, that even a quick and militarily decisive war might not bring the fruits of victory. Modern societies may be even

the other could on occasion come to believe that a quick victory was possible. Indeed, for many years most American officials have believed not only that the Soviets could win a conventional war in Europe or the Persian Gulf, but that they could do so at low cost. Were the United States to be pushed off the continent, the considerations Mueller gives might well lead it to make peace rather than pay the price of refighting World War II. Thus, extended deterrence could be more difficult without nuclear weapons. Of course, in their absence, NATO might build up a larger army and better defenses, but each side would continually explore new weapons and tactics that might permit a successful attack. At worst, such efforts would succeed. At best, they would heighten arms competition, national anxiety, and international tension. If both sides were certain that any new conventional war would last for years, the chances of war would be slight. But we should not be too quick to assume that conventional war with modern societies and weapons is synonymous with wars of attrition.

The length of the war is important in a related way as well. The fact that a war of attrition is slow makes a difference. It is true, as George Quester notes, that for some purposes all that matters is the amount of costs and pain the state has to bear, not the length of time over which it is spread.[21] But a conventional war would have to last a long time to do an enormous amount of damage; and it would not *necessarily* last a long time. Either side can open negotiations or make concessions during the war if the expected costs of continued fighting seem intolerable. Obviously, a timely termination is not guaranteed—the fitful attempts at negotiation during World War II and the stronger attempts during World War I were not fruitful. But the possibility of ending the war before the costs become excessive is never foreclosed. Of course, states can believe that a nuclear war would be prolonged, with relatively little damage being done each day, thus permitting intra-war bargaining. But no one can overlook the possibility that at any point the war could escalate to all-out destruction. Unlike the past, neither side could be certain that there would be a prolonged period for negotiation and intimidation. This blocks another path which statesmen in nonnuclear eras could see as a route to meaningful victory.

Furthermore, the possibility that escalation could occur even though neither side desires this outcome—what Schelling calls "the threat that leaves something to chance"[22]—induces caution in crises

---

harder to conquer than are modern governments. A high degree of civilian cooperation is required if the victor is to reach many goals. We should not assume it will be forthcoming. See Gene Sharp, *Making Europe Unconquerable* (Cambridge, Mass.: Ballinger, 1985).

[21] George Quester, "Crisis and the Unexpected," *Journal of Interdisciplinary History*, 18, no. 3 (Spring 1988): 701–3.

[22] Thomas Schelling, *The Strategy of Conflict* (Cambridge: Harvard University

as well. The fact that sharp confrontations can get out of control, leading to the eventual destruction of both sides, means that states will trigger them only when the incentives to do so are extremely high. Of course, crises in the conventional era also could escalate, but the possibility of quick and total destruction means that the risk, while struggling near the brink, of falling into the abyss is greater and harder to control than it was in the past. Fears of this type dominated the bargaining during the Cuban missile crisis: Kennedy's worry was "based on fear, not of Khrushchev's intention, but of human error, of something going terribly wrong down the line." Thus when Kennedy was told that a U-2 had made a navigational error and was flying over Russia, he commented: "There is always some so-and-so who doesn't get the word."[23] The knowledge of these dangers—which does not seem lacking on the Soviet side as well[24]—is a powerful force for caution.

Empirical findings on deterrence failure in the nuclear era confirm this argument. George and Smoke show that: "The initiator's belief that the risks of his action are calculable and that the unacceptable risks of it can be controlled and avoided is, with very few exceptions, a necessary (though not sufficient) condition for a decision to challenge deterrence."[25] The possibility of rapid escalation obviously does not make such beliefs impossible, but it does discourage them. The chance of escalation means that local military advantage cannot be confidently and safely employed to drive the defender out of areas in which its interests are deeply involved. Were status quo states able to threaten only a war of attrition, extended deterrence would be more difficult.

GENERAL STABILITY

But is very much deterrence needed? Is either superpower strongly driven to try to change the status quo? On these points I agree with much of Mueller's argument—the likely gains from war are now relatively low, thus producing what he calls general stability.[26] The set of transformations that go under the heading of

Press, 1960), 187–203; Schelling, *Arms and Influence*, 92–125. Also see Jervis, *The Illogic of American Nuclear Strategy* (Ithaca, N.Y.: Cornell University Press, 1984), ch. 5; Jervis, "'MAD is a Fact, not a Policy': Getting the Arguments Straight," in Jervis, *Meaning of the Nuclear Revolution* (Ithaca, N.Y.: Cornell University Press, 1989); and Robert Powell, "The Theoretical Foundations of Strategic Nuclear Deterrence," *Political Science Quarterly*, 100, no. 1 (Spring 1985): 75–96.

[23] Arthur M. Schlesinger, Jr., *Robert Kennedy and His Times* (Boston: Houghton Mifflin, 1978), 529; quoted in Roger Hilsman, *To Move A Nation* (Garden City, N.Y.: Doubleday, 1964), 221.

[24] See Benjamin Lambeth, "Uncertainties for the Soviet War Planner," *International Security*, 7, no. 3 (Winter 1982/83): 139–66.

[25] Alexander L. George and Richard Smoke, *Deterrence in American Foreign Policy* (New York: Columbia University Press, 1974), 529.

[26] Mueller, "Essential Irrrelevance," 69–70; also see Waltz, *Theory of International Politics*, 190.

"modernization" have not only increased the costs of war, but have created alternative paths to established goals, and, more profoundly, have altered values in ways that make peace more likely. Our focus on deterrence and, even more narrowly, on matters military has led to a distorted view of international behavior. In a parallel manner, it has adversely affected policy prescriptions. We have not paid sufficient attention to the incentives states feel to change the status quo, or to the need to use inducements and reassurance, as well as threats and deterrence.[27]

States that are strongly motivated to challenge the status quo may try to do so even if the military prospects are bleak and the chances of destruction considerable. Not only can rational calculation lead such states to challenge the status quo, but people who believe that a situation is intolerable feel strong psychological pressures to conclude that it can be changed.[28] Thus nuclear weapons by themselves—and even mutual second-strike capability—might not be sufficient to produce peace. Contrary to Waltz's argument, proliferation among strongly dissatisfied countries would not necessarily recapitulate the Soviet-American pattern of stability.[29]

The crucial questions in this context are the strength of the Soviet motivation to change the status quo and the effect of American policy on Soviet drives and calculations. Indeed, differences of opinion on these matters explain much of the debate over the application of deterrence strategies toward the USSR.[30] Most of this dispute is beyond our scope here. Two points, however, are not. I think Mueller is correct to stress that not only Nazi Germany, but Hitler himself, was exceptional in the willingness to chance an enormously destructive war in order to try to dominate the world. While of course such a leader could recur, we should not let either our theories or our policies be dominated by this possibility.

A second point is one of disagreement: Even if Mueller is correct to believe that the Soviet Union is basically a satisfied power—and I share his conclusion—war is still possible. Wars have broken out in the past between countries whose primary goal was to preserve

---

[27] For discussions of this topic, see George, Hall, and Simons, *Limits of Coercive Diplomacy;* George and Smoke, *Deterrence in American Foreign Policy;* Richard Ned Lebow, *Between Peace and War* (Baltimore: Johns Hopkins University Press, 1981); Robert Jervis, "Deterrence Theory Revisited," *World Politics,* 31, no. 2 (January 1979): 289–324; Jervis, Lebow, and Janice Gross Stein, *Psychology and Deterrence* (Baltimore: Johns Hopkins University Press, 1985); David Baldwin, "The Power of Positive Sanctions," *World Politics,* 24, no. 1 (October 1971): 19–38; and Janice Gross Stein, "Deterrence and Reassurance," in Philip E. Tetlock, et al., eds., *Behavior, Society and Nuclear War,* vol. 2 (New York: Oxford University Press, 1991).

[28] George and Smoke, *Deterrence in American Foreign Policy;* Lebow, *Between Peace and War;* Jervis, Lebow, and Stein, *Psychology and Deterrence.*

[29] Waltz, *Spread of Nuclear Weapons.*

[30] See Robert Jervis, *Perception and Misperception in International Politics* (Princeton: Princeton University Press, 1976), chap. 3.

the status quo. States' conceptions of what is necessary for their security often clash with one another. Because one state may be able to increase its security only by making others less secure, the premise that both sides are basically satisfied with the status quo does not lead to the conclusion that the relations between them will be peaceful and stable. But here too nuclear weapons may help. As long as all-out war means mutual devastation, it cannot be seen as a path to security. The general question of how nuclear weapons make mutual security more feasible than it often was in the past is too large a topic to engage here. But I can at least suggest that they permit the superpowers to adopt military doctrines and bargaining tactics that make it possible for them to take advantage of their shared interest in preserving the status quo. Winston Churchill was right: "Safety [may] be the sturdy child of terror."

Deterrence in the Post-Cold War Era

JEAN-LOUIS GERGORIN

DETERRENCE AND ITS FUTURE

The concept of deterrence dates back to the Hammurabi Code, the most ancient penal code in the world (3000 B.C.). To deter is to attempt to prevent a person or group of people from committing certain kinds of actions by persuading them that if they do so, they will be so severely punished that the disadvantages of the act will outweigh its advantages (as in having a hand cut off for stealing, for example). All penal systems are therefore systems of deterrence.

Before the emergence of nuclear weapons, were there any defence policies based on deterrence? Yes and no. Yes, in that all defence policies contain an element of deterrence which implies: 'Should you attack me, I am strong enough not only to prevent you from succeeding, but to crush you'. No, because the message of deterrence is concealed in offensive as well as defensive military attitudes, and besides has apparently prevented very few conflicts during the course of history. It is worth noting, however, that belligerents did not use chemical weapons during World War II apparently more out of fear of retaliation in kind than because of any great respect for existing international conventions.

The specificity of nuclear deterrence arose from the horror inspired by the destruction of Hiroshima with a *single* bomb. (The bombing of Dresden was equally or probably even more horrifying, but did not qualify as a 'technological strategic novelty'.) Certainly the first (and, happily, until now the only) nuclear strikes were intended as coercion, or the reverse of deterrence: to force an individual or collective agent, in this case Japan, to do something, in this case, capitulate; and failing that, to submit to an exorbitant punishment, in this case, further nuclear bombardments. Soon thereafter, the Cold War and the conventional imbalance on the Eurasian continent persuaded American strategists to make nuclear deterrence a key element in the relationship between East and West forces. At the same time, the Soviets developed their own nuclear weapons, initially very much with operational intentions. But pro-

From *Adelphi Papers*, No. 266, Winter 1991/92. © The International Institute for International Studies. Reprinted by permission.

gressively, especially thanks to the SALT talks, they were won over, at least partly, to deterrence.

What are the objectives of the deterrence policies among the nuclear powers today? Until now, the United States' nuclear strategy has been based largely on deterring two major and complementary Soviet threats:

—a first, disarming strike on key American military targets (silos and command centres);
—a massive attack (conventional and potentially chemical and/or nuclear) against Western Europe, the Gulf or Japan, against which conventional means of defence would prove ineffectual.

Within the concept of a flexible response, American nuclear doctrine has undergone all sorts of modulations, all connected with changes in technology and the strategic environment. Two of the most recent shifts are:

—On one hand, increasing emphasis on surgical strikes against specific targets, whose destruction would paralyse the Soviet political-military establishment (command, communication and detection centres, 'bunkers' of the leaders of the Party, the Army and the KGB).
—On the other hand, the 'last resort' concept adopted by NATO members (with the exception of France) during the London summit in June 1990. It implies resorting to nuclear arms as late as possible in the case of Soviet aggression against Western Europe.

Until the changes brought about by perestroika and the INF and START agreements, Soviet nuclear forces had two main missions:

—to neutralize major strategic targets in Western Europe (notably its nuclear potential) and in Japan, within the context of a general offensive against either one of these objectives;
—to deter a first strike on the part of the Americans, or the perpetration of limited nuclear strikes against Soviet objectives by the potential for pre-emptive destruction of demographic and, above all, military objectives (like silos), on US territory.

And, of course, to all this should be added a deterrent (and certainly here as well, potentially pre-emptive) capability directed against China.

Since the acceleration of perestroika in 1988, the Soviet leadership, including military leaders, has suggested a reorientation towards a minimal deterrence policy. However, even though the INF agreement has brought about the destruction of the SS-20s, and the START Treaty in July 1991 provided for the near elimination of all

Soviet anti-silo capabilities, the remaining 20,000 theatre nuclear weapons and 5,000 strategic missiles do not match the concept of minimal deterrence.

British nuclear strategy forms an integral part of NATO strategy, even though the UK government reserves the right to use its nuclear capabilities for the protection of the country's vital interests as it sees fit. It should be noted that the *Polaris* missiles that constitute the core of the UK's strategic deterrence are not very accurate. The *Tridents*, which will come into service within the decade, will provide something of a counter-force capability, but only the choice of an air-to-ground missile, in co-operation with the American or the French, could, if the missile were designed with this end in mind, put surgical destruction within Britain's grasp.

France, a member of NATO, but not part of its integrated military organization, and whose nuclear planning and means are totally independent, has based its nuclear strategy on two major objectives:

—to deter an aggression (implicitly Soviet) against the country's vital interests by the threat of a massive response against the potential aggressor's major cities (a threat made credible largely by the second-strike capability of French strategic submarines);
—to reinforce the credibility of this threat through the capacity to strike (Soviet) military targets by ground-to-ground (*Hadès*) or air-to-ground (*ASMP*) missiles, known as 'pre-strategic'. It should be noted that from 1988, that is, before the radical upheavals in Eastern Europe, President Mitterrand introduced the possibility that targets might not be restricted to the then eastern satellite countries, but might involve Soviet territory itself.

Little is known of Chinese nuclear strategy, but it is plausible that it aims above all at deterring Soviet aggression by the threat of reprisals against Soviet cities within reach of Chinese missiles. Or could Vietnam, India, Japan, even the United States be targets as well? We simply don't know.

Likewise, one can only guess at the nuclear strategies (current or potential) of India, the sixth-ranking declared nuclear power, of Israel, South Africa and Pakistan, which have secretly manufactured or are capable of constructing in a short time nuclear weapons or delivery systems. It is likely that the military missions of countries involved in regional conflicts, are (or could be) of two kinds:

—those designed to deter a conventional or ballistic attack (nuclear or chemical) endangering the country's survival by a potential for anti-city reprisals and/or tactical nuclear destruction of the invading forces;
—to have the capability of destroying in a pre-emptive manner the

nuclear, chemical or ballistic arsenal of potential regional adversaries.

To this description of the security objectives of nuclear states' deterrence strategies, a significant political objective should be added: the *status* linked to the possession of nuclear arms is an important element in international influence and diplomatic prestige. And this has been proven all the more true in that the nuclear balance was a key element in the East–West confrontation that formed the axis of the international system. The fact that the five permanent members of the UN Security Council (the US, the UK, China, France and the Soviet Union) are the same five declared military nuclear powers (India has the bomb but denies an operational nuclear military capability), has doubly reinforced the perception that nuclear deterrence is a major element in 'international standing'.

THE IMPACT OF THE NEW INTERNATIONAL ENVIRONMENT

The crumbling of the Soviet bloc in less than two years, followed by the collapse of the USSR itself, is obviously a phenomenon of major importance. Whatever the internal evolution of the USSR, three points are already clear:

—First, the conjunction of the loss of Eastern Europe as a glacis for the Soviets, the on-going evacuation of Soviet forces in these countries, and the CFE agreement on conventional forces reduction in Europe renders practically impossible any conventional aggression with the potential reinforcement of massive nuclear and chemical surprise attacks as NATO feared: a scenario which has in fact recently been confirmed as having been high on the Warsaw Pact's military agenda.
—Second, should the USSR retain a considerable nuclear arsenal despite the INF and START agreements, the combination of the already agreed reductions, the inevitable technological and operational consequences of its internal crisis (which has lasted for three years and is still continuing), and the dynamism of American technology will tilt the strategic balance increasingly in favour of the United States. Technically, in these conditions it will be increasingly difficult for Soviet or 'post-Soviet' leaders to launch a surprise nuclear attack against Western Europe or the United States that would not be absolutely suicidal.
—Lastly, and perhaps most importantly, the total eradication of Marxist-Leninist ideology, and notably of its international component, 'the worldwide class struggle', removes the principal factor that pushed the USSR from 1945 to 1987 into a strategy of permanent political and military expansion and made not com-

pletely implausible the possibility of its launching a major aggression, conventional or nuclear.

Because of these three changes the probability of this kind of massive aggression in the next ten to 15 years is virtually nil.

The failure of the August 1991 putsch and the constitutional revolution which ensued opened up three main possible directions which 'post-Soviet' military strategy might take:

—The most likely prospect appears to be that the Soviet Army is restructured and diminished, but conserves the maximum nuclear and conventional arsenals authorized by the START and INF agreements. The supervision of this army will be shared by the 'centre', that is, a new confederation's weak executive power and by Russia. National guards have been created in the confederate republics, but no nuclear weapons are available to them. This scenario brings one to the same conclusion as the preceding analysis regarding the Gorbachevian USSR of July 1991: the probability of an aggressive strategy *vis-à-vis* the West in the next ten or 15 years is essentially non-existent.
—A second possibility is that of a voluntarist policy of accelerated, and especially nuclear, disarmament. Recent declarations by Boris Yeltsin point in that direction. This disarmament would probably be partly unilateral, partly negotiated with the West, but more in return for financial advantages than for reductions on the part of the United States and its allies. The 'post-USSR' would thus be in possession of a minimal deterrent capability.
—The third scenario is that the economic crisis would, in the short or medium term, incur the downfall of the democratic forces and the imposition of a nationalist, authoritarian and autarkical group somewhat like those of Alkhnis or Jirinovski at Russia's helm, with more or less control over the other republics. To survive, this kind of regime would have to be largely autarkic, for the West would withdraw all aid. But were it to succeed in holding power for some length of time, we would witness some rearming in two areas:
  • strategic nuclear arms, to impress the West and persuade it not to interfere with internal repression and the eventual intimidation of its neighbours;
  • conventional weapons, which could be used to regain the territories of the former Soviet Union, risking border conflicts with the Baltic republics, Romania and perhaps even Poland.

In terms of this hypothesis, and in light of the fanatic nationalism of the new leadership, we could not completely exclude the possibility of an East–West conflict, which would be a sort of Cuban Missile Crisis in reverse: the neo-USSR would invade one or two of its neighbours, probably the Baltic states, which would receive Western military support. Although possible, this hypothesis hardly seems credible (would Europeans and Americans be willing to die for Vilnius, and would even fanatical Russian nationalists run the risk of a nuclear conflict?).

—The last scenario, which has been frequently mentioned of late, is that of a more or less anarchic evolution in the ex-USSR, which would go from a seizure of nuclear weapons by various republics or by uncontrolled groups to a civil war with opposing camps controlling and even using nuclear arms. In these various anarchic scenarios, the principal risk for the West is one of 'nuclear blackmail', either by one faction to obtain benevolent neutrality or economic aid from Western countries, or by an anonymous, uncontrolled group to secure a huge financial ransom.

The preceding analysis on the evolution of what was until recently the 'Soviet threat' can be summed up as follows:

—The probability of nuclear or conventional aggression against the West in the next ten to 15 years has become extremely low (probably even slighter than that of a Chinese aggression).

—The only slight risk of a Western–Soviet nuclear conflict would be in the case of Western intervention on behalf of a neighbour attacked by a nationalist neo-Russia, an attack which would be considered by the victim as a violation of its national sanctuary.

—A more probable risk is that of nuclear blackmail by groups having seized nuclear systems in a situation of anarchy or civil war.

THE EVOLUTION OF THE SOUTH

The second tendency of the international system which will weigh heavily on the future of deterrence is the proliferation of ballistic, nuclear, chemical and, potentially, biological weapons. Paradoxically, the end of East-West competition and the crumbling of Soviet communism will favour such proliferation. Some of the more radical countries consider that the collapse of the USSR (which until now played the role of moderating overseer for some of them) makes the acquisition of sophisticated weapons a necessity in order to compensate for the new tip of the scales in favour of 'imperialism' and 'Zionism'. Other more moderate countries might pursue similar efforts, either to protect themselves against their radical neighbours, or simply out of hunger for status and influence.

Iraq is an interesting case, in that it pursued a secret and systematic proliferation policy for more than 15 years. This policy was developed in four directions simultaneously:

—ballistic, by the acquisition and improvement of Soviet *Scud* missiles and participation in the secret *Condor* project;

—chemical, by the construction of plants for manufacturing these weapons, which were used at the end of the Iran-Iraq War and against the Kurds in 1988;

—biological, by means of the now acknowledged research programme, which was, fortunately, apparently in its infancy;

—nuclear, by a secret programme to manufacture fissionable materials (plutonium, treated in specially-equipped laboratories, and, above all, uranium enriched by centrifuges) and to acquire the equipment necessary for the production of fission bombs.

As to how it acquired the necessary equipment and technology, Iraq's effort is remarkable for its diversity and the complementarity of its sources (foreign training for its scientists, official co-operation or purchase agreements, clandestine acquisitions or secret co-operation with other proliferating countries) and the variety of its partners (the USSR and its then satellite countries, other Third World countries like its two partners in the *Condor* project, and even the principal Western states).

Needless to say, it is particularly noteworthy that this significant nuclear effort was carried out despite the fact that Iraq was a signatory to the NPT and subject to the IAEA's periodic inspections. This says a great deal about the efficiency of these controls in various other countries.

On a strategic level, prejudice against Iraq aside, the objectives pursued by Saddam in these programmes seem clear:

—Above all, to protect Iraq from a new Israeli operation on the lines of the raid against the Osirak nuclear reactor in July 1981, which was aimed at neutralizing Iraq's installations for the development of non-conventional arms. This goal was stated in Saddam's apparently absurdly provocative declaration at the beginning of 1990, threatening to destroy half of Israel with chemical weapons should the Israelis raid Iraq.

—More generally, to sanctuarize Iraq against Western actions aimed at preventing the pursuit of a strategy of regional expansion. One need only imagine the Western coalition's hesitations had the invasion of Kuwait taken place *after* Iraq had produced its own nuclear arms to understand Saddam's interest in conducting this kind of strategy.

—Lastly, confronted with Israel, which is most likely a nuclear power, and the United States, Iraq wished to appear as the leader and spokesman for the Arab world. In this regard, the debate over Saddam Hussein's intentions is immaterial (once his nuclear potential was fulfilled, did he intend to launch a surprise attack against Israel? This appears unlikely, as the Iraqi dictator is anything but suicidal). Strategic influence is a function of objective capabilities, not subjective intentions.

The Gulf War revealed much about the limits of this kind of proliferation strategy, though it was clearly far from having attained all its objectives, especially its nuclear ones:

—like the V-1s and V-2s at the end of World War II, the effect of the *Scuds* with conventional warheads was less military than political in their urban destruction (which even then was rather limited given the *Scuds'* capabilities). Nonetheless, the difficulty in locating the mobile launchers and the relative success of the *Patriots* in *Scud* interception, whatever their actual performance, revive the debate concerning deterrence or defence against such ballistic threats.
—Iraq did not use chemical arms either against Israel or the coalition forces. In the first case, it is unclear whether it was due to a technical inability to adapt chemical warheads to the *Scuds,* or more probably, to the fear of nuclear retaliation by the Israelis. But on the other hand, in the second case, it is by now certain that the Iraqi leadership voluntarily renounced the use of their impressive chemical arsenal, of which they talked so freely, out of fear of a matching allied response, against which they feared they could not sufficiently protect themselves. In addition, Anglo-American allusions to the possibility of a nuclear response appear to have suitably impressed them—which proves that one form of deterrence did work.

Despite obligatory international efforts, it appears certain that ballistic, chemical, nuclear and even biological proliferation is bound to continue, even if international action slows it down. It is impossible to halt the dissemination of basic scientific and technical knowledge, or to place all countries under suspicion under a regime of limited sovereignty, such as that which was imposed on Iraq under particular circumstances. Besides, instability in the 'post-Soviet' territory could be a factor in proliferation, either through the recruitment of mercenary Soviet technicians, or even by the theft of tactical nuclear warheads, more than 15,000 of which are in Soviet Army stockpiles.

From the Western viewpoint, three types of measures resulting from this proliferation should be kept in mind:

—First, the at least partial sanctuarization of powers seeking to practise regional expansionism without the intervention of the great powers and the international community. This was Iraqi policy until the Gulf War, and it would appear that it is still the policy of North Korea, to mention but one example.
—Second, an attempt at direct intimidation of the Western countries, *a priori* European, by radical countries wishing to extort economic or political advantages.

—Third, blackmail, even nuclear terrorism. To see how certain states manipulate groups incorrectly termed uncontrolled, and encourage the implementation of so-called 'anonymous terrorist attacks', like that at Lockerbie, or the destruction of the UTA DC-10; it is not hard to imagine how the acquisition of nuclear weapons could be used by these states or the terrorist movements they at least partially control.

THE CONSEQUENCES FOR DETERRENCE

To sum up the preceding analyses, in the next 15 years Western deterrence must focus on three main types of threats in order of increasing probability.

First, the Soviet threat as it has dominated Western strategic thinking over the last four decades has practically disappeared, at least in the form of the risk of a surprise attack. For the Western countries, there remains the necessity to continue to balance the Soviet/Russian potential that is left, and to be prepared to deter a new aggressive strategy which, in light of the events of the past four years, is nonetheless not capable of reappearing within the next ten.

Second, as we have seen, in the next decade, the danger of terrorist nuclear blackmail, slight until now, runs the risk of increasing, either by the uncontrolled dissemination of Soviet nuclear weapons, or as a natural consequence of technological proliferation.

Lastly, the primary risk is that of regional destabilization by countries having attained a significant level of ballistic, chemical or nuclear proliferation; a civil war in the post-USSR could be linked to this category of risks.

WHAT CAN BE DONE?

Confronted with the radical modification of the nature and probability of the main threat they have faced in the past, Western democracies now hesitate between two opposing alternatives in the formulation of their deterrence strategies.

The first consists of acting as if little had changed in the nature and probability of the threats, and to maintain deterrence strategies identical to those of the past. In the case of a successor state to the USSR pursuing the implementation of a major unilateral reduction in nuclear armament, there would be the paradox of American, French and British strategic nuclear submarine patrols sliding silently through the oceans, with hundreds, even thousands of missile heads aimed permanently at obsolete Soviet targets—obsolete for both military and political reasons—because, for example, many of these sites would be under the control of denuclearized republics and not the new union. The same could be said (whilst they remain deployed) of the vast majority of short-range nuclear weapons in Europe.

The opposite extreme would be in assuming that in the new

international environment nuclear deterrence had become obsolete, a benefit of economic deterrence, and consequently allowing existing arsenals to wither away without any strategy of modernization or replacement.

To this it should be answered that economic deterrence is very often ineffective with regard to totalitarian regimes: Iraq is an excellent case in point. On the other hand, the Gorbachevian USSR has become sensitive to Western economic pressure precisely because it has abandoned totalitarianism. Any new threats would be the fruit of totalitarian or fanatical powers.

In the new international environment, Western democracies must therefore elaborate and establish a new deterrence strategy, which could consist of three elements:

—First, to maintain sufficient deterrence in the face of the Russo-Soviet potential, while of course adjusting the level of sufficiency (which also obviously depends on the different doctrines of the three Western powers) to the level of the Russo-Soviet strategic offensive and defensive potential. This adjustment should also take into account the decline of the risk of a surprise attack.
—Second, to have available adequate space-based, airborne, electronic and human intelligence gathering, in order to identify and locate, if possible *before* operational deployment, new proliferation threats (the manufacturing and deployment sites of nuclear, ballistic, chemical and biological weapons, and the command posts of the leaders controlling these weapons).
—Third, to equip themselves with the capacity to destroy surgically these sites, while keeping to a minimum collateral damage. This last point is essential and represents one of the main limitations of current Western nuclear means for deterring or neutralizing proliferation threats.

This capacity would consist of dual-capable delivery systems, 'stealth' aircraft, cruise missiles or very accurate ballistic missiles, combining penetration and precision capacities. The warheads should be conventional whenever it is sufficient, and nuclear with very low yield and used only in retaliation to the actual use of weapons of mass destruction. These weapons fall within the framework of a somewhat enlarged concept of deterrence. They would, in effect, have a triple role:

—to deter nuclear blackmailers by the threat of the destruction of their command centres, and thus their leaders, in the event of aggression;
—in the event that such an aggression appears imminent, to neutralize its means as a pre-emptive measure;
—more generally, the existence of such capacities, which would be

much more credible than traditional nuclear systems in regional conflicts, must deter countries tempted to use ballistic, chemical and nuclear arms for regional expansion or in civil wars.

It is now possible to evaluate to what degree the principal nuclear powers have the means for this kind of evolution in their deterrence policies.

For the United States, the answer is certainly positive. The challenge for American planners will be to identify, preserve and develop the elements of this kind of specific deterrence in their enormous nuclear and conventional arsenals, which will certainly be reduced as Soviet disarmament proceeds. Flexible response will surely have to evolve further, particularly in its short-range nuclear component. This kind of policy would equally make a great deal of sense for a democratic post-USSR Russia, notably because of proliferation threats on the periphery of, and even within, the Union. Here, many ingredients are also already present in the Soviet arsenal, but the fact that some electronic and especially computer equipment is a little out of date could slow down such an evolution.

France and the UK probably have a great deal of work ahead of them to approach this kind of capacity. In effect, their deterrence strategies, formulated in response to the traditional Soviet threat, are above all anti-demographic, either by policy or by the nature of the strategic arms available. As for their tactical nuclear arms, for the most part they correspond, with different variations, to the hypothesis of a major aggression against Western Europe. And this, as we have already seen, has become extremely unlikely.

Nonetheless, France has assets which point in the right direction: a military space intelligence programme, the priority of which has just been reinforced by the current Defence Minister Pierre Joxe, as well as technical capabilities in the fields of tactical 'stealth' cruise missiles and ram jet missiles. Other significant similar or complementary assets exist in the UK. There is little doubt that had the two countries a common political will, they could establish as a complement to their basic deterrence a co-ordinated system of specific deterrence aimed at the new threats, preserving the decision-making independence of each partner, but which eventually, as a complement to the American system, could endow the West European political union with the capacity to deter the new proliferation threats.

In conclusion, it should be noted that if a significant partial nuclear disarmament in the wake of the START agreement is likely, the emergence of new threats will maintain the need for deterrence, in new and evolving forms. Certainly, in an ideal world, there should be a single means of deterrence, in the hands of the permanent

Military Staff of a United Nations Security Council formed exclusively of democratic and peaceful nations. But this goal is not yet within reach, and for many years to come the peace and stability of the world will depend on the deterrence capabilities of the great democratic powers.

Part IV
Military Issues in the
Post–Cold War Era

The end of the Cold War and the breakup of the Soviet Union raise four central questions about the role of military power in the current era of international politics. First, should the United States continue to use its military power globally for its own interests and those of other nations? Second, how much of a danger is the spread of weapons of mass destruction and how can their spread be limited? Third, should the United States, as the most technologically advanced military power, deploy limited defenses against ballistic missile attack for itself and its close allies? Fourth, what are the alternatives to national ownership and use of military power and how viable are they? The four sections of Part IV treat these questions.

In the first section, Kenneth N. Waltz points out the dangers of unbridled use of American military power. Robert W. Tucker and David Hendrickson call for a restrained use of it. And Robert J. Art undertakes an analysis of the post-Cold War goals of American foreign policy and the ways in which military power can serve them.

In the second section, Lewis Dunn points out the dangers to world peace of the spread of nuclear weapons, while Waltz questions the conventional wisdom about nuclear proliferation by arguing that the measured spread of nuclear forces may enhance international stability and peace. In the third section, Michael Krepon and Matthew Bunn argue the pros and cons of deploying limited defenses against ballistic missile attack. In the last section, Thomas C. Schelling lays out the requirements and consequences of international disarmament, and Sir Brian Urquhart sets forth what must be done if the United Nations is to serve as a true international collective security agency.

America as a Model for the World?
A Foreign Policy Perspective

KENNETH N. WALTZ

THE IMPLICATIONS OF UNBALANCED POWER

Francoise Fénélon, who lived from 1651 to 1715, was a French theologian and political adviser and one of the first to understand balance of power as a general phenomenon rather than as merely a particular condition. He argued that a country disposing of greater power than others do cannot long be expected to behave with decency and moderation.[1] His theorem has been well illustrated by such powerful rulers as Charles V, Louis XIV, Napoleon, and Kaiser Wilhelm II. There was not necessarily something wrong with the character of those rulers or of their countries. At a minimum, it was a surplus of power that tempted them to arbitrary and arrogant behavior.

So long as the world was bipolar, the United States and the Soviet Union held each other in check. With the crumbling of the Soviet Union, no country or set of countries can presently restore a balance. One expects two results to follow. Despite abundant good intentions, the United States will often act in accordance with Fénélon's theorem. Balance of power theory leads one to predict that other states, if they have a choice, will flock to the weaker side, for it is the stronger side that threatens them.

In recent years have we seen what theory leads us to expect? A few examples will help to answer the question. President Reagan, when asked at a press conference how long we would continue to support the Contra's effort to overthrow the Nicaraguan government, began to give a fumbling answer. Then, impatient with himself, he said: Oh well, until they say "uncle." Vice President Bush in February of 1985 explained the meaning of "uncle." He laid seven stipulations upon the Nicaraguan government, which in sum amounted to saying that until Nicaragua developed a government and society much like ours we would continue to support the opposition.[2]

From *PS: Political Science & Politics*, December 1991, pp. 667–670. Published by the American Political Science Association. Reprinted by permission. Portions of the text have been omitted.

[1] Herbert Butterfield, "The Balance of Power," in Butterfield and Martin Wight, eds., *Diplomatic Investigations* (London: George Allen & Unwin, 1966), p. 140.
[2] "Excerpts from Remarks by Vice President George Bush," Press Release, Austin, Texas, February 18, 1985.

Senior officials in the Reagan administration elevated the right to intervene to the level of general principle. As one of them said, we "debated whether we had the right to dictate the form of another country's government. The bottom line was yes, that some rights are more fundamental than the right of nations to nonintervention, like the rights of individual people. . . . [W]e don't have the right to subvert a democratic government but we do have the right against an undemocratic one."[3] In managing so much of the world's business for so long, the United States developed a rage to rule, which our position in the world now enables us to indulge. Thus, Charles Krauthammer looks forward to an overwhelmingly powerful America "unashamedly laying down the rules of world order and being prepared to enforce them."[4] Seeming to reflect the same spirit, President Bush, in a speech of August 2, 1990, a speech lost in the excitement of Iraq's invasion of Kuwait, announced that we would prepare for regional threats "in whatever corner of the globe they may occur." But how do threats arising in odd corners of the globe constitute dangers for us, and how many threats of what sort would we need to prepare to meet if our concern were to protect only our vital interests?

The powerful state may, and the United States does, think of itself as acting for the sake of peace, justice, and well-being in the world. But these terms will be defined to the liking of the powerful, which may conflict with the preferences and the interests of others. In international politics, overwhelming power repels and leads others to try to balance against it. With benign intent, the United States has behaved, and until its power is brought into a semblance of balance, will continue to behave in ways that annoy and frighten others.

America's management of the war against Iraq, and the subsequent reaction of others, provide telling examples. The United States skillfully forged a wide coalition of states in opposition to Iraq's invasion of Kuwait, but the United States opposed the efforts of France and others to find a peaceful settlement along the way. The United States pressed other states to agree that the embargo would expire on January 15, unless Iraq complied with the United Nations' resolutions, when many other states preferred to give the embargo more time to work. The United States chose the day when the war should begin and determined how it be fought, raining well more destruction from the air than immediate military objectives required.

Many states reacted as one would expect to America's making

[3] Quoted in Robert W. Tucker, *Intervention and the Reagan Doctrine*, (New York: Council on Religion and International Affairs, 1985), p. 5.
[4] In Christopher Layne, "The Unipolar Illusion: American Foreign Policy in the Post Cold War World." Presented to the Washington Strategy Seminar, April 25, 1991, p. 21.

the decisions. I give only a few examples. Philippine foreign minister Raul Manglapus called the United States "constable of the world" and wondered whether "it was necessary or even if it is just" for America to impose a new world order. Professor Sakuji Yoshimura of Waseda University expressed his distress this way: "America is a mighty country—and a frightening one . . . for better or worse the Gulf war built a new world order with America at the head . . . this will be fine as long as the rest of the world accepts its role as America's underlings." An opposition member of the Diet, Masao Kunihiro, observed that the "feeling that America is a fiercesome country is growing in Japan."[5] In France, fears of American imperialism were widely expressed and debated. In early September of 1991 foreign minister Roland Dumas remarked that "America might reign without balancing weight," and Jacques Delors, president of the European Community Commission, cautioned that the United States must not take charge of the world. Both of them called on the United Nations and the European Community to counterbalance American influence.[6]

Professor Michael Doyle has shown that rarely do democracies fight democracies, but adds rightly that they fight plenty of wars against undemocratic states. The first generalization is not as strong as many have thought it to be. Not only was Germany a democracy in 1914 but also its being a democracy helped to explain the outbreak of war. As Chancellor Bethmann Hollweg lamented before the event, interests supporting the ruling majority pushed for policies sure to accumulate enemies for Germany. Junkers in the east demanded a tariff against Russian grain. Industrial interests in the northwest supported the Berlin to Baghdad railroad and the building of a battlefleet that could challenge the British navy. Russia and Britain were annoyed and frightened by German policies that helped to forge and strengthen the Triple Entente, which in turn made German political and military leaders entertain thoughts of fighting a preventive war before the enemies of Germany would become still stronger. One might add that in 1812 the United States chose to fight a war against the only other country that could then be called democratic, and that later in the century the northern American democracy fought the southern one.

Still, peace has prevailed much more reliably among democratic countries than elsewhere. On external as well as on internal grounds, I hope that more countries will become democratic.

CONCLUSION

Yet for all of the reasons given above, we cannot take America or any other country as a model for the world. We might remind

---

[5] Quotations are from *ibid.*, pp. 21–22.
[6] *New York Times*, "France to U.S.: Don't Rule," September 3, 1991, p. A8 (no byline).

ourselves that in the past decade alone we have initiated three wars beginning with the one against Grenada and ending with the one against Iraq. In the intervening war against Panama, we not only violated international law but we violated laws that we had largely written: namely, the charter of the Organization of American States. I believe that America is better than most nations, I fear that it is not as much better as many Americans believe. In international politics, unbalanced power constitutes a danger even when it is American power that is out of balance.

The Imperial Temptation

ROBERT W. TUCKER AND DAVID C. HENDRICKSON

Writing in the midst of the Mexican War, and on the occasion of the death of John Quincy Adams, William Seward argued that "All nations must perpetually renovate their virtues and their constitutions, or perish." Never, Seward added, "was there more need to renovate ours than now, when we seem to be passing from the safe old policy of peace and moderation into a career of conquest and martial renown."[1] Seward's emphasis on "renovation," by which he meant the return to, and renewal of, first principles, was a theme continually articulated by the generation of statesmen who succeeded the Founding Fathers. The theme was in fact much older, being an essential element of the classical republican tradition from which the founders themselves drew so much of their own thought. It assumed that every republic stood in danger of a corruption in which public virtue was lost and purpose was betrayed. There were, and are, many variations on this theme. In the late eighteenth century, some of the most important agencies of this corruption were thought to be a burdensome public debt, overweening executive power, and standing military forces—phenomena, it was thought, that were both the cause and consequence of war.

The founders of the American state, it may be thought, ought to exercise no special hold on our outlook; the earth, as Jefferson said, belongs to the living. At the least, however, it is sobering to reflect that the nation has assumed many of the very traits that it was founded to escape. It enjoys the possession of military forces of far greater reach and power than any empire known to history. Its president lays claim to the authority not only to dispatch American military forces wherever he wishes in the world but to commit them to war on his own authority. It has contracted the habit of taxing the future to pay for its present needs, so much so, indeed, that at the present time the gap between its revenues and expenditures is larger than what it spends on a military establishment that is superior to any on earth.

From Robert W. Tucker and David C. Hendrickson, *The Imperial Temptation*, published by the Council on Foreign Relations Press, 1992, pp. 198–211. Reprinted by permission.

[1] William H. Seward, *Life and Public Services of John Quincy Adams* (Port Washington, N.Y.: Kennikat Press, 1971 [1849]), p. 360.

It is true that this formidable colossus of power was brought into being for the best of reasons. The old policy of isolation from Europe had reached a dead end in the 1930s, both in its commercial and political aspects. The Smoot-Hawley tariff of 1930, together with the neutrality legislation later in the decade, represented the hypertrophy of the old isolationist tradition in circumstances that justified its partial abandonment. Before the hostility and strength of the totalitarian great powers, the traditional emphasis on the power of example appeared as a cruel delusion; before that hostility and strength, American security was placed in serious danger. America abandoned isolationism not simply because a fascist victory was thought to threaten the nation's physical security. A fascist victory was also seen to threaten the nation's historic purpose, since such victory carried the prospect of a world in which American ideas of international order and, of course, American institutions would be rejected. In this world, the American example and American influence would become irrelevant. It was also feared that in such a world the integrity of the nation's institutions and the quality of its domestic life would be seriously jeopardized.

The profound revolution in American foreign policy that attended the defeat of the Axis powers and the containment of the Soviet Union was thus a necessary revolution; largely the same may be said of the creation of the national security state that was its inevitable accompaniment. Under the shield provided by American military power, and by virtue of enlightened measures of economic statesmanship, the peoples of Europe and Northeast Asia gave play to the creative and constructive impulses that had decayed under the shadow of war. The economic miracle that resulted was accompanied by a political miracle as Europe and Japan purged their internal demons and built constitutional democracies that offered their citizens just and stable frameworks of government unknown to the lost generation. This accomplishment, which entailed a vast enlargement of the sphere of ordered liberty, represented the real greatness of the postwar American *imperium*.

The renovation of American policy today must surely take account of this accomplishment. It would be foolish to surrender the advantages of alliances with Western Europe and Japan because they represent commitments against which the founders warned. Though the United States might reasonably look forward to the day when a federated Europe assumes sole responsibility for its own defense, that day has not yet arrived. It is even more distant in the case of Japan. In both cases, the key problem remains the nuclear status of the defeated states of World War II. For the foreseeable future, we must reckon with the possibility that an American withdrawal from either alliance would create pressures not otherwise arising for Germany and Japan to acquire nuclear weapons, a development there is no reason to encourage. A nuclear Germany and Japan would not only awaken old fears in Europe and east Asia; the instability that might follow such a portentous move might also threaten the stability of the global trading system. In the case of Japan, it might very well foster a degree of antagonism in the American-Japanese relationship that, added to the elements of discord now existing, could endanger the security of both countries.

Then, too, a decision to acquire nuclear weapons by Germany and Japan would inevitably affect antiproliferation efforts generally. That decision, however acquiesced in by the other nuclear powers, would set a precedent that could not but gravely prejudice such efforts. The present international system may remain one marked by great inequalities, but it is also one committed as never before to the principle of equality. To encourage in the cases of Germany and Japan what is forbidden in the cases of other, though far less advantaged, aspirants to nuclear status would surely go far in stripping an antiproliferation regime of such legitimacy as it might possess. Under the circumstances, the course of wisdom would seem to dictate the retention of the alliances with Western Europe and Japan, a central part of which has always been the American nuclear guarantee, while also adjusting defense policy to reflect the fact that the security of this community of the advanced industrialized democracies is achievable at far less cost than was paid during the years of the cold war.[2]

The case for preserving as much continuity in the Western

---

[2] It may of course be argued that Japan and Germany cannot be great powers without nuclear weapons, that the disparity between their economic status and their military status is an anomaly that cannot be sustained indefinitely, and that eventually they must move to surmount this disparity. Under current circumstances, however, their motives for taking such a step do not appear strong. The reality in Europe and Asia today is not only the emergence of a powerful Germany and Japan but of states that, so long as they eschew the old and disastrous ways, are likely to have few constraints placed on their freedom. The acquisition of nuclear weapons would seriously handicap the pursuit of an ever larger economic and political role. Nor is it likely that Germany and Japan will go nuclear in response to a precipitating event that suddenly reveals a threat to security only nuclear weapons can effectively counter. In the past, the existence of such a threat posed by the Soviet Union did not prompt either power to seek an independent nuclear capability, despite persistent fears over the credibility of the American deterrent. With the end of the cold war, there is less reason today to question the credibility of the American nuclear deterrent than there has been in decades.

A much more likely route to a nuclear capability would be a decision made in response to a lengthy train of events during which national pride and self-respect have been wounded once too often. In the case of both countries, it is the United States that is capable of inflicting the gravest of such wounds. The gulf war afforded the first object lesson of a process that might well result in the nuclear armament of the defeated states of World War II. If Germany and Japan are to pay the military bills of the new world order and to suffer slights to their national dignity while doing so, to have little or no say in how the new world order is implemented, the response might be to acquire nuclear weapons. That response, in turn, would lead in all likelihood to a policy disposition incompatible with the maintenance of the alliance structure over which America has presided since the immediate post–World War II years.

alliance as changed circumstances permit reflects the assumption that the nations comprising these alliances continue to embody the nation's principal interests in the world. It also reflects the assumption that the periphery of American policy during the cold war remains the periphery in the wake of the cold war. The latter assumption, however, has been challenged today by a vision that, if put into practice, would extend an American security guarantee to virtually the entire world. In pursuit of this vision of a new world order, the nation is to exercise a police power which confers the right to prevent states of the developing world from acquiring certain weapons, and which imposes the duty to guarantee the territorial integrity of the members of the international community. In pursuit of this vision we are to maintain powerful interventionary forces capable of instantly responding, and on a large scale if need be, to "multiple contingencies" on the periphery.

Although the vision of a new world order has been set forth as novel, it is in fact the latest manifestation of an outlook that found periodic expression during the decades of the contest with the Soviet Union. Then, it took the form of global containment which proclaimed the need to resist the expansion of Soviet power and influence, if necessary by force, wherever and however this expansion occurred. Global containment rested on the assumptions that in the contest between the Soviet Union and the United States lines could not be drawn; that we could not pick and choose those places where we had to contain Soviet expansion; that the periphery if neglected would soon become the center; and that when engaged in a conflict for global stakes, what appeared as a marginal interest was all too often invested with critical significance, for almost any challenge was likely to be seen by the adversary making the challenge and by third parties as a test of one's will.

Global containment led us into Vietnam, just as global containment kept us there long after the dangers attending the intervention had become apparent. Vietnam taught, or should have taught, the difficulty of applying the precepts of a conventional—and conservative—statecraft to the policy of global containment, for the prudence of the one is not the prudence of the other. Whether global containment was supported by geopolitical considerations or justified on ideological grounds—and it was compatible with either rationale—the result was the same. In either case, the reconciliation of interest and power proved elusive. Whereas power is always limited, the interest informing global containment was not. The ever threatening disparity between interest and power could not be bridged simply by an act of will—a will ever triumphant because of the interest or purpose it reflected. Eventually, as in the case of Vietnam, the conviction of an ever triumphant will was bound to overtax power and to betray interest.

Yet what once proved elusive no longer appears so. What once constrained our actions no longer appears to do so. In the wake of the cold war and the gulf war, American military power seems virtually unlimited, particularly with respect to the vast region of the developing world. The gulf war provided a vivid demonstration of the effectiveness of this power, and at only a modest cost. In these novel and unexpected circumstances, an interest possessing the scope of global containment may readily take on an attractiveness it would never have otherwise possessed. That this interest does not respond to the reasonable security requirements of the nation, that it does not even have the security justification global containment could legitimately claim, need not prove decisive for its purposes. Given the protean character of security, policies justified in its name may usually be given a semblance of plausibility. Besides, for those who are not satisfied with justifying the use of American power in terms of an international order that is equated with the nation's security, there is always the additional justification seemingly provided by purpose. Although the world has been made safer for democracy than at any time in this century, the argument can be and is put forth that it may be made still safer.

Given the favorable power circumstances in which the Bush administration would today pursue its vision of world order, a policy that is the functional equivalent of global containment for the post–cold war world has evident attractions. The nation has succumbed to these attractions before, at times to its bitter regret. The experience we have had with the developing world stands in sharp contrast to our experience with Europe and Japan. In the developing world vast disparities in power and in institutional forms have made impossible what was achieved in our relations with the advanced industrialized democracies, an ethic of mutual cooperation and a sense of comity. Whereas our relations with the nations that formed the core of American postwar policy often brought out what was very nearly the best in us, our relations with the nations that formed the periphery of American policy often evoked what was close to the worst in us. Nor is there reason to believe that this experience will now change for the better. If anything, it is likely that, with the end of the cold war, it will grow still worse now that a principal incentive for restrained behavior on our part has been removed. When the opportunity provided by the end of the cold war is joined with the ostensible lesson of the gulf war, the result could well be a greater disposition to intervene in the developing world. That disposition, if acted upon, will prove as corrupting to the nation in the future as it has proven in the past.

* * *

These strictures against intervention in the periphery would be worth observing even if the United States enjoyed the kind of economic surpluses it once did, but those surpluses are a thing of the past. It is true that military spending is not the sole cause of the inability of the nation to live within its means; it is equally apparent, however, that this inability reflects profound structural causes that pose a serious, long-term threat to the well-being of Americans and to the stability of the world financial system. The continuing budget deficits represent a profound disorder within the American body politic, a fundamental disequilibrium between the wants of the people and their willingness to sustain the sacrifices necessary to secure those wants. As a consequence of this disorder, interest payments on the debt have been far and away the most explosive expenditure of government in the 1980s. Although there is no reason to suppose that the needs of future generations will be any less exigent than our own, we persist in a policy of financial profligacy that can be defended only on this assumption.

Next to the existence of a formidable national security establishment itself, no feature of our current position would have so astonished and mortified the statesmen of the late eighteenth and nineteenth centuries as this propensity, in a period of peace, to run ceaselessly into debt. That propensity, unless reversed, will lead, sooner or later, to "great and convulsive revolutions of empire"[3]— revolutions that will adversely affect the core, as opposed to the peripheral, interests of the nation. Under the circumstances, it seems evident that military expenditures should meet the test of necessity. If current military expenditures were subjected to a rule in which both wars and the preparation for war were considered as something to be paid out of current expenditures, so that avarice might calculate the expenses of ambition, we would be in a far better position to judge the weight of these necessities and the value of these ambitions.

* * *

There is no reason today why a skepticism about military intervention may not coexist with a stance that is internationalist in other respects—one that recognizes the necessity of cooperation among the great representative democracies to preserve an open global trading system and to contend with a host of other functional problems. At the same time, however, and more disturbingly, there is also no reason to suppose that an increasingly nationalistic public, resolutely opposed to foreign aid and increasingly attracted by protectionism, will also be opposed to the use of American military power. As long as interventions, on the model of the gulf war, promise to be relatively painless in blood and treasure, they might well enjoy substantial support from a public that is otherwise growing more isolationist.

Concern over the fate of free institutions and the conditions of

---

[3] Alexander Hamilton, "Second Report on the Public Credit," January 20, 1795, *Papers on Public Credit, Commerce, and Finance,* Samuel McKee, Jr., and J. Harview Williams, eds. (Indianapolis: Bobbs-Merrill, 1957), p. 151.

world order will certainly continue to inform the American approach to foreign policy. Given the role that order and liberty have always played in reflections on the American purpose, such concern is both inevitable and appropriate. In pursuit of this concern, however, military power has assumed a role that is excessive in the light of traditional conceptions of the national purpose. In making force the primary basis of our power and influence in the world we risk betraying the distinctive purpose of America. The progressive expansion of the ends on behalf of which force is threatened or employed, whether on behalf of world order, as with Bush, or the extension of freedom, as with Reagan, is a corruption of the original understanding.

This disproportionate emphasis on military power is nowhere more apparent than in the gross disparity between the amount the nation spends on "defense" and the good work it performs to assist nations struggling to make the transition to representative democracy and market systems. Even with the reduction in military forces planned by the Bush administration, the national defense budget authority the administration plans to request between fiscal 1992 and 1996 (in 1992 dollars) amounts to $1,361.7 billion.[4] The economic aid that might make the most significant contribution to the establishment and growth of free institutions, however, is scrutinized by the public with near fanatical intensity. Billions for defense, it tells the politicians, not one cent for philanthropy. The public consents to these large military expenditures because it is persuaded that they are necessary for America's security, when in fact the greater part is necessary only if it is thought that the nation ought to undertake a vast philanthropic enterprise to order the world through its military power. Insofar as there is an obligation to engage in such philanthropy, however, it might be far better expressed by assisting in the development of the institutions of civil society among those peoples who have given clear evidence of a willingness to make the transition.

That such an opportunity presents itself today is clear. The waves of democratization that have swept across Eastern Europe, the Soviet Union, and Latin America offer a chance, which may prove fleeting, to solidify and stabilize free institutions through peaceful measures.[5] Sadly, however, the nation appears unwilling to make the tangible commitments of resources that would assist in the reconstruction of these economies and thus support their experiments in freedom. Given the scale of our own domestic problems,

    [4] See William W. Kaufmann and John D. Steinbruner, *Decisions for Defense: Prospects for a New Order* (Washington, D.C.: The Brookings Institution, 1991), pp. 37–38.
    [5] See James Schlesinger, "New Instabilities, New Priorities," *Foreign Policy*, No. 85 (Winter, 1991–92), pp. 3–24. Schlesinger recommends that priority in reconstruction aid be given to Eastern Europe.

such an attitude is surely understandable, even if regrettable. Less understandable, and even harder to justify, is the belief that our new calling, under the novel circumstances created by the end of the cold war, is to create a universal alliance against aggression, enforced by American military power. To refuse both tasks, under the exigent pressures of domestic crisis, would at least give consistency to the rejection of internationalism. But to refuse the one, while embracing the other, can only be deplored.

The outlook that informs American foreign policy today, of which Bush's vision of a new world order is a vivid expression, assumes that aggression, wherever it might occur, is a disease to which this nation must supply the antidote. A more detached view would allow us to see that aggression normally generates powerful opposing forces among those most immediately threatened by it. Rare are the occasions in which a hegemonic power, in the manner of Napoleon or Hitler, either aspires to or has a chance of realizing the mastery of the state system. It is not generally true, as Harry Truman said in 1951, that "if history has taught us anything, it is that aggression anywhere in the world is a threat to peace everywhere in the world."[6] It is not generally true, as George Bush said in 1990, that "every act of aggression unpunished . . . strengthens the forces of chaos and lawlessness that, ultimately, threaten us all."[7] This kind of universalism is the bane of American foreign policy in the twentieth century. If history has taught us anything, it is precisely the contrary of the lesson drawn by those who urge us to be the world's policeman. It is that peace is normally divisible and that conflicts, whatever their origin, are normally of merely local or regional significance. To convert a lesson drawn from America's experience with the totalitarian great powers of this century into a general rule applicable to smaller powers is an altogether misleading basis of national security policy.

The rejection of a *Pax Universalis* does not require a return to the rule of nonentanglement characteristic of nineteenth century American diplomacy. It need not, in particular, entail a withdrawal from the security commitments with which the United States encumbered itself during the cold war. Power does entail responsibility. If the architects of the new world order, who have often recurred to this maxim, have forgotten that one of these responsibilities is a restrained and moderate attitude toward the use of force, the maxim does nevertheless contain an important truth.

The principal aim of American security policy today ought to be a devolution of substantial responsibilities to alliance partners,

[6] Address of April 11, 1951, excerpted in Thomas G. Paterson, ed., *Major Problems in American Foreign Policy, Vol. II: Since 1914* (Lexington, Mass.: D. C. Heath, 1989), p. 408.

[7] President Bush, "Remarks at a Fundraising Luncheon for Rep. Bill Grant, Sept. 6, 1990, *Weekly Compilation of Presidential Documents* 26, no. 36, p. 1331.

together with the retention of existing security commitments. Such a devolution of power was presumably a principal aim of American policy during much of the cold war. If it was deemed a sensible aspiration in the midst of a hegemonial conflict, it is difficult to see why it should be rejected today. The expectation of American policy would be that the states with which we have security commitments are not thereby relieved of the obligation to assume primary responsibility for their own defense. Such an aim would make possible a far more substantial reduction in defense expenditures than that contemplated by the Bush administration, but it would not gratuitously introduce elements of instability where stability now prevails.

Though the Bush administration has not repudiated the principle of devolution in theory, its attitude in practice has been far more ambivalent. During the Iraqi crisis, it made little effort to find even a partial substitute for American power in the capabilities of regional states. It has looked with skepticism and a thinly veiled disapproval on the formation of a joint Franco-German force within the confines of the Western European Union, seeing such a force as a threat to American predominance in NATO. In its plans for rapidly deployable forces, there is little hint of the desirability of introducing policies, on the model of the Nixon Doctrine, that have as their aim either a division of labor or a devolution of responsibility. A *Pax Universalis*, after all, could hardly be sustained on the basis of such modest aspirations.

* * *

It is not only the traditional attitude toward world order and American security that might be partially rehabilitated in current circumstances, but the nation's traditional outlook toward the spread of free institutions. Such a renovation of American policy would represent a difficult undertaking; there is today a widespread consensus that it is our duty to demand of foreign states far-reaching reforms in their domestic policy on behalf of human rights. The main difference arises over the means by which this end may be pursued. A coup in Haiti, repression in China, apartheid in South Africa, communism in Cuba—all call forth the impulse to punish, whether that punishment takes the form of economic sanctions, the withholding (or withdrawal) of diplomatic recognition, or even, in some circumstances, the use of force. This impulse is not the exclusive possession of either the Right or Left in this country. On several occasions, the Democrats have outbid the Republicans in their denunciations of wrongdoing by foreign states, though they have shied away from forcible measures. Just as the proponents of the new world order have appropriated the Hamiltonian tradition of military preparedness and corrupted it through the lavish expansion (or universalization) of the American security frontier, so the proponents of nonforcible sanctions on behalf of human rights have also corrupted the Jeffersonian tradition of peaceable coercion.

Although Jefferson did look forward to the subversive effects that the example of free institutions would have on other peoples, he never linked economic sanctions and nonrecognition by them to changes in the internal character of foreign states. That link was first made by Woodrow Wilson.

A policy of economic sanctions on behalf of human rights today carries four main dangers. First, the infliction of severe economic deprivation on other states may give rise to widespread suffering, objectionable on humanitarian grounds particularly when resorted to with such readiness by the rich against the poor. Second, such suffering hardly seems commensurate with the benefits gained in promoting liberalization.[8] Third, such policies may lead to consequences we are unwilling to address, as it did in 1991 when intervention in Haiti produced refugees the administration had no intention of receiving (until temporarily forced to do so by a federal court). Finally, the demand that foreign states conform to a liberal or democratic standard may ultimately lead to war if nonforcible methods fail. These considerations may not justify in all cases a return to the rules governing recognition and intervention in the internal affairs of other states characteristic of nineteenth century American diplomacy; they do, however, justify a far more skeptical attitude toward the now well-nigh irresistible call for economic sanctions on behalf of liberty.

The traditional outlook was admittedly austere. It accorded recognition to foreign governments if they met the test of effectiveness and adhered to their international obligations. It refrained from intervention in the internal affairs of other states. It assumed an obligation to teach by example, thus directing primary attention to reforming the ills of American society while aiming for the "high, plain, yet dizzy ground that separates influence from intervention."[9] It was universalist in the sense that it assumed that the philosophical assumptions underlying the institutions of civil freedom were in principal open to all humanity, if humanity would have the wit to

---

[8] Commercial contacts with repressive states, such as China and South Africa, do encourage liberalizing tendencies. Such tendencies are seldom powerful enough to sweep everything before them, but then neither are punitive economic sanctions. Though each case is sufficiently different that it is difficult to make generalizations, three general considerations may be urged on behalf of the maintenance of commercial contacts even with repressive states. One is that such contacts help build the foundations of a civil society in preparation for the day when the old regime falls apart or feels impelled to moderate its repressive conduct. A second is that such contacts increase the likelihood of peaceful as opposed to revolutionary change. The latter seldom issues in a civil society, even if the apparatus of repressive power is swept away in violent upheaval. A third is that such contacts normally give dissident groups a window on the world that a severing of such ties might otherwise deny them.

[9] Rufus Choate, "A Discourse Commemorative of Daniel Webster," July 27, 1853, *The Works of Rufus Choate*, Samuel Gilman Brown, ed. (Boston: Little, Brown and Co., 1862, 2 vols.), I, p. 520.

see them. But it went not abroad, in search of monsters to destroy. It understood that to do so would entail an insensible change in the fundamental maxims of American policy "from *liberty* to *force*."[10]

Our recent experience has not refuted the wisdom embodied in this traditional outlook. It was the example of a prosperous and free Western civilization, built on the basis of principles recognizably American, that ensured the doom of communism. A patient policy of military containment played a very important role in the success of this policy, but the efficient cause lay elsewhere, in the power of example. Silenced for a time by military power, that example proved in the end to be "elastic, irrepressible, and invulnerable to the weapons of ordinary warfare."[11]

The old method, however, no longer has the appeal it once did. The irony of the present moment is that, while our own maxims are in danger of changing from liberty to force, free institutions have captured the imagination of peoples throughout the world. We may indeed deceive ourselves in thinking that this development augurs the "end of history"—understood as the permanent ascendancy of liberal institutions and as the endpoint of mankind's ideological evolution—but there is little doubt that the ideas of representative democracy and of the system of natural liberty do have an extraordinary appeal and power in the world today. If seen from the perspective of the traditional conception of the American purpose, such a development must appear profoundly gratifying. Yet we are willing to offer very little to solidify this auspicious development, nor have we seen it as an opportunity to rid the nation of the real and imagined necessities acted upon during fifty years of struggle with the totalitarian powers. Instead, the end of the cold war, which both vindicated the traditional American purpose and sharply diminished threats to American security, is seen as an opportunity to create a putative universal alliance against aggression, enforced by American military power.

This enterprise, so often justified as a vindication of the American purpose, represents its betrayal. It prefigures, in fact, the end of American history. For though we may be assured that history as such will never end, particular histories end all the time. The momentary achievements of men and nations may live on in memory for a time, but in the normal course of events they are forgotten or survive only as objects of curiosity to antiquarians. The proud boast of American statecraft was once that we were different in this

[10] John Quincy Adams, *An Address Delivered at the Request of a Committee of the Citizens of Washington, on the Occasion of Reading the Declaration of Independence* (Washington, D.C.: Davis and Force, 1821), p. 29.

[11] Daniel Webster, "The Greek Revolution," January 19, 1824, in B. F. Tefft, ed., *The Speeches of Daniel Webster* (Philadelphia: Porter & Coates, 1854), p. 134.

respect, that we would not forget the admonitions of the Founding Fathers and their successors, nor suffer the basic principles of the American experiment to undergo corruption. American history will come to an end when these sentiments no longer animate our political life.

A Defensible Defense: America's Grand Strategy After the Cold War

ROBERT J. ART

The Cold War is over and the United States won it. Now, after its forty-five year battle with the Soviet Union, what should the United States do with its power?[1]

Should it promote a new era of world politics in which collective security really works? Should it use every means at its disposal, including military force, to spread democracy around the globe, now that communism is dead as an ideological alternative? Should it continue to combat the growing forces of economic nationalism and guard against the ever-present potential for the spread of nuclear weapons? Or should it instead forget about all those goals, retreat into an isolationist posture, bring all its troops home from overseas and, safe behind its nuclear shield, enjoy the benefits of the huge North American market and concentrate on its own pressing domestic problems and social ills? Exactly where on the continuum between the two grand alternatives—unbridled internationalism and constricted isolationism—should the United States draw the line?[2]

From *International Security*. Spring 1991 (Vol. 15, No. 4). © 1991 by the President and Fellows of Harvard College and of the Massachusetts Institute of Technology. Reprinted by permission of MIT Press, Cambridge, Massachusetts. Portions of the text and some footnotes have been omitted.

For their insightful comments, I am especially grateful to John J. Mearsheimer and Stephen Van Evera. I am also indebted to the participants at the conference on "America's Foreign Policy Towards the Year 2000," April 28–29, 1990, sponsored by Brandeis University's Center for International and Comparative Studies, where an early version of this paper was presented; and to the National Security Seminar of the Olin Institute for Strategic Studies, Center for International Affairs, Harvard University, which provided much food for thought about American grand strategy. For research support, I thank the United States Institute of Peace.

¹ One can date the formal end of the Cold War in the fall of 1990, when Germany was unified on October 3 and when, on November 18, the NATO Alliance and the Warsaw Pact signed the Treaty on Conventional Armed Forces in Europe at a meeting of the thirty-four-member Conference on Security and Cooperation in Europe (CSCE). See Craig R. Whitney, "The Legacy of Helsinki," *New York Times*, November 19, 1990, p. A6, for the terms of the treaty. The arguments I make in this article are predicated on the assumptions that the Cold War is over and that Soviet troops will completely withdraw from Germany and Eastern Europe in the next few years. My arguments will not be undercut if the Soviet Union becomes a right-wing military or civilian dictatorship that treats its citizens harshly or that brutally uses its army to hold the Soviet Union together, so long as such a dictatorship does not return to an aggressive, ideologically-driven, expansionist foreign policy. However, even though such harsh internal policies would not bring a return to the Cold War, they would certainly produce a marked deterioration in U.S.-Soviet relations.

² For a short statement of the traditional isolationist position, see Patrick J.

THE REALM OF GRAND STRATEGY

The best way to deal with all these questions is to decide what foreign policy goals the United States should pursue in the post–Cold War era; and then to determine the instruments best suited to attain them. In this article, I lay out a broad range of potential U.S. goals, but do not deal with all the instruments of statecraft. Instead, I concentrate solely on how America's military power, and especially a continuing U.S. military presence overseas, can facilitate the attainment of its goals. I thus take an internationalist, not an isolationist, posture.[3]

By analyzing the relation between American goals and U.S. military power, I enter the realm of what has properly been called "grand strategy"; but I do so in a way different from some other analysts. Some employ a restrictive definition of grand strategy that specifies only the threats to a state and the military means to deal with them.[4] Others use a broader definition that specifies the threats to a nation's security and then details the military, political and economic means to meet them.[5] In this article, I employ the term grand strategy in neither of these senses. Rather I use it, first, to specify the goals that a state should pursue, including both security and non-security goals, and, second, to delineate how military power can serve these goals.[6] Unlike the first definition, mine

---

Buchanan, "America First—and Second, and Third," *The National Interest,* No. 19 (Spring 1990), pp. 77–82. For a carefully argued, comprehensive statement why the United States can now safely revert to isolationism, see Eric A. Nordlinger, *Masterly Inactivity: A "National" Security Strategy* (forthcoming). For a statement of the liberal internationalist position, see Charles William Maynes, "America without the Cold War," *Foreign Policy,* No. 78 (Spring 1990), pp. 3–25. A most eloquent argument for a significantly diminished world role for the United States is Robert W. Tucker, "1989 and All That," in Nicholas X. Rizopoulos, ed., *Sea-Changes: American Foreign Policy in a World Transformed* (New York: Council on Foreign Relations, 1990), pp. 204–238. For a well-reasoned and balanced statement why the United States must continue to provide world leadership, see Joseph S. Nye, Jr., *Bound to Lead: The Changing Nature of American Power* (New York: Basic Books, 1990).

[3] In this essay, I use the term "isolationism" to define a situation in which the United States has no *peacetime* binding military alliances with other powers and has withdrawn its army and air power to its own territory. The U.S. navy would continue to show some presence around the world, although it would not maintain a constant presence in any given place. I do not, therefore, suggest by the term that the United States is uninvolved politically with the rest of the world, nor that it pursues economic autarky. This is consistent with the traditional use of the term: a military, not a political or economic, withdrawal to the nation's borders. It is in this sense that Robert W. Tucker employs the term for what remains the best published treatment of the pros and cons of an isolationist posture for the United States. See Tucker, *A New Isolationism: Threat or Promise?* (New York: Universe Books, 1972).

[4] This is the definition employed by John J. Mearsheimer in *Liddel Hart and the Weight of History* (Ithaca: Cornell University Press, 1988), p. 17.

[5] This is the meaning employed by Barry R. Posen in *The Sources of Military Doctrine: France, Britain, and Germany between the World Wars* (Ithaca: Cornell University Press, 1984), p. 13.

[6] Throughout this article, I use the word "security" to refer to the ability of the

includes goals other than simply security; unlike the second, my purview is restricted to military means. Non-military instruments are as important to statecraft as the military one, but I do not treat them as part of grand strategy, because I wish to preserve the useful distinction between grand strategy and foreign policy, which includes all of the goals and all of the instruments of statecraft.

Important questions have been raised about the role that military power can play in America's peacetime foreign policy (regardless of the recent U.S. and allied use of force against Iraq). More than a decade before the Cold War ended, many analysts held that U.S. military power had lost a great deal of its utility in America's relations with Western Europe and Japan.[7] The end of the Cold War, many argued, will devalue the role of U.S. military power even more, not only in America's relations with these nations, but with most other nations as well. With a severely diminished (or perhaps non-existent) Soviet military threat, states will have little need for American protection; consequently, the United States will no longer have the capacity to extract political leverage from its provision of security to others. This type of analysis leads to a compelling case for America's military retrenchment. But does it also lead to a compelling case for isolationism?

The proper way to answer this question and to set forth America's grand strategy after the Cold War is to answer four questions: (1) What interests does the United States have, now that its major adversary is defeated? (2) What threats to those interests can we now foresee? (3) What military strategies are best suited to counter the foreseeable threats? and (4) What military forces are required to execute these strategies?[8] In this article, I deal primarily with the first two questions and only secondarily with the third and fourth. Although I argue against an isolationist policy, I do prescribe retrenchment, because I call for a residual, not a warfighting, U.S. overseas military presence. Once America's broad interests and the

---

United States to protect its homeland from attack, invasion, conquest, or destruction. I use the term to mean the physical protection of a nation's homeland, and primarily in reference to those military capabilities sufficient for deterrence of an attack, or defense against one should it occur. Some may argue that this definition of security is too narrow, and that it should include items such as the economic health of the nation, its access to raw materials, the flowering of its ideological predispositions abroad, and so on. The problem with this usage, however, is that it empties the concept of security of any meaning. To say that practically everything is related to making a nation feel secure is to say that security includes practically anything. Restricting the term to the meaning I suggest gives it analytical clarity and policy utility.

[7] See, for example, Richard Rosecrance, *The Rise of The Trading State: Commerce and Conquest in the Modern World* (New York: Basic Books, 1986); and Robert O. Keohane and Joseph S. Nye, Jr., *Power and Interdependence* (Boston: Little, Brown, 1977), chap. 2.

[8] Steven E. Miller suggested this framework to me some time ago, and I continue to find it useful.

threats to them are defined, the general outlines of the proper military strategy and the requisite forces will become clear.

I make six arguments in this article:

First: for the indefinite future, the United States has five specific interests, summarized in Table 1. They are: (1) protection of the U.S. homeland from attack; (2) continued prosperity based in part on preservation of an open world economy; (3) assured access to Persian Gulf oil; (4) prevention of war among the great powers of Europe and the Far East, and preservation of the independence of Israel and South Korea; and (5) where feasible, the promotion of democratic governments and the overthrow of governments engaged in the mass murder of their citizenry.[9]

Table 1.   Interests, Threats, and a U.S. Presence Overseas.

U.S. Interest	Prime Threat to U.S. Interest	Major Purpose of Overseas Forces	Nature of the Argument for U.S. Forces Overseas
1. Protect U.S. homeland destruction	Spread of nuclear weapons	Selectively extend deterrence to retard spread	Based on high cost of low-probability events
2. Preserve prosperity based on international economic openness	Economic nationalism	Reduce others' relative gains worries to preserve stability	Hedge bets because of indeterminate arguments about today's interdependence
3. Assure access to Persian Gulf oil	Near-monopoly control by regional hegemon	Deter attack and/or conquest of others	Simple deterrence
4. Prevent certain wars	Great-power wars in Europe and Far East; conquest of Israel and South Korea	Deter attack and/or conquest of others	Added insurance for low-probability events
5. Where feasible, promote democratic institutions and certain humanitarian values abroad	Other governments mass-murdering their citizens	Intervention in other states' internal affairs	Humanitarian motives

[9] There is a sixth interest: protection of the global environment, particularly by slowing the rate of global warming (the "enhanced greenhouse effect") and by stopping the destruction of the ozone layer. I do not deal with the global environment in this article, because there is little that American military power or an overseas U.S. military presence can do to deal with either threat to the environment. But I do agree with those who hold that the projected effects of ozone depletion and global warming are severe. The most important thing the United States can do to stop the

Second: As a general rule, the United States does not have an interest in spreading democracy by intervening militarily in the internal affairs of states; nor should it seek to impose peace among all states in every region. Spreading democracy by forceful means can too easily become a blank check for unbridled military interventionism. Imposing peace, either through a global collective security system or through unilateral American action, is a surefire recipe for assumption of the global policeman role.

Third: Nuclear weapons have severed the connection between America's security and the balance of power on the Eurasian land mass and have thereby invalidated traditional geopolitical logic. The only serious threat to U.S. security, as I have defined the term, is the spread of nuclear weapons to crazy Third World statesmen or fanatical terrorists.[10] To help retard their spread, the United States should maintain a selective overseas military presence.

Fourth: There is a case for a U.S. military presence in the Far East and Europe to help preserve the open economic order among the rich industrialized nations. The rationale for this presence, however, rests more on a general argument for insurance and reassurance than on any definitive theory about the utility of military power for the preservation of international economic openness, or on any definitive conclusions about the resiliency of this era's economic interdependence.

Fifth: Assured access to Persian Gulf oil, the long-term protection of Israel, and the historical commitment to South Korea call for some type of American military presence in those areas. The nature of the American presence in the Gulf will depend on the postwar constellation of political-military forces in the region, but it should occur within a multinational United Nations format. To assure the security of South Korea from its northern counterpart, a much smaller U.S. military presence is all that is required. To provide better protection of Israel, the United States should sign a military

---

destruction of the ozone layer is to see that the 1987 Montreal Protocol on Substances that Deplete the Ozone Layer, and the 1990 amendments to it, are fully implemented. The most important things the United States can do to slow global warming are to increase energy efficiency, reduce reliance on fossil fuels that pour carbon dioxide into the atmosphere, and foster international measures that will enable and encourage other states to do likewise. The best source on the current state of scientific knowledge about global warming is the Intergovernmental Panel on Climate Change (IPCC), World Meteorological Organization and United Nations Environment Programme (J. T. Houghton, G. J. Jenkins, and J. J. Ephraums, eds.) *Climate Change— The IPCC Scientific Assessment* (Cambridge: Cambridge University Press, 1990).

[10] Throughout this discussion, I use the term "spread" rather than "proliferation" to avoid the latter's implication of rapid or quick multiplication. Because the number of states that could quickly go nuclear is not large, and because so few states have gone nuclear, "spread" is a more accurate description of what has happened and what could happen. In this choice of terms, I follow the convention set by Kenneth N. Waltz, *The Spread of Nuclear Weapons: More May Be Better*, Adelphi Paper No. 171 (London: International Institute of Strategic Studies [IISS], 1981), p. 1.

treaty with Israel, station a residual American force there, and then cause Israel to disgorge the West Bank and Gaza.

Sixth: Overall, the United States needs a much smaller peacetime overseas military presence than it has had. With the Cold War's demise, the United States will be providing to others primarily insurance, reassurance, and stability, not large amounts of security. But it must retain the capability to reinforce those forces rapidly should the need arise.

In the first part of this article, I analyze the security threats to the United States and how to deal with them; in the second part, I show how a continuing overseas U.S. presence can help preserve an open international economic order; in the third part, I define the limits that should be put on any future American military interventions; and in the conclusion, I lay out the general principles of the post-Cold War strategy.

ENSURING AMERICA'S SECURITY IN THREE ERAS

To assess how the United States should ensure its security in the future, it is important to analyze what threats it has faced and what actions it has taken in the past. Prior to 1990, the United States passed through two security eras. The first was the geopolitical era, which lasted from 1789 to 1945; the second, the Cold War era, lasted from 1945 to 1990. In the geopolitical era, the United States faced two potential threats: invasion and conquest by a Eurasian hegemon; or slow strangulation caused by a hegemon's imposition of a global blockade. After about 1900, the first geopolitical threat was highly improbable, and the second problematical. During the Cold War era, America's possession of nuclear weapons invalidated both these geopolitical threats, although many argued the contrary.[11] The only possible threat was nuclear attack from the Soviet Union, but this was never very likely.

After the formal ending of the Cold War in 1990, the United States entered its third security era. As in the Cold War period, the geopolitical threats remain insignificant, and the Soviet threat is markedly diminished. The only potential threats to U.S. security will come from "crazy" nuclear states or nuclear-armed terrorist groups. Although neither threat seems likely, some hedging against them is wise. These conclusions are summarized in Table 2.

Threats in the Cold War Era

During the Cold War era, the United States faced no geopolitical threats from resource aggregation or slow strangulation, but it acted

---

[11] George Kennan's writings in the late 1940s were excellent examples of the (mis-)application of geopolitical logic to the nuclear era. For Kennan's argument at the time, see John Lewis Gaddis, *Strategies of Containment: A Critical Appraisal of Postwar American National Security Policy* (New York: Oxford University Press, 1982), chap. 2.

Table 2. Threats to U.S. Security During Three Eras.

Type of Threat	The Geopolitical Era (Pre-1945)	The Cold War Era (1945–90)	The Post-Cold War Era (Post-1990)
1. Invasion and conquest	Quite difficult after 1900	Practically zero probability	Practically zero probability
2. Slow strangulation through a global blockade	Of indeterminate feasibility	Practically zero probability	Practically zero probability
3. Nuclear attack			
From the Soviet Union		Not probable	Highly improbable
From other nations or subnational groups		Highly improbable	Not probable

as if it did. It constructed military forces more suitable for geopolitical threats than for nuclear threats.

From 1950 to 1990, the United States maintained a huge military establishment with: (1) a large intercontinental strategic nuclear force having significant counterforce capabilities; (2) thousands of tactical nuclear weapons deployed in Eurasia; (3) a huge navy, far superior to anything that the Soviets ever deployed, that dominated the world's seas; (4) a standing army of over 750,000 troops, with a significant number of heavily armored divisions stationed in the heart of Central Europe to counter any possible Soviet thrust westward; (5) a formidable and versatile air force, much of it stationed overseas, capable of intercontinental bombing, deep interdiction, close air support on the battlefield, and preservation of air superiority; and (6) a sea and air power projection capability that enabled the United States to move its conventional forces with relative ease around the globe. The strategic nuclear forces provided significant counterforce capabilities to bolster the credibility of extended deterrence of Soviet conventional attacks on U.S. allies. The tactical nuclear forces were intended to counter the Soviet Union's perceived huge advantage in conventional forces. The large navy, air force, and army were deployed to fight a long conventional war in Central Europe to stalemate and thereby dissuade a Soviet conventional attack there. In constructing its forces during the Cold War era, the United States acted as if geopolitical logic was still at work.

Had the United States been concerned only with its own security, and not that of Western Europe and Japan, it would have needed only: (1) a relatively small strategic nuclear force, a reasonable portion of it invulnerable to destruction by a Soviet first strike;

(2) a modest air force and navy able to sink any Soviet surface ships that attacked across the Pacific; and (3) a small army to deal with any minor border incursions from hemispheric neighbors or other states. The nuclear forces would deter attack and could defend against a large one; the conventional forces could defend against small-scale attacks if they materialized.

Because the United States fought the Cold War to preserve the political independence of Western Europe and Japan, not its own, it chose the first rather than the second posture. Even if the United States had permitted the Soviet Union to dominate Eurasia, it could have remained secure. Its standard of living, however, would probably have been lower, because there would have been less trade with Europe and Japan; and its psychological comfort would have been less, because far fewer great power democracies would have existed. But in fact, America's security would not have suffered with isolationism, because it had nuclear weapons.

THE ABSENCE OF GEOPOLITICAL THREATS. Two traditional arguments have been offered for why the United States could not have pursued isolationism and why, therefore, it still had to balance power in Eurasia. The first involves power projection; the second, resource aggregation.

Some have argued that in the early postwar period, because the United States lacked long-range bombers, it needed Western Europe and Japan: they provided the bases from which to threaten the Soviets with nuclear retaliation. A modified form of geopolitical logic still obtained because the United States did not yet have a viable intercontinental capability. Others have argued that for its own long-term interests, the United States could not permit Europe and Japan to come under the domination of the Soviet Union, because then the Soviets would have had much of the world's industrial resources and, as a consequence, could have brought the United States ultimately to heel.

Both of these arguments are suspect. With regard to the basing argument: if, in the early postwar era, the United States lacked an adequate long-range retaliatory capability against the Soviet Union, so, too, did the Soviet Union against the United States. Neither could easily threaten the other with nuclear bombardment. Each had rudimentary intercontinental capabilities against the other only by launching suicidal, one-way nuclear bombing missions. The United States could have done so in 1945, four years earlier than the Soviet Union.[12] But mutual nuclear deterrence would work with

---

[12] As early as January 1950, the Joint Intelligence Committee (JIC) of the Joint Chiefs of Staff (JCS) estimated that "without refueling, the Tu-4s [Soviet bombers] can reach every important industrial, urban, and governmental control center in the United States on a one-way mission basis," and that "the Soviets would not hesitate to expend airplanes and crews as necessary to deliver atomic bombs on selected targets in the United States." Quoted in *Appendix B, JIC 5-2, 20 January 1950*, JCS

suicidal bombing missions, no less than with round-trip bombing missions. Before the United States acquired an intercontinental bombing capability, the bases in Europe made it easier for the United States to attack the Soviet Union and thereby gave it a relative advantage. But the advantage was not essential to America's security and was of import, in the final analysis, only because it was used to protect the Europeans and the Japanese from a potential Soviet conventional attack. In short, until the mid-1950s, when the United States finally began to deploy a reasonably reliable intercontinental retaliatory force, America's European bomber bases were for the Europeans, not the Americans.

With regard to the resource aggregation argument: Soviet domination of the Eurasian land mass would not have posed an immediate or even a medium-term security threat to the United States. U.S. forces could fairly easily have interdicted any Soviet conventional naval armada or bomber force directed against the American homeland. Spykman's argument that a combined German-Japanese invasion of the United States would have been quite difficult applies with even greater force to a potential Soviet invasion. An American nuclear attack could have wiped out any Soviet invasion armada in one fell swoop, and it would have carried little risk of Soviet nuclear retaliation, because it would have been an attack on maritime forces on the high seas, not military forces or population centers on Soviet territory. This type of nuclear defense would have been highly credible, devastatingly effective, and difficult to retaliate against. In short, during the early years of the Cold War, the United States could easily have deterred or defeated any attempted Soviet nuclear or conventional attack.

The only arguable geopolitical threat to America's security in both the early and late phases of the Cold War was strangulation, not invasion. But here, too, nuclear weapons made slow strangulation nearly impossible. Nuclear weapons make the cost of defense and deterrence easy and cheap, enabling states that have them to turn their energies to tasks more economically productive than building military forces. When the low costs of nuclear defense and deterrence are combined with the flexibility of a modern economy in finding substitutes for critical goods and raw materials (as the Germans dramatically demonstrated in World War II), the staying power of modern economies becomes formidable. Two more factors—America's abundance of natural resources and the combined oil resources of the western hemisphere (in Venezuela, Mexico, the United States, and Canada)—make Spykman's ultimate nightmare, of a Eurasian hegemon slowly strangling the United States by a

Files, 1948–50, pp. 26–27, National Security Archive, Washington, D.C. See also Robert J. Art, *Nuclear Weapons and U.S. Grand Strategy* (manuscript), chap. 3

global embargo, even more of a chimera. This does not mean that matters would have been rosy for the United States had the Soviet Union become a Eurasian hegemon after World War II, only that they would not likely have been catastrophic.

THE EFFICACY OF NUCLEAR DETERRENCE. From the outset of the nuclear age, the logic of nuclear deterrence gripped statesmen even if their military services, due to vested interests, were slow to follow suit. Truman viewed nuclear weapons as terror weapons of last resort, and there is no reason to believe that Stalin thought differently. The United States has been secure since 1945 because nuclear deterrence reduced the frequency of crises and de-escalated them when they occurred. It has been the fear that crises could get out of control and escalate to total nuclear war that has prevented them from doing so. Nuclear statesmen can have no illusions about what a general nuclear war would mean for their nation. As a consequence, they run scared, not safe.[13]

Even if one rejects this argument for the first ten to fifteen years of the Cold War, when geopolitical logic and nuclear logic coexisted uneasily and ambiguously, it is a much stronger argument for the period after 1960. By then, the United States no longer relied on overseas bases for retaliation, because it had deployed ballistic missile submarines and land-based intercontinental ballistic missiles. The overseas bases it retained served primarily as symbols of the American commitment to deter attack on others. They were hostages for America's allies, not the first line of defense for the United States.

A retrospective look at the Cold War era thus yields two important reconsiderations. First, the United States enjoyed a greater degree of security than is often thought. There were no real geopolitical threats. The period of perceived maximum danger (1947–62), when crises were more frequent between the Americans and the Soviets, coincided with a period of American nuclear superiority. The years of relative calm (1963–90) were free of severe direct U.S.-Soviet confrontation, except for a few days during the October 1973 Middle East war.

Second, the United States continued to provide security to the Germans and the Japanese long after their economic recovery had made it feasible for them to supply their own. The United States did so partly for historical reasons (to prevent the World War II aggressors from rearming without constraints); partly for stability reasons

[13] For more on this point, see Robert J. Art, "Between Assured Destruction and Nuclear Victory," *Ethics*, Vol. 95, No. 3 (April 1985), pp. 497–516; Robert Jervis, *The Meaning of the Nuclear Revolution: Statecraft and the Prospects for Armageddon* (Ithaca: Cornell University Press, 1989), chap. 1; Richard K. Betts, *Nuclear Blackmail and Nuclear Balance* (Washington, D.C.: Brookings, 1987); and Kenneth N. Waltz, "Nuclear Myths and Political Realities," *American Political Science Review*, Vol. 84, No. 3 (September 1990), pp. 731–745.

(to provide an American presence in Europe and the Far East to assuage the fears of Germany's and Japan's neighbors, and to help foster economic openness); and partly for nonproliferation reasons (to extend the American nuclear umbrella to Germany and Japan so they would not feel impelled to acquire their own nuclear weapons). All three reasons were important, but the third is the only one with any direct bearing on America's security. The American concern was that if Germany and Japan went nuclear, the precedent thereby set would dramatically enhance the likelihood of nuclear spread elsewhere. A nuclear-armed West Germany or Japan by itself would not have threatened the United States, especially if they remained allied with the United States; but the prospect that this might speed the spread of nuclear weapons to other states, which might not act responsibly, was unsettling. This spread, although always a possibility, did not proceed very far, and did so only to states that were viewed as responsible citizens, not crazy aggressors.

Thus, throughout the Cold War era, the United States could have deterred or defended against any assault on its own territory; it did not need the Germans, the Japanese, or anyone else to do this. It did not have to protect others out of geopolitical logic, even though it may have thought so at the time. It offered protection partly out of a misconception about the continuing relevance of geopolitical logic, but also out of historical memories, concerns for stability and economic openness, and worries about nuclear spread. If there is a case to be made for isolationism in the nuclear era, it is one that becomes valid nearly immediately after World War II, certainly by the mid-1950s, and definitely by the very early 1960s.

Threats in the Post-Cold War Era

Throughout the Cold War, geopolitical threats were absent; nuclear deterrence worked; and nuclear spread was minimal. As a consequence, the United States remained quite secure. For the post-Cold War era, the nightmares of geopolitics remain irrelevant. America's nuclear deterrent cannot be threatened through conventional means, and no nation would launch a conventional attack on a nuclear-armed United States. The notion of a global blockade by a successful Eurasian hegemon is fanciful because there is no likely candidate for this role. Geopolitical imbalances therefore pose no threat to the United States.

Nuclear threats, however, could imperil America's security. The nuclear menace from the Soviet Union will remain low: if nuclear deterrence worked when U.S.-Soviet tension was high, it will continue to work whether the tension rises again or declines. In the post-Cold War era, therefore, the United States has only to worry about the spread of nuclear weapons to crazy statesmen and ruthless terrorists. How worrisome is either threat?

THE DANGERS OF NUCLEAR SPREAD. If more states acquire nuclear weapons, goes the conventional argument, then the probability of a nuclear war increases and so, too, will the opportunities for terrorists to steal and use them. The chances of things going awry does increase as more people get into the act. In more sophisticated form, the conventional argument stresses five important points about the dangers of nuclear spread. The first two points, associated with the early stages of developing nuclear forces, are viewed as transitional problems that could, in theory, be managed; the third and fourth, dealing with the nature of the Third-World governments that might acquire them, are thought to be more intractable; the fifth, dealing with nuclear terrorism, appears downright frightening.

First, new nuclear forces are not likely to be as secure from preemptive attack as those of the mature nuclear states. Consequently, there will be windows of danger in which states might be tempted to launch preemptive first strikes against an adversary's nuclear forces in order to destroy them. Second, command and control arrangements in new nuclear states are not likely to be state-of-the-art. Consequently, the chances for unauthorized and accidental use will be greater. Third, many would-be Third-World nuclear states do not have governments as stable as those of the more mature nuclear powers. Consequently, this increases the risk that their nuclear weapons could fall into the hands of sub-national groups waging civil war, or terrorist groups taking advantage of political chaos. Fourth, many Third-World would-be nuclear states are involved in implacable regional confrontations in which reason and restraint have been far less prevalent than they have in U.S.-Soviet relations. Consequently, the politically restraining effects that nuclear ownership has imposed on the superpowers might not be strong enough to offset the ambitions, insecurities, hatreds, and fanaticisms that characterize many Third-World conflicts. These dangers all add up to a greater likelihood that nuclear weapons will be used in interstate wars if more states get them.

Fifth, for the case of nuclear terrorism, the argument is both simple and terrifying: terrorists are not "deterrable," only suicidal. They have become terrorists precisely because they have given up all other avenues of influencing the behavior of their adversaries. They consider their own lives and those of their adversaries to be cheap. Even if they do value life, terrorists are hard to identify and difficult to locate. If they cannot be struck, then the threat to retaliate against them becomes empty.

THE SAFETY OF NUCLEAR SPREAD. To this gloomy picture of nuclear spread, three counterarguments can be offered. First is that of Kenneth Waltz: the ownership of nuclear weapons changes the psychology of their possessors and makes them more careful, because they are unable to come up with a way to use the weapons for any benefit. Second is the argument advanced by Robert W. Tucker: even if nuclear wars are more likely, the United States would not necessarily be drawn into them.[14] To these arguments I add a third: to make an effective nuclear threat, terrorists must reveal their identities; and when they do, they can be targeted and therefore deterred. If nuclear spread makes new members of the nuclear club more careful, if the United States can remain outside of any nuclear wars that may occur, and if terrorists can, indeed, be targeted, then the further spread of nuclear weapons presents no additional threat to America's security. The United States can remain indifferent to how many states acquire nuclear weapons, and it has few, if any, security reasons to retain its military alliances and keep its troops overseas.

Waltz has argued that nuclear weapons make both nuclear and conventional war less probable. He asserts that nuclear states are less likely to go to war with one another than conventionally-armed states, because nuclear statesmen clearly understand that any conflict or war might get out of control and go nuclear.[15] Thus, the political caution induced by nuclear ownership operates powerfully, irrespective of the ideology, personal temperament, and political circumstances of a political leader. The fear of known results, if matters were to get out of hand, overwhelms all other factors. The ownership of nuclear weapons makes *all* possessors cautious. As more states acquire nuclear weapons, "they will feel the constraints that present nuclear states have experienced," and the zone of peace will enlarge. Consequently, says Waltz, "the measured spread of nuclear weapons is more to be welcomed than feared."[16]

Even if Waltz is wrong and the spread of nuclear weapons brought nuclear wars, Tucker is skeptical that the United States would be drawn into them. The crux of his argument is that "the effects of these weapons have been to make peace more divisible today than it has been in a very long time."[17] To say that peace is divisible is to say that a war threatens different states in different degrees, and some states not at all. Nuclear weapons are the ultimate divider of peace because they bring nearly absolute security to states that own them. Nuclear states can stay out of wars if they choose because, "in a system governed by balance of deterrent nuclear power . . . isolation and vulnerability to attack are no longer synonymous."[18] If Tucker's position is accepted, then the United States has little to fear about being dragged into other countries' nuclear wars.

Finally, it is not self-evident that an increase in the states possessing nuclear weapons will increase terrorists' chances to steal those weapons; or that if terrorists somehow obtained nuclear

---

[14] See Waltz, *The Spread of Nuclear Weapons*, pp. 10–25; and Tucker, *A New Isolationism*, pp. 39–54.

[15] Waltz, *The Spread of Nuclear Weapons*, p. 12.

[16] Ibid., p. 30.

[17] Tucker, *A New Isolationism*, pp. 55.

[18] Ibid., p. 55.

bombs, they would succeed in nuclear blackmail or nuclear use. Governments that have nuclear weapons have taken great pains to make certain that they are well protected.[19] Certainly there have been lapses; but the record to date is clear: nuclear bombs have not made their way into unauthorized hands. There is no reason to expect that new nuclear states would be so cavalier about their weapons that terrorists could easily capture them. Rather, we should expect precisely the opposite. New nuclear states will not have many bombs at the outset. Those they do have are likely to have been produced in great secrecy and under very tight control. Their delivery systems are likely at first to be vulnerable to preemptive strikes, prompting these governments to take even more extraordinary methods to protect them. It is therefore more probable that new nuclear states will exercise tight control over their nuclear forces.[20]

Even if terrorists somehow arm themselves with nuclear weapons, however, they could not blackmail nuclear states as easily as has been imagined. If a threat to blow up New York City came to the U.S. president as an unsigned message, with a deadline but with no demands to be met, it would hardly be credible. It would look like a crank note. To have credibility, a threat must state the group's political demands, spell out how it expects the demands to be met, and indicate a timetable for meeting the demands. But if a message does all this, would not the identity of the terrorist group—and more importantly the civilians whom it purports to represent—be immediately apparent? The president could make a credible counterthreat: "If New York City is destroyed, I shall destroy the entire group of people whom you claim to represent." Ruthless and coldblooded though it might sound, this threat is no different from what the Americans and the Russians have been saying to one another for forty years. If innocent civilians are not held hostage to nuclear retaliation, then nuclear deterrence will not work against either governments or terrorists. Because terrorists would have to identify themselves by the very act of making the terrorist threat, they make the groups they represent known and targetable, and the threat of retaliation credible.[21]

[19] If the United States drastically reduces the numbers of tactical nuclear weapons it has deployed abroad, as I argue below, they should be easier to protect and there will be far fewer for terrorists to steal.

[20] Nuclear-armed states need to protect their nuclear forces against terrorist or other unauthorized seizure, against unauthorized use, and against preemptive attack. All three are components of the command and control of nuclear forces. We can have confidence that new nuclear states will do as well at the first and second tasks as do mature nuclear states, even though they may not do as well at the third task.

[21] The counter to this argument is that the people represented by the terrorists could be so intermingled with others that they could not be discriminately targeted. Or they might live within a country that the United States would never want to strike. Armenian terrorist threats emanating from Turkey or the Soviet Union might look

Hedging Bets to Retard Nuclear Spread

Both sets of arguments about the effects of nuclear spread are persuasive. I give a slight edge to those who downplay its dangers, but others may lean toward those who worry about them. In an ambiguous situation like this, one hedges one's bets. For nuclear weapons spread, we are dealing with a special class of events: those whose probability of occurrence is quite small, but whose costs are potentially astronomical.[22] Prudent people would avoid taking the risk, albeit small, of the terrible consequences if those who told us that nuclear weapons spread was safe were wrong. Therefore, coping with the spread of nuclear weapons is the second-best solution; halting or retarding their spread is the first-best solution.

Since the advent of nuclear weapons, the United States has chosen the first-best solution and has played the world's leading role in working to prevent their spread. U.S. provision of security to selected states has been an important ingredient in this effort, but there have been many other means by which the United States has tried to retard their spread.[23] These include: extending the American nuclear umbrella to others so that nations do not see themselves vulnerable to nuclear blackmail; providing economic and military aid in order to persuade nations not to go nuclear; supplying peaceful nuclear energy in ways designed to make nations dependent on American nuclear fuel and hence subject to fuel cutoffs if they seek to stray from the nonproliferation path; creating, implementing, and monitoring a worldwide anti-proliferation regime; and policing and sanctioning renegade states, like Iraq, that refuse to give up the nuclear weapons quest.

Effective though all these measures have been, if the United States no longer extended nuclear deterrence over other states, would those states seek to acquire their own nuclear forces? Shorn of American protection but facing a more benign Soviet Union, would Germany and Japan, for example, feel more or less secure? Would Israel, no longer able to count on its tacit alliance with the United States, publicly brandish what it privately wields? Bereft of American troops, would the South Koreans acquire nuclear weapons, as they said they would in the 1980s? If these states went nuclear, would others follow suit, and if so, how quickly? Do we need to posit specific enemies for the states that presently have

---

Armenian terrorist threats emanating from Turkey or the Soviet Union might look different from terrorist threats emanating from Syria, Libya, Iraq, or Iran. One rule, suggested by Stephen Van Evera, is to hold a state responsible for the terrorism emanating from its territory. This is a tough rule, but it would make a government work hard to prevent terrorists from using its territory as a base of operations.

[22] If they occur, such events yield a large expected value, which is the probability of an event's occurrence multiplied by its cost.

[23] See Mitchell Reiss, *Without the Bomb: The Politics of Nuclear Nonproliferation* (New York: Columbia University Press, 1988).

none, like the Germans and the Japanese, to argue that the United States should continue to extend them deterrence? Or do we make the case on the grounds of reassurance and stability and on the proposition that these states would be seen by other would-be nuclear powers as key precedent-setters—dominoes—were they to "fall" to nuclear spread?

These are difficult questions to answer. What is clear is that America's extended deterrence efforts—and hence its ability to stop nuclear spread—have been most successful with those nations where American troops, or their close surrogates, have been stationed: Japan, South Korea, and the nonnuclear nations of Western Europe, especially Germany. Among its close allies, the one nation where extended deterrence has been least successful in stopping nuclear spread is the one in which there have been no American troops: Israel. With no American troops to bolster extended deterrence, Israel has developed nuclear weapons.[24] Thus, sufficient conventional forces symbolizing America's commitment appear to be useful for extending deterrence and for reducing the pressures for national nuclear ownership. American actions, including the stationing of troops overseas, have played a critical role in retarding nuclear weapons spread among key states. Why remove American troops completely from those states, when the consequences could be severe and when the cost of keeping the troops overseas can be relatively cheap?

To keep American troops in Germany and Japan does not mean that the United States should station troops in every nation that threatens to acquire nuclear weapons. That would put the United States into the position of being easily blackmailed and truly becoming the world's policeman. But the United States can provide residual security to those states that have the wherewithal to acquire nuclear forces quickly, to which it has provided security for the last forty-five years, and which would, if they went nuclear, set bad precedents for other would-be nuclear powers. Taking out additional insurance against nuclear weapons spread, then, is the prime, indeed the only, security rationale for a continuing military global role for the United States. It is to the non-security reasons that I now turn.

PRESERVING AN OPEN WORLD ECONOMY

If the first essential goal for the United States in the post–Cold War era is to ensure its security, the second is to preserve the

---

[24] During 1954–55, Israel asked the United States for a military alliance, but the United States refused. The motivations for Israel to go nuclear are not to be found solely in the lack of a formal military alliance with the United States, but surely its absence has played a role. Ensuring that Israel stays in its current ambiguous nuclear posture is one of the reasons why I favor a clear U.S. military alliance with Israel. I outline additional reasons below.

industrialized world's open international economic order. After
World War II, American power helped to create and sustain an
economic system that allowed the factors of production (raw materials, labor, capital, and technology) to move more easily among the
rich industrialized nations. As a consequence, they developed a high
degree of economic interdependence.[25] By enabling the factors of
production to move freely among states, openness led to greater
efficiency in their use and thereby increased the wealth of all nations
that participated in the system. Because it enhances American
prosperity, therefore, openness and the interdependence that results
from it remain vital U.S. interests to be protected.

Must America stay abroad militarily to help preserve this order?
Would economic closure accompany a complete American military
withdrawal from its overseas outposts? To answer these questions,
I look first at how the Cold War helped produce economic openness;
second, at how resilient today's interdependence is by comparing it
with the interdependence of the pre-1914 era; and, third, at how a
residual military presence abroad can help maintain openness.

The Cold War and Economic Openness

OPENNESS VERSUS CONTAINMENT. America's provision of security to its major postwar allies helped bring about the present relatively open economic order.[26] This order developed and matured

[25] I use the term "interdependence" in roughly the same sense that Kenneth N.
Waltz employs it. Waltz says that interdependence refers to the losses and gains that
states experience through their interactions, and to the equality with which the losses
and gains are distributed among them. See Waltz, *Theory of International Politics*
(Reading, Mass.: Addison-Wesley, 1979), pp. 143–144. Waltz, however, emphasizes
the costs of breaking ties; I emphasize the benefits of having ties. My emphasis is
therefore the obverse of his: interdependence is the size of the stake that a state
believes it has in seeing other states' economies prosper, so as to help its own
economy flourish too. Interdependence can be high or low. The higher the perceived
interdependence, the larger a state's stake in the economic well-being of the countries
with which it heavily interacts, and hence the greater the incentives to cooperate for
mutual gain. In a condition of low interdependence, there is little incentive for states
to cooperate because there is little perceived benefit in doing so; and so concerns
about relative gains overwhelm those about absolute gains. Even in a situation of
high interdependence, however, where the incentives to cooperate are strong, the
opportunity for absolute gain does not entirely supplant the concern for relative gain
because, in a condition of anarchy, a state never forgets about how it is doing relative
to others. Instead, in such situations, a state will sacrifice some of the benefits of
cooperation in order to protect its relative position. In situations of high interdependence, exactly how a state balances out its considerations about relative versus
absolute gains depends both on the merits of the particular issue and on how that
issue is thought to be linked to other issues that the state considers vital. For an
empirical demonstration that concerns about relative gains never go away, even
among close allies, see Joseph M. Grieco, *Cooperation Among Nations: Europe,
America, and Non-Tariff Barriers to Trade* (Ithaca: Cornell University Press, 1990).
[26] In analyzing the relation between military power and economic orders, I do not
argue that force is the most important instrument, only that it has some role to play.
It can be of greatest use only when employed with other tools of statecraft. Force is
a blunt instrument, better held at the ready than readily used. Precisely because it

under the American security umbrella because the Cold War facilitated economic integration within Western Europe and economic
openness among Western Europe, North America, and Japan.[27]
American military power was neither the sole nor perhaps even the
most important factor responsible for the present international
economic regime. Also crucial were the conversion of many governments to Keynesian economics; their overwhelming desire to avoid
the catastrophic experience of the great depression of the 1930s and
the global war that came in its wake; the lessons of the 1930s about
how non-cooperative, beggar-thy-neighbor policies ultimately re-
dound to the disadvantage of all; the willingness of the United States
to underwrite the economic costs of setting up the system and of
sustaining it; and the acceptance of the legitimacy of American
leadership by its allies. But even though all these factors were
important, where economic openness began and subsequently flour-
ished most was among the countries that were most closely allied
with the United States against the Soviet Union, that were considered most vital to American interests, and over which the United
States most visibly extended its security umbrella.

Shortly before the end of World War II, the United States, in
conjunction with the British, began to implement its plans for an
open economic order. These included fixed exchange rates and

---

works best when kept in the background but primed for use, its exact influence on
outcomes is never easy to trace. The political effect of military power is akin to a
gravitational field: it is constantly present; it affects all action, but does not predeter-
mine it; and its effects are hard to perceive precisely because it is ever-present. Apart
from waging war, playing chicken, or using force overtly to blackmail, military
power's best role is to back up a nation's political and economic instruments. They
are the tools most appropriate to most of the issues with which most governments
most of the time deal. I therefore take the position that military power is versatile, to
a degree; it can yield some leverage in non-military areas (this is what other analysts
refer to as the "fungibility" of military power). But for two good arguments against
this view, see David A. Baldwin, "Power Analysis and World Politics: New Trends
versus Old Tendencies," *World Politics,* Vol. 31, No. 2 (January 1979), pp. 161-195;
and Robert O. Keohane, "The Theory of Hegemonic Stability and Changes in
International Economic Regimes, 1967-1977," in Keohane, *International Institutions
and State Power* (Boulder, Colo.: Westview, 1989), pp. 74-101. For an argument that
supports my view, see Nye, *Bound to Lead,* pp. 189-190.

[27] For the basic argument about the links between security and economics during
this period, I have relied heavily on the best statement on the subject, Robert Gilpin's
*U.S. Power and the Multinational Corporation: The Political Economy of Direct
Investment* (New York: Basic Books, 1975), esp. chap. 4. For arguments that a
bipolar international system is more conducive to free trade among states than a
multipolar one, see Joanne Gowa, "Bipolarity, Multipolarity, and Free Trade,"
American Political Science Review, Vol. 83, No. 4 (December 1989), pp. 1245-1257.
For a good analysis of the links between economic and security factors in the first
few years of the Cold War, see Robert Pollard, *Economic Security and the Origins of
the Cold War, 1945-1950* (New York: Columbia University Press, 1985). In spite of
these excellent sources, however, little work has been done on the links between
American military power and the flowering of interdependence. This is a fruitful area
for research because it cuts across the national security and political economy
subfields of international relations.

freely convertible currencies to foster world trade; a World Bank to aid in postwar reconstruction; and an international agency (ultimately GATT, the General Agreement on Tariffs and Trade) to bring about reductions in tariffs on manufactured goods. By early 1947, however, the United States had shelved these plans at about the same time that the hard-line policy towards the Soviet Union had triumphed in Washington. By early 1947, the American government in general and President Truman in particular had concluded that only a hard line would limit Soviet aggressiveness, that long-term containment of Soviet power would be necessary, and that strong allies would be needed to assist the nation in these tasks. By early 1947, in addition, the United States had recognized that its allies were still too debilitated by the effects of World War II to proceed with the open economic order.[28]

The decision to contain the Soviets made it imperative to lay aside the postwar economic plans. Once the United States realized that openness would weaken its allies, it instead permitted them to adopt economically nationalist policies. Their need for economic recovery was overriding if they were to fend off internal communist challenges. By the early spring of 1947, then, openness had become one of the first casualties of the Cold War. Furthermore, after the United States began its massive rearmament in the wake of the attack on South Korea in 1950, it also concluded that an economically strong Western Europe and Japan were necessary to relieve the United States of part of the military burden of containing the Soviet Union. What had started out as a plan to foster world economic growth through freer trade was scrapped for a policy of economic nationalism to rebuild allies for the long struggle against the Soviet Union. Openness and containment became inextricably entangled at the outset of the Cold War and remained so throughout its duration.

In the late 1950s, the United States began once again to implement its plans for an open world order, only after the risk of fatally weakening its European and Japanese allies had passed. It started first with the Western Europeans, after the emergence of the European Economic Community in 1958 signaled their full recovery from World War II. It began to force openness on the Japanese, with mixed success, beginning in the 1970s, after Japan's neo-mercantilist strategy began to wreak its destructive effects on selected American industries. And after openness was put into practice, it was maintained, not simply because of the economic benefits it would

---

[28] See Richard N. Gardner, *Sterling-Dollar Diplomacy in Current Perspective* (New York: Columbia University Press, 1980), chap. 15, for the details on the retreat from the open economic system; and Deborah Welch Larson, *Origins of Containment: A Psychological Explanation* (Princeton: Princeton University Press, 1985), chap. 7, on Truman's final conversion to the hard-line policy towards the Soviet Union.

yield in its own right, but also because of the military benefits that strong allies would yield for the United States. In short, the primary goal of the United States was the creation and maintenance of strong allies. When openness threatened that goal, the United States scrapped it; when openness facilitated the goal, the United States resurrected it. During the Cold War, containment, not openness, was America's overriding obsession.

THE SOVIET THREAT AND THE U.S. NIGHT WATCHMAN. Once the foundations for economic openness were put into place, the Soviet threat, and the measures taken to counter it, including the presence of American forces overseas, helped foster interdependence among America's great power allies. It did so, as E. H. Carr reminds us, because markets do not exist in political vacuums: "the science of economics presupposes a given political order and cannot be profitably studied in isolation from politics."[29] The political framework that the United States provided, partly by its economic resources and its political leadership, but also by its provision of security to its major economic trading partners abroad—the West Europeans and the Japanese—facilitated the flowering of trade amongst them.

The overseas U.S. military presence facilitated economic openness in four ways. First, the security provided by the United States created the political stability that was crucial to the orderly development of trading relations. Markets work best when embedded in political frameworks that yield predictable expectations.[30] U.S. military power deployed in the Far East and in Europe brought these stable expectations by providing the Europeans and the Japanese with the necessary psychological reassurance to rebuild after World War II and then to grow during the Cold War. The prime reason NATO was formed was psychological, not military: to make the Europeans feel secure enough against the Soviets so that they would have the political will to rebuild themselves economically. Just like the American-Japanese defense treaty, NATO created a politically stable island in a turbulent international sea.

Second, America's provision of security to its allies in Europe and in the Far East dampened their respective concerns about the German and Japanese military rearmament that the United States favored in order to help contain the Soviets. The U.S. presence protected its allies not only from the Soviets, but also from the Germans and the Japanese. The military power of Germany and Japan was contained in U.S.-dominated alliances, and American

---

[29] E. H. Carr, *The Twenty Years' Crisis, 1919–1939,* 2d ed. (London: Macmillan, 1961), p. 117.

[30] Stephen D. Krasner and Janice E. Thomson argue that "the more stable the pattern of property rights the higher the level of economic transactions." See Krasner and Thomson, "Global Transactions and the Consolidation of Sovereignty," in Ernst-Otto Czempiel and James N. Rosenau, eds., *Global Changes and Theoretical Challenges* (Lexington, Mass.: Lexington Books, 1989), p. 198.

troops were deployed in each nation, so, although their neighbors did not forget the horrors they had suffered at the hands of Germany and Japan during World World II, they were not paralyzed from cooperating with them. The success of the European Economic Community owes as much to the presence of American military power on the continent of Europe as it does to the vision of its founders. The same can be said for the Far East, where America's military presence helped smooth the way for Japan's economic dominance.

Third, the U.S. military presence helped to dampen concerns about disparities in relative economic growth and about the vulnerabilities inherent in interdependence, both of which are heightened in an open economic order. Freer trade benefits all nations, but not all equally. The most efficient nations benefit the most; and economic efficiencies can be turned to military advantage. Interdependence brings mutual dependency that is all the greater, the more states specialize economically. In turn, dependency can mean vulnerability. Through its provision of military protection to its allies, the United States mitigated these security externalities of interdependence. It also enabled the neighbors of Germany and Japan to be brought into their economic orbits without fearing that military conquest or political domination would follow.

Fourth, America's overseas military presence helped maintain the sense of allied solidarity, which, in turn, had "spill-over effects" on allied economic relations.[31] The overseas presence did not create the solidarity; fear of the Soviets did that. But U.S. forces overseas were the crucial intervening variable between the Soviet threat and alliance solidarity; they were the cement holding the anti-Soviet alliance together. U.S. troops enhanced allied solidarity because they provided visible reassurance that the United States was a reliable protector, and this prevented defection from the alliance. In turn, the heightened sense of solidarity strengthened economic openness: the need to cooperate militarily against the Soviet Union strengthened the political goodwill to overcome the inevitable economic disputes that interdependence brought. The need to preserve a united front against the common enemy put limits on how far the United States and its allies would permit their economic disputes to go, and prevented the inherent frictions among close trading partners from deteriorating into economic nationalism. In short, by strengthening solidarity, the U.S. overseas presence helped circumscribe economic disputes.

---

[31] The phrase "spill-over effects" was coined by Ernst Haas. He used it to describe a situation whereby the cooperation achieved on economic matters among the Western European states could be transferred to political matters, leading ultimately to the political integration of Western Europe. I use the phrase in the sense that I believe that cooperation on military issues has facilitated cooperation on economic matters. See Haas, *Beyond the Nation State: Functionalism and International Organization* (Stanford: Stanford University Press, 1964), p. 48.

Interdependence before 1914 and Now

America's overseas military presence fostered an open economic order among its rich industrial allies. Once the order was in place, goods, capital, and technology flowed more freely among the allies; as a consequence, their economic interdependence began to grow and reached a moderately high level by the early 1980s. How broad, deep, and resilient is this order now, and can it survive without the American overseas military presence that helped foster it?

One way to assess whether openness can continue without its military underpinning is to gauge the resiliency of the interdependence that openness produced. Openness *per se* means little unless it gives states a big stake in the economic well-being of their trading partners. The best measure of that stake is the level of economic interdependence among states. If interdependence is high, then the stake should be large and presumably so, too, will be a state's willingness to engage in cooperative behavior to keep its trading partners prosperous. One means to appraise the interdependence of 1958–90 is to compare it to that of 1870–1914. Although the two eras differ significantly, the comparison will reveal unique features of today's interdependence.

SIMILARITIES. By one set of statistics, the current interdependence looks little different from the earlier one. If measured by exports plus imports as a percentage of gross national product (GNP), the industrialized nations since 1960 have about the same stake in foreign economic activity as they did in the forty years before World War II. Kenneth Waltz and Stephen Krasner have both shown that from 1870 to 1914, the European great powers and Japan had ratios of exports plus imports to gross national product of 33 to 50 percent, which is about the same as for 1960–90.[32] The ratios for the United States ranged from 11 to 14 percent from 1870 to 1914, and 7 to 17 percent from 1945 through the 1980s.[33] Stephen Krasner and Janice Thomson demonstrate that the recent rapid growth in world trade is not unique. In the years 1830 to 1913, just as in 1950 to 1980, the growth in world trade outstripped the growth in world GNP by roughly a factor of two. In addition, international capital movements of today, when measured as a percentage of capital flowing out of and into economies, are not dramatically different from those of the pre-1914 era.[34] What has increased is the absolute amount of capital moving abroad, largely because the GNPs of today's rich nations are so much larger than they were in the earlier era.

[32] See Kenneth N. Waltz, *Theory of International Politics* (Reading, Mass.: Addison-Wesley, 1979), p. 212; and Stephen D. Krasner, "State Power and the Structure of International Trade," *World Politics*, Vol. 28, No. 3 (April 1976), pp. 327 and 328.

[33] Waltz, *Theory of International Politics*, p. 212; Krasner, "State Power and the Structure of International Trade," p. 328; Nye, *Bound to Lead*, p. 163.

[34] Krasner and Thomson, "Global Transactions," pp. 198–206.

Thus, whether we are measuring exports and imports, rates of growth of world trade, or capital flows, the percentages do not appear dramatically different now from the decades before 1914. The industrially rich nations today apparently have no greater stake in foreign economic activity than those before 1914. If that is the case, then today's interdependence could be shattered as easily as that before 1914, this time not because of a great power war, but because of the destructive forces of economic nationalism.

DIFFERENCES. Other statistics, however, make a credible case that today's interdependence is more resilient than the pre-1914 case. First, more nations today participate in a system of lowered barriers to trade among manufactured goods than in the period before 1914. In 1990, there were over 100 members of GATT, which has been the principal mechanism since 1945 for lowering tariff and non-tariff barriers to trade in manufactured goods. By contrast, the much-heralded nineteenth-century era of free trade was not all that free, did not last all that long, and involved not all that many states. Neither the United States, Russia, nor Japan participated much, if at all, when tariff duties began to be lowered in 1860. The era of free trade was largely over by the late 1870s, when the Germans and then the French raised their tariffs again.[35] Moreover, before 1914, much of the trade by the rich nations was vertical: the industrial nations imported raw materials from the non-industrialized nations, selling them manufactured goods in exchange. By contrast, today's rich nations engage in a high level of intra-industry trade, selling to one another goods that are similar, such as automobiles, consumer electronics, and other finished goods.[36]

Second, as Richard Rosecrance argues, the international investments of today's interdependence look different from those of the previous era. Before 1914, most investment was of the portfolio type—holdings of foreign shares easily sold on stock exchanges. Direct investment—the actual majority ownership of a plant, mine, or piece of real estate—was only ten percent of total foreign investment. Today, direct investment represents a much larger percentage of total foreign investment among the industrialized rich nations; it is less liquid than the traditional portfolio investment of the nineteenth century, and therefore reflects "the greater stake that countries have in each other's well-being."[37] Direct investment has created stronger ties than indirect investment ever could. This stake is increased by the interpenetration of investment among Western Europe, the United States, and Japan, which had become relatively balanced by the end of the 1970s after having been dominated by

[35] See Fieldhouse, "Imperialism: An Historiographical Revision"; and Timothy J. McKeown, "Tarriffs and Hegemonic Stability Theory," *International Organization,* Vol. 37, No. 1 (Winter 1983), pp. 80–89.
[36] Rosecrance, *The Rise of the Trading State,* pp. 145–146.
[37] Ibid., pp. 146–147.

America's direct investment overseas in earlier decades. The large size of direct foreign investment has given the industrial economies a stake in one another's economic health that did not exist in the nineteenth century.[38] Finally, because each government is committed to full employment without inflation, they must work together to ensure one another's success.

Third, daily capital movements, not trade flows, dominate currency exchange rates and dwarf, by a large factor, the daily trade in goods. As Peter Drucker points out, "the London Eurodollar market, in which the world's financial institutions borrow from and lend to each other, turns over $300 billion each working day, or $75 trillion a year, a volume at least 25 times that of world trade."[39] With these huge flows of monies across their borders, "the capacity of national monetary authorities to influence their national money supplies, to affect their national exchange rates, or even to supervise their banking systems has been reduced to new low levels."[40] This is a far cry from the pre-1914 era, when the Bank of London and the City of London could exercise a great deal of centralized control over the flow of international funds.[41]

Hedging Bets to Maintain Interdependence

The interdependence of today, though not unique in all respects, is different from what the world experienced before 1914. It involves a larger number of states, immediately engages the livelihoods of larger numbers of people, has tighter, more extensive and more direct interlinkages, and more deeply enmeshes the economic fate of a country in how other countries are faring. States today act as if their stakes in economic openness are deep, broad, and wide.[42] But it is by no means obvious that today's economic interdependence is

[38] Ibid., p. 148. Helen V. Milner has pointed out that the forces for openness have become quite strong in the United States because of the growth in the number of firms, across a wide number of industries, that have a sizeable stake in exports. As industries have become more export oriented, their stakes in economic openness have risen. See Milner, *Resisting Protectionism: Global Industries and the Politics of International Trade* (Princeton: Princeton University Press, 1988).

[39] Peter F. Drucker, "The Changed World Economy," *Foreign Affairs*, Vol. 64, No. 4 (Spring 1986), p. 782.

[40] Raymond Vernon and Debora L. Spar, *Beyond Globalism: Remaking American Foreign Economic Policy* (New York: Free Press, 1989), p. 100.

[41] See Robert Gilpin, *The Political Economy of International Relations* (Princeton: Princeton University Press, 1987), pp. 122–127, for a description of how the Bank of England and the City of London managed the world's flow of capital in the 1870–1914 period.

[42] The extent to which states actually cooperate in economic matters is an important issue for investigation, but that they feel the need to cooperate should not be in doubt. For a careful analysis of how the countries of Western Europe, North America, and Japan perceived the need to collaborate if their own economic policies were to succeed, see Robert D. Putnam and Nicholas Bayne, *Hanging Together: Cooperation and Conflict in the Seven-Power Summits*, rev. and enl. ed. (Cambridge: Harvard University Press, 1987).

so resilient and so deeply rooted that it could not be shattered as the earlier one was in 1914.

If history cannot tell us the answer, perhaps logic can. The pre-1914 era of interdependence among the great powers ended in total war. War and conquest were then thought easy and legitimate. Today, the presence of nuclear weapons makes war and conquest among the great powers improbable. But they do not make economic nationalism less probable, and it could shatter interdependence as thoroughly as World War I did. Interdependence is a tricky affair, because, as Robert Gilpin reminds us, it requires that governments manage the "clash between domestic autonomy and international norms" by reconciling "Keynes at home and Smith abroad."[43] Participating in the international economy in order to reap its benefits, while at the same time trying to insulate the domestic economy from its inevitably disruptive effects, makes the management of interdependence delicate, if not downright shaky.

The retreat from openness in the waning days of the Cold War should make us cautious about how robust the open system is.[44] The fact is that we simply do not know whether the world's political economy would experience even greater movement towards economic closure and managed trade if the United States were to withdraw totally into "Fortress America." Our theories about the relation between economic openness and military power are not well developed. What we do know is that the current openness was forged during the waging of the Cold War and is a partial by-product of it; that America's provision of security helped bind Western Europe, Japan, and the United States together; and that today's economic openness has been associated with a global American military presence.

As the rich nations enter the 1990s, momentous economic changes are taking place. Europe is poised to deepen its common market and may even move toward political unity. Japan is seeking to bring the nations of East Asia into an even tighter link with its economy than before. The United States is doing the same with Canada and Mexico. A united Germany's economic power already dominates western Europe and will, in due course, dominate Eastern Europe as well. Japan's economic power will similarly continue to dominate East Asia and the western Pacific. The neighbors of Germany and Japan, increasingly drawn into their respective eco-

[43] Gilpin, *The Political Economy of International Relations*, p. 363.

[44] Gilpin concludes *The Political Economy of International Relations* with this observation: "The postwar age of multilateral liberalization is over and the world's best hope for economic stability is some form of benign mercantilism" (p. 408). For his evidence to support this conclusion, see ibid., pp. 204–209 and 381–406. See also Gilpin, "The Economic Dimension of International Security," discussion paper for the Working Group on International Economic Change, Institute for East-West Security Studies, September 1988.

nomic orbits, will inevitably develop the same love-hate relationship with German and Japanese economic power that the Western Europeans and the Japanese earlier had towards American economic power: the power is needed, respected, and admired, but not liked, and is certainly potentially feared for the loss of autonomy it brings. A greater American economic presence in Eastern Europe, and the considerable U.S. economic presence in the Far East, could help contain fears, resentments, and unease about German and Japanese dominance, should they arise. But it is not prudent to count on the U.S. economic presence alone to assuage these concerns. A precipitate American military withdrawal could cause these concerns to grow all the greater; a residual U.S. military presence can help dampen them, as it has done in the past.[45] Why, then, complicate the advancing economic integration of the Far East under Japanese leadership with a Japanese military power no longer counterchecked by the American military presence? Why, similarly, burden the considerable economic task that confronts Eastern Europe or the European Community on its march toward economic and political unification with potential fears about unchecked German military power? Political institutionalization of the magnitude planned by the European Community takes time. Political instability disrupts the process of institutionalization; stability fosters it. Stability is in turn fostered by the maintenance of an American military presence in Europe and the Far East.

There are no good reasons why the Germans and the Japanese should want the Americans to take their troops home. The presence of U.S. troops in both the Far East and Europe should help to keep those two fields fertile for Japanese and German economic dynamism. With the Soviet Union imploding, Germany and Japan no longer face a significant security threat. But they still must contend with other states' historical memories about them, and the resentments caused by their economic power. Hence, Germany and Japan should want to retain a residual American military presence in their

___

[45] Some reports indicate that the Europeans and the Far Easterners want the United States to remain. After Defense Secretary Dick Cheney announced cuts of 10 percent in American forces in the Far East on February 23, 1990, the *New York Times* reported: "Japanese officials say privately that they are worried that an overall reduction of the American presence in Asia would reawaken fears in other parts of the region about the growing influence of Japan. They say the United States is a healthy influence that reassures Asian countries that they need not fear the possibility of a Japanese military threat that would follow its expanding economic influence down the road." See Steven R. Weisman, "Japan Backs Cheney's Troop-Cut Plan," *New York Times*, February 23, 1990, p. A8. *New York Times* columnist Flora Lewis reported that: "The Europeans want NATO to continue and they want Americans in Europe. . . . There is strong evidence supporting Britain's Foreign Minister, Douglas Hurd, when he said in a newspaper interview: 'I've never known a time when there was less anti-Americanism in Europe, whether in Britain or on the Continent.' His judgment that 'American engagement is absolutely fundamental to stability' is widely shared." Flora Lewis, "U.S. Takes the Lead," *New York Times*, July 10, 1990, p. A19.

respective regions in order to allay whatever concerns their trading partners will have about their growing power. This can also help preserve the benefits of openness for the United States and give it political leverage to affect, to its advantage, the course of regional political and economic developments.

In sum, how much of a risk does the United States want to take that a complete American military withdrawal would exacerbate the movement towards economic nationalism currently in progress? Removing the cement of American military power might risk causing the entire edifice to crumble. The risk may only marginally increase, but that might be enough. Much like the nuclear spread issue, then, the case for a continuing overseas U.S. military presence to shore up economic interdependence is not iron-clad, only suggestive, and is based on the principle of hedging bets.

RESTRAINING AMERICA'S INTERVENTIONIST IMPULSES

Besides retarding nuclear spread and preserving economic openness, there are two other goals for which an overseas presence can be of help: spreading democracy and imposing peace. The United States should, however, be restrained about using military power for either objective.

Spreading Democracy: U.S. Power and Human Rights

The spread of democracy should not be one of the prime goals to be served by American military power. I favor the spread of democracy, but I am dubious about the efficacy of military power to produce it. The aim of spreading democracy around the globe, moreover, can too easily become a license for indiscriminate and unending U.S. military interventions in the internal affairs of others. Democracies are best produced, rather, by stalemating aggressor states, by providing a stable international framework that facilitates economic development and the emergence of a middle class within states, and by using economic and other types of leverage to encourage internal liberalization. As a rule, military force is of little use.

The most successful forceful conversions to democracy since 1945 clearly show the costs and limits of military power. The conversion of Germany and Japan in 1945–50 required a total war, total defeat, and extensive occupation. They show that extensive force is required for coerced conversion. The Eastern European revolutions of 1989–90, on which the evidence is not yet all in, required the withdrawal of Soviet support for repressive regimes. These transformations illustrate that stalemating imperial powers and bringing about their retreat is a long, expensive process. Swift transformation requires military conquest, always a bloody matter. Stalemate takes a long time and requires a great expenditure of resources, although it is preferable to a big war. With the collapse of the Soviet empire in Eastern Europe, stalemate is no longer an option, because there are no formal empires left to stalemate.

The cases of Nicaragua, Chile, Grenada, and Panama offer a different model of the transition to democracy. America did not directly employ its military forces against Nicaragua on a sustained basis; however, it did help field and supply an extensive rebel force whose pressure helped bring about free elections in 1990. But the cost in Nicaraguan lives and economic misery was high. Chile's 1989 return to the democratic fold took much longer because of American backing for the reprehensible Pinochet regime, but once the United States began to redirect its considerable political and economic resources, the combination of international pressure and internal demand for change produced results. Chile's long-standing democratic traditions made its return to democracy easier than in other cases, but it still serves as a useful model for what the proper combination of external and internal pressure can produce. Grenada and Panama both show how swift military interventions can be effective when four special conditions are present: the nation invaded is small and militarily weak, the intervention is welcomed by the bulk of the populace, the costs in American casualties are relatively low, and the probability of success is high. But these conditions are not easily found or duplicated outside of the Caribbean and Central America.

Therefore, the United States should restrain itself from intervening militarily in the internal affairs of states to make them democratic, unless the four conditions described above are present. The United States should consider other military interventions only when a government is engaged in the mass murder of its citizens, and again only when the above four conditions obtain.[46] This second type of intervention, then, becomes a matter of human rights, not democracy; and the two are not the same thing.[47]

Imposing Peace: Everywhere or Selectively?

If, as a rule, the United States should not intervene militarily to make other states democratic, should it interpose itself between states to keep them at peace, or go to war to punish aggressor states, as it has against Iraq? And if it should, then where and when? To answer these questions, I first look at the argument for preventing all wars and reject it, and second, outline why the United

[46] Stephen Van Evera makes this argument. See Van Evera, "Why Europe Matters, Why the Third World Doesn't: American Grand Strategy After the Cold War," *Journal of Strategic Studies*, Vol. 13, No. 2 (June 1990), pp. 30 and 32.

[47] The two best recent candidates for this type of intervention would have been Uganda under Idi Amin and Cambodia under Pol Pot. Some may argue that humanitarian interventions of a sort did take place in each case: Tanzania ultimately invaded Uganda to depose Amin, and Vietnam intervened in Cambodia, forcing Pol Pot into hiding.

States should confine its war-prevention efforts to the Middle East, Europe, and the Far East in a highly selective fashion.

GLOBAL COLLECTIVE SECURITY? The Iraqi aggression against Kuwait demonstrated the potential of collective security, and has helped resurrect the United Nations. The U.S. government justified its intervention partly on the basis of creating the "new world order" that President Bush hopes will succeed the Cold War. We should, however, be skeptical about whether the UN action against Iraq foreshadows a bright future for UN peacekeeping efforts.

Three special conditions, unlikely to be repeated, allowed much of the world to support economic and military measures against Iraq: (1) Iraq sat quite close to the largest proven reserves of the world's oil, upon which the industrialized economies depend to a critical extent, and this led to a uniquely strong shared interest; (2) Iraq's imports and exports were easy to blockade by sea because it has only one port and only three oil pipelines to the oceans; and (3) Iraq's leader, Saddam Hussein, was widely disliked and feared because of his grandiose ambitions and because of his ability, unless stopped, to use his oil earnings to acquire even larger military capabilities, even more chemical and biological weapons, and ultimately nuclear weapons. Combined with America's military mobility, which let it quickly set up a defensive barrier along the northern border of Saudi Arabia, these three factors explain the relative ease with which a collective security response initially was engineered by the United States in the United Nations. Because these special conditions will rarely be present, the UN action against Iraq in 1990–91 is not likely to be the model for future UN peacekeeping.

Any future collective United Nations actions will require: (1) the marshalling of overwhelming majorities in favor of sanctions, including the threat or actual use of military power; and (2) an effective military force operating in the name of the United Nations. Collective security systems can dissuade aggression only if all the member states pledge in advance to punish any aggressor state for its aggression regardless of its identity. Should dissuasion fail, the UN could attack the aggressor and roll it back. But if either the dissuasion or punishment of aggression is to be global in nature, then the United Nations must have at its disposal a military force of global reach; and, of necessity, in such a force America's military power will have to be a key ingredient. Today and for the foreseeable future, only the United States can operate globally, because it is the world's only true conventional superpower. But such an American commitment would bind the United States to fight potentially everywhere. It is difficult to imagine Congress agreeing to this police role for the United States, or the American public marching off to wherever the United Nations has voted it should go, especially if other states seek to pass the buck and allow the United States to do the fighting for them.

SELECTIVE WAR PREVENTION. The key question thus becomes: in which regions and under what circumstances should the United States use its military forces to deter or punish aggression? Given its historic ties and major interests, the United States should concentrate its military efforts in Europe, the Far East, and the Middle East.

In Europe and the Far East, only a war among the great powers should concern the United States. Such a war would wreak havoc on economic openness and would dramatically enhance the incentives for nuclear spread. In contrast, wars among lesser powers in either region (for example, a war between Hungary and Romania over Transylvania) would not require American involvement. Such wars may be tragic for the peoples involved, but their stakes for the United States are small, unless they would cause a great power war.

The one exception to this rule is a North Korean attack on South Korea. Through formal alliance, the United States has guaranteed the independence of South Korea for forty years. To scuttle that commitment now would significantly diminish the credibility of America's other political-military commitments and would likely prompt the South Koreans to acquire nuclear weapons. To dissuade a North Korean attack, the United States must retain a military presence in South Korea, but at a much lower level than the 44,000 American troops currently there.[48] If the two Koreas unify peacefully, then the United States can withdraw its protection.

Fortunately, small wars will not cause a great power war in either Europe or the Far East; and a great power war in either region is unlikely, even in the absence of smaller wars. The Europe of today is not the Europe of 1914 or 1939. Neither drives for territorial hegemony (as with Germany in 1939) nor fears of political isolation (as with Germany in 1914) are causes for concern. In 1914, ethnic rivalry and border disputes in Eastern Europe became the cause of war only because they threatened one great power with destruction (Austria-Hungary) and another with political isolation (Germany). Today, similar rivalries and disputes may cause civil or foreign wars in Eastern Europe, but it is hard to see how any of these wars could escalate to a great power war. The two great powers who would most likely be involved, Germany and the Soviet Union, are militarily secure and currently preoccupied with their respective internal problems. Their internal preoccupations may eventually decrease, but they will continue to remain secure. The Soviet Union, like

[48] Secretary of Defense Dick Cheney, *Annual Report to the President, January 1990* (Washington, D.C.: U.S. Government Printing Office [U.S. GPO], 1990), p. 74. In late February 1990, Secretary Cheney announced plans to reduce American forces in East Asia and the western Pacific by ten percent, which would reduce American forces to about 40,000 in South Korea. See Weisman, "Japan Backs Cheney's Troop-Cut Plan." I see no reason to keep more than 10,000 American troops in South Korea.

France and Britain, never need fear an attack by Germany or anyone else, because it has nuclear weapons. And if Germany continues to host a residual American presence on its soil, the Germans also do not need to fear attack.[49]

Similarly, in the Far East, no great power seeks territorial hegemony. With the exception of the two Koreas and Taiwan, borders are well defined and accepted. China has nuclear weapons and is secure; Japan can still count on the United States for whatever residual protection it may require. Its interest, moreover, lies in taking a low military profile so as not to engender political resistance to its ever-growing economic power in the region.

Because the probability of a great power war in Europe and the Far East is so low, the American presence in either region need not be large. Nuclear deterrence alone has not produced this condition of peace, but it will guarantee peace among the great powers if other peace-promoting factors disappear. A residual American presence in both regions adds insurance to two stable situations at a small price in order to hedge against a highly unlikely but terribly costly possibility.

In the Middle East, matters are not quite so simple. The United States has two clear interests: preservation of secure access to Persian Gulf oil, and protection of Israel. The first may require a semi-permanent American presence in the Persian Gulf area to deter a future Iraqi government, or any other self-aggrandizing power in the region, from trying to control access to a large share of Persian Gulf oil. It is not simply the price of oil that concerns the United States; it is also who controls access to the oil, and the ways in which that access could be manipulated. Those who control the access will have to sell the oil, but it is a mistake to underestimate the bargaining and blackmail leverage that control over oil reserves could give an ambitious aggressor like Saddam Hussein. Those who earlier argued that it was not important to have a military capability to intervene in the Gulf have had their arguments punctured. Control of access to Persian Gulf oil is a matter of power, pure and simple. Aggressive, erratic, and otherwise ill-disposed states that threaten to grab a large measure of control over the world's most economically vital raw material must be stopped, with military force if necessary. The United States must continue to act to prevent any potential regional hegemon, be it Iraq, Iran, or a Saudi Arabia turned unfriendly, from dominating access to Gulf oil.

[49] Figuring out the exact political formula that will make a residual American presence in Europe politically saleable is by no means easy. For an excellent discussion of the various institutional formulas and a persuasive recommendation for a modern-day Concert of Europe housed in the Conference on European Security and Cooperation (CSCE), see Charles A. Kupchan and Clifford A. Kupchan, "Concerts, Collective Security, and the Future of Europe" (manuscript). See also Malcolm Chalmers, "Beyond the Alliance System: The Case for a European Security Organization," *World Policy Journal*, Vol. 12, No. 2 (Spring 1990), pp. 215–251.

Through extensive economic and military aid, the United States has underwritten Israel's security for over twenty-five years. To cease assistance now would have the same damaging effects on perceptions of U.S. reliability as cancellation of the treaty with South Korea. Additional reasons to maintain these ties include preservation of a democracy, the long-standing moral commitment to statehood for the survivors of the Holocaust, and the preservation of Israel's current ambiguous nuclear status. But U.S. protection of Israel will be made easier if a lasting settlement of the Palestinian issue can be achieved. There are only three possible solutions: (1) Israel annexes the West Bank and Gaza and forcibly expels the Arab populations from them; (2) Israel annexes the West Bank and Gaza and either permanently rules over, or makes equal citizens of, the Arab populations; or (3) Israel withdraws from the West Bank and Gaza, with adequate security arrangements.

The first course would bring Israel even greater political isolation than it now experiences and most likely also economic collapse, because the United States would probably withdraw the economic and military aid without which Israel cannot survive. The second course either would destroy Israel's democratic character through permanent rule over Arabs who have been made second-class citizens, or would destroy the Jewish character of the state if it remains a democracy and enfranchises all the Arabs annexed. The reason is that the birth rates of the Arabs far exceed those of the Jews. Even the immigration of huge numbers of Russian Jews will not change the ultimate result, only defer for a brief time its arrival.[50] Thus, after a number of years, Jews in a "greater Israel" will find themselves a minority in their expanded state. But before that happens, the state would be corrupted from within. The signs are already apparent. Thus, if Israel retains the West Bank and Gaza and all the Arabs in them, demographic realities will force Israel to

[50] The demographic facts are stark. In Israel proper, together with the West Bank and Gaza, there are currently about 4 million Jews and 2.4 million Arabs (650,000 Arabs in Israel proper, 800,000 in Gaza, and 1,000,000 in the West Bank). The Jewish birth rate is 65 percent of that of the Arabs living in Israel, and 50 percent of that of the Arabs living in the West Bank and Gaza. Today, a majority of the children in all three areas combined are Arab. The best estimate of Israeli demographers is that every 100,000 Russian immigrants coming to Israel (of whom it is estimated that up to 30 percent are not Jewish) postpone by only one year the day of demographic reckoning when Jews become a minority in their own "greater state." Assuming a total of 500,000 Russian Jewish immigrants over the next 3–4 years, Jews will constitute 58 percent of the population in ten years, 54 percent in twenty years, and 50 percent in thirty years. (Today, 60 percent of the population between the Jordan river and the sea is Jewish.) I am indebted to Professor Ian Lustick of Dartmouth College for providing me with these figures, which come from a symposium held at the Van Lee Institute in Jerusalem, May 24, 1990, entitled "The Demographic Problems in Israel in the Wake of Soviet Jewish Immigration." For additional population figures, see Central Bureau of Statistics, *Statistical Abstract of Israel* (Jerusalem Hamakor Press, 1987), pp. 3 and 702.

make a harsh choice between remaining democratic or remaining Jewish.

The third alternative is the only chance for Israel to have a durable peace and normal relations with its neighbors and to remain both democratic and Jewish. In return for Israel's agreement to release the bulk of the occupied territories, therefore, the United States should sign a military alliance with Israel and station a residual American force there, either a ground-force division or tactical air power.[51] This course of action would test Arab and Palestinian proclamations that they would accept peace if Israel returned the lands captured in the 1967 war, and it would allow Israel to feel secure enough to trade land for peace.[52] If the Arabs and the Palestinians did not then make peace, Israel would have gained the political high ground, and would have the added security that a clear-cut U.S. presence would provide. In the last analysis, this third course carries minimal risk for Israel because she has the ultimate guarantor of her security in her own hands—nuclear weapons.

Wars elsewhere among smaller nations in Africa, Asia, Central America, or Latin America, though tragic for the peoples involved, do not threaten the core interests of the United States and certainly would not decrease its security.[53] Should the United States for some reason find it difficult to stay out, the cardinal principle should be: "Never go in alone." It is precisely because the temptation for the one nation that has a global military reach to employ it is so great that the United States generally should refrain from doing so.

[51] I do not underestimate the difficulty of getting Israel to trade land for peace even once it has an alliance with the United States and some American military presence. Even after the United States dispatched Patriot anti-missile batteries with American crews to Israel to defend it from Iraq's Scud missile attacks in the early days of the Gulf war, Ze'ev Schiff, military editor of Israel Ha'aretz newspaper and one of Israel's most prominent military columnists, cautioned: "I don't think America's action in recent days can ever be a substitute for territory. Yes, it shows the friendship of the United States and that it can be relied on. But we remember quite well how we were pushed aside during the last five months of this operation, and we still believe that when it comes to political issues Americans might be sometimes very naive about events in the Middle East. We remember your policy toward Iraq before August 2. You can make a big mistake and absorb it. We can't. So it's good to know that they can protect us sometimes, but don't look for any revolution in Israeli strategic thinking overnight." See Thomas L. Friedman, "Hard Times, Better Allies," New York Times, January 21, 1991, p. A9.

[52] I have sidestepped two thorny issues: the political status of the West Bank and Gaza once freed from Israeli rule, and the status of Jerusalem. Neither issue will be easy to resolve politically, but no start on either can be made unless Israel is prepared to trade land for peace. My point is only to argue that an American presence in Israel is the best way to bring Israel to the point where it will make the trade.

[53] Given the long-standing U.S. commitment to the independence of South Korea, an exception for it must be made. The United States should continue to maintain some residual presence there as long as it is wanted by the South Koreans in order to deter any residual North Korean threat, until a political solution can be found for the division of Korea.

Capability should not father policy. Because it is impossible to foresee all contingencies, there may be other cases in the future that will require an American military presence in these regions, but the burden must lie on those who favor it to demonstrate how such cases would adversely affect the American interests and why other nations in the region are not better placed to deal with them.

AMERICA'S POST-COLD WAR STRATEGY

In sum, the United States should retain some type of peacetime military presence abroad to prevent five adverse situations: (1) an acceleration of nuclear weapons spread that could increase the likelihood of nuclear wars into which the United States could be drawn, or that could bring terrorist nuclear threats against it; (2) a serious decline in economic cooperation among the rich industrialized nations, due to a growth of economic nationalism, such that world trade, and thus American prosperity, would suffer significantly; (3) a great power war in Europe or the Far East that could wreck economic openness and hasten nuclear weapons spread; (4) control by a regional hegemon over Persian Gulf oil reserves that could threaten access to them; and (5) the conquest or destruction of either Israel or South Korea, which could fatally weaken other states' belief in the reliability of the United States.

For the era we are just now entering, the ultimate case for some type of American overseas military presence is a preventive one. It is a case that calls for buying insurance and for proceeding gradually, out of the judgment that matters could unravel if America entirely cast off its global military presence. It is a realist position because it assumes that international cooperation proceeds best if some nation or group of nations is willing to stabilize the international political and military environment. It is a defensive position because it assumes that prevention is cheaper, easier, and ultimately more effective than cure. The purpose of a residual overseas American presence is, thus, insurance and reassurance.

How much insurance, then, should the United States buy and how much reassurance need it give? The functions that the overseas forces are to serve should dictate the type of forces that need to be retained. The forces should be for signaling, not warfighting, purposes; but the United States must retain the ability to deploy forces capable of fighting major wars. The forces that remain abroad are to show the flag, not to destroy "the enemy." Their function is to demonstrate America's commitment tangibly and to engage the United States politically by a presence that is more than merely token, but not so large that it becomes burdensome to the American public that pays for it or offensive to the nations that accept it. Above all else, the overseas presence must be politically sustainable and financially affordable.[54] Both considerations dictate drastic cuts from the current size of the U.S. overseas force.[55]

The largest of the permanent reductions should come in Europe, where the bulk of overseas U.S. forces are stationed. It is hard to find reasons for keeping more than 30,000–50,000 American troops on the European continent, once the Soviets take their troops out of what used to be East Germany and send them back to the Soviet Union. The smaller the American presence, the less offense it will give to the Germans, and the greater the likelihood that it will be politically acceptable over the long term. In addition, in order to counter the residual Soviet threat and thereby keep Germany's appetite for nuclear weapons at its present low level, some tactical nuclear presence on the continent is desirable, but there is no reason for these forces to exceed a few hundred. Since the early 1970s, the main rationale for having tactical nuclear weapons in Europe has been to maintain a capability for limited use to send a political signal to the Soviets that escalation to a big nuclear war was at hand, not for waging a tactical nuclear war against Soviet forces. Especially now that NATO has declared its nuclear forces to be "weapons of last resort," this purpose is better served with the smallest tactical nuclear force (primarily gravity bombs and air-to-ground missiles) that legitimate military considerations about survivability will permit. All other U.S. tactical nuclear weapons should be taken out of Europe.

Given the uncertainties about the future constellation of power in the Persian Gulf, it is difficult to prescribe what types and amounts of U.S. forces should be stationed in the region. Two considerations will need to be balanced: U.S. forces must be large enough to deter future aggressions, yet small enough to minimize the political disruptions that the forces might cause within those states that agree to host them. Had Kuwait agreed to some American military presence before August 2, 1990, Saddam Hussein would probably not have attacked, knowing beyond a doubt that if he did, he would have killed American troops and thereby directly engaged and

[54] Considerations of affordability dictate that those states with adequate resources should help defer a large percentage of the costs of American forces overseas: Germany and Japan for Europe and the Far East, Kuwait and Saudi Arabia for the Gulf if there is a sizeable American presence there.

[55] At the end of fiscal year (FY) 1989 (September 30, 1989), the United States had 510,000 troops stationed abroad as follows: Germany 249,000; other Europe, 71,000; Europe afloat, 21,000; South Korea, 44,000; Japan, 50,000; other Pacific, 16,000; Pacific afloat, 25,000; Latin America/Caribbean, 21,000; and miscellaneous foreign, 13,000. These sum to 341,000 for Europe; 135,000 for East Asia and the Pacific; and 34,000 other. Figures are taken from Secretary of Defense Cheney, *Annual Report to the President and Congress, January 1990*, p. 74. I have used FY 1989 as the peacetime base for comparison because this is likely to have been the high point of America's permanent peacetime overseas presence. The figures for 1990 and 1991 are affected by the permanent projected withdrawals from Europe and the deployment of substantial forces to the Persian Gulf, some of which came from Europe.

enraged the United States. The smaller the military capability that Iraq has after the war is over, the smaller the American presence needs to be. It is vital that the U.S. forces that remain in the Gulf be part of a multinational presence under UN auspices, so that the political responsibility for the military presence will be shared with many states.

The stationing of some American forces in Israel, of whatever the type and mix, will not sit well with the Israeli government, which prefers to have American aid and backing, but not American advice and restraints. An American military presence in Israel would inevitably constrain Israel's political and military freedom of action. But the Israeli government is kidding itself if it thinks that it is now or can be completely free of such restraints. The United States possesses this power by virtue of the economic and military aid it gives to Israel, without which the state could not survive; but U.S. governments have chosen not to exploit it fully. Israel should recognize that it is better to be constrained and secure than constrained and insecure.

In the Far East, the case for large cuts in overall U.S. forces is not compelling yet because the Soviet Union has not begun to draw down its forces there as it has in Europe. But the Soviets inevitably will do so, and it is in America's interest to match their cuts. The case for large cuts in U.S. troops in South Korea, however, is already strong because the South Koreans are not weak. Once mutual U.S.-Soviet reductions have been agreed to, the American presence in the Far East, apart from some ground forces in South Korea and Japan, should be largely a maritime and air power presence.[56]

In this article, my purpose has been to present the merits of this case for retaining an American military presence abroad, not to describe in detail what that presence should look like. The details of policy are important, because the details *are* the policy. But to determine the details requires direction from an organizing strategy. Without the vision of where to go and how to get there, policy will be made by the drift of events and by the exigencies of budgetary politics. The world and the United States both still need some residual U.S. global military presence. The guiding principles for that presence are that it should be politically acceptable to the nations who will continue to host the forces, that it should be

---

[56] If the United States cuts its European force to 50,000–70,000, including the forces afloat; reduces, when appropriate, its western Pacific and East Asian contingent to 50,000; and stations 5,000–10,000 forces in Israel, it would have an overseas force, exclusive of what may be needed in the Persian Gulf, of 150,000–175,000, compared to 510,000 at the end of FY 1989. The Bush administration is formally committed to reducing the European force to 200,000–225,000, and cutting the East Asian and Pacific force by 10,000–13,000 over the next few years.

financially affordable to the American people who will continue to pay for it, and that it should be capable of rapid reinforcement from the United States should the forces be attacked.

For the current era, the duration of which no one can be certain, circumstances dictate retrenchment, but not withdrawal.

What Difference Will It Make?

LEWIS DUNN

THE BREAKDOWN OF NUCLEAR PEACE

A number of analysts and observers, noting that predictions at the dawn of the nuclear age of a nuclear apocalypse have proved exaggerated, argue that there is little reason to fear the consequences of the further spread of nuclear weapons. Frequently at the core of such optimistic assessments is the belief that the very destructiveness of those weapons will both instill prudence in their new owners, making them less willing to use even minimal conventional force out of fear that conflict will escalate to use of nuclear weapons, and lead to stable deterrent relationships between previously hostile countries. But such a fear of nuclear war was only one of the underpinnings of the first decades' nuclear peace. Other equally significant geopolitical and technical supports may be absent in the conflict-prone regions to which nuclear weapons are now likely to spread.

A SPIRALING THREAT TO PEACE

With the spread of nuclear weapons to conflict-prone regions, the chances that those weapons will be used again increase greatly. The heightened stakes and lessened room for maneuver in conflict-prone regions, the volatile leadership and political instability of many of the next nuclear powers, and the technical deficiencies of many new nuclear forces all threaten the first decades' nuclear peace.

Not least to be feared is nuclear war caused by accident or miscalculation. During an intense crisis or the first stages of a conventional military clash, for example, an accidental detonation of a nuclear weapon—even within the country of origin—or an accidental missile launch easily might be misinterpreted as the first shot of a surprise attack. Pressures to escalate in a last-ditch attempt to disarm the opponent before he completes that attack will be intense. Similarly, a technical malfunction of a radar warning system or a human error in interpreting an ambiguous warning might trigger a nuclear clash. Or fear that escalation to nuclear conflict no longer could be avoided

From *Controlling the Bomb* by Lewis A. Dunn. Copyright © 1982 by Yale University Press, pp. 69-95. Reprinted by permission of the publisher, Yale University Press. Portions of the text and some footnotes have been omitted.

might lead to a country to get in the first blow, so as partly to disarm the opponent and to minimize damage.

Unauthorized use of nuclear weapons by the military also is a possibility. For example, faced with imminent conventional military defeat and believing there is little left to lose anyway, a few members of Pakistan's military could launch a nuclear strike against India to damage that country as much as possible. Or a few hard-line, fanatic Iraqi, Libyan, or even Egyptian officers might use their countries' newly acquired nuclear weapons in an attempt to "solve" the Israeli problem once and for all. These officers' emotional commitment to a self-ordained higher mission would overwhelm any fear of the adverse personal or national consequences. Aside from the initial destruction, such unauthorized use could provoke a full-scale nuclear conflict between the hostile countries.

But the first use of nuclear weapons since Nagasaki may be a carefully calculated policy decision. The bomb might be used intentionally on the battlefield to defend against invasion. For example, faced with oncoming North Korean troops, a nuclear-armed South Korea would be under great pressure to use nuclear weapons as atomic demolition land mines to close critical invasion corridors running the thirty miles from the border to Seoul. Similar military logic could lead to Israeli use of enhanced radiation weapons—so-called neutron bombs—in the next Arab-Israeli war.

A calculated disarming nuclear surprise attack to seize the military advantage also is possible in these high-stakes, escalation-prone regional conflicts, particularly when one side has a decided strategic advantage. For example, in the 1980s, internal political instability in Pakistan and simmering unrest in Kashmir could erupt into a conventional military clash between India and Pakistan. A nuclear-armed India then would be under intense pressure to attack the more rudimentary Pakistani nuclear force to prevent its use—whether by accident or intention—against India. In a nuclear Middle East, as well, fear of events getting out of hand would fuel arguments in favor of an Israeli first strike once a conflict had begun.

Aside from the increased threat of actual use of nuclear weapons, the nuclearization of conflict-prone regions may have other costly or dangerous consequences. Given the stakes, some new nuclear powers will think seriously about a preventive strike with conventional weapons to preserve their regional nuclear monopoly. Israel already has taken such military action against Iraq's nuclear weapons program and has stated its readiness to take further action as needed. And notwithstanding the limited Iraqi reaction to Israel's preventive strike—in large part due to Iraq's being tied down in its war with Iran—it might not be possible to prevent escalation after similar or larger future attacks.

Possession of nuclear weapons also may be used as an instrument of blackmail or coercion. A country with nuclear edge may implicitly or explicitly threaten the use of nuclear weapons to enforce its demands in regional crises or low-level confrontations. Just as U.S. strategic superiority contributed to the Soviet Union's decision to back down in the 1962 Cuban Missile Crisis, so might possession of nuclear weapons by Iraq, Israel, India, or South Korea affect the resolution of crises with weaker opponents.

In addition, tensions among the countries of newly nuclearized regions are likely to be exacerbated. Pakistan's nuclear weapons activities, for example, already have heightened India's suspicion and have slowed efforts to improve relations between the two countries. Pakistani testing and deployment of nuclear weapons would further worsen relations between India and Pakistan, not least because such activity would affront India's claim to regional preeminence. Should India step up its nuclear weapons activities in response and achieve clear-cut nuclear superiority, Pakistan's fears of Indian nuclear blackmail would be increased as well. Even the anticipation of a country's "going nuclear" can have adverse political effects. For example, Iraq's efforts to acquire nuclear weapons have heightened Israel's siege mentality and stimulated efforts by Syria, Saudi Arabia, and even Kuwait at least to master basic nuclear theory and know-how.

The greater the scope, the quicker the pace, and the higher the level of proliferation, the more severe will be the threat of nuclear conflict. As more countries acquire the bomb, the number of situations in which a political miscalculation, leadership failure, geographical propinquity, or technical mishap could lead to a nuclear clash will increase. As the pace of proliferation accelerates, the time available for countries to adjust to living with nuclear weapons will grow shorter. As countries move to the more advanced levels of proliferation—from untested bombs to full-fledged military deployment, there is more chance that some of these new nuclear forces will be technically deficient. Further, nuclear weapons will cease to be isolated symbols and will become an integral part of international relations within these volatile regions.

The initial outcroppings of more widespread proliferation in and of themselves also will call forth efforts to reduce the resultant threat of nuclear conflict. But few of the possible measures for mitigating the consequences of proliferation offer a high promise of success, while domestic and international constraints may hinder implementation of even these more limited measures. And the greater the scope, pace, and level of proliferation, the more difficult and complex management efforts will become. Thus, the spiraling risk of regional nuclear conflict will not be entirely offset by these management efforts.

THE GLOBAL SPILLOVERS

While more widespread proliferation most likely will not overturn the existing structure of world politics, it will adversely affect the superpowers, and their relationship, as well as the great powers. The optimism among some analysts about the benign consequences of further proliferation again is likely to be proved wrong.

LIMITS TO STRUCTURAL CHANGE

The Soviet Union and the United States are involved in nearly all of the regions to which nuclear weapons may spread in the 1980s, frequently supporting opposite sides in long-standing disputes. Neither is likely to sever alliance ties, drop clients and allies, or phase out economic and military involvement after nuclear weapons spread to these regions. In all probability, the leaders of both countries will continue to believe that compelling national interests—whether, for example, Western access to Middle East oil, expansion of Soviet power toward the Persian Gulf or its containment, the protection of traditional allies, and maintenance of the military balance in East Asia—outweigh any new or enhanced risks of continuing involvement. Besides, because of the competitive nature of the superpower relationship, officials in each country may be reluctant to disengage from these regions in the absence of reciprocal action by the other country lest the opponent be given a "free hand." And an unwillingness to sacrifice past investments made in pursuit of regional influence and military-political advantage is likely to buttress these arguments against disengagement.

It is equally doubtful that more widespread proliferation will lead to a Soviet-U.S. condominium to prevent the further spread of nuclear weapons, ban their use by new nuclear powers, and restore the superpowers' absolute domination of world politics. The competing political, economic, and military interests of the Soviet Union and the United States in regions such as South Asia and the Middle East are likely to take precedence over joint efforts to reduce the risk of local nuclear conflict. The superpowers' reliance on the nuclear threat in their own defense postures also may constrain joint action, particularly since the threat of escalation to nuclear conflict is critical to NATO's defense posture. The international costs—political, military, and economic—of an attempt to restore superpower domination of regional politics also would be high, and quite possibly thought by U.S. and Soviet leaders to be excessive. For many countries, including U.S. allies in Western Europe, a superpower condominium for nuclear peace would be a grave threat to their current freedom of action. It is also doubtful that the military problems of reasserting control would be manageable at an acceptable cost in light of increased local capabilities for resistance, as exemplified by the Soviet experience in Afghanistan. Moreover, in the Middle East, the economic penalties of intervention at least for the United States, could be great. And while the domestic political constraints on active interventionism abroad may be less for the Soviet leadership than for U.S. policymakers, in neither country can they be overlooked.

The restoration of a more multipolar global political structure is even less likely to result from the further spread of nuclear weapons. The net impact on superpower strategic dominance of the emergence of a group of lesser nuclear powers will be quite limited. Even the deployment of nuclear forces by Japan and West Germany need not fundamentally upset the existing structure: should the nuclear forces of Japan and West Germany be equivalent to those of France and the United Kingdom, there still would be a considerable gap between the threat they could pose to the superpowers and the threat the superpowers would pose in return. The United States and the Soviet Union also could raise the threshold nuclear capability necessary for Japan or West Germany to mount a serious threat to either of their homelands by renegotiating the 1972 Treaty between the United States of America and the Union of Soviet Socialist Republics on the Limitation of Anti-Ballistic Missile Systems (ABM) to permit Soviet and U.S. deployment of defenses against Japanese or West German ballistic missiles. Besides, it is quite unlikely in any case that these countries will decide to acquire nuclear weapons.

This conclusion that widespread proliferation will not overturn the existing structure of world politics rests most of all on the assumption that even in that changed environment the leaders of the United States and the Soviet Union will continue to pursue their distinct national interests and objectives, utilizing force or the threat of force and relying on prudence, crisis management, and marginal adjustment to deal with the new risks. However, it is possible that following the use of nuclear weapons by a new nuclear power—especially if that use almost produces a nuclear confrontation between them—the United States and the Soviet Union may be far more ready to negotiate about joint disengagement and other steps to isolate newly nuclear regions. Alternatively, leaders in the Soviet Union and the United States could seek to reassert their countries' capability to dictate the rules of the regional nuclear game. The likelihood of such major adjustments clearly will depend on whether the superpowers' assessment of the direct risks to themselves and of the adequacy of traditional crisis management changes markedly. But particularly in light of the limited success of recent U.S. and Soviet efforts to reach agreement on reciprocal strategic restraints as well as their conflicting global interests, ideologies, and national styles, even after one or more small-power nuclear exchanges, the two superpowers probably will continue to pursue only prudent ameliorative measures to reduce the risks of competitive involvement in newly nuclearized regions.

REDUCED SUPERPOWER FREEDOM OF ACTION

Periodically during the past decades, the United States has intervened militarily in regional confrontations, disputes, and limited conflicts outside of the European arena. The decision in 1980 to create the Rapid Deployment Joint Task Force for Middle East and Persian Gulf contingencies reflects a continued willingness to project U.S. power into conflict-prone regions in order to protect U.S. interests, allies, and friends. But the presence of nuclear weapons in some future contingencies will increase the military and political risks of intervention, reducing U.S. freedom of action.

Notwithstanding the threat of U.S. retaliation, nuclear weapons might be used against U.S. intervention forces. A desperate leader, thinking there was nothing left to lose, might launch a nuclear strike against landing troops or close-in off-shore naval operations, both of which would be vulnerable to even a few rudimentary nuclear weapons. Or, in the heat of battle, a breakdown of communications could result in the use of nuclear weapons by a lesser nuclear power. Also possible is an unauthorized attack on U.S. forces by the military of a new nuclear power. If needed adaptations of the tactics, training, and structure of these U.S. intervention.forces are not made, U.S. intervention could prove very costly, and U.S. forces might even suffer stunning reversals.

Admittedly, U.S. policymakers could launch a limited nuclear strike to disarm the hostile new nuclear power rather than seek to "work around" this regional nuclear threat and risk valuable military assets. But the regional and global political costs to the United States of such a strike are likely to be so high as to make policymakers very hesitant to authorize it.

These heightened risks also are likely to reinforce the lingering, although somewhat muted, national presumption against intervention derived from the Vietnam experience. Consequently, the stakes needed to justify involvement in a newly nuclearized region probably will be greater than in the past. U.S. policymakers may choose not to intervene militarily in some situations where they previously would have acted.

The risks and complexities of military intervention will increase for the Soviet Union as well. In the eyes of a Soviet leadership that has intervened militarily only when the balance of forces appeared clearly favorable, the possible use of nuclear weapons against Soviet troops in a newly nuclearized region could be an excessive risk. To illustrate, Yugoslav deployment of battlefield nuclear weapons might discourage Soviet military action in a future domestic political struggle in

Yugoslavia. Similarly, even a slight possibility that Israel or South Africa would use nuclear weapons against Soviet ground or naval forces might help deter Soviet military entanglement in those regions. And the political costs of a nuclear disarming attack on a new nuclear power are likely to appear nearly as excessive to the Soviet Union as to the United States.

The eventual development by a few new nuclear powers of even a limited last-resort capability to threaten the homeland of one or the other superpower with nuclear attack or retaliation also would reduce both Soviet and American freedom of action. For example, should Israel acquire the capability to strike Odessa, Kiev, and Baku, the Soviet leaders might not be as willing to risk direct military involvement in the Middle East to support their Arab clients. Such a capability in Yugoslav or South African hands might have a comparable restraining effect on the Soviets. Or, though less likely, a radical Arab government might threaten to destroy one or more American cities in an attempt to blackmail the United States into not resupplying Israel in the midst of the next Middle East war. Of course, the risk of carrying out such a threat to a superpower would be extraordinary. But neither superpower could ignore the possibility that a leader who thought he had nothing left to lose might do so.

However, this threat of direct attack by a new nuclear power is likely to be greater for the Soviet Union than for the United States. Hardly any of the next countries likely to acquire the bomb will seek to target the U.S. homeland. Moreover, the geographical remoteness of the United States from potentially hostile new nuclear powers in the Middle East and Persian Gulf, combined with the technological backwardness of these countries, makes American cities somewhat less vulnerable than Soviet cities to such a nuclear strike. At least in the 1980s, to attack a U.S. city, Iraq or Libya—the most plausible opponents—probably would either have to smuggle a weapon into the United States by plane or boat or use a converted Boeing 707 or 747 registered as a private or corporate jet to deliver a bomb, counting on subterfuge and the steady decline of U.S. air defenses to penetrate U.S. airspace. Though possibly feasible, such unconventional modes of attack would be less technically reliable, limited in magnitude, and subject to interception by intelligence agencies.

In contrast, Israel, Yugoslavia, and South Korea already possess long-range nuclear-capable aircraft that can reach the Soviet Union and may well be able to slip through Soviet air defenses. South Africa and Israel also are said to be developing a crude cruise missile that could increase their capability to hit Soviet cities. Should Japan or West Germany acquire nuclear weapons, they would have little trouble targeting Soviet cities. Barring unexpectedly rapid technological progress, the breakdown of current restraints on the sale of cruise missiles and advanced missile guidance systems, or widespread traffic in space-booster technology and boosters themselves, the United States will continue to be less vulnerable to nuclear attack by a new nuclear power than will the Soviet Union—at least into the 1990s.

The constraining effect of more widespread possession of nuclear weapons of the superpowers should not be exaggerated. The superpowers' readiness and capability to control events abroad have already been lessened by the decreased legitimacy of using force, rising nationalism, the difficulties of bringing applicable force to bear in limited disputes, the availability of advanced weapons systems to regional powers, and the strengthening of countervailing economic instruments of power. So viewed, the further spread of nuclear weapons only contributes to a continuing, longer-term relative decline of superpower freedom of action. Moreover, as long as the two superpowers are ready to pay the necessary price, they could preserve a significant gap between their military capabilities and those of any new medium and lesser nuclear powers, including even Japan and West Germany. Further, in those situations where U.S. or Soviet interests are seen to justify either the military costs of working around lesser nuclear forces or the political costs of suppressing them, the superpowers most probably will be impeded but not prevented from realizing their objectives.

INCREASED RISK OF SUPERPOWER CONFRONTATION

Continued U.S. and Soviet pursuit of their respective interests in these newly nuclear conflict-prone regions also will entail acceptance of a higher risk of a U.S.-Soviet political-military confrontation. With the acquisition of nuclear weapons by long-standing regional enemies, there will be many more flashpoints for such a superpower clash. For instance, a preventive attack with conventional weapons, a surprise disarming strike, use of nuclear weapons on the battlefield, nuclear blackmail, a conventional attack backed by the threat of recourse to nuclear weapons, in each case by one superpower's ally against an ally of the other, all could trigger superpower involvement and confrontation. Both the Soviet Union and the United States would be under great pressure to "do something" to help their allies. While aware of the risks, Soviet and U.S. leaders might nonetheless be drawn into the conflict for fear that otherwise their past political, military, and economic investments in the regions would be wasted, their interests sacrificed, and their "reputations for action" ruined. But by responding, the superpower could set in motion an upward spiral of response and counterresponse, of initial entanglement and increased commitment, that may result in a direct confrontation between them.

Though present already, the risk of miscalculation on the part of the two superpowers also may be higher in situations involving newly nuclearized regions—again enhancing the chances of unwanted confrontation. In this new environment, either superpower may modify in unexpected ways its traditional assessment of the stakes, its preferred responses, or its readiness to run risks. Thus, whatever lessons about the other superpower's thinking and responses have been learned from prior regional crises may no longer be fully applicable. And this uncertainty could be most pronounced and most dangerous in the uncharted territory after the next use of nuclear weapons.

But concern about even indirect entanglement in crises or confrontations that could involve the use of nuclear weapons may make policymakers in Western Europe more cautious in extending existing political, economic, or military ties. Domestic pressures against heightened involvement could grow as well. Moreover, because of this fear, these policymakers might be even more reluctant to support U.S. military initiatives and may not permit use of facilities and bases on their territories, or agree to reallocate or transship material and supplies, or provide military forces.

As well, these Western European countries might be the targets of nuclear blackmail intended to make them stand aside in such clashes or withdraw previously offered assistance. For example, in the midst of an Arab-Israeli conflict in the late 1980s, Egypt, Iraq, or Libya could anonymously threaten to detonate a nuclear weapon previously smuggled into Portugal unless that country rescinded landing rights at air bases in the Azores for U.S. planes on their way to Israel with needed military equipment. Or West Germany might be the target of such an anonymous nuclear threat in an indirect effort to prevent the United States from shipping military equipment from NATO stocks to the Middle East. Besides, once nuclear weapons are more widely available, it could be quite difficult to distinguish a hoax from a serious threat, and, thus, even a hoax might suffice to disrupt such U.S. operations for a time.

Under certain conditions further proliferation also would increase considerably the cost and difficulty for France and Britain of maintaining a credible nuclear deterrent against the Soviet Union. Confronted by a growing threat to their homelands from new nuclear powers, or believing that such a threat was likely to emerge by the 1990s, the superpowers might renegotiate the 1972 ABM Treaty and deploy ballistic missile defenses. But to counter that change, these medium nuclear powers would have to develop and deploy costly and technically demanding systems able to penetrate those more extensive Soviet missile defenses. Failure to do so would lead to the increasing obsolescence of the French and British nuclear forces.*

---

*China's nuclear force would be similarly threatened with obsolescence by a Soviet missile defense capability.

DOMESTIC POLITICAL REPERCUSSIONS
NUCLEAR-ARMED TERRORISTS, IRREDENTISTS, AND SEPARATISTS

A considerably greater risk that terrorist and dissident groups will gain access to nuclear weapons will be another adverse consequence of the further spread of nuclear weapons. As more countries seek to acquire a nuclear weapons option by initiating sensitive reprocessing or enrichment activities, or set up actual weapons programs, the number of sites from which these groups could steal nuclear weapons material for a bomb will increase. The ensuing transportation of such material between a growing number of sites will further increase the risk of theft. Once a group possesses nuclear weapons material, the technical hurdles of processing that material and fabricating a nuclear weapon still would have to be overcome, but at least for some groups these difficulties would not be insurmountable. More important, a subnational group might opt for stealing the bomb itself, taking advantage of the probably less-than-adequate physical security measures of some new nuclear forces.

Hit-and-run clandestine terrorist groups, such as the Japanese Red Army, extreme left-wing Palestinian factions, the Italian Red Brigade, the Irish Republican Army (IRA), or successors to the Baader-Meinhof gang, may well regard a nuclear weapon as a means of extorting money or political concessions from a government, much as taking hostages is now. The countries of Western Europe, Japan, and the United States will be especially vulnerable to terrorist threats or attack because of their open societies. A group such as the IRA, claiming to represent a legitimate alternative government and dependent on popular support, might stop short of carrying out a nuclear threat even if its demands were not met. But members of the more radical and nihilistic fringe movements, such as the successors to the Baader-Meinhof gang and the Japanese Red Army, might think otherwise. To them, carrying out the threat might appear justified as a means of bringing down corrupt bourgeois society in a spasm of violence. Or, in the eyes of the most extreme Palestinian groups, use of a nuclear weapon might be thought justified as a way of mortally wounding Israel. Yet again, with the police closing in on them, these more radical, isolated terrorists could conclude that, since all was lost, it would be preferable to fall in a nuclear *Götterdämmerung*. Such a decision would be consistent with the near-suicide mentality shown in some past terrorist actions.

In contrast, the theft and threatened use of nuclear weapons may not appear a worthwhile tactic to a group such as the Palestinian Liberation Organization (PLO). Even though the PLO's freedom of action has been reduced by the Lebanese civil war, it still controls territory, administers to its refugee population, has a military force, and has been recognized by international bodies and foreign governments.

Rather than enhancing the PLO's claim that it is a legitimate government in exile, possession of a few stolen nuclear weapons could have the opposite effect. Theft of nuclear weapons would reinforce the PLO's reputation for extremism and unwillingness to accept minimal norms of international behavior and would make it harder for those Western European governments moving closer to the PLO's position on the Middle East to sustain that shift. Besides, should Israeli intelligence manage to locate these nuclear weapons, pressures to carry out a preventive strike, disregarding the risk of Soviet counteraction, would be intense. If Israel could not locate the nuclear weapons but knew that the PLO had them, the result is not likely to be Israeli acceptance of the need for a Palestinian state but Israeli unwillingness to compromise on that PLO demand. On balance, therefore, the costs to the PLO of stealing nuclear weapons appear to outweigh the benefits. Still, that conclusion reflects a Western weighing of costs and gains, which may prove as unfounded in this instance of Middle East maneuverings as it has on earlier occasions.

Separatist movements such as the Kurds or Arabs in Iran, the Baluchis in Pakistan, the Bengalis in India, the Moslems in the Philippines, or even the Basques in Spain might be more inclined to steal and threaten to use a nuclear weapon. For example, a separatist Baluchi movement might threaten to use stolen Pakistani nuclear weapons if the Pakistani central government mounted a new military campaign to restore its authority. Though extreme, such a threat would not be out of line with the bitter fighting so characteristic of these struggles for greater autonomy. Fearful of the consequences of cracking down on the separatists and under international and domestic pressure to find a "reasonable" settlement, the central government might come to terms with that group. Conversely, the central government could conclude that the costs of yielding to the separatists' demands were so great that it had no choice but to strike back, even using its own nuclear weapons against those of the separatists. But with little to lose, the Baluchis—and other separatist groups in other countries—might be ready to take that chance.

THE NUCLEAR COUP d'ETAT

In the 1980s and early 1990s, politically unstable new nuclear powers—such as Argentina, Brazil, Chile, Egypt, Iran, Iraq, Libya, Nigeria, Pakistan, South Korea, and Syria—might be vulnerable to nuclear coups d'etat. Particularly if the balance of political and military power between the rebels and the government were unclear, control of nuclear weapons—as compelling a symbol and instrument of national power as control of the airport, capital city, or radio and television stations—could greatly enhance the rebels' bargaining position. Control of nuclear weapons would change the psychological climate and afford rebel groups a means not only of demoralizing opponents but also of rallying supporters. The specter of nuclear destruction—should the situation get out of hand—quite possibly might lead civilian and military fence-sitters to come out in favor of a coup and even change the minds of some anti-coup forces. Moreover, just a few nuclear weapons in rebel hands could suffice to deter attack against them, assuming that the government was both unwilling to overwhelm the rebels with conventional force lest they retaliate with nuclear weapons and reluctant to use nuclear weapons first on its own territory in a surprise disarming attack. Consequently, more so than in past coups, efforts to dislodge such rebels would remain a test of wills and bargaining strategy. Nevertheless, nuclear weapons might be employed, either intentionally, by accident, or out of contempt and hatred.

Already on at least one occasion during the first decades of the nuclear age, access to nuclear weapons has figured in a domestic political upheaval. In April 1961, French army forces stationed in Algiers rebelled, demanding that the government in Paris reverse its decision to grant independence to Algeria. At the time, French scientists were preparing to test a nuclear weapon at the French Saharan test site in Reganne, Algeria, not too far from Algiers. Noting the proximity of the rebellion, the scientists called on the general in charge at Reganne to authorize an immediate test and thus avoid the possibility that the nuclear device would be seized by the rebel troops and used for bargaining leverage. Three days after the outbreak of the revolt, the order to detonate the device came directly from French President de Gaulle; there was no attempt to undertake precise experiments, only to use up all the available fissionable material.

THE CORROSION OF LIBERAL DEMOCRACIES?

At least some of the measures required to deal with the threats of clandestine nuclear attack—whether from a terrorist group or a new nuclear power—and of nuclear black marketing will be in tension with or in outright violation of the civil liberties procedures and underlying values of Western liberal democracies. Because of the stakes, there will be strong pressures to circumvent or set aside—in the United States and elsewhere—various constitutional and legal restrictions on invasions of privacy or other traditional civil liberties. Unauthorized, warrantless emergency searches based on skimpy evidence or tips might be made. Or broad neighborhood—even city-wide—searches may become legitimate in these instances, although existing laws in many countries, particularly the Fourth and Fourteenth Amendments in the United States, prohibit searches without specific definition of the site and evidence sought. The use of informants, warrantless or illegal wiretaps, and the secret detention and questioning of suspects for days or even weeks might follow, all motivated by the need to acquire information as fast as possible.

However, it may prove possible to contain this challenge to liberal democratic procedures and values. Within the United States, both rigorous administrative supervision of any emergency measures and strict judical review after the fact would help prevent those measures from spilling over their boundaries and corrupting procedures in other areas of law enforcement. Authorizing legislation and official policy statements also could stress the extraordinary character of those restrictions as a response to an exceptional threat while reemphasizing the more basic American belief in the worth, dignity, and sanctity of the individual that underlies respect for particular civil liberties.

But if the frequency of proliferation-related threats grows, and if violations of traditional civil liberties cease to be isolated occurrences, it will become more difficult to check this corrosion of liberal democracy here and elsewhere. For that reason, as well, concern about the many adverse consequences of increasingly widespread nuclear weapons proliferation is well founded.

Toward Nuclear Peace*

KENNETH N. WALTZ

What will the spread of nuclear weapons do to the world? I say "spread" rather than "proliferation" because so far nuclear weapons have proliferated only vertically as the major nuclear powers have added to their arsenals. Horizontally, they have spread slowly across countries and the pace is not likely to change much. Sort-term candidates for the nuclear club are not very numerous, and they are not likely to rush into the nuclear business. One reason is that the United States works with some effect to keep countries from doing that. Nuclear weapons will nevertheless spread, with a new member occasionally joining the club. Counting India and Israel, membership grew to seven in the first 35 years of the nuclear age. A doubling of membership in the next decade would be surprising. Since rapid changes in international conditions can be unsettling, the slowness of the spread of the nuclear weapons is fortunate.

Someday the world will be populated by 10 or 12 or 18 nuclear-weapon states (hereafter referred to as nuclear states). What the further spread of nuclear weapons will do to the world is therefore a compelling question.

THE MILITARY LOGIC OF SELF-HELP SYSTEMS

The world has enjoyed more years of peace since 1945 than had been known in this century—if peace is defined as the absence of general war among the major states of the world. The Second World War followed the first one within twenty-one years. As of 1983, 38 years had elapsed since the Allies' victory over the Axis powers. Conflict marks all human affairs. In the past third of a century, conflict has generated hostility among states and has at times issued in violence among the weaker and smaller ones. Even though the more powerful states of the world have occasionally been direct participants, war has been confined geographically and limited militarily. Remarkably, general war has been avoided in a period of rapid and far-reaching changes—decolonization; the rapid economic growth of some states;

*A shortened and revised version of Waltz, *The Spread of Nuclear Weapons: More May Be Better*, Adelphi Papers, No. 171 (London: International Institute of Strategic Studies, 1981).

the formation, tightening, and eventual loosening of blocs; the development of new technologies, and the emergence of new strategies for fighting guerrilla wars and deterring nuclear ones. The prevalence of peace, together with the fighting of circumscribed wars, indicates a high ability of the postwar international system to absorb changes and to contain conflicts and hostility.

Presumably features found in the postwar system that were not present earlier account for the world's recent good fortune. The biggest changes in the postwar world are the shift from multipolarity to bipolarity and the introduction of nuclear weapons. In this paper I concentrate on the latter.

States coexist in a condition of anarchy. Self-help is the principle of action in an anarchic order, and the most important way in which states must help themselves is by providing for their own security. Therefore, in weighing the chances for peace, the first questions to ask are questions about the ends for which states use force and about the strategies and weapons they employ. The chances of peace rise if states can achieve their most important ends without actively using force. War becomes less likely as the costs of war rise in relation to possible gains. Strategies bring ends and means together. How nuclear weapons affect the chances for peace is seen by examining the different implications of defense and deterrence.

How can one state dissuade another state from attacking? In either or in some combination of two ways. One way to counter an intended attack is to build fortifications and to muster forces that look forbiddingly strong. To build defenses so patently strong that no one will try to destroy or overcome them would make international life perfectly tranquil. I call this the defensive ideal. The other way to inhibit a country's intended aggressive moves is to scare that country out of making them by threatening to visit unacceptable punishment upon it. "To deter" literally means to stop someone from doing something by frightening him. In contrast to dissuasion by defense, dissuasion by deterrence operates by frightening a state out of attacking, not because of the difficulty of launching an attack and carrying it home, but because the expected reaction of the opponent will result in one's own severe punishment. Defense and deterrence are often confused. One frequently hears statements like this: "A strong defense in Europe will deter a Russian attack." What is meant is that a strong defense will dissuade Russia from attacking. Deterrence is achieved not through the ability to defend but through the ability to punish. Purely deterrent forces provide no defense. The message of the strategy is this: "Although we are defenseless, if you attack we will punish you to an extent that more than cancels your gains." Second-strike nuclear forces serve that kind of strategy. Purely defensive forces provide no deterrence. They offer no means of punishment.

The message of the strategy is this: "Although we cannot strike back at you, you will find our defenses so difficult to overcome that you will dash yourself to pieces against them". The Maginot Line was to serve that kind of strategy.

Do nuclear weapons increase or decrease the chances of war? The answer depends on whether nuclear weapons permit and encourage states to deploy forces in ways that make the active use of force more or less likely and in ways that promise to be more or less destructive. If nuclear weapons make the offense more effective and the blackmailer's threat more compelling, then nuclear weapons are bad for the world—the more so the more widely diffused nuclear weapons become. If defense and deterrence are made easier and more reliable by the spread of nuclear weapons, we may expect the opposite result. To maintain their security states must rely on the means they can generate and the arrangements they can make for themselves. It follows that the quality of international life varies with the ease or the difficulty states experience in making themselves secure.

Weapons and strategies change the situation of states in ways that make them more or less secure, as Robert Jervis has brilliantly shown. (ref. Jervis article) If weapons are not well suited for conquest, neighbors have more peace of mind. We should expect war to become less likely when weaponry is such as to make conquest more difficult, to discourage preemptive and preventive war, and to make coercive threats less credible. Do nuclear weapons have those effects? Some answers can be found by considering how nuclear deterrence and nuclear defense improve the prospects for peace.

First, wars can be fought in the face of deterrent threats, but the higher the stakes and the closer a country moves toward winning them, the more surely that country invites retaliation and risks its own destruction. States are not likely to run major risks for minor gains. Wars between nuclear states may escalate as the loser uses larger and larger warheads. Fearing that, states will want to draw back. Not escalation but deescalation becomes likely. War remains possible, but victory in war is too dangerous to fight for. If states can score only small gains, because large ones risk retaliation, they have little incentive to fight.

Second, states act with less care if the expected costs of war are low and with more care if they are high. In 1853 and '54 Britain and France expected to win an easy victory if they went to war against Russia. Prestige abroad and political popularity at home would be gained, if not much else. The vagueness of their expectations was matched by the carelessness of their actions. In blundering into the Crimean War they acted hastily on scant information, pandered to their people's frenzy for war, showed more concern for an ally's whim than for the adversary's situation, failed to specify the changes in behavior that threats were supposed to bring, and inclined toward testing strength first and bargaining second. In sharp contrast, the presence of nuclear weapons makes states exceedingly cautious. Think of Kennedy and Khrushchev in the Cuban missile crisis. Why fight if you can't win much and might lose everything?

Third, the question demands a negative answer all the more insistently when the deterrent deployment of nuclear weapons contributes more to a country's security than does conquest of territory. A country with a deterrent strategy does not need the extent of territory required by a country relying on a conventional defense. A deterrent strategy makes it unnecessary for a country to fight for the sake of increasing its security, and this removes a major cause of war.

Fourth, deterrent effect depends both on one's capabilities and on the will one has to use them. The will of the attacked, striving to preserve its own territory, can ordinarily be presumed stronger than the will of the attacker, striving to annex someone else's territory. Knowing this, the would-be attacker is further inhibited.

Certainty about the relative strength of adversaries also makes war less likely. From the late nineteenth century onward the speed of technological innovation increased the difficulty of estimating relative strengths and predicting the course of campaigns. Since World War II, technology has advanced even faster, but short of a ballistic missile defense (BMD) breakthrough, this does not matter very much. It does not disturb the American-Russian military equilibrium, because one side's missiles are not made obsolete by improvements in the other side's missiles. In 1906 the British Dreadnought, with the greater range and fire power of its guns, made older battleships obsolete. This does not happen to missiles. As Bernard Brodie put it: "Weapons that do not have to fight their like do not become useless because of the advent of newer and superior types." They may have to survive their like, but that is a much simpler problem to solve.

Many wars might have been avoided had their outcomes been foreseen. "To be sure," Georg Simmel once said, "the most effective presupposition for preventing struggle, the exact knowledge of the comparative strength of the two parties, is very often only to be obtained by the actual fighting out of the conflict." Miscalculation causes wars. One side expects victory at an affordable price, while the other side hopes to avoid defeat. Here the differences between conventional and nuclear worlds are fundamental. In the former, states are too often tempted to act on advantages that are wishfully discerned and narrowly calculated. In 1914, neither Germany nor France tried very hard to avoid a general war. Both hoped for victory even though they believed their forces to be quite evenly matched. In 1941, Japan, in attacking the the United States, could hope for victory only if a series of events that were possible but not highly probable took place.

Japan would grab resources sufficient for continuing the conquest of China and then dig in to defend a limited perimeter. Meanwhile, the United States and Britain would have to deal with Germany, which, having defeated the Soviet Union, would be supreme in Europe. Japan could then hope to fight a defensive war for a year or two until America, her purpose weakened, became willing to make a compromise peace in Asia (ref. Sansom article).

Countries more readily run the risks of war when defeat, if it comes, is distant and is expected to bring only limited damage. Given such expectations, leaders do not have to be insane to sound the trumpet and urge their people to be bold and courageous in the pursuit of victory. The outcome of battles and the course of campaigns are hard to foresee because so many things affect them. Predicting the result of conventional wars has proved difficult.

Uncertainty about outcomes does not work decisively against the fighting of wars in conventional worlds. Countries armed with conventional weapons go to war knowing that even in defeat their suffering will be limited. Calculations about nuclear war are differently made. A nuclear world calls for and encourages a different kind of reasoning. If countries armed with nuclear weapons go to war, they do so knowing that their suffering may be unlimited. Of course, it also may not be. But that is not the kind of uncertainty that encourages anyone to use force. In a conventional world, one is uncertain about winning or losing. In a nuclear world, one is uncertain about surviving or being annihilated. If force is used, and not kept within limits, catastrophe will result. That prediction is easy to make because it does not require close estimates of opposing forces. The number of one's cities that can be severely damaged is at least equal to the number of strategic warheads an adversary can deliver. Variations of number mean little within wide ranges. The expected effect of the deterrent achieves an easy clarity because wide margins of error in estimates of the damage one may suffer do not matter. Do we expect to lose one city or two, two cities or ten? When these are the pertinent questions, we stop thinking about running risks and start worrying about how to avoid them. In a conventional world, deterrent threats are ineffective because the damage threatened is distant, limited, and problematic. Nuclear weapons make military miscalculation difficult and politically pertinent prediction easy.

Dissuading a would-be attacker by throwing up a good-looking defense may be as effective as dissuading him through deterrence. Beginning with President Kennedy and Secretary of Defense McNamara in the early 1960s, we have asked how we can avoid, or at least postpone, using nuclear weapons rather than how we can mount the most effective defense. NATO's attempts to keep a defensive war conventional in its initial stage may guarantee that nuclear weapons, if used, will be used in a losing cause and in ways that multiply destruction without promising victory. Early use of very small warheads may stop escalation. Defensive deployment, if it should fail to dissuade, would bring small nuclear weapons into use before the physical, political, and psychological environment had deteriorated. The chances of de-escalation are high if the use of nuclear weapons is carefully planned and their use is limited to the battlefield. We have rightly put strong emphasis on strategic deterrence, which makes large wars less likely, and wrongly slighted the question of whether nuclear weapons of low yield can effectively be used for defense, which would make any war at all less likely still.*

An unassailable defense is fully dissuasive. Dissuasion is what is wanted whether by defense or by deterrence. The likelihood of war decreases as deterrent and defensive capabilities increase. Nuclear weapons and an appropriate doctrine for their use may make it possible to approach the defensive-deterrent ideal, a condition that would cause the chances of war to dwindle. Concentrating attention on the destructive power of nuclear weapons has obscured the important benefits they promise to states trying to coexist in a self-help world.

WHAT WILL THE SPREAD OF NUCLEAR WEAPONS DO TO THE WORLD?

Contemplating the nuclear past gives grounds for hoping that the world will survive if further nuclear powers join today's six or seven. This tentative conclusion is called into question by the widespread belief that the infirmities of some new nuclear states and the delicacy of their nuclear forces will work against the preservation of peace and for the fighting of nuclear wars. The likelihood of avoiding destruction as more states become members of the nuclear club is often coupled with the question of *who* those states will be. What are the likely differences in situation and behavior of new as compared to old nuclear powers?

NUCLEAR WEAPONS AND DOMESTIC STABILITY

What are the principal worries? Because of the importance of controlling nuclear weapons—of keeping them firmly in the hands of reliable officials—rulers of nuclear states may become more authoritarian and ever more given to secrecy. Moreover, some potential nuclear states are not politically strong and stable enough to ensure control of the weapons and control of the decision to use them. If neighboring, hostile, unstable states are armed with nuclear weapons, each will fear attack by the other. Feelings of insecurity may lead to arms races that subordinate civil needs to military necessities. Fears are compounded by the danger of internal coups in which the control

---

* I shall concentrate on nuclear deterrence and slight nuclear defense.

of nuclear weapons may be the main object of struggle and the key to political power. Under these fearful circumstances, to maintain governmental authority and civil order may be impossible. The legitimacy of the state and the loyalty of its citizenry may dissolve because the state is no longer thought to be capable of maintaining external security and internal order. The first fear is that states become tyrannical; the second, that they lose control. Both fears may be realized either in different states or in the same state at different times (ref. Dunn article). What can one say? Four things primarily. First, possession of nuclear weapons may slow arms races down, rather than speed them up, a possibility considered later. Second, for less developed countries to build nuclear arsenals requires a long lead time. Nuclear power and nuclear weapons programs, like population policies, require administrative and technical teams able to formulate and sustain programs of considerable cost that pay off only in the long run. The more unstable a government, the shorter becomes the attention span of its leaders. They have to deal with today's problems and hope for the best tomorrow. In countries where political control is most difficult to maintain, governments are least likely to initiate nuclear-weapons programs. In such states, soldiers help to maintain leaders in power or try to overthrow them. For those purposes nuclear weapons are not very useful. Soldiers who have political clout or want it are not interested in nuclear weapons. They are not scientists and technicians. They like to command troops and squadrons. Their vested interests are in the military's traditional trappings.

Third, although highly unstable states are unlikely to initiate nuclear projects, such projects, begun in stable times, may continue through periods of political turmoil and succeed in producing nuclear weapons. A nuclear state may be unstable or may become so. But what is hard to comprehend is why, in an internal struggle for power, the contenders should start using nuclear weapons. Who would they aim at? How would they use them as instruments for maintaining or gaining control? I see little more reason to fear that one faction or another in some less developed country will fire atomic weapons in a struggle for political power than that they will be used in a crisis of succession in the Soviet Union or China. One or another nuclear state will experience uncertainty of succession, fierce struggles for power, and instability of regime. Those who fear the worst have not very plausibly shown how those expected events may lead to the use of nuclear weapons. Fourth, the possibility of one side in a civil war firing a nuclear warhead at its opponent's stronghold nevertheless remains. Such an act would produce a national tragedy, not an international one. This question then arises: Once the weapon is fired, what happens next? The domestic use of nuclear weapons is, of all the uses imaginable, least likely to lead to escalation and to threaten the stability of the central balance.

NUCLEAR WEAPONS AND REGIONAL STABILITY

Nuclear weapons are not likely to be used at home. Are they likely to be used abroad? As nuclear weapons spread, what new causes may bring effects different from and worse than those known earlier in the nuclear age? This section considers five ways in which the new world is expected to differ from the old and then examines the prospects for, and the consequences of, new nuclear states using their weapons for blackmail or for fighting an offensive war.

In what ways may the actions and interactions of new nuclear states differ from those of old nuclear powers? First, new nuclear states may come in hostile pairs and share a common border. Where states are bitter enemies one may fear that they will be unable to resist using their nuclear weapons against each other. This is a worry about the future that the past does not disclose. The Soviet Union and the United States, and the Soviet Union and China, are hostile enough; and the latter pair share a long border. Nuclear weapons have caused China and the Soviet Union to deal cautiously with each other. But bitterness among some potential nuclear states, so it is said, exceeds that experienced by the old ones. Playing down the bitterness sometimes felt by the United States, the Soviet Union, and China requires a creative reading of history. Moreover, those who believe that bitterness causes wars assume a close association that is seldom found between bitterness among nations and their willingness to run high risks.

Second, some new nuclear states may have governments and societies that are not well rooted. If a country is a loose collection of hostile tribes, if its leaders form a thin veneer atop a people partly nomadic and with an authoritarian history, its rulers may be freer of constraints than, and have different values from, those who rule older and more fully developed polities. Idi Amin and Muammar el-Qaddafi fit these categories, and they are favorite examples of the kinds of rulers who supposedly cannot be trusted to manage nuclear weapons responsibly. Despite wild rhetoric aimed at foreigners, however, both of these "irrational" rulers became cautious and modest when punitive actions against them might have threatened their ability to rule. Even though Amin lustily slaughtered members of tribes he disliked, he quickly stopped goading Britain once the sending of her troops appeared to be a possibility. Qaddafi has shown similar restraint. He and Anwar Sadat were openly hostile. In July of 1977 both launched commando attacks and air raids, including two large air strikes by Egypt on Libya's el Adem airbase. Neither side let the attacks get out of hand. Qaddafi showed himself to be forbearing and amenable to mediation by other Arab leaders. Shai Feldman uses these and other examples to argue that Arab leaders are deterred from taking inordinate risks not because they engage in intricate rational calculations but simply because they, like other rulers, are "sensitive to costs."

Many Westeners who write fearfully about a future in which third-world countries have nuclear weapons seem to view their people in the once familiar imperial manner as "lesser breeds without the law." As is usual with ethnocentric views, speculation takes the place of evidence. How do we know, someone has asked, that a nuclear-armed and newly hostile Egypt or a nuclear-armed and still hostile Syria would not strike to destroy Israel at the risk of Israeli bombs falling on some of their cities? More than a quarter of Egypt's people live in four cities: Cairo, Alexandria, Giza, and Aswan. More than a quarter of Syria's live in three: Damascus, Aleppo, and Homs. What government would risk sudden losses of such proportion or indeed of much lesser proportion? Rulers want to have a country that they can continue to rule. Some Arab country might wish that some other Arab country would risk its own destruction for the sake of destroying Israel, but there is no reason to think that any Arab country would do so. One may be impressed that, despite ample bitterness, Israelis and Arabs have limited their wars and accepted constraints placed on them by others. Arabs did not marshal their resources and make an all-out effort to destroy Israel in the years before Israel could strike back with nuclear warheads. We cannot expect countries to risk more in the presence of nuclear weapons than they have in their absence.

Third, many fear that states that are radical at home will recklessly use their nuclear weapons in pursuit of revolutionary ends abroad. States that are radical at home, however, may not be radical abroad. Few states have been radical in the conduct of their foreign policy, and fewer have remained so for long. Think of the Soviet Union and the People's Republic of China. States coexist in a competitive arena. The pressures of competition cause them to behave in ways that make the threats they face manageable, in ways that enable them to get along. States can remain radical in foreign policy only if they are overwhelmingly strong—as none of the new nuclear states will be—or if their radical acts fall short of damaging vital interests of nuclear powers. States that acquire nuclear weapons will not be regarded with indifference. States that want to be freewheelers have to stay out of the nuclear business. A nuclear Libya, for example, would have to show caution, even in rhetoric, lest she suffer retaliation in response to someone else's anonymous attack on a third state. That state, ignorant of who attacked, might claim that its intelligence agents had identified Libya as the culprit and take the opportunity to silence her by striking a conventional blow. Nuclear weapons induce caution, especially in weak states.

Fourth, while some worry about nuclear states coming in hostile pairs, others worry that the bipolar pattern will not be reproduced regionally in a world populated by larger numbers of nuclear states. The simplicity of relations that obtains when one party has to concentrate its worry on only one other, and the ease of calculating forces and estimating the dangers they pose, may be lost. The structure of international politics, however, will remain bipolar so long as no third state is able to compete militarily with the great powers. Whatever the structure, the relations of states run in various directions. This applied to relations of deterrence as soon as Britain gained nuclear capabilities. It has not weakened deterrence at the center and need not do so regionally. The Soviet Union now has to worry lest a move made in Europe cause France and Britain to retaliate, thus possibly setting off American forces. Such worries at once complicate calculations and strengthen deterrence.

Fifth, in some of the new nuclear states civil control of the military may be shaky. Nuclear weapons may fall into the hands of military officers more inclined than civilians to put them to offensive use. This again is an old worry. I can see no reason to think that civil control of the military is secure in the Soviet Union, given the occasional presence of serving officers in the Politburo and some known and some surmised instances of military intervention in civil affairs at critical times. And in the People's Republic of China military and civil branches of government are not separated but fused. Although one may prefer civil control, preventing a highly destructive war does not require it. What is required is that decisions be made that keep destruction within bounds, whether decisions are made by civilians or soldiers. Soldiers may be more cautious than civilians. Generals and admirals do not like uncertainty, and they do not lack patriotism. They do not like to fight conventional wars under unfamiliar conditions. The offensive use of nuclear weapons multiplies uncertainties. Nobody knows what a nuclear battlefield would look like, and nobody knows what happens after the first city is hit. *Uncertainty* about the course that a nuclear war might follow, along with the *certainty* that destruction can be immense, strongly inhibits the first use of nuclear weapons.

Examining the supposedly unfortunate characteristics of new nuclear states removes some of one's worries. One wonders why their civil and military leaders should be less interested in avoiding their own destruction than leaders of other states have been. Nuclear weapons have never been used in a world in which two or more states possessed them. Still, one's feeling that something awful will emerge as new nuclear powers are added to the present group is not easily quieted. The fear remains that one state or another will fire its new nuclear weapons in a coolly calculated preemptive strike, or fire them in a moment of panic, or use them to launch a preventive war. These possibilities are examined in the next section. Nuclear weapons may also be set off anonymously, or back a policy of blackmail, or be used in a combined conventional-nuclear attack.

Some have feared that a radical Arab state might fire a nuclear warhead anonymously at an Israeli city in order to block a peace settlement. But the state exploding the warhead could not be certain of remaining unidentified. Even if a country's leaders persuade themselves that chances of retaliation are low, who would run the risk? Nor would blackmail be easy to accomplish, despite one instance of seeming success. In 1953 Russia and China may have been convinced by Eisenhower and Dulles that they would widen the Korean war and raise the level of violence by using nuclear weapons if a settlement were not reached. In Korea we had gone so far that the threat to go further was plausible. The blackmailer's threat is not a cheap way of working one's will. The threat is simply incredible unless a considerable investment has already been made. Dulles's speech of January 12, 1954, seemed to threaten massive retaliation in response to mildly bothersome actions by others. The successful siege of Dien Bien Phu in the spring of that year showed the limitations of such threats. Capabilities foster policies that employ them. But monstrous capabilities foster monstrous policies, which when contemplated are seen to be too horrible to carry through. Moreover, once two or more countries have nuclear weapons, the execution of nuclear threats risks retaliation. This compounds the problem of establishing credibility.

Although nuclear weapons are poor instruments for blackmail, would they not provide a cheap and decisive offensive force when used against a conventionally armed enemy? Some people think that South Korea wants, and that earlier the Shah's Iran had wanted, nuclear weapons for offensive use. Yet one cannot say why South Korea would use nuclear weapons against fellow Koreans while trying to reunite them nor how she could use nuclear weapons against the North, knowing that China and Russia might retaliate. And what goals might a conventionally strong Iran have entertained that would have tempted her to risk using nuclear weapons? A country that takes the nuclear offensive has to fear a punishing blow from someone. Far from lowering the expected cost of aggression, a nuclear offense even against a non-nuclear state raises the possible costs of aggression to uncalculable heights because the aggressor cannot be sure of the reaction of other nuclear powers.

Nuclear weapons do not make nuclear war a likely prospect, as history has so far shown. The point made when discussing the possible internal use of nuclear weapons, however, bears repeating. No one can say that nuclear weapons will never be used. Their use, although unlikely, is always possible. In asking what the spread of nuclear weapons will do to the world, we are asking about the effects to be expected as a larger number of relatively weak states get nuclear weapons. If such states use nuclear weapons, the world will not end. The use of nuclear weapons by lesser powers would hardly trigger them elsewhere, with the United States and the Soviet Union becoming involved in ways that might shake the central balance.

DETERRENCE WITH SMALL NUCLEAR FORCES

A number of problems are thought to attend the efforts of minor powers to use nuclear weapons for deterrence. In this section, I ask how hard these problems are for new nuclear states to solve.

The forces required for deterrence. In considering the physical requirements of deterrent forces, we should remark the difference between prevention and preemption. A preventive war is launched by a stronger state against a weaker one that is thought to be gaining in strength. Aside from the balance of forces, a preemptive strike is launched by one state when another state's offensive forces are seen to be vulnerable.

The first danger posed by the spread of nuclear weapons would seem to be that each new nuclear state may tempt an old one to strike preventively in order to destroy an embryonic nuclear capability before it can become militarily effective. Because of America's nuclear arsenal, the Soviet Union could hardly have destroyed the budding forces of Britain and France; but the United States could have struck the Soviet Union's early nuclear facilities, and the United States and the Soviet Union could have struck China's. Long before Israel struck Iraq's reactor, preventive strikes were treated as more than abstract possibilities. When Francis P. Matthews was President Truman's Secretary of the Navy, he made a speech that seemed to favor our waging a preventive war. The United States, he urged, should be willing to pay "even the price of instituting a war to compel cooperation for peace." Moreover, preventive strikes against nuclear installations can be made by non-nuclear states and have sometimes been threatened. Thus President Nasser warned Israel in 1960 that Egypt would attack if she were sure that Israel was building a bomb. "It is inevitable," he said, "that we should attack the base of aggression even if we have to mobilize four million to destroy it."

The uneven development of the forces of potential and of new nuclear states creates occasions that seem to permit preventive strikes and may seem to invite them. Two stages of nuclear development should be distinguished. First, a country may be in an early stage of nuclear development and be obviously unable to make nuclear weapons. Second, a country may be in an advanced stage of nuclear development, and whether or not it has some nuclear weapons may not be surely known. All of the present nuclear countries went through both stages, yet until Israel struck Iraq's nuclear facility in June of 1981 no one had launched a preventive strike. A number of reasons combined may account for the reluctance of states to strike in order to prevent adversaries from developing nuclear forces. A preventive strike would seem to be most promising during the first stage of nuclear development. A state could strike without fearing that the country it attacked would return a nuclear blow. But would one strike so hard as to destroy the very potential for future nuclear development? If not, the country struck could simply resume its nuclear career. If the blow struck is less than devastating, one must be prepared to repeat it or to occupy and control the country. To do either would be difficult and costly.

In striking Iraq, Israel showed that a preventive strike can be made, something that was not in doubt. Israel's act and its consequences, however, make clear that the likelihood of useful accomplishment is low. Israel's strike increased the determination of Arabs to produce nuclear weapons. Israel's strike, far from foreclosing Iraq's nuclear future, gained her the support of some other Arab states in pursuing it. And despite Prime Minister Begin's vow to strike as often as need be, the risks in doing so would rise with each occasion.

A preventive strike during the second stage of nuclear development is even less promising than a preventive strike during the first stage. As more countries acquire nuclear weapons, and as more countries gain nuclear competence through power projects, the difficulties and dangers of making preventive strikes increase. To know for sure that the country attacked has not already produced or otherwise acquired some deliverable warheads becomes increasingly difficult. If the country attacked has even a rudimentary nuclear capability, one's own severe punishment becomes possible. Fission bombs may work even though they have not been tested, as was the case with the bomb dropped on Hiroshima. Israel has apparently not tested weapons, yet Egypt cannot know whether Israel has zero, ten, or twenty warheads. And if the number is zero and Egypt can be sure of that, she would still not know how many days or hours are required for assembling components that may be on hand.

Preventive strikes against states that have, or may have, nuclear weapons are hard to imagine, but what about preemptive ones? The new worry in a world in which nuclear weapons have spread is that states of limited and roughly similar capabilities will use them against one another. They do not want to risk nuclear devastation anymore than we do. Preemptive strikes nevertheless seem likely because we assume that their forces will be "delicate." With delicate forces, states are tempted to launch disarming strikes before their own forces can be struck and destroyed.

To be effective a deterrent force must meet three requirements. First, a part of the force must appear to be able to survive an attack and launch one of its own. Second, survival of the force must not require early firing in response to what may be false alarms. Third, weapons must not be susceptible to accidental and unauthorized use.

Nobody wants vulnerable, hair-trigger, accident-prone forces. Will new nuclear states find ways to hide their weapons, to deliver them, and to control them? Will they be able to deploy and manage nuclear weapons in ways that meet the physical requirements of deterrent forces?

Deterrent forces are seldom delicate because no state wants delicate forces and nuclear forces can easily be made sturdy. Nuclear weapons are fairly small and light. They are easy to hide and to move. Early in the nuclear age, people worried about atomic bombs being concealed in packing boxes and placed in the hold of ships to be exploded when a signal was given. Now more than ever people worry about terrorists stealing nuclear warheads because various states have so many of them. Everybody seems to believe that terrorists are capable of hiding bombs. Why should states be unable to do what terrorist gangs are thought to be capable of?

It is sometimes claimed that the few bombs of a new nuclear state create a greater danger of nuclear war than additional thousands for the United States and the Soviet Union. Such statements assume that preemption of a small force is easy. It is so only if the would-be attacker knows that the intended victim's warheads are few in number, knows their exact number and locations, and knows that they will not be moved or fired before they are struck. To know all of these things, and to know that you know them for sure, is exceedingly difficult. How can military advisers promise the full success of a disarming first strike when the penalty for slight error may be so heavy? In 1962, Tactical Air Command promised that an American strike against Soviet missiles in Cuba would certainly destroy 90 percent of them but would not guarantee 100 percent. In the best case a first strike destroys all of a country's deliverable weapons. In the worst case, some survive and can be delivered.

If the survival of nuclear weapons requires their dispersal and concealment, do not problems of command and control become harder to solve? Americans think so because we think in terms of large nuclear arsenals. Small nuclear powers will neither have them nor need them. Lesser nuclear states might deploy, say, ten real weapons and ten dummies, while permitting other countries to infer that the numbers are larger. The adversary need only believe that some warheads may survive his attack and be visited on him. That belief should not be hard to create without making command and control unreliable. All nuclear countries must live through a time when their forces are crudely designed. All countries have so far been able to control them. Relations between the United States and the Soviet Union, and later among the United States, the Soviet Union, and China, were at their bitterest just when their nuclear forces were in early stages of development, were unbalanced, were crude and presumably hard to control. Why should we expect new nuclear states to experience greater difficulties than the old ones were able to cope with? Moreover, although some of the new nuclear states may be economically and technically backward, they will either have an expert and highly trained group of scientists and engineers or they will not produce nuclear weapons. Even if they buy the weapons, they will have to hire technicians to maintain and control them. We do not have to wonder whether they will take good care of their weapons. They have every incentive to do so. They will not want to risk retaliation because one or more of their warheads accidentally strikes another country.

Hiding nuclear weapons and keeping them under control are tasks for which the ingenuity of numerous states is adequate. Nor are means of delivery difficult to devise or procure. Bombs can be driven in by trucks from neighboring countries. Ports can be torpedoed by small boats lying offshore. Moreover, a thriving arms trade in ever more sophisticated military equipment provides ready access to what may be wanted, including planes and missiles suited to nuclear warhead delivery.

Lesser nuclear states can pursue deterrent strategies effectively. Deterrence requires the ability to inflict unacceptable damage on another country. "Unacceptable damage" to the Soviet Union was variously defined by Robert McNamara as requiring the ability to destroy a fifth to a fourth of her population and a half to two-thirds of her industrial capacity. American estimates of what is required for deterrence have been absurdly high. To deter, a country need not appear to be able to destroy a fourth or a half of another country, although in some cases that might be easily done. Would Libya try to destroy Israel's nuclear weapons at the risk of two bombs surviving to fall on Tripoli and Bengazi? And what would be left of Israel if Tel Aviv and Haifa were destroyed?

The weak can deter one another. But can the weak deter the strong? Raising the question of China's ability to deter the Soviet Union highlights the issue. The population and industry of most states concentrate in a relatively small number of centers. This is true of the Soviet Union. A major attack on the top ten cities of the Soviet Union would get 25 percent of its industrial capacity and 25 percent of its urban population. Geoffrey Kemp in 1974 concluded that China would probably be able to strike on that scale. And, I emphasize again, China need only appear to be able to do it. A low probability of carrying a highly destructive attack home is sufficient for deterrence. A force of an imprecisely specifiable minimum capacity is nevertheless needed.

In a 1979 study, Justin Galen (pseud.) wondered whether the Chinese had a force physically capable of deterring the Soviet Union. He estimated that China had 60 to 80 medium range and 60 to 80 intermediate range missiles of doubtful reliability and accuracy and 80 obsolete bombers. He rightly pointed out that the missiles may miss their targets even if fired at cities and that the bombers may not get through the Soviet Union's defenses. Moreover, the Russians may be able to preempt, having almost certainly "located virtually every Chinese missile, aircraft, weapons storage area and production facility." But surely Russian leaders put these things the other way around. To locate virtually all missiles and aircraft is not good enough. Despite inaccuracies, a few Chinese missiles *may* hit Russian cities, and some bombers *may* get through. Not much is required to deter. What political-military objective is worth risking Vladivostok, Novosibirsk, and Tomsk, with no way of being sure that Moscow will not go as well?

The credibility of small deterrent forces. The credibility of weaker countries' deterrent threats has two faces. The first is physical. Will such countries be able to construct and protect a deliverable force? We have found that they can quite readily do so. The second is psychological. Will deterrent threats that are physically feasible be psychologically plausible? Will an adversary believe that the retaliation that is threatened will be carried out?

Deterrent threats backed by second-strike nuclear forces raise the expected costs of war to such heights that war becomes unlikely. But deterrent threats may not be credible. In a world where two or more countries can make them, the prospect of *mutual* devastation makes it difficult, or irrational, to execute threats should the occasion for doing so arise. Would it not be senseless to risk suffering further destruction once a deterrent force had failed to deter? Believing that it would be, an adversary may attack counting on the attacked country's unwillingness to risk initiating a devastating exchange by its own retaliation. Why retaliate once a threat to do so has failed? If one's policy is to rely on forces designed to deter, then an attack that is nevertheless made shows that one's reliance was misplaced. The course of wisdom may be to pose a new question: What is the best policy now that deterrence has failed? One gains nothing by destroying an enemy's cities. Instead, in retaliating, one may prompt the enemy to unleash more warheads. A ruthless aggressor may strike believing that the leaders of the attacked country are capable of following such a "rational" line of thought. To carry out the threat that was "rationally" made may be "irrational." This old worry achieved new prominence as the strategic capabilities of the Soviet Union approached those of the United States in the middle 1970s. The Soviet Union, some feared, might believe that the United States would be self-deterred (ref. Nitze article).

Much of the literature on deterrence emphasizes the problem of achieving the credibility on which deterrence depends and the danger of relying on a deterrent of uncertain credibility. One earlier solution of the problem was found in Thomas Schelling's notion of "the threat that leaves something to chance." No state can know for sure that another state will refrain from retaliating even when retaliation would be irrational. No state can bet heavily on another state's rationality. Bernard Brodie put the thought more directly, while avoiding the slippery notion of rationality. Rather than ask what it may be rational or irrational for governments to do, the question he repeatedly asked was this: How do governments behave in the presence of awesome dangers? His answer was "very carefully."

To ask why a country should carry out its deterrent threat once deterrence has failed is to ask the wrong question. The question suggests that an aggressor may attack believing that the attacked country may not retaliate. This invokes the conventional logic that analysts find so hard to forsake. In a conventional world, a country can sensibly attack if it believes that success is probable. In a nuclear world, a country cannot sensibly attack unless it believes that success is assured. An attacker is deterred even if he believes only that the attacked *may* retaliate. Uncertainty of response, not certainty, is required for deterrence because, if retaliation occurs, one risks losing all. In a nuclear world, we should look less at the retaliator's conceivable inhibitions and more at the challenger's obvious risks.

One may nevertheless wonder, as Americans recently have, whether retaliatory threats remain credible if the strategic forces of the attacker are superior to those of the attacked. Will an unsuccessful defender in a conventional war have the courage to unleash its deterrent force, using nuclear weapons first against a country having superior strategic forces? Once more this asks the wrong question. The previous paragraph urged the importance of shifting attention from the defender's possible inhibitions to the aggressor's unwillingness to run extreme risks. This paragraph urges the importance of shifting attention from the defender's courage to the different valuations that defenders and attackers place on the stakes. An attacked country will ordinarily value keeping its own territory more highly than an attacker will value gaining some portion of it. Given second-strike capabilities, it is not the balance of forces but the courage to use them that counts. The balance or imbalance of strategic forces affects neither the calculation of danger nor the question of whose will is the stronger. Second-strike forces have to be seen in absolute terms. The question of whose interests are paramount will then determine whose will is perceived as being the stronger.

Emphasizing the importance of the "balance of resolve," to use Glenn Snyder's apt phrase, raises questions about what a deterrent force covers and what it does not. In answering these questions, we can learn something from the experience of the last three decades. The United States and the Soviet Union have limited and modulated their provocative acts, the more carefully so when major values for one side or the other were at issue. This can be seen both in what they have and in what they have not done. Whatever support the Soviet Union gave to North Korea's initial attack on the South was given after Secretary of State Acheson, the Joint Chiefs of Staff, General MacArthur, and the Chairman of the Senate Foreign Relations Committee all explicitly excluded both South Korea and Taiwan from America's defense perimeter. The United States, to take another example, could fight for years on a large scale in Southeast Asia because neither success nor failure mattered much internationally. Victory would not have made the world one of American hegemony. Defeat would not have made the world one of Russian hegemony. No vital interest of either super-power was at stake, as both Kissinger and Brezhnev made clear at the time (Stoessinger, 1976, ch. 8). One can fight without fearing escalation only where little is at stake. And that is where the deterrent does not deter.

Actions at the periphery can safely be bolder than actions at the center. In contrast, where much is at stake for one side, the other side moves with care. Trying to win where winning would bring the central balance into question threatens escalation and becomes too risky to contemplate. The United States is circumspect when East European crises impend. Thus Secretary of State Dulles assured the Soviet Union when Hungarians rebelled in October of 1956 that we would not interfere with efforts to suppress them. And the Soviet Union's moves in the center of Europe are carefully controlled. Thus her probes in Berlin have been tentative, reversible, and ineffective. Strikingly, the long border between East and West Europe—drawn where borders earlier proved unstable—has been free even of skirmishes in all of the years since the Second World War.

Contemplating American and Russian postwar behavior, and inter-preting it in terms of nuclear logic, suggests that deterrence extends to vital interests beyond the homeland more easily than many have thought. The United States cares more about Western Europe than the Soviet Union does. The Soviet Union cares more about Eastern Europe than the United States does. Communicating the weight of one side's concern as compared to the other side's has been easily enough done when the matters at hand affect the United States and the Soviet Union directly. For this reason, West European anxiety about the coverage it gets from our strategic forces, while understand-able, is exaggerated. The United States might well retaliate should the Soviet Union make a major military move against a NATO country, and that is enough to deter.

The problem of extended deterrence. How far from the homeland does deterrence extend? One answers that question by defining the conditions that must obtain if deterrent threats are to be credited. First, the would-be attacker must be made to see that the deterrer considers the interests at stake to be vital. One cannot assume that countries will instantly agree on the question of whose interests are vital. Nuclear weapons, however, strongly incline them to grope for *de facto* agreement on the answer rather than to fight over it.

Second, political stability must prevail in the area that the deterrent is intended to cover. If the threat to a regime is in good part from internal factions, then an outside power may risk supporting one of them even in the face of deterrent threats. The credibility of a deterrent force requires both that interests be seen to be vital and that it is the attack from outside that threatens them. Given these conditions, the would-be attacker provides both the reason to retaliate and the target for retaliation. Deterrence gains in credibility the more highly valued the interests covered appear to be.

The problem of stretching a deterrent, which has so agitated the western alliance, is not a problem for lesser nuclear states. Their problem is to protect not others but themselves. Many have feared that lesser nuclear states would be the first ones to break the nuclear taboo and that they would use their weapons irresponsibly. I expect just the opposite. Weak states find it easier than strong states to establish their credibility. Not only are they not trying to stretch their deterrent forces to cover others but also their vulnerability to conventional attack lends credence to their nuclear threats. Because in a conventional war they can lose so much so fast, it is easy to believe that they will unleash a deterrent force even at the risk of receiving a nuclear blow in return. With deterrent forces, the party that is absolutely threatened prevails (Feldman 1980, ch. 1). Use of nuclear weapons by lesser states will come only if survival is at stake. And this should be called not irresponsible but responsible use.

An opponent who attacks what is unambiguously mine risks suffering great distress if I have second-strike forces. This statement has important implications for both the deterrer and the deterred. Where territorial claims are shadowy and disputed, deterrent writs do not run. As Steven J. Rosen has said: "It is difficult to imagine Israel committing national suicide to hold on to Abu Rudeis or Hebron or Mount Hermon." Establishing the credibility of a deterrent force requires moderation of territorial claims on the part of the would-be deterred. For modest states, weapons whose very existence works strongly against their use are just what is wanted.

In a nuclear world, conservative would-be attackers will be prudent, but will would-be attackers be conservative? A new Hitler is not unimaginable. Would the presence of nuclear weapons have moderated Hitler's behavior? Hitler did not start World War II in order to destroy the Third Reich. Indeed, he was surprised and dismayed by British and French declarations of war on Poland's behalf. After all, the western democracies had not come to the aid of a geographically defensible and militarily strong Czechoslovakia. Why then should they have declared war on behalf of a less defensible Poland and against a Germany made stronger by the incorporation of Czechoslovakia's armor? From the occupation of the Rhineland in 1936 to the invasion of Poland in 1939, Hitler's calculations were realistically made. In those years, Hitler would probably have been deterred from acting in ways that immediately threatened massive death and widespread destruction in Germany. And, if Hitler had not been deterred, would his generals have obeyed his commands? In a nuclear world, to act in blatantly offensive ways is madness. Under the circumstances, how many generals would obey the commands of a madman? One man alone does not make war.

To believe that nuclear deterrence would have worked against Germany in 1939 is easy. It is also easy to believe that in 1945, given the ability to do so, Hitler and some few around him would have fired nuclear warheads at the United States, Great Britain, and the Soviet Union as their armies advanced, whatever the consequences for Germany. Two considerations, however, work against this possibility. When defeat is seen to be inevitable, a ruler's authority may vanish. Early in 1945 Hitler apparently ordered the initiation of gas warfare, but no one responded (ref. Brown article). The first consideration applies in a conventional world; the second in a nuclear world. In the latter, no country will press another to the point of decisive defeat. In the desperation of defeat desperate measures may be taken, but the last thing anyone wants to do is to make a nuclear nation desperate. The unconditional surrender of a nuclear nation cannot be demanded. Nuclear weapons affect the deterrer as well as the deterred. All of the parties involved are constrained to be moderate because one's immoderate behavior makes the nuclear threats of others credible.

Arms races among new nuclear states. One may easily believe that American and Russian military doctrines set the pattern that new nuclear states will follow. One may then also believe that they will suffer the fate of the United States and the Soviet Union, that they will compete in building larger and larger nuclear arsenals while continuing to accumulate conventional weapons. These are doubtful beliefs. One can infer the future from the past only insofar as future situations may be like present ones for the actors involved. For three main reasons, new nuclear states are likely to decrease rather than to increase their military spending.

First, nuclear weapons alter the dynamics of arms races. In a competition of two or more parties, it may be hard to say who is pushing and who is being pushed, who is leading and who is following. If one party seeks to increase its capabilities, it may seem that the other(s) must too. The dynamic may be built into the competition and may unfold despite a mutual wish to resist it. But need this be the case in a strategic competition between nuclear countries? It need not be if the conditions of competition make deterrent logic dominant. Deterrent logic dominates if the conditions of competition make it nearly impossible for any of the competing parties to achieve a first-strike capability. Early in the nuclear age, the implications of deterrent strategy were clearly seen. "When dealing with the absolute weapon," as William T. R. Fox put it, "arguments based on relative advantage lose their point." The United States has sometimes designed its forces according to that logic. Donald A. Quarles argued when he was Eisenhower's Secretary of the Air Force that "sufficiency of air power" is determined by "the force required to accomplish the mission assigned." Avoidance of total war then does not depend on the *"relative* strength of the two opposed forces." Instead, it depends on the *"absolute* power in the hands of each, and in the substantial invulnerability of this power to interdiction." To repeat: If no state can launch a disarming attack with high confidence, force comparisons are irrelevant. Strategic arms races are then pointless. Deterrent strategies offer this great advantage: Within wide ranges neither side need respond to increases in the other side's military capabilities.

Those who foresee nuclear arms racing among new nuclear states fail to make the distinction between war-fighting and war-deterring capabilities. War-fighting forces, because they threaten the forces of others, have to be compared. Superior forces may bring victory to one country; inferior forces may bring defeat to another. Force requirements vary with strategies and not just with the characteristics of weapons. With war-fighting strategies, arms races become difficult, if not impossible, to avoid. Forces designed for deterring war need not be compared. As Harold Brown said when he was Secretary of Defense, purely deterrent forces "can be relatively modest, and their size can perhaps be made substantially, though not completely, insensitive to changes in the posture of an opponent." With deterrent strategies, arms races make sense only if a first-strike capability is within reach. Because thwarting a first strike is easy, deterrent forces are quite cheap to build and maintain. With deterrent forces, the question is not whether one country has more than another but whether it has the capability of inflicting "unacceptable damage" on another, with unacceptable damage sensibly defined. Once that capability is assured, additional strategic weapons are useless. More is not better if less is enough.

Deterrent balances are inherently stable. If one can say how much is enough, then within wide limits one state can be insensitive to changes in its adversaries' forces. This is the way French leaders have thought. France, as President Giscard d'Estaing said, "fixes its security at the level required to maintain, regardless of the way the strategic situation develops in the world, the credibility—in other words, the effectiveness—of its deterrent force." With deterrent forces securely established, no military need presses one side to try to surpass the other. Human error and folly may lead some parties involved in deterrent balances to spend more on armaments than is needed, but other parties need not increase their armaments in response, because such excess spending does not threaten them. The logic of deterrence eliminates incentives for strategic arms racing. This should be easier for lesser nuclear states to understand than it has been for the United States and the Soviet Union. Because most of them are economically hard pressed, they will not want to have more than enough.

Allowing for their particular circumstances, lesser nuclear states confirm these statements in their policies. Britain and France are relatively rich countries, and they tend to overspend. Their strategic forces are nevertheless modest enough when one considers that their purpose is to deter the Soviet Union rather than states with capabilities comparable to their own. China of course faces the same task. These three countries show no inclination to engage in nuclear arms races with anyone. India appears content to have a nuclear military capability that may or may not have produced deliverable warheads, and Israel maintains her ambiguous status. New nuclear states are likely to conform to these patterns and aim for a modest sufficiency rather than vie with one another for a meaningless superiority.

Second, because strategic nuclear arms races among lesser powers are unlikely, the interesting question is not whether they will be run but whether countries having strategic nuclear weapons can avoid running conventional races. No more than the United States or the Soviet Union will new nuclear states want to rely on executing the deterrent threat that risks all. And will not their vulnerability to conventional attack induce them to continue their conventional efforts?

American policy as it has developed since the early 1960s again teaches lessons that mislead. For two decades, we have emphasized the importance of having a continuum of forces that would enable the United States and her allies to fight at any level from irregular to strategic nuclear warfare. A policy that decreases reliance on deterrence increases the chances that wars will be fought. This was well appreciated in Europe when we began to place less emphasis on deterrence and more on defense. The worries of many Europeans were well expressed by a senior British general, in the following words: "McNamara is practically telling the Soviets that the worst they need expect from an attack on West Germany is a conventional counterattack." Why risk one's own destruction if one is able to fight on the ground and forego the use of strategic weapons?

The policy of flexible response lessened reliance on strategic deterrence and increased the chances of fighting a war. New nuclear states are not likely to experience this problem. The expense of mounting conventional defenses, and the difficulties and dangers of fighting conventional wars, will keep most nuclear states from trying to combine large war-fighting forces with deterrent forces. Disjunction within their forces will enhance the value of deterrence.

Israeli policy seems to contradict these propositions. From 1971 through 1978, both Israel and Egypt spent from 20 to 40 percent of their GNPs on arms. Israel's spending on conventional arms remains high, although it has decreased since 1978. The decrease followed from the making of peace with Egypt and not from increased reliance on nuclear weapons. The seeming contradiction in fact bears out deterrent logic. So long as Israel holds the West Bank and the Gaza Strip she has to be prepared to fight for them. Since they are by no means unambiguously hers, deterrent threats, whether implicit or explicit, will not cover them. Moreover, while America's large subsidies continue, economic constraints will not drive Israel to the territorial settlement that would shrink her borders sufficiently to make a deterent policy credible.

From previous points it follows that nuclear weapons are likely to decrease arms racing and reduce military costs for lesser nuclear states in two ways. Conventional arms races will wither if countries shift emphasis from conventional defense to nuclear deterrence. For Pakistan, for example, acquiring nuclear weapons is an alternative to running a ruinous conventional race with India. And, of course, deterrent strategies make nuclear arms races pointless.

Finally, arms races in their ultimate form—the fighting of offensive wars designed to increase national security—also become pointless. The success of a deterrent strategy does not depend on the extent of territory a state holds, a point made earlier. It merits repeating because of its unusual importance for states whose geographic limits lead them to obsessive concern for their security in a world of ever more destructive conventional weapons.

The frequency and intensity of war. The presence of nuclear weapons makes war less likely. One may nevertheless oppose the spread of nuclear weapons on the ground that they would make war, however unlikely, unbearably intense should it occur. Nuclear weapons have not been fired in anger in a world in which more than one country has them. We have enjoyed over three decades of nuclear peace and may enjoy many more. But we can never have a guarantee. We may be grateful for decades of nuclear peace and for the discouragement of conventional war among those who have nuclear weapons. Yet the fear is widespread, and naturally so, that if they ever go off, we may all be dead. People as varied as the scholar Richard Smoke, the arms controller Paul Warnke, and former Defense Secretary Harold Brown all believe that if any nuclear weapons go off, many will. Although this seems the least likely of all the unlikely possibilities, unfortunately it is not impossible. What makes it so unlikely is that, even if deterrence should fail, the prospects for rapid deescalation are good.

McNamara asked himself what fractions of the Soviet Union's population and industry the United States should be able to destroy in order to deter her. For military, although not for budgetary, strategy this was the wrong question. States are not deterred because they expect to suffer a certain amount of damage but because they cannot know how much damage they will suffer. Near the dawn of the nuclear age Bernard Brodie put the matter simply: "The prediction is more important than the fact." The prediction, that is, that attacking the vital interests of a country having nuclear weapons may bring the attacker untold losses. As Patrick Morgan more recently put it: "To attempt to compute the cost of a nuclear war is to miss the point."

States are deterred by the prospect of suffering severe damage and by their physical inability to do much to limit it. Deterrence works because nuclear weapons enable one state to punish another state severely without first defeating it. "Victory" in Thomas Schelling's words, "is no longer a prerequisite for hurting the enemy." Countries armed with only conventional weapons can hope that their military forces will be able to limit the damage an attacker can do. Among countries armed with strategic nuclear forces, the hope of avoiding heavy damage depends mainly on the attacker's restraint and little on one's own efforts. Those who compare expected deaths through strategic exchanges of nuclear warheads with casualties suffered by the Soviet Union in World War II overlook this fundamental difference between conventional and nuclear worlds.

Deterrence rests on what countries *can* do to each other with strategic nuclear weapons. From this statement, one easily leaps to the wrong conclusion: that deterrent strategies, if they have to be carried through, will produce a catastrophe. That countries are able to annihilate each other means neither that deterrence depends on their threatening to do so nor that they will do so if deterrence fails. Because countries heavily armed with strategic nuclear weapons can carry war to its ultimate intensity, the control of force, in wartime as in peacetime, becomes the primary objective. If deterrence fails, leaders will have the strongest incentives to keep force under control and limit damage rather than launching genocidal attacks. If the Soviet Union should attack Western Europe, NATO's objectives would be to halt the attack and end the war. The United States has long had the ability to place hundreds of warheads precisely on targets in the Soviet Union. Surely we would strike military targets before striking industrial targets and industrial targets before striking cities. The intent to do so is sometimes confused with a war-fighting strategy, which it is not. It would not significantly reduce the Soviet

Union's ability to hurt us. It is a deterrent strategy, resting initially on the threat to punish. The threat, if it fails to deter, is appropriately followed not by spasms of violence but by punishment administered in ways that convey threats to make the punishment more severe.

A war between the United States and the Soviet Union that got out of control would be catastrophic. If they set out to destroy each other, they would greatly reduce the world's store of developed resources while killing millions outside of their own borders through fallout. Even while destroying themselves, states with few weapons would do less damage to others. As ever, the biggest international dangers come from the strongest states. Fearing the world's destruction, one may prefer a world of conventional great powers having a higher probability of fighting less destructive wars to a world of nuclear great powers having a lower probability of fighting more destructive wars. But that choice effectively disappeared with the production of atomic bombs by the United States during World War II. Since the great powers are unlikely to be drawn into the nuclear wars of others, the added global dangers posed by the spread of nuclear weapons are small.

The spread of nuclear weapons threatens to make wars more intense at the local and not at the global level, where wars of the highest intensity have been possible for a number of years. If their national existence should be threatened, weaker countries, unable to defend at lesser levels of violence, may destroy themselves through resorting to nuclear weapons. Lesser nuclear states will live in fear of this possibility. But this is not different from the fear under which the United States and the Soviet Union have lived for years. Small nuclear states may experience a keener sense of desperation because of extreme vulnerability to conventional as well as to nuclear attack, but, again, in desperate situations what all parties become most desperate to avoid is the use of strategic nuclear weapons. Still, however improbable the event, lesser states may one day fire some of their weapons. Are minor nuclear states more or less likely to do so than major ones? The answer to this question is vitally important because the existence of some states would be at stake even if the damage done were regionally confined.

For a number of reasons, then, deterrent strategies promise less damage than war-fighting strategies. First, deterrent strategies induce caution all around and thus reduce the incidence of war. Second, wars fought in the face of strategic nuclear weapons must be carefully limited because a country having them may retaliate if its vital interests are threatened. Third, prospective punishment need only be proportionate to an adversary's expected gains in war after those gains are discounted for the many uncertainties of war. Fourth, should deterrence fail, a few judiciously delivered warheads are likely to produce sobriety in the leaders of all of the countries involved and thus bring rapid deescalation. Finally, war-fighting strategies offer no clear place to stop short of victory for some and defeat for others. Deterrent strategies do, and that place is where one country threatens another's vital interests. Deterrent strategies lower the probability that wars will begin. If wars start nevertheless, deterrent strategies lower the probability that they will be carried very far.

Nuclear weapons may lessen the intensity as well as the frequency of wars among their possessors. For fear of escalation, nuclear states do not want to fight long or hard over important interests—indeed, they do not want to fight at all. Minor nuclear states have even better reasons than major ones to accommodate one another peacefully and to avoid any fighting. Worries about the intensity of war among nuclear states have to be viewed in this context and against a world in which conventional weapons become even costlier and more destructive.

CONCLUSION

The conclusion is in two parts. After saying what follows for American policy from my analysis, I briefly state the main reasons for believing that the slow spread of nuclear weapons will promote peace and reinforce international stability.

IMPLICATIONS FOR AMERICAN POLICY

I have argued that the gradual spread of nuclear weapons is better than either no spread or rapid spread. We do not face a set of happy choices. We may prefer that countries have conventional weapons only, do not run arms races, and do not fight. Yet the alternative to nuclear weapons for some countries may be ruinous arms races with high risk of their becoming engaged in debilitating conventional wars.

Countries have to care for their own security with or without the help of others. If a country feels highly insecure and believes that nuclear weapons would make it more secure, America's policy of opposing the spread of nuclear weapons will not easily prevail. Any slight chance of bringing the spread of nuclear weapons to a full stop exists only if the United States and the Soviet Union constantly and strenuously try to achieve that end. To do so carries costs measured in terms of their other interests. The strongest means by which the United States can persuade a country to forego nuclear weapons is a guarantee of its security, especially if the guarantee is made credible by the presence of American troops. But how many commitments do we want to make, and how many countries do we want to garrison? We are wisely reluctant to give guarantees, but we then should not expect to decide how other countries are to provide for their security. As a neighbor of China, India no doubt feels more secure, and can behave more reasonably, with a nuclear-weapons capability than without it. The thought applies as well to Pakistan as India's neighbor. We damage our relations with such countries by badgering them about nuclear weapons while being unwilling to guarantee their security. Under such circumstances they, not we, should decide what their national interests require.

Some have feared that weakening opposition to the spread of nuclear weapons will lead numerous states to make them because it may seem that "everyone is doing it." Why should we think that if we relax, numerous states will begin to make nuclear weapons? Both the United States and the Soviet Union were more relaxed in the past, and these effects did not follow. The Soviet Union initially supported China's nuclear program. The United States continues to help Britain maintain her deterrent forces. By 1968 the CIA had informed President Johnson of the existence of Israeli nuclear weapons, and in July of 1970 Richard Helms, Director of the CIA, gave this information to the Senate Foreign Relations Committee. These and later disclosures were not followed by censure of Israel or by reductions of assistance to her. And in September of 1980 the Executive Branch, against the will of the House of Representatives but with the approval of the Senate, continued to do nuclear business with India despite her explosion of a nuclear device and despite her unwillingness to sign the Nuclear Non-Proliferation Treaty.

Assisting some countries in the development of nuclear weapons and failing to oppose others has not caused a nuclear stampede. Is the more recent leniency toward India likely to? One reason to think so is that more countries now have the ability to make their own nuclear weapons, more than forty of them according to Joseph Nye.

Many more countries can than do. One can believe that American opposition to nuclear arming stays the deluge only by overlooking the complications of international life. Any state has to examine many conditions before deciding whether or not to develop nuclear weapons. Our opposition is only one factor and is not likely to be the decisive one. Many states feel fairly secure living with their neighbors. Why should they want nuclear weapons? Some countries, feeling threatened, have found security through their own strenuous efforts and through arrangements made with others. South Korea is an outstanding example. Many South Korean officials believe that South Korea would lose more in terms of American support if she acquired nuclear weapons than she would gain by having them. Further, on occasion we might slow the spread of nuclear weapons by *not* opposing the nuclear weapons program of some countries. When we oppose Pakistan's nuclear program, we are saying that we disapprove of countries developing nuclear weapons no matter what their neighbors do. Failing to oppose Pakistan's efforts also sends a signal to potential nuclear states, suggesting that if a country develops nuclear weapons, a regional rival may do so as well and may do so without opposition from us. This message may give pause to some of the countries that are tempted to acquire nuclear weapons. After all, Argentina is to Brazil as Pakistan is to India.

Neither the gradual spread of nuclear weapons nor American and Russian acquiescence in this has opened the nuclear floodgates. Nations attend to their security in ways they think best. The fact that so many more countries can make nuclear weapons than do make them says more about the hesitation of countries to enter the nuclear military business than about the effectiveness of American policy. We can sensibly suit our policy to individual cases, sometimes bringing pressure against a country moving toward nuclear-weapons capability and sometimes quietly acquiescing. No one policy is right for all countries. We should ask what our interests in regional stability require in particular instances. We should also ask what the interests of other countries require before putting pressure on them. Some countries are likely to suffer more in cost and pain if they remain conventional states than if they become nuclear ones. The measured and selective spread of nuclear weapons does not run against our interests and can increase the security of some states at a price they can afford to pay.

It is not likely that nuclear weapons will spread with a speed that exceeds the ability of their new owners to adjust to them. The spread of nuclear weapons is something that we have worried too much about and tried too hard to stop.

THE NUCLEAR FUTURE

What will a world populated by a larger number of nuclear states look like? I have drawn a picture of such a world that accords with experience throughout the nuclear age. Those who dread a world with more nuclear states do little more than assert that more is worse and claim without substantiation that new nuclear states will be less responsible and less capable of self control than the old ones have been. They feel fears that many felt when they imagined how a nuclear China would behave. Such fears have proved unfounded as nuclear weapons have slowly spread. I have found many reasons for believing that with more nuclear states the world will have a promising future. I have reached this unusual conclusion for five main reasons.

First, international politics is a self-help system, and in such systems the principal parties do most to determine their own fate, the fate of other parties, and the fate of the system. This will continue to be so, with the United States and the Soviet Union filling their customary roles. For the United States and the Soviet Union to achieve nuclear maturity and to show this by behaving sensibly is more important than preventing the spread of nuclear weapons.

Second, given the massive numbers of American and Russian warheads, and given the impossibility of one side destroying enough of the other side's missiles to make a retaliatory strike bearable, the balance of terror is indestructible. What can lesser states do to disrupt the nuclear equilibrium if even the mighty efforts of the United States and the Soviet Union cannot shake it? The international equilibrium will endure.

Third, nuclear weaponry makes miscalculation difficult because it is hard not to be aware of how much damage a small number of warheads can do. Early in this century Norman Angell argued that war could not occur because it would not pay (1914). But conventional wars have brought political gains to some countries at the expense of others. Among nuclear countries, possible losses in war overwhelm possible gains. In the nuclear age Angell's dictum, broadly interpreted, becomes persuasive. When the active use of force threatens to bring great losses, war becomes less likely. This proposition is widely accepted but insufficiently emphasized. Nuclear weapons have reduced the chances of war between the United States and the Soviet Union and between the Soviet Union and China. One may expect them to have similar effects elsewhere. Where nuclear weapons threaten to make the cost of wars immense, who will dare to start them? Nuclear weapons make it possible to approach the deterrent ideal.

Fourth, nuclear weapons can be used for defense as well as for deterrence. Some have argued that an apparently impregnable nuclear defense can be mounted. The Maginot Line has given defense a bad name. It nevertheless remains true that the incidence of wars decreases as the perceived difficulty of winning them increases. No one attacks a defense believed to be impregnable. Nuclear weapons may make it possible to approach the defensive ideal. If so, the spread of nuclear weapons will further help to maintain peace.

Fifth, new nuclear states will confront the possibilities and feel the constraints that present nuclear states have experienced. New nuclear states will be more concerned for their safety and more mindful of dangers than some of the old ones have been. Until recently, only the great and some of the major powers have had nuclear weapons. While nuclear weapons have spread, conventional weapons have proliferated. Under these circumstances, wars have been fought not at the center but at the periphery of international politics. The likelihood of war decreases as deterrent and defensive capabilities increase. Nuclear weapons, responsibly used, make wars hard to start. Nations that have nuclear weapons have strong incentives to use them responsibly. These statements hold for small as for big nuclear powers. Because they do, the measured spread of nuclear weapons is more to be welcomed than feared.

Ballistic Missiles and Weapons of Mass Destruction: What is the Threat? What Should be Done?

STEVE FETTER

Iraqi missile attacks against cities in Israel and Saudi Arabia have focused attention on the continuing proliferation of ballistic missile technology throughout the Third World. According to the Stockholm International Peace Research Institute 25 countries have acquired or are trying to acquire ballistic missiles, either through purchase or indigenous production. All but a few are developing countries, and the list encompasses some of the most volatile regions of the world. The greatest concentration is in the Middle East, where nine nations have missile programs. Missiles have also spread to other hot spots, including India and Pakistan, North and South Korea, Brazil and Argentina, Taiwan, and South Africa.

What are these missiles for, and why do countries want them? In particular, what types of warheads are emerging missile forces likely to be armed with? What capabilities will these missiles provide to their possessors, and what threats to international security will they pose? How should the United States and its allies respond to minimize these threats?

Since their invention in the 1930s, guided ballistic missiles have been used extensively in war only four times: the Germans launched over 2000 V-2 missiles against urban British and European targets during World War II; Iraq and Iran together launched nearly 1000 missiles against each other's cities during the 1980–88 Iran-Iraq war; the Kabul government fired over 1000 Soviet-made Scud missiles against *Mujahideen* guerrillas in the Afghanistan civil war; and Iraq launched about 80 modified Scud missiles against cities in Israel and Saudi Arabia in the 1991 Persian Gulf war. Three of these four cases occurred in the last decade, and in all four cases the missiles were armed solely with conventional (i.e., high-explosive) warheads. Moreover, these missiles were used mainly for strategic attacks against cities, perhaps because they lacked the accuracy necessary to strike even soft military targets such as airfields.

From *International Security*, summer 1991 (Vol. 16, No. 1), pp. 3–42, "Ballistic Missiles and Weapons of Mass Destruction." Reprinted by permission of The MIT Press, Cambridge, Massachusetts. © by the President and Fellows of Harvard College and of the Massachusetts Institute of Technology. Footnotes and portions of the text have been omitted.

Ballistic missiles with ranges greater than a few hundred kilometers are, however, an exceptionally inefficient vehicle for the delivery of conventional munitions. This has long been recognized by the nuclear powers, which rely on ballistic missiles almost exclusively for the delivery of nuclear warheads. The inefficiency of conventionally armed missiles seems to be well understood by the new missile states as well, since most of them are also actively seeking nuclear, chemical, and biological weapons. A missile armed with a Hiroshima-sized nuclear weapon is roughly 10,000 times more deadly than the same missile armed with high explosives. Fortunately, the development of nuclear weapons is expensive, easy to detect, and relatively easy to thwart with export controls. Chemical warheads, on the other hand, are far easier to acquire, and while they may be far less deadly than nuclear warheads, they could kill as many people as dozens or even hundreds of conventionally armed missiles. Even worse, biological warheads that dispense anthrax spores offer the possibility of inflicting casualties on the scale of small nuclear weapons.

As missile ranges increase, the civilian populations of U.S. allies (and eventually the United States itself) will become increasingly vulnerable to weapons of mass destruction. Responding to this threat should be a major preoccupation of the United States, just as ameliorating the Soviet nuclear threat has been a major policy goal for more than four decades. In fact, emerging missile arsenals may be an even greater menace, since the probability of inadvertent or accidental use is likely to be much higher, crisis instabilities are likely to be more severe, and several of these states are less politically stable than the Soviet Union has been.

Policy responses might include carrots (security guarantees and arms control), sticks (export controls, deterrence, or preventive war), and defenses (missile, aircraft, and civil defenses). The United States has tried each of these in a somewhat haphazard manner, with mixed success. Security guarantees cannot be extended to every state, and arms control is often unappealing to rogue states or their neighbors. Export controls are notoriously difficult to enforce, and are undercut by Third World suppliers and by the similarity of military and peaceful activities. Preventive war can be highly effective, but the risks and costs it entails (combined with the international environment it fosters) make it of very limited use as an instrument of national policy. Defenses are unlikely to be effective for a variety of reasons, and deterrence may not work in many situations. Nonetheless it is imperative, despite these shortcomings, that we weave these policy threads into a coherent and self-consistent fabric to protect civilians from weapons of mass destruction.

WHY SHOULD WE CARE ABOUT PROLIFERATION?

There are five reasons that we should be at least as concerned about the proliferation of weapons of mass destruction in the future as we have been about nuclear proliferation in the past: (1) proliferation complicates U.S. foreign policy; (2) crisis instabilities are likely to be more severe; (3) the probability of inadvertent or accidental use is likely to be greater; (4) transfers to terrorist or subnational groups are more likely; and (5) at least some of the future possessor nations are likely to be politically unstable, aggressive, and difficult to deter.

To see how missile proliferation, coupled with unconventional warheads, might complicate foreign policy, consider how the response to the Iraqi invasion of Kuwait might have been different if Iraq had possessed the capability to launch chemical, biological, or nuclear weapons against Paris or London. In the face of such a threat, would France and the United Kingdom have joined the United States in attacking Iraq? Indeed, if Iraq threatened to hold European cities "hostage," would even the United States have risked an attack? And if Iraq carried out threats to launch such weapons at the first notice of an allied attack, how would the United States and its allies have responded? The result would not necessarily be total paralysis; in the case of Iraq, for example, the United States could have preemptively destroyed the missile sites, as it did in the war. If weapons were launched nevertheless, massive conventional attacks would have been adequate to punish and defeat Iraq.

With regard to crisis instability, Third World weapons are more vulnerable to preemptive attack than are the forces of the nuclear powers, whether based on missiles or aircraft. The short distances separating nations in the Middle East make airbases and missile launch sites tempting targets for preemptive strikes; ballistic missiles, either with more accurate or with more powerful warheads, make it possible to attack such targets in just a few minutes. While light-weight missiles such as the Scud are readily mobile and thus can be difficult to destroy if dispersed throughout the countryside, longer-range missiles weighing more than ten or twenty tonnes are too heavy to be truly mobile and probably would be launched from a few (perhaps hardened) fixed sites. Missiles have the advantage of not requiring visible facilities such as airstrips, but, unlike aircraft, missiles cannot escape attack without being used offensively.

Although missiles themselves might not significantly worsen the vulnerability problem, weapons of mass destruction might, because the benefits that could be derived from a successful first strike would be much greater. Just as the early U.S. and Soviet nuclear forces were vulnerable to preemptive attack, so may emerging arsenals of mass destruction in the Third World create instability. If, during a crisis, one side believes that war is inevitable, it may try to preemptively destroy the other side's vulnerable but valuable weapons of mass destruction. Even if both sides prefer not to preempt, each may fear that the other side will; consequently, both may decide to launch at the first (perhaps false) indication of an attack. This crisis-stability problem is even worse than the one faced by the superpowers, because warning of an attack will be shorter, because of the shorter range, and much less reliable, because of the primitive intelligence-gathering capabilities of most Third World nations. The United States and the Soviet Union have managed to keep their nuclear forces on constant alert for three decades without an accidental launch. It is open to question whether the new missile states, lacking the wealth, technology, and political stability of the superpowers, can be expected to compile as good a record.

The possibility of unauthorized use or accident also creates dangers. Although political control over weapon systems may be very strong in authoritarian states, unauthorized use and accidental launches are not physically prevented by sophisticated permissive action links and environmental sensing devices, such as those used in U.S. nuclear weapons. A group of military officers might use or threaten to use such weapons on their own authority, either to satisfy an overzealous hatred of the enemy or to blackmail their own civilian government.

The probability of large-scale attacks by sub-national or terrorist organizations will become far more worrisome as weapons of mass destruction spread to Third World countries that sponsor acts of terrorism, such as Iran, Iraq, Libya, North Korea, and Syria. If the supplier of such weapons is known, victim nations could respond by retaliating against the supplier nation; but if the supplier cannot be positively identified, a forceful response to an anonymous attack could trigger widespread resentment, especially if the suspected supplier can plausibly deny its involvement. Terrorist attacks might also be calculated to catalyze war between two states.

With the possible exception of the Soviet Union in recent times, the nuclear powers exhibit an exceptional degree of internal political stability. Many of the potential proliferators listed in Table 2 do not enjoy the same degree of stability. Some states, such as Afghanistan, Iraq, and South Africa, have deep internal divisions. Other pairs of states, such as India and Pakistan, North and South Korea, and Israel and various Arab states, have deep religious, ideological, or cultural animosities, often combined with active border disputes, that weaken deterrence. Some authoritarian states are ruled by aggressive dictators, such as Libya's Muammar Qaddafi or Iraq's Saddam Hussein, who have little regard for international norms of behavior. Many of the new missile states are not happy with the status quo, and may look upon their newly acquired capabilities for mass destruction as instruments of intimidation and change. The probability of conflict within and among the new missile states will be substantially higher than has been the case with the present nuclear powers, which increases the probability that weapons of mass destruction will be used. Even if the United States or it allies would not be directly threatened, we should still be concerned because of the human suffering that would result from the use of such weapons.

WHAT CAN WE DO ABOUT PROLIFERATION?

The United States has a declaratory policy of preventing the proliferation of weapons of mass destruction, but this policy has been applied rather unevenly over time and among nations. Many of these inconsistencies have resulted from balancing the goal of nonproliferation against other goals of U.S. policy, such as containing the Soviet Union, supporting the state of Israel, or balancing the trade deficit. In most cases nonproliferation has taken a back seat to these other goals. It is time to give nonproliferation higher priority.

Possible policy responses fall into four broad categories: carrots, sticks, defenses, and management. *Carrots* include security guarantees and arms control arrangements designed to reassure states that are worried that they might need missiles or unconventional weapons for their defense. *Sticks* include export controls, deterrence through the threat of retaliation, economic sanctions, and the threat of preventive war, all of which are intended to thwart or deter proliferation. *Defenses,* both active and passive, seek to insulate the United States (and possibly its allies) from the effects of proliferation. *Management* refers to measures designed to cope with proliferation in a cooperative fashion by, for example, transferring technology or information that decreases the probability of accident, misuse, or instability.

Security Guarantees

Promising to defend a country if it is attacked can alleviate its desires for advanced weaponry, but this strategy has obvious limitations. The U.S. commitment to defend South Korea and Taiwan, not to mention Germany and Japan, may have averted the development of nuclear weapons by each of these nations. It is extremely difficult, however, to identify additional nations among those listed in Table 2 to which the United States could extend security guarantees. Even in the case of moderate Arab states such as Egypt and Saudi Arabia, guarantees would encounter strong opposition from supporters of Israel. Collective security guarantees, in which large groups of nations (e.g., the United Nations) agree to come to the aid of any member under attack, are more appealing, but for most nations collective security does not seem sufficiently reliable to forestall the desire to acquire advanced weapons.

Arms Control

Chemical, biological, and nuclear weapons have been the subject of multilateral arms control treaties; missiles have not. Although arms control treaties cannot prevent proliferation, they can provide a mechanism whereby nations that prefer not to develop certain types of weapons can be reassured that their rivals are also not developing them. If a nation believes that it would be better off if both it *and* its rivals refrained from acquiring certain weapons, then arms control should be an attractive solution. Unfortunately, it is not always so simple. For example, although India might be worse off if both it and Pakistan had ballistic missiles or nuclear weapons, India also faces another rival—China—which already has both and shows no interest in giving them up. Moreover, some nations (e.g., Israel) probably believe that they are better off if they possess weapons of mass destruction, even if it means that their rivals are free to develop the same weapons, for otherwise inferiorities in conventional weaponry or manpower could threaten their survival.

The 1925 Geneva Protocol prohibits the use (or, as interpreted by some countries, the first use) of chemical and biological weapons in war, but not the production or stockpiling of such weapons. Virtually all nations support a verified worldwide ban on chemical weapons, and negotiations on a Chemical Weapons Convention (CWC) are continuing in the multilateral Conference on Disarmament in Geneva. Although the widespread commercial uses of chemicals make a ban notoriously difficult to verify, the verification procedures under consideration are impressive, and it appears that, through a combination of continuous monitoring and on-site inspection, nonproduction by parties to a treaty can be adequately verified.

Although the Bush administration strongly supports the goals of the CWC, it has argued that the United States must retain a small stockpile of chemical weapons for deterrent purposes until all other states capable of manufacturing chemical weapons have joined the treaty. As might be expected, this position has come under heavy criticism by those who claim that it smacks of the division between the "haves" and the "have nots" that undermined adherence to the nuclear Non-Proliferation Treaty (NPT). The administration claims that this clause will be an incentive for potential holdouts to join the treaty. The administration's argument highlights the main problem with all multilateral arms control: what about states that will not sign the treaty? Since chemical weapons appear to be the main instrument by which some Arab states (e.g., Syria and Iraq) hope to offset the Israeli nuclear arsenal, it is unlikely that chemical weapons will disappear completely any time soon. Other states with powerfully armed neighbors may draw similar conclusions. There is always the hope that nonsignatories will heed world opinion and observe the taboo on the use of chemicals, but it is wise not to put too much faith in the power of international norms, especially those that have been broken in the recent past. The CWC will not prevent proliferation, but that is too high a standard to set for arms control. The appropriate question is whether the world will be a better place with a treaty than without one; in the case of the CWC, the answer is clearly "yes."

The development, production, stockpiling, and transfer of biological weapons is banned by the Biological Weapons Convention (BWC) of 1972, but the verification provisions of the BWC are limited. Parties to the BWC agree to cooperate with UN investigations, but such investigations must be approved by the Security Council, subject to the veto power of its permanent members. Various confidence-building measures have been adopted at the BWC review conferences, but these measures fall far short of the continuous monitoring and on-site inspections contemplated for the CWC. Since chemical agents are more likely to proliferate, because they are easier to produce and disseminate and their effects are more predictable, the lack of stringent BWC verification may not be worrisome now. But if the CWC makes chemical weapons far more difficult to acquire, then biological weapons may come to be seen as an attractive alternative, and their proliferation may become more of a problem.

In a recent trip to the Middle East, U.S. Secretary of State James Baker reportedly found "a lot of sympathy" among Persian Gulf states for a regional ban on weapons of mass destruction, and even found "considerable interest" in the idea in Israel. Although these discussions are commendable, there is little reason to believe that such an agreement could be achieved without solving the larger political problems in the Middle East, especially the Palestinian problem and the question of the occupied territories. If progress is not made along this front, the connection between Israeli nuclear weapons and Arab chemical (and possibly biological) weapons may create difficulties for the NPT as well as for the CWC. The final NPT review conference is scheduled for 1995, at which time the duration of the NPT will be decided. At least seven potential adversaries of Israel are signatories of the NPT: Egypt, Iran, Iraq, Libya, Saudi Arabia, Syria, and Yemen. Israel is not. All except Saudi Arabia and Yemen are strongly suspected of stockpiling chemical weapons; all but Yemen have acquired or are trying to acquire missiles capable of striking Israel. It is likely that the final NPT review conference will be used as a forum in which this group of countries, perhaps joined by other non-aligned nations, will insist that Israel join the NPT. Indeed, it is not inconceivable that these countries may tie their continued adherence to the NPT, as well as their support for the CWC, to Israeli accession to the NPT (or other equivalent steps). This situation would present the United States with a difficult management problem for which it should be prepared.

Export Controls

Controls on the export of key technologies and materials can slow proliferation, but such controls work much better and engender less resentment if they are coupled with a comprehensive arms control regime. In the NPT, for example, exports to signatories are accompanied by "safeguards" to verify that the exports (e.g., nuclear reactors) are not being used for military purposes. Supplier nations that are party to the NPT must require safeguards on all such exports, even to nations that are not parties to the Treaty. This coupling between arms control and export controls may be an important reason for the relatively slow pace of nuclear proliferation. Unfortunately, no comparable arrangements yet exist for the control of exports of chemical, biological, and ballistic-missile technology or materials. In general, export controls in these areas have been adopted only after proliferation problems were widely recognized. Even after controls are adopted, competition among suppliers and illegal exports often undermine their effectiveness.

Multilateral export controls were recently extended to missile technology through the Missile Technology Control Regime (MTCR). Although the MTCR has slowed missile programs in several countries, the regime is "too little, too late." One important flaw in the MTCR is that several current and potential future exporters of missile technology are not part of the regime, including China, India, Israel, North and South Korea, Taiwan, Brazil, and Argentina. Without the cooperation of all important suppliers, export controls can slow, but cannot stop, proliferation. Another major flaw is that the MTCR allows exports of missile technology for use in civilian applications such as space launch vehicles, even though the same technologies can be used in weapons. Even if the MTCR required safeguards to verify that exports were only being used in civilian applications (which it does not), the knowledge and experience gained would alone be sufficient in many cases to greatly aid military programs. And even if missile technologies were only exported to nations without military programs, sounding rockets and space launch vehicles developed for peaceful uses could quickly and easily be converted into ballistic missiles.

The prospects for export controls on chemical and biological warfare capabilities are not much brighter. The Australia Group, a loosely knit group of 23 countries including the United States, has for some time limited the export to certain countries of selected equipment and chemicals that can be used in the production of chemical agents, and yet chemical weapons have spread, with key technologies often slipping through the export controls of U.S. allies. The United States recently expanded its export restrictions, but this will be of little help unless most other supplier nations follow suit. Once again, a large part of the problem is that many of the chemicals and production techniques required for chemical and biological weapons have legitimate civilian uses. Many of the items whose export the United States limits are used to make plastics, pharmaceuticals, and fertilizers. Nerve agents, for example, are chemically similar to common organophosphate pesticides. Fermenters can be used to produce antibiotics as well as pathogens. Industrialized nations will find it difficult to deny technologies essential for the production of goods such as pesticides and antibiotics, even to the growing list of countries with a suspected interest in developing chemical or biological weapons; yet it is difficult, if not impossible, to ensure that such exports would not or could not be used for military purposes.

The power of export controls by the industrialized nations is waning. Several Third World countries, such as India and Brazil, have thriving chemical industries of their own, and they are highly unlikely ever to join the Australia Group or similar supplier groups. The only hope of enlisting the cooperation of such states is to embed export restrictions in an arms control framework that makes no distinctions between western and eastern, nuclear and non-nuclear, or industrialized and developing nations. In the case of nuclear weapons, chemical weapons, and ballistic missiles, the United States has been unwilling to go this far.

Deterrence, Sanctions, and Preventive War

Deterrence and preventive war represent the dark side of nonproliferation policy. Deterrence through threat of retaliation in kind is widely credited with preventing the use of chemical weapons in World War II, as well as the non-use of nuclear weapons since the end of World War II. Some claim that during the 1991 Gulf war, it was the possession of chemical weapons by the United States and the implicit threat to use these weapons that deterred Iraq from using its chemical weapons against allied ground troops, but this is far from obvious. First, Iraq apparently did not stockpile chemical weapons in Kuwait, and could not do so once the air war began destroying its supply lines. Iraqi forces might have used chemicals if they were available. Second, although most high-level officials were careful to say that the United States would consider all options if U.S. troops were attacked with chemical agents, others made it clear that the United States would not respond in kind. Indeed, the United States did not even have chemical weapons available for use in the Middle East.

It is theoretically impossible to prove that deterrence works, since it is always possible that the other side had no intention of using that which they were supposedly deterred from using. Only failures of deterrence can be verified. If one has faith in the power of the threat of retaliation in kind, then maintaining chemical arsenals might be better than a CWC that does not enjoy universal adherence. Some states or some leaders may not be deterrable, however. Moreover, the United States can deal militarily with most of the emerging unconventional threats by means of overwhelming conventional force, thus obviating the need for "in kind" retaliation.

The war against Iraq was a preventive war in the minds of many Americans. A primary goal of the war was to destroy Iraq's potential to make and deliver nuclear, chemical, and biological weapons—to make war now, rather than later when Iraq might be armed with long-range weapons of mass destruction. The destruction of the Iraqi Osiraq reactor by Israel is another example of a preventive use of force. The use of force, especially on the scale of U.S. actions in Iraq, will generally be limited to the most exceptional circumstances and the most obviously aggressive and nefarious governments. The use of economic sanctions is far more palatable, but sanctions by the United States alone are insufficient. However, the United Nations may be able to make more widespread use of sanctions to punish nations that use or threaten to use weapons of mass destruction, thereby deterring others from following the same path.

Defense

Even if arms control and export controls are reasonably effective, weapons of mass destruction will likely be acquired by a handful of determined states. Should the United States and its allies rely on the threat of retaliation to deter the use of such weapons, or should they pursue the development of defensive systems that could render such weapons "impotent and obsolete"? When this question was raised by President Reagan in 1983 in the context of the Soviet nuclear threat, general agreement emerged among defense analysts that the goal of a perfect defense was unattainable, and that the benefits of less-than-perfect defenses were unclear, and might well be negative. The use of Scud missiles in the Persian Gulf War and the apparent success of the Patriot system in shooting them down has rekindled the debate about the desirability of ballistic missile defenses. Now that perceptions of a Soviet threat have dimmed, should the United States develop defensive systems capable of shooting down missiles launched by Third World countries? I do not think so.

The Patriot is a ground-launched interceptor initially designed to shoot down aircraft, which has some capability to intercept short-range ballistic missiles (which travel at relatively low speeds) in their terminal or reentry phase. Although intercepting faster, longer-range missile warheads is far more challenging (especially at ranges of several thousand kilometers), it should be possible to build a system capable of destroying long-range missile warheads with non-nuclear interceptors in the near future. But a major problem with terminal systems is that they can only defend a limited area ("footprint" or area of coverage). The Patriot system, which has a small footprint, could be successful because the number of targets within range of Iraqi missiles was small. Defending cities from longer-range missiles would not only require a more sophisticated interceptor, but would require far more interceptor sites to defend all possible targets within range of the missile.

In designing terminal defenses against chemically armed missiles, care must be taken that warhead destruction will be high in the atmosphere. If the agent is released as a fine aerosol at altitudes of a few hundred meters or more, it will be sufficiently diluted by the time the cloud reaches the ground that doses will be inconsequential. If, on the other hand, the high explosive in the chemical warhead is not detonated, the agent may be released as relatively large droplets which rain quickly onto the ground (similar to the way in which agent is released from Soviet chemical warheads). The lethal area formed by such a release would, however, be much smaller than that resulting from a successful missile attack.

Even a highly effective terminal defense is unlikely to destroy more than 90 percent of incoming targets, but if only one nuclear or biological warhead penetrates the defenses of a city, thousands of people will die. Even the penetration of a single chemical warhead could result in hundreds of deaths and generate widespread panic in an unprepared population. Military planners are not likely to be satisfied with a 10 percent probability of penetration, however. Rather, it is probable that the deployment of defenses will prompt the search for offensive countermeasures (e.g., decoys, chaff, multiple warheads, maneuvering warheads, etc.), triggering an offense-defense arms race that leaves both sides less secure. It was the avoidance of just this sort of situation that lead the United States and the Soviet Union to limit strategic missile defenses in the Anti-Ballistic Missile (ABM) Treaty.

Only intercontinental-range missiles could threaten the U.S. homeland (except, possibly, from Cuba). Outside of the five declared nuclear powers, only Israel and India could strike the United States in the near future. However, important U.S. allies, such as the United Kingdom, France, Germany, and Japan, may soon be within range of the missile forces of several countries, and the United States might wish to protect its allies from attack. But space-based systems intended to intercept missiles in their boost phase, such as the SDI "brilliant pebbles" proposal, will not be able to engage short-range missiles or intermediate-range ballistic missiles that fly slightly depressed trajectories. Such systems might be able to destroy ICBMs, but their benefits are unclear, given how few countries will possess ICBMs, and given that any country sophisticated enough to develop ICBMs could certainly find other ways to deliver nuclear, chemical, and biological weapons if faced with an effective missile defense. Indeed, cruise missiles—about which SDI-type systems can do very little—may in the not-too-distant future prove to be far more effective delivery systems for emerging nuclear, chemical, and biological arsenals than ballistic missiles. Cruise missiles are extremely difficult to defend against.

Deployment of almost any type of defense against long-range missiles or the transfer of relevant technologies to U.S. allies would violate provisions of the ABM Treaty. Under the ABM Treaty, the United States and the Soviet Union are permitted to deploy no more than 100 ground-launched missiles, all at a single, fixed site. Mobile or space-based systems are prohibited, and neither country may transfer ABM technologies to third parties. Any system capable of efficiently destroying intermediate-range missiles would have some capability against strategic missiles, which may violate the Treaty. In contemplating defenses against longer-range Third World missiles, the United States must judge whether the benefits afforded by such a defense would be worth jeopardizing the ABM Treaty and the two decades of U.S.-Soviet arms control efforts that are based upon it. The United States and the Soviet Union could agree to deploy defenses in a cooperative fashion to defend against third-party missiles, but this is highly unlikely in the foreseeable future.

Management

As noted above, Third World missiles and weapons of mass destruction are likely to be far more vulnerable to crisis instability, accidents, and intentional misuse than U.S. and Soviet nuclear arsenals have been. While this is undoubtedly a good reason to avoid proliferation in the first place, additional nations will acquire such weapons despite our best efforts at dissuasion. Should the United States quietly offer to help improve the safety and stability of their weapons? It seems illogical to spend billions of dollars ensuring the safety and security of our own weapons, while doing nothing to ensure the safety and security of weapons that may be pointed at us or our allies. If crisis stability becomes a major problem, the United States could extend warnings or assurances as to missile attack, in hopes of preventing inadvertent launches and deterring preemptive strikes. Such measures might be in the best interest of the United States and the world community in general, but it is extremely difficult for a government to command this degree of flexibility in foreign policy. Moreover, such behavior on our part would be interpreted by other Third World nations as a "wink and a nod" to successful proliferators, and this would inevitably undermine the even more important task of preventing the spread of such weapons to additional states.

CONCLUSIONS

Ballistic missile proliferation continues, with several nations seeking ever-longer ranges. It is only a matter of time before cruise-missile technology proliferates in similar fashion. Long-range ballistic missiles armed with conventional warheads do not make military sense. This simple fact seems to be well understood, since many of these same nations are also actively pursuing nuclear, chemical, and biological weapons. Nuclear weapons are by far the most difficult to acquire; the requisite technologies to produce nuclear materials are expensive and export controls are relatively effective. Chemical weapons are much easier to acquire, and a missile armed with a chemical warhead could kill as many people as dozens or even hundreds of conventionally armed missiles. Biological weapons are more difficult to produce and more unpredictable in their effects, but could inflict casualties on the scale of small nuclear weapons. Therefore, it should not be surprising if the future of missile prolif-eration points in the direction of chemical and biological weaponry, since for many states these are the only weapons that could consti-tute a strategic threat or a strategic deterrent.

In dealing with this emerging threat, the United States and its allies should resist calls to develop ballistic missile defenses or to rely on deterrence or threat of military force. Defenses would be costly and imperfect; they would trigger offensive countermeasures and endanger superpower arms control; and they would address only one of the ways in which weapons of mass destruction could be delivered (and probably the least likely way they would be delivered to the United States). While deterrence may work among the nuclear powers, it is an unreliable foundation for Third World security, due to the increased probability of accidents, unauthorized use, crisis instability, political instability, and transfers to terrorist or sub-national groups.

The best approach lies in the creation of a comprehensive arms control regime that covers all of these weapons, and which incor-porates safeguards to ensure that exports—even to nonsignatories—are used only for peaceful purposes, coupled with the expanded use of the United Nations to foster collective security in the longer term. Comprehensive arms control regimes are unlikely to be created, however, if the superpowers continue to be viewed by Third World nations as "advocating water, but drinking wine." The superpowers are unlikely to command much authority in their efforts to limit nuclear weapons or ballistic missiles if they continue to develop, test, and deploy new types of nuclear weapons and missiles that they claim are essential for their security. Nor are they likely to muster much support for a "ban" on chemical weapons that permits the superpowers to retain small stockpiles for their own security. Nor are Third World countries likely to support treaties that permit their enemies to possess (or even use) weapons of mass destruction with impunity. The United States should promote the United Nations as the appropriate forum for addressing security and prolif-eration concerns. In particular, more use should be made of global economic sanctions to punish nations that violate agreed international norms, such as using or threatening to use weapons of mass destruction.

During the Cold War, efforts to stem proliferation often took a back seat to superpower confrontation, as illustrated by the U.S. decision to extend aid to Pakistan in support of *Mujahideen* guerrillas in Afghanistan, rather than cut it off in response to Pakistan's nuclear developments. Perhaps with the end of the Cold War and the Persian Gulf War, the United States and its allies can focus their attention firmly on the proliferation problem. A coherent, self-consistent, and high-priority effort is urgently needed if the United States and its allies are to avert the growing vulnerability of civilian populations to attacks with weapons of mass destruction.

Limited ABM Defense: A Prudent Step

MICHAEL KREPON

Specialists in European security are taking a whole new look at their discipline. Cold Warriors are starting with a clean slate and arguing about just causes for military intervention. The Soviet Union is trying to figure out what to call itself, how to reorganize its economy and political system, and how much of its internal empire can be saved. With so much re-evaluation going on, the time has come for the arms control community to review its basic principles and reassess how best to serve them.

We need this review, if only because we have been repeating ourselves for a very long time. Maybe we have been prophetically correct all along. If so, our friendly, in-house review of first principles and policy prescriptions will do no harm. After a thorough "zero-based" evaluation, we can continue to argue forcefully for the ideas that have long seemed right and just.

Alternately, our honest reappraisal may suggest some second thoughts. Few of us can hope to achieve perfect wisdom in this lifetime; those with a chance of reaching that lofty plateau usually stay far away from debates over throw-weight and on-site inspections. Vaclav Havel's admonition applies to us, no less than to others: "Follow those who seek the truth; flee those who have found it."

We are now engaged in a new debate over the future of the Antiballistic Missile (ABM) Treaty. . . . Senator Sam Nunn (D-GA) who, along with Senators John Warner (R-VA), William Cohen (R-ME), and others, has proposed that the United States deploy "one or an adequate additional number" of ground-based ABM sites, along with improved space-based sensors, to defend against limited ballistic missile attacks. This proposal . . . approved by the [Congress in 1991] . . . calls for these changes to take place in the context of negotiations with the Soviet Union to amend the ABM Treaty.

Many in the arms control community have heatedly denounced this plan as a threat to the future of strategic arms control and an attempt to gut the ABM Treaty. In this view, even modest amendments to the treaty will inevitably lead the United States onto a

From *Arms Control Today*, Vol. 21, No. 8, October 1991, pp. 15, 19–20. Reprinted by permission. Portions of the text have been omitted.

slippery slope paving the way for space-based interceptors, the "brilliant pebbles" so dear to the hearts of Strategic Defense Initiative (SDI) enthusiasts.

THE ABM TREATY

To address these concerns, it is first necessary to go back to the basic objectives and purposes of the ABM Treaty, as enunciated by the Nixon administration during the 1972 Senate ratification debate. According to this testimony, the basic purposes of the SALT I agreements were to maintain and enhance a sound U.S. strategic posture and to reach a more stable strategic relationship with the Soviet Union. The ABM Treaty's prohibition against territorial defenses was the agreed means toward these ends. Ground-based defenses in limited number do not undermine these basic objectives and purposes: 200 interceptor missiles were permitted by the ABM Treaty, a figure that was halved two years later by mutual agreement.

In the nearly 20 years that have elapsed since the ABM Treaty entered into force, the United States has learned to live comfortably with such deployments by the Soviet Union. These limited defenses cannot blunt a concerted retaliatory attack, and thus do not impair the nuclear standoff that helped avoid the use of nuclear weapons during the Cold War. Given this fact, ground-based interceptors in treaty-limited numbers have not generated new requirements for offensive forces, another legitimate concern of the arms control community. The rationales and impetus for strategic modernization programs have been driven by other considerations.

Nor have limited deployments of ground-based defenses lent very much credence to the anxieties of opponents of arms control. Die-hard ABM Treaty critics have worried that even modest defenses in being could lay the groundwork for a one-sided, sudden "break-out" from treaty constraints, actions that could place the United States at a disadvantage. These fears, so prominent in the Reagan administration's critiques of Soviet treaty compliance, have now been dismissed by the Bush administration, which has concluded that the military risks associated with ABM Treaty compliance concerns range "from minor to none."

In sum, the record of the past 20 years suggests that the basic objectives and purposes of the ABM Treaty remain sound. In the late 1960s, at the outset of the huge growth in strategic arsenals that resulted from multiple-warhead missiles, territorial ground-based defenses were very likely to drive up requirements for offensive forces, leading to an unstable situation and foreclosing the possibility of agreements on offensive or defensive forces. But now that offensive forces have grown so unnecessarily on both sides, ground-based defenses in limited numbers cannot threaten strategic stability and need not threaten a long-term process of arms reductions. After all, with 8,000 or 10,000 deliverable strategic warheads permitted under the Strategic Arms Reduction Treaty (START), 100 or 300 or even 600 ground-based interceptors can hardly affect the balance of terror. The crux of the debate over limited, ground-based defenses therefore revolves around costs and benefits, not strategic stability.

The same cannot be said for space-based interceptors, which raise even more problems than ground-based defenses did in the late 1960s. If brilliant pebbles can work as advertised, these interceptors could destroy missiles before they unleash their payload of multiple warheads. Ground-based missiles could then perform mop-up action, leaving whoever controls Soviet nuclear forces at a deadly disadvantage.

At a time when the United States needs to nurture constructive political change and the downsizing of military forces in what remains of the Soviet Union, it would be most unwise to press forward with space-based interceptor deployments. These activities are likely to fuel concerns over U.S. strategic intentions, help hardline elements to regroup, and sour U.S. political relations with both the Union leadership and the Russian republic.

A disorganized Soviet or revitalized Russian political leadership cannot stand idly by while it perceives that the United States is moving to gain overwhelming strategic nuclear superiority. As soon as they were able, they would pursue countermeasures to make sure that their worst fears were alleviated. The deployment of brilliant pebbles would be directly contrary to the basic objectives and purposes of the ABM Treaty, a sure-fire way to kill prospects for truly significant arms reductions, and an impediment to the transformation of political-military relations between the two nuclear superpowers.

For the foreseeable future, forging a new cooperative security relationship with the new Union leadership and the Russian republic is far more important and necessary than pushing ahead with space-based interceptors. At some point in the future, U.S. relations with the Union and with the Russian republic might be so firmly cooperative and secure, and other foreign threats might be so severe, that the two sides might agree to deploy a small number of brilliant pebbles-like interceptors, along with highly intrusive cooperative measures to provide assurance against breakout scenarios and other fears. But this scenario appears very remote at this point. The ABM Treaty's distinction between ground-based interceptors, which are permitted in agreed numbers, and space-based missiles, which are prohibited, remains crucial.

The Nunn-Warner proposal calls for the deployment of a single, 100-interceptor ABM site at Grand Forks, North Dakota, beginning by 1996, and for negotiations to permit additional ABM sites, additional interceptors, space-based battle-management sensors, and increased flexibility for advanced ABM testing, and to clarify existing treaty restrictions. The SDI Organization has pointed out that deployment of 100 interceptor missiles at one site, as permitted by the 1974 ABM Protocol, or even 200 interceptors at two sites, as the original treaty allowed, would only be useful against accidental or unauthorized launches of small numbers of missiles. To guard against "worst case" scenarios of unauthorized launches, such as the rogue submarine commander who steals up to our shores and fires a salvo of 20 10-warhead missiles, some have proposed four to six ground-based radar and missile sites. Precise cost estimates for these proposed deployments are difficult to find. Cost estimates for a 100-interceptor deployment at Grand Forks begin at around $10 billion.

It would be far less expensive to share U.S. technologies for maintaining strict control against unauthorized use of nuclear weapons with Union and Russian officials. Command destruct mechanisms that are employed for test missiles could also be used for missiles carrying nuclear weapons. These ideas are worth pursuing, despite prospective difficulties in their implementation. Since the damage from even a single nuclear detonation could be devastating, however, multiple solutions to this potential problem are warranted.

In addition to such improved safety and security measures, is it wise to spend money on limited ground-based defenses? We in the arms control community have come to understand the likelihood of unexpected occurrences, since they have continually set back nuclear negotiations. Accidents may also happen in the command and control of nuclear weapons, despite all of the concerted efforts made to prevent them and to foreclose unauthorized use.

The Earth's inhabitants have been extraordinarily fortunate that, during the first 46 years of the nuclear age, no nuclear weapon has been used against the United States or the Soviet Union, and none has gone off accidentally. Maybe we will all be this lucky for the next 46 years. After all, the probability of a ballistic missile warhead detonation is surely less than that of a tree falling on one's house.

Should we buy a ground-based insurance policy against unlikely but potentially devastating nuclear mishaps? Like other decisions to buy insurance, the answer depends on costs and risks. Insurance policies that cover every contingency are extremely expensive and rare. Those who are still fortunate enough to have insurance opt to pay premiums even though we are not covered against every possible misfortune.

With so many important domestic needs that are unmet, and with severe budget deficits stretching out as far as the eye can see, it is hard to make the case for new insurance premiums. But there is good reason to believe that the funds that now seem likely to be spent on SDI will not be transferred to domestic accounts. Therefore, as an arms controller who believes in Murphy's Law, facing a [former] Soviet Union that will be in a chaotic state for the foreseeable future, I believe it makes sense to purchase a modest ground-based insurance policy. The premiums can be paid even within decreased congressional appropriations for SDI.

It is still too early, however, to commit the United States to ground-based ABM sites beyond the terms of the ABM Treaty. . . .

It has taken us four decades of national debate to dismiss the worst-case threat of a Soviet "bolt-out-of-the-blue" attack; we do not need to repeat this syndrome for the threat of unauthorized launches. If we are wise enough to avoid the trap of planning on the basis of worst-case threats, we can take prudent steps to defend ourselves at modest cost without undercutting the objectives and purposes of the ABM Treaty.

At this point, simple prudence suggests the deployment of 100 interceptor missiles at the Grand Forks, North Dakota ABM site permitted by the ABM Treaty. Simple prudence also suggests the use of "pop-up" optical sensors, devices based in space, or other types of sensors to improve the performance of the single ABM site. These need not be destabilizing as long as both sides refrain from deploying interceptor missiles in space. When pressed, SDI officials acknowledge that with such tracking devices, the Grand Forks site could provide modest protection of the entire continental United States.

The deployment of such additional sensors would require a minor amendment to the treaty, if they were fully capable of substituting for an ABM radar. In any case, bilateral discussions would be needed over their capabilities and number. It is also necessary, at long last, to develop common understandings about the dividing line between theater and strategic ballistic missile defenses, and permitted and prohibited tests of new defensive concepts.

Ultimately, it may be necessary to deploy more than one land-based ABM missile site, but this decision need not be made now. We have several years to assess efforts to implement improved command and control procedures, such as command destruct mechanisms for ICBMs and submarine-launched ballistic missiles, and to review events in what once were the constituent republics of the Soviet Union. If, over time, we find it prudent to deploy more than one site, Union or Russian leaders may well be inclined to go down this path, since they, more than we, face third-country missile threats.

Will this process automatically lead to a slippery slope endangering not only the ABM Treaty but the entire process of strategic arms control? Not if the clear dividing line between ground-based and space-based interceptors is maintained. . . .

The best insurance policy against this eventuality is the ABM Treaty itself, which has served the cause of strategic stability and arms reductions in the past, and should continue to do so in the future. Amendments to the treaty, if they are warranted at all in the near term, should deal with ground-based deployments and sensors, not with the basic prohibition against space-based interceptors. The basic objectives and purposes of this 20-year-old treaty still remain valid, and they are entirely compatible with modest ground-based defenses.

Star Wars Redux: Limited Defenses,
Unlimited Dilemmas

MATTHEW BUNN

In his State of the Union address, President Bush pointed to the apparent success of the Patriot missile in the Gulf War and called for a revitalized Strategic Defense Initiative (SDI) program with a scaled-back mission—protecting against "limited strikes, whatever their source." Rather than intercepting less than half of a large-scale, well-coordinated Soviet strike, the previous SDI goal, the revised concept is to intercept essentially all of a small missile attack—a handful of missiles launched by a fanatic Third World dictator, perhaps, or by a deranged Soviet missile commander.

The Pentagon quickly put forward a new plan for this new mission, a downsized version of the previous "early deployment" plan, dubbed Global Protection Against Limited Strikes (GPALS). But when examined closely, this new SDI approach is little different from its predecessors—an ill-considered scheme to meet ill-defined threats that would cost tens of billions of dollars, force the United States to abrogate the Antiballistic Missile (ABM) Treaty, doom prospects for the offensive nuclear cutbacks called for in the nearly complete Strategic Arms Reduction Talks (START) treaty, and probably touch off a dangerous and costly competition between missile defenses and offensive forces.

Indeed, the ostensible scaling-back of SDI plans may be less than meets the eye, for while the initial GPALS concept does include fewer interceptors than earlier near-term deployment schemes, the Strategic Defense Initiative Organization (SDIO) has suggested that it sees GPALS as only the camel's nose under the tent, emphasizing that it would "provide options to expand our defense deployments" should circumstances warrant.

THE MORE THINGS CHANGE . . .

Despite the profoundly different mission President Bush has given the SDI program, the GPALS system is quite similar to the previous "Phase I" plan. The revised design has essentially all the same elements, but fewer of them. The system would include

From *Arms Control Today*, Vol. 21, No. 11, May 1991, pp. 12–18. Reprinted by permission of the publisher. Portions of the text and some footnotes have been omitted.

roughly 1,000 space-based "brilliant pebbles" interceptors—small, potentially autonomous orbiting rockets, designed to home in on target missiles with infrared and other sensors and destroy them by direct collision—as opposed to over 4,000 in the previous plan.

These would be backed up by 750–1,000 long-range, ground-based rockets, half the number called for in earlier early deployment designs. The ground-based layer would consist of one or both of two types of rockets—one designed to intercept warheads while they were still in space, and another that could, in theory, intercept them either in space or within the atmosphere, after drag had stripped away many of the warhead-mimicking decoys that might accompany them. The first system, which SDIO believes would be cheaper, is known as the ground-based interceptor (GBI), a follow-on to the Exoatmospheric Reentry-vehicle Interceptor System (ERIS). The dual-mode idea is known as the Exoatmospheric/Endoatmospheric Interceptor (E^2I), successor to the High Endoatmospheric Defense Interceptor (HEDI).

These interceptors would be supported by a command system and a network of sensors, which include ground-based radars, rocket-launched infrared probes, and a constellation of roughly 50 satellites based on brilliant pebbles technology, known as "brilliant eyes"—an adaptation of the earlier Space Surveillance and Tracking System (SSTS) concept. (SDI, unfortunately, is an alphabet-soup world of ever-changing acronyms.)

In addition to these systems for protection against long-range strategic missiles, antitactical ballistic missiles (ATBMs)—upgraded versions of the Patriot and a variety of potential follow-on systems—would be deployed to protect U.S. forces and allies around the world.

SDIO estimates GPALS' total cost at $41 billion (in 1988 dollars), of which $32 billion would be for strategic defenses, and $9 billion for ATBM systems. SDIO hopes to begin deploying the tactical defenses in the mid-1990s, and the strategic systems just before the turn of the century.

SHIFTING MISSIONS

President Reagan's vision of a Star Wars umbrella that would protect the American people from a massive Soviet missile attack "just as a roof protects a family from rain" was never feasible. Even the far more limited goal of intercepting less than half of a first-wave Soviet attack of several thousand warheads—since 1987, the official goal of initial missile defenses—was highly problematic.

But as the Patriot showed in the Gulf War, available technology can at least make a good beginning on the dramatically simpler task of protecting against small numbers of conventionally armed, slow-moving tactical ballistic missiles. Similarly, while some of SDIO's claims for its new system remain highly questionable—such as its alleged ability to provide global protection against all ballistic missiles with ranges of more than a "few hundred miles"—there is little doubt that it is technically possible to defend the United States against a handful of long-range ballistic missiles launched by accident, a mad commander, or a Third World country. The key reason that previous defense schemes "wouldn't work," in the often simplistic vernacular of the SDI debate, was not that it is impossible to shoot down a missile, but that defenses could be easily overcome by a wide array of countermeasures in a large, well-coordinated attack (as were Iraq's air defenses). But if the mission is only to defend against a handful of missiles, most such problems are far less relevant.

The key issues in the new SDI debate, therefore, focus not so much on technical feasibility as on costs and benefits. Is there really a substantial threat of limited missile attacks? Are ballistic missiles really the means a Third World fanatic would choose to attack or intimidate the United States? Is accomplishing SDI's new mission worth the enormous expense of the proposed system? Is it worth destroying the ABM Treaty, sacrificing the START agreement and hopes for further nuclear reductions, and potentially restarting an offense-defense arms competition? Are there alternative ways of addressing the same security threats?

THIRD WORLD MISSILES

In the aftermath of the Gulf War, the possibility of a Third World missile attack has gained a higher political profile than ever before. The technology of short-range ballistic missiles is undeniably spreading: Director of Central Intelligence William Webster has predicted that by the year 2000, 15 developing countries will be producing their own ballistic missiles. But these countries are investing in the short- and medium-range missiles needed to threaten their regional rivals, not in intercontinental missiles designed to attack the United States. Against such tactical missiles, ground-based ATBMs like the Patriot and planned follow-ons—which are permitted by the ABM Treaty, and have received strong congressional support, in contrast to SDI's other early deployment plans—can provide an effective defense.

Building a ballistic missile with the intercontinental range needed to threaten the United States poses fundamentally more difficult technological problems that are likely to take many years and billions of dollars to resolve. Even the superpowers required over a decade to move from acquiring German V-2 technology (similar to Iraq's Soviet-designed Scuds) in the aftermath of World War II to launching their first ICBMs. While developing nations will not have to invent ICBM technology for the first time, as the superpowers did, they will not have anything like the resources of the superpowers to devote to the problem. China, which was supplied with Soviet

Scud-type missiles in the late 1950s, required well over a decade to build and deploy an intermediate-range missile capable of reaching Moscow, and more than two decades to field a full-range ICBM capable of reaching the mainland United States, despite having a far better indigenous technical base than most other Third World countries possess. Hence, as former Secretary of Defense Harold Brown has recently predicted, China is likely to remain the only developing nation capable of threatening the United States with a ballistic missile for at least the next decade.[1]

Indeed, though Star Wars supporters often argue that the ABM Treaty is a relic of an extinct bipolar world, no longer relevant in an age of missile proliferation, the fact is that when the treaty was negotiated, a predicted near-term ICBM threat from China had already been the focus of a major U.S. ABM program—the Sentinel—and two decades later, that Chinese threat remains the only foreseeable Third World missile threat to U.S. territory.

In addition, since a land-based ballistic missile attack, unlike most terrorist acts, can easily be traced to its origin, only leaders willing to face a devastating retaliation from the full military power of the United States could contemplate a missile attack on U.S. territory. Particularly with Iraq now having accepted cease-fire terms requiring inspected dismantlement of its primitive missile capabilities, it is difficult to identify a plausible candidate for a "terrorist state" that might someday have both the motive and the means to attack the United States with a ballistic missile.

In any case, whatever the real risk of attack by a potential "terrorist state," a defense against ballistic missiles alone would not solve the problem. As Brown put it, "the argument that SDI would protect us from such potential nuclear-armed fanatics does not stand up under critical examination," as such weapons "are far more likely to be delivered by aircraft, ships sailed into our harbors, or packing crates smuggled across our borders than by ballistic missiles." SDI proponents often frame the issue as whether America will remain defenseless; but the fact is that we will be defenseless against these more likely threats whether we build a defense against the less plausible ICBM threat or not.

Ultimately, frustrating and imperfect though they may be, a combination of deterrence and international efforts to stem the spread of nuclear, chemical, and biological weapons, along with various means of delivery, will remain the mainstay of protection against these potential dangers.

ACCIDENTS AND MAD COMMANDERS

Another oft-cited hazard is the possibility that a missile might be launched by accident, or by a mad commander without authoriza-

---

[1] Harold Brown, "Yes on Patriot, No on SDI," *The Washington Post*, March 27, 1991.

tion. Here too, the real magnitude of the risks should not be overestimated. A truly "accidental" launch of a long-range nuclear missile is extremely unlikely. Rather than potentially resulting from the failure of one or more systems—hardly an unknown event in the annals of high technology—an accidental launch would require several independent systems to do their jobs correctly at the same time without being told to do so: opening the silo door, igniting the rocket engine, arming the warhead (which requires the insertion of a special code), and so on.

The more realistic concern is the possibility of unauthorized launch. Fortunately, however, both superpowers have devoted considerable attention to both procedural and mechanical safeguards to minimize this risk, carefully screening the personnel involved, setting up procedures under which it is impossible for any single officer to launch a long-range missile, and in the case of bombers and land-based missiles, installing electronic locks that make it physically impossible for the launch officers to arm and launch the weapons without receiving a code from higher authority. The Soviet Union has traditionally demonstrated even greater concern for maintaining central control over any use of nuclear weapons; in the 1950s and 1960s, Soviet missile warheads were reportedly stored entirely separate from the missiles themselves, under the control of the KGB. Even today, Soviet missiles reportedly cannot be launched unless the order is confirmed through two separate lines of authority: the military and the KGB. . . .

To the extent that accidental or unauthorized launches remain a possibility, there are other approaches to reducing the risk that may offer more foolproof protection at a lower cost than missile defenses. Both superpowers should undertake high-level reviews of existing safeguards, and the electronic locks used on land-based missiles should be extended to submarine-launched systems as well. In addition, as Senate Armed Services Committee Chairman Sam Nunn (D-GA) has suggested, serious consideration should be given to installing "command destruct" systems on existing missiles, so that a missile launched by accident or without authorization could be destroyed in flight—with appropriate attention devoted to providing assurance that such systems could not be used by an adversary to disable U.S. missiles.

LOOKING FOR THE PRICE TAG

The need for GPALS, in short, is far less urgent than proponents have made it seem. The costs and risks of building such a system, however, would be enormous.

Most obvious is the direct price tag of the system itself. As mentioned above, SDIO now estimates that GPALS would cost $41 billion. Far from the "affordable defensive capability" SDIO touts, that cost is far higher than the amount yet to be spent on any other strategic program, even the B-2 bomber whose price tag Congress is choking on. With the Pentagon now going through the painful process of culling hundreds of billions of dollars from past spending plans, and even Powell acknowledging that defense budgets will continue to decline, it is difficult to see where the money could be found, without drastic cuts in conventional defense programs.

Yet the $41 billion figure is highly misleading; it is set in 1988 dollars (to be comparable with past Phase I cost estimates), and excludes many of the substantial costs involved, including the billions already spent on SDI and the costs of continuing operations and support. As the 1,000 brilliant pebbles would each have a planned operational life of 10 years, "support" would include launching 100 new ABM satellites every year in perpetuity just to keep the system operational.

Moreover, many outside observers believe that even for what it does include, SDIO's cost estimate—which has not yet been approved by Pentagon cost analysts, let alone independent ones—is extremely optimistic. The price of brilliant pebbles is already spiralling rapidly upward. When the concept was first introduced three years ago, advocates estimated that development and deployment of 100,000 pebbles would cost only $10 billion; now, with a deployment only one percent as large, the estimated price remains the same. Yet current estimates of about $1.5 million per interceptor remain far below the nearly $50 million-per-satellite cost of NAV-STAR, the cheapest satellite currently in the Air Force inventory. Studies of other weapon systems suggest that the final cost is often roughly two-and-a-half times the cost estimated at this early stage of development. Ultimately, the cost of the GPALS system could well reach or even exceed $100 billion.

A NEW ARMS COMPETITION

The direct economic cost of GPALS would be only the beginning. Pursuing GPALS would soon require the United States to abrogate the ABM Treaty, potentially igniting an expensive and dangerous new race between ever-improving missiles and missile defenses, and short-circuiting prospects for nuclear arms control.

SPACING OUT

One of the oddest aspects of GPALS is its similarity to past plans, despite its radically different mission. On closer examination, the GPALS design appears to be more the result of a quick rewrite of the previous early deployment script than of any serious study of the most cost-effective way to meet SDI's new, limited goals.

Why SDIO continues its almost obsessive emphasis on space . . . is a particular mystery. When SDI began, it focused on space because the ground-based systems of the past could handle only a limited number of missiles. To defend against a massive attack, one had to extend the "battle space" back toward the missiles' launch sites. But when massive attack is no longer an issue, space is no longer necessary. Ground-based systems could do an adequate job of protecting the United States against a limited number of long-range missiles, without the expense, complexity, potential vulnerabilities, and treaty issues raised by space basing.

Against the shorter-range missiles that threaten U.S. forces and allies elsewhere in the world, ground-based ATBMs like the Patriot and planned follow-ons could be reasonably effective—and space-based interceptors would not, despite Cooper's remarkable claims that brilliant pebbles would provide protection even against "modified Scuds of the sort that are attacking Tel Aviv."[2] Brilliant pebbles cannot effectively intercept short-range missiles in the boost phase, as short-range systems are natural "fast-burn boosters," typically burning out in less than 100 seconds, before brilliant pebbles could realistically reach them.

SDIO now argues that brilliant pebbles can be modified to attack such missiles in the midcourse phase of flight instead. This would raise difficult new sensor problems, particularly as the relatively cold missile body and warhead would have to be detected and tracked looking down against a bright, warm Earth background, rather than looking up against the cold blackness of space.

But even if that problem could be solved, brilliant pebbles would still be ineffective against theater-range missiles, as the space rockets could easily be underflown. Cooper has acknowledged that atmospheric heating of their sensitive sensors would prevent brilliant pebbles from operating below 100 kilometers; short-range missiles naturally fly below that altitude, and intermediate-range missiles could easily be reprogrammed to do so, for a small penalty in range. . . . Indeed, even SDIO's own director of tactical missile defense, Colonel Harold Richardson, has acknowledged that interceptors such as brilliant pebbles would be "contributors" only against "very long-range missile threats that flew quite high."[3]

The Pentagon's arguments for its emphasis on space—presented by Assistant Secretary of Defense for International Security Policy Stephen Hadley at a February 12 press briefing—do not stand up to critical scrutiny.

First, Hadley argued that space-based sensors could be helpful to ground-based missile defenses. True enough; but that hardly justifies spending billions and tearing up major treaties for space-based *weapons*. Nor is it clear that a huge investment in new space-based sensors is needed, since current early warning satellites were already providing "cueing" to the Patriot in the Gulf War, with considerable success and without raising any ABM Treaty issues.

---

[2] Quoted in *Aviation Week and Space Technology*, February 4, 1991, p. 19.
[3] Quoted in *Inside the Pentagon*, February 7, 1991, p. 15.

The benefits, costs, and risks of adding an entirely new set of prohibited ABM-capable space sensors, as SDIO proposes, cry out for independent review.

Second, Hadley contended that space-based interceptors, being "always in position," could protect U.S. forces from theater missile threats as the forces arrived in a crisis area, before they could set up defenses of their own. But as noted above, such interceptors will not provide protection against short- and intermediate-range missile threats—and at the same briefing, SDIO Director Cooper pointed out that work is underway on air-based and ship-based ATBMs to solve this very problem.

Third, Hadley claimed that only space-based systems provide "global protection," and that it would be prohibitively expensive to deploy ground-based ATBMs everywhere a U.S. ally or U.S. forces might be threatened. But again, brilliant pebbles could not do the job either, against the theater-range missiles that pose the major threat. And if the goal is to protect U.S. allies, they should first be asked how they wish to be protected: Every major European NATO country has voiced emphatic support for maintaining the ABM Treaty, which serves their security interest in arms control and East-West relations, and eases Britain and France's tasks in maintaining independent nuclear deterrents. Indeed, the United States has sometimes stood alone in the entire world in opposing U.N. resolutions calling for agreements to prevent an arms race in outer space—precisely what a GPALS deployment would almost certainly provoke. And will U.S. allies help pay for this system ostensibly designed for their protection? . . .

More generally, SDI advocates argue that space would improve the effectiveness of defenses by adding an additional layer, and that space-based systems would actually be cheaper than ground-based defenses. The first claim is true, at least for long-range missiles, but in a time of fiscal stringency not every cake can have icing. The second claim, however, is simply absurd: few serious engineers would argue that a system that had to be designed to operate for years in the hostile environment of space, without repair or adjustment, and that had to be lifted into orbit, would be cheaper overall than doing the same job from the ground—if a ground-based system would serve.

In short, there is simply no plausible rationale for SDIO's obsession with space-based brilliant pebbles. By contrast, the ABM Treaty's absolute ban on development, testing, and deployment of such space-based ABM components—along with all other mobile ABM systems and components—is based on a carefully thought-out effort to provide maximum assurance that neither side could rapidly break out of the agreement and build a nationwide missile defense. Space-based systems inherently cannot be limited to the single permitted ABM site, and could be deployed relatively rapidly (with no site preparation) once developed and tested—particularly with the Soviet Union's enormous heavy-lift rockets. Removing the prohibition on space-based systems would eviscerate the treaty's critical protection against potential Soviet ABM breakout, leaving the agreement a "dead letter," in the words of chief U.S. negotiator Gerard Smith.

BACK TO BASICS

In sum, GPALS should be put on the shelf. The cost is daunting; the need is questionable; and the risks are substantial. The new, more limited mission of SDI simply cannot justify a near-term deployment of partly space-based defenses costing tens of billions of dollars, which would require abrogating the ABM Treaty. . . . Potential Third World threats to U.S. territory are more likely to come from sources other than ballistic missiles, while the risk of accidental or unauthorized launches is already low and can be dealt with through improved safeguards. Brilliant pebbles are not needed to protect U.S. territory against small numbers of long-range missiles, and would not be effective against short-range missiles; against the latter, straightforward technical considerations make ground-based systems such as the Patriot the clear choice. . . .

The United States should pursue ground-based ATBM technologies to provide protection against the short-range missiles that are proliferating in the developing world. But for the foreseeable future, that portion of SDI devoted to defense against long-range missiles should remain a research program, consistent with the traditional interpretation of the ABM Treaty, at a comparatively low level of funding. That sensible path is the course reportedly recommended by the Joint Chiefs of Staff when the Bush administration conducted its strategic review two years ago. . . . Research on defense options for limited threats should focus on ground-based approaches, abandoning SDIO's misguided emphasis on space. . . .

Stability in a Disarmed World

THOMAS C. SCHELLING

THE PROBLEM OF STABILITY IN A DISARMED WORLD

Much of the interest in arms control among people concerned with military policy became focused in the early 1960s on the stability of mutual deterrence. Many writers on arms control were more concerned about the character of strategic weapons than the quantity, and where quantity was concerned their overriding interest was the effect of the number of weapons on the incentives to initiate war, rather than on the extent of destruction if war should ensue. A fairly sharp distinction came to be drawn between "arms control" and "disarmament." The former seeks to reshape military incentives and capabilities with a view to stabilizing mutual deterrence; the latter, it is alleged, eliminates military incentives and capabilities.

But the success of either depends on mutual deterrence and on the stability of that deterrence. Military stability is just as crucial in relations between unarmed countries as between armed ones. Short of universal brain surgery, nothing can erase the memory of weapons and how to build them. If "total disarmament" could make war unlikely, it would have to be by reducing incentives. It could not eliminate the potential. The most primitive war could be modernized by rearmament, once it got started.

If war breaks out a nation can rearm, unless its capacity to rearm is destroyed at the outset and kept destroyed by enemy military action. By the standards of 1944, the United States was fairly near to total disarmament when World War II broke out. Virtually all munitions later expended by the United States forces were nonexistent in September 1939. "Disarmament" did not preclude U.S. participation; it merely slowed it down.

As we eliminate weapons, warning systems, vehicles, and bases, we change the standards of military effectiveness. Airplanes count more if missiles are banned, complex airplanes are needed less if complex defenses are banned. Since weapons themselves are the most urgent targets in war, to eliminate a weapon eliminates a target and changes the requirements for attack. A country may indeed be

From *Arms and Influence* by Thomas C. Schelling. Copyright © 1966 by Yale University, pp. 248–259. Reprinted by permission of the publisher, Yale University Press. Portions of the text have been omitted.

safer if it is defenseless, or without means of retaliation, on condition its potential enemies are equally disarmed; but if so it is not because it is physically safe from attack. Security would depend on its being able to mobilize defenses, or means of retaliation, faster than an enemy could mobilize the means to overcome it, and on the enemy's knowing it.

The difficulty cannot be avoided by banning weapons of attack and keeping those of defense. If, again, nations were islands, coastal artillery would seem useless for aggression and a valuable safeguard against war and the fear of war. But most are not. And in the present era "defensive" weapons often embody equipment or technology that is superbly useful in attack and invasion. Moreover, a prerequisite of successful attack is some ability to defend against retaliation or counterattack; in a disarmed world, whatever lessens the scale of retaliation reduces the risk a nation runs in starting war. Defenses against retaliation are close substitutes for offensive power.

Disarmament would not preclude the eruption of crisis; war and rearmament could seem imminent. Even without possessing complex weapons, a nation might consider initiating war with whatever resources it had, on grounds that delay would allow an enemy to strike or to mobilize first. If a nation believed its opponent might rush to rearm to achieve military preponderance, it might consider "preventive war" to forestall its opponent's dominance. Or, if confidence in the maintenance of disarmament were low and if war later, under worse conditions, seemed at all likely, there could be motives for "preventive ultimatum," or for winning a short war through coercion with illicitly retained nuclear weapons, or for using force to impose a more durable disarmament arrangement. As with highly armed countries, the decision to attack might be made reluctantly, motivated not toward profit or victory but by the danger in not seizing the initiative. Motives to undertake preventive or preemptive war might be as powerful under disarmament as with today's weapons, or even stronger.

In a disarmed world, as now, the objective would probably be to destroy the enemy's ability to bring war into one's homeland, and to "win"sufficiently to prevent his subsequent buildup as a military menace. The urgent targets would be the enemy's available weapons of mass destruction (if any), his means of delivery, his equipment that could be quickly converted for strategic use, and the components, standby facilities, and cadres from which he could assemble a capability for strategic warfare. If both sides had nuclear weapons, either by violating the agreement or because the disarmament agreement permitted it, stability would depend on whether the attacker, improvising a delivery capability, could forestall the assembly or improvisation of the victim's retaliatory vehicles or his nuclear stockpile. This would depend on the technology of "disarmed" warfare, and on how well each side planned its "disarmed" retaliatory potential.

If an aggressor had nuclear weapons but the victim did not, the latter's response would depend on how rapidly production could be resumed, on how vulnerable the productive facilities were to enemy action, and whether the prospect of interim nuclear damage would coerce the victim into surrender.

In the event that neither side had nuclear weapons, asymmetrical lead times in nuclear rearmament could be decisive. Whether it took days or months, the side that believed it could be first to acquire a few dozen megatons through a crash program of rearmament would expect to dominate its opponent.

This advantage would be greatest if nuclear facilities themselves were vulnerable to nuclear bombardment; the first few weapons produced would be used to spoil the opponent's nuclear rearmament. Even if facilities were deep under the ground, well disguised or highly dispersed, a small difference in the time needed to acquire a few score megatons might make the war unendurable for the side that was behind. It might not be essential to possess nuclear weapons in order to destroy nuclear facilities. High explosives, commandos, or saboteurs could be effective. "Strategic warfare" might reach a purity not known in this century: like the king in chess, nuclear facilities would be the overriding objective. Their protection would have absolute claim on defense. In such a war the object would be to preserve one's mobilization base and to destroy the enemy's. To win a war would not require overcoming the enemy's defenses—just winning the rearmament race.

Such a war might be less destructive than war under present conditions, not primarily because disarmament had reduced the attacker's capability for destruction but because, with the victim unable to respond, the attacker could adopt a more measured pace that allowed time to negotiate a ceasefire before he had reduced his victim to rubble. Victory, of course, might be achieved without violence; if one side appeared to have an advantage so convincingly decisive as to make the outcome of mobilization and war inevitable, it might then deliver not weapons but an ultimatum.

AN INTERNATIONAL MILITARY AUTHORITY

Some kind of international authority is generally proposed as part of an agreement on total disarmament. If militarily superior to any combination of national forces, an international force implies (or is) some form of world government. To call such an arrangement "disarmament" is about as oblique as to call the Constitution of the United States "a Treaty for Uniform Currency and Interstate Commerce." The authors of the Federalist Papers were under no illusion as to the far-reaching character of the institution they were discussing, and we should not be either.

One concept deserves mention in passing: that the projected police force should aim to control persons rather than nations. Its weapons would be squad cars, tear gas, and pistols; its intelligence system would be phone taps, lie detectors, and detectives; its mission would be to arrest people, not to threaten war on governments. Here, however, we shall concentrate on the concept of an International Force to police nations—and all nations, not just small ones. The most intriguing questions are those that relate to the Force's technique or strategy for deterring and containing the former nuclear powers.

The mission of the Force would be to police the world against war and rearmament. It might be authorized only to stop war; but some kinds of rearmament would be clear signals of war, obliging the Force to take action. There might be, explicitly or implicitly, a distinction between the kinds of rearmament that call for intervention and the kinds that are not hostile.

The operations of the Force raise a number of questions. Should it try to contain aggression locally, or to invade the aggressor countries (or all parties to the conflict) and to disable them militarily? Should it use long-range strategic weapons to disable the country militarily? Should it rely on the threat of massive punitive retaliation? Should it use the threat or, if necessary, the practice of limited nuclear reprisal as a coercive technique? In the case of rearmament, the choices would include invasion or threats of invasion, strategic warfare, reprisal or the threat of reprisal; "containment" could not forestall rearmament unless the country were vulnerable to blockade.

Is the Force intended to do the job itself or to head a worldwide alliance against transgressors? In case of aggression, is the victim to participate in his own defense? If the Indians take Tibet, or the Chinese encourage armed homesteading in Siberia, the Force would have to possess great manpower unless it was prepared to rely on nuclear weapons. A force could not be maintained on a scale sufficient to "contain" such excursions by a nation with a large population unless it relied on the sudden mobilization of the rest of the world or on superior weaponry—nuclear weapons if the defense is to be confined to the area of incursion. . . . A country threatened by invasion might rather capitulate than be defended in that fashion. Moreover, the Force might require logistical facilities, infrastructure, and occasional large-scale maneuvers in areas where it expects to be called upon. . . .

A sizable intervention of the Force between major powers is not, of course, something to be expected often in a disarmed world. Nevertheless, if the Force is conceived of as superseding . . . [Russian] and American reliance on their own nuclear capabilities, it needs to have some plausible capability to meet large-scale aggression; if it hasn't, the major powers may still be deterred, but it is not the Force that deters them.

A capability for massive or measured nuclear punishment is probably the easiest attribute with which to equip the Force. But it is not evident that the Force could solve the problems of "credibility" or of collective decision any better than can the United States alone . . . at the present time. This does not mean that it could not solve them—just that they are not automatically solved when a treaty is signed. If the Force is itself stateless, it may have no "homeland" against which counter-reprisal could be threatened by a transgressor nation; but if it is at all civilized, it will not be wholly immune to the counter-deterrent threats of a transgressor to create civil damage in other countries. These could be either explicit threats of reprisal or implicit threats of civil destruction collateral to the bombardment of the Force's own mobilization base. (The Force presumably produces or procures its weaponry in the industrial nations, and cannot be entirely housed in Antarctica, on the high seas, or in outer space.)

If it should appear technically impossible to police the complete elimination of nuclear weapons, then we should have to assume that at least minimal stockpiles had been retained by the major powers. In that case, the Force might not be a great deal more than one additional deterrent force; it would not enjoy the military monopoly generally envisaged.

One concept needs to be disposed of—that the Force should be strong enough to defeat a coalition of aggressors but not so strong as to impose its will against universal opposition. Even if the world had only the weapons of Napoleon, the attempt to calculate such a delicate power balance would seem impossible. With concepts like preemption, retaliation, and nuclear blackmail, any arithmetical solution is out of the question.

The knottiest strategic problem for an International Force would be to halt the unilateral rearmament of a major country. The credibility of its threat to employ nuclear weapons whenever some country renounces the agreement and begins to rearm itself would seem to be very low indeed.

The kind of rearmament would make a difference. If a major country openly arrived at a political decision to abandon the agreement and to recover the security it felt it had lost by starting to build a merely retaliatory capability and sizable home-defense forces, it is hard to envisage a civilized International Force using weapons of mass destruction on a large scale to stop it. Limited nuclear reprisals might be undertaken in an effort to discourage the transgressor from his purpose. But unless the rearmament program is accompanied by some overt aggressive moves, perhaps in limited war, the cool and restrained introduction of nuclear or other unconventional weapons into the country's population centers does not seem plausible, unless nonlethal chemical or biological weapons could be used.

Invasion might offer a more plausible sanction, perhaps with paratroops armed with small nuclear weapons for their own defense; their objective would be to paralyze the transgressor's government and mobilization. But if this should be considered the most feasible technique for preventing rearmament, we have to consider two implications. We have provided the Force a bloodless way of taking over national governments. And a preemptive invasion of this kind might require the Force to act with a speed and secrecy inconsistent with political safeguards.

There is also the question of what kinds of rearmament or political activity leading to rearmament should precipitate occupation by the Force. In our country, could the Republicans or Democrats campaign on a rearmament platform, go to the polls and win, wait to be inaugurated, denounce the agreement, and begin orderly rearmament? If the Force intervenes, should it do so after rearmament is begun, or after a party has introduced a rearmament resolution in Congress? The illustration suggests that one function of the Force, or the political body behind it, would be to attempt first to negotiate with a potential rearming country rather than to intervene abruptly at some point in these developments.

Again, the character of rearmament would make a difference. Suppose the President presented a well-designed plan to build an obviously second-strike retaliatory force of poor preemptive capability against either the International Force or other countries, but relatively secure from attack. If he justified it on the grounds that the current military environment was susceptible to sudden overturn by technological developments, political upheavals, irrepressible international antagonism, the impotence of the Force for decisive intervention, the corruption or subversion of the Force, or other such reasons, then the authorization of a drastic intervention by the Force in the United States would be less likely than if the President ordered a crash program to assemble nuclear weapons, trained crews, and long-range aircraft. It would make a considerable difference, too, whether rearmament occurred at a time of crisis, perhaps with a war going on, or in calmer times.

The point of all this is simply that even an international military authority with an acknowledged sole right in the possession of major weapons will have strategic problems that are not easy.[1] This is, of

---

[1] Max Lerner, in the book cited earlier, exemplifies the common tendency to confuse the solution of a problem with its replacement by another, in his haste to make the case for drastic disarmament. "If there were an outlawry of aggressive war in any form, enforced by an international authority, a good deal of what is dangerous about total disarmament could be remedied" (pp. 259–60). But so would it if the outlawry were enforced by the United States, the NATO alliance, or the fear of God; and if such outlawry of "aggressive war" could be enforced by a potent *and* decisive *and* credible authority (immune to the dangers of an opponent's "irrationality" that Lerner, as mentioned earlier, thinks may spoil deterrence), we might settle equally well for something more modest, less unsettling, than "total disarmament." Who cares about arms, much, if we can reliably rule out all modes of aggressive warfare (and self-defensive, preventive, inadvertent, or mischievous warfare)? It may be

course, aside from the even more severe problems of political control of the "executive branch" and "military establishment" of the world governing body. If we hope to turn all our international disputes over to a formal procedure of adjudication and to rely on an international military bureaucracy to enforce decisions, we are simply longing for government without politics. We are hoping for the luxury, which most of us enjoy municipally, of turning over our dirtiest jobs—especially those that require strong nerves—to some specialized employees. That works fairly well for burglary, but not so well for school integration, general strikes, or Algerian independence. We may achieve it if we create a sufficiently potent and despotic ruling force; but then some of us would have to turn around and start plotting civil war, and the Force's strategic problems would be only beginning.[2]

DESIGNING DISARMAMENT FOR STABILITY

A stable military environment, in other words, would not result automatically from a ban on weapons and facilities to make them. War, even nuclear war, remains possible no matter how much it is slowed down by the need to mobilize and even to produce the weapons.[3] The two modes of instability that worry armed countries now (or ought to worry them) would be just as pertinent for disarmed countries. The timing of war and rearmament, and the role of speed and initiative, would remain critically important in a world in which the pace of war was initially slowed for lack of modern weapons. There would remain, even in the design of "total disarmament," the difficult choice between minimizing war's destructiveness and minimizing its likelihood. If disarmament is to discourage the initiation of war, to remove the incentives toward preemptive and preventive war, and to remove the danger of unstable mobilization races, it has to be designed to do that. Disarmament does not eliminate military potential; it changes it.

The essential requirement is for some stable situation of "rearmament parity." If disarmament is to be durable, it must be so designed that the disadvantages of being behind in case an arms race should resume are not too great and so that, in the face of

---

easier for some "authority" to manage its job if all its opponents are "totally disarmed" but this depends on analysis, not assertion. One cannot disagree with Lerner, only question whether he had said anything.

[2] For a more extensive, and somewhat more constructive if equally discouraging, treatment of the "Strategic Problems of an International Armed Force," see the author's article by that title in *International Organization, 17* (1963), 465–85, reprinted in Lincoln P. Bloomfield, ed., *International Military Forces* (Boston: Little, Brown, 1964).

[3] This was proved in World War II when the United States not only produced nuclear weapons while the war was on but invented them! Next time it would be easier.

ambiguous evidence of clandestine rearmament or overt evidence of imminent rearmament, nations can react without haste. The straightforward elimination of so-called "military production facilities" might, by sheer coincidence, provide the stability; but stability is more likely if there is a deliberately designed system of "stable equal readiness for rearmament." It is impossible to eliminate the ability to rearm; one can only hope to stretch the time required to reach, from the word "go," any specified level of rearmament, and try to make defensive or retaliatory rearmament easier than offensive or preemptive rearmament. One can try to take the profit out of being ahead and the penalty out of being slow and to minimize the urge of either side, in a renewed arms race, to consolidate its advantage (or to minimize its disadvantage) by launching war itself.

It is not certain that maximizing the time required to rearm is a way to deter it. Lengthening the race course does not necessarily lessen the incentive to be first under the wire. It may, however, reduce the advantage of a small headstart; it may allow time to renegotiate before the race has too much momentum; and it may reduce the confidence of a fast starter that he could win if he called for a race.

The likelihood of war, then, or of a rearmament race that could lead to war, depends on the character of the disarmament. If mobilization potentials are such that a head start is not decisive and the race course is long, preemptive action may be delayed until motives are clear. Important elements for stability in a disarmed world would be the dispersal and duplication of standby facilities for rearmament and of reserve personnel or cadres around which rearmament could be mobilized. Dispersal could be important because of the interaction between rearmament and war itself. If a nation could achieve just enough production of weapons to disrupt its opponent's rearmament, it might gain a decisive advantage. Once the race were on, a few easily located facilities for producing nuclear weapons might invite a preventive and very limited war.

The argument here is not that disarmament would be especially unstable, or less stable than the present world of armament. It is that disarmament could be *either* more stable *or* less stable militarily than an armed world, according to how the existing military potential loaded the dice in favor of speed, surprise, and initiative or instead made it safe to wait, safe to be second in resuming an arms race or second in launching attack, and on whether the easiest directions of rearmament tended toward stable or unstable armaments.

It should not be expected that reduced tensions would be the natural consequence of a disarmament agreement, making the existing military potential irrelevant. Not everyone would be confident that disarmament provided a viable military environment or promised the political atmosphere most conducive to peace and good relations. It is hard to believe that any sober person under any conceivable world arrangement could come to believe with confidence that war had at last been banished from human affairs until there had been at the very least some decades of experience. There would be surprises, rumors, and sharp misunderstandings, as well as the usual antagonisms among countries. It is not even out of the question that if something called "general and complete disarmament" were achieved, responsible governments might decide that international apprehensions would be reduced if they possessed more secure, more diversified, and more professionally organized mobilization bases or weapon systems, with more freedom to improve them, drill them, and discuss the strategy of their use. It might be that moderate though expensive modern weapon systems, professionally organized and segregated from the main population centers, would provide less—not more—military interference in everyday life than a "total" disarmament agreement under which every commercial pilot carried emergency mobilization instructions in his briefcase.

Stability, in other words, of the two kinds discussed in this chapter, is relevant to any era and to any level of armament or disarmament. It is just not true that if only disarmament is "total" enough we can forget about deterrence and all that. It would be a mistake to suppose that under "total" disarmament there would be no military potential to be controlled, balanced, or stabilized. If disarmament were to work, it would have to stabilize deterrence. The initiation of war would have to be made unprofitable. It cannot be made impossible.

It is sometimes argued that to perpetuate military deterrence is to settle for a peace based on fear. But the implied contrast between stabilized deterrence and total disarmament is not persuasive. What would deter rearmament in a disarmed world, or small wars that could escalate into large ones, would be the apprehension of a resumed arms race and war. The extent of the "fear" involved in any arrangement—total disarmament, negotiated mutual deterrence, or stable weaponry achieved unilaterally by conscious design—is a function of confidence. If the consequences of transgression are plainly bad—bad for all parties, little dependent on who transgresses first, and not helped by rapid mobilization—we can take the consequences for granted and call it a "balance of prudence."

The United Nations: From Peace-keeping to a Collective System?

SIR BRIAN URQUHART

INTRODUCTION

During the Gulf crisis harsh reality was accompanied by a good deal of rhetoric. There was talk of 'turning points' and 'defining moments', but the phrase likely to resound the longest was the 'new world order'. What exactly was meant by this term has not yet been made clear by those who used it. It seems doubtful that it was intended to apply to a revitalized United Nations.

At the end of World War II in 1945, the Charter of the United Nations was supposed to be the blueprint for a world organization and system which was 'to save succeeding generations from the scourge of war', and 46 years later remains the sole global framework for maintaining international peace and security. The possibility of making the UN an effective central mechanism for maintaining international peace and security in the post-Cold War period therefore needs to be analysed.

Even before the Gulf crisis, the end of the Cold War had already contributed to a considerable revitalization of the UN Security Council. For the first time in the Council's history, the five permanent members had begun to work regularly together for the solution of major problems, and the results were fairly impressive. Soviet forces withdrew from Afghanistan under a plan negotiated by the Secretary-General. The Iran–Iraq War came to an end on the basis of a resolution of the Security Council devised by the five permanent members. The long-delayed independence of Namibia was successfully and peacefully effected on the basis of a 1978 resolution. The Cubans withdrew from Angola, and the civil war in that country has recently come to an end. UN peace-keeping and good offices were applied with growing effect in Central America. The five permanent members developed a plan for the peaceful future of Cambodia. The problem of Western Sahara is to be resolved by a UN-controlled plebiscite. These are considerable successes for the techniques of peace-keeping and conflict resolution.

The invasion of Kuwait by Iraq on 2 August 1990 challenged the Security Council on its original and primary function, dealing with

From *Adelphi Papers*, No. 266, Winter 1991/92. © The International Institute for Strategic Studies. Reprinted by permission.

threats to the peace and acts of aggression. The Council's response and the forced withdrawal of Iraq from Kuwait were a unique exercise in collective action and enforcement under the previously little used Chapter VII of the UN Charter. How much does this experience, as well as those of the previous two years, tell us about developing an effective international security system? The United Nations has so far not provided a *system* for peace and security so much as a last resort, or safety net. Although sometimes the organization was able to mount a peace-keeping force as a kind of sheriff's posse when things had already got out of hand, its approach was spasmodic and reactive. The basic question is whether, in the new international climate, the nations of the world are capable of the effort to create and maintain a *system* based on vigilance, consensus, common interest, collective action and international law. Ideally such a system would keep a permanent watch on international peace and security around the world, seek peaceful solutions and mediate disputes, pre-empt or prevent conflict, assure the protection of the weak, and deal authoritatively with aggressors or would-be aggressors.

The creation of a reliable system for international peace and security involves more than reacting, however forcefully, to a crisis that has already broken out. It necessitates both the creation of conditions in which peace can be maintained, and the capacity to anticipate and to prevent breaches of the peace. It requires respect for, confidence in, and the capacity to enforce the decisions of the Security Council and the findings of international law. That respect and confidence were eroded in the 40 years of the Cold War, as became very clear in Iraq's response to the Security Council at the outset of the recent crisis. It will take time and effort to restore respect and to make sure that confidence in the Security Council is shared by the UN members generally. Governments will also have to be prepared to support and put adequate resources behind both global and regional security systems. Peacekeeping, particularly, will need a much more solid logistical, financial and training basis.

THE GULF CRISIS AS A PROTOTYPE

It would be unwise to base thinking about the future of international security—or indeed of the United Nations—too much on the Gulf experience. It is highly unlikely that such a clear case of aggression will occur in the near future in an area where the stakes are so high for the major powers, or that its perpetrator and the manner of its perpetration will cause such almost universal outrage as did Saddam Hussein and his assault on Kuwait. The Gulf crisis did, however, demonstrate both the possibility of the international use of force and the limitations of such a use of force. It also provided a useful measure of the strength and weakness of the United Nations, and especially of the Security Council.

The crises of the future are likely to arise from more ambiguous situations in which it will usually be impossible to agree on defining, let alone denouncing, the aggressor. We are probably entering a period of great instability in the world. Many long-standing international rivalries and resentments persist and are compounded by ethnic and religious factors. Domestic disintegration threatens a number of sovereign states, and there is an increasing demand for international intervention in humanitarian emergencies and human rights violations. Poverty and deep economic inequities are dramatized by instant worldwide communication. Population pressures, vast economic migrations, natural and ecological disasters, and imminent scarcities of essential natural resources all contribute to instability.

If the international system is to play a helpful role in the disorders of the future, its members will not simply have to improve its performance and its capacity to intervene constructively. Governments will also have to consider how, and how far, to modify the existing rules of the game, especially as regards national sovereignty and the sacrosanct nature of domestic jurisdiction.

CREATING THE CONDITIONS FOR PEACE AND STABILITY

Any international system will continue to flounder and will often be irrelevant, unless a major effort is made to deal with some of the basic causes of conflict and to create the conditions for a more stable and less violent world. This Paper will only mention a few examples of major problems which need to be tackled if we are to be serious about a 'new world order'.

The most obvious of these is the flow of arms, especially to the developing world. It is no small irony that the five permanent members of the UN Security Council, whose newly found cordiality is now supposed to be the best hope for peace, are also the world's five largest arms exporters. The question inevitably arises whether a great power can sell arms and deter aggression at the same time. In their first capacity the five permanent members are now meeting to discuss curbing the transfer of arms, while in their second, trade is booming. The immense sums of money involved at all levels of the arms trade make it, like the drug traffic, particularly hard to control or reduce. Perhaps in the end only a huge worldwide public outcry will have any real effect. In the meantime, one of the great lessons of World War II, that massive national arms build-ups are an invitation to war and must give way to collective security and disarmament, seems, for the moment at any rate, to have been forgotten.

Economic determinism has long gone out of fashion, but there can be no doubt that a world dramatically divided into a rich minority and a desperately poor majority can never, especially in this age of mass communication, be a stable one. Marxist thinkers used to prophesy that this trend would result in a global class war. That has not happened, but sufficient despair and deprivation harnessed to demagoguery, ideology or militant religion, and modern terrorist technology could present formidable possibilities. Large international programmes to deal with poverty and achieve sustainable development seem, in many parts of the world, to be fighting a losing battle. They need to be sustained and made more effective. Much more attention also needs to be given to economic, social and environmental developments which may, even now, be generating future conflicts.

The Gulf crisis gave an instructive example of the connection between the lack of democracy and gross human rights abuses on the one hand, and the propensity for aggression and other sorts of international irresponsibility on the other. The spread of democracy, and a respect for human rights, if necessary internationally monitored, is an indispensable foundation of a more stable, less violent world. It is becoming increasingly obvious that we cannot have equitable development, peace or justice without democracy and a respect for human rights.

These are only the most obvious items of the 'hidden agenda' of collective security. They present an immense challenge to international organizations and to their members as issues which will, to a large extent, determine the culture of human beings on this planet. Their treatment will also affect the possibilities of maintaining international peace and security of which they are an indivisible part. And without a vastly improved system of peace and security, neither the will nor the resources will be available to tackle the great global issues that will determine our fate.

STRENGTHENING THE DEVELOPMENT OF THE UN AS A PEACE-KEEPING AND PEACEMAKING AGENCY

Any improvement in the performance of the UN in maintaining peace and security will have to be based on a coherent approach to the various phases of the process of conflict resolution. If these phases could be linked to one another, the resulting degree of automatic reaction to particular crises or threats to the peace would give new life and credibility to the Security Council.

Vigilance and Evaluation

The first phase to be considered is a constant watch on the world situation and the evaluation of its impact on international peace and security. In retrospect it seems extraordinary that Saddam Hussein took the world by surprise on 2 August 1990. He had a disproportionately large and diversified military establishment for a relatively small country. He had already invaded one of his neighbours. He had an appalling domestic record of tyranny, cruelty and ruthlessness. His megalomania and overwhelming ambition were well known. He had a well publicized dispute on several matters of great importance to Iraq with a small, defenceless, but immensely rich neighbour, Kuwait. And yet on the day of the invasion, the Security Council met in an atmosphere of shock and surprise.

Obviously, there is a great deal to be done in the UN, both to heighten vigilance and to improve the evaluation of available information. A department (the Office for Research and the Collection of Information—ORCI), whose task it is to observe events around the world, has already been formed. The Secretary-General, with his responsibility under Article 99 of the Charter 'to bring to the attention of the Security Council any matter which in his opinion may threaten the maintenance of international peace and security', has traditionally tried to warn the Council of impending crises, but, at least during the period of the Cold War, he was usually a sentry whose alarms generally went unheeded. The five permanent members of the Security Council have access to the world's largest intelligence agencies, while the Military Staff Committee (MSC), composed, in theory at least, of the Chiefs of Staff of the five permanent members, has access to the best military intelligence. If recent proposals for a UN register for arms transfers become a reality, another indicator of sinister intentions will become available. What seems to be lacking is a system of watch and evaluation and the will to use it.

It seems likely that Saddam Hussein was able to take the world by surprise not so much because of lack of information as because of the attitudes of the governments concerned, their short-term interests, and the absence of a forceful, independent, critical evaluation of the facts and figures. Serious preventive diplomacy and action has to be based on an evaluation of a situation which is not influenced by special interests and which starts with a worst-case analysis. Preventive diplomacy is also more likely to work if there is a precedent, such as now exists, for aggression being strongly dealt with.

Another factor in the lack of effective evaluation is a lack of focus at the UN on regional instability, as well as a lack of active contact with regional organizations on the evaluation of the local situation. In the case of Iraq, regional organizations themselves seem to have been living in as much of a fool's paradise as the UN Security Council.

The problem is not so much a question of gathering intelligence and information, as evaluating and acting upon it. An objective but active high-level evaluation team, with access to all the various sources of information described above, and with direct access to the Secretary-General and the Security Council, might save the Security Council (and the world) a lot of trouble and embarrassment in the future.

Preventive Action

It is axiomatic that preventive action is preferable, more effective and cheaper than reacting to a crisis or a conflict which is already in progress. Nonetheless, the Security Council has tended to adopt a reactive role in past years, although successive Secretaries-General have, on frequent occasions, engaged in preventive efforts in a variety of situations.

If the vigilance and evaluation function in the UN could be made more effective, it would be logical to link it automatically to efforts to prevent conflict before a situation has reached crisis stage. Such efforts can take a variety of forms, all of which would be strengthened by the authoritative backing of the Security Council and by an enhancement of the status and authority thereof. Indeed, it seems likely that its record during the Gulf crisis will result in a considerable increase in the Council's authority and stature.

Many forms of preventive diplomatic action go on all the time. Governments, especially the more powerful ones, frequently engage in preventive bilateral diplomacy. In fact, it can be argued that only major powers wield the real instruments of preventive diplomacy, such as control of the flow of arms or of international trade.

Regional organizations do their best to resolve differences among their members before they reach a flashpoint. The Security Council provides a forum where differences can be put on the table and resolved peacefully. There are various places, both within and outside the United Nations, where economic and other differences can be, and are, discussed and solutions sought. Resort to the International Court of Justice can also sometimes provide a peaceful way out of a dangerous dispute.

The Secretary-General provides his good offices each year in scores of cases where governments need an intermediary to settle a problem. He also undertakes good offices missions formalized by the Security Council, as in Cyprus, or Western Sahara, or during the Iran–Iraq War. On occasion he appoints special representatives to carry out these tasks for him.

More operational forms of preventive action include peace-keeping and observer missions and fact-finding missions, but peace-keeping missions and observer missions have so far tended to be deployed only after conflict has already broken out, as part of a cease-fire arrangement.

If current intentions to strengthen the UN are to have practical meaning, two features of past practice will have to change. In the first place, the Security Council should try consistently, by preventive action, to pre-empt a crisis before it develops, instead of acting only after the worst has occurred. Secondly, the different phases of maintaining peace and security should be linked by an element of automaticity. That is to say, a seriously negative evaluation of a situation should trigger off appropriate preventive action within or outside the Security Council. On occasion it might be decided to deploy a peace-keeping presence in an unstable area as a source of objective information, as a symbol of international concern, and as a warning that further UN action will be taken if one or other of the parties concerned oversteps the lines laid down by the Security Council. Such advanced stationing of trip-wire peace-keeping units, even on one side of a national border, would be a major step in enhancing the preventive capacity of the Security Council.

Collective Action

Preventive and peace-keeping measures will in all probability remain the mainstays of the Security Council's efforts. If, however, such measures prove to be of no avail, that failure should be linked to a different sort of international action. In Charter terms, this would be the transition from Chapter VI (Pacific Settlement of Disputes) to Chapter VII (Action with Respect to Threats to the Peace, Breaches of the Peace, and Acts of Aggression). Until now, such transitions have been rare, and never automatic. When a Council resolution was rebuffed or a peace-keeping force swept aside, as in Cyprus in 1974 or South Lebanon in 1982, there was no arrangement for, or even any talk of, moving to enforcement action.

Is it possible that with the new co-operation of the five permanent members and with the example of the Council's firm stand on the Kuwaiti crisis, this transition may become the accepted practice rather than the exception? If peace-keeping operations or other forms of preventive action were equipped with a trip-wire clause— that is to say that their demise in certain circumstances would automatically trigger a pre-planned collective action—preventive action and deterrence might begin to have more effect. The decisions of the Security Council would certainly also command a far greater degree of respect. Lack of respect for, and enforceability of, its resolution has, hitherto, been the Achilles heel of the Security Council.

The linking of the different phases of action—from evaluation to pacific settlement to preventive measures to peace-keeping to enforcement—would require a far greater degree of consistency in the work of the Security Council. It would also require serious and continuous staff work and contingency planning, including the availability of forces (Article 43), command structure and logistics. There is already serious concern about systematising peace-keeping and giving it a better basis of financing, logistics, training, readiness and standby arrangements. So far, at any rate, no similar efforts seem to be envisaged for measures required by Chapter VII—embargoes, sanctions, enforcement measures, and so on.

Sanctions

In the Gulf crisis the Council imposed sanctions and eventually authorized the use of force. The effectiveness of sanctions with regard to Iraq has still to be assessed. While sanctions did not force Iraq to leave Kuwait, they have been an important element of pressure in the implementation of Resolution 687, the Council's astonishingly detailed set of conditions for the cease-fire, especially in relation to Iraq's military establishment. At first glance it seems clear that sanctions are useful as a rallying point for the international system. It also seems obvious that they can cause pain without necessarily changing governments' behaviour. It seems entirely possible that sanctions do not work with megalomaniacal dictators, but that they are a necessary step in the escalation to the actual use of force. In the Gulf there was never a precise determination that sanctions would not work. The whole history of UN sanctions, including those imposed on Iraq, needs to be reviewed and evaluated, including the highly sensitive question of their humanitarian implications.

The Use of Force

The use of force in the Gulf was not consistent with the letter of Chapter VII of the Charter. The Security Council, lacking any mechanisms for enforcement, chose to achieve its goals, which were consistent with the Charter, through improvised means, that is, by authorizing the US-led coalition to use force. Given that the clarity of Iraq's aggression against Kuwait is unlikely to be replicated, does Chapter VII of the Charter still provide an appropriate basis for future action?

Because Chapter VII was a chapter of which the founding fathers were particularly proud, provision was made in the Charter for staff work to support it by the establishment of the MSC. That Committee was an early casualty of the Cold War. It played no role at all in the Gulf crisis. Can it usefully be revived? That question brings us to the great political changes that have been taking place since 1945, and the sort of obstacles which may well stand in the way of strengthening the performance of the Security Council.

Current Attitudes and the Future

During and after the Gulf crisis there was considerable criticism and resentment, especially in the developing world, of the dominant role of the five permanent members, and especially the United States, during the crisis. Although it is hard to see how such an enterprise could have succeeded without strong leadership and an extraordinary demonstration of military power and technology, the fact remains that the institution of the veto-wielding five permanent members, including the MSC, is regarded in some quarters as an offensive anachronism and therefore an unsound basis for collective action in the future. Further suspicion and resentment arise from the anomaly that, due to the veto power, no collective action can be taken by the Security Council directed in any way at the actions or the interests of any one of the five permanent members. This leaves a very large hole in what is supposed to be a universal system of collective security.

Yet another source of unease is the new enthusiasm of some of the permanent members (see again the G-7 London Declaration) for UN intervention in humanitarian and human rights situations regardless of national sovereignty and of Article 2, paragraph 7 of the Charter, which debars the UN from intervening in matters within the domestic jurisdiction of member states. This trend is regarded in some parts of the world as a new cloak for great power interventionism and is likely to be resisted as such.

The Gulf crisis was a very clear case of aggression in a region of great importance, especially to the industrialized powers. Any system of global security—or new world order—worthy of the name must have both the will and the capacity to deal with far less clear or economically significant situations, especially those involving the defence of the weak. Who will take the lead or make the necessary resources available in such situations? The answer can only lie in strengthening the basis of enforceable international law in international relations and in establishing a systematic, and to some extent automatic, mechanism for maintaining international peace and security. It will be a long, frustrating job, but it is worth remembering that such a system came into being in well-governed nation-states only relatively recently when injustice, oppression, disorder and anarchy had become dangerous to the survival of the state and intolerable to the majority. Similar conditions new exist at the international level.

STEPS TOWARDS A FUTURE SYSTEM

Can the UN's capacity for collective action as outlined in the Charter be modified both to work better in future and to overcome some of these obstacles?

On the diplomatic front, a more comprehensive and systematic consultation with governments outside the Security Council on peace and security matters would be valuable, both psychologically and for building support for the Council's actions. A far better system of informing other governments of the Council's actions and intentions is needed, especially during times of crisis. For example, it is not good enough for governments to learn for the first time through the public media of the imposition of mandatory sanctions, a step which is normally of great political and economic importance to them. As to contingency planning and related activities designed to improve the capacity for maintaining peace and security, it should be possible to open up the five permanent member arrangement without destroying it. (I shall not deal here with the complex question of changing or increasing the present number of permanent members.) For example, the MSC can invite any member of the UN to be associated with it 'when the efficient discharge of the Committee's responsibilities requires the participation of that member in its work' (Article 47, paragraph 1). It can also establish regional subcommittees (Article 47, paragraph 4). Whether such a broadening of participation would be sufficient to overcome the latent suspicion of the whole five permanent member concept remains to be seen. And, for the moment at least, the five permanent members themselves have shown little enthusiasm for reviving the moribund MSC.

In the early days of the UN, much importance was attached to agreements for making armed forces available to the Security Council, under Article 43, in order to contribute to the Council's task of maintaining international peace and security. However, during the Cold War period, no such agreements were ever concluded, and for this among other reasons, the Council, in responding to Iraq's aggression against Kuwait, had to resort to authorizing the use of force by a coalition under the leadership of the United States. It seems likely that, for the foreseeable future, some such arrangement will be the only feasible one in a major military confrontation. For crises involving a less serious military challenge, however, it might be worth considering the possibility of organizing a relatively small UN Rapid Deployment Force under the terms of Article 43.

New Possibilities

Are there other possibilities for providing the staff work and contingency planning essential for a more coherent and systematic approach to maintaining peace and security in the world? Should the Secretary-General be charged with establishing the necessary military and civilian framework to overcome the total lack of readiness which was evident on 2 August 1990? As has already been mentioned, a serious effort is under way to put peace-keeping on a firmer and more systematic basis. Can this effort be extended to the field of collective action, since the five permanent members do not seem willing, through the MSC, to do much about the matter themselves? Perhaps a start could be made with the Secretary-General and the Secretariat offices responsible for peace and security.

Secretariat Reorganization

A radical organization of the Secretariat is urgently needed for many reasons. One suggested plan is to replace the present cumbersome system, in which some 30 top-level officials report directly to the Secretary-General, with a grouping of functions under four deputy secretaries-general. One of these deputies would be in charge of political, security and peace affairs, bringing together all the different parts of the UN which at present deal separately with such matters. These include a worldwide watch on developments in peace and security, peace-keeping, peace-making and good offices, disarmament, arms control and regional security, the servicing of the Security Council and General Assembly on political and peace and security matters, and the MSC Secretariat.

To bring all these disparate elements together under a single deputy would certainly facilitate the work of the Secretary-General. It should also bring activities which are intrinsically related, though until now organizationally separate, into a far more coherent, mutually supportive pattern. It would, on the Secretariat side, provide the basis for that linking of different activities and different phases of operations which alone can transform the current, haphazard, *ex post facto* approach of the Security Council into something resembling a systematic approach to maintaining international peace and security.

Such a unified department would serve to keep the Secretary-General and, through him, the Security Council, alerted to possible conflicts or emergencies. It could develop recommendations for early initiatives by the Secretary-General in the use of good offices to resolve disputes. It would conduct contingency planning for possible emergencies. It would support the peace-making tasks of the Secretary-General, his representatives, or the Security Council, providing information, advice and staff as required. It would link peace-making to peace-keeping through a regular review of existing peace-keeping operations and peace-making efforts.

This comprehensive department could initiate operational planning for future missions in good time and with the full support of all relevant parts of the Secretariat, as well as supporting existing peace-keeping missions. It would maintain constant contact with contributors and potential contributors of troops and of other essential personnel and support, concerning readiness and availability, training and, as necessary, planning for actual operations. It would provide staff and support for the substantive work of the Security Council and the MSC, both in planning for a more efficient framework of collective security and on actual requirements for collective action such as sanctions, embargoes and other enforcement measures.

The new department would link the work of the Secretary-General and the Security Council to current developments in disarmament, arms control and regional security—that is, connect work on peace-making and peace-keeping to efforts to create the conditions in which peace and stability can be better maintained, with appropriate involvement of other organs of the UN system. It should study new types of operations such as supervision of elections, protection of humanitarian operations, rapid reaction to unconventional situations, and so on.

Such a reorganization would in no sense replace the need for revitalizing and systematizing the working of the Security Council itself, but it would at least provide a coherent servicing basis for it.

Financing and Other Support

The effectiveness and seriousness of UN efforts in the peace and security field are conditioned to an important extent by proper financial and logistic support. Until now there has been a significant double standard in the way in which governments view their obligations towards international peace-keeping (a relatively economical activity) and traditional 'defence' and military spending (an extremely expensive one). Two days of the cost of *Operation Desert Storm* would have comfortably supported all UN peace-keeping operations worldwide for a year. The former expenditure was never questioned; the latter is constantly haggled over and left in arrears.

It is a cliché that peace, and the preparations for it, are far less expensive than war. This is a factor that does not seem to influence the attitude of governments to financing international operations for preventive purposes or for peace-keeping. The deployment of vital operations has even had to be delayed, sometimes with serious consequences, as in Namibia, for lack of financial support. If governments cannot afford such support for what, in times of trouble, usually turn out to be vital operations, it may be advisable to look to other sources of financing, especially for peace-keeping and for emergency humanitarian operations. A small international levy on arms transactions, for example, might be an appropriate source to explore. Certainly, there must be a standing contingency fund to finance the start-up and early stages of urgent operations.

CONCLUSION

Realists may regard the establishment of a peace and security system that is consistent, comprehensive and, to some extent, automatic, as a utopian dream. Others may regard a profoundly insecure and unstable world—loaded with expensive and lethal weapons, floundering from crisis to crisis, split between rich and poor, and daily compromising its own ecological future—as the ultimate lack of realism.

What is certainly true is that the world now faces a series of urgent global problems. Our ability to deal with them is going to determine whether life on this planet will be worth living in a 100 years or so. It is not only nuclear or biological weapons that can now put an end to the human experiment. To tackle those problems effectively will require international co-operation and understanding, resources and leadership on a scale unknown in the past. Governments will have to make an extraordinary effort to raise their sights from short-term concerns to long-term interests. It is unlikely that this will happen if the world is preoccupied with, and its resources tied up in, uncertainties about peace and security. In such circumstances an international system that really does provide a reasonable degree of peace and security is quite literally vital.

Contributors

Bruce J. Allyn is a former Director of the Kennedy School-Soviet Project on Crisis Prevention at the Center for Science and International Affairs, Harvard University.

Robert J. Art is Herter Professor of International Relations at Brandeis University.

Barry M. Blechman is President of Defense Forecasts, Inc.

James G. Blight is Senior Research Fellow, Center for Foreign Policy Development, Brown University.

Bernard Brodie was affiliated with the RAND Corporation and was Professor of Political Science at the University of California at Los Angeles.

Frederic J. Brown served in the United States Army.

Harold Brown is a former Secretary of Defense under President Jimmy Carter.

McGeorge Bundy is a former National Security Advisor to President Kennedy and Professor of History at New York University.

Matthew Bunn is editor of *Arms Control Today* and Associate Director for Publications at the Arms Control Association.

John Foster Dulles was Secretary of State under President Dwight D. Eisenhower.

Lewis Dunn is Senior Analyst at Science Applications International Corporation.

Steve Fetter is an Assistant Professor in the School of Public Affairs at the University of Maryland.

Lawrence Freedman is a member of the Department of War Studies, King's College, London.

John Lewis Gaddis is Professor of History at Ohio University.

Jean-Louis Gergorin is Senior Vice President, Societe Matra, Paris.

Morton Halperin is Senior Associate at the Carnegie Endowment for International Peace.

Douglas M. Hart is a former defense analyst for the Pacific Sierra Corporation.

David C. Hendrickson is Associate Professor of Political Science at Colorado College.

Samuel P. Huntington is Eaton Professor of the Science of Government at Harvard University.

Robert Jervis is Professor of Political Science at Columbia University.

Efraim Karsh is a member of the Department of War Studies, King's College, London.

Edward L. Katzenbach, Jr. was Vice President of the University of Oklahoma.

Nikita Khrushchev was chairman of the Communist Party of the Soviet Union.

Andrei Kokoshin is Deputy Director of the Institute for USA and Canada Studies in Moscow.

Michael Krepon is President of the Henry L. Stimson Center in Washington, D.C.

Robert S. McNamara is a former Secretary of Defense under Presidents Kennedy and Johnson and former President of the World Bank.

Louis Morton was Professor of History at Dartmouth College.

John H. Mueller is Professor of Political Science at the University of Rochester.

Barry Posen is Professor of Political Science at the Massachusetts Institute of Technology.

Sir George Sansom was a writer and a British diplomat with extensive experience in the Far East.

Thomas C. Schelling is Professor of Economics at the University of Maryland.

James Schlesinger is a former Secretary of Defense under President Gerald Ford.

Glenn H. Snyder is Professor of Political Science at the University of North Carolina.

Robert W. Tucker is Professor Emeritus of American Foreign Policy at the School of Advanced International Studies, Johns Hopkins University.

Stephen Van Evera is Assistant Professor of Political Science at the Massachusetts Institute of Technology.

Sir Brian Urquhart is a former Undersecretary General for Special Political Affairs at the United Nations.

Kenneth N. Waltz is Ford Professor of Political Science at the University of California, Berkeley.

David Welch is on the faculty of the Political Science Department at the University of Toronto.